SELECTED WRITINGS OF
WASHINGTON IRVING

Introduction by
William P. Kelly
Queens College
The City University of New York

THE MODERN LIBRARY
NEW YORK

ADVISOR

Donald McQuade
Queens College
The City University of New York

First Edition

987654321

Copyright © 1984 by Random House, Inc.

Library of Congress Cataloging in Publication Data

Irving, Washington, 1783–1859.
  Selected writings of Washington Irving.

  Bibliography: p.
  I. Kelly, William P. II. Title.
PS2052.K44   1983   818'.209   83-2865
ISBN 0-394-33199-0

Cover design by Sara Eisenman

Contents

Introduction

On May 21, 1832, after a seventeen-year residence in Europe, Washington Irving returned to his native New York. His arrival was an event of some significance for his countrymen. As the first American writer to win a European audience, he had, during his absence, become a source of national pride and a symbol of his culture's advancing maturity. His fellow New Yorkers were particularly eager to celebrate his achievements. A committee of the most prominent social, political, and literary figures of the day greeted Irving, conducted him on a tour of the city's newest landmarks, and feted him at a six-hour banquet. The New York press hailed Irving as a favorite son, and in a series of flattering portraits and biographies, proclaimed his entry into the pantheon of world literature.

Soon after his arrival in New York, Irving embarked on an extensive tour of the young nation and discovered that his celebrity was by no means a local matter. In Philadelphia, he was lionized in drawing rooms and literary clubs. In Washington, he met with President Jackson, who sought his advice on European policy and tried unsuccessfully to interest him in a diplomatic post. In Cincinnati, in Saratoga, and ultimately in the garrisons of the trans-Mississippi west, Irving was entertained by local dignitaries and toasted as the founder of America's literary independence.

Irving was gratified but somewhat surprised by the warmth of his reception. He had assumed that his lengthy stay in Europe and his neglect of American material during that period would compromise his national popularity. Rather than being welcomed as a hero, he had half expected to be repudiated as a dilettante and an expatriate whose writing was at odds with the democratic spirit that was reshaping American life. Certainly those fears were not ungrounded. Irving had found his subject matter in European folklore, in the chronicles of Old World history, and in the traditions of the English gentry. His attachments were to the past; his affinities were primarily aristocratic. Nothing that he had written in Europe was consistent with the populist tenor of Jacksonian America. Irving's apparent alienation from that culture had, in fact, been previously remarked by a number of American reviewers who assailed both *Bracebridge Hall* (1822) and *Tales of a Traveller* (1824) as works which pandered to reactionary tastes and betrayed Irving's republican heritage. Irving's triumphant return to America was, however, largely unmarred by such nativist rhetoric. Indeed, the affection of his countrymen did not abate during his lifetime. Until his death in 1859, Irving continued to enjoy a level of regard rarely experienced by American writers.

Irving's appeal for a generation whose lives and values seem to us remote from the concerns of his writing was, to some degree, a product of his European reputation. As the author of *The Sketch Book* (1819), he had achieved considerable fame both in Britain and on the Continent. French and English critics, who were notoriously contemptuous of all things American, praised his work; Scott, Byron, and Dickens pronounced him a writer of rare talent; political and social luminaries held dinners in his honor. Despite their boastful chauvinism, Irving's contemporaries were still in the thrall of Old World opinion. Rather than regarding his success with suspicion, they perceived his European popularity as evidence of America's intellectual progress. Paradoxically, Irving's ability to gain the imprimatur of a cultural establishment antagonistic to republican principles enhanced his American stature.

But Irving's international renown does not fully explain the enthusiasm of his American readers. Fenimore Cooper had, for example, attracted a European following as extensive as Irving's, but when he returned to New York from London in 1833—seventeen months after Irving's arrival—Cooper met with considerable hostility. Although he had consistently defended the nation's values, he was branded a turncoat and exiled from the main currents of American life. The contrasting treatment accorded these two writers by their countrymen is somewhat difficult for the modern reader to understand. For us, Cooper's interest in the frontier, his efforts to impose form on the American past, and his investigations of democratic theory and practice speak more directly to the concerns of Jacksonian America than Irving's genteel accounts of European history and legend. But such was not the judgment of Irving's contemporaries. They discovered in his writing a chord which resonated in their lives and gave voice to their feelings. If we are to appreciate Irving's significance, and gain a richer conception of the formative era of our national history, we must pursue the nature of that attraction.

As difficult as it is to explain the fluctuations of literary reputation, we may begin to look for the sources of Irving's preeminence in his choice of subject matter. Throughout his career, Irving was obsessed with the relation of the past to the present. That concern held a particular attraction for his generation. As the immediate heirs of the Revolution, they understood that they had been liberated from the imperatives of Old World experience. But if they knew what they were not, they were less certain about what they were. Lacking a context against which to measure their achievements, they exulted in their freedom from the past as the only source of their identities. Implicit in this radical rejection of history, however, was a pervasive sense of estrangement. As they looked toward the past, Irving's generation confronted a vacuum of dramatic proportions. The Revolution had severed them from their European heritage; the brief duration of American history was insufficient to locate them in time. Denied the comforts of precedent, they were forced to invent themselves. Irving's writing both reflects and responds to this pressing quest for national identity. As we trace his halting steps toward American definition, Irving's stature as a major cultural spokesman becomes increasingly more apparent.

Irving was well placed to enact the role of a representative man. Born on April 3, 1783, five days after the cessation of the Revolutionary War, and named for the hero of that conflict, he was among the first of America's children. Although his father, William Irving, had supported the cause of independence, he was deeply rooted in the traditions of the British middle class. He imposed his stern Calvinism and his respect for commerce and thrift on his eight children by carefully supervising their education and moral development. But the Irving children came of age during a period of national transition and were exposed to influences alien to Deacon Irving's sensibility. Each of them repudiated their father's rigid theology for the more liberal tenets of the American Enlightenment. None of William Irving's sons entered the ministry as he had hoped they would, but chose instead to pursue the wide range of secular opportunities available in postwar America.

The youngest of the Irving children, Washington was pampered by his older brothers and sisters and insulated from his father's authority. He was educated at a series of private academies, and although he proved to be an indifferent scholar, he was engaged by literary and historical studies. He read books of travel and adventure with great enthusiasm and developed a lifelong attraction to folklore and romance. The New York of Irving's youth was ideally suited to his temperament. Its docks teemed with foreign travelers and seamen. Its British and Dutch heritage provided a rich source of local legend, and its newly established theaters and galleries nourished his interest in the arts. Irving's brothers were actively involved in the cultural life of the city. Stalwarts in literary clubs, partisans of New York's political factions, writers and editors, they were, despite their commercial origins, men of social significance. William Junior and Peter Irving, in particular, recognized Washington's precocious talent and sponsored his entry into New York society.

As attracted as he was by the prospect of becoming a man of letters, Irving recognized that in young America a literary career was an avocation and not a profession. He set himself, therefore, to the study of law. Irving's progress was plodding at best. He consistently looked for diversions from his duties as a legal clerk and could more readily be found in the city's theaters than in its courts. His brother Peter, who was as devoted to his medical practice as Washington was to the law, sympathized with his restlessness and invited him to write a column for his newspaper, the *Morning Chronicle*. Irving gratefully accepted and in 1802 wrote the first of nine essays which he subsequently collected as *The Letters of Jonathan Oldstyle.*

The name Irving chose for his persona in *The Letters* reflects, as the critic William Hedges has argued, the ambivalence of early American writers. As a "Jonathan," the generic nickname of the American national, Irving's narrator is a patriot who rejects his country's dependence on the cultural forms of Europe. But as an "Oldstyle," he also satirizes the barbarity of American society and offers instruction designed to redress its provinciality. In his first two letters, Jonathan Oldstyle ridicules the conventions of American dress and marriage; in the remaining seven essays of the series, he attacks every aspect of New York's theatrical establishment. The city's drama, he argues, is unoriginal and crude. New York actors are, for the most part, woeful buffoons. Their costumes are ill-conceived; the theaters in which they perform are devoid of taste. But it is the city's audiences who most offend Oldstyle's sensitivity. Theatergoers, he reports, drink and carouse during performances, respond to the basest forms of entertainment, and demonstrate no capacity for critical discrimination. Scorning the New York stage as beneath the contempt of a judicious commentator, Oldstyle, in his final letter, throws up his hands in disgust and calls for the "total reformation" of "the whole house, inside and out."

The Oldstyle Letters are, as the apprentice work of a nineteen-year-old writer, perhaps too fragile a vessel to bear sustained examination, but they are an informative preface to the rest of Irving's writing. Jonathan Oldstyle is a figure drawn from the tradition of eighteenth-century British satire, but unlike the personae of such writers as Addison and Goldsmith, he lacks, as a comic character, the authority to enforce his didactic intentions. Irving does employ him to attack American pretension and vulgarity, but at the same time he undercuts Oldstyle as a cranky anachronism whose proposed reforms would retard rather than advance national progress. Dissatisfied with the contemporary state of American life, and yet uncomfortable with the reactionary implications of his discontent, Irving parodies both his critic and the culture Oldstyle assails. Throughout the series, Irving's youthful wit disguises the cynicism implicit in *The Letters*. We are amused by Irving's burlesque and are thankful for the glimpse of turn-of-the-century New York which Jonathan Oldstyle provides. Inescapable, however, is the sense of detachment which lurks beneath the surface of Irving's text. There is a rootlessness in these letters which epitomizes the uncertainty of Irving's generation and anticipates the subsequent direction of his career.

Irving's satiric posture in *The Oldstyle Letters* was consistent with the literary tastes of his New York contemporaries. The absence of a constraining tradition had, in the final decade of the eighteenth century, spurred the energies of the city's artistic community. Theaters, literary clubs, salons, and magazines flourished as New Yorkers attempted to create a cultural environment appropriate to their city's growing wealth and prominence. These efforts were, however, impeded by a lack of context. Confused about their relation to the traditions within which they worked, local artists and writers vacillated between an exuberant nationalism and an uneasy reliance on the masterworks of Europe. Predictably, this tension generated a great vogue for satire. In growing numbers, the city's wits scorned both the jingoism of patriotic plays and poetry and the derivative quality of works inspired by Old World example. Like Irving's Jonathan Oldstyle, they rejected both a callow nationalism and a subservient dependence on the past as inadequate expressions of the national character. The victims of cultural flux, they drifted toward cynicism and alienation.

Soon after the publication of the final *Oldstyle Letter*, Irving was liberated from the boredom of his legal studies and the confines of New York society. His brothers were worried about his health and agreed to finance a two-year tour of Europe. Irving's travels are preserved for us in a series of notebooks in which he first recorded and then revised his impressions of the Old World. The content of these journals is unremarkable. Irving's judgments are, for the most part, derived from the guidebooks he read during his trip; his enthusiasms are consistent with those of other American tourists of the period. Irving's notebooks do, however, testify to his growing confidence as a writer and to the emergence of his characteristic literary perspective. He is, in these journals, an outsider, a voyeur whose involvement in the scenes he describes is entirely vicarious. Here the self-conscious detachment which marks *The Oldstyle Letters* becomes a deliberate stylistic strategy which Irving exploits independent of any satiric intent.

Irving did not immediately capitalize on his newly-won literary skills when he returned to New York in 1806 but resumed his desultory legal career. Accepting a position in the office of Judge Josiah Hoffman, he discharged the responsibilities of a law clerk with competence, if not enthusiasm. Occasionally, he found his duties to be of interest. He was, for example, delighted to assist Hoffman at Aaron Burr's trial for treason. But more often, he regarded his work as tedious. He did, however, find stimulation in an informal literary society, the self-styled "Lads of Kilkenny."

Meeting in taverns, in clubrooms, and at the New Jersey estate of Gouverneur Kemble, the "nine worthies" of the Kilkenny circle indulged their high spirits in drink and conversation. As Irving's commitment to the law continued to diminish, he conceived a plan for a journal which would reproduce the mirth of the Kilkenny gatherings. Enlisting the aid of his brother William and their friend James Kirk Paulding, he published in January, 1807, the first issue of *Salmagundi; or, The Whim-Whams and Opinions of Launcelot Langstaff, Esq., and Others*.

As its title suggests, *Salmagundi* was a kind of hash, an acerbic hodgepodge of political parody, literary reviews, social criticism, and sentimental essays. Writing under the names Launcelot Langstaff, Will Wizard, and Andrew Evergreen, Irving and his two collaborators turned a scattergun on New York society. Across the journal's twenty issues, the activities of the city's assembly, the fashions of its women, the failings of its theaters, and the indiscretions of its citizens all became grist for *Salmagundi*'s mill. Urbane and allusive, Irving's contributions to the journal considerably extend the range of *The Oldstyle Letters*, but the energy of his writing proceeds from an identical source. Like *The Letters*, *Salmagundi* is an exercise in both social satire and self-parody. Launcelot Langstaff and his colleagues begin their journal by pledging "to instruct the young, reform the old, correct the town, and castigate the age." But they freely acknowledge the futility of their ambition. *Salmagundi*'s perspective is resolutely ironic—from the editors' initial announcement that their journal will be "printed on hot-pressed vellum paper, as that is held in highest esteem for buckling up young ladies' hair" to Langstaff's subsequent admission that "after all our lectures, precepts, and excellent admonitions, the people of New

York are nearly as much given to backsliding and ill nature as ever." Mocking their attempts to reform their audience as consistently as they attack contemporary mores, the fictitious editors subvert the moral function of the satirist.

At a further remove, Irving undermines even the limited authority his personae might claim for themselves. Langstaff, Evergreen, and the other contributors to *Salmagundi* are satirized as insolent wags, characters as naive and as sentimental as the targets of their abuse. Again Irving's humor obscures his intent, but there is a method to the anarchy and madness of *Salmagundi*. By carefully locating the journal within the context of Augustan letters, by invoking the example of Addison, Steele, Fielding, Sterne, Smollett, and their myriad American imitators, Irving is not simply acknowledging a literary debt but is reducing to rubble the props which support that tradition. The viability of reform is *Salmagundi*'s true subject. Living in the culture which was itself the product of the Enlightenment's faith in human renewal, Irving parodies the very idea of progress. America has not, *Salmagundi* insists, realized the dreams of the Age of Reason but has become only another stage on which the human comedy is ceaselessly repeated. As a result, Irving implies, the satirist, the social commentator, the critic has no real function. The example of the past is useless to correct the present; the present offers no hope for the future. Self-irony becomes the writer's final resort. A laughter, which has its source in the absurd, is his only appropriate response.

Salmagundi temporarily exhausted Irving's powers of invention, but when the journal ceased publication in 1808, he was still unwilling to devote himself to the law. Abandoning, for all practical purposes, his legal practice, Irving began work on his third major project,

Diedrich Knickerbocker's A History of New York (1809). This comic chronicle of New York from the beginning of the world to the demise of the Dutch empire directly engages the historical concerns that are implicit in *The Oldstyle Letters* and *Salmagundi*. Irving initially conceived the *History* as a parody of Dr. Samuel Latham Mitchill's *The Picture of New York; or the Traveller's Guide through the Commercial Metropolis of the United States* (1807). Mitchill's somber account of the city's grandeur epitomized for Irving the unwarranted reverence New Yorkers had for their city's past and present glory. The mock-heroic tenor of Irving's language and the strained seriousness of his narrator ruthlessly prick that conceit by exposing the discrepancy between New York's aristocratic pretension and its prosaic heritage. Despite Diedrich Knickerbocker's desperate attempts to impose an epic form on their lives, the Dutch leaders whose careers he recounts remain stolid burghers for whom the pleasures of the table and the pipe greatly outweigh the laurels of the battlefield. As he unfolds the tragic fate of New Amsterdam, Knickerbocker is undone by an absence of chivalric incident. Grossly distorting the significance of his subject, he unwittingly reduces history to farce.

But as we might expect, Irving's satire is not directed exclusively toward the vanity of New York's leading citizens. *Knickerbocker's History* is also a parody of contemporary political figures, most notably Thomas Jefferson, who appears in the book as the splenetic Governor William Kieft. By recounting the failures of Kieft's administration, Irving types Jefferson as an indecisive bungler whose ineptitude is exceeded only by his arrogance. On a third level, the *History* is an indictment of American nationalists who persisted in romanticizing their culture's past and future. Irving was contemptuous of poets such as Timothy Dwight, Joel Barlow, and

Philip Freneau, who were attempting to recast American history in the heroic mode of the *Odyssey* and the *Aeneid*. In satirizing Diedrich Knickerbocker's epic aspirations, Irving clearly has these writers and their critical proponents in mind.

The *History's* enduring interest is not, however, a product of any of these satiric intentions. Its primary significance resides in Irving's consideration of the nature and function of history. In the course of his narrative, Irving defines history as a form of fiction, a self-serving exercise through which men endow their lives with meaning. Lost in the present, detached from any context, Diedrich Knickerbocker invents a Golden Age, and with it a role for himself as its heir and defender. The self-deluding nature of his enterprise is transparent. Knickerbocker is a fool and a pedant, a bankrupt antiquarian whose manuscript is seized in lieu of his back rent. His naivety is merely pathetic, but behind him stands the respected Dr. Mitchill, and behind Mitchill, every historian who has ever claimed objectivity for his writing. Their common attempt to bring order, dignity, and direction to the chaos of human experience is, for Irving, only a less obvious version of Knickerbocker's futile longing.

To some degree, Irving's attack on the legitimacy of historians is another indication of the cynicism that characterizes his early career. *Knickerbocker's History* is, however, a work of a more complex imaginative order than either *The Letters* or *Salmagundi*. Even as he disassociates himself from Diedrich Knickerbocker in particular, and from historians in general, Irving sympathizes with their ambition. Too self-conscious to embrace an imagined past as a source of identity, he recognizes nonetheless the appeal of tradition, however fabricated it may be. Irving cannot share Knickerbocker's vision of a coherent national history, but his detachment is as wistful as it is satiric. Both the subject of Irving's extended jest and the object of his envy, Diedrich Knickerbocker becomes, by the conclusion of his *History*, an American Quixote.

Both *Salmagundi* and *Knickerbocker's History* enjoyed considerable popular acclaim. Irving's position as New York's leading writer was secure. There was at last no necessity to return to the law. And yet, in the ten years that followed the publication of the *History*, Irving failed to produce any writing of consequence. From 1809 to 1815, he drifted through the social circles of New York, Washington, and Philadelphia. He did prepare, in 1810, a volume of Thomas Campbell's poetry and edited, from 1813 through 1814, *The Analectic*, a journal which reprinted excerpts from British magazines. But Irving's activities during this period were not primarily literary. He represented his brothers' importing business as a Washington lobbyist, served as an adjutant during the final year of the War of 1812, and half-heartedly pursued a political appointment. His restlessness was pronounced, but he could find no outlet for his energies.

Irving's lack of direction during these years has most frequently been attributed to the disappointment he experienced after the death in 1807 of Judge Hoffman's daughter Matilda. In letters and journal entries written several years after her death, Irving professed his love for Matilda and described her loss as a severe blow to his hopes. These accounts of his grief seem, however, more sentimental than genuine. Irving was an intimate of the Hoffman family, but his attachments there were primarily with Matilda's stepmother, Maria Fenno, and her older sister Ann. During her lifetime, Irving appears to have regarded Matilda as a charming younger sister, and in his correspondence gives little indication that he thought of her with anything more than fraternal affection. Moreover, a marriage at that point in Irving's life would have forced him to relinquish his literary pursuits for the security of a legal practice. As much as he may have been attracted to Matilda, Irving would most certainly have regarded such an expedient as an onerous sacrifice.

Yet there is a more compelling explanation for the precipitous decline in Irving's literary production. What, we may well ask, could Irving write about in 1810? Lacking both tradition and texture, American culture provided its writers with very little subject matter. In *The Oldstyle Letters* and *Salmagundi* Irving had exhausted the possibilities of social satire. In *Knickerbocker's History* he had eliminated the American past as a subject worthy of serious interest. The primary theme of his writing had been the futility of authorship. Jonathan Oldstyle had abandoned his critical role as pointless; Launcelot Langstaff had admitted his impotence; Diedrich Knickerbocker had disappeared as a failed historian. The logic of Irving's prior writing dictated his silence.

It was only after he left America in 1815 that Irving's paralysis began to ease. The ostensible purpose of his trip was to assist his brother Peter in managing the English office of the family's firm, but Irving hoped that a change of scene would reignite his writing. Initially that expectation was disappointed. He found Peter in ill health and his accounts in disarray. For three years Irving struggled to right the family's affairs, but a simultaneous decline in his brothers' American trade doomed his efforts to failure. In 1818 bankruptcy was declared and Irving was left virtually without financial resources. Returning, in some desperation, to writing, he began to mine his English notebooks for material that might be of interest to an American audience. In June 1819, the first of seven installments of *The Sketch Book of Geoffrey Crayon, Gent.*, appeared in New York; in February 1820, the first volume of *The Sketch Book* was published in England. The encouraging sales of that edition and the intervention of Walter Scott convinced John Murray, Britain's most prestigious publisher, to reissue Volume One and to release in July a second collection of Crayon's sketches.

The book was an immediate international success. Reviewers in New York and in London praised its elegance and applauded Irving as a writer of distinction. Their response was, we should note, not entirely free from extraliterary considerations. Irving's favorable treatment in the British press was aided by his friendships with Scott and Francis Jeffrey, the editor of the influential *Edinburgh Review*. More important, his obvious debts to the British sentimental essay, his affectionate descriptions of English scenes, and the gentlemanly demeanor of his persona, Geoffrey Crayon, endeared him to an English audience who had come to expect a more antagonistic tone from American writers. Clearly, British reaction to *The Sketch Book* was marked by condescension. Here at last, Irving's reviewers implied, was an American who wrote like an Englishman. In contrast, New York critics found in *The Sketch Book* an object of patriotic pride. Stung by the abuse of British writers—one had asked in 1820 "Who the world over reads an American book?"—Irving's countrymen were delighted by the collection's refinement and hailed it as a product of the nation's emerging genius.

Regardless of their motivation, *The Sketch Book*'s critics were justified in their praise. Irving's writing across the thirty-four essays that make up the two volumes of the collection is consistently engaging; his thematic intentions are, despite the diversity of *The Sketch Book*'s subject matter, consistent and fully realized. Irving concerns himself primarily with the nature of human identity. What, he asks, is man's relation to the past? How can he reconcile his reason and his emotion? What are the sources of his alienation? Although Irving is addressing universal concerns, his perspective is that of an American observer detached by the Revolution from the prior course of history. Geoffrey Crayon's struggle to insinuate himself within the British tradition is complicated by his nationality. Like Irving himself, Crayon, as a man of letters, has no place in the American present and no reference for his art in its past. He turns for comfort to the rich substance of English history, but as a citizen of the new republic, he finds himself an alien in his ancient home. Crayon's search for identity in a world repudiated by the founding fathers establishes *The Sketch Book* as a culturally specific work, the cornerstone of our literary tradition. The sense of cultural estrangement so insistent in Irving's essays clarifies for us the sensibility of his age and, at the same time, informs our reading of the work of American expatriates from Hawthorne and James to Pound and Hemingway.

Irving advances his argument in *The Sketch Book* on three separate fronts. In essays such as "The Country Church," "A Sunday in London," "Westminster Abbey," "The Angler," "John Bull," and the Christmas pieces, he provides a comprehensive survey of British manners. His attention is not, however, focused on the circumstances of contemporary life, but on the vanishing traditions of the past. Irving's accounts of rural life, holiday festivities, and representative cultural types are eulogies of a sort, memorials marked by a persistent melancholy. The Industrial Revolution was, as Irving wrote, continuing to reshape British society. He was not, as some of his critics have charged, indifferent to or unaware of the disruption of English life. He does not, it is true, address that transformation directly in *The Sketch Book*, but its force is implicit in each of his essays.

Irving sympathizes with Geoffrey Crayon's affection for Squire Bracebridge, his respect for the coherence of rural society, and his devotion to the rugged integrity of John Bull. But Crayon is, we must remember, a persona cast in the mold of Jonathan Oldstyle, Launcelot Langstaff and Diedrich Knickerbocker. Rather than employing Crayon as a vehicle for his own perceptions, Irving uses him as a literary device. He undercuts, for example, Crayon's attempts to preserve an ideal Britain in the same way that he parodies Diedrich Knickerbocker's description of Dutch New York as a Golden Age. The features of British life Crayon most admires are, Irving understands, the relics of a superseded era. He permits Crayon to align himself with the tradition he resuscitates, but he defines that attachment as illusory. The question Irving poses is not whether the British past is preferable to the British present, but whether any past can provide a source of personal and national identity.

Certainly, Crayon's connection to the scenes and characters he describes is vicarious. He is an outsider, an American traveler who must remain apart from the social order he finds so attractive. His immersion in the British tradition only emphasizes his isolation. But Englishmen themselves, Irving implies, are as remote as Crayon from their past. Their highly developed sense of their heritage is finally as groundless as Knickerbocker's conception of New Amsterdam. The country churchyards of *The Sketch Book* are disappearing, urban enclaves like Little Britain are giving way to change, John Bull and The Angler have become factory workers. In their place only legend and memory remain. Crayon and the English traditionalists he portrays do not recognize the futility of their efforts to root themselves within a historical continuum. Irving, on the other hand, is all too aware of history's kinship with fiction. He does not satirize Crayon's attraction to the English past, but neither does he participate in his enthusiasms. Crayon's desire to embrace a tradition beyond his grasp becomes a powerful metaphor of both the human condition and the precarious nature of an American identity.

A second group of essays in *The Sketch Book* are sentimental narratives which trade on the pleasures of melancholy. "The Wife," "The Pride of the Village," "The Broken Heart," and "The Widow and her Son" appear to be conventional exercises designed to invoke a cultivated tear. Modern readers have generally dismissed them as maudlin and outmoded pieces that demonstrate Irving's distance from the mainstream of nineteenth-century romanticism. But that response fails to account for Irving's use of the Crayon persona. Irving's narrator is unquestionably an heir of the sentimental school of the eighteenth century. Like Gray and Goldsmith, in particular, he relies on stock situations to elicit an emotional response from his readers. But Irving is not Crayon. He does not exploit a cliché in these essays, but addresses instead the contradictory impulses of our intellect and our feelings.

However remote from Crayon's melancholy we may imagine ourselves to be, our distance from him is only a matter of degree. We are, in a sense, trapped by Irving's narrative strategy. He invites us to reject Crayon's attraction to tales of disappointed love and premature death as naive and foolish, but if we do so, we define ourselves as either dehumanized or hypocritical. Our reason tells us that if we respond to the plight of fictional characters, as Crayon asks us to do, we are the victims of a confidence game. And yet, if we deny the involvement Crayon offers, we have lost an opportunity to affirm our membership in the brotherhood of man. Sentiment, Irving argues, is as irrational as history but the fictitious sense of community they both engender is essential for our survival. As extravagant as Crayon's sentimentality is, we ridicule it at our peril. Again, for Irving, the price of self-consciousness is high; its costs are measured in detachment and isolation.

Writing itself is the third major concern of *The Sketch Book*. In "The Author's Account of Himself," "The Voyage," and "L'Envoy," Crayon considers the personal significance of his authorship. In "The Art of Book Making," "The Mutability of Literature," "English Writers on America," "A Royal Poet," and "Stratford-on-Avon," he locates his work against the backdrop of literary history. In these essays Crayon examines two propositions: first, that a writer, regardless of his lack of a social or a historical context, can create an identity with his pen; and second, that an author's work secures his place in a literary tradition. For Crayon these are not abstract conceptions, but issues of fundamental importance. If, through his sketches, Crayon can both invent himself and establish a bond with past and future writers, his isolation will be broken.

But Crayon's hopes are dashed by Irving's corrosive irony. All writing, Crayon learns in "The Art of Book Making," is plagiarism. The originality authors claim for themselves is illusory. Rather than announcing its author's individuality, writing merely illustrates the burden of entailment under which men labor. More damaging still, Crayon discovers in "The Mutability of Literature" that his writing does not admit an author to membership in a literary tradition. Fame is, of course, ephemeral, but more important, our sense of a literary heritage is itself a fiction. Even a writer as distinguished as Shakespeare is subject to the revision and the neglect of his readers; his work is continually remade to suit the fashion of changing times. "Shakespeare," Crayon acknowledges, is a construct elaborated across the centuries and not a historical presence.

Irving's rejection of authorship as an agency of identity and context in these essays is conventional and heavy-handed. But in "Rip Van Winkle" and "The Legend of Sleepy Hollow," the two most familiar chapters of *The Sketch Book*, Irving describes the limitations and the attractions of writing with considerable power. Both Rip and Ichabod Crane are themselves traffickers in the realm of the imagination. Idlers in the past, they are aliens in the present. Rip's indolence separates him from the life of his village and ultimately denies him a role in the pageant of history. Ichabod's addiction to ghost stories and superstition renders him an inappropriate candidate for the hand of Katrina Van Tassel and results in his flight from Sleepy Hollow and the pragmatic Brom Van Brunt. Irving's response to these woolgathering characters is quite complex. He recognizes that society has a right to demand participation from its members and that Rip and Ichabod are useless men. Yet their attraction for him is undiminished. His sympathies are engaged by Rip's encounter with the crew of the *Half-Moon* and by Ichabod's affection for Cotton Mather's witchery. Irving's choice of a literary career documents his decision to side with Rip and Ichabod against the figures of commerce and progress who displace them. He retains, however, no illusions about that choice. He understands that, as a teller of tales, he occupies a social position as peripheral as that of his characters.

But Irving is not content to define writing as an activity remote from the business of life. By first acknowledging that both "Rip Van Winkle" and "The Legend of Sleepy Hollow" are retellings of German folklore and then presenting them as stories derived by Geoffrey Crayon from Dutch legends recorded in the notebooks of Diedrich Knickerbocker, Irving distances himself from their creation. His self-conscious detachment is all-embracing: as a writer of tales and sketches, he is a man apart from the world at large; as the reshaper of other writers' material, he has no place in the literary tradition. The quest for identity, on which Irving embarks in *The Sketch Book*, has come full circle. History, sentiment, and authorship provide only the illusion of personal attachment. By crediting them, we may, like Geoffrey Crayon, mask our alienation. Alternatively, we may, with Irving, recognize identity itself as a necessary fiction, an act of self-preservation.

The Sketch Book is the apex of Irving's achievement. In the seven years that followed its appearance, Irving traveled widely in Europe, reaping the rewards of his fame. He indulged himself in the social life of London, Paris, Dresden, and Vienna, tried his hand at writing and producing plays, and assembled an extensive collection of European folklore. The two books that he published during these years—*Bracebridge Hall* and *Tales of a Traveller*—are of interest to students of Irving's career, but neither of them recaptures the energy of *The Sketch Book*. There is a twice-told quality about them that suggests Irving's inability to discover a new source of inspiration. *Bracebridge Hall* extends Geoffrey Crayon's survey of English life, but its significance is that of a footnote to the major achievement of *The Sketch Book*.

Tales of a Traveller glosses Irving's consideration of the limits of authorship, but despite Irving's skill as a storyteller, the collection lacks the rich invention and the subtle ironies that distinguish his earlier writing.

Irving was well aware that his work had become stagnant and, as a result, was only too happy to accept in 1825 a ministerial appointment to the American legation in Spain. He was called to that post by Ambassador Alexander Everett, who hoped that Irving would agree to translate Martin Fernandez de Navarette's recently published history of the voyages of Christopher Columbus. That request appealed to Irving on three levels. First, he had, since his boyhood, been interested in Spanish history and in the career of Columbus. Second, his investments had miscarried, and he was in need of the royalties he expected the translation to generate. Third, and most important, he hoped that a residence in Spain would stimulate his moribund imagination. But Irving's initial enthusiam soon waned, and rather than translating Navarette's chronicle, he decided to prepare a biography of his own. Devoting himself to months of research, he collated Navarette's work with other accounts of Columbus and his times. For two years, Irving labored at his task, and in July 1827, completed *The Life and Voyages of Christopher Columbus*.

Irving's *Columbus* is of limited intrinsic interest. Although it is more lively than Navarette's monumental study, it lacks its insight and scholarly authority. But if this work is only a minor contribution to the history of the Age of Exploration, it does represent a turning point in Irving's career. Prior to *Columbus*, Irving consistently undermined the legitimacy of the historian's craft; here he abandons his skepticism to become a historian himself. Still, there are moments in his narrative when Irving's characteristic self-consciousness reasserts itself.

As Columbus pleads his case before Queen Isabella, as he confronts the doubts of his crew, and as he first sights land, we have a sense that Irving has become again a writer of fiction. In these episodes Columbus is less the subject of a biography than a mythic character involved in a romantic quest. But such incidents are subordinate to Irving's genuine commitment to the demands of accuracy and objectivity. The irony, the detachment, the consistent qualification that had been the hallmarks of his writing evaporate. Irving now claims for himself an authority that he had formerly rejected.

In the remaining thirty-one years of his life, Irving published twelve major works. His Spanish research yielded five books in addition to *Columbus*: *Conquest of Granada* (1829), *Voyages of the Companions of Columbus* (1831), *Tales of the Alhambra* (1835), *Legends of the Conquest of Spain* (1835), and *Mahomet and His Successors* (1850). Irving also produced three more biographies: *The Life of Oliver Goldsmith* (1840), *The Biography of Margaret Davidson* (1841), and *The Life of Washington* (1855–59); three studies of the American frontier: *A Tour on the Prairies* (1835), *Astoria* (1836), and *The Adventures of Captain Bonneville* (1837); two literary memoirs: *Abbotsford* (1835) and *Newstead Abbey* (1835); and a final collection of tales and sketches: *Woolfert's Roost* (1855). Irving's prose in all of these works is masterful, and many of them contain memorable passages. We admire, for example, Irving's painterly descriptions of the New West, his vivid accounts of Washington's leadership during the Revolution, and his skillful retellings of Spanish folklore. But—with the exception of *Tales of the Alhambra* and *A Tour on the Prairies*—none of these books captures our interest with the power of *Salmagundi* or *The Sketch Book*. They are at best workmanlike efforts which echo the stentorian tone of *Columbus*. No longer are we challenged by the twists of Irving's narrative strategies and the rigor of his caustic wit. The distance which he had carefully preserved between himself and Geoffrey Crayon has closed; the skeptical critic has become a genteel man of letters.

Irving's success played a major role in this transformation. His appointment to the Spanish Ministry was a watershed that marked his transition from a self-conscious voyeur to a public man. Following his stay in Madrid, Irving was summoned to London where he served as the Secretary of the American Legation. While he was at the Court of St. James, Irving was awarded a medal by the Royal Society of Literature and granted an honorary degree by the University of Oxford. His return to America in 1832 occasioned, as we have noted, a display of national homage—Irving had become America's first laureate. His opinion and support were solicited by aspiring writers; his friends urged him to run for Congress or for mayor; President Van Buren offered him a cabinet position as Secretary of the Navy. In 1842 he returned to Madrid as the American Ambassador and was elected to the Spanish Academy. At home again in 1846, he settled into a comfortable retirement at Sunnyside, his estate in Tarrytown, New York. There he supervised the publication of a revised edition of his works and completed his biography of George Washington.

Quite understandably, the sense of detachment which had shaped Irving's literary development was replaced by a commitment to his public station. Rather than rejecting tradition as an illusion, he devoted himself to its creation. Particularly in *Columbus*, the frontier books, and *The Life of Washington*, Irving attempts to bring design to the American past. The skepticism of *Knickerbocker's History* is forgotten as he plots a line of national descent that runs from Columbus through Washington to John Jacob Astor and Captain Bonneville.

Irving's new perspective was consistent with a change in the national temperament. The period between Irving's return to America in 1832 and his death in 1859 was a time of cultural consolidation. Although America still lacked an extensive history, its past was not as vacuous as it had been when Irving wrote *The Oldstyle Letters*. A second generation of American writers continued to probe the complex nature of America's relation to the past, but they now had no doubts about the legitimacy of either their writing or their culture. Although Irving's later work hardly rivals the startling achievements of Poe, Emerson, Hawthorne, and Melville, it proceeds from the same self-assertive spirit. Just as *Salmagundi* reflects the anxieties of the young republic, *The Life of Washington* recalls for us the pride and assurance of pre–Civil War America.

The second half of Irving's career is not, however, entirely undistinguished. *Tales of the Alhambra* and *A Tour on the Prairies* are significant works which extend the achievement of *The Sketch Book* and deserve a place among the major documents of the American Renaissance. *The Alhambra* was one of the products of Irving's residence in Spain. As he prepared his biography of Columbus, Irving had become increasingly more involved in the history and legend of Spain. He first explored that interest in *Conquest of Granada*, a history of the Moors. The *Conquest* is a leaden work which quickly passed into obscurity, but it did have the effect of bringing Irving to the Alhambra, the deteriorating fortress of the Moorish kings. During a four-month stay in one of its apartments, Irving conceived *Tales of the Alhambra*, a volume much closer in spirit to *The Sketch Book* than anything else he was to write.

The Alhambra is primarily a collection of Spanish folktales which Irving gathered in Madrid and Granada. He retells these legends in a compelling fashion, but they are not the major source of the book's interest. More important is the relation Irving crafts between the tales and their teller. Dismissing his accustomed use of a persona, Irving confronts his vulnerability as a writer of fiction and a compiler of antiquarian lore. As he describes his life at the Alhambra, Irving admits his kinship with Diedrich Knickerbocker, Rip Van Winkle, and Geoffrey Crayon. Like them he is an enthusiast more at home in the past than in the present. That proclivity is, Irving argues, irrational. He does not believe the legends he recounts, in fact he consistently undercuts their credibility. Nor does he imagine that his rummagings in Spanish history will result in a sharper sense of himself. He does not, however, feel any need to deny his attraction to these stories. Resigning the schizophrenic stance of his earlier, persona-narrated works, Irving arrives at a satisfactory rapprochement with himself. In "The Balcony," one of Irving's most interesting essays, for example, he mocks his inclination to romanticize experience and his attraction to a voyeur's perspective, but at the same time he grants a legitimacy to his imagination that had heretofore been beyond his power. Self-consciousness had finally become for Irving a source of comfort rather than pain.

Like *The Alhambra*, *A Tour on the Prairies* is an exercise in self-discovery. The first book Irving wrote after his return to America, it is the last of his works which does not bear the patriarch's stamp. The *Tour* is a diary of Irving's 1832 trip to the Oklahoma frontier, but it is also a record of his reconciliation with America. In his preface Irving quotes a passage from *The Sketch Book* in which he described the anxieties attendant to his 1815 departure from New York. He then characterizes his years in Europe as a period of mounting alienation during which he became convinced that his countrymen had forgotten or repudiated him. Those fears were dispelled, he continues, by the welcome he received, but his homecoming nonetheless provoked a sense of dislocation. New York's landscape had been transformed. His friends had grown old. The monuments of his youth were no more.

But unlike Rip Van Winkle, whose adventures this preface recalls, Irving did not retire to the shades of the Catskills but set off on a voyage of rediscovery. Although the *Tour* is an account of that journey, it is not, Irving concludes, the work that he expected it to be. Lacking romantic characters and dramatic incidents, it is hardly "a story" at all. But that is precisely the strength of the *Tour*. For the first time in his career, Irving is without the insulation of either a narrative persona or an alien subject matter. He confronts the nation he left seventeen years before with an uncharacteristic immediacy.

The *Tour*'s originality is not at first apparent. Like British tourists who viewed the American landscape through the frame of a Claude glass, Irving attempts to impose a European grid on the American west. His guide is "a kind of Gil Blas of the frontiers"; an Indian brave recalls "a wild Arab on the prowl"; a half-breed tracker has features "not unlike those of Napoleon." There is for Irving "something quite oriental in the appearance" of a party of Creek horsemen; light glancing through a grove of trees reminds him of "the effect of sunshine among the stained windows and clustering columns of a Gothic cathedral." The western inhabitants he meets are variously described as "an Adonis," "a Lycurgus," and "the hero of La Mancha." But as Irving's party presses further into the plains, his use of Old

World metaphors diminishes. The herds of buffalo and wild horses, the prairie fires, and the Indian alarms which enliven his journey cease to suggest literary analogues. Irving's language is chastened; rather than relying on convention, he crafts new conceits and images. The slaughter of wild game is stripped of romance and becomes "butchery." Indians are not picturesque "gypsies" but threatening figures who disrupt Irving's sleep. Nightfall on the plains is an occasion for anxiety rather than a time of tranquil meditation.

Irving's altered diction is not the only evidence of a shift in his perspective. His narrative frame also undergoes a significant change. In the first few chapters of the *Tour*, Irving is once again an outsider, a traveler whose sensibility is closer to that of his two European companions than to that of the border scouts and rangers who accompanied them. He is "a seeker of adventures," a "virtuoso" in search of stimulation and pleasure. The *Tour*, we expect, will be an American version of *The Sketch Book*, with Irving cast in the role of Geoffrey Crayon. The hardships of his journey do not, however, permit Irving the luxury of detachment. If he is to survive, he cannot remain an observer but must become a participant. Keenly aware of his altered circumstances, Irving abandons the structure of the *Tour*'s opening chapters and conceives the rest of his narrative as a rite of passage. Like the untrained rangers whose rash conduct repeatedly hazards the company's security, Irving is a neophyte on the plains. His progress demands the adoption of a vision adequate to the rigors of his environment. As he experiences deprivation and danger, as he is called upon to relinquish his reserve, Irving acquires a new perspective. In the book's climactic scene, he sets aside his notebooks and joins a buffalo hunt. The melancholy that engulfs him when he kills one of the herd has considerable resonance. Irving's innocence has died with the buffalo. The spilling of blood has compromised his detachment. In an almost archetypal manner, Irving gains an American identity, and with it an equal measure of guilt and exhilaration.

It is appropriate that Irving begins the *Tour* with a citation from *The Sketch Book*. Together these two works suggest both the range of Irving's career and the progress of American literature during his lifetime. *The Sketch Book* is the product of an adolescent sensibility. Poised between a childhood he has outgrown and a maturity he can only imagine, Irving is caught between the past and the future, between the worlds of Europe and America. In the *Tour*, Irving hesitates for a moment at the brink of maturity and then commits himself to the violent energies of his homeland. His frontier experience has immersed him in the life of his culture. In killing a buffalo and in encountering the primitive urgings at the heart of his consciousness, Irving recapitulates the course of American history and comes to terms with the distinctive character of his heritage.

Certainly, a full appreciation of the *Tour*'s significance depends upon a reading of *The Sketch Book*, but it is also true that a consideration of Irving's career that limits itself to that work is incomplete. *The Sketch Book* teaches us that America's imagined freedom from the past is a source of anxiety as well as liberation, that independence implies emptiness as well as possibility. As crucial as that insight is to our understanding of our culture, it represents only one aspect of Irving's perspective. In the *Tour*, Irving explores historical presence rather than absence. By defining in that book the peculiar energies which have given shape and direction to American experience, Irving brings his search for a national identity to its conclusion. The trajectory of his career—

Irving's progress from the cynical wit of *The Oldstyle Letters* and *Salmagundi* to the celebratory prose of *The Life of Washington*, from the passive reserve of *The Sketch Book* to the active engagement of *A Tour on the Prairies*—not only charts the direction of his writing and of his age but refines as well our sense of the complex tensions inherent in our culture.

William P. Kelly
New York, New York
October, 1982

A Note on the Texts

The texts collected here derive from the Author's Uniform Revised Edition of *The Works of Washington Irving*, published originally in 1860–61 and reissued in 1881 by G. P. Putnam. All of the footnotes which appear in this volume are Irving's own, except for translations of two Latin passages supplied by Professor Catherine McKenna, which are marked off by square brackets.

Suggested Readings

A definitive edition of Irving's writing is currently being prepared by Twayne Publishers under the direction of Richard Dilworth Rust. Most of the series is now available; the edition is scheduled for completion in 1986. Each of the Twayne volumes includes a well-documented introductory essay. Stanley T. Williams' *The Life of Washington Irving* (Oxford University Press, 1935) remains the standard biography. Although Williams' appraisal of Irving was unduly influenced by the political context of the American thirties, his book is a work of exceptional scholarship. For another perspective on Irving's life and career, see Edward Wagenknecht's *Washington Irving: Moderation Displayed* (Oxford University Press, 1962).

The most comprehensive and insightful analysis of Irving's major works is William L. Hedges' *Washington Irving: An American Study, 1802–1832* (Johns Hopkins University Press, 1965). Donald Ringe's *The Pictorial Mode: Space and Time in the Art of Bryant, Irving, and Cooper* (University of Kentucky Press, 1971) locates Irving within the aesthetic context of his time; Martin Roth's *Comedy and America: The Lost World of Washington Irving* (Kennikat Press, 1976) considers the sources of Irving's humor, particularly as it is manifested in *Knickerbocker's History*. Essays of considerable merit include: Terence Martin, "Rip, Ichabod, and the Ameri-

tion," *American Literature*, 30, 1959; Philip Young, "Fallen from Time: The Mythic Rip Van Winkle," *Kenyon Review*, 22, 1960; Wayne R. Kine, "The Completeness of Washington Irving's *A Tour on the Prairies*," *Western American Literature*, 8, 1973; Allen Guttman, "Washington Irving and the Conservative Imagination," *American Literature*, 36, 1964; and William Bedford Clark, "Irving's Comic Inversion of the Westering Myth in *A Tour on the Prairies*," *American Literature*, 50, 1978. Andrew B. Myer has edited two excellent collections of essays devoted to Irving's life and work: *Washington Irving: A Tribute* (Sleepy Hollow Restorations, 1972) and *A Century of Commentary on the Works of Washington Irving* (Sleepy Hollow Restorations, 1976).

The Sketch Book of Geoffrey Crayon, Gent.
(1819–1820)

I have no wife nor children, good or bad, to provide for.
A mere spectator of other men's fortunes and adventures, and how they play their parts, which, methinks,
are diversely presented unto me, as from a common
theatre or scene.

BURTON

THE AUTHOR'S ACCOUNT
OF HIMSELF

"I am of this mind with Homer, that as the snaile that crept out of her shel was turned eftsoons into a toad, and thereby was forced to make a stoole to sit on; so the traveller that stragleth from his owne country is in a short time transformed into so monstrous a shape, that he is faine to alter his mansion with his manners, and to live where he can, not where he would."

LYLY'S EUPHUES

I WAS always fond of visiting new scenes, and observing strange characters and manners. Even when a mere child I began my travels, and made many tours of discovery into foreign parts and unknown regions of my native city, to the frequent alarm of my parents, and the emolument of the town-crier. As I grew into boyhood, I extended the range of my observations. My holiday afternoons were spent in rambles about the surrounding country. I made myself familiar with all its places famous in history or fable. I knew every spot where a murder or robbery had been committed, or a ghost seen. I visited the neighboring villages, and added greatly to my stock of knowledge, by noting their habits and customs, and conversing with their sages and great men. I even journeyed one long summer's day to the summit of the most distant hill, whence I stretched my eye over many a mile of terra incognita, and was astonished to find how vast a globe I inhabited.

This rambling propensity strengthened with my years. Books of voyages and travels became my passion, and in devouring their contents, I neglected the regular exercises of the school. How wistfully would I wander about the pierheads in fine weather, and watch the parting ships, bound to distant climes—with what longing eyes would I gaze after their lessening sails, and waft myself in imagination to the ends of the earth!

Further reading and thinking, though they brought this vague inclination into more reasonable bounds, only served to make it more decided. I visited various parts of my own country; and had I been merely a lover of fine scenery, I should have felt little desire to seek elsewhere its gratification, for on no country have the charms of nature been more prodigally lavished. Her mighty lakes, like oceans of liquid silver; her mountains, with their bright aerial tints; her valleys, teeming with wild fertility; her tremendous cataracts, thundering in their solitudes; her boundless plains, waving with spontaneous verdure; her broad deep rivers, rolling in solemn silence to the ocean; her trackless forests, where vegetation puts forth all its magnificence; her skies, kindling with the magic of summer clouds and glorious sunshine;—no, never need an American look beyond his own country for the sublime and beautiful of natural scenery.

But Europe held forth the charms of storied and poetical association. There were to be seen the masterpiece of art, the refinements of highly-cultivated society, the quaint peculiarities of ancient and local custom. My native country was full of youthful promise: Europe was rich in the accumulated treasures of age. Her very ruins told the history of times gone by, and every mouldering stone was a chronicle. I longed to wander over the scenes of renowned achievement—to tread, as it were, in the footsteps of antiquity—to loiter about the ruined castle—to meditate on the falling tower—to escape, in short, from the common-place realities of the present, and lose myself among the shadowy grandeurs of the past.

I had, beside all this, an earnest desire to see the great

men of the earth. We have, it is true, our great men in
America: not a city but has an ample share of them. I
have mingled among them in my time, and been almost
withered by the shade into which they cast me; for there
is nothing so baleful to a small man as the shade of a
great one, particularly the great man of a city. But I was
anxious to see the great men of Europe; for I had read
in the works of various philosophers, that all animals
degenerated in America, and man among the number.
A great man of Europe, thought I, must therefore be as
superior to a great man of America, as a peak of the
Alps to a highland of the Hudson; and in this idea I was
confirmed, by observing the comparative importance
and swelling magnitude of many English travellers
among us, who, I was assured, were very little people in
their own country. I will visit this land of wonders,
thought I, and see the gigantic race from which I am
degenerated.

It has been either my good or evil lot to have my
roving passion gratified. I have wandered through
different countries, and witnessed many of the shifting
scenes of life. I cannot say that I have studied them with
the eye of a philosopher; but rather with the sauntering
gaze with which humble lovers of the picturesque stroll
from the window of one print-shop to another; caught
sometimes by the delineations of beauty, sometimes by
the distortions of caricature, and sometimes by the
loveliness of landscape. As it is the fashion for modern
tourists to travel pencil in hand, and bring home their
portfolios filled with sketches, I am disposed to get up a
few for the entertainment of my friends. When, however, I look over the hints and memorandums I have taken
down for the purpose, my heart almost fails me at
finding how my idle humor has led me aside from the
great objects studied by every regular traveller who

would make a book. I fear I shall give equal disappointment with an unlucky landscape painter, who had travelled on the continent, but, following the bent of his vagrant inclination, had sketched in nooks, and corners, and by-places. His sketch-book was accordingly crowded with cottages, and landscapes, and obscure ruins; but he had neglected to paint St. Peter's, or the Coliseum; the cascade of Terni, or the bay of Naples; and had not a single glacier or volcano in his whole collection.

THE VOYAGE

Ships, ships, I will descrie you
   Amidst the main,
I will come and try you,
What you are protecting,
   And projecting,
      What's your end and aim.
One goes abroad for merchandise and trading,
Another stays to keep his country from invading,
A third is coming home with rich and wealthy lading.
   Hallo! my fancie, whither wilt thou go?

OLD POEM

TO AN American visting Europe, the long voyage he has to make is an excellent preparative. The temporary absence of worldly scenes and employments produces a state of mind peculiarly fitted to receive new and vivid impressions. The vast space of waters that separates the hemispheres is like a blank page in existence. There is no gradual transition, by which, as in Europe, the features and population of one country blend almost imperceptibly with those of another. From the moment you lose sight of the land you have left all is vacancy until you step on the opposite shore, and are launched at once into the bustle and novelties of another world.

In travelling by land there is a continuity of scene and a connected succession of persons and incidents, that carry on the story of life, and lessen the effect of absence and separation. We drag, it is true, "a lengthening chain," at each remove of our pilgrimage; but the chain is unbroken: we can trace it back link by link; and we feel that the last still grapples us to home. But a wide sea voyage severs us at once. It makes us conscious of being cast loose from the secure anchorage of settled life, and sent adrift upon a doubtful world. It interposes a gulf, not merely imaginary, but real, between us and our homes—a gulf subject to tempest, and fear, and uncertainty, rendering distance palpable, and return precarious.

Such, at least, was the case with myself. As I saw the last blue line of my native land fade away like a cloud in the horizon, it seemed as if I had closed one volume of the world and its concerns, and had time for meditation, before I opened another. That land, too, now vanishing from my view, which contained all most dear to me in life; what vicissitudes might occur in it—what changes might take place in me, before I should visit it again! Who can tell, when he sets forth to wander, whither he may be driven by the uncertain currents of existence; or when he may return; or whether it may ever be his lot to revisit the scenes of his childhood?

I said that at sea all is vacancy; I should correct the expression. To one given to day-dreaming, and fond of losing himself in reveries, a sea voyage is full of subjects for meditation; but then they are the wonders of the deep, and of the air, and rather tend to abstract the mind from worldly themes. I delighted to loll over the quarter-railing, or climb to the main-top, of a calm day, and muse for hours together on the tranquil bosom of a summer's sea; to gaze upon the piles of golden clouds just peering above the horizon, fancy them some fairy realms, and people them with a creation of my own;—to watch the gentle undulating billows, rolling their silver volumes, as if to die away on those happy shores.

There was a delicious sensation of mingled security and awe with which I looked down from my giddy height, on the monsters of the deep at their uncouth gambols. Shoals of porpoises tumbling about the bow of the ship; the grampus slowly heaving his huge form above the surface; or the ravenous shark, darting, like a spectre, through the blue waters. My imagination would conjure up all that I had heard or read of the watery world beneath me; of the finny herds that roam its fathomless valleys; of the shapeless monsters that lurk among the very foundations of the earth; and of those wild phantasms that swell the tales of fishermen and sailors.

Sometimes a distant sail, gliding along the edge of the ocean, would be another theme of idle speculation. How interesting this fragment of a world, hastening to rejoin the great mass of existence! What a glorious monument of human invention; which has in a manner triumphed over wind and wave; has brought the ends of the world into communion; has established an interchange of blessings, pouring into the sterile regions of the north all the luxuries of the south; has diffused the light of knowledge and the charities of cultivated life; and has thus bound together those scattered portions of the human race, between which nature seemed to have thrown an insurmountable barrier.

We one day descried some shapeless object drifting at a distance. At sea, everything that breaks the monotony of the surrounding expanse attracts attention. It proved to be the mast of a ship that must have been completely wrecked; for there were the remains of handkerchiefs, by which some of the crew had fastened themselves to this spar, to prevent their being washed off by the waves. There was no trace by which the name of the ship could be ascertained. The wreck had evidently drifted about for many months; clusters of shell-fish had fastened about it, and long sea-weeds flaunted at its sides. But where, thought I, is the crew? Their struggle has long been over—they have gone down amidst the roar of the tempest—their bones lie whitening among the caverns of the deep. Silence, oblivion, like the waves, have closed over them, and no one can tell the story of their end. What sighs have been wafted after that ship! what prayers offered up at the deserted fireside of home! How often has the mistress, the wife, the mother, pored over the daily news, to catch some casual intelligence of this rover of the deep! How has expectation darkened into anxiety—anxiety into dread—and dread into despair! Alas! not one memento may ever return for love to cherish. All that may ever be known, is, that she sailed from her port, "and was never heard of more!"

The sight of this wreck, as usual, gave rise to many dismal anecdotes. This was particularly the case in the evening, when the weather, which had hitherto been fair, began to look wild and threatening, and gave indications of one of those sudden storms which will sometimes break in upon the serenity of a summer voyage. As we sat round the dull light of a lamp in the cabin, that made the gloom more ghastly, every one had his tale of shipwreck and disaster. I was particularly struck with a short one related by the captain.

"As I was once sailing," said he, "in a fine stout ship across the banks of Newfoundland, one of those heavy fogs which prevail in those parts rendered it impossible

for us to see far ahead even in the daytime; but at night
the weather was so thick that we could not distinguish
any object at twice the length of the ship. I kept lights at
the mast-head, and a constant watch forward to look out
for fishing smacks, which are accustomed to lie at
anchor on the banks. The wind was blowing a smacking
breeze, and we were going at a great rate through the
water. Suddenly the watch gave the alarm of 'a sail
ahead!'—it was scarcely uttered before we were upon
her. She was a small schooner, at anchor, with her
broadside towards us. The crew were all asleep, and had
neglected to hoist a light. We struck her just amid-ships.
The force, the size, and weight of our vessel bore her
down below the waves; we passed over her and were
hurried on our course. As the crashing wreck was
sinking beneath us, I had a glimpse of two or three half-
naked wretches rushing from her cabin; they just
started from their beds to be swallowed shrieking by the
waves. I heard their drowning cry mingling with the
wind. The blast that bore it to our ears swept us out of all
farther hearing. I shall never forget that cry! It was
some time before we could put the ship about, she was
under such headway. We returned, as nearly as we could
guess, to the place where the smack had anchored. We
cruised about for several hours in the dense fog. We
fired signal guns, and listened if we might hear the
halloo of any survivors: but all was silent—we never saw
or heard anything of them more."

I confess these stories, for a time, put an end to all my
fine fancies. The storm increased with the night. The
sea was lashed into tremendous confusion. There was a
fearful, sullen sound of rushing waves, and broken
surges. Deep called unto deep. At times the black
volume of clouds over head seemed rent asunder by
flashes of lightning which quivered along the foaming

billows, and made the succeeding darkness doubly terrible. The thunders bellowed over the wild waste of waters, and were echoed and prolonged by the mountain waves. As I saw the ship staggering and plunging among these roaring caverns, it seemed miraculous that she regained her balance, or preserved her buoyancy. Her yards would dip into the water: her bow was almost buried beneath the waves. Sometimes an impending surge appeared ready to overwhelm her, and nothing but a dexterous movement of the helm preserved her from the shock.

When I retired to my cabin, the awful scene still followed me. The whistling of the wind through the rigging sounded like funereal wailings. The creaking of the masts, the straining and groaning of bulk-heads, as the ship labored in the weltering sea, were frightful. As I heard the waves rushing along the sides of the ship, and roaring in my very ear, it seemed as if Death were raging round this floating prison, seeking for his prey: the mere starting of a nail, the yawning of a seam, might give him entrance.

A fine day, however, with a tranquil sea and favoring breeze, soon put all these dismal reflections to flight. It is impossible to resist the gladdening influence of fine weather and fair wind at sea. When the ship is decked out in all her canvas, every sail swelled, and careering gayly over the curling waves, how lofty, how gallant she appears—how she seems to lord it over the deep!

I might fill a volume with the reveries of a sea voyage for with me it is almost a continual reverie—but it is time to get to shore.

It was a fine sunny morning when the thrilling cry of "land!" was given from the mast-head. None but those who have experienced it can form an idea of the delicious throng of sensations which rush into an

American's bosom, when he first comes in sight of Europe. There is a volume of associations with the very name. It is the land of promise, teeming with every thing of which his childhood has heard, or on which his studious years have pondered.

From that time until the moment of arrival, it was all feverish excitement. The ships of war, that prowled like guardian giants along the coast; the headlands of Ireland, stretching out into the channel; the Welsh mountains, towering into the clouds; all were objects of intense interest. As we sailed up the Mersey, I reconnoitred the shores with a telescope. My eye dwelt with delight on neat cottages, with their trim shrubberies and green grass plots. I saw the mouldering ruin of an abbey overrun with ivy, and the taper spire of a village church rising from the brow of a neighboring hill—all were characteristic of England.

The tide and wind were so favorable that the ship was enabled to come at once to the pier. It was thronged with people; some, idle lookers-on, others, eager expectants of friends or relatives. I could distinguish the merchant to whom the ship was consigned. I knew him by his calculating brow and restless air. His hands were thrust into his pockets; he was whistling thoughtfully, and walking to and fro, a small space having been accorded him by the crowd, in deference to his temporary importance. There were repeated cheerings and salutations interchanged between the shore and the ship, as friends happened to recognize each other. I particularly noticed one young woman of humble dress, but interesting demeanor. She was leaning forward from among the crowd; her eye hurried over the ship as it neared the shore, to catch some wished-for countenance. She seemed disappointed and agitated; when I heard a faint voice call her name. It was from a poor sailor who had been ill all the voyage, and had excited the sympathy of every one on board. When the weather was fine, his messmates had spread a mattress for him on deck in the shade, but of late his illness had so increased, that he had taken to his hammock, and only breathed a wish that he might see his wife before he died. He had been helped on deck as we came up the river, and was now leaning against the shrouds, with a countenance so wasted, so pale, so ghastly, that it was no wonder even the eye of affection did not recognize him. But at the sound of his voice, her eye darted on his features; it read, at once, a whole volume of sorrow; she clasped her hands, uttered a faint shriek, and stood wringing them in silent agony.

All now was hurry and bustle. The meetings of acquaintances—the greetings of friends—the consultations of men of business. I alone was solitary and idle. I had no friend to meet, no cheering to receive. I stepped upon the land of my forefathers—but felt that I was a stranger in the land.

ROSCOE

> ———In the service of mankind to be
> A guardian god below; still to employ
> The mind's brave ardor in heroic aims,
> Such as may raise us o'er the grovelling herd,
> And make us shine for ever—that is life.
>
> THOMSON

ONE OF the first places to which a stranger is taken in Liverpool is the Athenæum. It is established on a liberal and judicious plan; it contains a good library, and spacious reading-room, and is the great literary resort of the place. Go there at what hour you may, you are sure to find it filled with grave-looking personages, deeply absorbed in the study of newspapers.

As I was once visiting this haunt of the learned, my attention was attracted to a person just entering the room. He was advanced in life, tall, and of a form that might once have been commanding, but it was a little bowed by time—perhaps by care. He had a noble Roman style of countenance; a head that would have pleased a painter; and though some slight furrows on his brow showed that wasting thought had been busy there, yet his eye still beamed with the fire of a poetic soul. There was something in his whole appearance that indicated a being of a different order from the bustling race around him.

I inquired his name, and was informed that it was Roscoe. I drew back with an involuntary feeling of veneration. This, then, was an author of celebrity; this was one of those men, whose voices have gone forth to the ends of the earth; with whose minds I have communed even in the solitudes of America. Accustomed, as we are in our country, to know European writers only by their works, we cannot conceive of them, as of other men, engrossed by trivial or sordid pursuits, and jostling with the crowd of common minds in the dusty paths of life. They pass before our imaginations like superior beings, radiant with the emanations of their genius, and surrounded by a halo of literary glory.

To find, therefore, the elegant historian of the Medici, mingling among the busy sons of traffic, at first shocked my poetical ideas; but it is from the very circumstances and situation in which he has been placed, that Mr. Roscoe derives his highest claims to admiration. It is interesting to notice how some minds seem almost to create themselves, springing up under every disadvantage, and working their solitary but irresistible way through a thousand obstacles. Nature seems to delight in disappointing the assiduities of art, with which it would rear legitimate dullness to maturity; and to glory in the vigor and luxuriance of her chance productions. She scatters the seeds of genius to the winds, and though some may perish among the stony places of the world, and some be choked by the thorns and brambles of early adversity, yet others will now and then strike root even in the clefts of the rock, struggle bravely up into sunshine, and spread over their sterile birthplace all the beauties of vegetation.

Such has been the case with Mr. Roscoe. Born in a place apparently ungenial to the growth of literary talent; in the very market-place of trade; without fortune, family connections, or patronage; self-prompted, self-sustained, and almost self-taught, he has conquered every obstacle, achieved his way to eminence, and, having become one of the ornaments of the nation, has turned the whole force of his talents and influence to advance and embellish his native town.

Indeed, it is this last trait in his character which has given him the greatest interest in my eyes, and induced me particularly to point him out to my countrymen. Eminent as are his literary merits, he is but one among the many distinguished authors of this intellectual nation. They, however, in general, live but for their own fame, or their own pleasures. Their private history presents no lesson to the world, or, perhaps, a humiliating one of human frailty and inconsistency. At best, they are prone to steal away from the bustle and common-place of busy existence; to indulge in the selfishness of lettered ease; and to revel in scenes of mental, but exclusive enjoyment.

Mr. Roscoe, on the contrary, has claimed none of the

accorded privileges of talent. He has shut himself up in no garden of thought, nor elysium of fancy; but has gone forth into the highways and thoroughfares of life; he has planted bowers by the way-side, for the refreshment of the pilgrim and the sojourner, and has opened pure fountains, where the laboring man may turn aside from the dust and heat of the day, and drink of the living streams of knowledge. There is a "daily beauty in his life," on which mankind may meditate and grow better. It exhibits no lofty and almost useless, because inimitable, example of excellence; but presents a picture of active, yet simple and imitable virtues, which are within every man's reach, but which, unfortunately, are not exercised by many, or this world would be a paradise.

But his private life is peculiarly worthy the attention of the citizens of our young and busy country, where literature and the elegant arts must grow up side by side with the coarser plants of daily necessity; and must depend for their culture, not on the exclusive devotion of time and wealth, nor the quickening rays of titled patronage, but on hours and seasons snatched from the pursuit of worldly interests, by intelligent and public-spirited individuals.

He has shown how much may be done for a place in hours of leisure by one master spirit, and how completely it can give its own impress to surrounding objects. Like his own Lorenzo de' Medici, on whom he seems to have fixed his eye as on a pure model of antiquity, he has interwoven the history of his life with the history of his native town, and has made the foundations of its fame the monuments of his virtues. Wherever you go in Liverpool, you perceive traces of his footsteps in all that is elegant and liberal. He found the tide of wealth flowing merely in the channels of traffic; he has diverted from it invigorating rills to refresh the garden of literature. By his own example and constant exertions he has effected that union of commerce and the intellectual pursuits, so eloquently recommended in one of his latest writings:* and has practically proved how beautifully they may be brought to harmonize, and to benefit each other. The noble institutions for literary and scientific purposes, which reflect such credit on Liverpool, and are giving such an impulse to the public mind, have mostly been originated, and have all been effectively promoted, by Mr. Roscoe; and when we consider the rapidly increasing opulence and magnitude of that town, which promises to vie in commercial importance with the metropolis, it will be perceived that in awakening an ambition of mental improvement among its inhabitants, he has effected a great benefit to the cause of British literature.

In America, we know Mr. Roscoe only as the author— in Liverpool he is spoken of as the banker; and I was told of his having been unfortunate in business. I could not pity him, as I heard some rich men do. I considered him far above the reach of pity. Those who live only for the world, and in the world, may be cast down by the frowns of adversity; but a man like Roscoe is not to be overcome by the reverses of fortune. They do but drive him in upon the resources of his own mind; to the superior society of his own thoughts; which the best of men are apt sometimes to neglect, and to roam abroad in search of less worthy associates. He is independent of the world around him. He lives with antiquity and posterity; with antiquity, in the sweet communion of studious retirement; and with posterity, in the generous aspirings after future renown. The solitude of such a mind is its state of highest enjoyment. It is then visited

* Address on the opening of the Liverpool Institution.

by those elevated meditations which are the proper aliment of noble souls, and are, like manna, sent from heaven, in the wilderness of this world.

While my feelings were yet alive in the subject, it was my fortune to light on further traces of Mr. Roscoe. I was riding out with a gentleman, to view the environs of Liverpool, when he turned off, through a gate, into some ornamented grounds. After riding a short distance, we came to a spacious mansion of freestone, built in the Grecian style. It was not in the purest taste, yet it had an air of elegance, and the situation was delightful. A fine lawn sloped away from it, studded with clumps of trees, so disposed as to break a soft fertile country into a variety of landscapes. The Mersey was seen winding a broad quiet sheet of water through an expanse of green meadow-land; while the Welsh mountains, blended with clouds, and melting into distance, bordered the horizon.

This was Roscoe's favorite residence during the days of his prosperity. It had been the seat of elegant hospitality and literary retirement. The house was now silent and deserted. I saw the windows of the study, which looked out upon the soft scenery I have mentioned. The windows were closed—the library was gone. Two or three ill-favored beings were loitering about the place, whom my fancy pictured into retainers of the law. It was like visiting some classic fountain, that had once welled its pure waters in a sacred shade, but finding it dry and dusty, with the lizard and the toad brooding over the shattered marbles.

I inquired after the fate of Mr. Roscoe's library, which had consisted of scarce and foreign books, from many of which he had drawn the materials for his Italian histories. It had passed under the hammer of the auctioneer, and was dispersed about the country. The good people of the vicinity thronged like wreckers to get some part of the noble vessel that had been driven on shore. Did such a scene admit of ludicrous associations, we might imagine something whimsical in this strange irruption in the regions of learning. Pigmies rummaging the armory of a giant, and contending for the possession of weapons which they could not wield. We might picture to ourselves some knot of speculators, debating with calculating brow over the quaint binding and illuminated margin of an obsolete author; of the air of intense, but baffled sagacity, with which some successful purchaser attempted to dive into the black-letter bargain he had secured.

It is a beautiful incident in the story of Mr. Roscoe's misfortunes, and one which cannot fail to interest the studious mind, that the parting with his books seems to have touched upon his tenderest feelings, and to have been the only circumstance that could provoke the notice of his muse. The scholar only knows how dear these silent, yet eloquent, companions of pure thoughts and innocent hours become in the seasons of adversity. When all that is worldly turns to dross around us, these only retain their steady value. When friends grow cold, and the converse of intimates languishes into vapid civility and commonplace, these only continue the unaltered countenance of happier days, and cheer us with that true friendship which never deceived hope, nor deserted sorrow.

I do not wish to censure; but, surely, if the people of Liverpool had been properly sensible of what was due to Mr. Roscoe and themselves, his library would never have been sold. Good worldly reasons may, doubtless, be given for the circumstance, which it would be difficult to combat with others that might seem merely fanciful; but it certainly appears to me such an opportunity as seldom occurs, of cheering a noble mind struggling under misfortunes, by one of the most delicate, but most expressive tokens of public sympathy. It is difficult, however, to estimate a man of genius properly who is daily before our eyes. He becomes mingled and confounded with other men. His great qualities lose their novelty, we become too familiar with the common materials which form the basis even of the loftiest character. Some of Mr. Roscoe's townsmen may regard him merely as a man of business; others as a politician; all find him engaged like themselves in ordinary occupations, and surpassed, perhaps, by themselves on some points of worldly wisdom. Even that amiable and unostentatious simplicity of character, which gives the nameless grace to real excellence, may cause him to be undervalued by some coarse minds, who do not know that true worth is always void of glare and pretension. But the man of letters, who speaks of Liverpool, speaks of it as the residence of Roscoe. The intelligent traveller who visits it inquires where Roscoe is to be seen. He is the literary landmark of the place, indicating its existence to the distant scholar. He is, like Pompey's column at Alexandria, towering alone in classic dignity.

The following sonnet, addressed by Mr. Roscoe to his books on parting with them, is alluded to in the preceding article. If any thing can add effect to the pure feeling and elevated thought here displayed, it is the conviction, that the whole is no effusion of fancy, but a faithful transcript from the writer's heart.

TO MY BOOKS

As one who, destined from his friends to part,
   Regrets his loss, but hopes again erewhile
    To share their converse and enjoy their smile,
And tempers as he may affliction's dart;

Thus, loved associates, chiefs of elder art,
    Teachers of wisdom, who could once beguile
    My tedious hours, and lighten every toil,
I now resign you; nor with fainting heart;

For pass a few short years, or days, or hours,
    And happier seasons may their dawn unfold,
    And all your sacred fellowship restore:
When, freed from earth, unlimited its powers,
    Mind shall with mind direct communion hold,
        And kindred spirits meet to part no more.

THE WIFE

The treasures of the deep are not so precious
As are the conceal'd comforts of a man
Locked up in woman's love. I scent the air
Of blessings, when I come but near the house.
What a delicious breath marriage sends forth . . .
The violet bed's not sweeter.

MIDDLETON

I HAVE often had occasion to remark the fortitude with which women sustain the most overwhelming reverses of fortune. Those disasters which break down the spirit of a man, and prostrate him in the dust, seem to call forth all the energies of the softer sex, and give such intrepidity and elevation to their character, that at times it approaches to sublimity. Nothing can be more touching than to behold a soft and tender female, who had been all weakness and dependence, and alive to every trivial roughness, while treading the prosperous paths of life, suddenly rising in mental force to be the comforter and support of her husband under misfortune, and abiding, with unshrinking firmness, the bitterest blasts of adversity.

As the vine, which has long twined its graceful foliage about the oak, and been lifted by it into sunshine, will, when the hardy plant is rifted by the thunderbolt, cling round it with its caressing tendrils, and bind up its shattered boughs; so is it beautifully ordered by Providence, that woman, who is the mere dependent and ornament of man in his happier hours, should be his stay and solace when smitten with sudden calamity; winding herself into the rugged recesses of his nature, tenderly supporting the drooping head, and binding up the broken heart.

I was once congratulating a friend, who had around him a blooming family, knit together in the strongest affection. "I can wish you no better lot," said he, with enthusiasm, "than to have a wife and children. If you are prosperous, there they are to share your prosperity; if otherwise, there they are to comfort you." And, indeed, I have observed that a married man falling into misfortune is more apt to retrieve his situation in the world than a single one; partly because he is more stimulated to exertion by the necessities of the helpless and beloved beings who depend upon him for subsistence; but chiefly because his spirits are soothed and relieved by domestic endearments, and his self-respect kept alive by finding, that though all abroad is darkness and humiliation, yet there is still a little world of love at home, of which he is the monarch. Whereas a single man is apt to run to waste and self-neglect; to fancy himself lonely and abandoned, and his heart to fall to ruin like some deserted mansion, for want of an inhabitant.

These observations call to mind a little domestic story, of which I was once a witness. My intimate friend, Leslie, had married a beautiful and accomplished girl, who had been brought up in the midst of fashionable life. She had, it is true, no fortune, but that of my friend was ample; and he delighted in the anticipation of indulging her in every elegant pursuit, and administering to those delicate tastes and fancies that spread a kind of witchery about the sex. "Her life," said he, "shall be like a fairy tale."

The very difference in their characters produced an harmonious combination: he was of a romantic and somewhat serious cast; she was all life and gladness. I have often noticed the mute rapture with which he would gaze upon her in company, of which her sprightly powers made her the delight; and how, in the midst of applause, her eye would still turn to him, as if there alone she sought favor and acceptance. When leaning on his arm, her slender form contrasted finely with his tall manly person. The fond confiding air with which she looked up to him seemed to call forth a flush of triumphant pride and cherishing tenderness, as if he doted on his lovely burden for its vast helplessness. Never did a couple set forward on the flowery path of early and well-suited marriage with a fairer prospect of felicity.

It was the misfortune of my friend, however, to have embarked his property in large speculations; and he had not been married many months, when, by a succession of sudden disasters, it was swept from him, and he found himself reduced almost to penury. For a time he kept his situation to himself, and went about with a haggard countenance, and a breaking heart. His life was but a protracted agony; and what rendered it more insupportable was the necessity of keeping up a smile in the presence of his wife; for he could not bring himself to overwhelm her with the news. She saw, however, with the quick eyes of affection, that all was not well with him. She marked his altered looks and stifled sighs, and was not to be deceived by his sickly and vapid attempts at cheerfulness. She tasked all her sprightly powers and tender blandishments to win him back to happiness; but she only drove the arrow deeper into his soul. The more he saw cause to love her, the more torturing was the thought that he was soon to make her wretched. A little while, thought he, and the smile will vanish from that cheek—the song will die away from those lips—the lustre of those eyes will be quenched with sorrow; and the happy heart, which now beats lightly in that bosom, will be weighed down like mine, by the cares and miseries of the world.

At length he came to me one day, and related his whole situation in a tone of the deepest despair. When I heard him through I inquired, "Does your wife know all this?"—At the question he burst into an agony of tears. "For God's sake!" cried he, "if you have any pity on me, don't mention my wife; it is the thought of her that drives me almost to madness!"

"And why not?" said I. "She must know it sooner or later: you cannot keep it long from her, and the intelligence may break upon her in a more startling manner, than if imparted by yourself; for the accents of those we love soften the harshest tidings. Besides, you are depriving yourself of the comforts of her sympathy; and not merely that, but also endangering the only bond that can keep hearts together—an unreserved community of thought and feeling. She will soon perceive that something is secretly preying upon your mind; and true love will not brook reserve; it feels undervalued and outraged, when even the sorrows of those it loves are concealed from it."

"Oh, but, my friend! to think what a blow I am to give to all her future prospects—how I am to strike her very soul to the earth, by telling her that her husband is a beggar! that she is to forego all the elegancies of life—all the pleasures of society—to shrink with me into indigence and obscurity! To tell her that I have dragged her down from the sphere in which she might have continued to move in constant brightness—the light of every eye—the admiration of every heart!—How can she bear poverty? she has been brought up in all the refinements of opulence. How can she bear neglect? she has been the idol of society. Oh! it will break her heart—it will break her heart!"

I saw his grief was eloquent, and I let it have its flow; for sorrow relieves itself by words. When his paroxysm had subsided, and he had relapsed into moody silence, I resumed the subject gently, and urged him to break his situation at once to his wife. He shook his head mournfully, but positively.

"But how are you to keep it from her? It is necessary she should know it, that you may take the steps proper to the alteration of your circumstances. You must change your style of living——nay," observing a pang to pass across his countenance, "don't let that afflict you. I am sure you have never placed your happiness in outward show—you have yet friends, warm friends, who will not think the worse of you for being less splendidly lodged: and surely it does not require a palace to be happy with Mary——"

"I could be happy with her," cried he, convulsively, "in a hovel!—I could go down with her into poverty and the dust!—I could—I could—God bless her!—God bless her!" cried he, bursting into a transport of grief and tenderness.

"And believe me, my friend," said I, stepping up, and grasping him warmly by the hand, "believe me she can be the same with you. Ay, more: it will be a source of pride and triumph to her—it will call forth all the latent energies and fervent sympathies of her nature; for she will rejoice to prove that she loves you for yourself. There is in every true woman's heart a spark of heavenly fire, which lies dormant in the broad daylight of prosperity; but which kindles up, and beams and blazes in the dark hour of adversity. No man knows what the wife of his bosom is—no man knows what a ministering angel she is—until he has gone with her through the fiery trials of this world."

There was something in the earnestness of my manner, and the figurative style of my language, that caught the excited imagination of Leslie. I knew the auditor I had to deal with; and following up the impression I had made, I finished by persuading him to go home and unburden his sad heart to his wife.

I must confess, notwithstanding all I had said, I felt some little solicitude for the result. Who can calculate on the fortitude of one whose life has been a round of pleasures? Her gay spirits might revolt at the dark downward path of low humility suddenly pointed out before her, and might cling to the sunny regions in which they had hitherto revelled. Besides, ruin in fashionable life is accompanied by so many galling mortifications, to which in other ranks it is a stranger. In short, I could not meet Leslie the next morning without trepidation. He had made the disclosure.

"And how did she bear it?"

"Like an angel! It seemed rather to be a relief to her mind, for she threw her arms round my neck, and asked if this was all that had lately made me unhappy. But, poor girl," he added, "she cannot realize the change we must undergo. She has no idea of poverty but in the abstract; she has only read of it in poetry, where it is allied to love. She feels as yet no privation; she suffers no loss of accustomed conveniencies nor elegancies.

When we come practically to experience its sordid cares, its paltry wants, its petty humiliations—then will be the real trial."

"But," said I, "now that you have got over the severest task, that of breaking it to her, the sooner you let the world into the secret the better. The disclosure may be mortifying; but then it is a single misery, and soon over: whereas you otherwise suffer it, in anticipation, every hour in the day. It is not poverty so much as pretense, that harasses a ruined man—the struggle between a proud mind and an empty purse—the keeping up a hollow show that must soon come to an end. Have the courage to appear poor and you disarm poverty of its sharpest sting." On this point I found Leslie perfectly prepared. He had no false pride himself, and as to his wife, she was only anxious to conform to their altered fortunes.

Some days afterward he called upon me in the evening. He had disposed of his dwelling house, and taken a small cottage in the country, a few miles from town. He had been busied all day in sending out furniture. The new establishment required few articles, and those of the simplest kind. All the splendid furniture of his late residence had been sold, excepting his wife's harp. That, he said, was too closely associated with the idea of herself; it belonged to the little story of their loves; for some of the sweetest moments of their courtship were those when he had leaned over that instrument, and listened to the melting tones of her voice. I could not but smile at this instance of romantic gallantry in a doting husband.

He was now going out to the cottage, where his wife had been all day superintending its arrangement. My feelings had become strongly interested in the progress of this family story, and, as it was a fine evening, I offered to accompany him.

He was wearied with the fatigues of the day, and, as he walked out, fell into a fit of gloomy musing.

"Poor Mary!" at length broke, with a heavy sigh, from his lips.

"And what of her?" asked I, "has any thing happened to her?"

"What," said he, darting an impatient glance, "is it nothing to be reduced to this paltry situation—to be caged in a miserable cottage—to be obliged to toil amost in the menial concerns of her wretched habitation?"

"Has she then repined at the change?"

"Repined! she has been nothing but sweetness and good humor. Indeed, she seems in better spirits than I have ever known her; she has been to me all love, and tenderness, and comfort!"

"Admirable girl!" exclaimed I. "You call yourself poor, my friend; you never were so rich—you never knew the boundless treasures of excellence you possess in that woman."

"Oh! but, my friend, if this first meeting at the cottage were over, I think I could then be comfortable. But this is her first day of real experience; she has been introduced into a humble dwelling—she has been employed all day in arranging its miserable equipments—she has, for the first time, known the fatigues of domestic employment—she has, for the first time, looked round her on a home destitute of every thing elegant,—almost of every thing convenient; and may now be sitting down, exhausted and spiritless, brooding over a prospect of future poverty."

There was a degree of probability in this picture that I could not gainsay, so we walked on in silence.

After turning from the main road up a narrow lane,

so thickly shaded with forest trees as to give it a complete air of seclusion, we came in sight of the cottage. It was humble enough in its appearance for the most pastoral poet; and yet it had a pleasing rural look. A wild vine had overrun one end with a profusion of foliage; a few trees threw their branches gracefully over it; and I observed several pots of flowers tastefully disposed about the door, and on the grassplot in front. A small wicket gate opened upon a footpath that wound through some shrubbery to the door. Just as we approached, we heard the sound of music—Leslie grasped my arm; we paused and listened. It was Mary's voice singing, in a style of the most touching simplicity, a little air of which her husband was peculiarly fond.

I felt Leslie's hand tremble on my arm. He stepped forward to hear more distinctly. His step made a noise on the gravel walk. A bright beautiful face glanced out at the window and vanished—a light footstep was heard—and Mary came tripping forth to meet us: she was in a pretty rural dress of white; a few wild flowers were twisted in her fine hair; a fresh bloom was on her cheek; her whole countenance beamed with smiles—I had never seen her look so lovely.

"My dear George," cried she, "I am go glad you are come! I have been watching and watching for you; and running down the lane, and looking out for you. I've set out a table under a beautiful tree behind the cottage; and I've been gathering some of the most delicious strawberries, for I know you are fond of them—and we have such excellent cream—and every thing is so sweet and still here—Oh!" said she, putting her arm within his, and looking up brightly in his face, "Oh, we shall be so happy!"

Poor Leslie was overcome. He caught her to his bosom—he folded his arms round her—he kissed her again and again—he could not speak, but the tears gushed into his eyes; and he has often assured me, that though the world has since gone prosperously with him, and his life has, indeed, been a happy one, yet never has he experienced a moment of more exquisite felicity.

RIP VAN WINKLE

A POSTHUMOUS WRITING OF DIEDRICH KNICKERBOCKER

By Woden, God of Saxons,
From whence comes Wensday, that is Wodensday.
Truth is a thing that ever I will keep
Unto thylke day in which I creep into
My sepulchre——

CARTWRIGHT

[The following Tale was found among the papers of the late Diedrich Knickerbocker, an old gentleman of New York, who was very curious in the Dutch history of the province, and the manners of the descendants from its primitive settlers. His historical researches, however, did not lie so much among books as among men; for the former are lamentably scanty on his favorite topics; whereas he found the old burghers, and still more their wives, rich in that legendary lore, so invaluable to true history. Whenever, therefore, he happened upon a genuine Dutch family, snugly shut up in its low-roofed farmhouse, under a spreading sycamore, he looked upon it as a little clasped volume of black-letter, and studied it with the zeal of a book-worm.

The result of all these researches was a history of the province during the reign of the Dutch governors, which he published some years since. There have been various opinions as to the literary character of his work, and, to tell the truth, it is not a whit better than it should be. Its chief merit is its scrupulous accuracy, which indeed was a little questioned on its first appearance, but has since been completely established; and it is now admitted into all historical collections, as a book of unquestionable authority.

The old gentleman died shortly after the publication of his work, and now that he is dead and gone, it cannot do much harm to his memory to say that his time might have been much better employed in weightier labors. He, however, was apt to ride his hobby his own way; and though it did now and then kick up the dust a little in the eyes of his neighbors, and grieve the spirit of some friends, for whom he felt the truest deference and affection; yet his errors and follies are remembered "more in sorrow than in anger," and it begins to be suspected, that he never intended to injure or offend. But however his memory may be appreciated by critics, it is still held dear by many folk, whose good opinion is well worth having; particularly by certain biscuitbakers, who have gone so far as to imprint his likeness on their new-year cakes; and have thus given him a chance for immortality, almost equal to being stamped on a Waterloo Medal, or a Queen Anne's Farthing.]

WHOEVER has made a voyage up the Hudson must remember the Kaatskill mountains. They are a dismembered branch of the great Appalachian family, and are seen away to the west of the river, swelling up to a noble height, and lording it over the surrounding country. Every change of season, every change of weather, indeed, every hour of the day, produces some change in the magical hues and shapes of these mountains, and they are regarded by all the good wives, far and near, as perfect barometers. When the weather is fair and settled, they are clothed in blue and purple, and print their bold outlines on the clear evening sky; but, sometimes, when the rest of the landscape is cloudless, they will gáther a hood of gray vapors about their summits, which, in the last rays of the setting sun, will glow and light up like a crown of glory.

At the foot of these fairy mountains, the voyager may have descried the light smoke curling up from a village, whose shingle-roofs gleam among the trees, just where the blue tints of the upland melt away into the fresh green of the nearer landscape. It is a little village, of great antiquity, having been founded by some of the Dutch colonists, in the early times of the province, just about the beginning of the government of the good Peter Stuyvesant, (may he rest in peace!) and there were some of the houses of the original settlers standing within a few years, built of small yellow bricks brought from Holland, having latticed windows and gable fronts, surmounted with weather-cocks.

In that same village, and in one of these very houses (which, to tell the precise truth, was sadly time-worn and weather-beaten), there lived many years since, while the country was yet a province of Great Britain, a simple good-natured fellow, of the name of Rip Van Winkle. He was a descendant of the Van Winkles who figured so gallantly in the chivalrous days of Peter Stuyvesant, and accompanied him to the siege of Fort Christina. He inherited, however, but little of the martial character of his ancestors. I have observed that he was a simple good-natured man; he was, moreover, a kind neighbor, and an obedient, hen-pecked husband. Indeed, to the latter circumstance might be owing that meekness of spirit which gained him such universal popularity; for those men are most apt to be obsequious and conciliating abroad, who are under the discipline of shrews at home. Their tempers, doubtless, are rendered pliant and malleable in the fiery furnace of domestic tribulation;

and a curtain lecture is worth all the sermons in the world for teaching the virtues of patience and long-suffering. A termigant wife may, therefore, in some respects, be considered a tolerable blessing; and if so, Rip Van Winkle was thrice blessed.

Certain it is, that he was a great favorite among all the good wives of the village, who, as usual, with the amiable sex, took his part in all family squabbles; and never failed, whenever they talked those matters over in their evening gossipings, to lay all the blame on Dame Van Winkle. The children of the village, too, would shout with joy whenever he approached. He assisted at their sports, made their playthings, taught them to fly kites and shoot marbles, and told them long stories of ghosts, witches, and Indians. Whenever he went dodging about the village, he was surrounded by a troop of them, hanging on his skirts, clambering on his back, and playing a thousand tricks on him with impunity; and not a dog would bark at him throughout the neighborhood.

The great error in Rip's composition was an insuperable aversion to all kinds of profitable labor. It could not be from the want of assiduity or perseverance; for he would sit on a wet rock, with a rod as long and heavy as a Tartar's lance, and fish all day without a murmur, even though he should not be encouraged by a single nibble. He would carry a fowling-piece on his shoulder for hours together, trudging through woods and swamps, and up hill and down dale, to shoot a few squirrels or wild pigeons. He would never refuse to assist a neighbor even in the roughest toil, and was a foremost man at all country frolics for husking Indian corn, or building stone-fences; the women of the village, too, used to employ him to run their errands, and to do such little odd jobs as their less obliging husbands would not do for them. In a word Rip was ready to attend to anybody's business but his own; but as to doing family duty, and keeping his farm in order, he found it impossible.

In fact, he declared it was of no use to work on his farm; it was the most pestilent little piece of ground in the whole country; everything about it went wrong, and would go wrong, in spite of him. His fences were continually falling to pieces; his cow would either go astray, or get among the cabbages; weeds were sure to grow quicker in his fields than anywhere else; the rain always made a point of setting in just as he had some out-door work to do; so that though his patrimonial estate had dwindled away under his management, acre by acre, until there was little more left than a mere patch of Indian corn and potatoes, yet it was the worst conditioned farm in the neighborhood.

His children, too, were as ragged and wild as if they belonged to nobody. His son Rip, an urchin begotten in his own likeness, promised to inherit the habits, with the old clothes of his father. He was generally seen trooping like a colt at his mother's heels, equipped in a pair of his father's cast-off galligaskins, which he had much ado to hold up with one hand, as a fine lady does her train in bad weather.

Rip Van Winkle, however, was one of those happy mortals, of foolish, well-oiled dispositions, who take the world easy, eat white bread or brown, whichever can be got with least thought or trouble, and would rather starve on a penny than work for a pound. If left to himself, he would have whistled life away in perfect contentment; but his wife kept continually dinning in his ears about his idleness, his carelessness, and the ruin he was bringing on his family. Morning, noon, and night, her tongue was incessantly going, and every thing he said or did was sure to produce a torrent of household eloquence. Rip had but one way of replying to all lectures of the kind, and that, by frequent use, had grown into a habit. He shrugged his shoulders, shook his head, cast up his eyes, but said nothing. This, however, always provoked a fresh volley from his wife; so that he was fain to draw off his forces, and take to the outside of the house—the only side which, in truth, belongs to a hen-pecked husband.

Rip's sole domestic adherent was his dog Wolf, who was as much hen-pecked as his master; for Dame Van Winkle regarded them as companions in idleness, and even looked upon Wolf with an evil eye, as the cause of his master's going so often astray. True it is, in all points of spirit befitting an honorable dog, he was as courageous an animal as ever scoured the woods—but what courage can withstand the ever-during and all-besetting terrors of a woman's tongue! The moment Wolf entered the house his crest fell, his tail drooped to the ground, or curled between his legs, he sneaked about with a gallows air, casting many a sidelong glance at Dame Van Winkle, and at the least flourish of a broomstick or ladle, he would fly to the door with yelping precipitation.

Times grew worse and worse with Rip Van Winkle as years of matrimony rolled on; a tart temper never mellows with age, and a sharp tongue is the only edged tool that grows keener with constant use. For a long while he used to console himself, when driven from home, by frequenting a kind of perpetual club of the sages, philosophers, and other idle personages of the village; which held its sessions on a bench before a small inn, designated by a rubicund portrait of His Majesty George the Third. Here they used to sit in the shade through a long lazy summer's day, talking listlessly over village gossip, or telling endless sleepy stories about nothing. But it would have been worth any statesman's money to have heard the profound discussions that sometimes took place, when by chance an old newspaper fell into their hands from some passing traveller. How solemnly they would listen to the contents, as drawled out by Derrick Van Bummel, the schoolmaster, a dapper learned little man, who was not to be daunted by the most gigantic word in the dictionary; and how sagely they would deliberate upon public events some months after they had taken place.

The opinions of this junto were completely controlled by Nicholas Vedder, a patriarch of the village, and landlord of the inn, at the door of which he took his seat from morning till night, just moving sufficiently to avoid the sun and keep in the shade of a large tree; so that the neighbors could tell the hour by his movements as accurately as by a sun-dial. It is true he was rarely heard to speak, but smoked his pipe incessantly. His adherents, however (for every great man has his adherents), perfectly understood him, and knew how to gather his opinions. When any thing that was read or related displeased him, he was observed to smoke his pipe vehemently, and to send forth short, frequent and angry puffs; but when pleased, he would inhale the smoke slowly and tranquilly, and emit it in light and placid clouds; and sometimes, taking the pipe from his mouth, and letting the fragrant vapor curl about his nose, would gravely nod his head in token of perfect approbation.

From even this stronghold the unlucky Rip was at length routed by his termagant wife, who would suddenly break in upon the tranquillity of the assemblage and call the members all to naught; nor was that august personage, Nicholas Vedder himself, sacred from the daring tongue of this terrible virago, who charged him outright with encouraging her husband in habits of idleness.

Poor Rip was at last reduced almost to despair; and his

only alternative, to escape from the labor of the farm and clamor of his wife, was to take gun in hand and stroll away into the woods. Here he would sometimes seat himself at the foot of a tree, and share the contents of his wallet with Wolf, with whom he sympathized as a fellow-sufferer in persecution. "Poor Wolf," he would say, "thy mistress leads thee a dog's life of it; but never mind, my lad, whilst I live thou shalt never want a friend to stand by thee!" Wolf would wag his tail, look wistfully in his master's face, and if dogs can feel pity I verily believe he reciprocated the sentiment with all his heart.

In a long ramble of the kind on a fine autumnal day, Rip had unconsciously scrambled to one of the highest parts of the Kaatskill mountains. He was after his favorite sport of squirrel shooting, and the still solitudes had echoed and reechoed with the reports of his gun. Panting and fatigued, he threw himself, late in the afternoon, on a green knoll, covered with mountain herbage, that crowned the brow of a precipice. From an opening between the trees he could overlook all the lower country for many a mile of rich woodland. He saw at a distance the lordly Hudson, far, far below him, moving on its silent but majestic course, with the reflection of a purple cloud, or the sail of a lagging bark, here and there sleeping on its glassy bosom, and at last losing itself in the blue highlands.

On the other side he looked down into a deep mountain glen, wild, lonely, and shagged, the bottom filled with fragments from the impending cliffs, and scarcely lighted by the reflected rays of the setting sun. For some time Rip lay musing on this scene; evening was gradually advancing; the mountains began to throw their long blue shadows over the valleys; he saw that it would be dark long before he could reach the village, and he heaved a heavy sigh when he thought of encountering the terrors of Dame Van Winkle.

As he was about to descend, he heard a voice from a distance, hallooing, "Rip Van Winkle! Rip Van Winkle!" He looked round, but could see nothing but a crow winging its solitary flight across the mountain. He thought his fancy must have deceived him, and turned again to descend, when he heard the same cry ring through the still evening air; "Rip Van Winkle! Rip Van Winkle!"—at the same time Wolf bristled up his back, and giving a low growl, skulked to his master's side, looking fearfully down into the glen. Rip now felt a vague apprehension stealing over him; he looked anxiously in the same direction, and perceived a strange figure slowly toiling up the rocks, and bending under the weight of something he carried on his back. He was surprised to see any human being in this lonely and unfrequented place, but supposing it to be some one of the neighborhood in need of his assistance, he hastened down to yield it.

On nearer approach he was still more surprised at the singularity of the stranger's appearance. He was a short, square-built old fellow, with thick bushy hair, and a grizzled beard. His dress was of the antique Dutch fashion—a cloth jerkin strapped round the waist— several pair of breeches, the outer one of ample volume, decorated with rows of buttons down the sides, and bunches at the knees. He bore on his shoulder a stout keg, that seemed full of liquor, and made signs for Rip to approach and assist him with the load. Though rather shy and distrustful of this new acquaintance, Rip complied with his usual alacrity; and mutually relieving one another, they clambered up a narrow gully, apparently the dry bed of a mountain torrent. As they ascended, Rip every now and then heard long rolling peals, like distant thunder, that seemed to issue out of a deep ravine, or rather cleft, between lofty rocks, toward which their rugged path conducted. He paused for an instant, but supposing it to be the muttering of one of those transient thunder-showers which often take place in mountain heights, he proceeded. Passing through the ravine, they came to a hollow, like a small amphitheatre, surrounded by perpendicular precipices, over the brinks of which impending trees shot their branches, so that you only caught glimpses of the azure sky and the bright evening cloud. During the whole time Rip and his companion had labored on in silence; for though the former marvelled greatly what could be the object of carrying a keg of liquor up this wild mountain, yet there was something strange and incomprehensible about the unknown, that inspired awe and checked familiarity.

On entering the amphitheatre, new objects of wonder presented themselves. On a level spot in the centre was a company of odd-looking personages playing at nine-pins. They were dressed in a quaint outlandish fashion; some wore short doubtlets, others jerkins, with long knives in their belts, and most of them had enormous breeches, of similar style with that of the guide's. Their visages, too, were peculiar: one had a large beard, broad face, and small piggish eyes: the face of another seemed to consist entirely of nose, and was surmounted by a white sugar-loaf hat, set off with a little red cock's tail. They all had beards, of various shapes and colors. There was one who seemed to be the commander. He was a stout old gentleman, with a weather-beaten countenance; he wore a laced doublet, broad belt and hanger, high crowned hat and feather, red stockings, and high-heeled shoes, with roses in them. The whole group reminded Rip of the figures in an old Flemish painting, in the parlor of Dominie Van Shaick, the village parson, and which had been brought over from Holland at the time of the settlement.

What seemed particularly odd to Rip was, that though these folks were evidently amusing themselves, yet they maintained the gravest faces, the most mysterious silence, and were, withal, the most melancholy party of pleasure he had ever witnessed. Nothing interrupted the stillness of the scene but the noise of the balls, which, whenever they were rolled, echoed along the mountains like rumblng peals of thunder.

As Rip and his companion approached them, they suddenly desisted from their play, and stared at him with such fixed statue-like gaze, and such strange, uncouth, lack-lustre countenances, that his heart turned within him, and his knees smote together. His companion now emptied the contents of the keg into large flagons, and made signs to him to wait upon the company. He obeyed with fear and trembling; they quaffed the liquor in profound silence, and then returned to their game.

By degrees Rip's awe and apprehension subsided. He even ventured, when no eye was fixed upon him, to taste the beverage, which he found had much of the flavor of excellent Hollands. He was naturally a thirsty soul, and was soon tempted to repeat the draught. One taste provoked another; and he reiterated his visits to the flagon so often that at length his senses were overpowered, his eyes swam in his head, his head gradually declined, and he fell into a deep sleep.

On waking, he found himself on the green knoll whence he had first seen the old man of the glen. He rubbed his eyes—it was a bright sunny morning. The birds were hopping and twittering among the bushes, and the eagle was wheeling aloft, and breasting the pure mountain breeze. "Surely," thought Rip, "I have not slept here all night." He recalled the occurrences before he fell asleep. The strange man with a keg of liquor—the mountain ravine—the wild retreat among the rocks—the wobegone party at nine-pins—the flagon—"Oh! that flagon! that wicked flagon!" thought Rip—"what excuse shall I make to Dame Van Winkle!"

He looked round for his gun, but in place of the clean well-oiled fowling-piece, he found an old firelock lying by him, the barrel incrusted with rust, the lock falling off, and the stock worm-eaten. He now suspected that the grave roysters of the mountain had put a trick upon him, and, having dosed him with liquor, had robbed him of his gun. Wolf, too, had disappeared, but he might have strayed away after a squirrel or partridge. He whistled after him and shouted his name, but all in vain; the echoes repeated his whistle and shout, but no dog was to be seen.

He determined to revisit the scene of the last evening's gambol, and if he met with any of the party, to demand his dog and gun. As he rose to walk, he found himself stiff in the joints, and wanting in his usual activity. "These mountain beds do not agree with me," thought Rip, "and if this frolic should lay me up with a fit of the rheumatism, I shall have a blessed time with Dame Van Winkle." With some difficulty he got down into the glen: he found the gully up which he and his companion had ascended the preceding evening; but to his astonishment a mountain stream was now foaming down it, leaping from rock to rock, and filling the glen with babbling murmurs. He, however, made shift to scramble up its sides, working his toilsome way through thickets of birch, sassafras, and witch-hazel, and sometimes tripped up or entangled by the wild grapevines that twisted their coils or tendrils from tree to tree, and spread a kind of network in his path.

At length he reached to where the ravine had opened through the cliffs to the amphitheatre; but no traces of such opening remained. The rocks presented a high impenetrable wall over which the torrent came tumbling in a sheet of feathery foam, and fell into a broad deep basin, black from the shadows of the surrounding forest. Here, then, poor Rip was brought to a stand. He again called and whistled after his dog; he was only answered by the cawing of a flock of idle crows, sporting high in the air about a dry tree that overhung a sunny precipice: and who, secure in their elevation, seemed to look down and scoff at the poor man's perplexities. What was to be done? the morning was passing away, and Rip felt famished for want of his breakfast. He grieved to give up his dog and gun; he dreaded to meet his wife; but it would not do to starve among the mountains. He shook his head, shouldered the rusty firelock, and, with a heart full of trouble and anxiety, turned his steps homeward.

As he approached the village he met a number of people, but none whom he knew, which somewhat surprised him, for he had thought himself acquainted with every one in the country round. Their dress, too, was of a different fashion from that to which he was accustomed. They all stared at him with equal marks of surprise, and whenever they cast their eyes upon him, invariably stroked their chins. The constant recurrence of this gesture induced Rip, involuntarily, to do the same, when, to his astonishment, he found his beard had grown a foot long!

He had now entered the skirts of the village. A troop of strange children ran at his heels, hooting after him, and pointing at his gray beard. The dogs, too, not one of which he recognized for an old acquaintance, barked at him as he passed. The very village was altered; it was larger and more populous. There were rows of houses which he had never seen before, and those which had been his familiar haunts had disappeared. Strange names were over the doors—strange faces at the windows—every thing was strange. His mind now misgave him; he began to doubt whether both he and the world around him were not bewitched. Surely this was his native village, which he had left but the day before. There stood the Kaatskill mountains—there ran the silver Hudson at a distance—there was every hill and dale precisely as it had always been—Rip was sorely perplexed—"That flagon last night," thought he, "has addled my poor head sadly!"

It was with some difficulty that he found the way to his own house, which he approached with silent awe, expecting every moment to hear the shrill voice of Dame Van Winkle. He found the house gone to decay—the roof fallen in, the windows shattered, and the doors off the hinges. A half-starved dog that looked like Wolf was skulking about it. Rip called him by name, but the cur snarled, showed his teeth, and passed on. This was an unkind cut indeed—"My very dog," sighed poor Rip, "has forgotten me!"

He entered the house, which, to tell the truth, Dame Van Winkle had always kept in neat order. It was empty, forlorn, and apparently abandoned. This desolateness overcame all his connubial fears—he called loudly for his wife and children—the lonely chambers rang for a moment with his voice, and then all again was silence.

He now hurried forth, and hastened to his old resort, the village inn—but it too was gone. A large rickety wooden building stood in its place, with great gaping windows, some of them broken and mended with old hats and petticoats, and over the door was painted, "the Union Hotel, by Jonathan Doolittle." Instead of the great tree that used to shelter the quiet little Dutch inn of yore, there now was reared a tall naked pole, with something on the top that looked like a red night-cap, and from it was fluttering a flag, on which was a singular assemblage of stars and stripes—all this was strange and incomprehensible. He recognized on the sign, however, the ruby face of King George, under which he had smoked so many a peaceful pipe; but even this was singularly metamorphosed. The red coat was changed for one of blue and buff, a sword was held in the hand instead of a sceptre, the head was decorated with a cocked hat, and underneath was painted in large characters, GENERAL WASHINGTON.

There was, as usual, a crowd of folk about the door, but none that Rip recollected. The very character of the people seemed changed. There was a busy, bustling disputatious tone about it, instead of the accustomed phlegm and drowsy tranquillity. He looked in vain for the sage Nicholas Vedder, with his broad face, double chin, and fair long pipe, uttering clouds of tobacco-smoke instead of idle speeches; or Van Bummel, the schoolmaster, doling forth the contents of an ancient newspaper. In place of these, a lean, bilious-looking fellow, with his pockets full of handbills, was haranguing vehemently about rights of citizens—elections—members of congress—liberty—Bunker's Hill—heroes of seventy-six—and other words, which were a perfect Babylonish jargon to the bewildered Van Winkle.

The appearance of Rip, with his long grizzled beard, his rusty fowling-piece, his uncouth dress, and an army of women and children at his heels, soon attracted the attention of the tavern politicians. They crowded round him, eyeing him from head to foot with great curiosity. The orator bustled up to him, and, drawing him partly aside, inquired "on which side he voted?" Rip stared in vacant stupidity. Another short but busy little fellow pulled him by the arm, and, rising on tiptoe, inquired in his ear, "Whether he was Federal or Democrat?" Rip was equally at a loss to comprehend the question; when a knowing, self-important old gentleman, in a sharp cocked hat, made his way through the crowd, putting them to the right and left with his elbows as he passed, and planting himself before Van Winkle, with one arm akimbo, the other resting on his cane, his keen eyes and sharp hat penetrating, as it were, into his very soul, demanded in an austere tone, "what brought him to the election with a gun on his shoulder, and a mob at his heels, and whether he meant to breed a riot in the village?"—"Alas! gentlemen," cried Rip, somewhat dismayed, "I am a poor quiet man, a native of the place, and a loyal subject of the king, God bless him!"

Here a general shout burst from the by-standers—"A tory! a tory! a spy! a refugee! hustle him! away with him!" It was with great difficulty that the self-important man in the cocked hat restored order; and, having assumed a tenfold austerity of brow, demanded again of the unknown culprit, what he came there for, and whom he was seeking? The poor man humbly assured him that he meant no harm, but merely came there in search of some of his neighbors, who used to keep about the tavern.

"Well—who are they?—name them."

Rip bethought himself a moment, and inquired, "Where's Nicholas Vedder?"

There was a silence for a little while, when an old man replied, in a thin piping voice, "Nicholas Vedder! why, he is dead and gone these eighteen years! There was a wooden tombstone in the church-yard that used to tell all about him, but that's rotten and gone too."

"Where's Brom Dutcher?"

"Oh, he went off to the army in the beginning of the war; some say he was killed at the storming of Stony Point—others say he was drowned in a squall at the foot of Anthony's Nose. I don't know—he never came back again."

"Where's Van Bummel, the schoolmaster?"

"He went off to the wars too, was a great militia general, and is now in congress."

Rip's heart died away at hearing of these sad changes in his home and friends, and finding himself thus alone in the world. Every answer puzzled him too, by treating of such enormous lapses of time, and of matters which he could not understand: war—congress—Stony Point;—he had no courage to ask after any more friends, but cried out in despair, "Does nobody here know Rip Van Winkle?"

"Oh, Rip Van Winkle!" exclaimed two or three, "Oh, to be sure! that's Rip Van Winkle yonder, leaning against the tree."

Rip looked, and beheld a precise counterpart of himself, as he went up the mountain: apparently as lazy, and certainly as ragged. The poor fellow was now completely confounded. He doubted his own identity, and whether he was himself or another man. In the midst of his bewilderment, the man in the cocked hat demanded who he was, and what was his name?

"God knows," exclaimed he, at his wit's end; "I'm not myself—I'm somebody else—that's me yonder—no—that's somebody else got into my shoes—I was myself last night, but I fell asleep on the mountain, and they've changed my gun, and every thing's changed, and I'm changed, and I can't tell what's my name, or who I am!"

The by-standers began now to look at each other, nod, wink significantly, and tap their fingers against their foreheads. There was a whisper, also, about securing the gun, and keeping the old fellow from doing mischief, at the very suggestion of which the self-important man in the cocked hat retired with some precipitation. At this critical moment a fresh comely woman pressed through the throng to get a peep at the gray-bearded man. She had a chubby child in her arms, which, frightened at his looks, began to cry. "Hush, Rip," cried she, "hush, you little fool; the old man won't hurt you." The name of the child, the air of the mother, the tone of her voice, all awakened a train of recollections in his mind. "What is your name, my good woman?" asked he.

"Judith Gardenier."

"And your father's name?"

"Ah, poor man, Rip Van Winkle was his name, but it's twenty years since he went away from home with his gun, and never has been heard of since—his dog came home without him; but whether he shot himself, or was carried away by the Indians, nobody can tell. I was then but a little girl."

Rip had but one question more to ask; but he put it with a faltering voice:

"Where's your mother?"

"Oh, she too had died but a short time since; she broke a blood-vessel in a fit of passion at a New-England peddler."

There was a drop of comfort, at least, in this intelligence. The honest man could contain himself no longer. He caught his daughter and her child in his arms. "I am your father!" cried he—"Young Rip Van Winkle once—old Rip Van Winkle now!—Does nobody know poor Rip Van Winkle?"

All stood amazed, until an old woman, tottering out from among the crowd, put her hand to her brow, and peering under it in his face for a moment, exclaimed, "Sure enough! it is Rip Van Winkle—it is himself!

Welcome home again, old neighbor—Why, where have you been these twenty long years?"

Rip's story was soon told, for the whole twenty years had been to him but as one night. The neighbors stared when they heard it; some were seen to wink at each other, and put their tongues in their cheeks: and the self-important man in the cocked hat, who, when the alarm was over, had returned to the field, screwed down the corners of his mouth, and shook his head—upon which there was a general shaking of the head throughout the assemblage.

It was determined, however, to take the opinion of old Peter Vanderdonk, who was seen slowly advancing up the road. He was a descendant of the historian of that name, who wrote one of the earliest accounts of the province. Peter was the most ancient inhabitant of the village, and well versed in all the wonderful events and traditions of the neighborhood. He recollected Rip at once, and corroborated his story in the most satisfactory manner. He assured the company that it was a fact, handed down from his ancestor the historian, that the Kaatskill mountains had always been haunted by strange beings. That it was affirmed that the great Hendrick Hudson, the first discoverer of the river and country, kept a kind of vigil there every twenty years, with his crew of the *Half-moon*; being permitted in this way to revisit the scenes of his enterprise, and keep a guardian eye upon the river, and the great city called by his name. That his father had once seen them in their old Dutch dresses playing at nine-pins in a hollow of the mountain; and that he himself had heard, one summer afternoon, the sound of their balls, like distant peals of thunder.

To make a long story short, the company broke up, and returned to the more important concerns of the election. Rip's daughter took him home to live with her;

she had a snug, well-furnished house, and a stout cheery farmer for a husband, whom Rip recollected for one of the urchins that used to climb upon his back. As to Rip's son and heir, who was the ditto of himself, seen leaning against the tree, he was employed to work on the farm; but evinced an hereditary disposition to attend to any thing else but his business.

Rip now resumed his old walks and habits; he soon found many of his former cronies, though all rather the worse for the wear and tear of time; and preferred making friends among the rising generation, with whom he soon grew into great favor.

Having nothing to do at home, and being arrived at that happy age when a man can be idle with impunity, he took his place once more on the bench at the inn door, and was reverenced as one of the patriarchs of the village, and a chronicle of the old times "before the war." It was some time before he could get into the regular track of gossip, or could be made to comprehend the strange events that had taken place during his torpor. How that there had been a revolutionary war—that the country had thrown off the yoke of old England—and that, instead of being a subject of his Majesty George the Third, he was now a free citizen of the United States. Rip, in fact, was no politician; the changes of states and empires made but little impression on him; but there was one species of despotism under which he had long groaned, and that was—petticoat government. Happily that was at an end; he had got his neck out of the yoke of matrimony, and could go in and out whenever he pleased, without dreading the tyranny of Dame Van Winkle. Whenever her name was mentioned, however, he shook his head, shrugged his shoulders, and cast up his eyes; which might pass either for an expression of resignation to his fate, or joy at his deliverance.

He used to tell his story to every stranger that arrived at Mr. Doolittle's hotel. He was observed, at first, to vary on some points every time he told it, which was, doubtless, owing to his having so recently awaked. It at last settled down precisely to the tale I have related, and not a man, woman, or child in the neighborhood, but knew it by heart. Some always pretended to doubt the reality of it, and insisted that Rip had been out of his head, and that this was one point on which he always remained flighty. The old Dutch inhabitants, however, almost universally gave it full credit. Even to this day they never hear a thunderstorm of a summer afternoon about the Kaatskill, but they say Hendrick Hudson and his crew are at their game of nine-pins; and it is a common wish of all henpecked husbands in the neighborhood, when life hangs heavy on their hands, that they might have a quieting draught out of Rip Van Winkle's flagon.

NOTE

The foregoing Tale, one would suspect, had been suggested to Mr. Knickerbocker by a little German superstition about the Emperor Frederick *der Rothbart*, and the Kypphaüser mountain: the subjoined note, however, which he had appended to the tale, shows that it is an absolute fact, narrated with his usual fidelity:

"The story of Rip Van Winkle may seem incredible to many, but nevertheless I give it my full belief, for I know the vicinity of our old Dutch settlements to have been very subject to marvellous events and appearances. Indeed, I have heard many stranger stories than this, in the villages along the Hudson; all of which were too well authenticated to admit of a doubt. I have even talked with Rip Van Winkle myself, who, when last I saw him, was a very venerable old man, and so perfectly rational and consistent on every other point, that I think no conscientious person could refuse to take this into the bargain; nay, I have seen a certificate on the subject taken before a country justice and signed with a cross, in the justice's own handwriting. The story, therefore, is beyond the possibility of doubt.

D. K."

POSTSCRIPT

The following are travelling notes from a memorandum-book of Mr. Knickerbocker:

The Kaatsberg, or Catskill Mountains, have always been a region full of fable. The Indians considered them the abode of spirits, who influenced the weather, spreading sunshine or clouds over the landscape, and sending good or bad hunting seasons. They were ruled by an old squaw spirit, said to be their mother. She dwelt on the highest peak of the Catskills, and had charge of the doors of day and night to open and shut them at the proper hour. She hung up the new moons in the skies, and cut up the old ones into stars. In times of drought, if properly propitiated, she would spin light summer clouds out of cobwebs and morning dew, and send them off from the crest of the mountain, flake after flake, like flakes of carded cotton, to float in the air; until, dissolved by the heat of the sun, they would fall in gentle showers, causing the grass to spring, the fruits to ripen, and the corn to grow an inch an hour. If displeased, however, she would brew up clouds black as ink, sitting in the midst of them like a bottle-bellied spider in the midst of its web; and when these clouds broke, wo betide the valleys!

In old times, say the Indian traditions, there was a kind of Manitou or Spirit, who kept about the wildest recesses of the Catskill Mountains, and took a mischievous pleasure in wreaking all kinds of evils and vexations upon the red men. Sometimes he would assume the form of a bear, a panther, or a deer, lead the bewildered hunter a weary chase through tangled forests and among ragged rocks; and then spring off with a loud ho! ho! leaving him aghast on the brink of a beetling precipice or raging torrent.

The favorite abode of this Manitou is still shown. It is a great rock or cliff on the loneliest part of the mountains, and, from the flowering vines which clamber about it, and the wild flowers which abound in its neighborhood, is known by the name of the Garden Rock. Near the foot of it is a small lake, the haunt of the solitary bittern, with water-snakes basking in the sun on the leaves of the pond-lilies which lie on the surface. This place was held in great awe by the Indians, insomuch that the boldest hunter would not pursue his game within its precincts.

Once upon a time, however, a hunter who had lost his way, penetrated to the garden rock, where he beheld a number of gourds placed in the crotches of trees. One of these he seized and made off with it, but in the hurry of his retreat he let it fall among the rocks, when a great stream gushed forth, which washed him away and swept him down precipices, where he was dashed to pieces, and the stream made its way to the Hudson, and continues to flow to the present day; being the identical stream known by the name of the Kaaters-kill.

ENGLISH WRITERS ON AMERICA

"Methinks I see in my mind a noble and puissant nation, rousing herself like a strong man after sleep, and shaking her invincible locks: methinks I see her as an eagle, mewing her mighty youth, and kindling her endazzled eyes at the full midday beam."

MILTON ON THE LIBERTY OF THE PRESS

I T IS with feelings of deep regret that I observe the literary animosity daily growing up between England and America. Great curiosity has been awakened of late with respect to the United States, and the London press has teemed with volumes of travels through the Republic; but they seem intended to diffuse error rather than knowledge; and so successful have they been, that, notwithstanding the constant intercourse between the nations, there is no people concerning whom the great mass of the British public have less pure information, or entertain more numerous prejudices.

English travellers are the best and the worst in the world. Where no motives of pride or interest intervene, none can equal them for profound and philosophical views of society, or faithful and graphical descriptions of external objects; but when either the interest or reputation of their own country comes in collision with that of another, they go to the opposite extreme, and forget their usual probity and candor, in the indulgence of splenetic remark, and an illiberal spirit of ridicule.

Hence, their travels are more honest and accurate, the more remote the country described. I would place implicit confidence in an Englishman's descriptions of the regions beyond the cataracts of the Nile; of unknown islands in the Yellow Sea; of the interior of India; or of any other tract which other travellers might be apt to picture out with the illusions of their fancies; but I would cautiously receive his account of his immediate neighbors, and of those nations with which he is in habits of most frequent intercourse. However I might be disposed to trust his probity, I dare not trust his prejudices.

It has also been the peculiar lot of our country to be visited by the worst kind of English travellers. While men of philosophical spirit and cultivated minds have been sent from England to ransack the poles, to penetrate the deserts, and to study the manners and customs of barbarous nations, with which she can have no permanent intercourse of profit or pleasure; it has been left to the broken-down tradesman, the scheming adventurer, the wandering mechanic, the Manchester and Birmingham agent, to be her oracles respecting America. From such sources she is content to receive her information respecting a country in a singular state of moral and physical development; a country in which one of the greatest political experiments in the history of the world is now performing; and which presents the most profound and momentous studies to the statesman and the philosopher.

That such men should give prejudicial accounts of America is not a matter of surprise. The themes it offers for contemplation are too vast and elevated for their capacities. The national character is yet in a state of fermentation; it may have its frothiness and sediment, but its ingredients are sound and wholesome; it has already given proofs of powerful and generous qualities; and the whole promises to settle down into something substantially excellent. But the causes which are operating to strengthen and ennoble it, and its daily indications of admirable properties, are all lost upon these purblind observers; who are only affected by the little asperities incident to its present situation. They are capable of judging only of the surface of things; of those matters which come in contact with their private interests and personal gratifications. They miss some of the snug conveniences and petty comforts which belong to an old, highly-finished, and over-populous state of society; where the ranks of useful labor are crowded, and many earn a painful and servile subsistence by studying the very caprices of appetite and self-indulgence. These minor comforts, however, are all-important in the estimation of narrow minds; which either do not perceive, or will not acknowledge, that they are more than counterbalanced among us by great and generally diffused blessings.

They may, perhaps, have been disappointed in some unreasonable expectation of sudden gain. They may have pictured America to themselves an El Dorado, where gold and silver abounded, and the natives were lacking in sagacity; and where they were to become strangely and suddenly rich, in some unforeseen, but easy manner. The same weakness of mind that indulges absurd expectations produces petulance in disappointment. Such persons become embittered against the country on finding that there, as everywhere else, a man must sow before he can reap; must win wealth by industry and talent; and must contend with the common difficulties of nature, and the shrewdness of an intelligent and enterprising people.

Perhaps, through mistaken, or ill-directed hospitality, or from the prompt disposition to cheer and countenance the stranger, prevalent among my countrymen, they may have been treated with unwonted respect in America; and having been accustomed all their lives to consider themselves below the surface of good society, and brought up in a servile feeling of inferiority, they become arrogant on the common boon of civility: they attribute to the lowliness of others their own elevation; and underrate a society where there are no artificial distinctions, and where, by any chance, such individuals as themselves can rise to consequence.

One would suppose, however, that information coming from such sources, on a subject where the truth is so desirable, would be received with caution by the censors of the press; that the motives of these men, their veracity, their opportunities of inquiry and observation, and their capacities for judging correctly, would be rigorously scrutinized before their evidence was admitted, in such sweeping extent, against a kindred nation. The very reverse, however, is the case, and it furnishes a striking instance of human inconsistency. Nothing can surpass the vigilance with which English critics will examine the credibility of the traveller who publishes an account of some distant, and comparatively unimportant country. How warily will they compare the measurements of a pyramid, or the descriptions of a ruin; and how sternly will they censure any inaccuracy in these contributions of merely curious knowledge: while they will receive, with eagerness and unhesitating faith, the gross misrepresentations of coarse and obscure writers, concerning a country with which their own is placed in the most important and delicate relations. Nay, they will even make these apocryphal volumes text-books, on which to enlarge with a zeal and an ability worthy of a more generous cause.

I shall not, however, dwell on this irksome and hackneyed topic; nor should I have adverted to it, but for the undue interest apparently taken in it by my countrymen, and certain injurious effects which I apprehended it might produce upon the national feeling. We attach too much consequence to these attacks. They cannot do us any essential injury. The tissue of misrepresentations attempted to be woven round us are like cobwebs woven round the limbs of an infant giant. Our country continually outgrows them. One falsehood after another falls off of itself. We have but to live on, and every day we live a whole volume of refutation.

All the writers of England united, if we could for a moment suppose their great minds stooping to so unworthy a combination, could not conceal our rapidly-growing importance, and matchless prosperity. They could not conceal that these are owing, not merely to physical and local, but also to moral causes—to the political liberty, the general diffusion of knowledge, the prevalence of sound moral and religious principles, which give force and sustained energy to the character of a people; and which, in fact, have been the acknowledged and wonderful supporters of their own national power and glory.

But why are we so exquisitely alive to the aspersions of England? Why do we suffer ourselves to be so affected by the contumely she has endeavored to cast upon us? It is not in the opinion of England alone that honor lives, and reputation has its being. The world at large is the arbiter of a nation's fame; with its thousand eyes it witnesses a nation's deeds, and from their collective testimony is national glory or national disgrace established.

For ourselves, therefore, it is comparatively of but little importance whether England does us justice or not; it is, perhaps, of far more importance to herself. She is instilling anger and resentment into the bosom of a youthful nation, to grow with its growth and strengthen with its strength. If in America, as some of her writers are laboring to convince her, she is hereafter to find an invidious rival, and a gigantic foe, she may thank those very writers for having provoked rivalship and irritated hostility. Every one knows the all-pervading influence of literature at the present day, and how much the opinions and passions of mankind are under its control. The mere contests of the sword are temporary; their wounds are but in the flesh, and it is the pride of the generous to forgive and forget them; but the slanders of the pen pierce to the heart; they rankle longest in the noblest spirits; they dwell ever present in the mind, and render it morbidly sensitive to the most trifling collision. It is but seldom that any one overt act produces hostilities between two nations; there exists, most commonly, a previous jealousy and ill-will; a predisposition to take offence. Trace these to their cause, and how often will they be found to originate in the mischievous effusions of mercenary writers; who, secure in their closets, and for ignominious bread, concoct and circulate the venom that is to inflame the generous and the brave.

I am not laying too much stress upon this point; for it applies most emphatically to our particular case. Over no nation does the press hold a more absolute control than over the people of America; for the universal education of the poorest classes makes every individual a reader. There is nothing published in England on the subject of our country that does not circulate through every part of it. There is not a calumny dropped from English pen, nor an unworthy sarcasm uttered by an English statesman, that does not go to blight good-will, and add to the mass of latent resentment. Possessing, then, as England does, the fountain-head whence the literature of the language flows, how completely it is in her power, and how truly it is her duty, to make it the medium of amiable and magnanimous feeling—a stream where the two nations might meet together, and drink in peace and kindness. Should she, however, persist in turning it to waters of bitterness, the time may come when she may repent her folly. The present friendship of America may be of but little moment to her; but the future destinies of that country do not admit of a doubt; over those of England there lower some shadows of uncertainty. Should, then, a day of gloom arrive; should these reverses overtake her, from which the proudest empires have not been exempt; she may look back with regret at her infatuation, in repulsing from her side a nation she might have grappled to her bosom, and thus destroying her only chance for real friendship beyond the boundaries of her own dominions.

There is a general impression in England, that the people of the United States are inimical to the parent country. It is one of the errors which have been diligently propagated by designing writers. There is, doubtless, considerable political hostility, and a general soreness at the illiberality of the English press; but, generally speaking, the prepossessions of the people are strongly in favor of England. Indeed, at one time, they amounted, in many parts of the Union, to an absurd degree of bigotry. The bare name of Englishman was a passport to the confidence and hospitality of every family, and too often gave a transient currency to the worthless and the ungrateful. Throughout the country there was something of enthusiasm connected with the idea of England. We looked to it with a hallowed feeling of tenderness and veneration, as the land of our forefathers—the august repository of the monuments and antiquities of our race—the birthplace and mausoleum of the sages and heroes of our parental history. After our own country, there was none in whose glory we more delighted—none whose good opinion we were more anxious to possess—none towards which our hearts yearned with such throbbings of warm consanguinity. Even during the late war, whenever there was the least opportunity for kind feelings to spring forth, it was the delight of the generous spirits of our country to show that, in the midst of hostilities, they still kept alive the sparks of future friendship.

Is all this to be at an end? Is this golden band of kindred sympathies, so rare between nations, to be broken for ever? Perhaps it is for the best—it may dispel an illusion which might have kept us in mental vassalage; which might have interfered occasionally with our true interests, and prevented the growth of proper national pride. But it is hard to give up the kindred tie! and there are feelings dearer than interest—closer to the heart than pride—that will still make us cast back a look of regret, as we wander farther and farther from the paternal roof, and lament the waywardness of the parent that would repel the affections of the child.

Short-sighted and injudicious, however, as the conduct of England may be in this system of aspersion, recrimination on our part would be equally ill-judged. I speak not of a prompt and spirited vindication of our country, nor the keenest castigation of her slanderers—but I allude to a disposition to retaliate in kind; to retort sarcasm, and inspire prejudice; which seems to be spreading widely among our writers. Let us guard particularly against such a temper, for it would double the evil instead of redressing the wrong. Nothing is so easy and inviting as the retort of abuse and sarcasm; but it is a paltry and an unprofitable contest. It is the alternative of a morbid mind, fretted into petulance, rather than warmed into indignation. If England is willing to permit the mean jealousies of trade, or the rancorous animosities of politics, to deprave the integrity of her press, and poison the fountain of public opinion, let us beware of her example. She may deem it her interest to diffuse error, and engender antipathy, for the purpose of checking emigration; we have no purpose of the kind to serve. Neither have we any spirit of national jealousy to gratify, for as yet, in all our rivalships with England, we are the rising and the gaining party. There can be no end to answer, therefore, but the gratification of resentment—a mere spirit of retaliation; and even that is impotent. Our retorts are never republished in England; they fall short, therefore, of their aim; but they foster a querulous and peevish temper among our writers; they sour the sweet flow of our early literature, and sow thorns and brambles among its blossoms. What is still worse, they circulate through our own country, and, as far as they have effect, excite virulent national prejudices. This last is the evil most especially to be deprecated. Governed, as we are, entirely by public opinion, the utmost care should be taken to preserve the purity of the public mind. Knowledge is power, and truth is knowledge; whoever, therefore, knowingly propagates a prejudice, willfully saps the foundation of his country's strength.

The members of a republic, above all other men, should be candid and dispassionate. They are, individually, portions of the sovereign mind and sovereign will, and should be enabled to come to all questions of national concern with calm and unbiased judgments. From the peculiar nature of our relations with England, we must have more frequent questions of a difficult and delicate character with her than with any other nation; questions that affect the most acute and excitable feelings; and as, in the adjusting of these, our national measures must ultimately be determined by popular sentiment, we cannot be too anxiously attentive to purify it from all latent passion or prepossession.

Opening, too, as we do, an asylum for strangers from every portion of the earth, we should receive all with impartiality. It should be our pride to exhibit an example of one nation, at least, destitute of national antipathies, and exercising not merely the overt acts of hospitality, but those more rare and noble courtesies which spring from liberality of opinion.

What have we to do with national prejudices? They are the inveterate diseases of old countries, contracted in rude and ignorant ages, when nations knew but little of each other, and looked beyond their own boundaries with distrust and hostility. We, on the contrary, have sprung into national existence in an enlightened and philosophic age, when the different parts of the habitable world, and the various branches of the human family, have been indefatigably studied and made known to each other; and we forego the advantages of our birth, if we do not shake off the national prejudices, as we would the local superstitions of the old world.

But above all let us not be influenced by any angry feelings, so far as to shut our eyes to the perception of what is really excellent and amiable in the English character. We are a young people, necessarily an imitative one, and must take our examples and models, in a great degree, from the existing nations of Europe.

There is no country more worthy of our study than England. The spirit of her constitution is most analogous to ours. The manners of her people—their intellectual activity—their freedom of opinion—their habits of thinking on those subjects which concern the dearest interests and most sacred charities of private life, are all congenial to the American character; and, in fact, are all intrinsically excellent; for it is in the moral feeling of the people that the deep foundations of British prosperity are laid; and however the superstructure may be time-worn, or overrun by abuses, there must be something solid in the basis, admirable in the materials, and stable in the structure of an edifice, that so long has towered unshaken amidst the tempests of the world.

Let it be the pride of our writers, therefore, discarding all feelings of irritation, and disdaining to retaliate the illiberality of British authors, to speak of the English nation without prejudice, and with determined candor. While they rebuke the indiscriminating bigotry with which some of our countrymen admire and imitate every thing English, merely because it is English, let them frankly point out what is really worthy of approbation. We may thus place England before us as a perpetual volume of reference, wherein are recorded sound deductions from ages of experience; and while we avoid the errors and absurdities which may have crept into the page, we may draw thence golden maxims of practical wisdom, wherewith to strengthen and to embellish our national character.

RURAL LIFE IN ENGLAND

Oh! friendly to the best pursuits of man,
Friendly to thought, to virtue, and to peace,
Domestic life in rural pleasures past!

COWPER

THE stranger who would form a correct opinion of
the English character must not confine his observations to the metropolis. He must go forth into the
country; he must sojourn in villages and hamlets; he
must visit castles, villas, farm-houses, cottages; he must
wander through parks and gardens; along hedges and
green lanes; he must loiter about country churches;
attend wakes and fairs, and other rural festivals; and
cope with the people in all their conditions, and all their
habits and humors.

In some countries the large cities absorb the wealth
and fashion of the nation; they are the only fixed abodes
of elegant and intelligent society, and the country is
inhabited almost entirely by boorish peasantry. In England, on the contrary, the metropolis is a mere gather-
ing-place, or general rendezvous, of the polite classes,
where they devote a small portion of the year to a hurry
of gaiety and dissipation, and, having indulged this
kind of carnival, return again to the apparently more
congenial habits of rural life. The various orders of
society are therefore diffused over the whole surface of
the kingdom, and the most retired neighborhoods
afford specimens of the different ranks.

The English, in fact, are strongly gifted with the rural
feeling. They possess a quick sensibility to the beauties
of nature, and a keen relish for the pleasures and
employments of the country. This passion seems inherent in them. Even the inhabitants of cities, born and

brought up among brick walls and bustling streets, enter with facility into rural habits, and evince a tact for rural occupation. The merchant has his snug retreat in the vicinity of the metropolis, where he often displays as much pride and zeal in the cultivation of his flower-garden, and the maturing of his fruits, as he does in the conduct of his business, and the success of a commercial enterprise. Even those less fortunate individuals, who are doomed to pass their lives in the midst of din and traffic, contrive to have something that shall remind them of the green aspect of nature. In the most dark and dingy quarters of the city, the drawing-room window resembles frequently a bank of flowers; every spot capable of vegetation has its grass-plot and flower-bed; and every square its mimic park, laid out with picturesque taste, and gleaming with refreshing verdure.

Those who see the Englishman only in town are apt to form an unfavorable opinion of his social character. He is either absorbed in business, or distracted by the thousand engagements that dissipate time, thought, and feeling in this huge metropolis. He has, therefore, too commonly a look of hurry and abstraction. Wherever he happens to be, he is on the point of going somewhere else; at the moment he is talking on one subject, his mind is wandering to another; and while paying a friendly visit, he is calculating how he shall economize time so as to pay the other visits alloted in the morning. An immense metropolis, like London, is calculated to make men selfish and uninteresting. In their casual and transient meetings, they can but deal briefly in commonplaces. They present but the cold superficies of character—its rich and genial qualities have no time to be warmed into a flow.

It is in the country that the Englishman gives scope to his natural feelings. He breaks loose gladly from the cold formalities and negative civilities of town; throws off his habits of shy reserve, and becomes joyous and free-hearted. He manages to collect round him all the conveniences and elegancies of polite life, and to banish its restraints. His country-seat abounds with every requisite, either for studious retirement, tasteful gratification, or rural exercise. Books, paintings, music, horses, dogs, and sporting implements of all kinds, are at hand. He puts no constraint either upon his guests or himself, but in the true spirit of hospitality provides the means of enjoyment, and leaves every one to partake according to his inclination.

The taste of the English in the cultivation of land, and in what is called landscape gardening, is unrivalled. They have studied nature intently, and discover an exquisite sense of her beautiful forms and harmonious combinations. Those charms, which in other countries she lavishes in wild solitudes, are here assembled round the haunts of domestic life. They seem to have caught her coy and furtive graces, and spread them, like witchery, about their rural abodes.

Nothing can be more imposing than the magnificence of English park scenery. Vast lawns that extend like sheets of vivid green, with here and there clumps of gigantic trees, heaping up rich piles of foliage: the solemn pomp of groves and woodland glades, with the deer trooping in silent herds across them; the hare, bounding away to the covert; or the pheasant, suddenly bursting upon the wing: the brook, taught to wind in natural meanderings or expand into a glassy lake: the sequestered pool, reflecting the quivering trees, with the yellow leaf sleeping on its bosom, and the trout roaming fearlessly about its limpid waters; while some rustic temple or sylvan statue, grown green and dank with age, gives an air of classic sanctity to the seclusion.

These are but a few of the features of park scenery; but what most delights me, is the creative talent with which the English decorate the unostentatious abodes of middle life. The rudest habitation, the most unpromising and scanty portion of land, in the hands of an Englishman of taste, becomes a little paradise. With a nicely discriminating eye, he seizes at once upon its capabilities, and pictures in his mind the future landscape. The sterile spot grows into loveliness under his hand; and yet the operations of art which produce the effect are scarcely to be perceived. The cherishing and training of some trees; the cautious pruning of others; the nice distribution of flowers and plants of tender and graceful foliage; the introduction of a green slope of velvet turf; the partial opening to a peep of blue distance, or silver gleam of water: all these are managed with a delicate tact, a pervading yet quiet assiduity, like the magic touchings with which a painter finishes up a favorite picture.

The residence of people of fortune and refinement in the country has diffused a degee of taste and elegance in rural economy, that descends to the lowest class. The very laborer, with his thatched cottage and narrow slip of ground, attends to their embellishment. The trim hedge, the grassplot before the door, the little flower-bed bordered with snug box, the woodbine trained up against the wall, and hanging its blossoms about the lattice, the pot of flowers in the window, the holly, providently planted about the house, to cheat winter of its dreariness, and to throw in a semblance of green summer to cheer the fireside: all these bespeak the influence of taste, flowing down from high sources, and pervading the lowest levels of the public mind. If ever Love, as poets sing, delights to visit a cottage, it must be the cottage of an English peasant.

The fondness for rural life among the higher classes of the English has had a great and salutary effect upon the national character. I do not know a finer race of men than the English gentlemen. Instead of the softness and effeminacy which characterize the men of rank in most countries, they exhibit a union of elegance and strength, a robustness of frame and freshness of complexion, which I am inclined to attribute to their living so much in the open air, and pursuing so eagerly the invigorating recreations of the country. These hardy exercises produce also a healthful tone of mind and spirits, and a manliness and simplicity of manners, which even the follies and dissipations of the town cannot easily pervert, and can never entirely destroy. In the country, too, the different orders of society seem to approach more freely, to be more disposed to blend and operate favorably upon each other. The distinctions between them do not appear to be so marked and impassable as in the cities. The manner in which property has been distributed into small estates and farms has established a regular gradation from the nobleman, through the classes of gentry, small landed proprietors, and substantial farmers, down to the laboring peasantry; and while it has thus banded the extremes of society together, has infused into each intermediate rank a spirit of independence. This, it must be confessed, is not so universally the case at present as it was formerly; the larger estates having, in late years of distress, absorbed the smaller, and, in some parts of the country, almost annihilated the sturdy race of small farmers. These, however, I believe, are but casual breaks in the general system I have mentioned.

In rural occupation there is nothing mean and debasing. It leads a man forth among scenes of natural grandeur and beauty; it leaves him to the workings of his own mind, operated upon by the purest and most elevating of external influences. Such a man may be simple and rough, but he cannot be vulgar. The man of refinement, therefore, finds nothing revolting in an intercourse with the lower orders in rural life, as he does when he casually mingles with the lower orders of cities. He lays aside his distance and reserve, and is glad to waive the distinctions of rank, and to enter into the honest, heartfelt enjoyments of common life. Indeed the very amusements of the country bring men more and more together; and the sound of hound and horn blend all feelings into harmony. I believe this is one great reason why the nobility and gentry are more popular among the inferior orders in England than they are in any other country; and why the latter have endured so many excessive pressures and extremities, without repining more generally at the unequal distribution of fortune and privilege.

To this mingling of cultivated and rustic society may also be attributed the rural feeling that runs through British literature; the frequent use of illustrations from rural life; those incomparable descriptions of nature that abound in the British poets, that have continued down from "the Flower and the Leaf" of Chaucer, and have brought into our closets all the freshness and fragrance of the dewy landscape. The pastoral writers of other countries appear as if they had paid nature an occasional visit, and become acquainted with her general charms; but the British poets have lived and revelled with her—they have wooed her in her most secret haunts—they have watched her minutest caprices. A spray could not tremble in the breeze—a leaf could not rustle to the ground—a diamond drop could not patter in the stream—a fragrance could not exhale from the humble violet, nor a daisy unfold its crimson tints to the morning, but it has been noticed by these impassioned and delicate observers, and wrought up into some beautiful morality.

The effect of this devotion of elegant minds to rural occupations has been wonderful on the face of the country. A great part of the island is rather level, and would be monotonous, were it not for the charms of culture: but it is studded and gemmed, as it were, with castles and palaces, and embroidered with parks and gardens. It does not abound in grand and sublime prospects, but rather in little home scenes of rural repose and sheltered quiet. Every antique farm-house and moss-grown cottage is a picture: and as the roads are continually winding, and the view is shut in by groves and hedges, the eye is delighted by a continual succession of small landscapes of captivating loveliness.

The great charm, however, of English scenery is the moral feeling that seems to pervade it. It is associated in the mind with ideas of order, of quiet, of sober well-established principles, of hoary usage and reverent custom. Every thing seems to be the growth of ages of regular and peaceful existence. The old church of remote architecture, with its low massive portal; its gothic tower; its windows rich with tracery and painted glass, in scrupulous preservation; its stately monuments of warriors and worthies of the olden time, ancestors of the present lords of the soil; its tombstones, recording successive generations of sturdy yeomanry, whose progeny still plough the same fields, and kneel at the same altar—the parsonage, a quaint irregular pile, partly antiquated, but repaired and altered in the tastes of various ages and occupants—the stile and footpath leading from the churchyard, across pleasant fields, and along shady hedge-rows, according to an immemorial right of way—the neighboring village, with its venerable cottages, its public green sheltered by trees, under which the forefathers of the present race have sported—the antique family mansion, standing apart in some little rural domain, but looking down with a protecting air on the surrounding scene: all these common features of English landscape evince a calm and settled security, and hereditary transmission of homebred virtues and local attachments, that speak deeply and touchingly for the moral character of the nation.

It is a pleasing sight of a Sunday morning, when the bell is sending its sober melody across the quiet fields, to behold the peasantry in their best finery, with ruddy faces and modest cheerfulness, thronging tranquilly along the green lanes to church; but it is still more pleasing to see them in the evenings, gathering about their cottage doors, and appearing to exult in the humble comforts and embellishments which their own hands have spread around them.

It is this sweet home-feeling, this settled repose of affection in the domestic scene, that is, after all, the parent of the steadiest virtues and purest enjoyments; and I cannot close these desultory remarks better, than by quoting the words of a modern English poet, who has depicted it with remarkable felicity:

> Though each gradation, from the castled hall,
> The city dome, the villa crown'd with shade,
> But chief from modest mansions numberless,
> In town or hamlet, shelt'ring middle life,
> Down to the cottaged vale, and straw roof'd shed;
> This western isle hath long been famed for scenes
> Where bliss domestic finds a dwelling-place;
> Domestic bliss, that, like a harmless dove,
> (Honor and sweet endearment keeping guard,)
> Can centre in a little quiet nest
> All that desire would fly for through the earth;
> That can, the world eluding, be itself

A world enjoy'd; that wants no witnesses
But its own sharers, and approving heaven;
That, like a flower deep hid in rocky cleft,
Smiles, though 'tis looking only at the sky.*

THE BROKEN HEART

> I never heard
> Of any true affection, but 'twas nipt
> With care, that, like the caterpillar, eats
> The leaves of the spring's sweetest book, the rose.
>
> MIDDLETON

I T IS a common practice with those who have outlived the susceptibility of early feeling, or have been brought up in the gay heartlessness of dissipated life, to laugh at all love stories, and to treat the tales of romantic passion as mere fictions of novelists and poets. My observations on human nature have induced me to think otherwise. They have convinced me, that however the surface of the character may be chilled and frozen by the cares of the world, or cultivated into mere smiles by the arts of society, still there are dormant fires lurking in the depths of the coldest bosom, which, when once enkindled, become impetuous, and are sometimes desolating in their effects. Indeed, I am a true believer in the blind deity, and go to the full extent of his doctrines. Shall I confess it?—I believe in broken hearts, and the possibility of dying of disappointed love. I do not, however, consider it a malady often fatal to my own sex; but I firmly believe that it withers down many a lovely woman into an early grave.

Man is the creature of interest and ambition. His

*From a Poem on the death of the Princess Charlotte, by the Reverend Rann Kennedy, A. M.

nature leads him forth into the struggle and bustle of the world. Love is but the embellishment of his early life, or a song piped in the intervals of the acts. He seeks for fame, for fortune, for space in the world's thought, and dominion over his fellow-men. But a woman's whole life is a history of the affections. The heart is her world: it is there her ambition strives for empire; it is there her avarice seeks for hidden treasures. She sends forth her sympathies on adventure; she embarks her whole soul in the traffic of affection; and if shipwrecked, her case is hopeless—for it is a bankruptcy of the heart.

To a man the disappointment of love may occasion some bitter pangs: it wounds some feelings of tenderness—it blasts some prospects of felicity; but he is an active being—he may dissipate his thoughts in the whirl of varied occupation, or may plunge into the tide of pleasure; or, if the scene of disappointment be too full of painful associations, he can shift his abode at will, and taking as it were the wings of the morning, can "fly to the uttermost parts of the earth, and be at rest."

But woman's is comparatively a fixed, a secluded, and meditative life. She is more the companion of her own thoughts and feelings; and if they are turned to ministers of sorrow, where shall she look for consolation? Her lot is to be wooed and won; and if unhappy in her love, her heart is like some fortress that has been captured, and sacked, and abandoned, and left desolate.

How many bright eyes grow dim—how many soft cheeks grow pale—how many lovely forms fade away into the tomb, and none can tell the cause that blighted their loveliness! As the dove will clasp its wings to its side, and cover and conceal the arrow that is preying on its vitals, so is it the nature of woman to hide from the world the pangs of wounded affection. The love of a delicate female is always shy and silent. Even when fortunate, she scarcely breathes it to herself; but when otherwise, she buries it in the recesses of her bosom, and there lets it cower and brood among the ruins of her peace. With her the desire of the heart has failed. The great charm of existence is at an end. She neglects all the cheerful exercises which gladden the spirits, quicken the pulses, and send the tide of life in healthful currents through the veins. Her rest is broken—the sweet refreshment of sleep is poisoned by melancholy dreams— "dry sorrow drinks her blood," until her enfeebled frame sinks under the slightest external injury. Look for her, after a little while, and you find friendship weeping over her untimely grave, and wondering that one, who but lately glowed with all the radiance of health and beauty, should so speedily be brought down to "darkness and the worm." You will be told of some wintry chill, some casual indisposition, that laid her low;—but no one knows of the mental malady which previously sapped her strength, and made her so easy a prey to the spoiler.

She is like some tender tree, the pride and beauty of the grove; graceful in its form, bright in its foliage, but with the worm preying at its heart. We find it suddenly withering, when it should be most fresh and luxuriant. We see it drooping its branches to the earth, and shedding leaf by leaf, until, wasted and perished away, it falls even in the stillness of the forest; and as we muse over the beautiful ruin, we strive in vain to recollect the blast or thunderbolt that could have smitten it with decay.

I have seen many instances of women running to waste and self-neglect, and disappearing gradually from the earth, almost as if they had been exhaled to heaven; and have repeatedly fancied that I could trace their death through the various declensions of consumption, cold, debility, languor, melancholy, until I reached the first symptom of disappointed love. But an instance of the kind was lately told to me; the circumstances are well known in the country where they happened, and I shall but give them in the manner in which they were related.

Every one must recollect the tragical story of young E——, the Irish patriot; it was too touching to be soon forgotten. During the troubles in Ireland, he was tried, condemned, and executed, on a charge of treason. His fate made a deep impression on public sympathy. He was so young—so intelligent—so generous—so brave—so everything that we are apt to like in a young man. His conduct under trial, too, was so lofty and intrepid. The noble indignation with which he repelled the charge of treason against his country—the eloquent vindication of his name—and his pathetic appeal to posterity, in the hopeless hour of condemnation—all these entered deeply into every generous bosom, and even his enemies lamented the stern policy that dictated his execution.

But there was one heart, whose anguish it would be impossible to describe. In happier days and fairer fortunes, he had won the affections of a beautiful and interesting girl, the daughter of a late celebrated Irish barrister. She loved him with the disinterested fervor of a woman's first and early love. When every worldly maxim arrayed itself against him; when blasted in fortune, and disgrace and danger darkened around his name, she loved him the more ardently for his very sufferings. If, then, his fate could awaken the sympathy even of his foes, what must have been the agony of her, whose whole soul was occupied by his image! Let those tell who have had the portals of the tomb suddenly closed between them and the being they most loved on earth—who have sat at its threshold, as one shut out in a cold and lonely world, whence all that was most lovely and loving had departed.

But then the horrors of such a grave! so frightful, so dishonored! there was nothing for memory to dwell on that could soothe the pang of separation—none of those tender though melancholy circumstances, which endear the parting scene—nothing to melt sorrow into those blessed tears, sent like the dews of heaven, to revive the heart in the parting hour of anguish.

To render her widowed situation more desolate, she had incurred her father's displeasure by her unfortunate attachment, and was an exile from the paternal roof. But could the sympathy and kind offices of friends have reached a spirit so shocked and driven in by horror, she would have experienced no want of consolation, for the Irish are a people of quick and generous sensibilities. The most delicate and cherishing attentions were paid her by families of wealth and distinction. She was led into society, and they tried by all kinds of occupation and amusement to dissipate her grief, and wean her from the tragical story of her loves. But it was all in vain. There are some strokes of calamity which scathe and scorch the soul—which penetrate to the vital seat of happiness—and blast it, never again to put forth bud or blossom. She never objected to frequent the haunts of pleasure, but was as much alone there as in the depths of solitude; walking about in a sad reverie, apparently unconscious of the world around her. She carried with her an inward woe that mocked at all the blandishments of friendship, and "heeded not the song of the charmer, charm he never so wisely."

The person who told me her story had seen her at a masquerade. There can be no exhibition of far-gone wretchedness more striking and painful than to meet it in such a scene. To find it wandering like a spectre, lonely and joyless, where all around is gay—to see it dressed out in the trappings of mirth, and looking so wan and wobegone, as if it had tried in vain to cheat the poor heart into a momentary forgetfulness of sorrow. After strolling through the splendid rooms and giddy crowd with an air of utter abstraction, she sat herself down on the steps of an orchestra, and, looking about for some time with a vacant air, that showed her insensibility to the garish scene, she began, with the capriciousness of a sickly heart, to warble a little plaintive air. She had an exquisite voice; but on this occasion it was so simple, so touching, it breathed forth such a soul of wretchedness, that she drew a crowd mute and silent around her, and melted every one into tears.

The story of one so true and tender could not but excite great interest in a country remarkable for enthusiasm. It completely won the heart of a brave officer, who paid his addresses to her, and thought that one so true to the dead could not but prove affectionate to the living. She declined his attentions, for her thoughts were irrevocably engrossed by the memory of her former lover. He, however, persisted in his suit. He solicited not her tenderness, but her esteem. He was assisted by her conviction of his worth, and her sense of her own destitute and dependent situation, for she was existing on the kindness of friends. In a word, he at length succeded in gaining her hand, though with the solemn assurance, that her heart was unalterably another's.

He took her with him to Sicily, hoping that a change of scene might wear out the remembrance of early woes. She was an amiable and exemplary wife, and made an effort to be a happy one; but nothing could cure the silent and devouring melancholy that had entered into her very soul. She wasted away in a slow, but hopeless decline, and at length sunk into the grave, the victim of a broken heart.

It was on her that Moore, the distinguished Irish poet, composed the following lines:

> She is far from the land where her young hero sleeps,
>   And lovers around her are sighing:
> But coldly she turns from their gaze, and weeps,
>   For her heart in his grave is lying.
>
> She sings the wild songs of her dear native plains,
>   Every note which he loved awaking—
> Ah! little they think, who delight in her strains,
>   How the heart of the minstrel is breaking!
>
> He had lived for his love—for his country he died,
>   They were all that to life had entwined him—
> Nor soon shall the tears of his country be dried,
>   Nor long will his love stay behind him!
>
> Oh! make her a grave where the sunbeams rest,
>   When they promise a glorious morrow;
> They'll shine o'er her sleep, like a smile from the west,
>   From her own loved island of sorrow!

THE ART OF
BOOK-MAKING

"If that severe doom of Synesius be true—'It is a greater offence to steal dead men's labor, than their clothes,' what shall become of most writers?"

BURTON'S ANATOMY OF MELANCHOLY

I HAVE often wondered at the extreme fecundity of the press, and how it comes to pass that so many heads, on which nature seemed to have inflicted the curse of barrenness, should teem with voluminous productions. As a man travels on, however, in the journey of life, his objects of wonder daily diminish, and he is continually finding out some very simple cause for some great matter of marvel. Thus have I chanced, in my peregrinations about this great metropolis, to blunder upon a scene which unfolded to me some of the mysteries of the book-making craft, and at once put an end to my astonishment.

I was one summer's day loitering through the great saloons of the British Museum, with that listlessness with which one is apt to saunter about a museum in warm weather; sometimes lolling over the glass cases of minerals, sometimes studying the hieroglyphics on an Egyptian mummy, and sometimes trying, with nearly equal success, to comprehend the allegorical paintings on the lofty ceilings. Whilst I was gazing about in this idle way, my attention was attracted to a distant door, at the end of a suite of apartments. It was closed, but every now and then it would open, and some strange-favored being, generally clothed in black, would steal forth, and glide through the rooms, without noticing any of the surrounding objects. There was an air of mystery about this that piqued my languid curiosity, and I determined

to attempt the passage of that strait, and to explore the
unknown regions beyond. The door yielded to my
hand, with that facility with which the portals of
enchanted castles yield to the adventurous knight-
errant. I found myself in a spacious chamber, surrounded with great cases of venerable books. Above the
cases, and just under the cornice, were arranged a great
number of black-looking portraits of ancient authors.
About the room were placed long tables, with stands for
reading and writing, at which sat many pale, studious
personages, poring intently over dusty volumes, rummaging among mouldy manuscripts, and taking copious
notes of their contents. A hushed stillness reigned
through this mysterious apartment, excepting that you
might hear the racing of pens over sheets of paper, or
occasionally, the deep sigh of one of these sages, as he
shifted his position to turn over the page of an old folio;
doubtless arising from that hollowness and flatulency
incident to learned research.

Now and then one of these personages would write
something on a small slip of paper, and ring a bell,
whereupon a familiar would appear, take the paper in
profound silence, glide out of the room, and return
shortly loaded with ponderous tomes, upon which the
other would fall tooth and nail with famished voracity. I
had no longer a doubt that I had happened upon a body
of magi, deeply engaged in the study of occult sciences.
The scene reminded me of an old Arabian tale, of a
philosopher shut up in an enchanted library, in the
bosom of a mountain, which opened only once a year;
where he made the spirits of the place bring him books
of all kinds of dark knowledge, so that at the end of the
year, when the magic portal once more swung open on
its hinges, he issued forth so versed in forbidden lore,

as to be able to soar above the heads of the multitude, and to control the powers of nature.

My curiosity being now fully aroused, I whispered to one of the familiars, as he was about to leave the room, and begged an interpretation of the strange scene before me. A few words were sufficient for the purpose. I found that these mysterious personages, whom I had mistaken for magi, were principally authors, and in the very act of manufacturing books. I was, in fact, in the reading-room of the great British Library—an immense collection of volumes of all ages and languages, many of which are now forgotten, and most of which are seldom read: one of these sequestered pools of obsolete literature, to which modern authors repair, and draw buckets full of classic lore, or "pure English, undefiled," wherewith to swell their own scanty rills of thought.

Being now in possession of the secret, I sat down in a corner, and watched the process of this book manufactory. I noticed one lean, bilious-looking wight, who sought none but the most worm-eaten volumes, printed in black-letter. He was evidently constructing some work of profound erudition, that would be purchased by every man who wished to be thought learned, placed upon a conspicuous shelf of his library, or laid open upon his table; but never read. I observed him, now and then, draw a large fragment of biscuit out of his pocket, and gnaw; whether it was his dinner, or whether he was endeavoring to keep off that exhaustion of the stomach produced by much pondering over dry works, I leave to harder students than myself to determine.

There was one dapper little gentleman in bright-colored clothes, with a chirping, gossiping expression of countenance, who had all the appearance of an author on good terms with his bookseller. After considering him attentively, I recognized in him a diligent getter-up of miscellaneous works, which bustled off well with the trade. I was curious to see how he manufactured his wares. He made more stir and show of business than any of the others; dipping into various books, fluttering over the leaves of manuscripts, taking a morsel out of one, a morsel out of another, "line upon line, precept upon precept, here a little and there a little." The contents of his book seemed to be as heterogeneous as those of the witches' caldron in Macbeth. It was here a finger and there a thumb, toe of frog and blind-worm's sting, with his own gossip poured in like "baboon's blood," to make the medley "slab and good."

After all, thought I, may not this pilfering disposition be implanted in authors for wise purposes; may it not be the way in which Providence has taken care that the seeds of knowledge and wisdom shall be preserved from age to age, in spite of the inevitable decay of the works in which they were first produced? We see that nature has wisely, though whimsically, provided for the conveyance of seeds from clime to clime, in the maws of certain birds; so that animals, which in themselves, are little better than carrion, and apparently the lawless plunderers of the orchard and the cornfield, are, in fact, nature's carriers to disperse and perpetuate her blessings. In like manner, the beauties and fine thoughts of ancient and obsolete authors are caught up by these flights of predatory writers, and cast forth again to flourish and bear fruit in a remote and distant tract of time. Many of their works, also, undergo a kind of metempsychosis, and spring up under new forms. What was formerly a ponderous history revives in the shape of a romance—an old legend changes into a modern play—and a sober philosophical treatise furnishes the body for a whole series of bouncing and sparkling essays. Thus it is in the clearing of our American woodlands; where we burn down a forest of stately pines, a progeny of dwarf oaks start up in their place: and we never see the prostrate trunk of a tree mouldering into soil, but it gives birth to a whole tribe of fungi.

Let us not, then, lament over the decay and oblivion into which ancient writers descend; they do but submit to the great law of nature, which declares that all sublunary shapes of matter shall be limited in their duration, but which decrees, also, that their elements shall never perish. Generation after generation, both in animal and vegetable life, passes away, but the vital principle is transmitted to posterity, and the species continue to flourish. Thus, also, do authors beget authors, and having produced a numerous progeny, in a good old age they sleep with their fathers, that is to say, with the authors who proceded them—and from whom they had stolen.

Whilst I was indulging in these rambling fancies, I had leaned my head against a pile of reverend folios. Whether it was owing to the soporific emanations from these works; or to the profound quiet of the room; or to the lassitude arising from much wandering; or to an unlucky habit of napping at improper times and places, with which I am grievously afflicted, so it was, that I fell into a doze. Still, however, my imagination continued busy, and indeed the same scene remained before my mind's eye, only a little changed in some of the details. I dreamt that the chamber was still decorated with the portraits of ancient authors, but that the number was increased. The long tables had disappeared, and, in place of the sage magi, I beheld a ragged, threadbare throng, such as may be seen plying about the great repository of cast-off clothes, Monmouth-street. Whenever they seized upon a book, by one of those incongruities common to dreams, methought it turned into a garment of foreign or antique fashion, with which they proceeded to equip themselves. I noticed, however, that no one pretended to clothe himself from any particular suit, but took a sleeve from one, a cape from another, a skirt from a third, thus decking himself out piecemeal, while some of his original rags would peep out from among his borrowed finery.

There was a portly, rosy, well-fed parson, whom I observed ogling several mouldy polemical writers through an eye-glass. He soon contrived to slip on the voluminous mantle of one of the old fathers, and, having purloined the gray beard of another, endeavored to look exceedingly wise; but the smirking commonplace of his countenance set at naught all the trappings of wisdom. One sickly-looking gentleman was busied embroidering a very flimsy garment with gold thread drawn out of several old court-dresses of the reign of Queen Elizabeth. Another had trimmed himself magnificently from an illuminated manuscript, had stuck a nosegay in his bosom, culled from "The Paradise of Daintie Devices," and having put Sir Philip Sidney's hat on one side of his head, strutted off with an exquisite air of vulgar elegence. A third, who was but of puny dimensions, had bolstered himself out bravely with the spoils from several obscure tracts of philosophy, so that he had a very imposing front; but he was lamentably tattered in rear, and I perceived that he had patched his small-clothes with scraps of parchment from a Latin author.

There were some well-dressed gentlemen, it is true, who only helped themselves to a gem or so, which sparkled among their own ornaments, without eclipsing them. Some, too, seemed to contemplate the costumes of the old writers, merely to imbibe their principles of taste, and to catch their air and spirit; but I grieve to say, that too many were apt to array themselves from top to toe in the patchwork manner I have mentioned. I shall not omit to speak of one genius, in drab breeches and gaiters, and an Arcadian hat, who had a violent propensity to the pastoral, but whose rural wanderings had been confined to the classic haunts of Primrose Hill, and the solitudes of the Regent's Park. He had decked himself in wreaths and ribbons from all the old pastoral poets, and, hanging his head on one side, went about with a fantastical lack-a-daisical air, "babbling about green fields." But the personage that most struck my attention was a pragmatical old gentleman, in clerical robes, with a remarkably large and square, but bald head. He entered the room wheezing and puffing, elbowed his way through the throng, with a look of sturdy self-confidence, and having laid hands upon a thick Greek quarto, clapped it upon his head, and swept majestically away in a formidable frizzled wig.

In the height of this literary masquerade, a cry suddenly resounded from every side, of "Thieves! thieves!" I looked, and lo! the portraits about the wall became animated! The old authors thrust out, first a head, then a shoulder, from the canvas, looked down curiously, for an instant, upon the motley throng, and then descended with fury in their eyes, to claim their rifled property. The scene of scampering and hubbub that ensued baffles all description. The unhappy culprits endeavored in vain to escape with their plunder. On one side might be seen half a dozen old monks, stripping a modern professor; on another, there was sad devastation carried into the ranks of modern dramatic writers. Beaumont and Fletcher, side by side, raged round the field like Castor and Pollux, and sturdy Ben Jonson enacted more wonders than when a volunteer with the army in Flanders. As to the dapper little compiler of farragos, mentioned some time since, he had arrayed himself in as many patches and colors as Harlequin, and there was as fierce a contention of claimants about him, as about the dead body of Patroclus. I was grieved to see many men, to whom I had been accustomed to look up with awe and reverence, fain to steal off with scarce a rag to cover their nakedness. Just then my eye was caught by the pragmatical old gentleman in the Greek grizzled wig, who was scrambling away in sore affright with half a score of authors in full cry after him! They were close upon his haunches: in a twinkling off went his wig; at every turn some strip of raiment was peeled away; until in a few moments, from his domineering pomp, he shrunk into a little, pursy, "chopped bald shot," and made his exit with only a few tags and rags fluttering at his back.

There was something so ludicrous in the catastrophe of this learned Theban, that I burst into an immoderate fit of laughter, which broke the whole illusion. The tumult and the scuffle were at an end. The chamber resumed its usual appearance. The old authors shrunk back into their picture-frames, and hung in shadowy solemnity along the walls. In short, I found myself wide awake in my corner, with the whole assemblage of bookworms gazing at me with astonishment. Nothing of the dream had been real but my burst of laughter, a sound never before heard in that grave sanctuary, and so abhorrent to the ears of wisdom, as to electrify the fraternity.

The librarian now stepped up to me, and demanded whether I had a card of admission. At first I did not comprehend him, but I soon found that the library was a kind of literary "preserve," subject to game-laws, and that no one must presume to hunt there without special license and permission. In a word, I stood convicted of being an arrant poacher, and was glad to make a precipitate retreat, lest I should have a whole pack of authors let loose upon me.

A ROYAL POET

Though your body be confined,
  And soft love a prisoner bound.
Yet the beauty of your mind
  Neither check nor chain hath found,
    Look out nobly, then, and dare
    Even the fetters that you wear.
                                        FLETCHER

ON A soft, sunny morning in the genial month of May, I made an excursion to Windsor Castle. It is a place full of storied and poetical associations. The very external aspect of the proud old pile is enough to inspire high thought. It rears its irregular walls and massive towers, like a mural crown, round the brow of a lofty ridge, waves its royal banner in the clouds, and looks down, with a lordly air, upon the surrounding world.

On this morning the weather was of that voluptuous vernal kind, which calls forth all the latent romance of a man's temperament, filling his mind with music, and disposing him to quote poetry and dream of beauty. In wandering through the magnificent saloons and long echoing galleries of the castle, I passed with indifference by whole rows of portraits of warriors and statesmen, but lingered in the chamber, where hang the likenesses of the beauties which graced the gay court of Charles the Second; and as I gazed upon them, depicted with amorous, half-dishevelled tresses, and the sleepy eye of love, I blessed the pencil of Sir Peter Lely, which had thus enabled me to bask in the reflected rays of beauty. In traversing also the "large green courts," with sunshine beaming on the gray walls, and glancing along the velvet turf, my mind was engrossed with the image of the tender, the gallant, but hapless Surrey, and his account of his loiterings about them in his stripling days, when enamored of the Lady Geraldine—

> "With eyes cast up unto the maiden's tower,
> With easie sighs, such as men draw in love,"

In this mood of mere poetical susceptibility, I visited the ancient Keep of the Castle, where James the First of Scotland, the pride and theme of Scottish poets and historians, was for many years of his youth detained a prisoner of state. It is a large gray tower, that has stood the brunt of ages, and is still in good preservation. It stands on a mound, which elevates it above the other parts of the castle, and a great flight of steps leads to the interior. In the armory, a Gothic hall, furnished with weapons of various kinds and ages, I was shown a coat of armor hanging against the wall, which had once belonged to James. Hence I was conducted up a staircase to a suite of apartments of faded magnificence, hung with storied tapestry, which formed his prison, and the scene of that passionate and fanciful amour, which has woven into the web of his story the magical hues of poetry and fiction.

The whole history of this amiable but unfortunate prince is highly romantic. At the tender age of eleven he was sent from home by his father, Robert III, and destined for the French court, to be reared under the eye of the French monarch, secure from the treachery and danger that surrounded the royal house of Scotland. It was his mishap in the course of his voyage to fall into the hands of the English, and he was detained prisoner by Henry IV, notwithstanding that a truce existed between the two countries.

The intelligence of his capture, coming in the train of many sorrows and disasters, proved fatal to his unhappy father. "The news," we are told, "was brought to him while at supper, and did so overwhelm him with grief, that he was almost ready to give up the ghost into the hands of the servant that attended him. But being carried to his bed-chamber, he abstained from all food, and in three days died of hunger and grief at Rothesay."*

James was detained in captivity above eighteen years; but though deprived of personal liberty, he was treated with the respect due to his rank. Care was taken to instruct him in all the branches of useful knowledge cultivated at that period, and to give him those mental and personal accomplishments deemed proper for a prince. Perhaps, in this respect, his imprisonment was an advantage, as it enabled him to apply himself the more exclusively to his improvement, and quietly to imbibe that rich fund of knowledge, and to cherish those elegant tastes, which have given such a lustre to his memory. The picture drawn of him in early life, by the Scottish historians, is highly captivating, and seems rather the description of a hero of romance, than of a character in real history. He was well learned, we are told, "to fight with the sword, to joust, to tournay, to wrestle, to sing and dance; he was an expert mediciner, right crafty in playing both of lute and harp, and sundry other instruments of music, and was expert in grammar, oratory, and poetry."†

With this combination of manly and delicate accom-

*Buchanan.
†Ballenden's Translation of Hector Boyce.

plishments, fitting him to shine both in active and elegant life, and calculated to give him an intense relish for joyous existence; it must have been a severe trial, in an age of bustle and chivalry, to pass the spring-time of his years in monotonous captivity. It was the good fortune of James, however, to be gifted with a powerful poetic fancy, and to be visited in his prison by the choicest inspirations of the muse. Some minds corrode and grow inactive, under the loss of personal liberty; others grow morbid and irritable; but it is the nature of the poet to become tender and imaginative in the loneliness of confinement. He banquets upon the honey of his own thoughts, and, like the captive bird, pours forth his soul in melody.

> Have you not seen the nightingale,
>   A pilgrim coop'd into a cage,
> How doth she chant her wonted tale,
>   In that her lonely hermitage!
> Even there her charming melody doth prove
> That all her boughs are trees, her cage a grove.*

Indeed, it is the divine attribute of the imagination, that it is irrepressible, unconfinable; that when the real world is shut out, it can create a world for itself, and with a necromantic power, can conjure up glorious shapes and forms, and brilliant visions, to make solitude populous, and irradiate the gloom of the dungeon. Such was the world of pomp and pageant that lived round Tasso in his dismal cell at Ferrara, when he conceived the splendid scenes of his Jerusalem; and we may consider the "King's Quair," composed by James, during his captivity at Windsor, as another of those beautiful breakings-forth of the soul from the restraint and gloom of the prison house.

*Roger L'Estrange.

The subject of the poem is his love for the Lady Jane Beaufort, daughter of the Earl of Somerset, and a princess of the blood royal of England, of whom he became enamored in the course of his captivity. What gives it a peculiar value, is that it may be considered a transcript of the royal bard's true feelings, and the story of his real loves and fortunes. It is not often that sovereigns write poetry, or that poets deal in fact. It is gratifying to the pride of a common man, to find a monarch thus suing, as it were, for admission into his closet, and seeking to win his favor by administering to his pleasures. It is a proof of the honest equality of intellectual competition, which strips off all the trappings of factitious dignity, brings the candidate down to a level with his fellowmen, and obliges him to depend on his own native powers for distinction. It is curious, too, to get at the history of a monarch's heart, and to find the simple affections of human nature throbbing under the ermine. But James had learnt to be a poet before he was a king: he was schooled in adversity, and reared in the company of his own thoughts. Monarchs have seldom time to parley with their hearts, or to meditate their minds into poetry; and had James been brought up amidst the adulation and gayety of a court, we should never, in all probability, have had such a poem as the Quair.

I have been particularly interested by those parts of the poem which breathe his immediate thoughts concerning his situation, or which are connected with the apartment in the tower. They have thus a personal and local charm, and are given with such circumstantial truth, as to make the reader present with the captive in his prison, and the companion of his meditations.

Such is the account which he gives of his weariness of

spirit, and of the incident which first suggested the idea of writing the poem. It was the still midwatch of a clear moonlight night; the stars, he says, were twinkling as fire in the high vault of heaven: and "Cynthia rinsing her golden locks in Aquarius." He lay in bed wakeful and restless, and took a book to beguile the tedious hours. The book he chose was Boethius' *Consolations of Philosophy*, a work popular among the writers of that day, and which had been translated by his great prototype Chaucer. From the high eulogium in which he indulges, it is evident this was one of his favorite volumes while in prison: and indeed it is an admirable text-book for meditation under adversity. It is the legacy of a noble and enduring spirit, purified by sorrow and suffering, bequeathing to its successors in calamity the maxims of sweet morality, and the trains of eloquent but simple reasoning, by which it was enabled to bear up against the various ills of life. It is a talisman, which the unfortunate may treasure up in his bosom, or, like the good King James, lay upon his nightly pillow.

After closing the volume, he turns its contents over in his mind, and gradually falls into a fit of musing on the fickleness of fortune, the vicissitudes of his own life, and the evils that had overtaken him even in his tender youth. Suddenly he hears the bell ringing to matins; but its sound, chiming in with his melancholy fancies, seems to him like a voice exhorting him to write his story. In the spirit of poetic errantry he determines to comply with this intimation: he therefore takes pen in hand, makes with it a sign of the cross to implore a benediction, and sallies forth into the fairy land of poetry. There is something extremely fanciful in all this, and it is interesting as furnishing a striking and beautiful instance of the simple manner in which whole trains of poetical thought are sometimes awakened, and literary enterprises suggested to the mind.

In the course of his poem he more than once bewails the peculiar hardness of his fate; thus doomed to lonely and inactive life, and shut up from the freedom and pleasure of the world, in which the meanest animal indulges unrestrained. There is a sweetness, however, in his very complaints; they are the lamentations of an amiable and social spirit at being denied the indulgence of its kind and generous propensities; there is nothing in them harsh nor exaggerated; they flow with a natural and touching pathos, and are perhaps rendered more touching by their simple brevity. They contrast finely with those elaborate and iterated repinings, which we sometimes meet with in poetry;—the effusions of morbid minds sickening under miseries of their own creating, and venting their bitterness upon an unoffending world. James speaks of his privations with acute sensibility, but having mentioned them passes on, as if his manly mind disdained to brood over unavoidable calamities. When such a spirit breaks forth into complaint, however brief, we are aware how great must be the suffering that extorts the murmur. We sympathize with James, a romantic, active, and accomplished prince, cut off in the lustihood of youth from all the enterprise, the noble uses, and vigorous delights of life; as we do with Milton, alive to all the beauties of nature and glories of art, when he breathes forth brief, but deep-toned lamentations over his perpetual blindness.

Had not James evinced a deficiency of poetic artifice, we might almost have suspected that these lowerings of gloomy reflection were meant as preparative to the brightest scene of his story; and to contrast with that refulgence of light and loveliness, that exhilarating accompaniment of bird and song, and foliage and flower, and all the revel of the year, with which he ushers in the lady of his heart. It is this scene, in particular, which throws all the magic of romance about the old Castle Keep. He had risen, he says, at daybreak, according to custom, to escape from the dreary meditations of a sleepless pillow. "Bewailing in his chamber thus alone," despairing of all joy and remedy, "fortired of thought and wobegone," he had wandered to the window, to indulge the captive's miserable solace of gazing wistfully upon the world from which he is excluded. The window looked forth upon a small garden which lay at the foot of the tower. It was a quiet, sheltered spot, adorned with arbors and green alleys, and protected from the passing gaze by trees and hawthorn hedges.

> Now was there made, fast by the tower's wall,
>   A garden faire, and in the corners set
> An arbour green with wandis long and small
>   Railed about, and so with leaves beset
> Was all the place and hawthorn hedges knet,
>   That lyf* was none, walkyng there forbye
>   That might within scarce any wight espye.
>
> So thick the branches and the leves grene,
>   Beshaded all the alleys that there were,
> And midst of every arbour might be sene
>   The sharpe, grene, swete juniper,
> Growing so fair, with branches here and there,
>   That as it seemed to a lyf without,
>   The boughs did spread the arbour all about.
>
> And on the small grene twistis† set
>   The lytel swete nightingales, and sung
> So loud and clear, the hymnis consecrate
>   Of lovis use, now soft, now loud among,
> That all the garden and the wallis rung
> Right of their song——

Lyf, Person.   †*Twistis*, small boughs or twigs.

It was the month of May, when everything was in bloom; and he interprets the song of the nightingale into the language of his enamored feeling:

> Worship, all ye that lovers be, this May,
>   For of your bliss the kalends are begun,
> And sing with us, away, winter, away,
>   Come, summer, come, the sweet season and sun.

As he gazes on the scene, and listens to the notes of the birds, he gradually relapses into one of those tender and undefinable reveries, which fill the youthful bosom in this delicious season. He wonders what this love may be, of which he has so often read, and which thus seems breathed forth in the quickening breath of May, and melting all nature into ecstasy and song. If it really be so great a felicity, and if it be a boon thus generally dispensed to the most insignificant beings, why is he alone cut off from its enjoyments?

> Oft would I think, O Lord, what may this be,
>   That love is of such noble myght and kynde?
> Loving his folke, and such prosperitee
>   Is it of him, as we in books do find:
>   May he oure hertes setten* and unbynd:
> Hath he upon our hertes such maistrye?
> Or is all this but feynit fantasye?
>
> For giff he be of so grete excellence,
>   That he of every wight hath care and charge,
> What have I gilt† to him, or done offense,
>   That I am thral'd, and birdis go at large?

In the midst of his musing, as he casts his eye downward, he beholds "the fairest and the freshest young floure" that ever he seen. It is the lovely Lady Jane, walking in the garden to enjoy the beauty of that "fresh May

Setten, incline.
†*Gilt*, what injury have I done, etc.

morrowe." Breaking thus suddenly upon his sight, in the moment of loneliness and excited susceptibility, she at once captivates the fancy of the romantic prince, and becomes the object of his wandering wishes, the sovereign of his ideal world.

There is, in this charming scene, an evident resemblance to the early part of Chaucer's *Knight's Tale;* where Palamon and Arcite fall in love with Emilia, whom they see walking in the garden of their prison. Perhaps the similarity of the actual fact to the incident which he had read in Chaucer may have induced James to dwell on it in his poem. His description of the Lady Jane is given in the picturesque and minute manner of his master; and being doubtless taken from the life, is a perfect portrait of a beauty of that day. He dwells, with the fondness of a lover, on every article of her apparel, from the net of pearl, splendent with emeralds and sapphires, that confined her golden hair, even to the "goodly chaine of small orfeverye"* about her neck, whereby there hung a ruby in shape of a heart, that seemed, he says, like a spark of fire burning upon her white bosom. Her dress of white tissue was looped up to enable her to walk with more freedom. She was accompanied by two female attendants, and about her sported a little hound decorated with bells; probably the small Italian hound of exquisite symmetry, which was a parlor favorite and pet among the fashionable dames of ancient times. James closes his description by a burst of general eulogium:

> In her was youth, beauty, with humble port,
>   Bounty, richesse, and womanly feature;
> God better knows then my pen can report,
>   Wisdom, largesse,† estate,‡ and cunning§ sure,
> In every point so guided her measure,
>   In word, in deed, in shape, in countenance,
>   That nature might no more her child advance.

*Wrought gold.   †*Largesse,* bounty.
‡*Estate,* dignity.   §*Cunning,* discretion.

The departure of the Lady Jane from the garden puts an end to this transient riot of the heart. With her departs the amorous illusion that had shed a temporary charm over the scene of his captivity, and he relapses into loneliness, now rendered tenfold more intolerable by this passing beam of unattainable beauty. Through the long and weary day he repines at his unhappy lot, and when evening approaches, and Phœbus, as he beautifully expresses it, had "bade farewell to every leaf and flower," he still lingers at the window, and, laying his head upon the cold stone, gives vent to a mingled flow of love and sorrow, until, gradually lulled by the mute melancholy of the twilight hour, he lapses, "half sleeping, half swoon," into a vision, which occupies the remainder of the poem, and in which is allegorically shadowed out the history of his passion.

When he wakes from his trance, he rises from his stony pillow, and, pacing his apartment, full of dreary reflections, questions his spirit, whither it has been wandering; whether, indeed, all that has passed before his dreaming fancy has been conjured up by preceding circumstances; or whether it is a vision, intended to comfort and assure him in his despondency. If the latter, he prays that some token may be sent to confirm the promise of happier days, given him in his slumbers. Suddenly, a turtle dove, of the purest whiteness, comes flying in at the window, and alights upon his hand, bearing in her bill a branch of red gilliflower, on the leaves of which is written, in letters of gold, the following sentence:

> Awake! awake! I bring, lover, I bring
> The newis glad that blissful is, and sure
> Of thy comfort; now laugh, and play, and sing,
> For in the heaven decretit is thy cure.

He receives the branch with mingled hope and dread; reads it with rapture: and this, he says, was the first token of his succeeding happiness. Whether this is a mere poetic fiction, or whether the Lady Jane did actually send him a token of her favor in this romantic way, remains to be determined according to the faith or fancy of the reader. He concludes his poem, by intimating that the promise conveyed in the vision and by the flower is fulfilled, by his being restored to liberty, and made happy in the possession of the sovereign of his heart.

Such is the poetical account given by James of his love adventures in Windsor Castle. How much of it is absolute fact, and how much the embellishment of fancy, it is fruitless to conjecture: let us not, however, reject every romantic incident as incompatible with real life; but let us sometimes take a poet at his word. I have noticed merely those parts of the poem immediately connected with the tower, and have passed over a large part, written in the allegorical vein, so much cultivated at that day. The language, of course, is quaint and antiquated, so that the beauty of many of its golden phrases will scarcely be perceived at the present day; but it is impossible not to be charmed with the genuine sentiment, the delightful artlessness and urbanity, which prevail throughout it. The descriptions of nature too, with which it is embellished, are given with a truth, a discrimination, and a freshness, worthy of the most cultivated periods of the art.

As an amatory poem, it is edifying in these days of coarser thinking, to notice the nature, refinement, and exquisite delicacy which pervade it; banishing every gross thought or immodest expression, and presenting female loveliness, clothed in all its chivalrous attributes of almost supernatural purity and grace.

James flourished nearly about the time of Chaucer and Gower, and was evidently an admirer and studier of their writings. Indeed, in one of his stanzas he acknowledges them as his masters; and, in some parts of his poem, we find traces of similarity to their productions, more especially to those of Chaucer. There are always, however, general features of resemblance in the works of contemporary authors, which are not so much borrowed from each other as from the times. Writers, like bees, toll their sweets in the wide world; they incorporate with their own conception the anecdotes and thoughts current in society; and thus each generation has some features in common, characteristic of the age in which it lived.

James belongs to one of the most brilliant eras of our literary history, and establishes the claims of his country to a participation in its primitive honors. Whilst a small cluster of English writers are constantly cited as the fathers of our verse, the name of their great Scottish compeer is apt to be passed over in silence; but he is evidently worthy of being enrolled in that little constellation of remote but neverfailing luminaries, who shine in the highest firmament of literature, and who, like morning stars, sang together at the bright dawning of British poesy.

Such of my readers as may not be familiar with Scottish history (though the manner in which it has of late been woven with captivating fiction has made it a universal study), may be curious to learn something of the subsequent history of James, and the fortunes of his love. His passion for the Lady Jane, as it was the solace of his captivity, so it facilitated his release, it being imagined by the court that a connection with the blood royal of England would attach him to its own interests. He was ultimately restored to his liberty and crown, having previously espoused the Lady Jane, who accompanied him to Scotland, and made him a most tender and devoted wife.

He found his kingdom in great confusion, the feudal chieftains having taken advantage of the troubles and irregularities of a long interregnum to strengthen themselves in their possessions, and place themselves above the power of the laws. James sought to find the basis of his power in the affections of his people. He attached the lower orders to him by the reformation of abuses, the temperate and equable administration of justice, the encouragement of the arts of peace, and the promotion of every thing that could diffuse comfort, competency, and innocent enjoyment through the humblest ranks of society. He mingled occasionally among the common people in disguise; visited their firesides; entered into their cares, their pursuits, and their amusements; informed himself of the mechanical arts, and how they could best be patronized and improved; and was thus an all-pervading spirit, watching with a benevolent eye over the meanest of his subjects. Having in this generous manner made himself strong in the hearts of the common people, he turned himself to curb the power of the factious nobility; to strip them of those dangerous immunities which they had usurped; to punish such as had been guilty of flagrant offences; and to bring the whole into proper obedience to the crown. For some time they bore this with outward submission, but with secret impatience and brooding resentment. A conspiracy was at length formed against his life, at the head of which was his own uncle, Robert Stewart, Earl of Athol, who, being too old himself for the perpetration of the deed of blood, instigated his grandson Sir Robert Stewart, together with Sir Robert Graham, and others of less note, to commit the deed. They broke into his bedchamber at the Dominican Convent near Perth, where he was residing, and barbarously murdered him by oft-repeated wounds. His faithful queen, rushing to throw her tender body between him and the sword, was twice wounded in the ineffectual attempt to shield him from the assassin; and it was not until she had been forcibly torn from his person, that the murder was accomplished.

It was the recollection of this romantic tale of former times, and of the golden little poem which had its birthplace in this Tower, that made me visit the old pile with more than common interest. The suit of armor hanging up in the hall, richly gilt and embellished, as if to figure in the tournay, brought the image of the gallant and romantic prince vividly before my imagination. I paced the deserted chambers where he had composed his poem; I leaned upon the window, and endeavored to persuade myself it was the very one where he had been visited by his vision; I looked out upon the spot where he had first seen the Lady Jane. It was the same genial and joyous month; the birds were again vying with each other in strains of liquid melody; every thing was bursting into vegetation, and budding forth the tender promise of the year. Time, which delights to obliterate the sterner memorials of human pride, seems to have passed lightly over this little scene of poetry and love, and to have withheld his desolating hand. Several centuries have gone by, yet the garden still flourishes at the foot of the Tower. It occupies what was once the moat of the Keep; and though some parts have been separated by dividing walls, yet others have still their arbors and shaded walks, as in the days of James, and the whole is sheltered, blooming, and retired. There is a charm about a spot that has been printed by the footsteps of departed beauty, and consecrated by the inspirations of the poet, which is heightened, rather than impaired, by the lapse of ages. It is, indeed, the gift of poetry to hallow every place in which it moves; to breathe around nature an odor more exquisite than the perfume of the rose, and to shed over it a tint more magical than the blush of morning.

Others may dwell on the illustrious deeds of James as a warrior and a legislator; but I have delighted to view him merely as the companion of his fellow-men, the benefactor of the human heart, stooping from his high estate to sow the sweet flowers of poetry and song in the paths of common life. He was the first to cultivate the vigorous and hardy plant of Scottish genius, which has since become so prolific of the most wholesome and highly-flavored fruit. He carried with him into the sterner regions of the north all the fertilizing arts of southern refinement. He did every thing in his power to win his countrymen to the gay, the elegant, and gentle arts, which soften and refine the character of a people, and wreathe a grace round the loftiness of a proud and warlike spirit. He wrote many poems, which, unfortunately for the fulness of his fame, are now lost to the world; one, which is still preserved, called "Christ's Kirk of the Green," shows how diligently he made himself acquainted with the rustic sports and pastimes, which constitute such a source of kind and social feeling among the Scottish peasantry; and with what simple and happy humor he could enter into their enjoyments. He contributed greatly to improve the national music; and traces of his tender sentiment, and elegant taste, are said to exist in those witching airs, still piped among the wild mountains and lonely glens of Scotland. He has thus connected his image with whatever is most gracious and endearing in the national character; he has embalmed his memory in song, and floated his name to after ages in the rich streams of Scottish melody. The recollection of these things was kindling at my heart as I paced the silent scene of his imprisonment. I have visited Vaucluse with as much enthusiasm as a pilgrim would visit the shrine at Loretto; but I have never felt more poetical devotion than when contemplating the old Tower and the little garden at Windsor, and musing over the romantic loves of the Lady Jane and the Royal Poet of Scotland.

THE COUNTRY CHURCH

A gentleman!
What, o' the woolpack? or the sugar-chest?
Or lists of velvet? which is't, pound, or yard,
You vend your gentry by?
BEGGAR'S BUSH

THERE are few places more favorable to the study of character than an English country church. I was once passing a few weeks at the seat of a friend, who resided in the vicinity of one, the appearance of which particularly struck my fancy. It was one of those rich morsels of quaint antiquity which give such a peculiar charm to English landscape. It stood in the midst of a country filled with ancient families, and contained, within its cold and silent aisles, the congregated dust of many noble generations. The interior walls were incrusted with monuments of every age and style. The light streamed through windows dimmed with armorial bearings, richly emblazoned in stained glass. In various parts of the church were tombs of knights, and high-born dames, of gorgeous workmanship, with their effigies in colored marble. On every side the eye was struck with some instance of aspiring mortality; some haughty memorial which human pride had erected over its kindred dust, in this temple of the most humble of all religions.

The congregation was composed of the neighboring people of rank, who sat in pews, sumptuously lined and cushioned, furnished with richly-gilded prayer-books, and decorated with their arms upon the pew doors; of the villagers and peasantry, who filled the back seats, and a small gallery beside the organ; and of the poor of the parish, who were ranged on benches in the aisles.

The service was performed by a snuffling well-fed vicar, who had a snug dwelling near the church. He was a privileged guest at all the tables of the neighborhood, and had been the keenest fox-hunter in the country; until age and good living had disabled him from doing anything more than ride to see the hounds throw off, and make one at the hunting dinner.

Under the ministry of such a pastor, I found it impossible to get into the train of thought suitable to the time and place: so, having, like many other feeble Christians, compromised with my conscience, by laying the sin of my own delinquency at another person's threshold, I occupied myself by making observations on my neighbors.

I was as yet a stranger in England, and curious to notice the manners of its fashionable classes. I found, as usual, that there was the least pretension where there was the most acknowledged title to respect. I was particularly struck, for instance, with the family of a nobleman of high rank, consisting of several sons and daughters. Nothing could be more simple and unassuming than their appearance. They generally came to church in the plainest equipage, and often on foot. The young ladies would stop and converse in the kindest

manner with the peasantry, caress the children, and
listen to the stories of the humble cottagers. Their
countenances were open and beautifully fair, with an
expression of high refinement, but, at the same time, a
frank cheerfulness, and an engaging affability. Their
brothers were tall, and elegantly formed. They were
dressed fashionably, but simply; with strict neatness and
propriety, but without any mannerism or foppishness.
Their whole demeanor was easy and natural, with that
lofty grace, and noble frankness, which bespeak
freeborn souls that have never been checked in their
growth by feelings of inferiority. There is a healthful
hardiness about real dignity, that never dreads contact
and communion with others, however humble. It is only
spurious pride that is morbid and sensitive, and shrinks
from every touch. I was pleased to see the manner in
which they would converse with the peasantry about
those rural concerns and field-sports, in which the
gentlemen of this country so much delight. In these
conversations there was neither haughtiness on the one
part, nor servility on the other; and you were only
reminded of the difference of rank by the habitual
respect of the peasant.

In contrast to these was the family of a wealthy citizen,
who had amassed a vast fortune; and, having purchased
the estate and mansion of a ruined nobleman in the
neighborhood, was endeavoring to assume all the style
and dignity of an hereditary lord of the soil. The family
always came to church *en prince*. They were rolled
majestically along in a carriage emblazoned with arms.
The crest glittered in silver radiance from every part of
the harness where a crest could possibly be placed. A fat
coachman, in a three-cornered hat, richly laced, and a
flaxen wig, curling close round his rosy face, was seated
on the box, with a sleek Danish dog beside him. Two

footmen, in gorgeous liveries, with huge bouquets, and gold-headed canes, lolled behind. The carriage rose and sunk on its long springs with peculiar stateliness of motion. The very horses champed their bits, arched their necks, and glanced their eyes more proudly than common horses; either because they had caught a little of the family feeling, or were reined up more tightly than ordinary.

I could not but admire the style with which this splendid pageant was brought up to the gate of the church-yard. There was a vast effect produced at the turning of an angle of the wall;—a great smacking of the whip, straining and scrambling of horses, glistening of harness, and flashing of wheels through gravel. This was the moment of triumph and vain-glory to the coachman. The horses were urged and checked until they were fretted into a foam. They threw out their feet in a prancing trot, dashing about pebbles at every step. The crowd of villagers sauntering quickly to church, opened precipitately to the right and left, gaping in vacant admiration. On reaching the gate, the horses were pulled up with a suddenness that produced an immediate stop, and almost threw them on their haunches.

There was an extraordinary hurry of the footman to alight, pull down the steps, and prepare every thing for the descent on earth of this august family. The old citizen first emerged his round, red face from out the door, looking about him with the pompous air of a man accustomed to rule on 'Change, and shake the Stock Market with a nod. His consort, a fine, fleshy, comfortable dame, followed him. There seemed, I must confess, but little pride in her composition. She was the picture of broad, honest, vulgar enjoyment. The world went well with her; and she liked the world. She had fine clothes, a fine house, a fine carriage, fine children, every thing was fine about her: it was nothing but driving about, and visiting and feasting. Life was to her a perpetual revel; it was one long Lord Mayor's day.

Two daughters succeeded to this goodly couple. They certainly were handsome; but had a supercilious air, that chilled admiration, and disposed the spectator to be critical. They were ultra-fashionable in dress; and, though no one could deny the richness of their decorations, yet their appropriateness might be questioned amidst the simplicity of a country church. They descended loftily from the carriage, and moved up the line of peasantry with a step that seemed dainty of the soil it trod on. They cast an excursive glance around, that passed coldly over the burly faces of the peasantry, until they met the eyes of the nobleman's family, when their countenances immediately brightened into smiles, and they made the most profound and elegant courtesies, which were returned in a manner that showed they were but slight acquaintances.

I must not forget the two sons of this aspiring citizen, who came to church in a dashing curricle, with outriders. They were arrayed in the extremity of the mode, with all that pedantry of dress which marks the man of questionable pretensions to style. They kept entirely by themselves, eyeing every one askance that came near them, as if measuring his claims to respectability; yet they were without conversation, except the exchange of an occasional cant phrase. They even moved artificially; for their bodies, in compliance with the caprice of the day, had been disciplined into the absence of all ease and freedom. Art had done every thing to accomplish them as men of fashion, but nature had denied them the nameless grace. They were vulgarly shaped, like men formed from the common purposes of life, and had that air of supercilious assumption which is never seen in the true gentleman.

I have been rather minute in drawing the pictures of these two families, because I considered them specimens of what is often to be met with in this country—the unpretending great, and the arrogant little. I have no respect for titled rank, unless it be accompanied with true nobility of soul; but I have remarked in all countries where artificial distinctions exist, that the very highest classes are always the most courteous and unassuming. Those who are well assured of their own standing are least apt to trespass on that of others: whereas nothing is so offensive as the aspirings of vulgarity, which thinks to elevate itself by humiliating its neighbor.

As I have brought these families into contrast, I must notice their behavior in church. That of the nobleman's family was quiet, serious, and attentive. Not that they appeared to have any fervor of devotion, but rather a respect for sacred things, and sacred places, inseparable from good breeding. The others, on the contrary, were in a perpetual flutter and whisper; they betrayed a continual consciousness of finery, and a sorry ambition of being the wonders of a rural congregation.

The old gentleman was the only one really attentive to the service. He took the whole burden of family devotion upon himself, standing bolt upright, and uttering the responses with a loud voice that might be heard all over the church. It was evident that he was one of those thorough church and king men, who connect the idea of devotion and loyalty; who consider the Deity, somehow or other, of the government party, and religion "a very excellent sort of thing, that ought to be countenanced and kept up."

When he joined so loudly in the service, it seemed

more by way of example to the lower orders, to show
them that, though so great and wealthy, he was not
above being religious; as I have seen a turtle-fed
alderman swallow publicly a basin of charity soup,
smacking his lips at every mouthful, and pronouncing it
"excellent food for the poor."

When the service was at an end, I was curious to
witness the several exits of my groups. The young
noblemen and their sisters, as the day was fine, preferred strolling home across the fields, chatting with the
country people as they went. The others departed as
they came, in grand parade. Again were the equipages
wheeled up to the gate. There was again the smacking of
whips, the clattering of hoofs, and the glittering of
harness. The horses started off almost at a bound; the
villagers again hurried to right and left; the wheels
threw up a cloud of dust; and the aspiring family was
rapt out of sight in a whirlwind.

THE WIDOW AND HER SON

Pittie olde age, within whose silver haires
Honour and reverence evermore have rain'd.
MARRLOWE'S TAMBURLAINE

THOSE who are in the habit of remarking such
matters, must have noticed the passive quiet of an
English landscape on Sunday. The clacking of the mill,
the regularly recurring stroke of the flail, the din of the
blacksmith's hammer, the whistling of the ploughman,
the rattling of the cart, and all other sounds of rural
labor are suspended. The very farm dogs bark less
frequently, being less disturbed by passing travellers. At

such times I have almost fancied the winds sunk into quiet, and that the sunny landscape, with its fresh green tints melting into blue haze, enjoyed the hallowed calm.

> Sweet day, so pure, so calm, so bright,
> The bridal of the earth and sky.

Well was it ordained that the day of devotion should be a day of rest. The holy repose which reigns over the face of nature, has its moral influence; every restless passion is charmed down, and we feel the natural religion of the soul gently springing up within us. For my part, there are feelings that visit me, in a country church, amid the beautiful serenity of nature, which I experience nowhere else; and if not a more religious, I think I am a better man on Sunday than on any other day of the seven.

During my recent residence in the country, I used frequently to attend at the old village church. Its shadowy aisles; its mouldering monuments; its dark oaken panelling, all reverend with the gloom of departed years, seemed to fit it for the haunt of solemn meditation; but being in a wealthy aristocratic neighborhood, the glitter of fashion penetrated even into the sanctuary; and I felt myself continually thrown back upon the world by the frigidity and pomp of the poor worms around me. The only being in the whole congregation who appeared thoroughly to feel the humble and prostrate piety of a true Christian was a poor decrepit old woman, bending under the weight of years and infirmities. She bore the traces of something better than abject poverty. The lingerings of decent pride were visible in her appearance. Her dress, though humble in the extreme, was scrupulously clean. Some trivial respect, too, had been awarded her, for she did not take her seat among the village poor, but sat alone on the steps of the altar. She seemed to have survived all love, all friendship, all society; and to have nothing left her but the hopes of heaven. When I saw her feebly rising and bending her aged form in prayer; habitually conning her prayer-book, which her palsied hand and failing eyes would not permit her to read, but which she evidently knew by heart; I felt persuaded that the faltering voice of that poor woman arose to heaven far before the responses of the clerk, the swell of the organ, or the chanting of the choir.

I am fond of loitering about country churches, and this was so delightfully situated, that it frequently attracted me. It stood on a knoll, round which a small stream made a beautiful bend, and then wound its way through a long reach of soft meadow scenery. The church was surrounded by yew-trees which seemed almost coeval with itself. Its tall Gothic spire shot up lightly from among them, with rooks and crows generally wheeling about it. I was seated there one still sunny morning, watching two laborers who were digging a grave. They had chosen one of the most remote and neglected corners of the church-yard; where, from the number of nameless graves around, it would appear that the indigent and friendless were huddled into the earth. I was told that the new-made grave was for the only son of a poor widow. While I was meditating on the distinctions of worldly rank, which extend thus down into the very dust, the toll of the bell announced the approach of the funeral. They were the obsequies of poverty, with which pride had nothing to do. A coffin of the plainest materials, without pall or other covering, was borne by some of the villagers. The sexton walked before with an air of cold indifference. There were no mock mourners in the trappings of affected woe; but there was one real mourner who feebly tottered after the corpse. It was the aged mother of the deceased—the poor old woman whom I had seen seated on the steps of the altar. She was supported by a humble friend, who was endeavoring to comfort her. A few of the neighboring poor had joined the train, and some children of the village were running hand in hand, now shouting with unthinking mirth, and now pausing to gaze, with childish curiosity, on the grief of the mourner.

As the funeral train approached the grave, the parson issued from the church porch, arrayed in the surplice, with prayer-book in hand, and attended by the clerk. The service, however, was a mere act of charity. The deceased had been destitute, and the survivor was penniless. It was shuffled through, therefore, in form, but coldly and unfeelingly. The well-fed priest moved but a few steps from the church door; his voice could scarcely be heard at the grave; and never did I hear the funeral service, that sublime and touching ceremony, turned into such a frigid mummery of words.

I approached the grave. The coffin was placed on the ground. On it were inscribed the name and age of the deceased—"George Somers, aged 26 years." The poor mother had been assisted to kneel down at the head of it. Her withered hands were clasped, as if in prayer, but I could perceive by a feeble rocking of the body, and a convulsive motion of her lips, that she was gazing on the last relics of her son, with the yearnings of a mother's heart.

Preparations were made to deposit the coffin in the earth. There was that bustling stir which breaks so harshly on the feelings of grief and affection; directions given in the cold tones of business: the striking of spades into sand and gravel; which, at the grave of those we love, is, of all sounds, the most withering. The bustle around seemed to waken the mother from a wretched reverie. She raised her glazed eyes, and looked about with a faint wildness. As the men approached with cords to lower the coffin into the grave, she wrung her hands, and broke into an agony of grief. The poor woman who attended her took her by the arm, endeavoring to raise her from the earth, and to whisper something like consolation—"Nay, now—nay, now—don't take it so sorely to heart." She could only shake her head and wring her hands, as one not to be comforted.

As they lowered the body into the earth, the creaking of the cords seemed to agonize her; but when, on some accidental obstruction, there was a justling of the coffin, all the tenderness of the mother burst forth; as if any harm could come to him who was far beyond the reach of worldly suffering.

I could see no more—my heart swelled into my throat—my eyes filled with tears—I felt as if I were acting a barbarous part in standing by, and gazing idly on this scene of maternal anguish. I wandered to another part of the church-yard, where I remained until the funeral train had dispersed.

When I saw the mother slowly and painfully quitting the grave, leaving behind her the remains of all that was dear to her on earth, and returning to silence and destitution, my heart ached for her. What, thought I, are the distresses of the rich! they have friends to soothe—pleasures to beguile—a world to divert and dissipate their griefs. What are the sorrows of the young! Their growing minds soon close above the wound—their elastic spirits soon rise beneath the pressure—their green and ductile affections soon twine round new objects. But the sorrows of the poor, who have no outward appliances to soothe—the sorrows of the aged, with whom life at best is but a wintry day, and who can look for no after-growth of joy—the sorrows of a widow, aged, solitary, destitute, mourning over an only son, the last solace of her years; these are indeed sorrows which make us feel the impotency of consolation.

It was some time before I left the church-yard. On my way homeward I met with the woman who had acted as comforter: she was just returning from accompanying the mother to her lonely habitation, and I drew from her some particulars connected with the affecting scene I had witnessed.

The parents of the deceased had resided in the village from childhood. They had inhabited one of the neatest cottages, and by various rural occupations, and the assistance of a small garden, had supported themselves creditably and comfortably, and led a happy and a blameless life. They had one son, who had grown up to be the staff and pride of their age.—"Oh, sir!" said the good woman, "he was such a comely lad, so sweet-tempered, so kind to every one around him, so dutiful to his parents! It did one's heart good to see him of a Sunday, dressed out in his best, so tall, so straight, so cheery, supporting his old mother to church—for she was always fonder of leaning on George's arm, than on her good man's; and, poor soul, she might well be proud of him, for a finer lad there was not in the country round."

Unfortunately, the son was tempted, during a year of scarcity and agricultural hardship, to enter into the service of one of the small craft that plied on a neighboring river. He had not been long in this employ when he was entrapped by a press-gang, and carried off to sea. His parents received tidings of his seizure, but beyond that they could learn nothing. It was the loss of their main prop. The father, who was already infirm, grew heartless and melancholy, and sunk into his grave. The widow, left lonely in her age and feebleness, could no longer support herself, and came upon the parish. Still there was a kind feeling toward her throughout the village, and a certain respect as being one of the oldest inhabitants. As no one applied for the cottage, in which she had passed so many happy days, she was permitted to remain in it, where she lived solitary and almost helpless. The few wants of nature were chiefly supplied from the scanty productions of her little garden, which the neighbors would now and then cultivate for her. It was but a few days before the time at which these circumstances were told me, that she was gathering some vegetables for her repast, when she heard the cottage door which faced the garden suddenly opened. A stranger came out, and seemed to be looking eagerly and wildly around. He was dressed in seaman's clothes, was emaciated and ghastly pale, and bore the air of one broken by sickness and hardships. He saw her, and hastened toward her, but his steps were faint and faltering; he sank on his knees before her, and sobbed like a child. The poor woman gazed upon him with a vacant and wandering eye—"Oh, my dear, dear mother! don't you know your son? your poor boy, George?" It was indeed the wreck of her once noble lad, who, shattered by wounds, by sickness and foreign imprisonment, had, at length, dragged his wasted limbs homeward, to repose among the scenes of his childhood.

I will not attempt to detail the particulars of such a meeting, where joy and sorrow were so completely blended: still he was alive! he was come home! he might yet live to comfort and cherish her old age! Nature, however, was exhausted in him; and if any thing had been wanting to finish the work of fate, the desolation of his native cottage would have been sufficient. He stretched himself on the pallet on which his widowed mother had passed many a sleepless night, and he never rose from it again.

The villagers, when they heard that George Somers had returned, crowded to see him, offering every comfort and assistance that their humble means afforded. He was too weak, however, to talk—he could only look his thanks. His mother was his constant attendant; and he seemed unwilling to be helped by any other hand.

There is something in sickness that breaks down the pride of manhood; that softens the heart, and brings it back to the feelings of infancy. Who that has languished, even in advanced life, in sickness and despondency; who that has pined on a weary bed in the neglect and loneliness of a foreign land; but has thought on the mother "that looked on his childhood," that smoothed his pillow, and administered to his helplessness? Oh! there is an enduring tenderness in the love of a mother to her son that transcends all other affections of the heart. It is neither to be chilled by selfishness, nor daunted by danger, nor weakened by worthlessness, nor stifled by ingratitude. She will sacrifice every comfort to his convenience; she will surrender every pleasure to his enjoyment; she will glory in his fame, and exult in his prosperity:—and, if misfortune overtake him, he will be the dearer to her from misfortune; and if disgrace settle upon his name, she will still love and cherish him in spite of his disgrace; and if all the world beside cast him off, she will be all the world to him.

Poor George Somers had known what it was to be in sickness, and none to soothe—lonely and in prison, and none to visit him. He could not endure his mother from his sight; if she moved away, his eye would follow her. She would sit for hours by his bed, watching him as he slept. Sometimes he would start from a feverish dream, and look anxiously up until he saw her bending over him; when he would take her hand, lay it on his bosom, and fall asleep, with the tranquillity of a child. In this way he died.

My first impulse on hearing this humble tale of affliction was to visit the cottage of the mourner, and administer pecuniary assistance, and, if possible, comfort. I found, however, on inquiry, that the good feelings of the villagers had prompted them to do every thing that the case admitted: and as the poor know best how to console each other's sorrows, I did not venture to intrude.

The next Sunday I was at the village church; when to my surprise, I saw the poor old woman tottering down the aisle to her accustomed seat on the steps of the altar.

She had made an effort to put on something like mourning for her son; and nothing could be more touching than this struggle between pious affection and utter poverty: a black ribbon or so—a faded black handkerchief, and one or two more such humble attempts to express by outward signs that grief which passes show. When I looked round upon the storied monuments, the stately hatchments, the cold marble pomp, with which grandeur mourned magnificently over departed pride, and turned to this poor widow, bowed down by age and sorrow, at the altar of her god, and offering up the prayers and praises of a pious, though a broken heart, I felt that this living monument of real grief was worth them all.

I related her story to some of the wealthy members of the congregation, and they were moved by it. They exerted themselves to render her situation more comfortable, and to lighten her afflictions. It was, however, but smoothing a few steps to the grave. In the course of a Sunday or two after, she was missed from her usual seat at church, and before I left the neighborhood, I heard, with a feeling of satisfaction, that she had quietly breathed her last, and had gone to rejoin those she loved, in that world where sorrow is never known, and friends are never parted.

A SUNDAY IN LONDON*

IN A preceding paper I have spoken of an English Sunday in the country, and its tranquillizing effect upon the landscape; but where is its sacred influence more strikingly apparent than in the very heart of that great Babel, London? On this sacred day, the gigantic monster is charmed into repose. The intolerable din and struggle of the week are at an end. The shops are shut. The fires of forges and manufactories are extinguished; and the sun, no longer obscured by murky clouds of smoke, pours down a sober, yellow radiance into the quiet streets. The few pedestrians we meet, instead of hurrying forward with anxious countenances, move leisurely along; their brows are smoothed from the wrinkles of business and care; they have put on their Sunday looks, and Sunday manners, with their Sunday clothes, and are cleansed in mind as well as in person.

And now the melodious clangor of bells from church towers summons their several flocks to the fold. Forth issues from his mansion the family of the decent tradesman, the small children in the advance; then the citizen and his comely spouse, followed by the grown-up daughters, with small morocco-bound prayer-books laid in the folds of their pocket-handkerchiefs. The house-maid looks after them from the window, admiring the finery of the family, and receiving, perhaps, a nod and

*Part of a sketch omitted in the preceding editions.

smile from her young mistresses, at whose toilet she has assisted.

Now rumbles along the carriage of some magnate of the city, peradventure an alderman or a sheriff; and now the patter of many feet announces a procession of charity scholars, in uniforms of antique cut, and each with a prayer-book under his arm.

The ringing of bells is at an end; the rumbling of the carriage has ceased; the pattering of feet is heard no more; the flocks are folded in ancient churches, cramped up in by-lanes and corners of the crowded city, where the vigilant beadle keeps watch, like the shepherd's dog, round the threshold of the sanctuary. For a time every thing is hushed; but soon is heard the deep, pervading sound of the organ, rolling and vibrating through the empty lanes and courts; and the sweet chanting of the choir making them resound with melody and praise. Never have I been more sensible of the sanctifying effect of church music, than when I have heard it thus poured forth, like a river of joy, through the inmost recesses of this great metropolis, elevating it, as it were, from all the sordid pollutions of the week; and bearing the poor world-worn soul on a tide of triumphant harmony to heaven.

The morning service is at an end. The streets are again alive with the congregations returning to their homes, but soon again relapse into silence. Now comes on the Sunday dinner, which, to the city tradesman, is a meal of some importance. There is more leisure for social enjoyment at the board. Members of the family can now gather together, who are separated by the laborious occupations of the week. A school-boy may be permitted on that day to come to the paternal home; an old friend of the family takes his accustomed Sunday seat at the board, tells over his well-known stories, and rejoices young and old with his well-known jokes.

On Sunday afternoon the city pours forth its legions to breathe the fresh air and enjoy the sunshine of the parks and rural environs. Satirists may say what they please about the rural enjoyments of a London citizen on Sunday, but to me there is something delightful in beholding the poor prisoner of the crowded and dusty city enabled thus to come forth once a week and throw himself upon the green bosom of nature. He is like a child restored to the mother's breast; and they who first spread out these noble parks and magnificent pleasure-grounds which surround this huge metropolis, have done at least as much for its health and morality, as if they had expended the amount of cost in hospitals, prisons, and penitentiaries.

THE BOAR'S HEAD TAVERN, EASTCHEAP

A SHAKESPEAREAN RESEARCH

"A tavern is the rendezvous, the exchange, the staple of good fellows. I have heard my great-grandfather tell, how his great-great-grandfather should say, that it was an old proverb when his great-grandfather was a child, that 'it was a good wind that blew a man to the wine.'"

MOTHER BOMBIE

IT IS a pious custom, in some Catholic countries, to honor the memory of saints by votive lights burnt before their pictures. The popularity of a saint, therefore, may be known by the number of these offerings.

One, perhaps, is left to moulder in the darkness of his little chapel; another may have a solitary lamp to throw its blinking rays athwart his effigy; while the whole blaze of adoration is lavished at the shrine of some beatified father of renown. The wealthy devotee brings his huge luminary of wax; the eager zealot his seven-branched candlestick, and even the mendicant pilgrim is by no means satisfied that sufficient light is thrown upon the deceased, unless he hangs up his little lamp of smoking oil. The consequence is, that in the eagerness to enlighten, they are often apt to obscure; and I have occasionally seen an unlucky saint almost smoked out of countenance by the officiousness of his followers.

In like manner has it fared with the immortal Shakespeare. Every writer considers it his bounden duty to light up some portion of his character or works, and to rescue some merit from oblivion. The commentator, opulent in words, produces vast tomes of dissertations; the common herd of editors send up mists of obscurity from their notes at the bottom of each page; and every casual scribbler brings his farthing rushlight of eulogy or research, to swell the cloud of incense and of smoke.

As I honor all established usages of my brethren of the quill, I thought it but proper to contribute my mite of homage to the memory of the illustrious bard. I was for some time, however, sorely puzzled in what way I should discharge this duty. I found myself anticipated in every attempt at a new reading; every doubtful line had been explained a dozen different ways, and perplexed beyond the reach of elucidation; and as to fine passages, they had all been amply praised by previous admirers; nay, so completely had the bard, of late, been overlarded with panegyric by a great German critic, that it was difficult now to find even a fault that had not been argued into a beauty.

In this perplexity, I was one morning turning over his pages, when I casually opened upon the comic scenes of Henry IV, and was, in a moment, completely lost in the madcap revelry of the Boar's Head Tavern. So vividly and naturally are these scenes of humor depicted, and with such force and consistency are the characters sustained, that they become mingled up in the mind with the facts and personages of real life. To few readers does it occur, that these are all ideal creations of a poet's brain, and that, in sober truth, no such knot of merry roysters ever enlivened the dull neighborhood of Eastcheap.

For my part, I love to give myself up to the illusions of poetry. A hero of fiction that never existed is just as valuable to me as a hero of history that existed a thousand years since, and, if I may be excused such an insensibility to the common ties of human nature, I would not give up fat Jack for half the great men of ancient chronicle. What have the heroes of yore done for me, or men like me? They have conquered countries of which I do not enjoy an acre; or they have gained laurels of which I do not inherit a leaf; or they have furnished examples of hair-brained prowess, which I have neither the opportunity nor the inclination to follow. But, old Jack Falstaff!—kind Jack Falstaff!—sweet jack Falstaff!—has enlarged the boundaries of human enjoyment; he has added vast regions of wit and good humor, in which the poorest man may revel; and has bequeathed a never-failing inheritance of jolly laughter, to make mankind merrier and better to the latest posterity.

A thought suddenly struck me: "I will make a pilgrimage to Eastcheap," said I, closing the book, "and see if the old Boar's Head Tavern still exists. Who knows but I may light upon some legendary traces of Dame Quickly and her guests; at any rate, there will be a kindred pleasure, in treading the halls once vocal with their mirth, to that the toper enjoys in smelling to the empty cask once filled with generous wine."

The resolution was no sooner formed than put in execution. I forbear to treat of the various adventures and wonders I encountered in my travels; of the haunted regions of Cock Lane; of the faded glories of Little Britain, and the parts adjacent; what perils I ran in Cateaton-street and old Jewry; of the renowned Guild-hall and its two stunted giants, the pride and wonder of the city, and the terror of all unlucky urchins; and how I visited London Stone, and struck my staff upon it, in imitation of that arch rebel, Jack Cade.

Let it suffice to say, that I at length arrived in merry Eastcheap, that ancient region of wit and wassail, where the very names of the streets relished of good cheer, as Pudding Lane bears testimony even at the present day. For Eastcheap, says old Stowe, "was always famous for its convivial doings. The cookes cried hot ribbes of beef roasted, pies well baked, and other victuals: there was clattering of pewter pots, harpe, pipe, and sawtrie." Alas! how sadly is the scene changed since the roaring days of Falstaff and old Stowe! The madcap royster has given place to the plodding tradesman; the clattering of pots and the sound of "harpe and sawtrie" to the din of carts and the accursed dinging of the dustman's bell; and no song is heard, save, haply, the strain of some siren from Billinsgate, chanting the eulogy of deceased mackerel.

I sought, in vain, for the ancient abode of Dame Quickly. The only relic of it is a boar's head, carved in relief in stone, which formerly served as the sign, but at present is built into the parting line of two houses, which stand on the site of the renowned old tavern.

For the history of this little abode of good fellowship, I was referred to a tallow-chandler's widow, opposite, who had been born and brought up on the spot, and was looked up to as the indisputable chronicler of the neighborhood. I found her seated in a little back parlor, the window of which looked out upon a yard about eight feet square, laid out as a flowergarden; while a glass door opposite afforded a distant peep of the street, through a vista of soap and tallow candles: the two views, which comprised, in all probability, her prospects in life, and the little world in which she had lived, and moved, and had her being, for the better part of a century.

To be versed in the history of Eastcheap, great and little, from London Stone even unto the Monument, was doubtless, in her opinion, to be acquainted with the history of the universe. Yet, with all this, she possessed the simplicity of true wisdom, and that liberal communicative disposition, which I have generally remarked in intelligent old ladies, knowing in the concerns of their neighborhood.

Her information, however, did not extend far back into antiquity. She could throw no light upon the history of the Boar's Head, from the time that Dame Quickly espoused the valiant Pistol, until the great fire of London, when it was unfortunately burnt down. It was soon rebuilt, and continued to flourish under the old name and sign, until a dying landlord, struck with remorse for double scores, bad measures, and other iniquities, which are incident to the sinful race of publicans, endeavored to make his peace with heaven, by bequeathing the tavern to St. Michael's Church, Crooked Lane, towards the supporting of a chaplain. For some time the vestry meetings were regularly held there; but it was observed that the old Boar never held up his head under church government. He gradually declined, and finally gave his last gasp about thirty years since. The tavern was then turned into shops; but she informed me that a picture of it was still preserved in St. Michael's Church, which stood just in the rear. To get a sight of this picture was now my determination; so, having informed myself of the abode of the sexton, I took my leave of the venerable chronicler of Eastcheap, my visit having doubtless raised greatly her opinion of her legendary lore, and furnished an important incident in the history of her life.

It cost me some difficulty, and much curious inquiry, to ferret out the humble hanger-on to the church. I had to explore Crooked Lane, and divers little alleys, and elbows, and dark passages, with which this old city is perforated, like an ancient cheese, or a worm-eaten chest of drawers. At length I traced him to a corner of a small court surrounded by lofty houses, where the inhabitants enjoy about as much of the face of heaven, as a community of frogs at the bottom of a well.

The sexton was a meek, acquiescing little man, of a bowing, lowly habit: yet he had a pleasant twinkling in his eye, and, if encouraged, would now and then hazard a small pleasantry; such as a man of his low estate might venture to make in the company of high churchwardens, and other mighty men of the earth. I found him in company with the deputy organist, seated apart, like Milton's angels, discoursing, no doubt, on high doctrinal points, and settling the affairs of the church over a friendly pot of ale—for the lower classes of English seldom deliberate on any weighty matter without the assistance of a cool tankard to clear their understandings. I arrived at the moment when they had finished their ale and their argument, and were about to repair to the church to put it in order; so having made known my wishes, I received their gracious permission to accompany them.

The church of St. Michael's, Crooked Lane, standing a short distance from Billingsgate, is enriched with the tombs of many fishmongers of renown; and as every profession has its galaxy of glory, and its constellation of great men, I presume the monument of a mighty fishmonger of the olden time is regarded with as much reverence by succeeding generations of the craft, as poets feel on contemplating the tomb of Virgil, or soldiers the monument of a Marlborough or Turenne.

I cannot but turn aside, while thus speaking of illustrious men, to observe that St. Michael's, Crooked Lane, contains also the ashes of that doughty champion, William Walworth, knight, who so manfully clove down the sturdy wight, Wat Tyler, in Smithfield; a hero worthy of honorable blazon, as almost the only Lord Mayor on record famous for deeds of arms:—the sovereigns of Cockney being generally renowned, as the most pacific of all potentates.*

*The following was the ancient inscription on the monument of this worthy; which, unhappily, was destroyed in the great conflagration.

> Hereunder lyth a man of Fame,
> William Walworth callyd by name;
> Fishmonger he was in lyfftime here,
> And twise Lord Maior, as in books appere;
> Who, with courage stout and manly myght,
> Slew Jack Straw in Kyng Richard's sight.
> For which act done, and trew entent,
> The Kyng made him knyght incontinent;
> And gave him armes, as here you see,
> To declare his fact and chivaldrie.
> He left this lyff the yere of our God
> Thirteen hundred forescore and three odd.

An error in the foregoing inscription has been corrected by the venerable Stowe. "Whereas," saith he, "it hath been far spread abroad by vulgar opinion, that the rebel smitten down so manfully by Sir William Walworth, the then worthy Lord Maior, was named Jack Straw, and not Wat Tyler, I thought good to reconcile this rash-

Adjoining the church, in a small cemetery, immediately under the back window of what was once the Boar's Head, stands the tombstone of Robert Preston, whilom drawer at the tavern. It is now nearly a century since this trusty drawer of good liquor closed his bustling career, and was thus quietly deposited within call of his customers. As I was clearing away the weeds from his epitaph, the little sexton drew me on one side with a mysterious air, and informed me in a low voice, that once upon a time, on a dark wintry night, when the wind was unruly, howling, and whistling, banging about doors and windows, and twirling weathercocks, so that the living were frightened out of their beds, and even the dead could not sleep quietly in their graves, the ghost of honest Preston, which happened to be airing itself in the church-yard, was attracted by the well-known call of "waiter" from the Boar's Head, and made its sudden appearance in the midst of a roaring club, just as the parish clerk was singing a stave from the "mirre garland of Captain Death;" to the discomfiture of sundry train-band captains, and the conversion of an infidel attorney, who became a zealous Christian on the spot, and was never known to twist the truth afterwards, except in the way of business.

I beg it may be remembered, that I do not pledge myself for the authenticity of this anecdote; though it is well known that the church-yards and by-corners of this old metropolis are very much infested with perturbed spirits; and every one must have heard of the Cock Lane ghost, and the apparition that guards the regalia in the

---

conceived doubt by such testimony as I find in ancient and good records. The principal leaders, or captains, of the commons, were Wat Tyler, as the first man; the second was John, or Jack, Straw," etc., etc.
STOWE'S LONDON

Tower, which has frightened so many bold sentinels almost out of their wits.

Be all this as it may, this Robert Preston seems to have been a worthy successor to the nimble-tongued Francis, who attended upon the revels of Prince Hal; to have been equally prompt with his "anon, anon, sir;" and to have transcended his predecessor in honesty; for Falstaff, the veracity of whose taste no man will venture to impeach, flatly accuses Francis of putting lime in his sack; whereas honest Preston's epitaph lauds him for the sobriety of his conduct, the soundness of his wine, and the fairness of his measure.* The worthy dignitaries of the church, however, did not appear much captivated by the sober virtues of the tapster; the deputy organist, who had a moist look out of the eye, made some shrewd remark on the abstemiousness of a man brought up among full hogsheads; and the little sexton corroborated his opinion by a significant wink, and a dubious shake of the head.

Thus far my researches, though they threw much light of the history of tapsters, fishmongers, and Lord Mayors, yet disappointed me in the great object of my quest, the picture of the Boar's Head Tavern. No such painting was to be found in the church of St. Michael.

---

* As this inscription is rife with excellent morality, I transcribe it for the admonition of delinquent tapsters. It is, no doubt, the production of some choice spirit, who once frequented the Boar's Head.

> Bacchus, to give the toping world surprise,
> Produced one sober son, and here he lies.
> Though rear'd among full hogsheads, he defy'd
> The charms of wine, and every one beside.
> O reader, if to justice thou'rt inclined,
> Keep honest Preston daily in thy mind.
> He drew good wine, took care to fill his pots,
> Had sundry virtues that excused his faults.
> You that on Bacchus have the like dependance,
> Pray copy Bob in measure and attendance.

"Marry and amen!" said I, "here endeth my research!"
So I was giving the matter up, with the air of a baffled
antiquary, when my friend the sexton, perceiving me to
be curious in every thing relative to the old tavern,
offered to show me the choice vessels of the vestry,
which had been handed down from remote times, when
the parish meetings were held at the Boar's Head. These
were deposited in the parish club-room, which had been
transferred, on the decline of the ancient establishment,
to a tavern in the neighborhood.

A few steps brought us to the house, which stands No.
12 Miles Lane, bearing the title of The Mason's Arms,
and is kept by Master Edward Honeyball, the "bully-
rock" of the establishment. It is one of those little
taverns which abound in the heart of the city, and form
the centre of gossip and intelligence of the neighborhood. We entered the bar-room, which was narrow and
darkling; for in these close lanes but rays of reflected
light are enabled to struggle down to the inhabitants,
whose broad day is at best but a tolerable twilight. The
room was partitioned into boxes, each containing a table
spread with a clean white cloth, ready for dinner. This
showed that the guests were of the good old stamp, and
divided their day equally, for it was but just one o'clock.
At the lower end of the room was a clear coal fire, before
which a breast of lamb was roasting. A row of bright
brass candlesticks and pewter mugs glistened along the
mantlepiece, and an old-fashioned clock ticked in one
corner. There was something primitive in this medley of
kitchen, parlor, and hall, that carried me back to earlier
times, and pleased me. The place, indeed, was humble,
but every thing had that look of order and neatness,
which bespeaks the superintendence of a notable English housewife. A group of amphibious-looking beings,
who might be either fishermen or sailors, were regaling

themselves in one of the boxes. As I was a visitor of rather higher pretensions, I was ushered into a little misshapen backroom, having at least nine corners. It was lighted by a skylight, furnished with antiquated leathern chairs, and ornamented with the portrait of a fat pig. It was evidently appropriated to particular customers, and I found a shabby gentleman, in a red nose and oil-cloth hat, seated in one corner, meditating on a half-empty pot of porter.

The old sexton had taken the landlady aside, and with an air of profound importance imparted to her my errand. Dame Honeyball was a likely, plump, bustling little woman, and no bad substitute for that paragon of hostesses, Dame Quickly. She seemed delighted with an opportunity to oblige; and hurrying up stairs to the archives of her house, where the precious vessels of the parish club were deposited, she returned, smiling and courtesying, with them in her hands.

The first she presented me was a japanned iron tobacco-box, of gigantic size, out of which, I was told, the vestry had smoked at their stated meetings, since time immemorial; and which was never suffered to be profaned by vulgar hands, or used on common occasions. I received it with becoming reverence; but what was my delight, at beholding on its cover the identical painting of which I was in quest! There was displayed the outside of the Boar's Head Tavern, and before the door was to be seen the whole convivial group, at table, in full revel; pictured with that wonderful fidelity and force, with which the portraits of renowned generals and commodores are illustrated on tobacco-boxes, for the benefit of posterity. Lest, however, there should be any mistake, the cunning limner had warily inscribed the names of Prince Hal and Falstaff on the bottoms of their chairs.

On the inside of the cover was an inscription, nearly obliterated, recording that this box was the gift of Sir Richard Gore, for the use of the vestry meetings at the Boar's Head Tavern, and that it was "repaired and beautified by his successor, Mr. John Packard, 1767." Such is a faithful description of this august and venerable relic; and I question whether the learned Scriblerius contemplated his Roman shield, or the Knights of the Round Table the long-sought san-greal, with more exultation.

While I was meditating on it with enraptured gaze, Dame Honeyball, who was highly gratified by the interest it excited, put in my hands a drinking cup or goblet, which also belonged to the vestry, and was descended from the old Boar's Head. It bore the inscription of having been the gift of Francis Wythers, knight, and was held, she told me, in exceeding great value, being considered very "antyke." This last opinion was strengthened by the shabby gentleman in the red nose and oil-cloth hat, and whom I strongly suspected of being a lineal descendant from the valiant Bardolph. He suddenly roused from his mediation on the pot of porter, and, casting a knowing look at the goblet, exclaimed, "Ay, ay! the head don't ache now that made that there article!"

The great importance attached to this memento of ancient revelry by modern churchwardens at first puzzled me; but there is nothing sharpens the apprehension so much as antiquarian research; for I immediately perceived that this could be no other than the identical "parcel-gilt goblet" on which Falstaff made his loving, but faithless vow to Dame Quickly; and which would, of course, be treasured up with care among the regalia of her domains, as a testimony of that solemn contract.*

Mine hostess, indeed, gave me a long history how the goblet had been handed down from generation to generation. She also entertained me with many particulars concerning the worthy vestrymen who have seated themselves thus quietly on the stools of the ancient roysters of Eastcheap, and, like so many commentators, utter clouds of smoke in honor of Shakespeare. These I forbear to relate, lest my readers should not be as curious in these matters as myself. Suffice it to say, the neighbors, one and all, about Eastcheap, believe that Falstaff and his merry crew actually lived and revelled there. Nay, there are several legendary anecdotes concerning him still extant among the oldest frequenters of the Mason's Arms, which they give as transmitted down from their forefathers; and Mr. M'Kash, an Irish hairdresser, whose shop stands on the site of the old Boar's Head, has several dry jokes of Fat Jack's, not laid down in the books, with which he makes his customers ready to die of laughter.

I now turned to my friend the sexton to make some further inquiries, but I found him sunk in pensive meditation. His head had declined a little on one side; a deep sigh heaved from the very bottom of his stomach; and, though I could not see a tear trembling in his eye, yet a moisture was evidently stealing from a corner of his mouth. I followed the direction of his eye through

* Thou didst swear to me upon a *parcel-gilt goblet*, sitting in my Dolphin chamber, at the round table, by a sea-coal fire, on Wednesday, in Whitsunweek, when the prince broke thy head for likening his father to a singing man at Windsor; thou didst swear to me then, as I was washing thy wound, to marry me, and make me my lady, thy wife. Canst thou deny it?—*Henry IV, Part 2*

the door which stood open, and found it fixed wistfully on the savory breast of lamb, roasting in dripping richness before the fire.

I now called to mind that, in the eagerness of my recondite investigation, I was keeping the poor man from his dinner. My bowels yearned with sympathy, and, putting in his hand a small token of my gratitude and goodness, I departed, with a hearty benediction on him, Dame Honeyball, and the Parish Club of Crooked Lane;—not forgetting my shabby, but sententious friend, in the oil-cloth hat and copper nose.

Thus have I given a "tedious brief" account of this interesting research, for which, if it prove too short and unsatisfactory, I can only plead my inexperience in this branch of literature, so deservedly popular at the present day. I am aware that a more skillful illustrator of the immortal bard would have swelled the materials I have touched upon, to a good merchantable bulk; comprising the biographies of William Walworth, Jack Straw, and Robert Preston; some notice of the eminent fishmongers of St. Michael's; the history of Eastcheap, great and little; private anecdotes of Dame Honeyball, and her pretty daughter, whom I have not even mentioned; to say nothing of a damsel tending the breast of lamb, (and whom, by the way, I remarked to be a comely lass, with a neat foot and ankle;)—the whole enlivened by the riots of Wat Tyler, and illuminated by the great fire of London.

All this I leave, as a rich mine, to be worked by future commentators; nor do I despair of seeing the tobacco-box, and the "parcel-gilt goblet," which I have thus brought to light, the subjects of future engravings, and almost as fruitful of voluminous dissertations and disputes as the shield of Achilles, or the far-famed Portland vase.

THE MUTABILITY OF LITERATURE

A COLLOQUY IN WESTMINSTER ABBEY

> I know that all beneath the moon decays,
> And what by mortals in this world is brought,
> In time's great period shall return to nought.
> I know that all the muse's heavenly lays,
> With toil of sprite which are so dearly bought,
> As idle sounds, of few or none are sought,
> That there is nothing lighter than mere praise.
>
> DRUMMOND OF HAWTHORNDEN

THERE are certain half-dreaming moods of mind, in which we naturally steal away from noise and glare, and seek some quiet haunt, where we may indulge our reveries and build our air castles undisturbed. In such a mood I was loitering about the old gray cloisters of Westminster Abbey, enjoying that luxury of wandering thought which one is apt to dignify with the name of reflection; when suddenly an interruption of madcap boys from Westminster School, playing at football, broke in upon the monastic stillness of the place, making the vaulted passages and mouldering tombs echo with their merriment. I sought to take refuge from their noise by penetrating still deeper into the solitudes of the pile, and applied to one of the vergers for admission to the library. He conducted me through a portal rich with the crumbling sculpture of former ages, which opened upon a gloomy passage leading to the chapter-house and the chamber in which doomsday book is deposited. Just within the passage is a small door on the left. To this the verger applied a key; it was double locked, and opened with some difficulty, as if seldom used. We now ascended a dark narrow staircase, and, passing through a second door, entered the library.

I found myself in a lofty antique hall, the roof supported by massive joists of old English oak. It was soberly lighted by a row of Gothic windows at a considerable height from the floor, and which apparently opened upon the roofs of the cloisters. An ancient picture of some reverend dignitary of the church in his robes hung over the fireplace. Around the hall and in a small gallery were the books, arranged in carved oaken cases. They consisted principally of old polemical writers, and were much more worn by time than use. In the centre of the library was a solitary table with two or three books on it, an inkstand without ink, and a few pens parched by long disuse. The place seemed fitted for quiet study and profound meditation. It was buried deep among the massive walls of the abbey, and shut up from the tumult of the world. I could only hear now and then the shouts of the school-boys faintly swelling from the cloisters, and the sound of a bell tolling for prayers, echoing soberly along the roofs of the abbey. By degrees the shouts of merriment grew fainter and fainter, and at length died away; the bell ceased to toll, and a profound silence reigned through the dusky hall.

I had taken down a little thick quarto, curiously bound in parchment, with brass clasps, and seated myself at the table in a venerable elbow-chair. Instead of reading, however, I was beguiled by the solemn monastic air, and lifeless quiet of the place, into a train of musing. As I looked around upon the old volumes in their mouldering covers, thus ranged on the shelves, and apparently never disturbed in their repose, I could not but consider the library a kind of literary catacomb, where authors, like mummies, are piously entombed, and left to blacken and moulder in dusty oblivion.

How much, thought I, has each of these volumes, now thrust aside with such indifference, cost some aching head! how many weary days! how many sleepless nights! How have their authors buried themselves in the solitude of cells and cloisters; shut themselves up from the face of man, and the still more blessed face of nature; and devoted themselves to painful research and intense reflection! And all for what! to occupy an inch of dusty shelf—to have the title of their works read now and then in a future age, by some drowsy churchman or casual straggler like myself; and in another age to be lost, even to remembrance. Such is the amount of this boasted immortality. A mere temporary rumor, a local sound; like the tone of that bell which has just tolled among these towers, filling the ear for a moment—lingering transiently in echo—and then passing away like a thing that was not!

While I sat half murmuring, half meditating these unprofitable speculations with my head resting on my hand, I was thrumming with the other hand upon the quarto, until I accidently loosened the clasps; when, to my utter astonishment, the little book gave two or three yawns, like one awakening from a deep sleep; then a husky hem; and at length began to talk. At first its voice was very hoarse and broken, being much troubled by a cobweb which some studious spider had woven across it; and having probably contracted a cold from long exposure to the chills and damps of the abbey. In a short time, however, it became more distinct, and I soon found it an exceedingly fluent conversable little tome. Its language, to be sure, was rather quaint and obsolete, and its pronunciation, what, in the present day, would be deemed barbarous; but I shall endeavor, as far as I am able, to render it in modern parlance.

It began with railings about the neglect of the world—

about merit being suffered to languish in obscurity, and other such commonplace topics of literary repining, and complained bitterly that it had not been opened for more than two centuries. That the dean only looked now and then into the library, sometimes took down a volume or two, trifled with them for a few moments, and then returned them to their shelves. "What a plague do they mean," said the little quarto, which I began to perceive was somewhat choleric, "what a plague do they mean by keeping several thousand volumes of us shut up here, and watched by a set of old vergers, like so many beauties in a harem, merely to be looked at now and then by the dean? Books were written to give pleasure and to be enjoyed; and I would have a rule passed that the dean should pay each of us a visit at least once a year; or if he is not equal to the task, let them once in a while turn loose the whole school of Westminster among us, that at any rate we may now and then have an airing."

"Softly, my worthy friend," replied I, "you are not aware how much better you are off than most books of your generation. By being stored away in this ancient library, you are like the treasured remains of those saints and monarchs, which lie enshrined in the adjoining chapels; while the remains of your contemporary mortals, left to the ordinary course of nature, have long since returned to dust."

"Sir," said the little tome, ruffling his leaves and looking big, "I was written for all the world, not for the bookworms of an abbey. I was intended to circulate from hand to hand, like other great contemporary works; but here have I been clasped up for more than two centuries, and might have silently fallen a prey to these worms that are playing the very vengeance with my intestines, if you had not by chance given me an opportunity of uttering a few last words before I go to pieces."

"My good friend," rejoined I, "had you been left to the circulation of which you speak, you would long ere this have been no more. To judge from your physiognomy, you are now well stricken in years: very few of your contemporaries can be at present in existence; and those few owe their longevity to being immured like yourself in old libraries; which, suffer me to add, instead of likening to harems, you might more properly and gratefully have compared to those infirmaries attached to religious establishments, for the benefit of the old and decrepit, and where, by quiet fostering and no employment, they often endure to an amazingly good-for-nothing old age. You talk of your contemporaries as if in circulation—where do we meet with their works? what do we hear of Robert Groteste, of Lincoln? No one could have toiled harder than he for immortality. He is said to have written nearly two hundred volumes. He built, as it were, a pyramid of books to perpetuate his name: but, alas! the pyramid has long since fallen, and only a few fragments are scattered in various libraries, where they are scarcely disturbed even by the antiquarian. What do we hear of Giraldus Cambrensis, the historian, antiquary, philosopher, theologian, and poet? He declined two bishoprics, that he might shut himself up and write for posterity; but posterity never inquires after his labors. What of Henry of Huntingdon, who, besides a learned history of England, wrote a treatise on the contempt of the world, which the world has revenged by forgetting him? What is quoted of Joseph of Exeter, styled the miracle of his age in classical composition? Of his three great heroic poems one is lost forever, excepting a mere fragment; the others are known only to a few of the curious in literature; and as to his love verses and epigrams, they have entirely disappeared. What is in current use of John Wallis, the Franciscan, who acquired the name of the tree of life? Of William of Malmsbury;—of Simeon of Durham;—of Benedict of Peterborough;—of John Hanvill of St. Albans;—of——?"

"Prithee, friend," cried the quarto, in a testy tone, "how old do you think me? You are talking of authors that lived long before my time, and wrote either in Latin or French, so that they in a manner expatriated themselves, and deserved to be forgotten;* but I, sir, was ushered into the world from the press of the renowned Wynkyn De Worde. I was written in my own native tongue, at a time when the language had become fixed; and indeed I was considered a model of pure and elegant English."

(I should observe that these remarks were couched in such intolerably antiquated terms, that I have had infinite difficulty in rendering them into modern phraseology.)

"I cry your mercy," said I, "for mistaking your age; but it matters little: almost all the writers of your time have likewise passed into forgetfulness; and De Worde's publications are mere literary rarities among bookcollectors. The purity and stability of language, too, on which you found your claims of perpetuity, have been the fallacious dependence of authors of every age, even back to the times of the worthy Robert of Gloucester, who wrote his history in rhymes of mongrel Saxon.†

---

*In Latin and French hath many soueraine wittes had great delyte to endite, and have many noble thinges fulfilde, but certes there ben some that speaken their poisye in French, of which speche the Frenchmen have as good a fantasye as we have in hearying of Frenchmen's Englishe.—*Chaucer's Testament of Love.*

†Holinshed, in his Chronicle, observes, "afterwards, also, by deligent travell of Geffry Chaucer and of John Gowre, in the time of

Even now many talk of Spenser's 'well of pure English undefiled,' as if the language ever sprang from a well or fountain-head, and was not rather a mere confluence of various tongues, perpetually subject to changes and intermixtures. It is this which has made English literature so extremely mutable, and the reputation built upon it so fleeting. Unless thought can be committed to something more permanent and unchangeable than such a medium, even thought must share the fate of everything else, and fall into decay. This should serve as a check upon the vanity and exultation of the most popular writer. He finds the language in which he has embarked his fame gradually altering, and subject to the dilapidations of time and the caprice of fashion. He looks back and beholds the early authors of his country, once the favorites of their day, supplanted by modern writers. A few short ages have covered them with obscurity, and their merits can only be relished by the quaint taste of the bookworm. And such, he anticipates, will be the fate of his own work, which, however it may be admired in its day, and held up as a model of purity, will in the course of years grow antiquated and obsolete; until it shall become almost as unintelligible in its native land as an Egyptian obelisk, or one of those Runic inscriptions said to exist in the deserts of Tartary. I declare," added I, with some emotion, "when I contemplate a modern library, filled with new works, in all the bravery of rich gilding and binding, I feel disposed to sit

Richard the Second, and after them of John Scogan and John Lydgate, monke of Berrie, our said toong was brought to an excellent passe, notwithstanding that it never came unto the type of perfection until the time of Queen Elizabeth, wherein John Jewell, Bishop of Sarum, John Fox, and sundrie learned and excellent writers, have fully accomplished the ornature of the same, to their great praise and immortal commendation."

down and weep; like the good Xerxes, when he surveyed his army, pranked out in all the splendor of military array, and reflected that in one hundred years not one of them would be in existence!"

"Ah," said the little quarto, with a heavy sigh, "I see how it is; these modern scribblers have superseded all the good old authors. I suppose nothing is read now-a-days but Sir Philip Sidney's *Arcadia*, Sackville's stately plays, and *Mirror for Magistrates*, or the fine-spun euphuisms of the 'unparalleled John Lyly.'"

"There you are again mistaken," said I; "the writers whom you suppose in vogue, because they happened to be so when you were last in circulation, have long since had their day. Sir Philip Sidney's *Arcadia*, the immortality of which was so fondly predicted by his admirers,* and which, in truth, is full of noble thoughts, delicate images, and graceful turns of language, is now scarcely ever mentioned. Sackville has strutted into obscurity; and even Lyly, though his writings were once the delight of a court, and apparently perpetuated by a proverb, is now scarcely known even by name. A whole crowd of authors who wrote and wrangled at the time, have likewise gone down, with all their writings and their controversies. Wave after wave of succeeding literature has rolled over them, until they are buried so deep, that it is only now and then that some industrious diver after fragments of antiquity brings up a specimen for the gratification of the curious.

"For my part," I continued, "I consider this mutability

---

*Live ever sweete booke; the simple image of his gentle witt, and the golden-pillar of his noble courage; and ever notify unto the world that thy writer was the secretary of eloquence, the breath of the muses, the honey-bee of the daintyest flowers of witt and arte, the pith of morale and intellectual virtues, the arme of Bellona in the field, the tonge of Suada in the chamber, the sprite of Practise in esse, and the paragon of excellency in print.—*Harvey Pierce's Supererogation.*

of language a wise precaution of Providence for the benefit of the world at large, and of authors in particular. To reason from analogy, we daily behold the varied and beautiful tribes of vegetables springing up, flourishing, adorning the fields for a short time, and then fading into dust, to make way for their successors. Were not this the case, the fecundity of nature would be a grievance instead of a blessing. The earth would groan with rank and excessive vegetation, and its surface become a tangled wilderness. In like manner the works of genius and learning decline, and make way for subsequent productions. Language gradually varies, and with it fade away the writings of authors who have flourished their allotted time; otherwise, the creative powers of genius would overstock the world, and the mind would be completely bewildered in the endless mazes of literature. Formerly there were some restraints on this excessive multiplication. Works had to be transcribed by hand, which was a slow and laborious operation; they were written either on parchment, which was expensive, so that one work was often erased to make way for another; or on papyrus, which was fragile and extremely perishable. Authorship was a limited and unprofitable craft, pursued chiefly by monks in the leisure and solitude of their cloisters. The accumulation of manuscripts was slow and costly, and confined almost entirely to monasteries. To these circumstances it may, in some measure, be owing that we have not been inundated by the intellect of antiquity; that the fountains of thought have not been broken up, and modern genius drowned in the deluge. But the inventions of paper and the press have put an end to all these restraints. They have made every one a writer, and enabled every mind to pour itself into print, and diffuse itself over the whole intellectual world. The consequences are alarming. The stream of literature has swollen into a torrent—augmented into a river—expanded into a sea. A few centuries since, five or six hundred manuscripts constituted a great library; but what would you say to libraries such as actually exist, containing three or four hundred thousand volumes; legions of authors at the same time busy; and the press going on with fearfully increasing activity, to double and quadruple the number? Unless some unforseen mortality should break out among the progeny of the muse, now that she has become so prolific, I tremble for posterity. I fear the mere fluctuation of langage will not be sufficient. Criticism may do much. It increases with the increase of literature, and resembles one of those salutary checks on population spoken of by economists. All possible encouragement, therefore, should be given to the growth of critics, good or bad. But I fear all will be in vain; let criticism do what it may, writers will write, printers will print, and the world will inevitably be overstocked with good books. It will soon be the employment of a lifetime merely to learn their names. Many a man of passable information, at the present day, reads scarcely anything but reviews; and before long a man of erudition will be little better than a mere walking catalogue."

"My very good sir," said the little quarto, yawning most drearily in my face, "excuse my interrupting you, but I perceive you are rather given to prose. I would ask the fate of an author who was making some noise just as I left the world. His reputation, however, was considered quite temporary. The learned shook their heads at him, for he was a poor half-educated varlet, that knew little of Latin, and nothing of Greek, and had been obliged to run the country for deer-stealing. I think his name was Shakespeare. I presume he soon sunk into oblivion."

"On the contrary," said I, "it is owing to that very man that the literature of his period has experienced a duration beyond the ordinary term of English literature. There rise authors now and then, who seem proof against the mutability of language, because they have rooted themselves in the unchanging principles of human nature. They are like gigantic trees that we sometimes see on the banks of a stream; which, by their vast and deep roots, penetrating through the mere surface, and laying hold on the very foundations of the earth, preserve the soil around them from being swept away by the ever-flowing current, and hold up many a neighboring plant, and, perhaps, worthless weed, to perpetuity. Such is the case with Shakespeare, whom we behold defying the encroachments of time, retaining in modern use the language and literature of his day, and giving duration to many an indifferent author, merely from having flourished in his vicinity. But even he, I grieve to say, is gradually assuming the tint of age, and his whole form is overrun by a profusion of commentators, who, like clambering vines and creepers, almost bury the noble plant that upholds them."

Here the little quarto began to heave his sides and chuckle, until at length he broke out in a plethoric fit of laughter that had well nigh choked him, by reason of his excessive corpulency. "Mighty well!" cried he, as soon as he could recover breath, "mighty well! and so you would persuade me that the literature of an age is to be perpetuated by a vagabond deer-stealer! by a man without learning; by a poet, forsooth—a poet!" And here he wheezed forth another fit of laughter.

I confess that I felt somewhat nettled at his rudeness, which, however, I pardoned on account of his having flourished in a less polished age. I determined, nevertheless, not to give up my point.

"Yes," resumed I, positively, "a poet; for of all writers he has the best chance of immortality. Others may write from the head, but he writes from the heart, and the heart will always understand him. He is the faithful portrayer of nature, whose features are always the same, and always interesting. Prose writers are voluminous and unwieldy; their pages are crowded with commonplaces, and their thoughts expanded into tediousness. But with the true poet every thing is terse, touching, or brilliant. He gives the choicest thoughts in the choicest language. He illustrates them by everything that he sees most striking in nature and art. He enriches them by pictures of human life, such as it is passing before him. His writings, therefore, contain the spirit, the aroma, if I may use the phrase, of the age in which he lives. They are caskets which enclose within a small compass the wealth of the language—its family jewels, which are thus transmitted in a portable form to posterity. The setting may occasionally be antiquated, and require now and then to be renewed, as in the case of Chaucer; but the brilliancy and intrinsic value of the gems continue unaltered. Cast a look back over the long reach of literary history. What vast valleys of dullness, filled with monkish legends and academical controversies! what bogs of theogical speculations! what dreary wastes of metaphysics! Here and there only do we behold the heaven-illuminated bards, elevated like beacons on their widely-separate heights, to transmit the pure light of poetical intelligence from age to age."*

*Thorow earth and waters deepe,
  The pen by skill doth passe:
And featly nyps the worldes abuse,
  And shoes us in a glasse,
The vertu and the vice
  Of every wight alyve;
The honey comb that bee doth make

I was just about to launch forth into eulogiums upon the poets of the day, when the sudden opening of the door caused me to turn my head. It was the verger, who came to inform me that it was time to close the library. I sought to have a parting word with the quarto, but the worthy little tome was silent; the clasps were closed: and it looked perfectly unconscious of all that had passed. I have been to the library two or three times since, and have endeavored to draw it into further conversation, but in vain; and whether all this rambling colloquy actually took place, or whether it was another of those odd day-dreams to which I am subject, I have never to this moment been able to discover.

RURAL FUNERALS

Here's a few flowers! but about midnight more:
The herbs that have on them cold dew o' the night;
Are strewings fitt'st for graves—
You were as flowers now wither'd; even so
These herblets shall, which we upon you strow.
                                    CYMBELINE

AMONG the beautiful and simple-hearted customs of rural life which still linger in some parts of England, are those of strewing flowers before the funerals, and planting them at the graves of departed friends. These, it is said, are the remains of some of the rites of the primitive church; but they are of still higher

Is not so sweet in hyve,
As are the golden leves
  That drop from poet's head!
Which doth surmount our common talke
  As farre as dross doth lead.
                        Churchyard

antiquity, having been observed among the Greeks and Romans, and frequently mentioned by their writers, and were, no doubt, the spontaneous tributes of unlettered affection, originating long before art had tasked itself to modulate sorrow into song, or story it on the monument. They are now only to be met with in the most distant and retired places of the kingdom, where fashion and innovation have not been able to throng in, and trample out all the curious and interesting traces of the olden time.

In Glamorganshire, we are told, the bed whereon the corpse lies is covered with flowers, a custom alluded to in one of the wild and plaintive ditties of Ophelia:

> White his shroud as the mountain snow
>   Larded all with sweet flowers;
> Which be-wept to the grave did go,
>   With true love showers.

There is also a most delicate and beautiful rite observed in some of the remote villages of the south, as the funeral of a female who has died young and unmarried. A chaplet of white flowers is borne before the corpse by a young girl nearest in age, size, and resemblance, and is afterwards hung up in the church over the accustomed seat of the deceased. These chaplets are sometimes made of white paper, in imitation of flowers, and inside of them is generally a pair of white gloves. They are intended as emblems of the purity of the deceased, and the crown of glory which she has received in heaven.

In some parts of the country, also, the dead are carried to the grave with the singing of psalms and hymns: a kind of triumph, "to show," says Bourne, "that they have finished their course with joy, and are become conquerors." This, I am informed, is observed in some of the northern counties, particularly in Northumberland, and it has a pleasing, though melancholy effect, to hear, of a still evening, in some lonely country scene, the mournful melody of a funeral dirge swelling from a distance, and to see the train slowly moving along the landscape.

> Thus, thus, and thus, we compass round
> Thy harmlesse and unhaunted ground,
> And as we sing thy dirge, we will
> > The daffodill
> And other flowers lay upon
> The altar of our love, thy stone.
>
> > HERRICK

There is also a solemn respect paid by the traveller to the passing funeral in these sequestered places; for such spectacles, occurring among the quiet abodes of nature, sink deep into the soul. As the mourning train approaches, he pauses, uncovered, to let it go by; he then follows silently in the rear; sometimes quite to the grave, at other times for a few hundred yards, and, having paid this tribute of respect to the deceased, turns and resumes his journey.

The rich vein of melancholy which runs through the English character, and gives it some of its most touching and ennobling graces, is finely evidenced in these pathetic customs, and in the solicitude shown by the common people for an honored and a peaceful grave. The humblest peasant, whatever may be his lowly lot while living, is anxious that some little respect may be paid to his remains. Sir Thomas Overbury, describing the "faire and happy milkmaid," observes, "thus lives she, and all her care is, that she may die in the spring-time, to have store of flowers stucke upon her winding-sheet." The poets, too, who always breathe the feeling of a nation, continually advert to this fond solicitude about the grave. In "The Maid's Tragedy," by Beaumont and Fletcher, there is a beautiful instance of the kind, describing the capricious melancholy of a broken-hearted girl:

> When she sees a bank
> Stuck full of flowers, she, with a sigh, will tell
> Her servants, what a pretty place it were
> To bury lovers in; and make her maids
> Pluck 'em, and strew her over like a corse.

The custom of decorating graves was once universally prevalent; osiers were carefully bent over them to keep the turf uninjured, and about them were planted evergreens and flowers. "We adorn their graves," says Evelyn, in his *Sylva*, "with flowers and redolent plants, just emblems of the life of man, which has been compared in Holy Scriptures to those fading beauties, whose roots being buried in dishonor, rise again in glory." This usage has now become extremely rare in England; but it may still be met with in the churchyards of retired villages, among the Welsh mountains; and I recollect an instance of it at the small town of Ruthen, which lies at the head of the beautiful vale of Clewyd. I have been told also by a friend, who was present at the funeral of a young girl in Glamorganshire, that the female attendants had their aprons full of flowers, which, as soon as the body was interred, they stuck about the grave.

He noticed several graves which had been decorated in the same manner. As the flowers had been merely stuck in the ground, and not planted, they had soon withered, and might be seen in various states of decay; some drooping, others quite perished. They were afterwards to be supplanted by holly, rosemary, and other evergreens; which on some graves had grown to great luxuriance, and overshadowed the tombstones.

There was formerly a melancholy fancifulness in the arrangement of these rustic offerings, that had something in it truly poetical. The rose was sometimes blended with the lily, to form a general emblem of frail mortality. "This sweet flower," said Evelyn, "borne on a branch set with thorns, and accompanied with the lily, are natural hieroglyphics of our fugitive, umbratile, anxious, and transitory life, which, making so fair a show for a time, is not yet without its thorns and crosses." The nature and color of the flowers, and of the ribbons with which they were tied, had often a particular reference to the qualities or story of the deceased, or were expressive of the feelings of the mourner. In an old poem, entitled "Corydon's Doleful Knell," a lover specifies the decorations he intends to use:

> A garland shall be framed
>   By art and nature's skill,
> Of sundry-colored flowers,
>   In token of good-will.
>
> And sundry-color'd ribands
>   On it I will bestow;
> But chiefly blacke and yellowe
>   With her to grave shall go.
>
> I'll deck her tomb with flowers,
>   The rarest ever seen;
> And with my tears as showers,
>   I'll keep them fresh and green.

The white rose, we are told, was planted at the grave of a virgin; her chaplet was tied with white ribbons, in token of her spotless innocence; though sometimes black ribbons were intermingled, to bespeak the grief of the survivors. The red rose was occasionally used in remembrance of such as had been remarkable for benevolence; but roses in general were appropriated to the graves of lovers. Evelyn tells us that the custom was not altogether extinct in his time, near his dwelling in the county of Surrey, "where the maidens yearly planted and decked the graves of their defunct sweethearts with rose-bushes." And Camden likewise remarks, in his Britannia: "Here is also a certain custom, observed time out of mind, of planting rose-trees upon the graves, especially by the young men and maids who have lost their loves; so that this church-yard is now full of them."

When the deceased had been unhappy in their loves, emblems of a more gloomy character were used, such as the yew and cypress; and if flowers were strewn, they were of the most melancholy colors. Thus, in poems by Thomas Stanley, Esq. (published in 1651), is the following stanza:

> Yet strew
> Upon my dismall grave
> Such offerings as you have,
>   Forsaken cpyresse and sad yewe;
> For kinder flowers can take no birth
> Or growth from such unhappy earth.

In "The Maid's Tragedy," a pathetic little air is introduced, illustrative of this mode of decorating the funerals of females who had been disappointed in love:

> Lay a garland on my hearse,
>   Of the dismall yew,
> Maidens, willow branches wear,
>   Say I died true.
>
> My love was false, but I was firm,
>   From my hour of birth,
> Upon my buried body lie
>   Lightly, gentle earth.

The natural effect of sorrow over the dead is to refine and elevate the mind; and we have a proof of it in the purity of sentiment and the unaffected elegance of thought which pervaded the whole of these funeral observances. Thus, it was an especial precaution that none but sweet-scented evergreens and flowers should be employed. The intention seems to have been to soften the horrors of the tomb, to beguile the mind from brooding over the disgraces of perishing mortality, and to associate the memory of the deceased with the most delicate and beautiful objects in nature. There is a dismal process going on in the grave, ere dust can return to its kindred dust, which the imagination shrinks from contemplating; and we seek still to think of the form we have loved, with those refined associations which it awakened when blooming before us in youth and beauty. "Lay her i' the earth," says Laertes, of his virgin sister,

> And from her fair and unpolluted flesh
> May violets spring!

Herrick, also, in his "Dirge of Jephtha," pours forth a fragrant flow of poetical thought and image, which in a manner embalms the dead in the recollections of the living.

> Sleep in thy peace, thy bed of spice,
> And make this piace all Paradise:
> May sweets grow here! and smoke from hence
> > Fat frankincense.
> Let balme and cassia send their scent
> From out thy maiden monument.
>
> *   *   *   *   *   *
>
> May all shie maids at wonted hours
> Come forth to strew thy tombe with flowers!
> May virgins, when they come to mourn,
> > Male incense burn
> Upon thine altar! then return
> And leave thee sleeping in thine urn.

I might crowd my pages with extracts from the older British poets who wrote when these rites were more prevalent, and delighted frequently to allude to them; but I have already quoted more than is necessary. I cannot however refrain from giving a passage from

Shakespeare, even though it should appear trite; which illustrates the emblematical meaning often conveyed in these floral tributes; and at the same time possesses that magic of language and appositeness of imagery for which he stands pre-eminent.

> With fairest flowers,
> Whilst summer lasts, and I live here, Fidele,
> I'll sweeten thy sad grave; thou shalt not lack
> The flower that's like thy face, pale primrose; nor
> The azured harebell, like thy veins; no, nor
> The leaf of eglantine; whom not to slander,
> Outsweeten'd not thy breath.

There is certainly something more affecting in these prompt and spontaneous offerings of nature, than in the most costly monuments of art; the hand strews the flower while the heart is warm, and the tear falls on the grave as affection is binding the osier round the sod; but pathos expires under the slow labor of the chisel, and is chilled among the cold conceits of sculptured marble.

It is greatly to be regretted, that a custom so truly elegant and touching has disappeared from general use, and exists only in the most remote and insignificant villages. But it seems as if poetical custom always shuns the walks of cultivated society. In proportion as people grow polite they cease to be poetical. They talk of poetry, but they have learnt to check its free impulses, to distrust its sallying emotions, and to supply its most affecting and picturesque usages, by studied form and pompous ceremonial. Few pageants can be more stately and frigid than an English funeral in town. It is made up of show and gloomy parade; mourning carriages, mourning horses, mourning plumes, and hireling mourners, who make a mockery of grief. "There is a grave digged," says Jeremy Taylor, "and a solemn mourning, and a great talk in the neighborhood, and when the daies are finished, they shall be, and they shall be remembered no more." The associate in the gay and crowded city is soon forgotten; the hurrying succession of new intimates and new pleasures effaces him from our minds, and the very scenes and circles in which he moved are incessantly fluctuating. But funerals in the country are solemnly impressive. The stroke of death makes a wider space in the village circle, and is an awful event in the tranquil uniformity of rural life. The passing bell tolls its knell in every ear; it steals with its pervading melancholy over hill and vale, and saddens all the landscape.

The fixed and unchanging features of the country also perpetuate the memory of the friend with whom we once enjoyed them; who was the companion of our most retired walks, and gave animation to every lonely scene. His idea is associated with every charm of nature; we hear his voice in the echo which he once delighted to awaken; his spirit haunts the grove which he once frequented; we think of him in the wild upland solitude, or amidst the pensive beauty of the valley. In the freshness of joyous morning, we remember his beaming smiles and bounding gayety; and when sober evening returns with its gathering shadows and subduing quiet, we call to mind many a twilight hour of gentle talk and sweet-souled melancholy.

> Each lonely place shall him restore,
>   For him the tear be duly shed;
> Beloved, till life can charm no more;
>   And mourn'd till pity's self be dead.

Another cause that perpetuates the memory of the deceased in the country is that the grave is more immediately in sight of the survivors. They pass it on their way to prayer, it meets their eyes when their hearts are softened by the exercises of devotion; they linger about it on the Sabbath, when the mind is disengaged from worldly cares, and most disposed to turn aside from present pleasures and present loves, and to sit down among the solemn mementos of the past. In North Wales the peasantry kneel and pray over the graves of their deceased friends, for several Sundays after the interment; and where the tender rite of strewing and planting flowers is still practised, it is always renewed on Easter, Whitsuntide, and other festivals, when the season brings the companion of former festivity more vividly to mind. It is also invariably performed by the nearest relatives and friends; no menials nor hirelings are employed; and if a neighbor yields assistance, it would be deemed an insult to offer compensation.

I have dwelt upon this beautiful rural custom, because, as it is one of the last, so is it one of the holiest offices of love. The grave is the ordeal of true affection. It is there that the divine passion of the soul manifests its superiority to the instinctive impulse of mere animal attachment. The latter must be continually refreshed and kept alive by the presence of its object; but the love that is seated in the soul can live on long remembrance. The mere inclinations of sense languish and decline with the charms which excited them, and turn with shuddering disgust from the dismal precincts of the tomb; but it is thence that truly spiritual affection rises, purified from every sensual desire, and returns, like a holy flame, to illumine and sanctify the heart of the survivor.

The sorrow for the dead is the only sorrow from which we refuse to be divorced. Every other wound we seek to heal—every other affliction to forget; but this wound we consider it a duty to keep open—this affliction we cherish and brood over in solitude. Where is the mother who would willingly forget the infant that perished like a blossom from her arms, though every recollection is a pang? Where is the child that would willingly forget the most tender of parents, though to remember be but to lament? Who, even in the hour of agony, would forget the friend over whom he mourns? Who, even when the tomb is closing upon the remains of her he most loved; when he feels his heart, as it were, crushed in the closing of its portal; would accept of consolation that must be bought by forgetfulness?—No, the love which survives the tomb is one of the noblest attributes of the soul. If it has its woes, it has likewise its delights; and when the overwhelming burst of grief is calmed into the gentle tear of recollection; when the sudden anguish and the convulsive agony over the present ruins of all that we most loved, is softened away into pensive meditation on all that it was in the days of its loveliness—who would root out such a sorrow from the heart? Though it may sometimes throw a passing cloud over the bright hour of gayety, or spread a deeper sadness over the hour of gloom, yet who would exchange it even for the song of pleasure, or the burst of revelry? No, there is a voice from the tomb sweeter than song. There is a remembrance of the dead to which we turn even from the charms of the living. Oh, the grave!—the grave!—It buries every error—covers every defect—extinguishes every resentment! From its peaceful bosom spring none but fond regrets and tender recollections. Who can look down upon the grave even of an enemy, and not feel a compunctious throb, that he should ever have warred with the poor handful of earth that lies mouldering before him.

But the grave of those we loved—what a place for meditation! There it is that we call up in long review the whole history of virtue and gentleness, and the thousand endearments lavished upon us almost unheeded in the daily intercourse of intimacy—there it is that we dwell upon the tenderness, the solemn, awful tenderness of the parting scene. The bed of death, with all its stifled griefs—its noiseless attendance—its mute, watchful assiduities. The last testimonies of expiring love! The feeble, fluttering, thrilling—oh! how thrilling!—pressure of the hand! The faint, faltering accents, struggling in death to give one more assurance of affection! The last fond look of the glazing eye, turned upon us even from the threshold of existence!

Aye, go to the grave of buried love, and meditate! There settle the account with thy conscience for every past benefit unrequited—every past endearment unregarded, of that departed being, who can never—never—never return to be soothed by thy contrition!

If thou art a child, and hast ever added a sorrow to the soul, or a furrow to the silvered brow of an affectionate parent—if thou art a husband, and hast ever caused the fond bosom that ventured its whole happiness in thy arms to doubt one moment of thy kindness or thy truth—if thou art a friend, and hast ever wronged, in thought, or word, or deed, the spirit that generously confided in thee—if thou art a lover, and hast ever given one unmerited pang to that true heart which now lies cold and still beneath thy feet; then be sure that every unkind look, every ungracious word, every ungentle action, will come thronging back upon thy memory, and knocking dolefully at thy soul—then be sure that thou wilt lie down sorrowing and repentant on the grave, and utter the unheard groan, and pour the unavailing tear; more deep, more bitter, because unheard and unavailing.

Then weave thy chaplet of flowers, and strew the beauties of nature about the grave; console thy broken spirit, if thou canst, with these tender, yet futile tributes of regret; but take warning by the bitterness of this thy contrite affliction over the dead, and henceforth be more faithful and affectionate in the discharge of thy duties to the living.

In writing the preceding article, it was not intended to give a full detail of the funeral customs of the English peasantry, but merely to furnish a few hints and quotations illustrative of particular rites, to be appended, by way of note, to another paper, which has been withheld. The article swelled insensibly into its present form, and this is mentioned as an apology for so brief and casual a notice of these usages, after they have been amply and learnedly investigated in other works.

I must observe, also, that I am well aware that this custom of adorning graves with flowers prevails in other countries besides England. Indeed, in some it is much more general, and is observed even by the rich and fashionable; but it is then apt to lose its simplicity, and to degenerate into affectation. Bright, in his travels in Lower Hungary, tells of monuments of marble, and recesses formed for retirement, with seats placed among bowers of greenhouse plants; and that the graves generally are covered with the gayest flowers of the season. He gives a casual picture of filial piety, which I cannot but transcribe; for I trust it is as useful as it is delightful, to illustrate the amiable virtues of the sex. "When I was at Berlin," says he, "I followed the celebrated Iffland to the grave. Mingled with some pomp, you might trace much real feeling. In the midst of the ceremony, my attention was attracted by a young woman, who stood on a mound of earth, newly covered with turf, which she anxiously protected from the feet of the passing crowd. It was the tomb of her parent; and the figure of this affectionate daughter presented a monument more striking than the most costly work of art."

I will barely add an instance of sepulchral decoration that I once met with among the mountains in Switzerland. It was at the village of Gersau, which stands on the borders of the Lake of Lucerne, at the foot of Mount Rigi. It was once the capital of a miniature republic, shut up between the Alps and the Lake, and accessible on the land side only by foot-paths. The whole force of the republic did not exceed six hundred fighting men; and a few miles of circumference, scooped out as it were from the bosom of the mountains, comprised its territory. The village of Gersau seemed separated from the rest of the world, and retained the golden simplicity of a purer age. It had a small church, with a burying-ground adjoining. At the heads of the graves were placed crosses of wood or iron. On some were affixed miniatures, rudely executed, but evidently attempts at likenesses of the deceased. On the crosses were hung chaplets of flowers, some withering, others fresh, as if occasionally renewed. I paused with interest at this scene; I felt that I was at the source of poetical description, for these were the beautiful but unaffected offerings of the heart which poets are fain to record. In a gayer and more populous place, I should have suspected them to have been suggested by factitious sentiment, derived from books; but the good people of Gersau knew little of books; there was not a novel nor a love poem in the village; and I question whether any peasant of the place dreamt, while he was twining a fresh chaplet for the grave of his mistress, that he was fulfilling one of the most fanciful rites of poetical devotion, and that he was practically a poet.

THE INN KITCHEN

Shall I not take mine ease in mine inn?
FALSTAFF

DURING a journey that I once made through the Netherlands, I had arrived one evening at the *Pomme d' Or*, the principal inn of a small Flemish village. It was after the hour of the *table d'hôte*, so that I was obliged to make a solitary supper from the relics of its ampler board. The weather was chilly; I was seated alone in one end of a great gloomy dining-room, and, my repast being over, I had the prospect before me of a long dull evening, without any visible means of enlivening it. I summoned mine host, and requested something to read; he brought me the whole literary stock of his household, a Dutch family Bible, an almanac in the same language, and a number of old Paris newspapers. As I sat dozing over one of the latter, reading old and stale criticisms, my ear was now and then struck with bursts of laughter which seemed to proceed from the kitchen. Every one that has travelled on the continent must know how favorite a resort the kitchen of a country inn is to the middle and inferior order of travellers; particularly in that equivocal kind of weather, when a fire becomes agreeable toward evening. I threw aside the newspaper, and explored my way to the kitchen, to take a peep at the group that appeared to be so merry. It was composed partly of travellers who had arrived some hours before in a diligence, and partly of the usual attendants and hangers-on of inns. They were seated round a great burnished stove, that might have been mistaken for an altar, at which they were worshipping. It was covered with various kitchen vessels of resplendent brightness; among which steamed and hissed a huge copper tea-kettle. A large lamp threw a strong mass of light upon the group, bringing out many odd features in strong relief. Its yellow rays partially illumined the spacious kitchen, dying duskily away into remote corners; except where they settled in mellow radiance on the broad side of a flitch of bacon, or were reflected back from well-scoured utensils, that gleamed from the midst of obscurity. A strapping Flemish lass, with long golden pendants in her ears, and a necklace with a golden heart suspended to it, was the presiding priestess of the temple.

Many of the company were furnished with pipes, and most of them with some kind of evening potation. I found their mirth was occasioned by anecdotes, which a little swarthy Frenchman, with a dry weazen face and large whiskers, was giving of his love adventures; at the end of each of which there was one of those bursts of honest unceremonious laughter, in which a man indulges in that temple of true liberty, an inn.

As I had no better mode of getting through a tedious blustering evening, I took my seat near the stove, and listened to a variety of traveller's tales, some very extravagant, and most very dull. All of them, however, have faded from my treacherous memory except one, which I will endeavor to relate. I fear, however, it derived its chief zest from the manner in which it was told, and the peculiar air and appearance of the narrator. He was a corpulent old Swiss, who had the look of a veteran traveller. He was dressed in a tarnished green travelling-jacket, with a broad belt round his waist, and a pair of overalls, with buttons from the hips to the ankles. He was of a full, rubicund countenance, with a double chin, aquiline nose, and a pleasant, twinkling eye. His hair was light, and curled from under an old green velvet travelling-cap stuck on one side of his head. He was interrupted more than once by the arrival of guests, or the remarks of his auditors; and paused now and then to replenish his pipe; at which times he had generally a roguish leer, and a sly joke for the buxom kitchen-maid.

I wish my readers could imagine the old fellow lolling in a huge arm-chair, one arm akimbo, the other holding a curiously twisted tobacco pipe, formed of genuine *écume de mer*, decorated with silver chain and silken tassel—his head cocked on one side, and a whimsical cut of the eye occasionally, as he related the following story.

———————

THE SPECTRE BRIDEGROOM

A TRAVELLER'S TALE*

> He that supper for is dight,
> He lyes full cold, I trow, this night!
> Yestreen to chamber I him led,
> This night Gray-Steel has made his bed.
>   SIR EGER, SIR GRAHAME, AND SIR GRAY-STEEL

O N THE summit of one of the heights of the Odenwald, a wild and romantic tract of Upper Germany, that lies not far from the confluence of the Main and the Rhine, there stood, many, many years since, the Castle of the Baron Von Landshort. It is now quite fallen to decay, and almost buried among beech trees and dark firs; above which, however, its old watch-tower may still be seen, struggling, like the former

———————

*The erudite reader, well versed in good-for-nothing lore, will perceive that the above Tale must have been suggested to the old Swiss by a little French anecdote, a circumstance said to have taken place at Paris.

possessor I have mentioned, to carry a high head, and look down upon the neighboring country.

The baron was a dry branch of the great family of Katzenellenbogen,* and inherited the relics of the property, and all the pride of his ancestors. Though the warlike disposition of his predecessors had much impaired the family possessions, yet the baron still endeavored to keep up some show of former state. The times were peaceable, and the German nobles, in general, had abandoned their inconvenient old castles, perched like eagles' nests among the mountains, and had built more convenient residences in the valleys: still the baron remained proudly drawn up in his little fortress, cherishing with hereditary inveteracy, all the old family feuds; so that he was on ill terms with some of his nearest neighbors, on account of disputes that had happened between their great-great-grandfathers.

The baron had but one child, a daughter; but nature, when she grants but one child, always compensates by making it a prodigy; and so it was with the daughter of the baron. All the nurses, gossips, and country cousins, assured her father that she had not her equal for beauty in all Germany; and who should know better than they? She had, moreover, been brought up with great care under the superintendence of two maiden aunts, who had spent some years of their early life at one of the little German courts, and were skilled in all the branches of knowledge necessary to the education of a fine lady. Under their instructions she became a miracle of accomplishments. By the time she was eighteen, she could embroider to admiration, and had worked whole histories of the saints in tapestry, with such strength of

---

*i. e., CAT'S-ELBOW. The name of a family of those parts very powerful in former times. The appellation, we are told, was given in compliment to a peerless dame of the family, celebrated for her fine arm.

expression in their countenances, that they looked like so many souls in purgatory. She could read without great difficulty, and had spelled her way through several church legends, and almost all the chivalric wonders of the Heldenbuch. She had even made considerable proficiency in writing; could sign her own name without missing a letter, and so legibly, that her aunts could read it without spectacles. She excelled in making little elegant good-for-nothing lady-like nicknacks of all kinds; was versed in the most abstruse dancing of the day; played a number of airs on the harp and guitar; and knew all the tender ballads of the Minnie-lieders by heart.

Her aunts, too, having been great flirts and coquettes in their younger days, were admirably calculated to be vigilant guardians and strict censors of the conduct of their niece; for there is no duenna so rigidly prudent, and inexorably decorous, as a superannuated coquette. She was rarely suffered out of their sight; never went beyond the domains of the castle, unless well attended, or rather well watched; had continual lectures read to her about strict decorum and implicit obedience; and, as to the men—pah!—she was taught to hold them at such a distance, and in such absolute distrust, that, unless properly authorized, she would not have cast a glance upon the handsomest cavalier in the world—no, not if he were even dying at her feet.

The good effects of this system were wonderfully apparent. The young lady was a pattern of docility and correctness. While others were wasting their sweetness in the glare of the world, and liable to be plucked and thrown aside by every hand, she was coyly blooming into fresh and lovely womanhood under the protection of those immaculate spinsters, like a rose-bud blushing forth among guardian thorns. Her aunts looked upon her with pride and exultation, and vaunted that though all the other young ladies in the world might go astray, yet, thank Heaven, nothing of the kind could happen to the heiress of Katzenellenbogen.

But, however scantily the Baron Von Landshort might be provided with children, his household was by no means a small one; for Providence had enriched him with abundance of poor relations. They, one and all, possessed the affectionate disposition common to humble relatives; were wonderfully attached to the baron, and took every possible occasion to come in swarms and enliven the castle. All family festivals were commemorated by these good people at the baron's expense; and when they were filled with good cheer, they would declare that there was nothing on earth so delightful as these family meetings, these jubilees of the heart.

The baron, though a small man, had a large soul, and it swelled with satisfaction at the consciousness of being the greatest man in the little world about him. He loved to tell long stories about the dark old warriors whose portraits looked grimly down from the walls around, and he found no listeners equal to those who fed at his expense. He was much given to the marvellous, and a firm believer in all those supernatural tales with which every mountain and valley in Germany abounds. The faith of his guests exceeded even his own: they listened to every tale of wonder with open eyes and mouth, and never failed to be astonished, even though repeated for the hundredth time. Thus lived the Baron Von Landshort, the oracle of his table, the absolute monarch of his little territory, and happy, above all things, in the persuasion that he was the wisest man of the age.

At the time of which my story treats, there was a great family gathering at the castle, on an affair of the utmost importance: it was to receive the destined bridegroom of the baron's daughter. A negotiation had been carried on between the father and an old nobleman of Bavaria, to unite the dignity of their houses by the marriage of their children. The preliminaries had been conducted with proper punctilio. The young people were betrothed without seeing each other; and the time was appointed for the marriage ceremony. The young Count Von Altenburg had been recalled from the army for the purpose, and was actually on his way to the baron's to receive his bride. Missives had even been received from him, from Wurtzburg, where he was accidentally detained, mentioning the day and hour when he might be expected to arrive.

The castle was in a tumult of preparation to give him a suitable welcome. The fair bride had been decked out with uncommon care. The two aunts had superintended her toilet, and quarrelled the whole morning about every article of her dress. The young lady had taken advantage of their contest to follow the bent of her own taste; and fortunately it was a good one. She looked as lovely as youthful bridegroom could desire; and the flutter of expectation heightened the lustre of her charms.

The suffusions that mantled her face and neck, the gentle heaving of the bosom, the eye now and then lost in reverie, all betrayed the soft tumult that was going on in her little heart. The aunts were continually hovering around her; for maiden aunts are apt to take great interest in affairs of this nature. They were giving her a world of staid counsel how to deport herself, what to say, and in what manner to receive the expected lover.

The baron was no less busied in preparation. He had, in truth, nothing exactly to do: but he was naturally a fuming bustling little man, and could not remain passive when all the world was in a hurry. He worried from top to bottom of the castle with an air of infinite anxiety; he continually called the servants from their work to exhort them to be diligent; and buzzed about every hall and chamber, as idly restless and importunate as a blue-bottle fly on a warm summer's day.

In the mean time the fatted calf had been killed; the forests had rung with the clamor of the huntsmen; the kitchen was crowded with good cheer; the cellars had yielded up whole oceans of *Rhein-wein* and *Ferne-wein;* and even the great Heidelburg tun had been laid under contribution. Every thing was ready to receive the distinguished guest with *Saus und Braus* in the true spirit of German hospitality—but the guest delayed to make his appearance. Hour rolled after hour. The sun, that had poured his downward rays upon the rich forest of the Odenwald, now just gleamed along the summits of the mountains. The baron mounted the highest tower, and strained his eyes in hope of catching a distant sight of the count and his attendants. Once he thought he beheld them; the sound of horns came floating from the valley, prolonged by the mountain echoes. A number of horsemen were seen far below, slowly advancing along the road; but when they had nearly reached the foot of the mountain, they suddenly struck off in a different direction. The last ray of sunshine departed—the bats began to flit by in the twilight—the road grew dimmer and dimmer to the view; and nothing appeared stirring in it but now and then a peasant lagging homeward from his labor.

While the old castle of Landshort was in this state of perplexity, a very interesting scene was transacting in a different part of the Odenwald.

The young Count Von Altenburg was tranquilly pursuing his route in that sober jog-trot way, in which a man travels toward matrimony when his friends have taken all the trouble and uncertainty of courtship off his hands, and a bride is waiting for him, as certainly as a dinner at the end of his journey. He had encountered at Wurtzburg, a youthful companion in arms, with whom he had seen some service on the frontiers; Herman Von Starkenfaust, one of the stoutest hands, and worthiest hearts, of German chivalry, who was now returning from the army. His father's castle was not far distant from the old fortress of Landshort, although an hereditary feud rendered the families hostile, and strangers to each other.

In the warm-hearted moment of recognition, the young friends related all their past adventures and fortunes, and the count gave the whole history of his intended nuptials with a young lady whom he had never seen, but of whose charms he had received the most enrapturing descriptions.

As the route of the friends lay in the same direction, they agreed to perform the rest of their journey together; and, that they might do it the more leisurely, set off from Wurtzburg at an early hour, the count having given directions for his retinue to follow and overtake him.

They beguiled their wayfaring with recollections of their military scenes and adventures; but the count was apt to be a little tedious, now and then, about the reputed charms of his bride, and the felicity that awaited him.

In this way they had entered among the mountains of the Odenwald, and were traversing one of its most lonely and thickly-wooded passes. It is well known that the forests of Germany have always been as much infested by robbers as its castles by spectres; and, at this time, the former were particularly numerous, from the hordes of disbanded soldiers wandering about the country. It will not appear extraordinary, therefore, that the cavaliers were attacked by a gang of these stragglers, in the midst of the forest. They defended themselves with bravery, but were nearly overpowered, when the count's retinue arrived to their assistance. At sight of them the robbers fled, but not until the count had received a mortal wound. He was slowly and carefully conveyed back to the city of Wurtzburg, and a friar summoned from a neighboring convent, who was famous for his skill in administering to both soul and body, but half of his skill was superfluous; the moments of the unfortunate count were numbered.

With his dying breath he entreated his friend to repair instantly to the castle of Landshort, and explain the fatal cause of his not keeping his appointment with his bride. Though not the most ardent of lovers, he was one of the most punctilious of men, and appeared earnestly solicituous that his mission should be speedily and courteously executed. "Unless this is done," said he, "I shall not sleep quietly in my grave!" He repeated these last words with peculiar solemnity. A request, at a moment so impressive, admitted no hesitation. Starkenfaust endeavored to soothe him to calmness; promised faithfully to execute his wish, and gave him his hand in solemn pledge. The dying man pressed it in acknowledgment, but soon lapsed into delirium—raved about his bride—his engagements—his plighted word; ordered his horse, that he might ride to the castle of Landshort; and expired in the fancied act of vaulting into the saddle.

Starkenfaust bestowed a sigh and a soldier's tear on the untimely fate of his comrade; and then pondered on the awkward mission he had undertaken. His heart was heavy, and his head perplexed; for he was to present himself an unbidden guest among hostile people, and to damp their festivity with tidings fatal to their hopes. Still there were certain whisperings of curiosity in his bosom to see this far-famed beauty of Katzenellenbogen, so cautiously shut up from the world; for he was a passionate admirer of the sex, and there was a dash of eccentricity and enterprise in his character that made him fond of all singular adventure.

Previous to his departure he made all due arrangements with the holy fraternity of the convent for the funeral solemnities of his friend, who was to be buried in the cathedral of Wurtzburg, near some of his illustrious relatives; and the mourning retinue of the count took charge of his remains.

It is now high time that we should return to the ancient family of Katzenellenbogen, who were impatient for their guest, and still more for their dinner; and to the worthy little baron, whom we left airing himself on the watch-tower.

Night closed in, but still no guest arrived. The baron descended from the tower in despair. The banquet, which had been delayed from hour to hour, could no longer be postponed. The meats were already overdone; the cook in an agony; and the whole household had the look of a garrison that had been reduced by famine. The baron was obliged reluctantly to give orders for the feast without the presence of the guest. All were seated at table, and just on the point of commencing, when the sound of a horn from without the gate gave notice of the approach of a stranger. Another long blast filled the old courts of the castle with its echoes, and was answered by the warder from the walls. The baron hastened to receive his future son-in-law.

The drawbridge had been let down, and the stranger was before the gate. He was a tall, gallant cavalier, mounted on a black steed. His countenance was pale, but he had a beaming, romantic eye, and an air of stately melancholy. The baron was a little mortified that he should have come in this simple, solitary style. His dignity for a moment was ruffled, and he felt disposed to consider it a want of proper respect for the important occasion, and the important family with which he was to be connected. He pacified himself, however, with the conclusion, that it must have been youthful impatience which had induced him thus to spur on sooner than his attendants.

"I am sorry," said the stranger, "to break in upon you thus unseasonably——"

Here the baron interrupted him with a world of compliments and greetings; for, to tell the truth, he prided himself upon his courtesy and eloquence. The stranger attempted, once or twice, to stem the torrent of words, but in vain, so he bowed his head and suffered it to flow on. By the time the baron had come to a pause, they had reached the inner court of the castle; and the stranger was again about to speak, when he was once more interrupted by the appearance of the female part of the family, leading forth the shrinking and blushing bride. He gazed on her for a moment as one entranced; it seemed as if his whole soul beamed forth in the gaze, and rested upon that lovely form. One of the maiden aunts whispered something in her ear; she made an effort to speak; her moist blue eye was timidly raised; gave a shy glance of inquiry on the stranger; and was cast again to the ground. The words died away; but there was a sweet smile playing about her lips, and a soft dimpling of the cheek that showed her glance had not been unsatisfactory. It was impossible for a girl of the fond age of eighteen, highly predisposed for love and matrimony, not to be pleased with so gallant a cavalier.

The late hour at which the guests had arrived left no time for parley. The baron was peremptory, and deferred all particular conversation until the morning, and led the way to the untasted banquet.

It was served up in the great hall of the castle. Around the walls hung the hard-favored portraits of the heroes of the house of Katzenellenbogen, and the trophies which they had gained in the field and in the chase. Hacked corslets, splintered jousting spears, and tattered banners, were mingled with the spoils of sylvan warfare; the jaws of the wolf, and the tusks of the boar, grinned horribly among cross-bows and battle-axes, and a huge pair of antlers branched immediately over the head of the youthful bridegroom.

The cavalier took but little notice of the company or the entertainment. He scarcely tasted the banquet, but seemed absorbed in admiration of his bride. He conversed in a low tone that could not be overheard—for the language of love is never loud; but where is the female ear so dull that it cannot catch the softest whisper of the lover? There was a mingled tenderness and gravity in his manner, that appeared to have a powerful effect upon the young lady. Her color came and went as she listened with deep attention. Now and then she made some blushing reply, and when his eye was turned away, she would steal a sidelong glance at his romantic countenance, and heave a gentle sigh of tender happiness. It was evident that the young couple were completely enamored. The aunts, who were deeply versed in the mysteries of the heart, declared that they had fallen in love with each other at first sight.

The feast went on merrily, or at least noisily, for the guests were all blessed with those keen appetites that attend upon light purses and mountain air. The baron told his best and longest stories, and never had he told

them so well, or with such great effect. If there was any
thing marvellous, his auditors were lost in astonishment;
and if any thing facetious, they were sure to laugh
exactly in the right place. The baron, it is true, like most
great men, was too dignified to utter any joke but a dull
one; it was always enforced, however, by a bumper of
excellent Hockheimer; and even a dull joke, at one's own
table, served up with jolly old wine, is irresistible. Many
good things were said by poorer and keener wits, that
would not bear repeating, except on similar occasions;
many sly speeches whispered in ladies' ears, that almost
convulsed them with suppressed laughter; and a song or
two roared out by a poor, but merry and broad-faced
cousin of the baron, that absolutely made the maiden
aunts hold up their fans.

Amidst all this revelry, the stranger guest maintained
a most singular and unseasonable gravity. His countenance assumed a deeper cast of dejection as the evening
advanced; and, strange as it may appear, even the
baron's jokes seemed only to render him the more
melancholy. At times he was lost in thought, and at times
there was a perturbed and restless wandering of the eye
that bespoke a mind but ill at ease. His conversations
with the bride became more and more earnest and
mysterious. Lowering clouds began to steal over the fair
serenity of her brow, and tremors to run through her
tender frame.

All this could not escape the notice of the company.
Their gayety was chilled by the unaccountable gloom of
the bridegroom; their spirits were infected; whispers
and glances were interchanged, accompanied by shrugs
and dubious shakes of the head. The song and the laugh
grew less and less frequent; there were dreary pauses in
the conversation, which were at length succeeded by
wild tales and supernatural legends. One dismal story

produced another still more dismal, and the baron nearly frightened some of the ladies into hysterics with the history of the goblin horseman that carried away the fair Leonora; a dreadful story, which has since been put into excellent verse, and is read and believed by all the world.

The bridegroom listened to this tale with profound attention. He kept his eyes steadily fixed on the baron, and, as the story drew to a close, began gradually to rise from his seat, growing taller and taller, until, in the baron's entranced eye, he seemed almost to tower into a giant. The moment the tale was finished, he heaved a deep sigh, and took a solemn farewell of the company. They were all amazement. The baron was perfectly thunder-struck.

"What! going to leave the castle at midnight? why, every thing was prepared for his reception; a chamber was ready for him if he wished to retire."

The stranger shook his head mournfully and mysteriously; "I must lay my head in a different chamber to-night!"

There was something in this reply, and the tone in which it was uttered, that made the baron's heart misgive him; but he rallied his forces, and repeated his hospitable entreaties.

The stranger shook his head silently, but positively, at every offer; and, waving his farewell to the company, stalked slowly out of the hall. The maiden aunts were absolutely petrified—the bride hung her head, and a tear stole to her eye.

The baron followed the stranger to the great court of the castle, where the black charger stood pawing the earth, and snorting with impatience. When they had reached the portal, whose deep archway was dimly lighted by a cresset, the stranger paused, and addressed the baron in a hollow tone of voice, which the vaulted roof rendered still more sepulchral.

"Now that we are alone," said he, "I will impart to you the reason of my going. I have a solemn, an indispensable engagement—"

"Why?" said the baron, "cannot you send some one in your place?"

"It admits of no substitute—I must attend it in person—I must away to Wurtzburg cathedral—"

"Ay," said the baron, plucking up spirit, "but not until to-morrow—to-morrow you shall take your bride there."

"No! no!" replied the stranger, with tenfold solemnity, "my engagement is with no bride—the worms! the worms expect me! I am a dead man—I have been slain by robbers—my body lies at Wurtzburg—at midnight I am to be buried—the grave is waiting for me—I must keep my appointment!"

He sprang on his black charger, dashed over the drawbridge, and the clattering of his horse's hoofs was lost in the whistling of the night blast.

The baron returned to the hall in the utmost consternation, and related what had passed. Two ladies fainted outright, others sickened at the idea of having banqueted with a spectre. It was the opinion of some, that this might be the wild huntsman, famous in German legend. Some talked of mountain sprites, of wood-demons, and of other supernatural beings, with which the good people of Germany had been so grievously harassed since time immemorial. One of the poor relations ventured to suggest that it might be some sportive evasion of the young cavalier, and that the very gloominess of the caprice seemed to accord with so melancholy a personage. This, however, drew on him the indignation of the whole company, and especially of the baron, who looked upon him as little better than an infidel; so that he was fain to abjure his heresy as speedily as possible, and come into the faith of the true believers.

But whatever may have been the doubts entertained, they were completely put to an end by the arrival, next day, of regular missives, confirming the intelligence of the young count's murder, and his interment in Wurtzburg cathedral.

The dismay at the castle may well be imagined. The baron shut himself up in his chamber. The guests, who had come to rejoice with him, could not think of abandoning him in his distress. They wandered about the courts, or collected in groups in the hall, shaking their heads and shrugging their shoulders, at the troubles of so good a man; and sat longer than ever at table, and ate and drank more stoutly than ever, by way of keeping up their spirits. But the situation of the widowed bride was the most pitiable. To have lost a husband before she had even embraced him—and such a husband! if the very spectre could be so gracious and noble, what must have been the living man. She filled the house with lamentations.

On the night of the second day of her widowhood, she had retired to her chamber, accompanied by one of her aunts, who insisted on sleeping with her. The aunt, who was one of the best tellers of ghost stories in all Germany, had just been recounting one of her longest, and had fallen asleep in the very midst of it. The chamber was remote, and overlooked a small garden. The niece lay pensively gazing at the beams of the rising moon, as they trembled on the leaves of an aspen-tree before the lattice. The castle clock had just tolled midnight, when a soft strain of music stole up from the garden. She rose hastily from her bed, and stepped lightly to the window. A tall figure stood among the shadows of the trees. As it raised its head, a beam of moonlight fell upon the countenance. Heaven and earth! she beheld the Spectre Bridegroom! A loud shriek at that moment burst upon her ear, and her aunt, who had been awakened by the music, and had followed her silently to the window, fell into her arms. When she looked again, the spectre had disappeared.

Of the two females, the aunt now required the most soothing, for she was perfectly beside herself with terror. As to the young lady, there was something, even in the spectre of her lover, that seemed endearing. There was still the semblance of manly beauty; and though the shadow of a man is but little calculated to satisfy the affections of a love-sick girl, yet, where the substance is not to be had, even that is consoling. The aunt declared she would never sleep in that chamber again; the niece, for once, was refractory, and declared as strongly that she would sleep in no other in the castle: the consequence was, that she had to sleep alone: but she drew a promise from her aunt not to relate the story of the spectre, lest she should be denied the only melancholy pleasure left her on earth—that of inhabiting the chamber over which the guardian shade of her lover kept its nightly vigils.

How long the good old lady would have observed this promise is uncertain, for she dearly loved to talk of the marvellous, and there is a triumph in being the first to tell a frightful story; it is, however, still quoted in the neighborhood, as a memorable instance of female secrecy, that she kept it to herself for a whole week; when she was suddenly absolved from all further restraint, by intelligence brought to the breakfast table one morning that the young lady was not to be found.

Her room was empty—the bed had not been slept in—the window was open, and the bird had flown!

The astonishment and concern with which the intelligence was received, can only be imagined by those who have witnessed the agitation which the mishaps of a great man cause among his friends. Even the poor relations paused for a moment from the indefatigable labors of the trencher; when the aunt, who had at first been struck speechless, wrung her hands, and shrieked out, "The goblin! the goblin! she's carried away by the goblin."

In a few words she related the fearful scene of the garden, and concluded that the spectre must have carried off his bride. Two of the domestics corroborated the opinion, for they had heard the clattering of a horse's hoofs down the mountain about midnight, and had no doubt that it was the spectre on his black charger, bearing her away to the tomb. All present were struck with the direful probability; for events of the kind are extremely common in Germany, as many well authenticated histories bear witness.

What a lamentable situation was that of the poor baron! What a heart-rending dilemma for a fond father, and a member of the great family of Katzenellenbogen! His only daughter had either been rapt away to the grave, or he was to have some wood-demon for a son-in-law, and, perchance, a troop of goblin grandchildren. As usual, he was completely bewildered, and all the castle in an uproar. The men were ordered to take horse, and scour every road and path and glen of the Odenwald. The baron himself had just drawn on his jack-boots, girded on his sword, and was about to mount his steed to sally forth on the doubtful quest, when he was brought to a pause by a new apparition. A lady was seen approaching the castle, mounted on a palfrey, attended by a cavalier on horseback. She galloped up to the gate, sprang from her horse, and falling at the baron's feet, embraced his knees. It was his lost daughter—and her companion—the Spectre Bridegroom! The baron was astounded. He looked at his daughter, then at the spectre, and almost doubted the evidence of his senses. The latter, too, was wonderfully improved in his appearance since his visit to the world of spirits. His dress was splendid, and set off a noble figure of manly symmetry. He was no longer pale and melancholy. His fine countenance was flushed with the glow of youth, and joy rioted in his large dark eye.

The mystery was soon cleared up. The cavalier (for, in truth, as you must have known all the while, he was no goblin) announced himself as Sir Herman Von Starkenfaust. He related his adventure with the young count. He told how he had hastened to the castle to deliver the unwelcome tidings, but that the eloquence of the baron had interrupted him in every attempt to tell his tale. How the sight of the bride had completely captivated him, and that to pass a few hours near her, he had tacitly suffered the mistake to continue. How he had been sorely perplexed in what way to make a decent retreat, until the baron's goblin stories had suggested his eccentric exit. How, fearing the feudal hostility of the family, he had repeated his visits by stealth—had haunted the garden beneath the young lady's window—had wooed—had won—had borne away in triumph—and, in a word, had wedded the fair.

Under any other circumstances the baron would have been inflexible, for he was tenacious of paternal authority, and devoutly obstinate in all family feuds; but he loved his daughter; he had lamented her as lost; he rejoiced to find her still alive; and, though her husband was of a hostile house, yet, thank Heaven, he was not a goblin. There was something, it must be acknowledged, that did not exactly accord with his notions of strict veracity, in the joke the knight had passed upon him of his being a dead man; but several old friends present, who had served in the wars, assured him that every stratagem was excusable in love, and that the cavalier was entitled to especial privilege, having lately served as a trooper.

Matters, therefore, were happily arranged. The baron pardoned the young couple on the spot. The revels at the castle were resumed. The poor relations overwhelmed this new member of the family with loving kindness; he was so gallant, so generous—and so rich. The aunts, it is true, were somewhat scandalized that their system of strict seclusion, and passive obedience should be so badly exemplified, but attributed it all to their negligence in not having the windows grated. One of them was particularly mortified at having her marvellous story marred, and that the only spectre she had ever seen should turn out a counterfeit: but the niece seemed perfectly happy at having found him substantial flesh and blood—and so the story ends.

WESTMINSTER ABBEY

When I behold, with deep astonishment,
To famous Westminster how there resorte
Living in brasse or stoney monument,
The princes and the worthies of all sorte;
Doe not I see reformde nobilitie,
Without contempt, or pride, or ostentation,
And looke upon offenselesse majesty,
Naked of pomp or earthly domination?
And how a play-game of a painted stone
Contents the quiet now and silent sprites,
Whome all the world which late they stood upon
Could not content or quench their appetites.
    Life is a frost of cold felicitie,
    And death the thaw of all our vanitie.

CHRISTOLERO'S EPIGRAMS, BY T. B. 1598

ON ONE of those sober and rather melancholy days, in the latter part of Autumn, when the shadows of morning and evening almost mingle together, and throw a gloom over the decline of the year, I passed several hours in rambling about Westminster Abbey. There was something congenial to the season in the mournful magnificence of the old pile; and, as I passed its threshold, seemed like stepping back into the regions of antiquity, and losing myself among the shades of former ages.

I entered from the inner court of Westminster School, through a long, low, vaulted passage, that had an almost subterranean look, being dimly lighted in one part by circular perforations in the massive walls. Through this dark avenue I had a distant view of the cloisters, with the figure of an old verger, in his black gown, moving along their shadowy vaults, and seeming like a spectre from one of the neighboring tombs. The approach to the abbey through these gloomy monastic remains prepares the mind for its solemn contemplation. The cloisters still retain something of the quiet and seclusion of former days. The gray walls are discolored by damps, and crumbling with age; a coat of hoary moss has gathered over the inscriptions of the mural monuments, and obscured the death's heads, and other funereal emblems. The sharp touches of the chisel are gone from the rich tracery of the arches; the roses which adorned the keystones have lost their leafy beauty; every thing bears marks of the gradual dilapidations of time, which yet has something touching and pleasing in its very decay.

The sun was pouring down a yellow autumnal ray into the square of the cloisters; beaming upon a scanty plot of grass in the centre, and lighting up an angle of the vaulted passage with a kind of dusty splendor. From between the arcades, the eye glanced up to a bit of blue sky or a passing cloud; and beheld the sun-gilt pinnacles of the abbey towering into the azure heaven.

As I paced the cloisters, sometimes contemplating this mingled picture of glory and decay, and sometimes endeavoring to decipher the inscriptions on the tombstones, which formed the pavement beneath my feet, my eye was attracted to three figures, rudely carved in relief, but nearly worn away by the footsteps of many generations. They were the effigies of three of the early abbots; the epitaphs were entirely effaced; the names alone remained, having no doubt been renewed in later times. (Vitalis Abbas. 1082, and Gislebertus Crispinus. Abbas. 1114, and Laurentius. Abbas. 1176.) I remained some little while, musing over these casual relics of antiquity, thus left like wrecks upon this distant shore of time, telling no tale but that such beings had been, and had perished; teaching no moral but the futility of that pride which hopes still to exact homage in its ashes, and to live in an inscription. A little longer, and even these faint records will be obliterated, and the monument will cease to be a memorial. Whilst I was yet looking down upon these grave-stones, I was roused by the sound of the abbey clock, reverberating from buttress to buttress, and echoing among the cloisters. It is almost startling to hear this warning of departed time sounding among the tombs, and telling the lapse of the hour, which, like a billow, has rolled us onward towards the grave. I pursued my walk to an arched door opening to the interior of the abbey. On entering here, the magnitude of the building breaks fully upon the mind, contrasted with the vaults of the cloisters. The eyes gaze with wonder at clustered columns of gigantic dimensions, with arches springing from them to such an amazing height; and man wandering about their bases, shrunk into insignificance in comparison with his own handiwork. The spaciousness and gloom of this vast edifice produce a profound and mysterious awe. We step cautiously and softly about, as if fearful of disturbing the hallowed silence of the tomb; while every footfall whispers along the walls, and chatters among the sepulchres, making us more sensible of the quiet we have interrupted.

It seems as if the awful nature of the place presses down upon the soul, and hushes the beholder into noiseless reverence. We feel that we are surrounded by the congregated bones of the great men of past times, who have filled history with their deeds, and the earth with their renown.

And yet it almost provokes a smile at the vanity of human ambition, to see how they are crowded together and jostled in the dust; what parsimony is observed in doling out a scanty nook, a gloomy corner, a little portion of earth, to those, whom, when alive, kingdoms could not satisfy; and how many shapes, and forms, and artifices, are devised to catch the casual notice of the passenger, and save from forgetfulness, for a few short years, a name which once aspired to occupy ages of the world's thought and admiration.

I passed some time in Poet's Corner, which occupies an end of one of the transepts or cross aisles of the abbey. The monuments are generally simple; for the lives of literary men afford no striking themes for the sculptor. Shakespeare and Addison have statues erected to their memories; but the greater part have busts, medallions, and sometimes mere inscriptions. Notwithstanding the simplicity of these memorials, I have always observed that the visitors to the abbey remained longest about them. A kinder and fonder feeling takes place of that cold curiosity or vague admiration with which they gaze on the splendid monuments of the great and the heroic. They linger about these as about the tombs of friends and companions; for indeed there is something of companionship between the author and the reader. Other men are known to posterity only through the medium of history, which is continually growing faint and obscure: but the intercourse between the author and his fellow-men is ever new, active, and immediate. He has lived for them more than for himself; he has sacrificed surrounding enjoyments, and shut himself up from the delights of social life, that he might the more intimately commune with distant minds and distant ages. Well may the world cherish his renown; for it has been purchased, not by deeds of violence and blood, but by the diligent dispensation of pleasure. Well may posterity be grateful to his memory; for he has left it an inheritance, not of empty names and sounding actions, but whole treasures of wisdom, bright gems of thought, and golden veins of language.

From Poet's Corner I continued my stroll towards that

part of the abbey which contains the sepulchres of the kings. I wandered among what once were chapels, but which are now occupied by the tombs and monuments of the great. At every turn I met with some illustrious name; or the cognizance of some powerful house renowned in history. As the eye darts into these dusky chambers of death, it catches glimpses of quaint effigies; some kneeling in niches, as if in devotion; others stretched upon the tombs, with hands piously pressed together: warriors in armor, as if reposing after battle; prelates with crosiers and mitres; and nobles in robes and coronets, lying as it were in state. In glancing over this scene, so strangely populous, yet where every form is so still and silent, it seems almost as if we were treading a mansion of that fabled city, where every being had been suddenly transmuted into stone.

I paused to contemplate a tomb on which lay the effigy of a knight in complete armor. A large buckler was on one arm; the hands were pressed together in supplication upon the breast: the face was almost covered by the morion; the legs were crossed, in token of the warrior's having been engaged in the holy war. It was the tomb of a crusader; of one of those military enthusiasts, who so strangely mingled religion and romance, and whose exploits form the connecting link between fact and fiction; between the history and the fairy tale. There is something extremely picturesque in the tombs of these adventurers, decorated as they are with rude armorial bearings and Gothic sculpture. They comport with the antiquated chapels in which they are generally found; and in considering them, the imagination is apt to kindle with the legendary associations, the romantic fiction, the chivalrous pomp and pageantry, which poetry has spread over the wars for the sepulchre of Christ. They are the relics of times utterly gone by; of beings passed from recollection; of customs and manners with which ours have no affinity. They are like objects from some strange and distant land, of which we have no certain knowledge, and about which all our conceptions are vague and visionary. There is something extremely solemn and awful in those effigies on Gothic tombs, extended as if in the sleep of death, or in the supplication of the dying hour. They have an effect infinitely more impressive on my feelings than the fanciful attitudes, the overwrought conceits, and allegorical groups, which abound on modern monuments. I have been struck, also, with the superiority of many of the old sepulchral inscriptions. There was a noble way, in former times, of saying things simply, and yet saying them proudly; and I do not know an epitaph that breathes a loftier consciousness of family worth and honorable lineage, than one which affirms, of a noble house, that "all the brothers were brave, and all the sisters virtuous."

In the opposite transept to Poet's Corner stands a monument which is among the most renowned achievements of modern art; but which to me appears horrible rather than sublime. It is the tomb of Mrs. Nightingale, by Roubillac. The bottom of the monument is represented as throwing open its marble doors, and a sheeted skeleton is starting forth. The shroud is falling from his fleshless frame as he launches his dart at his victim. She is sinking into her affrighted husband's arms, who strives, with vain and frantic effort, to avert the blow. The whole is executed with terrible truth and spirit; we almost fancy we hear the gibbering yell of triumph bursting from the distended jaws of the spectre. But why should we thus seek to clothe death with unnecessary terrors, and to spread horrors round the tomb of those we love? The grave should be surrounded by every thing that might inspire tenderness and veneration for the dead; or that might win the living to virtue. It is the place, not of disgust and dismay, but of sorrow and meditation.

While wandering about these gloomy vaults and silent aisles, studying the records of the dead, the sound of busy existence from without occasionally reaches the ear; the rumbling of the passing equipage; the murmur of the multitude; or perhaps the light laugh of pleasure. The contrast is striking with the deathlike repose around: and it has a strange effect upon the feelings, thus to hear the surges of active life hurrying along, and beating against the very walls of the sepulchre.

I continued in this way to move from tomb to tomb, and from chapel to chapel. The day was gradually wearing away; the distant tread of loiterers about the abbey grew less and less frequent; the sweet-tongued bell was summoning to evening prayers; and I saw at a distance the choristers, in their white surplices, crossing the aisle and entering the choir. I stood before the entrance to Henry the Seventh's chapel. A flight of steps lead up to it, through a deep and gloomy, but magnificent arch. Great gates of brass, richly and delicately wrought, turn heavily upon their hinges, as if proudly reluctant to admit the feet of common mortals into this most gorgeous of sepulchres.

On entering, the eye is astonished by the pomp of architecture, and the elaborate beauty of sculptured detail. The very walls are wrought into universal ornament, incrusted with tracery, and scooped into niches, crowded with the statues of saints and martyrs. Stone seems, by the cunning labor of the chisel, to have been robbed of its weight and density, suspended aloft, as if by magic, and the fretted roof achieved with the wonderful minuteness and airy security of a cobweb.

Along the sides of the chapel are the lofty stalls of the Knights of the Bath, richly carved of oak, though with the grotesque decorations of Gothic architecture. On the pinnacles of the stalls are affixed the helmets and crests of the knights, with their scarfs and swords; and above them are suspended their banners, emblazoned with armorial bearings, and contrasting the splendor of gold and purple and crimson, with the cold gray fretwork of the roof. In the midst of this grand mausoleum stands the sepulchre of its founder, his effigy, with that of his queen, extended on a sumptuous tomb, and the whole surrounded by a superbly-wrought brazen railing.

There is a sad dreariness in this magnificence; this strange mixture of tombs and trophies; these emblems of living and aspiring ambition, close beside mementos which show the dust and oblivion in which all must sooner or later terminate. Nothing impresses the mind with a deeper feeling of loneliness, than to tread the silent and deserted scene of former throng and pageant. On looking round on the vacant stalls of the knights and their esquires, and on the rows of dusty but gorgeous banners that were once borne before them, my imagination conjured up the scene when this hall was bright with the valor and beauty of the land; glittering with the splendor of jewelled rank and military array; alive with the tread of many feet and the hum of an admiring multitude. All had passed away; the silence of death had settled again upon the place, interrupted only by the casual chirping of birds, which had found their way into the chapel, and built their nests among its friezes and pendants—sure signs of solitariness and desertion.

When I read the names inscribed on the banners, they

were those of men scattered far and wide about the world; some tossing upon distant seas; some under arms in distant lands; some mingling in the busy intrigues of courts and cabinets; all seeking to deserve one more distinction in this mansion of shadowy honors: the melancholy reward of a monument.

Two small aisles on each side of this chapel present a touching instance of the equality of the grave; which brings down the oppressor to a level with the oppressed, and mingles the dust of the bitterest enemies together. In one is the sepulchre of the haughty Elizabeth; in the other is that of her victim, the lovely and unfortunate Mary. Not an hour in the day but some ejaculation of pity is uttered over the fate of the latter, mingled with indignation at her oppressor. The walls of Elizabeth's sepulchre continually echo with the sighs of sympathy heaved at the grave of her rival.

A peculiar melancholy reigns over the aisle where Mary lies buried. The light struggles dimly through windows darkened by dust. The greater part of the place is in deep shadow, and the walls are stained and tinted by time and weather. A marble figure of Mary is stretched upon the tomb, round which is an iron railing, much corroded, bearing her national emblem—the thistle. I was weary with wandering, and sat down to rest myself by the monument, revolving in my mind the chequered and disastrous story of poor Mary.

The sound of casual footsteps had ceased from the abbey. I could only hear, now and then, the distant voice of the priest repeating the evening service, and the faint responses of the choir; these paused for a time, and all was hushed. The stillness, the desertion and obscurity that were gradually prevailing around, gave a deeper and more solemn interest to the place:

For in the silent grave no conversation,
No joyful tread of friends, no voice of lovers,
No careful father's counsel—nothing's heard,
For nothing is, but all oblivion,
Dust, and an endless darkness.

Suddenly the notes of the deep-laboring organ burst upon the ear, falling with doubled and redoubled intensity, and rolling, as it were, huge billows of sound. How well do their volume and grandeur accord with this mighty building! With what pomp do they swell through its vast vaults, and breathe their awful harmony through these caves of death, and make the silent sepulchre vocal! And now they rise in triumph and acclamation, heaving higher and higher their accordant notes, and piling sound on sound. And now they pause, and the soft voices of the choir break out into sweet gushes of melody; they soar aloft, and warble along the roof, and seem to play about these lofty vaults like the pure airs of heaven. Again the pealing organ heaves its thrilling thunders, compressing air into music, and rolling it forth upon the soul. What long-drawn cadences! What solemn sweeping concords! It grows more and more dense and powerful—it fills the vast pile, and seems to jar the very walls—the ear is stunned—the senses are overwhelmed. And now it is winding up in full jubilee— it is rising from the earth to heaven—the very soul seems rapt away and floated upwards on this swelling tide of harmony!

I sat for some time lost in that kind of reverie which a strain of music is apt sometimes to inspire: the shadows of evening were gradually thickening round me; the monuments began to cast deeper and deeper gloom; and the distant clock again gave token of the slowly waning day.

I rose and prepared to leave the abbey. As I descended the flight of steps which lead into the body of the building, my eye was caught by the shrine of Edward the Confessor, and I ascended the small staircase that conducts to it, to take from thence a general survey of this wilderness of tombs. The shrine is elevated upon a kind of platform, and close around it are the sepulchres of various kings and queens. From this eminence the eye looks down between pillars and funeral trophies to the chapels and chambers below, crowded with tombs; where warriors, prelates, courtiers and statesmen, lie mouldering in their "beds of darkness." Close by me stood the great chair of coronation, rudely carved of oak, in the barbarous taste of a remote and Gothic age. The scene seemed almost as if contrived, with theatrical artifice, to produce an effect upon the beholder. Here was a type of the beginning and the end of human pomp and power; here it was literally but a step from the throne to the sepulchre. Would not one think that these incongruous mementos had been gathered together as a lesson to living greatness?—to show it, even in the moment of its proudest exaltation, the neglect and dishonor to which it must soon arrive; how soon that crown which encircles its brow must pass away, and it must lie down in the dust and disgraces of the tomb, and be trampled upon by the feet of the meanest of the multitude. For, strange to tell, even the grave is here no longer a sanctuary. There is a shocking levity in some natures, which leads them to sport with awful and hallowed things; and there are base minds, which delight to revenge on the illustrious dead the abject homage and grovelling servility which they pay to the living. The coffin of Edward the Confessor has been broken open, and his remains despoiled of their funereal ornaments; the sceptre has been stolen from the hand of the imperious Elizabeth, and the effigy of Henry the

Fifth lies headless. Not a royal monument but bears some proof how false and fugitive is the homage of mankind. Some are plundered; some mutilated; some covered with ribaldry and insult—all more or less outraged and dishonored!

The last beams of day were now faintly streaming through the painted windows in the high vaults above me; the lower parts of the abbey were already wrapped in the obscurity of twilight. The chapels and aisles grew darker and darker. The effigies of the kings faded into shadows; the marble figures of the monuments assumed strange shapes in the uncertain light; the evening breeze crept through the aisles like the cold breath of the grave; and even the distant footfall of a verger, traversing the Poet's Corner, had something strange and dreary in its sound. I slowly retraced my morning's walk, and as I passed out at the portal of the cloisters, the door, closing with a jarring noise behind me, filled the whole building with echoes.

I endeavored to form some arrangement in my mind of the objects I had been contemplating, but found they were already fallen into indistinctness and confusion. Names, inscriptions, trophies, had all become confounded in my recollection, though I had scarcely taken my foot from off the threshold. What, thought I, is this vast assemblage of sepulchres but a treasury of humiliation; a huge pile of reiterated homilies on the emptiness of renown, and the certainty of oblivion! It is, indeed, the empire of death; his great shadowy palace, where he sits in state, mocking at the relics of human glory, and spreading dust and forgetfulness on the monuments of princes. How idle a boast, after all, is the immortality of a name! Time is ever silently turning over his pages; we are too much engrossed by the story of the present, to think of the characters and anecdotes that gave interest to the past; and each age is a volume thrown aside to be speedily forgotten. The idol of to-day pushes the hero of yesterday out of our recollection; and will, in turn, be supplanted by his successor of to-morrow. "Our fathers," says Sir Thomas Brown, "find their graves in our short memories, and sadly tell us how we may be buried in our survivors." History fades into fable; fact becomes clouded with doubt and controversy; the inscription moulders from the tablet; the statue falls from the pedestal. Columns, arches, pyramids, what are they but heaps of sand; and their epitaphs, but characters written in the dust? What is the security of a tomb, or the perpetuity of an embalmment? The remains of Alexander the Great have been scattered to the wind, and his empty sarcophagus is now the mere curiosity of a museum. "The Egyptian mummies, which Cambyses or time hath spared, avarice now consumeth; Mizraim cures wounds, and Pharaoh is sold for balsams."*

What then is to insure this pile which now towers above me from sharing the fate of mightier mausoleums? The time must come when its gilded vaults, which now spring so loftily, shall lie in rubbish beneath the feet; when, instead of the sound of melody and praise, the wind shall whistle through the broken arches, and the owl hoot from the shattered tower—when the garish sunbeam shall break into these gloomy mansions of death, and the ivy twine round the fallen column; and the fox-glove hand its blossoms about the nameless urn, as if in mockery of the dead. Thus man passes away; his name perishes from record and recollection; his history is as a tale that is told, and his very monument becomes a ruin.

* Sir T. Brown.

CHRISTMAS

But is old, old, good old Christmas gone? Nothing but the hair of his good, gray old head and beard left? Well, I will have that, seeing I cannot have more of him.

HUE AND CRY AFTER CHRISTMAS.

A man might then behold
  At Christmas, in each hall
Good fires to curb the cold,
  And meat for great and small.
The neighbors were friendly bidden,
  And all had welcome true,
The poor from the gates were not chidden
  When this old cap was new.

OLD SONG

NOTHING in England exercises a more delightful spell over my imagination, than the lingerings of the holiday customs and rural games of former times. They recall the pictures my fancy used to draw in the May morning of life, when as yet I only knew the world through books, and believed it to be all that poets had painted it; and they bring with them the flavor of those honest days of yore, in which, perhaps, with equal fallacy, I am apt to think the world was more homebred, social, and joyous than at present. I regret to say that they are daily growing more and more faint, being gradually worn away by time, but still more obliterated by modern fashion. They resemble those picturesque morsels of Gothic architecture, which we see crumbling in various parts of the country, partly dilapidated by the waste of ages, and partly lost in the additions and alterations of later days. Poetry, however, clings with cherishing fondness about the rural game and holiday revel, from which it has derived so many of its themes— as the ivy winds its rich foliage about the Gothic arch and mouldering tower, gratefully repaying their support, by clasping together their tottering remains, and, as it were, embalming them in verdure.

Of all the old festivals, however, that of Christmas awakens the strongest and most heartfelt associations. There is a tone of solemn and sacred feeling that blends with our conviviality, and lifts the spirit to a state of hallowed and elevated enjoyment. The services of the church about this season are extremely tender and inspiring. They dwell on the beautiful story of the origin of our faith, and the pastoral scenes that accompanied its announcement. They gradually increase in fervor and pathos during the season of Advent, until they break forth in full jubilee on the morning that brought peace and good-will to men. I do not know a grander effect of music on the moral feelings, than to hear the full choir and the pealing organ performing a Christmas anthem in a cathedral, and filling every part of the vast pile with triumphant harmony.

It is a beautiful arrangement, also, derived from days of yore, that this festival, which commemorates the announcement of the religion of peace and love, has been made the season for gathering together of family connections, and drawing closer again those bands of kindred hearts, which the cares and pleasures and sorrows of the world are continually operating to cast loose; of calling back the children of a family, who have launched forth in life, and wandered widely asunder, once more to assemble about the paternal hearth, that rallying place of the affections, there to grow young and loving again among the endearing mementos of childhood.

There is something in the very season of the year that gives a charm to the festivity of Christmas. At other times we derive a great portion of our pleasures from

the mere beauties of nature. Our feelings sally forth and
dissipate themselves over the sunny landscape, and we
"live abroad and everywhere." The song of the bird, the
murmur of the stream, the breathing fragrance of
spring, the soft voluptuousness of summer, the golden
pomp of autumn; earth with its mantle of refreshing
green, and heaven with its deep delicious blue and its
cloudy magnificence, all fill us with mute but exquisite
delight, and we revel in the luxury of mere sensation.
But in the depth of winter, when nature lies despoiled of
every charm, and wrapped in her shroud of sheeted
snow, we turn for our gratifications to moral sources.
The dreariness and desolation of the landscape, the
short gloomy days and darksome nights, while they
circumscribe our wanderings, shut in our feelings also
from rambling abroad, and make us more keenly
disposed for the pleasure of the social circle. Our
thoughts are more concentrated; our friendly sympathies more aroused. We feel more sensibly the charm
of each other's society, and are brought more closely
together by dependence on each other for enjoyment.
Heart calleth unto heart; and we draw our pleasures
from the deep wells of loving-kindness, which lie in the
quiet recesses of our bosoms; and which, when resorted
to, furnish forth the pure element of domestic felicity.

The pitchy gloom without makes the heart dilate on
entering the room filled with the glow and warmth of
the evening fire. The ruddy blaze diffuses an artificial
summer and sunshine through the room, and lights up
each countenance in a kindlier welcome. Where does
the honest face of hospitality expand into a broader and
more cordial smile—where is the shy glance of love
more sweetly eloquent—than by the winter fireside? and
as the hollow blast of wintry wind rushes through the
hall, claps the distant door, whistles about the casement,

and rumbles down the chimney, what can be more grateful than that feeling of sober and sheltered security, with which we look round upon the comfortable chamber and the scene of domestic hilarity?

The English, from the great prevalence of rural habit throughout every class of society, have always been fond of those festivals and holidays which agreeably interrupt the stillness of country life; and they were, in former days, particularly observant of the religious and social rites of Christmas. It is inspiring to read even the dry details which some antiquaries have given of the quaint humors, the burlesque pageants, the complete abandonment to mirth and good-fellowship, with which this festival was celebrated. It seemed to throw open every door, and unlock every heart. It brought the peasant and the peer together, and blended all ranks in one warm, generous flow of joy and kindness. The old halls of castles and manor-houses resounded with the harp and the Christmas carol, and their ample boards groaned under the weight of hospitality. Even the poorest cottage welcomed the festive season with green decorations of bay and holly—the cheerful fire glanced its rays through the lattice, inviting the passengers to raise the latch, and join the gossip knot huddled round the hearth, beguiling the long evening with legendary jokes and oft-told Christmas tales.

One of the least pleasing effects of modern refinement is the havoc it has made among the hearty old holiday customs. It has completely taken off the sharp touchings and spirited reliefs of these embellishments of life, and has worn down society into a more smooth and polished, but certainly a less characteristic surface. Many of the games and ceremonials of Christmas have entirely disappeared, and, like the sherris sack of old Falstaff, are become matters of speculation and dispute among commentators. They flourished in times full of spirit and lustihood, when men enjoyed life roughly, but heartily and vigorously; times wild and picturesque, which have furnished poetry with its richest materials, and the drama with its most attractive variety of characters and manners. The world has become more worldly. There is more of dissipation, and less of enjoyment. Pleasure has expanded into a broader, but a shallower stream; and has forsaken many of those deep and quiet channels where it flowed sweetly through the calm bosom of domestic life. Society has acquired a more enlightened and elegant tone; but it has lost many of its strong local peculiarities, its homebred feelings, its honest fireside delights. The traditionary customs of golden-hearted antiquity, its feudal hospitalities, and lordly wassailings, have passed away with the baronial castles and stately manor-houses in which they were celebrated. They comported with the shadowy hall, the great oaken gallery, and the tapestried parlor, but are unfitted to the light showy saloons and gay drawing-rooms of the modern villa.

Shorn, however, as it is, of its ancient and festive honors, Christmas is still a period of delightful excitement in England. It is gratifying to see that home feeling completely aroused which holds so powerful a place in every English bosom. The preparations making on every side for the social board that is again to unite friends and kindred; the presents of good cheer passing and repassing, those tokens of regard, and quickeners of kind feelings; the evergreens distributed about houses and churches, emblems of peace and gladness; all these have the most pleasing effect in producing fond associations, and kindling benevolent sympathies. Even the sound of the Waits, rude as may be their minstrelsy, breaks upon the midwatches of a winter night with the effect of perfect harmony. As I have been awakened by them in that still and solemn hour, "when deep sleep falleth upon man," I have listened with a hushed delight, and, connecting them with the sacred and joyous occasion, have almost fancied them into another celestial choir, announcing peace and good-will to mankind.

How delightfully the imagination, when wrought upon by these moral influences, turns every thing to melody and beauty! The very crowing of the cock, heard sometimes in the profound repose of the country, "telling the night watches to his feathery dames," was thought by the common people to announce the approach of this sacred festival.

> "Some say that ever 'gainst that season comes
> Wherein our Saviour's birth is celebrated,
> This bird of dawning singeth all night long;
> And then, they say, no spirit dares stir abroad;
> The nights are wholesome—then no planets strike.
> No fairy takes, no witch hath power to charm,
> So hallow'd and so gracious is the time."

Amidst the general call to happiness, the bustle of the spirits, and stir of the affections, which prevail at this period, what bosom can remain insensible? It is, indeed, the season of regenerated feeling—the season for kindling, not merely the fire of hospitality in the hall, but the genial flame of charity in the heart.

The scene of early love again rises green to memory beyond the sterile waste of years; and the idea of home, fraught with the fragrance of home-dwelling joys, reanimates the drooping spirit; as the Arabian breeze will sometimes waft the freshness of the distant fields to the weary pilgrim of the desert.

Stranger and sojourner as I am in the land—though for me no social hearth may blaze, no hospitable roof throw open its doors, nor the warm grasp of friendship welcome me at the threshold—yet I feel the influence of the season beaming into my soul from the happy looks of those around me. Surely happiness is reflective, like the light of heaven; and every countenance, bright with smiles, and glowing with innocent enjoyment, is a mirror transmitting to others the rays of a supreme and ever-shining benevolence. He who can turn churlishly away from contemplating the felicity of his fellow-beings, and can sit down darkling and repining in his loneliness when all around is joyful, may have his moments of strong excitement and selfish gratification, but he wants the genial and social sympathies which constitute the charm of a merry Christmas.

THE STAGE COACH

> Omne bené
> Sine pœnâ
> Tempus est ludendi.
> Venit hora
> Absque morâ
> Libros deponendi.*
> OLD HOLIDAY SCHOOL SONG

IN THE preceding paper I have made some general observations on the Christmas festivities of England, and am tempted to illustrate them by some anecdotes of a Christmas passed in the country; in perusing which I would most courteously invite my reader to lay aside the austerity of wisdom, and to put on that genuine holiday

*[It's time to play
  Full happily, without punishment.
  The hour has come
  To put aside books without delay.]

spirit which is tolerant of folly, and anxious only for amusement.

In the course of a December tour in Yorkshire, I rode for a long distance in one of the public coaches, on the day preceding Christmas. The coach was crowded, both inside and out, with passengers, who, by their talk, seemed principally bound to the mansions of relations or friends, to eat the Christmas dinner. It was loaded also with hampers of game, and baskets and boxes of delicacies; and hares hung dangling their long ears about the coachman's box, presents from distant friends for the impending feast. I had three fine rosy-cheeked boys for my fellow-passengers inside, full of the buxom health and manly spirit which I have observed in the children of this country. They were returning home for the holidays in high glee, and promising themselves a world of enjoyment. It was delightful to hear the gigantic plans of the little rogues, and the impracticable feats they were to perform during their six weeks' emancipation from the abhorred thraldom of book, birch, and pedagogue. They were full of anticipations of the meeting with the family and household, down to the very cat and dog; and of the joy they were to give their little sisters by the presents with which their pockets were crammed; but the meeting to which they seemed to look forward with the greatest impatience was with Bantam, which I found to be a pony, and, according to their talk, possessed of more virtues than any steed since the days of Bucephalus. How he could trot! how he could run! and then such leaps as he would take—there was not a hedge in the whole country that he could not clear.

They were under the particular guardianship of the coachman, to whom, whenever an opportunity presented, they addressed a host of questions, and pronounced him one of the best fellows in the world. Indeed, I could not but notice the more than ordinary air of bustle and importance of the coachman, who wore his hat a little on one side, and had a large bunch of Christmas greens stuck in the button-hole of his coat. He is always a personage full of mighty care and business, but he is particularly so during this season, having so many commissions to execute in consequence of the great interchange of presents. And here, perhaps, it may not be unacceptable to my untravelled readers, to have a sketch that may serve as a general representation of this very numerous and important class of functionaries, who have a dress, a manner, a language, an air, peculiar to themselves, and prevalent throughout the fraternity; so that, wherever an English stage coachman may be seen, he cannot be mistaken for one of any other craft or mystery.

He has commonly a broad, full face, curiously mottled with red, as if the blood had been forced by hard feeding into every vessel of the skin; he is swelled into jolly dimensions by frequent potations of malt liquors, and his bulk is still further increased by a multiplicity of coats, in which he is buried like a cauliflower, the upper one reaching to his heels. He wears a broad-brimmed, low-crowned hat; a huge roll of colored handkerchief about his neck, knowingly knotted and tucked in at the bosom; and has in summer time a large bouquet of flowers in his button-hole; the present, most probably, of some enamored country lass. His waistcoat is commonly of some bright color, striped, and his small clothes extend far below the knees, to meet a pair of jockey boots which reach about half way up his legs.

All this costume is maintained with much precision; he has a pride in having his clothes of excellent materials; and, notwithstanding the seeming grossness of his appearance, there is still discernible that neatness and propriety of person, which is almost inherent in an Englishman. He enjoys great consequence and consideration along the road; has frequent conferences with the village housewives, who look upon him as a man of great trust and dependence; and he seems to have a good understanding with every bright-eyed country lass. The moment he arrives where the horses are to be changed, he throws down the reins with something of an air, and abandons the cattle to the care of the hostler; his duty being merely to drive from one stage to another. When off the box, his hands are thrust into the pockets of his great coat, and he rolls about the inn yard with an air of the most absolute lordliness. Here he is generally surrounded by an admiring throng of hostlers, stable-boys, shoeblacks, and those nameless hangers-on, that infest inns and taverns, and run errands, and do all kind of odd jobs, for the privilege of battening on the drippings of the kitchen and the leakage of the tap-room. These all look up to him as to an oracle; treasure up his cant phrases; echo his opinions about horses and other topics of jockey lore; and, above all, endeavor to imitate his air and carriage. Every ragamuffin that has a coat to his back, thrusts his hands in the pockets, rolls in his gait, talks slang, and is an embryo Coachey.

Perhaps it might be owing to the pleasing serenity that reigned in my own mind, that I fancied I saw cheerfulness in every countenance throughout the journey. A stage coach, however, carries animation always with it, and puts the world in motion as it whirls along. The horn, sounded at the entrance of a village, produces a general bustle. Some hasten forth to meet friends; some with bundles and bandboxes to secure places, and in the hurry of the moment can hardly take leave of the group that accompanies them. In the mean time, the coachman has a world of small commissions to execute. Sometimes he delivers a hare or pheasant; sometimes jerks a small parcel or newspaper to the door of a public house; and sometimes, with knowing leer and words of sly import, hands to some half-blushing, half-laughing housemaid an odd-shaped billet-doux from some rustic admirer. As the coach rattles through the village, every one runs to the windows, and you have glances on every side of fresh country faces and blooming giggling girls. At the corners are assembled juntos of village idlers and wise men, who take their stations there for the important purpose of seeing company pass; but the sagest knot is generally at the blacksmith's, to whom the passing of the coach is an event fruitful of much speculation. The smith, with the horse's heel in his lap, pauses as the vehicle whirls by; the cyclops round the anvil suspend their ringing hammers, and suffer the iron to grow cool; and the sooty spectre, in brown paper cap, laboring at the bellows, leans on the handle for a moment, and permits the asthmatic engine to heave a long-drawn sigh, while he glares through the murky smoke and sulphureous gleams of the smithy.

Perhaps the impending holiday might have given a more than usual animation to the country, for it seemed to me as if everybody was in good looks and good spirits. Game, poultry, and other luxuries of the table, were in brisk circulation in the villages; the grocers', butchers' and fruiterers' shops were thronged with customers. The housewives were stirring briskly about, putting their dwellings in order; and the glossy branches of holly, with their bright-red berries, began to appear at the windows. The scene brought to mind an old writer's account of Christmas preparations:—"Now capons and hens, beside turkeys, geese, and ducks, with beef and mutton—must all die—for in twelve days a multitude of people will not be fed with a little. Now plums and spice, sugar and honey, square it among pies and broth. Now or never must music be in tune, for the youth must dance and sing to get them a heat, while the aged sit by the fire. The country maid leaves half her market, and must be sent again, if she forgets a pack of cards on Christmas eve. Great is the contention of holly and ivy, whether master or dame wears the breeches. Dice and cards benefit the butler; and if the cook do not lack wit, he will sweetly lick his fingers."

I was roused from this fit of luxurious meditation, by a shout from my little travelling companions. They had been looking out of the coach windows for the last few miles, recognizing every tree and cottage as they approached home, and now there was a general burst of joy—"There's John! and there's old Carlo! and there's Bantam!" cried the happy little rogues, clapping their hands.

At the end of a lane there was an old sober-looking servant-in livery, waiting for them; he was accompanied by a superannuated pointer, and by the redoubtable Bantam, a little old rat of a pony, with a shaggy mane and long rusty tail, who stood dozing quietly by the road-side, little dreaming of the bustling times that awaited him.

I was pleased to see the fondness with which the little fellows leaped about the steady old footman, and hugged the pointer; who wriggled his whole body for joy. But Bantam was the great object of interest; all wanted to mount at once, and it was with some difficulty that John arranged that they should ride by turns, and the eldest should ride first.

Off they set at last; one on the pony, with the dog bounding and barking before him, and the others holding John's hands; both talking at once, and over-powering him with questions about home, and with school anecdotes. I looked after them with a feeling in which I do not know whether pleasure or melancholy predominated; for I was reminded of those days when, like them, I had neither known care nor sorrow, and a holiday was the summit of earthly felicity. We stopped a few moments afterwards to water the horses, and on resuming our route, a turn of the road brought us in sight of a neat country seat. I could just distinguish the forms of a lady and two young girls in the portico, and I saw my little comrades, with Bantam, Carlo, and old John, trooping along the carriage road. I leaned out of the coach window, in hopes of witnessing the happy meeting, but a grove of trees shut it from my sight.

In the evening we reached a village where I had determined to pass the night. As we drove into the great gateway of the inn, I saw on one side the light of a rousing kitchen fire beaming through a window. I entered, and admired, for the hundredth time, that picture of convenience, neatness, and broad honest enjoyment, the kitchen of an English inn. It was of spacious dimensions, hung round with copper and tin vessels highly polished, and decorated here and there with a Christmas green. Hams, tongues, and flitches of bacon, were suspended from the ceiling; a smoke-jack made its ceaseless clanking beside the fireplace, and a clock ticked in one corner. A well-scoured deal table extended along one side of the kitchen, with a cold round of beef, and other hearty viands upon it, over which two foaming tankards of ale seemed mounting guard. Travellers of inferior order were preparing to attack this stout repast, while others sat smoking and gossiping over their ale on two high-backed oaken settles beside the fire. Trim housemaids were hurrying backwards and forwards under the directions of a fresh, bustling landlady; but still seizing an occasional moment to exchange a flippant word, and have a rallying laugh, with the group round the fire. The scene completely realized Poor Robin's humble idea of the comforts of mid-winter:

> Now trees their leafy hats do bare
> To reverence Winter's silver hair;
> A handsome hostess, merry host,
> A pot of ale now and a toast,
> Tobacco and a good coal fire,
> Are things this season doth require.*

I had not been long at the inn when a post-chaise drove up to the door. A young gentleman stept out, and by the light of the lamps I caught a glimpse of a countenance which I thought I knew. I moved forward to get a nearer view, when his eye caught mine. I was not mistaken; it was Frank Bracebridge, a sprightly good-humored young fellow, with whom I had once travelled on the continent. Our meeting was extremely cordial, for the countenance of an old fellow-traveller always brings up the recollection of a thousand pleasant scenes, odd adventures, and excellent jokes. To discuss all these in a transient interview at an inn was impossible; and finding that I was not pressed for time, and was merely making a tour of observation, he insisted that I should give him a day or two at his father's country seat, to which he was going to pass the holidays, and which lay at a few miles distance. "It is better than eating a solitary Christmas dinner at an inn," said he, "and I can assure you of a hearty welcome in something of the old-fashioned style." His reasoning was cogent, and I must confess the preparation I had seen for universal festivity and social enjoyment had made me feel a little impatient

*Poor Robin's Almanac, 1684.

of my loneliness. I closed, therefore, at once, with his invitation: the chaise drove up to the door, and in a few moments I was on my way to the family mansion of the Bracebridges.

CHRISTMAS EVE

Saint Francis and Saint Benedight
Blesse this house from wicked wight;
From the night-mare and the goblin,
That is hight good fellow Robin;
Keep it from all evil spirits,
Fairies, weezels, rats, and ferrets:
From curfew time
To the next prime.

CARTWRIGHT

IT WAS a brilliant moonlight night, but extremely cold; our chaise whirled rapidly over the frozen ground; the postboy smacked his whip incessantly, and a part of the time his horses were on a gallop. "He knows where he is going," said my companion, laughing, "and is eager to arrive in time for some of the merriment and good cheer of the servants' hall. My father, you must know, is a bigoted devotee of the old school, and prides himself upon keeping up something of old English hospitality. He is a tolerable specimen of what you will rarely meet with nowadays in its purity, the old English country gentleman; for our men of fortune spend so much of their time in town, and fashion is carried so much into the country, that the strong rich peculiarities of ancient rural life are almost polished away. My father, however, from early years, took honest Peacham* for his text-book, instead of Chesterfield; he determined in his own

* Peacham's complete Gentleman, 1622.

mind, that there was no condition more truly honorable and enviable than that of a country gentleman on his paternal lands, and therefore passes the whole of his time on his estate. He is a strenuous advocate for the revival of the old rural games and holiday observances, and is deeply read in the writers, ancient and modern, who have treated on the subject. Indeed his favorite range of reading is among the authors who flourished at least two centuries since; who, he insists, wrote and thought more like true Englishmen than any of their successors. He even regrets sometimes that he had not been born a few centuries earlier, when England was itself, and had its peculiar manners and customs. As he lives at some distance from the main road, in rather a lonely part of the country, without any rival gentry near him, he has that most enviable of all blessings to an Englishman, an opportunity of indulging the bent of his own humor without molestation. Being representative of the oldest family in the neighborhood, and a great part of the peasantry being his tenants, he is much looked up to, and, in general, is known simply by the appellation of "The Squire;" a title which has been accorded to the head of the family since time immemorial. I think it best to give you these hints about my worthy old father, to prepare you for any eccentricities that might otherwise appear absurd."

We had passed for some time along the wall of a park, and at length the chaise stopped at the gate. It was in a heavy magnificent old style, of iron bars, fancifully wrought at top into flourishes and flowers. The huge square columns that supported the gate were surmounted by the family crest. Close adjoining was the porter's lodge, sheltered under dark fir-trees, and almost buried in shrubbery.

The postboy rang a large porter's bell, which resounded through the still frosty air, and was answered by the distant barking of dogs, with which the mansion-house seemed garrisoned. An old woman immediately appeared at the gate. As the moonlight fell strongly upon her, I had a full view of a little primitive dame, dressed very much in the antique taste, with a neat kerchief and stomacher, and her silver hair peeping from under a cap of snowy whiteness. She came courtesying forth, with many expressions of simple joy at seeing her young master. Her husband, it seemed, was up at the house keeping Christmas eve in the servants' hall; they could not do without him, as he was the best hand at a song and story in the household.

My friend proposed that we should alight and walk through the park to the hall, which was at no great distance, while the chaise should follow on. Our road wound through a noble avenue of trees, among the naked branches of which the moon glittered, as she rolled through the deep vault of a cloudless sky. The lawn beyond was sheeted with a slight covering of snow, which here and there sparkled as the moonbeams caught a frosty crystal; and at a distance might be seen a thin transparent vapor, stealing up from the low grounds and threatening gradually to shroud the landscape.

My companion looked around him with transport: "How often," said he, "have I scampered up this avenue, on returning home on school vacations! How often have I played under these trees when a boy! I feel a degree of filial reverence for them, as we look up to those who have cherished us in childhood. My father was always scrupulous in exacting our holidays, and having us around him on family festivals. He used to direct and superintend our games with the strictness that some parents do the studies of their children. He was very particular that we should play the old English games according to their original form; and consulted old books for precedent and authority for every 'merrie disport;' yet I assure you there never was pedantry so delightful. It was the policy of the good old gentleman to make his children feel that home was the happiest place in the world; and I value this delicious home-feeling as one of the choicest gifts a parent could bestow."

We were interrupted by the clamor of a troop of dogs of all sorts and sizes, "mongrel, puppy, whelp and hound, and curs of low degree," that, disturbed by the ring of the porter's bell and the rattling of the chaise, came bounding, open-mouthed, across the lawn.

> "——The little dogs and all,
> Tray, Blanch, and Sweetheart, see, they bark at me!"

cried Bracebridge, laughing. At the sound of his voice, the bark was changed into a yelp of delight, and in a moment he was surrounded and almost overpowered by the caresses of the faithful animals.

We had now come in full view of the old family mansion, partly thrown in deep shadow, and partly lit up by the cold moonshine. It was an irregular building, of some magnitude, and seemed to be of the architecture of different periods. One wing was evidently very ancient, with heavy stone-shafted bow windows jutting out and overrun with ivy, from among the foliage of which the small diamond-shaped panes of glass glittered with the moonbeams. The rest of the house was in the French taste of Charles the Second's time, having been repaired and altered, as my friend told me, by one of his ancestors, who returned with that monarch at the Restoration. The grounds about the house were laid out in the old formal manner of artificial flower-beds, clipped shrubberies, raised terraces, and heavy stone balustrades, ornamented with urns, a leaden statue or two, and a jet of water. The old gentleman, I was told, was extremely careful to preserve this obsolete finery in all its original state. He admired this fashion in gardening; it had an air of magnificence, was courtly and noble, and befitting good old family style. The boasted imitation of nature in modern gardening had sprung up with modern republican notions, but did not suit a monarchical government; it smacked of the levelling system—I could not help smiling at this introduction of politics into gardening, though I expressed some apprehension that I should find the old gentleman rather intolerant in his creed. Frank assured me, however, that it was almost the only instance in which he had ever heard his father meddle with politics; and he believed that he had got this notion from a member of parliament who once passed a few weeks with him. The squire was glad of any argument to defend his clipped yew-trees and formal terraces, which had been occasionally attacked by modern landscape gardeners.

As we approached the house, we heard the sound of music, and now and then a burst of laughter, from one end of the building. This, Bracebridge said, must proceed from the servants' hall, where a great deal of revelry was permitted, and even encouraged by the squire, throughout the twelve days of Christmas, provided every thing was done conformably to ancient usage. Here were kept up the old games of hoodman blind, shoe the wild mare, hot cockles, steal the white loaf, bob apple, and snap dragon: the Yule clog and Christmas candle were regularly burnt, and the mistletoe, with its white berries, hung up, to the imminent peril of all the pretty housemaids.*

So intent were the servants upon their sports that we had to ring repeatedly before we could make ourselves heard. On our arrival being announced, the squire came out to receive us, accompanied by his two other sons; one a young officer in the army, home on leave of absence; the other an Oxonian, just from the university. The squire was a fine healthy-looking old gentleman, with silver hair curling lightly round an open florid countenance; in which the physiognomist, with the advantage, like myself, of a previous hint or two, might discover a singular mixture of whim, and benevolence.

The family meeting was warm and affectionate; as the evening was far advanced, the squire would not permit us to change our travelling dresses, but ushered us at once to the company, which was assembled in a large old-fashioned hall. It was composed of different branches of a numerous family connection, where there were the usual proportion of old uncles and aunts, comfortable married dames, superannuated spinsters, blooming country cousins, half-fledged striplings, and bright-eyed boarding-school hoydens. They were variously occupied; some at a round game of cards; others conversing around the fireplace; at one end of the hall was a group of the young folks, some nearly grown up, others of a more tender and budding age, fully engrossed by a merry game; and a profusion of wooden horses, penny trumpets, and tattered dolls, about the floor, showed traces of a troop of little fairy beings, who, having frolicked through a happy day, had been carried off to slumber through a peaceful night.

*The mistletoe is still hung up in farmhouses and kitchens at Christmas; and the young men have the privilege of kissing the girls under it, plucking each time a berry from the bush. When the berries are all plucked, the privilege ceases.

While the mutual greetings were going on between young Bracebridge and his relatives, I had time to scan the apartment. I have called it a hall, for so it had certainly been in old times, and the squire had evidently endeavored to restore it to something of its primitive state. Over the heavy projecting fireplace was suspended a picture of a warrior in armor, standing by a white horse, and on the opposite wall hung a helmet, buckler, and lance. At one end an enormous pair of antlers were inserted in the wall, the branches serving as hooks on which to suspend hats, whips, and spurs; and in the corners of the apartment were fowling-pieces, fishing-rods, and other sporting implements. The furniture was of the cumbrous workmanship of former days, though some articles of modern convenience had been added, and the oaken floor had been carpeted; so that the whole presented an odd mixture of parlor and hall.

The grate had been removed from the wide over-whelming fireplace, to make way for a fire of wood, in the midst of which was an enormous log glowing and blazing, and sending forth a vast volume of light and heat: this I understood was the Yule clog, which the squire was particular in having brought in and illumined on a Christmas eve, according to ancient custom.*

*The *Yule clog* is a great log of wood, sometimes the root of a tree, brought into the house with great ceremony, on Christmas eve, laid in the fireplace, and lighted with the brand of last year's clog. While it lasted, there was great drinking, singing, and telling of tales. Some-times it was accompanied by Christmas candles; but in the cottages the only light was from the ruddy blaze of the great wood fire. The Yule clog was to burn all night; if it went out, it was considered a sign of ill luck.

Herrick mentions it in one of his songs:—

> Come, bring with a noise,
> My merrie, merrie boyes,
> The Christmas log to the firing;
> While my good dame, she
> Bids ye all be free,
> And drink to your hearts desiring.

It was really delightful to see the old squire seated in his hereditary elbow chair, by the hospitable fireside of his ancestors, and looking around him like the sun of a system, beaming warmth and gladness to every heart. Even the very dog that lay stretched at his feet, as he lazily shifted his position and yawned, would look fondly up in his master's face, wag his tail against the floor, and stretch himself again to sleep, confident of kindness and protection. There is an emanation from the heart in genuine hospitality which cannot be described, but is immediately felt, and puts the stranger at once at his ease. I had not been seated many minutes by the comfortable hearth of the worthy old cavalier, before I found myself as much at home as if I had been one of the family.

Supper was announced shortly after our arrival. It was served up in a spacious oaken chamber, the panels of which shone with wax, and around which were several family portraits decorated with holly and ivy. Besides the accustomed lights, two great wax tapers, called Christmas candles, wreathed with greens, were placed on a highly-polished beaufet among the family plate. The table was abundantly spread with substantial fare; but the squire made his supper of frumenty, a dish made of wheat cakes boiled in milk, with rich spices, being a standing dish in old times for Christmas eve.

I was happy to find my old friend, minced pie, in the retinue of the feast; and finding him to be perfectly orthodox, and that I need not be ashamed of my

---

The Yule clog is still burnt in many farmhouses and kitchens in England, particularly in the north, and there are several superstitions connected with it among the peasantry. If a squinting person come to the house while it is burning, or a person barefooted, it is considered an ill omen. The brand remaining from the Yule clog is carefully put away to light the next year's Christmas fire.

predilection, I greeted him with all the warmth wherewith we usually greet an old and very genteel acquaintance.

The mirth of the company was greatly promoted by the humors of an eccentric personage whom Mr. Bracebridge always addressed with the quaint appellation of Master Simon. He was a tight brisk little man, with the air of an arrant old bachelor. His nose was shaped like the bill of a parrot; his face slightly pitted with the smallpox, with a dry perpetual bloom on it, like a frostbitten leaf in autumn. He had an eye of great quickness and vivacity, with a drollery and lurking waggery of expression that was irresistible. He was evidently the wit of the family, dealing very much in sly jokes and inuendoes with the ladies, and making infinite merriment by harping upon old themes; which, unfortunately, my ignorance of the family chronicles did not permit me to enjoy. It seemed to be his great delight during supper to keep a young girl next him in a continual agony of stifled laughter, in spite of her awe of the reproving looks of her mother, who sat opposite. Indeed, he was the idol of the younger part of company, who laughed at everything he said or did, and at every turn of his countenance, I could not wonder at it; for he must have been a miracle of accomplishments in their eyes. He could imitate Punch and Judy; make an old woman of his hand, with the assistance of a burnt cork and pocket-handkerchief; and cut an orange into such a ludicrous caricature, that the young folks were ready to die with laughing.

I was let briefly into his history by Frank Bracebridge. He was an old bachelor, of a small independent income, which, by careful management, was sufficient for all his wants. He revolved through the family system like a vagrant comet in its orbit; sometimes visiting one branch, and sometimes another quite remote; as is often the case with gentlemen of extensive connections and small fortunes in England. He had a chirping buoyant disposition, always enjoying the present moment; and his frequent change of scene and company prevented his acquiring those rusty unaccommodating habits, with which old bachelors are so uncharitably charged. He was a complete family chronicle, being versed in the genealogy, history, and intermarriages of the whole house of Bracebridge, which made him a great favorite with the old folks; he was a beau of all the elder ladies and superannuated spinsters, among whom he was habitually considered rather a young fellow, and he was a master of the revels among the children; so that there was not a more popular being in the sphere in which he moved than Mr. Simon Bracebridge. Of late years, he had resided almost entirely with the squire, to whom he had become a factotum, and whom he particularly delighted by jumping with his humor in respect to old times, and by having a scrap of an old song to suit every occasion. We had presently a specimen of his last-mentioned talent, for no sooner was supper removed, and spiced wines and other beverages peculiar to the season introduced, than Master Simon was called on for a good old Christmas song. He bethought himself for a moment, and then, with a sparkle of the eye, and a voice that was by no means bad, excepting that it ran occasionally into a falsetto, like the notes of a split reed, he quavered forth a quaint old ditty.

> Now Christmas is come,
> Let us beat up the drum,
> And call all our neighbors together,
> And when they appear,
> Let us make them such cheer,
> As will keep out the wind and the weather, etc.

The supper had disposed every one to gaiety, and an old harper was summoned from the servants' hall, where he had been strumming all the evening, and to all appearance comforting himself with some of the squire's home-brewed. He was a kind of hanger-on, I was told, of the establishment, and, though ostensibly a resident of the village, was oftener to be found in the squire's kitchen than his own house, the old gentleman being fond of the sound of "harp in hall."

The dance, like most dances after supper, was a merry one; some of the older folks joined in it, and the squire himself figured down several couple with a partner, with whom he affirmed he had danced at every Christmas for nearly half a century. Master Simon, who seemed to be a kind of connecting link between the old times and the new, and to be withal a little antiquated in the taste of his accomplishments, evidently piqued himself on his dancing, and was endeavoring to gain credit by the heel and toe, rigadoon, and other graces of the ancient school; but he had unluckily assorted himself with a little romping girl from boarding-school, who, by her wild vivacity, kept him continually on the stretch, and defeated all his sober attempts at elegance:—such are the ill-assorted matches to which antique gentlemen are unfortunately prone!

The young Oxonian, on the contrary, had led out one of his maiden aunts, on whom the rogue played a thousand little knaveries with impunity: he was full of practical jokes, and his delight was to tease his aunts and cousins; yet, like all madcap youngsters, he was a universal favorite among the women. The most interesting couple in the dance was the young officer and a ward of the squire's, a beautiful blushing girl of seventeen. From several shy glances which I had noticed in the course of the evening, I suspected there was a little kindness growing up between them; and, indeed, the young soldier was just the hero to captivate a romantic girl. He was tall, slender, and handsome, and, like most young British officers of late years, had picked up various small accomplishments on the continent—he could talk French and Italian—draw landscapes, sing very tolerably—dance divinely; but, above all, he had been wounded at Waterloo—what girl of seventeen, well read in poetry and romance, could resist such a mirror of chivalry and perfection!

The moment the dance was over, he caught up a guitar, and, lolling against the old marble fireplace, in an attitude which I am half inclined to suspect was studied, began the little French air of the Troubadour. The squire, however, exclaimed against having any thing on Christmas eve but good old English; upon which the young minstrel, casting up his eye for a moment, as if in an effort of memory, struck into another strain, and, with a charming air of gallantry, gave Herrick's "Night-Piece to Julia."

> Her eyes the glow-worm lend thee,
> The shooting stars attend thee,
>   And the elves also,
>   Whose little eyes glow
> Like the sparks of fire, befriend thee.
>
> No Will o' the Wisp mislight thee;
> Nor snake nor slow-worm bite thee;
>   But on, on thy way,
>   Not making a stay,
> Since ghost there is none to affright thee.
>
> Then let not the dark thee cumber;
> What though the moon does slumber,
>   The stars of the night
>   Will lend thee their light,
> Like tapers clear without number.

Then, Julia, let me woo thee,
Thus, thus to come unto me,
And when I shall meet
Thy silvery feet,
My soul I'll pour into thee.

The song might or might not have been intended in
compliment to the fair Julia, for so I found his partner
was called; she, however, was certainly unconscious of
any such application, for she never looked at the singer,
but kept her eyes cast upon the floor. Her face was
suffused, it is true, with a beautiful blush, and there was
a gentle heaving of the bosom, but all that was doubtless
caused by the exercise of the dance; indeed, so great was
her indifference, that she amused herself with plucking
to pieces a choice bouquet of hot-house flowers, and by
the time the song was concluded the nosegay lay in ruins
on the floor.

The party now broke up for the night with the kind-
hearted old custom of shaking hands. As I passed
through the hall, on my way to my chamber, the dying
embers of the Yule clog still sent forth a dusky glow, and
had it not been the season when "no spirit dares stir
abroad," I should have been half tempted to steal from
my room at midnight, and peep whether the fairies
might not be at their revels about the hearth.

My chamber was in the old part of the mansion, the
ponderous furniture of which might have been fabricated in the days of the giants. The room was panelled
with cornices of heavy carved work, in which flowers
and grotesque faces were strangely intermingled; and a
row of black-looking portraits stared mournfully at me
from the walls. The bed was of rich, though faded
damask, with a lofty tester, and stood in a niche opposite
a bow window. I had scarcely got into bed when a strain
of music seemed to break forth in the air just below the

window. I listened, and found it proceeded from a band, which I concluded to be the waits from some neighboring village. They went round the house, playing under the windows. I drew aside the curtains to hear them more distinctly. The moonbeams fell through the upper part of the casement, partially lighting up the antiquated apartment. The sounds, as they receded, became more soft and aerial, and seemed to accord with the quiet and moonlight. I listened and listened—they became more and more tender and remote, and, as they gradually died away, my head sunk upon the pillow, and I fell asleep.

CHRISTMAS DAY

> Dark and dull night, flie hence away,
> And give the honor to this day
> That sees December turn'd to May.
>
> *   *   *   *   *   *   *
>
> Why does the chilling winter's morne
> Smile like a field beset with corn?
> Or smell like to a meade new-shorne,
> Thus on the sudden?—Come and see
> The cause why things thus fragrant be.
>
> HERRICK

WHEN I woke the next morning, it seemed as if all the events of the preceding evening had been a dream, and nothing but the identity of the ancient chamber convinced me of their reality. While I lay musing on my pillow, I heard the sound of little feet pattering outside of the door, and a whispering consultation. Presently a choir of small voices chanted forth an old Christmas carol, the burden of which was—

Rejoice, our Saviour he was born
On Christmas day in the morning.

I rose softly, slipt on my clothes, opened the door suddenly, and beheld one of the most beautiful little fairy groups that a painter could imagine. It consisted of a boy and two girls, the eldest not more than six, and lovely as seraphs. They were going the rounds of the house, and singing at every chamber door; but my sudden appearance frightened them into mute bashfulness. They remained for a moment playing on their lips with their fingers, and now and then stealing a shy glance from under their eyebrows, until, as if by one impulse, they scampered away, and as they turned an angle of the gallery, I heard them laughing in triumph at their escape.

Every thing conspired to produce kind and happy feelings in this strong-hold of old-fashioned hospitality. The window of my chamber looked out upon what in summer would have been a beautiful landscape. There was a sloping lawn, a fine stream winding at the foot of it, and a track of park beyond, with noble clumps of trees, and herds of deer. At a distance was a neat hamlet, with the smoke from the cottage chimneys hanging over it; and a church with its dark spire in strong relief against the clear, cold sky. The house was surrounded with evergreens, according to the English custom, which would have given almost an appearance of summer; but the morning was extremely frosty; the light vapor of the preceding evening had been precipitated by the cold, and covered all the trees and every blade of grass with its fine crystallizations. The rays of a bright morning sun had a dazzling effect among the glittering foliage. A robin, perched upon the top of a mountain ash that hung its clusters of red berries just before my window, was basking himself in the sunshine, and piping a few querulous notes; and a peacock was displaying all the glories of his train, and strutting with the pride and gravity of a Spanish grandee, on the terrace walk below.

I had scarcely dressed myself, when a servant appeared to invite me to family prayers. He showed me the way to a small chapel in the old wing of the house, where I found the principal part of the family already assembled in a kind of gallery, furnished with cushions, hassocks, and large prayer-books; the servants were seated on benches below. The old gentleman read prayers from a desk in front of the gallery, and Master Simon acted as clerk, and made the responses; and I must do him the justice to say that he acquitted himself with great gravity and decorum.

The service was followed by a Christmas carol, which Mr. Bracebridge himself had constructed from a poem of his favorite author, Herrick; and it had been adapted to an old church melody by Master Simon. As there were several good voices among the household, the effect was extremely pleasing; but I was particularly gratified by the exaltation of heart, and sudden sally of grateful feeling, with which the worthy squire delivered one stanza; his eye glistening, and his voice rambling out of all the bounds of time and tune:

> " 'Tis thou that crown'st my glittering hearth
>   With guiltlesse mirth.
>   And givest me Wassaile bowles to drink
>   Spiced to the brink:
>   Lord, 'tis thy plenty-dropping hand
>   That soiles my land:
>   And giv'st me for my bushell sowne,
>   Twice ten for one."

I afterwards understood that early morning service was read on every Sunday and saints' day throughout the year, either by Mr. Bracebridge or by some member of the family. It was once almost universally the case at the seats of the nobility and gentry of England, and it is much to be regretted that the custom is falling into neglect; for the dullest observer must be sensible of the order and serenity prevalent in those households, where the occasional exercise of a beautiful form of worship in the morning gives, as it were, the key-note to every temper for the day, and attunes every spirit to harmony.

Our breakfast consisted of what the squire denominated true old English fare. He indulged in some bitter lamentations over modern breakfasts of tea and toast, which he censured as among the causes of modern effeminacy and weak nerves, and the decline of old English heartiness; and though he admitted them to his table to suit the palates of his guests, yet there was a brave display of cold meats, wine, and ale, on the sideboard.

After breakfast I walked about the grounds with Frank Bracebridge and Master Simon, or, Mr. Simon, as he was called by every body but the squire. We were escorted by a number of gentlemanlike dogs, that seemed loungers about the establishment; from the frisking spaniel to the steady old stag-hound; the last of which was of a race that had been in the family time out of mind: they were all obedient to a dog-whistle which hung to Master Simon's button-hole, and in the midst of their gambols would glance an eye occasionally upon a small switch he carried in his hand.

The old mansion had a still more venerable look in the yellow sunshine than by pale moonlight; and I could not but feel the force of the squire's idea, that the formal terraces, heavily moulded balustrades, and clipped yew-trees, carried with them an air of proud aristocracy. There appeared to be an unusual number of peacocks about the place, and I was making some remarks upon what I termed a flock of them, that were basking under a sunny wall, when I was gently corrected in my phraseology by Master Simon, who told me that, according to the most ancient and approved treatise on hunting, I must say a *muster* of peacocks. "In the same way," added he, with a slight air of pedantry, "we say a flight of doves or swallows, a bevy of quails, a herd of deer, of wrens, or cranes, a skulk of foxes, or a building of rooks." He went on to inform me that, according to Sir Anthony Fitzherbert, we ought to ascribe to this bird "both understanding and glory; for, being praised, he will presently set up his tail, chiefly against the sun, to the intent you may the better behold the beauty thereof. But at the fall of the leaf, when his tail falleth, he will mourn and hide himself in corners, till his tail come again as it was."

I could not help smiling at this display of small erudition on so whimsical a subject; but I found that the peacocks were birds of some consequence at the hall; for Frank Bracebridge informed me that they were great favorites with his father, who was extremely careful to keep up the breed; partly because they belonged to chivalry, and were in great request at the stately banquets of the olden time; and partly because they had a pomp and magnificence about them, highly becoming an old family mansion. Nothing he was accustomed to say, had an air of greater state and dignity than a peacock perched upon an antique stone balustrade.

Master Simon had now to hurry off, having an appointment at the parish church with the village choristers, who were to perform some music of his selection. There was something extremely agreeable in the cheerful flow of animal spirits of the little man; and I confess I had been somewhat surprised at his apt quotations from authors who certainly were not in the range of every-day reading. I mentioned this last circumstance to Frank Bracebridge, who told me with a smile that Master Simon's whole stock of erudition was confined to some half a dozen old authors, which the squire had put into his hands, and which he read over and over, whenever he had a studious fit; as he sometimes had on a rainy day, or a long winter evening. Sir Anthony Fitzherbert's *Book of Husbandry*; Markham's *Country Contentments*; *The Tretyse of Hunting*, by Sir Thomas Cockayne, Knight; Izaac Walton's *Angler*, and two or three more such ancient worthies of the pen, were his standard authorities; and, like all men who know but a few books, he looked up to them with a kind of idolatry, and quoted them on all occasions. As to his songs, they were chiefly picked out of old books in the squire's library, and adapted to tunes that were popular among the choice spirits of the last century. His practical application of scraps of literature, however, had caused him to be looked upon as a prodigy of book knowledge by all the grooms, huntsmen, and small sportsmen of the neighborhood.

While we were talking we heard the distant tolling of the village bell, and I was told that the squire was a little particular in having his household at church on Christmas morning; considering it a day of pouring out of thanks and rejoicing; for, as old Tusser observed,

> "At Christmas be merry, *and thankful withal,*
>   And feast thy poor neighbors, the great with the small."

"If you are disposed to go to church," said Frank Bracebridge, "I can promise you a specimen of my cousin Simon's musical achievements. As the church is destitute of an organ, he has formed a band from the village amateurs, and established a musical club for their improvement; he has also sorted a choir, as he sorted my father's pack of hounds, according to the directions of Jervaise Markham, in his *Country Contentments*; for the bass he has sought out all the 'deep, solemn mouths,' and for the tenor the 'loud-ringing mouths,' among the country bumpkins; and for 'sweet mouths,' he has culled with curious taste among the prettiest lasses in the neighborhood; though these last, he affirms, are the most difficult to keep in tune; your pretty female singer being exceedingly wayward and capricious, and very liable to accident."

As the morning, though frosty, was remarkably fine and clear, the most of the family walked to the church, which was a very old building of gray stone, and stood near a village, about half a mile from the park gate. Adjoining it was a low snug parsonage, which seemed coeval with the church. The front of it was perfectly matted with a yew-tree, that had been trained against its walls, through the dense foliage of which, apertures had been formed to admit light into the small antique lattices. As we passed this sheltered nest, the parson issued forth and preceded us.

I had expected to see a sleek well-conditioned pastor, such as is often found in a snug living in the vicinity of a rich patron's table, but I was disappointed. The parson was a little, meagre, black-looking man, with a grizzled wig that was too wide, and stood off from each ear; so that his head seemed to have shrunk away within it, like a dried filbert in its shell. He wore a rusty coat, with great skirts, and pockets that would have held the church Bible and prayer book: and his small legs seemed still smaller, from being planted in large shoes, decorated with enormous buckles.

I was informed by Frank Bracebridge, that the parson had been a chum of his father's at Oxford, and had received this living shortly after the latter had come to his estate. He was a complete black-letter hunter, and would scarcely read a work printed in the Roman character. The editions of Caxton and Wynkin de Worde were his delight; and he was indefatigable in his researches after such old English writers as have fallen into oblivion from their worthlessness. In deference, perhaps, to the notions of Mr. Bracebridge, he had made diligent investigations into the festive rites and holiday customs of former times; and had been as zealous in the inquiry as if he had been a boon companion; but it was merely with that plodding spirit with which men of adust temperament follow up any track of study, merely because it is denominated learning; indifferent to its intrinsic nature, whether it be the illustration of the wisdom, or of the ribaldry and obscenity of antiquity. He had pored over these old volumes so intensely, that they seemed to have been reflected in his countenance; which, if the face be indeed an index of the mind, might be compared to a title-page of black-letter.

On reaching the church porch, we found the parson rebuking the gray-headed sexton for having used mistletoe among the greens with which the church was decorated. It was, he observed, an unholy plant, profoaned by having been used by the Druids in their mystic ceremonies; and though it might be innocently employed in the festive ornamenting of halls and kitchens, yet it had been deemed by the Fathers of the Church as unhallowed, and totally unfit for sacred purposes. So tenacious was he on this point, that the poor sexton was obliged to strip down a great part of the humble trophies of his taste, before the parson would consent to enter upon the service of the day.

The interior of the church was venerable but simple;

on the walls were several mural monuments of the Bracebridges, and just beside the altar was a tomb of ancient workmanship, on which lay the effigy of a warrior in armor, with his legs crossed, a sign of his having been a crusader. I was told it was one of the family who had signalized himself in the Holy Land, and the same whose picture hung over the fireplace in the hall.

During service, Master Simon stood up in the pew, and repeated the responses very audibly; evincing that kind of ceremonious devotion punctually observed by a gentleman of the old school, and a man of old family connections. I observed too that he turned over the leaves of a folio prayer-book with something of a flourish; possibly to show off an enormous seal-ring which enriched one of his fingers, and which had the look of a family relic. But he was evidently most solicitous about the musical part of the service, keeping his eye fixed intently on the choir, and beating time with much gesticulation and emphasis.

The orchestra was in a small gallery, and presented a most whimsical grouping of heads, piled one above the other, among which I particularly noticed that of the village tailor, a pale fellow with a retreating forehead and chin, who played on the clarinet, and seemed to have blown his face to a point; and there was another, a short pursy man, stooping and laboring at a bass-viol, so as to show nothing but the top of a round bald head, like the egg of an ostrich. There were two or three pretty faces among the female singers, to which the keen air of a frosty morning had given a bright rosy tint; but the gentlemen choristers had evidently been chosen, like old Cremona fiddles, more for tone than looks; and as several had to sing from the same book, there were clusterings of odd physiognomies, not unlike those groups of cherubs we sometimes see on country tomb-stones.

The usual services of the choir were managed tolerably well, the vocal parts generally lagging a little behind the instrumental, and some loitering fiddler now and then making up for lost time by travelling over a passage with prodigious celerity, and clearing more bars than the keenest fox-hunter to be in at the death. But the great trial was an anthem that had been prepared and arranged by Master Simon, and on which he had founded great expectation. Unluckily there was a blunder at the very outset; the musicians became flurried; Master Simon was in a fever; everything went on lamely and irregularly until they came to a chorus beginning "Now let us sing with one accord," which seemed to be a signal for parting company: all became discord and confusion; each shifted for himself, and got to the end as well, or, rather, as soon as he could, excepting one old chorister in a pair of horn spectacles, bestriding and pinching a long sonorous nose; who happened to stand a little apart, and, being wrapped up in his own melody, kept on a quavering course, wriggling his head, ogling his book, and winding all up by a nasal solo of at least three bars' duration.

The parson gave us a most erudite sermon on the rites and ceremonies of Christmas, and the propriety of observing it not merely as a day of thanksgiving, but of rejoicing; supporting the correctness of his opinions by the earliest usages of the church, and enforcing them by the authorities of Theophilus of Cesarea, St. Cyprian, St. Chrysostom, St. Augustine, and a cloud more of saints and fathers, from whom he made copious quotations. I was a little at a loss to perceive the necessity of such a mighty array of forces to maintain a point which no one present seemed inclined to dispute; but I soon found that the good man had a legion of ideal adversaries to contend with; having, in the course of his researches on the subject of Christmas, got completely embroiled in the sectarian controversies of the Revolution, when the Puritans made such a fierce assault upon the ceremonies of the church, and poor old Christmas was driven out of the land by proclamation of Parliament.* The worthy parson lived but with times past, and knew but little of the present.

Shut up among worm-eaten tomes in the retirement of his antiquated little study, the pages of old times were to him as the gazettes of the day; while the era of the Revolution was mere modern history. He forgot that nearly two centuries had elapsed since the fiery persecution of poor mince-pie throughout the land; when plum porridge was denounced as "mere popery," and roast-beef as anti-christian; and that Christmas had been brought in again triumphantly with the merry court of King Charles at the Restoration. He kindled into warmth with the ardor of his contest, and the host of imaginary foes with whom he had to combat; he had a stubborn conflict with old Prynne and two or three other forgotten champions of the Round Heads, on the subject of Christmas festivity; and concluded by urging his hearers, in the most solemn and affecting manner, to

---

*From the "Flying Eagle," a small Gazette, published December 24th, 1652—"House spent much time this day about the business of the Navy, for settling the affairs at sea, and before they rose, were presented with a terrible remonstrance against Christmas day, grounded upon divine Scriptures, 2 Cor. v. 16; 1 Cor. xv. 14, 17; and in honor of the Lord's Day, grounded upon these Scriptures, John xx. 1; Rev. i. 10; Psalm cxviii. 24; Lev. xxiii. 7, 11; Mark xv. 8; Psalm lxxxiv. 10, in which Christmas is called Anti-christ's masse, and those Massemongers and Papists who observe it, etc. In consequence of which Parliament spent some time in consultation about the abolition of Christmas day, passed orders to that effect, and resolved to sit on the following day, which was commonly called Christmas day."

stand to the traditional customs of their fathers, and feast and make merry on this joyful anniversary of the Church.

I have seldom known a sermon attended apparently with more immediate effects; for on leaving the church the congregation seemed one and all possessed with the gaiety of spirit so earnestly enjoined by their pastor. The elder folks gathered in knots in the church-yard, greeting and shaking hands; and the children ran about crying Ule! Ule! and repeating some uncouth rhymes,* which the parson, who had joined us, informed me had been handed down from days of yore. The villagers doffed their hats to the squire as he passed, giving him the good wishes of the season with every appearance of heartfelt sincerity, and were invited by him to the hall, to take something to keep out the cold of the weather; and I heard blessings uttered by several of the poor, which convinced me that, in the midst of his enjoyments, the worthy old cavalier had not forgotten the true Christmas virtue of charity.

On our way homeward his heart seemed overflowed with generous and happy feelings. As we passed over a rising ground which commanded something of a prospect, the sounds of rustic merriment now and then reached our ears: the squire paused for a few moments, and looked around with an air of inexpressible benignity. The beauty of the day was of itself sufficient to inspire philanthropy. Notwithstanding the frostiness of the morning, the sun in his cloudless journey had acquired sufficient power to melt away the thin covering of snow from every southern declivity, and to bring out the living green which adorns an English landscape even in mid-

*"Ule! Ule!
  Three puddings in a pule;
  Crack nuts and cry ule!"

winter. Large tracts of smiling verdure contrasted with the dazzling whiteness of the shaded slopes and hollows. Every sheltered bank, on which the broad rays rested, yielded its silver rill of cold and limpid water, glittering through the dripping grass; and sent up slight exhalations to contribute to the thin haze that hung just above the surface of the earth. There was something truly cheering in this triumph of warmth and verdure over the frosty thraldom of winter; it was, as the squire observed, an emblem of Christmas hospitality, breaking through the chills of ceremony and selfishness, and thawing every heart into a flow. He pointed with pleasure to the indications of good cheer reeking from the chimneys of the comfortable farmhouses, and low thatched cottages. "I love," said he, "to see this day well kept by rich and poor; it is a great thing to have one day in the year, at least, when you are sure of being welcome wherever you go, and of having, as it were, the world all thrown open to you; and I am almost disposed to join with Poor Robin, in his malediction on every churlish enemy to this honest festival

> "Those who at Christmas do repine
> And would fain hence dispatch him,
> May they with old Duke Humphry dine,
> Or else may Squire Ketch catch 'em."

The squire went on to lament the deplorable decay of the games and amusements which were once prevalent at this season among the lower orders, and countenanced by the higher; when the old halls of the castles and manor-houses were thrown open at daylight; when the tables were covered with brawn, and beef, and humming ale; when the harp and the carol resounded all day long, and when rich and poor were alike welcome to enter and make merry.* "Our old games and local customs," said he, "had a great effect in making the peasant fond of his home, and the promotion of them by the gentry made him fond of his lord. They made the times merrier, and kinder, and better, and I can truly say, with one of our old poets:

> 'I like them well—the curious preciseness
> And all-pretended gravity of those
> That seek to banish hence these harmless sports,
> Have thrust away much ancient honesty.'

"The nation," continued he, "is altered; we have almost lost our simple true-hearted peasantry. They have broken asunder from the higher classes, and seem to think their interests are separate. They have become too knowing, and begin to read newspapers, listen to ale-house politicians, and talk of reform. I think one mode to keep them in good humor in these hard times would be for the nobility and gentry to pass more time on their estates, mingle more among the country people, and set the merry old English games going again."

Such was the good squire's project for mitigating public discontent: and, indeed, he had once attempted to put his doctrine in practice, and a few years before had kept open house during the holidays in the old style. The country people, however, did not understand how to play their parts in the scene of hospitality; many uncouth circumstances occurred; the manor was over-

---

*"An English gentleman, at the opening of the great day, i. e. on Christmas day in the morning, had all his tenants and neighbors enter his hall by daybreak. The strong beer was broached, and the blackjacks went plentifully about with toast, sugar and nutmeg, and good Cheshire cheese. The Hackin (the great sausage) must be boiled by daybreak, or else two young men must take the maiden (i. e. the cook) by the arms, and run her round the market-place till she is shamed of her laziness."—*Round about our Sea-Coal Fire*

run by all the vagrants of the country, and more beggars drawn into the neighborhood in one week than the parish officers could get rid of in a year. Since then, he had contented himself with inviting the decent part of the neighboring peasantry to call at the hall on Christmas day, and with distributing beef, and bread, and ale, among the poor, that they might make merry in their own dwellings.

We had not been long home when the sound of music was heard from a distance. A band of country lads, without coats, their shirt sleeves fancifully tied with ribbons, their hats decorated with greens, and clubs in their hands, was seen advancing up the avenue, followed by a large number of villagers and peasantry. They stopped before the hall door, where the music struck up a peculiar air, and the lads performed a curious and intricate dance, advancing, retreating, and striking their clubs together, keeping exact time to the music; while one, whimsically crowned with a fox's skin, the tail of which flaunted down his back, kept capering round the skirts of the dance, and rattling a Christmas box with many antic gesticulations.

The squire eyed this fanciful exhibition with great interest and delight, and gave me a full account of its origin, which he traced to the times when the Romans held possession of the island; plainly proving that this was a lineal descendant of the sword dance of the ancients. "It was now," he said, "nearly extinct, but he had accidentally met with traces of it in the neighborhood, and had encouraged its revival; though, to tell the truth, it was too apt to be followed up by the rough cudgel play, and broken heads in the evening."

After the dance was concluded, the whole party was entertained with brawn and beef, and stout home-brewed. The squire himself mingled among the rustics, and was received with awkward demonstrations of deference and regard. It is true I perceived two or three of the younger peasants, as they were raising their tankards to their mouths, when the squire's back was turned, making something of a grimace, and giving each other the wink; but the moment they caught my eye they pulled grave faces, and were exceedingly demure. With Master Simon, however, they all seemed more at their ease. His varied occupations and amusements had made him well known throughout the neighborhood. He was a visitor at every farmhouse and cottage; gossiped with the farmers and their wives; romped with their daughters; and, like that type of a vagrant bachelor, the bumblebee, tolled the sweets from all the rosy lips of the country round.

The bashfulness of the guests soon gave way before good cheer and affability. There is something genuine and affectionate in the gaiety of the lower orders, when it is excited by the bounty and familiarity of those above them; the warm glow of gratitude enters into their mirth, and a kind word or a small pleasantry frankly uttered by a patron, gladdens the heart of the dependent more than oil and wine. When the squire had retired, the merriment increased, and there was much joking and laughter, particularly between Master Simon and a hale, ruddy-faced, white-headed farmer, who appeared to be the wit of the village; for I observed all his companions to wait with open mouths for his retorts, and burst into a gratuitous laugh before they could well understand them.

The whole house indeed seemed abandoned to merriment: as I passed to my room to dress for dinner, I heard the sound of music in a small court, and looking through a window that commanded it, I perceived a band of wandering musicians, with pandean pipes and tambourine; a pretty coquettish housemaid was dancing a jig with a smart country lad, while several of the other servants were looking on. In the midst of her sport the girl caught a glimpse of my face at the window, and, coloring up, ran off with an air of roguish affected confusion.

———————

THE CHRISTMAS DINNER

Lo, now is come our joyful'st feast!
  Let every man be jolly,
Eache roome with yvie leaves is drest,
  And every post with holly.
Now all our neighbours' chimneys smoke,
  And Christmas blocks are burning;
Their ovens they with bak't meats choke
  And all their spits are turning.
    Without the door let sorrow lie,
    And if, for cold, it hap to die,
    Wee'le bury 't in a Christmas pye,
    And evermore be merry.
                    WITHERS' JUVENILIA

I HAD finished my toilet, and was loitering with Frank Bracebridge in the library, when we heard a distant thwacking sound, which he informed me was a signal for the serving up of the dinner. The squire kept up old customs in kitchen as well as hall; and the rolling-pin, struck upon the dresser by the cook, summoned the servants to carry in the meats.

Just in this nick the cook knock'd thrice,
And all the waiters in a trice
  His summons did obey;
Each serving man, with dish in hand,
March'd boldly up, like our train band,
  Presented, and away.*

The dinner was served up in the great hall, where the squire always held his Christmas banquet. A blazing

*Sir John Suckling.

crackling fire of logs had been heaped on to warm the spacious apartment, and the flame went sparkling and wreathing up the wide-mouthed chimney. The great picture of the crusader and his white horse had been profusely decorated with greens for the occasion; and holly and ivy had likewise been wreathed round the helmet and weapons on the opposite wall, which I understood were the arms of the same warrior. I must own, by the by, I had strong doubts about the authenticity of the painting and armor as having belonged to the crusader, they certainly having the stamp of more recent days; but I was told that the painting had been so considered time out of mind; and that, as to the armor, it had been found in a lumber-room, and elevated to its present situation by the squire, who at once determined it to be the armor of the family hero; and as he was absolute authority on all such subjects in his own household, the matter had passed into current acceptation. A sideboard was set out just under this chivalric trophy, on which was a display of plate that might have vied (at least in variety) with Belshazzar's parade of the vessels of the temple: "flagons, cans, cups, beakers, goblets, basins, and ewers;" the gorgeous utensils of good companionship that had gradually accumulated through many generations of jovial housekeepers. Before these stood the two Yule candles, beaming like two stars of the first magnitude; other lights were distributed in branches, and the whole array glittered like a firmament of silver.

We were ushered into this banqueting scene with the sound of minstrelsy, the old harper being seated on a stool beside the fireplace, and twanging his instrument with a vast deal more power than melody. Never did Christmas board display a more goodly and gracious assemblage of countenances; those who were not handsome were, at least, happy; and happiness is a rare improver of your hard-favored visage. I always consider an old English family as well worth studying as a collection of Holbein's portraits or Albert Durer's prints. There is much antiquarian lore to be acquired; much knowledge of the physiognomies of former times. Perhaps it may be from having continually before their eyes those rows of old family portraits, with which the mansions of this country are stocked; certain it is, that the quaint features of antiquity are often most faithfully perpetuated in these ancient lines; and I have traced an old family nose through a whole picture gallery, legitimately handed down from generation to generation, almost from the time of the Conquest. Something of the kind was to be observed in the worthy company around me. Many of their faces had evidently originated in a Gothic age, and been merely copied by succeeding generations; and there was one little girl in particular, of staid demeanor, with a high Roman nose, and an antique vinegar aspect, who was a great favorite of the squire's, being, as he said, a Bracebridge all over, and the very counterpart of one of his ancestors who figured in the court of Henry VIII.

The parson said grace, which was not a short familiar one, such as is commonly addressed to the Deity in these unceremonious days; but a long, courtly, well-worded one of the ancient school. There was now a pause, as if something was expected; when suddenly the butler entered the hall with some degree of bustle: he was attended by a servant on each side with a large wax-light, and bore a silver dish, on which was an enormous pig's head, decorated with rosemary, with a lemon in its mouth, which was placed with great formality at the head of the table. The moment this pageant made its appearance, the harper struck up a flourish; at the conclusion of which the young Oxonian, on receiving a hint from the squire, gave, with an air of the most comic gravity, an old carol, the first verse of which was as follows:

> Caput apri defero
> Reddens laudes Domino.
> The boar's head in hand bring I,
> With garlands gay and rosemary.
> I pray you all synge merrily
> Qui estis in convivio.

Though prepared to witness many of these little eccentricities, from being apprised of the peculiar hobby of mine host; yet, I confess, the parade with which so odd a dish was introduced somewhat perplexed me, until I gathered from the conversation of the squire and the parson, that it was meant to represent the bringing in of the boar's head; a dish formerely served up with much ceremony and the sound of minstrelsy and song, at great tables, on Christmas day. "I like the old custom," said the squire, "not merely because it is stately and pleasing in itself, but because it was observed at the college at Oxford at which I was educated. When I hear the old song chanted, it brings to mind the time when I was young and gamesome—and the noble old college hall—and my fellow-students loitering about in their black gowns; many of whom, poor lads, are now in their graves!"

The parson, however, whose mind was not haunted by such associations, and who was always more taken up with the text than the sentiment, objected to the Oxonian's version of the carol; which he affirmed was different from that sung at college. He went on, with the dry perseverance of a commentator, to give the college reading, accompanied by sundry annotations; addressing himself at first to the company at large; but finding their attention gradually diverted to other talk and other objects, he lowered his tone as his number of

auditors diminished, until he concluded his remarks in
an under voice, to a fat-headed old gentleman next him,
who was silently engaged in the discussion of a huge
plateful of turkey.*

The table was literally loaded with good cheer, and
presented an epitome of country abundance, in this
season of overflowing larders. A distinguished post was
allotted to "ancient sirloin," as mine host termed it;
being, as he added, "the standard of old English
hospitality, and a joint of goodly presence, and full of
expectation." There were several dishes quaintly deco-

---

*The old ceremony of serving up the boar's head on Christmas day
is still observed in the hall of Queen's College, Oxford. I was favored
by the parson with a copy of the carol as now sung, and as it may be
acceptable to such of my readers as are curious in these grave and
learned matters, I give it entire.

> The boar's head in hand bear I,
> Bedeck'd with bays and rosemary;
> And I pray you, my masters, be merry
>   Quot estis in convivio.
>   Caput apri defero,
>   Reddens laudes domino.
> [Because you are at a banquet.
> I bear the boar's head,
> Giving praise to the Lord.]
>
> The boar's head, as I understand,
> Is the rarest dish in all this land,
> Which thus bedeck'd with a gay garland
>   Let us servire cantico.
>   Caput apri defero, etc.
> [Let us serve with song.
> I bear the boar's head, etc.]
>
> Our steward hath provided this
> In honor of the King of Bliss,
> Which on this day to be served is
>   In Reginensi Atrio.
>   Caput apri defero,
>   etc., etc., etc.
> [In the hall of Queen's.
> I bear the boar's head, etc.]

rated, and which had evidently something traditional in their embellishments; but about which, as I did not like to appear over curious, I asked no questions.

I could not, however, but notice a pie, magnificently decorated with peacock's feathers, in imitation of the tail of that bird, which overshadowed a considerable tract of the table. This, the squire confessed, with some little hesitation, was a pheasant pie, though a peacock pie was certainly the most authentical; but there had been such a mortality among the peacocks this season, that he could not prevail upon himself to have one killed.*

It would be tedious, perhaps, to my wiser readers, who may not have that foolish fondness for odd and obsolete things to which I am a little given, were I to mention the other make-shifts of this worthy old humorist, by which he was endeavoring to follow up, though at humble distance, the quaint customs of antiquity. I was pleased, however, to see the respect shown to his whims by his children and relatives; who, indeed, entered readily into the full spirit of them, and seemed all well versed in their parts; having doubtless been present at many a rehearsal. I was amused, too, at the air of profound gravity with which the butler and

*The peacock was anciently in great demand for stately entertainments. Sometimes it was made into a pie, at one end of which the head appeared above the crust in all its plumage, with the beak richly gilt; at the other end the tail was displayed. Such pies were served up at the solemn banquets of chivalry, when knights-errant pledged themselves to undertake any perilous enterprise, whence came the ancient oath, used by Justice Shallow, "by cock and pie."

The peacock was also an important dish for the Christmas feast; and Massinger, in his *City Madam*, gives some idea of the extravagance with which this, as well as other dishes, was prepared for the gorgeous revels of the olden times:—

Men may talk of Country Christmasses,
Their thirty pound butter'd eggs, their pies of carps' tongues;
Their pheasants drench'd with ambergris; *the carcases of three fat wethers bruised for gravy to make sauce for a single peacock.*

other servants executed the duties assigned them, however eccentric. They had an old-fashioned look; having,
for the most part, been brought up in the household,
and grown into keeping with the antiquated mansion,
and the humors of its lord; and most probably looked
upon all his whimsical regulations as the established laws
of honorable housekeeping.

When the cloth was removed, the butler brought in a
huge silver vessel of rare and curious workmanship,
which he placed before the squire. Its appearance was
hailed with acclamation; being the Wassail Bowl, so
renowned in Christmas festivity. The contents had been
prepared by the squire himself; for it was a beverage in
the skilful mixture of which he particularly prided
himself: alleging that it was too abstruse and complex
for the comprehension of an ordinary servant. It was a
potation, indeed, that might well make the heart of a
toper leap within him; being composed of the richest
and raciest wines, highly spiced and sweetened, with
roasted apples bobbing about the surface.*

The old gentleman's whole countenance beamed with
a serene look of indwelling delight, as he stirred this
mighty bowl. Having raised it to his lips, with a hearty
wish of a merry Christmas to all present, he sent it
brimming round the board, for every one to follow his
example, according to the primitive style; pronouncing

*The Wassail Bowl was sometimes composed of ale instead of wine;
with nutmeg, sugar, toast, ginger, and roasted crabs; in this way the
nut-brown beverage is still prepared in some old families, and round
the hearths of substantial farmers at Christmas. It is also called Lamb's
Wool, and is celebrated by Herrick in his *Twelfth Night*:

> Next crowne the bowle full
> With gentle Lamb's Wool;
> Add sugar, nutmeg, and ginger
> With store of ale too;
> And thus ye must doe
> To make the Wassaile a swinger.

it "the ancient fountain of good feeling, where all hearts met together."*

There was much laughing and rallying as the honest emblem of Christmas joviality circulated, and was kissed rather coyly by the ladies. When it reached Master Simon, he raised it in both hands, and with the air of a boon companion struck up an old Wassail chanson.

> The brown bowle,
> The merry brown bowle,
> As it goes round about-a,
>   Fill
>   Still,
> Let the world say what it will,
> And drink your fill all out-a.
> The deep canne,
> The merry deep canne,
> As thou dost freely quaff-a,
>   Sing
>   Fling,
> Be as merry as a king,
> And sound a lusty laugh-a.†

Much of the conversation during dinner turned upon family topics, to which I was a stranger. There was, however, a great deal of rallying of Master Simon about some gay widow, with whom he was accused of having a flirtation. This attack was commenced by the ladies; but it was continued throughout the dinner by the fat-headed old gentleman next the parson, with the persevering assiduity of a slow hound; being one of those long-winded jokers, who, though rather dull at starting game, are unrivalled for their talents in hunting it down. At every pause in the general conversation, he renewed his

*"The custom of drinking out of the same cup gave place to each having his cup. When the steward came to the doore with the Wassel, he was to cry three times, *Wassel, Wassel, Wassel,* and then the chappell (chaplein) was to answer with a song."—Archæologia

†From Poor Robin's Almanac.

bantering in pretty much the same terms; winking hard at me with both eyes, whenever he gave Master Simon what he considered a home thrust. The latter, indeed, seemed fond of being teased on the subject, as old bachelors are apt to be; and he took occasion to inform me, in an under tone, that the lady in question was a prodigiously fine woman, and drove her own curricle.

The dinner-time passed away in this flow of innocent hilarity, and, though the old hall may have resounded in its time with many a scene of broader rout and revel, yet I doubt whether it ever witnessed more honest and genuine enjoyment. How easy it is for one benevolent being to diffuse pleasure around him; and how truly is a kind heart a fountain of gladness, making every thing in its vicinity to freshen into smiles! The joyous disposition of the worthy squire was perfectly contagious; he was happy himself, and disposed to make all the world happy; and the little eccentricities of his humor did but season, in a manner, the sweetness of his philanthropy.

When the ladies had retired, the conversation, as usual, became still more animated; many good things were broached which had been thought of during dinner, but which would not exactly do for a lady's ear; and though I cannot positively affirm that there was much wit uttered, yet I have certainly heard many contests of rare wit produce much less laughter. Wit, after all, is a mighty tart, pungent ingredient, and much too acid for some stomachs; but honest good humor is the oil and wine of a merry meeting, and there is no jovial companionship equal to that where the jokes are rather small, and the laughter abundant.

The squire told several long stories of early college pranks and adventures, in some of which the parson had been a sharer; though in looking at the latter, it required some effort of imagination to figure such a little dark anatomy of a man into the perpetrator of a madcap gambol. Indeed, the two college chums pre-sented pictures of what men may be made by their different lots in life. The squire had left the university to live lustily on his paternal domains, in the vigorous enjoyment of prosperity and sunshine, and had flour-ished on to a hearty and florid old age; whilst the poor parson, on the contrary, had dried and withered away, among dusty tomes, in the silence and shadows of his study. Still there seemed to be a spark of almost extinguished fire, feebly glimmering in the bottom of his soul; and as the squire hinted at a sly story of the parson and a pretty milkmaid, whom they once met on the banks of the Isis, the old gentleman made an "alphabet of faces," which, as far as I could decipher his physiognomy, I verily believe was indicative of laughter; indeed, I have rarely met with an old gentleman that took absolute offence at the imputed gallantries of his youth.

I found the tide of wine and wassail fast gaining on the dry land of sober judgment. The company grew merrier and louder as their jokes grew duller. Master Simon was in as chirping a humor as a grasshopper filled with dew; his old songs grew of a warmer complexion, and he began to talk maudlin about the widow. He even gave a long song about the wooing of a widow, which he informed me he had gathered from an excellent black-letter work, entitled "Cupid's Solicitor for Love," containing store of good advice for bachelors, and which he promised to lend me: the first verse was to this effect:

> He that will woo a widow must not dally,
>   He must make hay while the sun doth shine;
> He must not stand with her, shall I, shall I,
>   But boldly say Widow, thou must be mine.

This song inspired the fat-headed old gentleman, who made several attempts to tell a rather broad story out of

Joe Miller, that was pat to the purpose; but he always stuck in the middle, everybody recollecting the latter part excepting himself. The parson, too, began to show the effects of good cheer, having gradually settled down into a doze, and his wig sitting most suspiciously on one side. Just at this juncture we were summoned to the drawing-room, and, I suspect, at the private instigation of mine host, whose joviality seemed always tempered with a proper love for decorum.

After the dinner table was removed, the hall was given up to the younger members of the family, who, prompted to all kind of noisy mirth by the Oxonian and Master Simon, made its old walls ring with their merriment, as they played at romping games. I delight in witnessing the gambols of children, and particularly at this happy holiday season, and could not help stealing out of the drawing-room on hearing one of their peals of laughter. I found them at the game of blindman's-buff. Master Simon, who was the leader of their revels, and seemed on all occasions to fulfil the office of that ancient potentate, the Lord of Misrule,* was blinded in the midst of the hall. The little beings were as busy about him as the mock fairies about Falstaff; pinching him, plucking at the skirts of his coat, and tickling him with straws. One fine blue-eyed girl of about thirteen, with her flaxen hair all in beautiful confusion, her frolic face in a glow, her frock half torn off her shoulders, a complete picture of a romp, was the chief tormentor; and, from the slyness with which Master Simon avoided the smaller game, and hemmed this wild little nymph in corners, and obliged her to jump shrieking over chairs, I

*At Christmasse there was in the Kinge's house, wheresoever hee was lodged, a lorde of misrule, or mayster of merre disportes, and the like had ye in the house of every nobleman of honor, or good worshippe, were he spirituall or temporall.—STOWE.

suspected the rogue of being not a whit more blinded than was convenient.

When I returned to the drawing-room, I found the company seated round the fire, listening to the parson, who was deeply ensconced in a high-backed oaken chair, the work of some cunning artificer of yore, which had been brought from the library for his particular accommodation. From this venerable piece of furniture, with which his shadowy figure and dark weazen face so admirably accorded, he was dealing out strange accounts of the popular superstitions and legends of the surrounding country, with which he had become acquainted in the course of his antiquarian researches. I am half inclined to think that the old gentleman was himself somewhat tinctured with superstition, as men are very apt to be who live a recluse and studious life in a sequestered part of the country, and pore over blackletter tracts, so often filled with the marvellous and supernatural. He gave us several anecdotes of the fancies of the neighboring peasantry, concerning the effigy of the crusader, which lay on the tomb by the church altar. As it was the only monument of the kind in that part of the country, it had always been regarded with feelings of superstition by the good wives of the village. It was said to get up from the tomb and walk the rounds of the church-yard in stormy nights, particularly when it thundered; and one old woman, whose cottage bordered on the church-yard, had seen it through the windows of the church, when the moon shone, slowly pacing up and down the aisles. It was the belief that some wrong had been left unredressed by the deceased, or some treasure hidden, which kept the spirit in a state of trouble and restlessness. Some talked of gold and jewels buried in the tomb, over which the spectre kept watch; and there was a story current of a sexton in old times, who endeavored to break his way to the coffin at night, but, just as he reached it, received a violent blow from the marble hand of the effigy, which stretched him senseless on the pavement. These tales were often laughed at by some of the sturdier among the rustics, yet, when night came on, there were many of the stoutest unbelievers that were shy of venturing alone in the footpath that led across the church-yard.

From these and other anecdotes that followed, the crusader appeared to be the favorite hero of ghost stories throughout the vicinity. His picture, which hung up in the hall, was thought by the servants to have something supernatural about it; for they remarked that, in whatever part of the hall you went, the eyes of the warrior were still fixed on you. The old porter's wife, too, at the lodge, who had been born and brought up in the family, and was a great gossip among the maid servants, affirmed, that in her young days she had often heard say, that on Midsummer eve, when it was well known all kinds of ghosts, goblins, and fairies become visible and walk abroad, the crusader used to mount his horse, come down from his picture, ride about the house, down the avenue, and so to the church to visit the tomb; on which occasion the church door most civilly swung open of itself; not that he needed it; for he rode through closed gates and even stone walls, and had been seen by one of the dairy maids to pass between two bars of the great park gate, making himself as thin as a sheet of paper.

All these superstitions I found had been very much countenanced by the squire, who, though not superstitious himself, was very fond of seeing others so. He listened to every goblin tale of the neighboring gossips with infinite gravity, and held the porter's wife in high favor on account of her talent for the marvellous. He was himself a great reader of old legends and romances, and often lamented that he could not believe in them; for a superstitious person, he thought, must live in a kind of fairy land.

Whilst we were all attention to the parson's stories, our ears were suddenly assailed by a burst of heterogeneous sounds from the hall, in which were mingled something like the clang of rude minstrelsy, with the uproar of many small voices and girlish laughter. The door suddenly flew open, and a train came trooping into the room, that might almost have been mistaken for the breaking up of the court of Fairy. That indefatigable spirit, Master Simon, in the faithful discharge of his duties as lord of misrule, had conceived the idea of a Chrtistmas mummery or masking; and having called in to his assistance the Oxonian and the young officer, who were equally ripe for anything that should occasion romping and merriment, they had carried it into instant effect. The old housekeeper had been consulted; the antique clothespresses and wardrobes rummaged, and made to yield up the relics of finery that had not seen the light for several generations; the younger part of the company had been privately convened from the parlor and hall, and the whole had been bedizened out, into a burlesque imitation of an antique mask.*

Master Simon led the van, as "Ancient Christmas," quaintly apparelled in a ruff, a short cloak, which had very much the aspect of one of the old housekeeper's petticoats, and a hat that might have served for a village steeple, and must indubitably have figured in the days of the Covenanters. From under this his nose curved

---

*Maskings or mummeries were favorite sports at Christmas in old times; and the wardrobes at halls and manor-houses were often laid under contribution to furnish dresses and fantastic disguisings. I strongly suspect Master Simon to have taken the idea of his from Ben Jonson's *Masque of Christmas.*

boldly forth, flushed with a frost-bitten bloom, that seemed the very trophy of a December blast. He was accompanied by the blue-eyed romp, dished up as "Dame Mince Pie," in the venerable magnificence of a faded brocade, long stomacher, peaked hat, and high-heeled shoes. The young officer appeared as Robin Hood, in a sporting dress of Kendal green, and a foraging cap with a gold tassel.

The costume, to be sure, did not bear testimony to deep research, and there was an evident eye to the picturesque, natural to a young gallant in the presence of his mistress. The fair Julia hung on his arm in a pretty rustic dress, as "Maid Marian." The rest of the train had been metamorphosed in various ways; the girls trussed up in the finery of the ancient belles of the Bracebridge line, and the striplings bewhiskered with burnt cork, and gravely clad in broad skirts, hanging sleeves, and full-bottomed wigs, to represent the character of Roast Beef, Plum Pudding, and other worthies celebrated in ancient maskings. The whole was under the control of the Oxonian, in the appropriate character of Misrule; and I observed that he exercised rather a mischievous sway with his wand over the smaller personages of the pageant.

The irruption of this motley crew, with beat of drum, according to ancient custom, was the consummation of uproar and merriment. Master Simon covered himself with glory by the stateliness with which, as Ancient Christmas, he walked a minuet with the peerless, though giggling, Dame Mince Pie. It was followed by a dance of all the characters, which from its medley of costumes, seemed as though the old family portraits had skipped down from their frames to join in the sport. Different centuries were figuring at cross hands and right and left; the dark ages were cutting pirouettes and rigadoons; and the days of Queen Bess jigging merrily down the middle, through a line of succeeding generations.

The worthy squire contemplated these fantastic sports, and this resurrection of his old wardrobe, with the simple relish of childish delight. He stood chuckling and rubbing his hands, and scarcely hearing a word the parson said, notwithstanding that the latter was discoursing most authentically on the ancient and stately dance at the Paon, or peacock, from which he conceived the minuet to be derived.* For my part, I was in a continual excitement from the varied scenes of whim and innocent gaiety passing before me. It was inspiring to see wild-eyed frolic and warm-hearted hospitality breaking out from among the chills and glooms of winter, and old age throwing off his apathy, and catching once more the freshness of youthful enjoyment. I felt also an interest in the scene, from the consideration that these fleeting customs were posting fast into oblivion, and that this was, perhaps, the only family in England in which the whole of them was still punctiliously observed. There was a quaintness, too, mingled with all this revelry, that gave it a peculiar zest: it was suited to the time and place; and as the old manor-house almost reeled with mirth and wassail, it seemed echoing back the joviality of long departed years.†

*Sir John Hawkins, speaking of the dance called the Pavon, from pavo, a peacock, says, "It is a grave and majestic dance; the method of dancing it anciently was by gentlemen dressed with caps and swords, by those of the long robe in their gowns, by the peers in their mantles, and by the ladies in gowns with long trains, the motion whereof, in dancing, resembled that of a peacock."—*History of Music.*

†At the time of the first publication of this paper, the picture of an old-fashioned Christmas in the country was pronounced by some as out of date. The author had afterwards an opportunity of witnessing almost all the customs above described, existing in unexpected vigor in the skirts of Derbyshire and Yorkshire, where he passed the Christmas holidays. The reader will find some notice of them in the author's account of his sojourn at Newstead Abbey.

But enough of Christmas and its gambols; it is time for me to pause in this garrulity. Methinks I hear the questions asked by my graver readers, "To what purpose is all this—how is the world to be made wiser by this talk?" Alas! is there not wisdom enough extant for the instruction of the world? And if not, are there not thousands of abler pens laboring for its improvement? It is so much pleasanter to please than to instruct, to play the companion rather than the preceptor.

What, after all, is the mite of wisdom that I could throw into the mass of knowledge; or how am I sure that my sagest deductions may be safe guides for the opinions of others? But in writing to amuse, if I fail, the only evil is in my own disappointment. If, however, I can by any lucky chance, in these days of evil, rub out one wrinkle from the brow of care, or beguile the heavy heart of one moment of sorrow; if I can now and then penetrate through the gathering film of misanthropy, prompt a benevolent view of human nature, and make my reader more in good humor with his fellow beings and himself, surely, surely, I shall not then have written entirely in vain.

LONDON ANTIQUES

—— I do walk
Methinks like Guido Vaux, with my dark lanthorn,
Stealing to set the town o' fire; i' th' country
I should be taken for William o' the Wisp,
Or Robin Goodfellow.

FLETCHER

I AM somewhat of an antiquity hunter, and am fond of exploring London in quest of the relics of old times. These are principally to be found in the depths of the city, swallowed up and almost lost in a wilderness of brick and mortar; but deriving poetical and romantic interest from the commonplace prosaic world around them. I was struck with an instance of the kind in the course of a recent summer ramble into the city; for the city is only to be explored to advantage in summer time, when free from the smoke and fog, and rain and mud of winter. I had been buffeting for some time against the current population setting through Fleet-street. The warm weather had unstrung my nerves, and made me sensitive to every jar and jostle and discordant sound. The flesh was weary, the spirit faint, and I was getting out of humor with the bustling busy throng through which I had to struggle, when in a fit of desperation I tore my way through the crowd, plunged into a by lane, and after passing through several obscure nooks and angles, emerged into a quaint and quiet court with a grassplot in the centre, overhung by elms, and kept perpetually fresh and green by a fountain with its sparkling jet of water. A student with book in hand was seated on a stone bench, partly reading, partly meditating on the movements of two or three trim nursery maids with their infant charges.

I was like an Arab, who had suddenly come upon an oasis amid the panting sterility of the desert. By degrees the quiet and coolness of the place soothed my nerves and refreshed my spirit. I pursued my walk, and came, hard by, to a very ancient chapel, with a low-browed Saxon portal of massive and rich architecture. The interior was circular and lofty, and lighted from above. Around were monumental tombs of ancient date, on which were extended the marble effigies of warriors in armor. Some had the hands devoutly crossed upon the breast; others grasped the pommel of the sword, menacing hostility even in the tomb—while the crossed legs of several indicated soldiers of the Faith who had been on crusades to the Holy Land.

I was, in fact, in the chapel of the Knights Templars, strangely situated in the very center of sordid traffic; and I do not know a more impressive lesson for the man of the world than thus suddenly to turn aside from the highway of busy money-seeking life, and sit down among these shadowy sepulchres, where all is twilight, dust, and forgetfulness.

In a subsequent tour of observation, I encountered another of these relics of a "foregone world" locked up in the heart of the city. I had been wandering for some time through dull monotonous streets, destitute of anything to strike the eye or excite the imagination, when I beheld before me a Gothic gateway of mouldering antiquity. It opened into a spacious quadrangle forming the court-yard of a stately Gothic pile, the portal of which stood invitingly open.

It was apparently a public edifice, and as I was antiquity hunting, I ventured in, though with dubious steps. Meeting no one either to oppose or rebuke my intrusion, I continued on until I found myself in a great hall, with a lofty arched roof and oaken gallery, all of Gothic architecture. At one end of the hall was an enormous fireplace, with wooden settles on each side; at the other end was a raised platform, or dais, the seat of state, above which was the portrait of a man in antique garb, with a long robe, a ruff, and a venerable gray beard.

The whole establishment had an air of monastic quiet and seclusion, and what gave it a mysterious charm was that I had not met with a human being since I had passed the threshold.

Encouraged by this loneliness, I seated myself in a recess of a large bow window, which admitted a broad flood of yellow sunshine, checkered here and there by tints from panes of colored glass; while an open casement let in the soft summer air. Here, leaning my head on my hand, and my arm on an old oaken table, I indulged in a sort of reverie about what might have been the ancient uses of this edifice. It had evidently been of monastic origin; perhaps one of those collegiate establishments built of yore for the promotion of learning, where the patient monk, in the ample solitude of the cloister, added page to page and volume to volume, emulating in the productions of his brain the magnitude of the pile he inhabited.

As I was seated in this musing mood, a small panelled door in an arch at the upper end of the hall was opened, and a number of gray-headed old men, clad in long black cloaks, came forth one by one; proceeding in that manner through the hall, without uttering a word, each turning a pale face on me as he passed, and disappearing through a door at the lower end.

I was singularly struck with their appearance; their black cloaks and antiquated air comported with the style of this most venerable and mysterious pile. It was as if the ghosts of the departed years, about which I had been musing, were passing in review before me. Pleasing myself with such fancies, I set out, in the spirit of romance, to explore what I pictured to myself a realm of shadows, existing in the very center of substantial realities.

My ramble led me through a labyrinth of interior courts, and corridors, and dilapidated cloisters, for the main edifice had many additions and dependencies, built at various times and in various styles; in one open space a number of boys, who evidently belonged to the establishment, were at their sports; but everywhere I observed those mysterious old gray men in black mantles, sometimes sauntering alone, sometimes conversing in groups: they appeared to be the pervading genii of the place. I now called to mind what I had read of certain colleges in old times, where judicial astrology, geomancy, necromancy, and other forbidden and magical sciences were taught. Was this an establishment of the kind, and were these black-cloaked old men really really professors of the black art?

These surmises were passing through my mind as my eye glanced into a chamber, hung round with all kinds of strange and uncouth objects; implements of savage warfare; strange idols and stuffed alligators; bottled serpents and monsters decorated the mantlepiece; while on the high tester of an old-fashioned bedstead grinned a human skull, flanked on each side by a dried cat.

I approached to regard more narrowly this mystic chamber, which seemed a fitting laboratory for a necromancer, when I was startled at beholding a human countenance staring at me from a dusky corner. It was that of a small, shrivelled old man, with thin cheeks, bright eyes, and gray wiry projecting eyebrows. I at first doubted whether it were not a mummy curiously preserved, but it moved, and I saw that it was alive. It was another of these black-cloaked old men, and, as I regarded his quaint physiognomy, his obsolete garb, and the hideous and sinister objects by which he was surrounded, I began to persuade myself that I had come upon the arch mago, who ruled over this magical fraternity.

Seeing me pausing before the door, he rose and invited me to enter. I obeyed, with singular hardihood, for how did I know whether a wave of his wand might not metamorphose me into some strange monster, or conjure me into one of the bottles on his mantelpiece? He proved, however, to be any thing but a conjuror, and his simple garrulity soon dispelled all the magic and mystery with which I had enveloped this antiquated pile and its no less antiquated inhabitants.

It appeared that I had made my way into the center of an ancient asylum for superannuated tradesmen and decayed householders, with which was connected a school for a limited number of boys. It was founded upwards of two centuries since on an old monastic establishment, and retained somewhat of the conventual air and character. The shadowy line of old men in black mantles who had passed before me in the hall, and whom I had elevated into magi, turned out to be the pensioners returning from morning service in the chapel.

John Hallum, the little collector of curiosities, whom I had made the arch magician, had been for six years a resident of the place, and had decorated this final nestling-place of his old age with relics and rarities picked up in the course of his life. According to his own account he had been somewhat of a traveller; having been once in France, and very near making a visit to Holland. He regretted not having visited the latter country, "as then he might have said he had been there." He was evidently a traveller of the simplest kind.

He was aristocratical too in his notions; keeping aloof, as I found, from the ordinary run of pensioners. His chief associates were a blind man who spoke Latin and

Greek, of both which languages Hallum was profoundly ignorant; and a broken-down gentleman who had run through a fortune of forty thousand pounds left him by his father, and ten thousand pounds, the marriage portion of his wife. Little Hallum seemed to consider it an indubitable sign of gentle blood as well as of lofty spirit to be able to squander such enormous sums.

P.S. The picturesque remnant of old times into which I have thus beguiled the reader is what is called the Charter House, originally the Chartreuse. It was founded in 1611, on the remains of an ancient convent, by Sir Thomas Sutton, being one of those noble charities set on foot by individual munificence, and kept up with the quaintness and sanctity of ancient times amidst the modern changes and innovations of London. Here eighty broken-down men, who have seen better days, are provided, in their old age, with food, clothing, fuel, and a yearly allowance for private expenses. They dine together as did the monks of old, in the hall which had been the refectory of the original convent. Attached to the establishment in a school for forty-four boys.

Stow, whose work I have consulted on the subject, speaking of the obligations of the gray-headed pensioners, says, "They are not to intermeddle with any business touching the affairs of the hospital, but to attend only to the service of God, and take thankfully what is provided for them, without muttering, murmuring, or grudging. None to wear weapon, long hair, colored boots, spurs or colored shoes, feathers in their hats, or any ruffian-like or unseemly apparel, but such as becomes hospital men to wear." "And in truth," adds Stow, "happy are they that are so taken from the cares and sorrows of the world, and fixed in so good a place as these old men are; having nothing to care for, but the good of their souls, to serve God and to live in brotherly love."

For the amusement of such as have been interested by the preceding sketch, taken down from my own observation, and who may wish to know a little more about the mysteries of London, I subjoin a modicum of local history, put into my hands by an odd-looking old gentleman in a small brown wig and a snuff-colored coat, with whom I became acquainted shortly after my visit to the Charter House. I confess I was a little dubious at first, whether it was not one of those apocryphal tales often passed off upon inquiring travellers like myself; and which have brought our general character for veracity into such unmerited reproach. On making proper inquiries, however, I have received the most satisfactory assurances of the author's probity; and, indeed, have been told that he is actually engaged in a full and particular account of the very interesting region in which he resides; of which the following may be considered merely as a foretaste.

LITTLE BRITAIN

What I write is most true * * * * I have a whole booke of cases lying by me which if I should sette foorth, some grave auntients (within the hearing of Bow bell) would be out of charity with me.

NASHE

IN THE centre of the great city of London lies a small neighborhood, consisting of a cluster of narrow streets and courts, of very venerable and debilitated houses, which goes by the name of LITTLE BRITAIN. Christ Church School and St. Bartholomew's Hospital bound it on the west; Smithfield and Long Lane on the north; Aldersgate Street, like an arm of the sea, divides it from the eastern part of the city; whilst the yawning gulf of Bull-and-Mouth Street separates it from Butcher Lane, and the regions of Newgate. Over this little territory, thus bounded and designated, the great dome of St. Paul's, swelling above the intervening houses of Paternoster Row, Amen Corner, and Ave Maria Lane, looks down with an air of motherly protection.

This quarter derives its appellation from having been, in ancient times, the residence of the Dukes of Brittany. As London increased, however, rank and fashion rolled off to the west, and trade creeping on at their heels, took possession of their deserted abodes. For some time Little Britain became the great mart of learning, and was peopled by the busy and prolific race of booksellers; these also gradually deserted it, and, emigrating beyond the great strait of Newgate Street, settled down in Paternoster Row and St. Paul's Church-Yard, where they continue to increase and multiply even at the present day.

But though thus fallen into decline, Little Britain still bears traces of its former splendor. There are several houses ready to tumble down, the fronts of which are magnificently enriched with old oaken carvings of hideous faces, unknown birds, beasts, and fishes, and fruits and flowers which it would perplex a naturalist to classify. There are also, in Aldersgate Street, certain remains of what were once spacious and lordly family mansions, but which have in latter days been subdivided into several tenements. Here may often be found the family of a petty tradesman, with its trumpery furniture, burrowing among the relics of antiquated finery, in great rambling time-stained apartments, with fretted ceilings, gilded cornices, and enormous marble fireplaces. The lanes and courts also contain many smaller houses, not on so grand a scale, but, like your small ancient gentry, sturdily maintaining their claims to equal antiquity. These have their gable ends to the street; great bow windows, with diamond panes set in lead, grotesque carvings, and low arched door-ways.*

In this most venerable and sheltered little nest have I passed several quiet years of existence, comfortably lodged in the second floor of one of the smallest but oldest edifices. My sitting-room is an old wainscoted chamber, with small panels, and set off with a miscellaneous array of furniture. I have a particular respect for three or four high-backed claw-footed chairs, covered with tarnished brocade, which bear the marks of having seen better days, and have doubtless figured in some of the old palaces of Little Britain. They seem to me to keep together, and to look down with sovereign contempt upon their leathern-bottomed neighbors; as I have seen decayed gentry carry a high head among the plebeian society with which they were reduced to associate. The whole front of my sitting-room is taken up with a bow window, on the panes of which are recorded the names of previous occupants for many generations, mingled with scraps of very indifferent gentleman-like poetry, written in characters which I can scarcely decipher, and which extol the charms of many a beauty of Little Britain, who has long, long since bloomed, faded, and passed away. As I am an idle personage, with no apparent occupation, and pay my bill regularly every week, I am looked upon as the only independent gentleman of the neighborhood; and, being curious to learn the internal state of a community so apparently shut up within itself, I have managed to work my way into all the concerns and secrets of the place.

Little Britain may truly be called the heart's core of the

*It is evident that the author of this interesting communication has included, in his general title of Little Britain, many of those little lanes and courts that belong immediately to Cloth Fair.

city; the strong-hold of true John Bullism. It is a fragment of London as it was in its better days, with its antiquated folks and fashions. Here flourish in great preservation many of the holiday games and customs of yore. The inhabitants most religiously eat pancakes on Shrove Tuesday, hot-cross-buns on Good Friday, and roast goose at Michaelmas; they send love-letters on Valentine's Day, burn the pope on the fifth of November, and kiss all the girls under the mistletoe at Christmas. Roast beef and plum-pudding are also held in superstitious veneration, and port and sherry maintain their grounds as the only true English wines; all others being considered vile outlandish beverages.

Little Britain has its long catalogue of city wonders, which its inhabitants consider the wonders of the world; such as the great bell of St. Paul's, which sours all the beer when it tolls; the figures that strike the hours at St. Dunstan's clock; the Monument; the lions in the Tower; and the wooden giants in Guildhall. They still believe in dreams and fortune-telling, and an old woman that lives in Bull-and-Mouth Street makes a tolerable subsistence by detecting stolen goods, and promising the girls good husbands. They are apt to be rendered uncomfortable by comets and eclipses; and if a dog howls dolefully at night, it is looked upon as a sure sign of a death in the place. There are even many ghost stories current, particularly concerning the old mansion-houses; in several of which it is said strange sights are sometimes seen. Lords and ladies, the former in full-bottomed wigs, hanging sleeves, and swords, the latter in lappets, stays, hoops, and brocade, have been seen walking up and down the great waste chambers, on moonlight nights; and are supposed to be the shades of the ancient proprietors in their court-dresses.

Little Britain has likewise its sages and great men. One of the most important of the former is a tall, dry old gentleman, of the name of Skryme, who keeps a small apothecary's shop. He has a cadaverous countenance, full of cavities and projections; with a brown circle round each eye, like a pair of horn spectacles. He is much thought of by the old women, who consider him as a kind of conjurer, because he has two or three stuffed alligators hanging up in his shop, and several snakes in bottles. He is a great reader of almanacs and newspapers, and is much given to pore over alarming accounts of plots, conspiracies, fires, earthquakes, and volcanic eruptions; which last phenomena he considers as signs of the time. He has always some dismal tale of the kind to deal out to his customers, with their doses; and thus at the same time puts both soul and body into an uproar. He is a great believer in omens and predictions; and has the prophecies of Robert Nixon and Mother Shipton by heart. No man can make so much out of an eclipse, or even an unusually dark day; and he shook the tail of the last comet over the heads of his customers and disciples until they were nearly frightened out of their wits. He has lately got hold of a popular legend or prophecy, on which he has been unusually eloquent. There has been a saying current among the ancient sibyls, who treasure up these things, that when the grasshopper on the top of the Exchange shook hands with the dragon on the top of Bow Church steeple, fearful events would take place. This strange conjunction, it seems, has as strangely come to pass. The same architect has been engaged lately on the repairs of the cupola of the Exchange, and the steeple of Bow Church; and, fearful to relate, the dragon and the grasshopper actually lie, cheek by jole, in the yard of his workshop.

"Others," as Mr. Skryme is accustomed to say, "may go star-gazing, and look for conjunctions in the heavens, but here is a conjunction on the earth, near at home, and under our own eyes, which surpasses all the signs and calculations of astrologers." Since these portentous weather-cocks have thus laid their heads together, wonderful events have already occurred. The good old king, notwithstanding that he had lived eighty-two years, had all at once given up the ghost; another king had mounted the throne; a royal duke had died suddenly— another, in France, had been murdered; there had been radical meetings in all parts of the kingdom; the bloody scenes at Manchester; the great plot in Cato Street; and, above all, the queen had returned to England! All these sinster events are recounted by Mr. Skryme, with a mysterious look, and a dismal shake of the head; and being taken with his drugs, and associated in the minds of his auditors with stuffed sea-monsters, bottled serpents, and his own visage, which is a title-page of tribulation, they have spread great gloom through the minds of the people of Little Britain. They shake their heads whenever they go by Bow Church, and observe, that they never expected any good to come of taking down that steeple, which in old times told nothing but glad tidings, as the history of Whittington and his Cat bears witness.

The rival oracle of Little Britain is a substantial cheesemonger, who lives in a fragment of one of the old family mansions, and is as magnificently lodged as a round-bellied mite in the midst of one of his own Cheshires. Indeed he is a man of no little standing and importance; and his renown extends through Huggin Lane, and Lad Lane, and even unto Aldermanbury. His opinion is very much taken in affairs of state, having read the Sunday papers for the last half century, together with the *Gentleman's Magazine, Rapin's History of England*, and the *Naval Chronicle*. His head is stored with invaluable maxims which have borne the test of time and use for centuries. It is his firm opinion that "it is a moral impossible," so long as England is true to herself, that any thing can shake her, and he has much to say on the subject of the national debt; which, somehow or other, he proves to be a great national bulwark and blessing. He passed the greater part of his life in the purlieus of Little Britain, until of late years, when, having become rich, and grown into the dignity of a Sunday cane, he begins to take his pleasure and see the world. He has therefore made several excursions to Hampstead, Highgate, and other neighboring towns, where he has passed whole afternoons in looking back upon the metropolis through a telescope, and endeavoring to descry the steeple of St. Bartholomew's. Not a stage-coachman of Bull-and-Mouth Street but touches his hat as he passes; and he is considered quite a patron at the coach-office of the Goose and Gridiron, St. Paul's Church-yard. His family have been very urgent for him to make an expedition to Margate, but he has great doubts of those new gimcracks, the steamboats, and indeed thinks himself too advanced in life to undertake sea-voyages.

Little Britain has occasionally its factions and divisions, and party spirit ran very high at one time in consequence of two rival "Burial Societies" being set up in the place. One held its meeting at the Swan and Horse Shoe, and was patronized by the cheesemonger; the other at the Cock and Crown, under the auspices of the apothecary: it is needless to say that the latter was the most flourishing. I have passed an evening or two at each, and have acquired much valuable information, as to the best mode of being buried, the comparative merits of church-yards, together with divers hints on the subject of patent-iron coffins. I have heard the question discussed in all its bearings as to the legality of prohibiting the latter on account of their durability. The feuds occasioned by these societies have happily died of late;

but they were for a long time prevailing themes of controversy, the people of Little Britain being extremely solicitous of funereal honors and of lying comfortably in their graves.

Besides these two funeral societies there is a third of quite a different cast, which tends to throw the sunshine of good-humor over the whole neighborhood. It meets once a week at a little old-fashioned house, kept by a jolly publican of the name of Wagstaff, and bearing for insignia a resplendent half-moon, with a most seductive bunch of grapes. The old edifice is covered with inscriptions to catch the eye of the thirsty wayfarer, such as "Truman, Hanbury, and Co.'s Entire," "Wine, Rum, and Brandy Vaults," "Old Tom, Rum and Compounds, etc." This indeed has been a temple of Bacchus and Momus from time immemorial. It has always been in the family of the Wagstaffs, so that its history is tolerably preserved by the present landlord. It was much frequented by the gallants and cavalieros of the reign of Elizabeth, and was looked into now and then by the wits of Charles the Second's day. But what Wagstaff principally prides himself upon is, that Henry the Eighth, in one of his nocturnal rambles, broke the head of one of his ancestors with his famous walking-staff. This however is considered as rather a dubious and vainglorious boast of the landlord.

The club which now holds its weekly sessions here goes by the name of "The Roaring Lads of Little Britain." They abound in old catches, glees, and choice stories, that are traditional in the place, and not to be met with in any other part of the metropolis. There is a mad-cap undertaker who is inimitable at a merry song; but the life of the club, and indeed the prime wit of Little Britain, is bully Wagstaff himself. His ancestors were all wags before him, and he has inherited with the inn a large stock of songs and jokes, which go with it from generation to generation as heir-looms. He is a dapper little fellow, with bandy legs and pot belly, a red face, with a moist merry eye, and a little shock of gray hair behind. At the opening of every club night he is called in to sing his "Confession of Faith," which is the famous old drinking trowl from Grammer Gurton's Needle. He sings it, to be sure, with many variations, as he received it from his father's lips; for it has been a standing favorite at the Half-Moon and Bunch of Grapes ever since it was written; nay, he affirms that his predecessors have often had the honor of singing it before the nobility and gentry at Christmas mummeries, when Little Britain was in all its glory.*

*As mine host of the Half-Moon's Confession of Faith may not be familiar to the majority of readers, and as it is a specimen of the current songs of Little Britain, I subjoin it in its original orthography. I would observe, that the whole club always join in the chorus with a fearful thumping on the table and clattering of pewter pots.

> I cannot eate but lytle meate,
>   My stomacke is not good,
> But sure I thinke that I can drinke
>   With him that weares a hood,
> Though I go bare, take ye no care,
>   I nothing am a colde,
> I stuff my skyn so full within,
>   Of joly good ale and olde.
> *Chorus.*   Backe and syde go bare, go bare,
>   Booth foote and hand go colde,
> But belly, God send thee good ale ynoughe
>   Whether it be new or olde.
>
> I have no rost, but a nut brawne toste,
>   And a crab laid in the fyre;
> A little breade shall do me steade,
>   Much breade I not desyre.
> No frost nor snow, nor winde, I trowe,
>   Can hurte mee, if I wolde,
> I am so wrapt and throwly lapt
>   Of joly good ale and olde.
> *Chorus.*   Backe and syde go bare, go bare, etc.
>
> And Tyb my wife, that, as her lyfe,
>   Loveth well good ale to seeke,

It would do one's heart good to hear, on a club night, the shouts of merriment, the snatches of song, and now and then the choral bursts of half a dozen discordant voices, which issue from this jovial mansion. At such times the street is lined with listeners, who enjoy a delight equal to that of gazing into a confectioner's window, or snuffing up the steams of a cookshop.

There are two annual events which produce great stir and sensation in Little Britain; these are St. Bartholomew's fair, and the Lord Mayor's day. During the time of the fair, which is held in the adjoining regions of Smithfield, there is nothing going on but gossiping and gadding about. The late quiet streets of Little Britain are overrun with an irruption of strange figures and faces; every tavern is a scene of rout and revel. The fiddle and the song are heard from the tap-room, morning, noon, and night; and at each window may be seen some group of boon companions, with half-shut eyes, hats on one side, pipe in mouth, and tankard in hand, fondling, and prosing, and singing maudlin songs over their liquor. Even the sober decorum of private families, which I

> Full oft drynkes shee, tyll ye may see,
> The teares run downe her cheeke.
> Then doth she trowle to me the bowle,
> Even as a mault-worme sholde,
> And sayth, sweete harte, I took my parte
> Of this joly good ale and olde.
> *Chorus.* Backe and syde go bare, go bare, etc.
>
> Now let them drynke, tyll they nod and winke,
> Even as goode fellowes sholde doe,
> They shall not mysse to have the blisse,
> Good ale doth bring men to;
> And all poore soules that have scowred bowles,
> Or have them lustily trolde,
> God save the lyves of them and their wives,
> Whether they be yonge or olde.
> *Chorus.* Backe and syde go bare, go bare, etc.

must say is rigidly kept up at other times among my neighbors, is no proof against this Saturnalia. There is no such thing as keeping maid-servants within doors. Their brains are absolutely set madding with Punch and the Puppet Show; the Flying Horses; Signior Polito; the Fire-Eater; the celebrated Mr. Paap; and the Irish Giant. The children too lavish all their holiday money in toys and gilt gingerbread, and fill the house with the Lilliputian din of drums, trumpets, and penny whistles.

But the Lord Mayor's day is the great anniversary. The Lord Mayor is looked up to by the inhabitants of Little Britain as the greatest potentate upon earth; his gilt coach with six horses as the summit of human splendor; and his procession, with all the Sheriffs and Aldermen in his train, as the grandest of earthly pageants. How they exult in the idea, that the King himself dare not enter the city, without first knocking at the gate of Temple Bar, and asking permission of the Lord Mayor: for if he did, heaven and earth! there is no knowing what might be the consequence. The man in armor who rides before the Lord Mayor, and is the city champion, has orders to cut down every body that offends against the dignity of the city; and then there is the little man with a velvet porringer on his head, who sits at the window of the state coach, and holds the city sword, as long as a pike-staff—Odd's blood! If he once draws that sword, Majesty itself is not safe!

Under the protection of this mighty potentate, therefore, the good people of Little Britain sleep in peace. Temple Bar is an effectual barrier against all interior foes; and as to foreign invasion, the Lord Mayor has but to throw himself into the Tower, call in the train bands, and put the standing army of Beef-eaters under arms, and he may bid defiance to the world!

Thus wrapped up in its own concerns, its own habits,

and its own opinions, Little Britain has long flourished as a sound heart to this great fungous metropolis. I have pleased myself with considering it as a chosen spot, where the principles of sturdy John Bullism were garnered up, like seed corn, to renew the national character, when it had run to waste and degeneracy. I have rejoiced also in the general spirit of harmony that prevailed throughout it; for though there might now and then be a few clashes of opinion between the adherents of the cheesemonger and the apothecary, and an occasional feud between the burial societies, yet these were but transient clouds, and soon passed away. The neighbors met with good-will, parted with a shake of the hand, and never abused each other except behind their backs.

I could give rare descriptions of snug junketing parties at which I have been present; where we played at All-Fours, Pope-Joan, Tom-come-tickle-me, and other choice old games; and where we sometimes had a good old English country dance to the tune of Sir Roger de Coverley. Once a year also the neighbors would gather together, and go on a gypsy party to Epping Forest. It would have done any man's heart good to see the merriment that took place here as we banqueted on the grass under the trees. How we made the woods ring with bursts of laughter at the songs of little Wagstaff and the merry undertaker! After dinner, too, the young folks would play at blind-man's-buff and hide-and-seek; and it was amusing to see them tangle among the briers, and to hear a fine romping girl now and then squeak from among the bushes. The elder folks would gather round the cheesemonger and the apothecary, to hear them talk politics; for they generally brought out a newspaper in their pockets, to pass away time in the country. They would now and then, to be sure, get a little warm in argument; but their disputes were always adjusted by reference to a worthy old umbrella maker in a double chin, who, never exactly comprehending the subject, managed somehow or other to decide in favor of both parties.

All empires, however, says some philosopher or historian, are doomed to changes and revolutions. Luxury and innovation creep in; factions arise; and families now and then spring up, whose ambition and intrigues throw the whole system into confusion. Thus in latter days has the tranquillity of Little Britain been grievously disturbed, and its golden simplicity of manners threatened with total subversion, by the aspiring family of a retired butcher.

The family of the Lambs had long been among the most thriving and popular in the neighborhood: the Miss Lambs were the belles of Little Britain, and everybody was pleased when Old Lamb had made money enough to shut up shop, and put his name on a brass plate on his door. In an evil hour, however, one of the Miss Lambs had the honor of being a lady in attendance on the Lady Mayoress, at her grand annual ball, on which occasion she wore three towering ostrich feathers on her head. The family never got over it; they were immediately smitten with a passion for high life; set up a one-horse carriage, put a bit of gold lace round the errand boy's hat, and have been the talk and detestation of the whole neighborhood ever since. They could no longer be induced to play at Pope-Joan or blindman's-bluff; they could endure no dances but quadrilles, which nobody had ever heard of in Little Britain; and they took to reading novels, talking bad French, and playing upon the piano. Their brother, too, who had been articled to an attorney, set up for a dandy and a critic, characters hitherto unknown in these parts;

and he confounded the worthy folks exceedingly by talking about Kean, the opera, and the *Edinburgh Review*.

What was still worse, the Lambs gave a grand ball, to which they neglected to invite any of their old neighbors; but they had a great deal of genteel company from Theobald's Road, Red-Lion Square, and other parts towards the west. There were several beaux of their brother's acquaintance from Gray's Inn Lane and Hatton Garden; and not less than three Aldermen's ladies with their daughters. This was not to be forgotten or forgiven. All Little Britain was in an uproar with the smacking of whips, the lashing of miserable horses, and the rattling and the jingling of hackney coaches. The gossips of the neighborhood might be seen popping their night-caps out at every window, watching the crazy vehicles rumble by; and there was a knot of virulent old cronies, that kept a look-out from a house just opposite the retired butcher's, and scanned and criticised every one that knocked at the door.

This dance was a cause of almost open war, and the whole neighborhood declared they would have nothing more to say to the Lambs. It is true that Mrs. Lamb, when she had no engagements with her quality acquaintance, would give little humdrum tea junketings to some of her old cronies, "quite," as she would say, "in a friendly way;" and it is equally true that her invitations were always accepted, in spite of all previous vows to the contrary. Nay, the good ladies would sit and be delighted with the music of the Miss Lambs, who would condescend to strum an Irish melody for them on the piano; and they would listen with wonderful interest to Mrs. Lamb's anecdotes of Alderman Plunket's family, of Portsokenward, and the Miss Timberlakes, the rich heiresses of Crutched-Friars; but then they relieved their consciences, and averted the reproaches of their confederates, by canvassing at the next gossiping convocation every thing that had passed, and pulling the Lambs and their rout all to pieces.

The only one of the family that could not be made fashionable was the retired butcher himself. Honest Lamb, in spite of the meekness of his name, was a rough, hearty old fellow, with the voice of a lion, a head of black hair like a shoe brush, and a broad face mottled like his own beef. It was in vain that the daughters always spoke of him as "the old gentleman," addressed him as "papa," in tones of infinite softness, and endeavored to coax him into a dressing-gown and slippers, and other gentlemanly habits. Do what they might, there was no keeping down the butcher. His sturdy nature would break through all their glozings. He had a hearty, vulgar good-humor that was irrepressible. His very jokes made his sensitive daughters shudder; and he persisted in wearing his blue cotton coat of a morning, dining at two o'clock, and having a "bit of sausage with his tea."

He was doomed, however, to share the unpopularity of his family. He found his old comrades gradually growing cold and civil to him; no longer laughing at his jokes; and now and then throwing out a fling at "some people," and a hint about "quality binding." This both nettled and perplexed the honest butcher; and his wife and daughters, with the consummate policy of the shrewder sex, taking advantage of the circumstance, at length prevailed upon him to give up his afternoon's pipe and tankard at Wagstaff's; to sit after dinner by himself, and take his pint of port—a liquor he detested—and to nod in his chair in solitary and dismal gentility.

The Miss Lambs might now be seen flaunting along the streets in French bonnets, with unknown beaux; and talking and laughing so loud that it distressed the nerves of every good lady within hearing. They even went so far as to attempt patronage, and actually induced a French dancing-master to set up in the neighborhood; but the worthy folks of Little Britain took fire at it, and did so persecute the poor Gaul, that he was fain to pack up fiddle and dancing-pumps, and decamp with such precipitaton, that he absolutely forgot to pay for his lodgings.

I had flattered myself, at first, with the idea that all this fiery indignation on the part of the community was merely the overflowing of their zeal for good old English manners, and their horror of innovation; and I applauded the silent contempt they were so vociferous in expressing, for upstart pride, French fashions, and the Miss Lambs. But I grieve to say that I soon perceived the infection had taken hold; and that my neighbors, after condemning, were beginning to follow their example. I overheard my landlady importuning her husband to let their daughters have one quarter at French and music, and that they might take a few lessons in quadrille. I even saw, in the course of a few Sundays, no less than five French bonnets, precisely like those of the Miss Lambs, parading about Little Britain.

I still had my hopes that all this folly would gradually die away; that the Lambs might move out of the neighborhood; might die, or might run away with attorneys' apprentices; and that quiet and simplicity might be again restored to the community. But unluckily a rival power arose. An opulent oilman died, and left a widow with a large jointure and a family of buxom daughters. The young ladies had long been repining in secret at the parsimony of a prudent father, which kept down all their elegant aspirings. Their ambition, being now no longer restrained, broke out into a blaze, and they openly took the field against the family of the butcher. It is true that the Lambs, having had the first start, had naturally an advantage of them in the fashionable career. They could speak a little bad French, play the piano, dance quadrilles, and had formed high acquaintances; but the Trotters were not to be distanced. When the Lambs appeared with two feathers in their hats, the Miss Trotters mounted four, and of twice as fine colors. If the Lambs gave a dance, the Trotters were not to be behindhand, and though they might not boast of as good company, yet they had double the number, and were twice as merry.

The whole community has at length divided itself into fashionable factions, under the banners of these two families. The old games of Pope-Joan and Tom-come-tickle-me are entirely discarded; there is no such thing as getting up an honest country dance; and on my attempting to kiss a young lady under the mistletoe last Christmas, I was indignantly repulsed; the Miss Lambs having pronounced it "shocking vulgar." Bitter rivalry has also broken out as to the most fashionable part of Little Britain; the Lambs standing up for the dignity of Cross-Keys Square, and the Trotters for the vicinity of St. Bartholomew's.

Thus is this little territory torn by factions and internal dissensions, like the great empire whose name it bears; and what will be the result would puzzle the apothecary himself, with all his talent at prognostics, to determine; though I apprehend that it will terminate in the total downfall of genuine John Bullism.

The immediate effects are extremely unpleasasnt to me. Being a single man, and, as I observed before, rather an idle good-for-nothing personage, I have been considered the only gentleman by profession in the place. I stand therefore in high favor with both parties, and have to hear all their cabinet councils and mutual backbitings. As I am too civil not to agree with the ladies on all occasions, I have committed myself most horribly with both parties, by abusing their opponents. I might manage to reconcile this to my conscience, which is a truly accommodating one, but I cannot to my apprehension—if the Lambs and Trotters ever come to a reconciliation, and compare notes, I am ruined!

I have determined, therefore, to beat a retreat in time, and am actually looking out for some other nest in this great city, where old English manners are still kept up; where French is neither eaten, drunk, danced, nor spoken; and where there are no fashionable families of retired tradesmen. This found, I will, like a veteran rat, hasten away before I have an old house about my ears; bid a long, though a sorrowful adieu to my present abode, and leave the rival factions of the Lambs and the Trotters to divide the distracted empire of LITTLE BRITAIN.

STRATFORD-ON-AVON

Thou soft-flowing Avon, by thy silver stream
Of things more than mortal sweet Shakespeare would dream;
The fairies by moonlight dance round his green bed,
For hallow'd the turf is which pillow'd his head.

                                                   GARRICK

T O A homeless man, who has no spot on this wide world which he can truly call his own, there is a momentary feeling of something like independence and territorial consequence, when, after a weary day's travel, he kicks off his boots, thrusts his feet into slippers, and stretches himself before an inn fire. Let the world without go as it may; let kingdoms rise or fall, so long as he has the wherewithal to pay his bill, he is, for the time being, the very monarch of all he surveys. The arm-chair is his throne, the poker his sceptre, and the little parlor, some twelve feet square, his undisputed empire. It is a morsel of certainty, snatched from the midst of the uncertainties of life; it is a sunny moment gleaming out kindly on a cloudy day; and he who has advanced some way on the pilgrimage of existence, knows the importance of husbanding even morsels and moments of enjoyment. "Shall I not take mine ease in mine inn?" thought I, as I gave the fire a stir, lolled back in my elbow-chair, and cast a complacent look about the little parlor of the Red Horse, at Stratford-on-Avon.

The words of sweet Shakespeare were just passing through my mind as the clock struck midnight from the tower of the church in which he lies buried. There was a gentle tap at the door, and a pretty chambermaid, putting in her smiling face, inquired, with a hesitating air, whether I had rung. I understood it as a modest hint that it was time to retire. My dream of absolute dominion was at an end; so abdicating my throne, like a prudent potentate, to avoid being deposed, and putting the Stratford *Guide Book* under my arm, as a pillow companion, I went to bed, and dreamt all night of Shakespeare, the jubilee, and David Garrick.

The next morning was one of those quickening mornings which we sometimes have in early spring; for it was about the middle of March. The chills of a long winter had suddenly given way; the north wind had spent its last gasp; and a mild air came stealing from the west, breathing the breath of life into nature, and wooing every bud and flower to burst forth into fragrance and beauty.

I had come to Stratford on a poetical pilgrimage. My

first visit was to the house where Shakespeare was born, and where, according to tradition, he was brought up to his father's craft of wool-combing. It is a small, mean-looking edifice of wood and plaster, a true nestling-place of genius, which seems to delight in hatching its offspring in by-corners. The walls of its squalid chambers are covered with names and inscriptions in every language, by pilgrims of all nations, ranks, and conditions, from the prince to the peasant; and present a simple, but striking instance of the spontaneous and universal homage of mankind to the great poet of nature.

The house is shown by a garrulous old lady, in a frosty red face, lighted up by a cold blue anxious eye, and garnished with artificial locks of flaxen hair, curling from under an exceedingly dirty cap. She was peculiarly assiduous in exhibiting the relics with which this, like all other celebrated shrines, abounds. There was the shat-tered stock of the very match-lock with which Shaks-peare shot the deer, on his poaching exploits. There, too, was his tobacco-box; which proves that he was a rival smoker of Sir Walter Raleigh; the sword also with which he played Hamlet; and the identical lantern with which Friar Laurence discovered Romeo and Juliet at the tomb! There was an ample supply also of Shake-speare's mulberry-tree, which seems to have as extraor-dinary powers of self-multiplication as the wood of the true cross; of which there is enough extant to build a ship of the line.

The most favorite object of curiosity, however, is Shakespeare's chair. It stands in the chimney nook of a small gloomy chamber, just behind what was his father's shop. Here he may many a time have sat when a boy, watching the slowly revolving spit with all the longing of an urchin; or of an evening, listening to the cronies and gossips of Stratford, dealing forth church-yard tales and legendary anecdotes of the troublesome times of England. In this chair it is the custom of every one that visits the house to sit: whether this be done with the hope of imbibing any of the inspiration of the bard I am at a loss to say, I merely mention the fact; and mine hostess privately assured me, that, though built of solid oak, such was the fervent zeal of devotees, that the chair had to be new bottomed at least once in three years. It is worthy of notice also, in the history of this extraordinary chair, that it partakes something of the volatile nature of the Santa Casa of Loretto, or the flying chair of the Arabian enchanter; for though sold some few years since to a northern princess, yet, strange to tell, it has found its way back again to the old chimney corner.

I am always of easy faith in such matters, and am ever willing to be deceived, where the deceit is pleasant and costs nothing. I am therefore a ready believer in relics, legends, and local anecdotes of goblins and great men; and would advise all travellers who travel for their gratification to be the same. What is it to us, whether these stories be true or false, so long as we can persuade ourselves into the belief of them, and enjoy all the charm of the reality? There is nothing like resolute good-humored credulity in these matters; and on this occasion I went even so far as willingly to believe the claims of mine hostess to a lineal descent from the poet, when, luckily, for my faith, she put into my hands a play of her own composition, which set all belief in her consanguinity at defiance.

From the birth-place of Shakespeare a few paces brought me to his grave. He lies buried in the chancel of the parish church, a large and venerable pile, mouldering with age, but richly ornamented. It stands on the banks of the Avon, on an embowered point, and separated by adjoining gardens from the suburbs of the town. Its situation is quiet and retired; the river runs murmuring at the foot of the church-yard, and the elms which grow upon its banks droop their branches into its clear bosom. An avenue of limes, the boughs of which are curiously interlaced, so as to form in summer an arched way of foliage, leads up from the gate of the yard to the church parlor. The graves are overgrown with grass; the gray tombstones, some of them nearly sunk into the earth, are half covered with moss, which has likewise tinted the reverend old building. Small birds have built their nests among the cornices and fissures of the walls, and keep up a continual flutter and chirping, and rooks are sailing and cawing about its lofty gray spire.

In the course of my rambles I met with the gray-headed sexton, Edmonds, and accompanied him home to get the key of the church. He had lived in Stratford, man and boy, for eighty years, and seemed still to consider himself a vigorous man, with the trivial exception that he had nearly lost the use of his legs for a few years past. His dwelling was a cottage, looking out upon the Avon and its bordering meadows; and was a picture of that neatness, order, and comfort, which pervade the humblest dwellings in this country. A low white-washed room, with a stone floor carefully scrubbed, served for parlor, kitchen and hall. Rows of pewter and earthen dishes glittered along the dresser. On an old oaken table, well rubbed and polished, lay the family Bible and prayer-book, and the drawer contained the family library, composed of about half a score of well-thumbed volumes. An ancient clock, that important article of cottage furniture, ticked on the opposite side of the room; with a bright warming-pan hanging on one side of it, and the old man's horn-handled Sunday cane on the other. The fireplace, as usual, was wide and deep enough to admit a gossip knot within its jambs. In one corner sat the old man's granddaughter sewing, a pretty blue-eyed girl,—and in the opposite corner was a superannuated crony, whom he addressed by the name of John Ange, and who, I found, had been his companion from childhood. They had played together in infancy; they had worked together in manhood; they were now tottering about and gossiping away the evening of life; and in a short time they will probably be buried together in the neighboring churchyard. It is not often that we see two streams of existence running thus evenly and tranquilly side by side; it is only in such quiet "bosom scenes" of life that they are to be met with.

I had hoped to gather some traditionary anecdotes of the bard from these ancient chroniclers; but they had nothing new to impart. The long interval during which Shakespeare's writings lay in comparative neglect has spread its shadow over his history; and it is his good or evil lot that scarcely any thing remains to his biographers but a scanty handful of conjectures.

The sexton and his companion had been employed as carpenters on the preparations for the celebrated Stratford jubilee, and they remembered Garrick, the prime mover of the fête, who superintended the arrangements, and, who, according to the sexton, was "a short punch man, very lively and bustling." John Ange had assisted also in cutting down Shakespeare's mulberry tree, of which he had a morsel in his pocket for sale; no doubt a sovereign quickener of literary conception.

I was grieved to hear these two worthy wights speak very dubiously of the eloquent dame who shows the Shakespeare house. John Ange shook his head when I mentioned her valuable collection of relics, particularly her remains of the mulberry tree; and the old sexton even expressed a doubt as to Shakespeare's having been born in her house. I soon discovered that he looked upon her mansion with an evil eye, as a rival to the poet's tomb; the latter having comparatively but few visitors. Thus it is that historians differ at the very outset, and mere pebbles make the stream of truth diverge into different channels even at the fountain head.

We approached the church through the avenue of limes, and entered by a Gothic porch, highly ornamented, with carved doors of massive oak. The interior is spacious, and the architecture and embellishments superior to those of most country churches. There are several ancient monuments of nobility and gentry, over some of which hang funeral escutcheons, and banners dropping piecemeal from the walls. The tomb of Shakespeare is in the chancel. The place is solemn and sepulchral. Tall elms wave before the pointed windows, and the Avon, which runs at a short distance from the walls, keeps up a low perpetual murmur. A flat stone marks the spot where the bard is buried. There are four lines inscribed on it, said to have been written by himself, and which have in them something extremely awful. If they are indeed his own, they show that solicitude about the quiet of the grave, which seems natural to fine sensibilities and thoughtful minds.

> Good friend, for Jesus' sake forbeare
> To dig the dust enclosed here.
> Blessed be he that spares these stones,
> And curst be he that moves my bones.

Just over the grave, in a niche of the wall, is a bust of Shakespeare, put up shortly after his death, and considered as a resemblance. The aspect is pleasant and serene, with a finely-arched forehead; and I thought I could read in it clear indications of that cheerful, social disposition, by which he was as much characterized among his contemporaries as by the vastness of his genius. The inscription mentions his age at the time of his decease—fifty-three years; an untimely death for the world; for what fruit might not have been expected from the golden autumn of such a mind, sheltered as it was from the stormy vicissitudes of life, and flourishing in the sunshine of popular and royal favor.

The inscription on the tombstone has not been without its effect. It has prevented the removal of his remains from the bosom of his native place to Westminster Abbey, which was at one time contemplated. A few years since also, as some laborers were digging to make an adjoining vault, the earth caved in, so as to leave a vacant space almost like an arch, through which one might have reached into his grave. No one, however, presumed to meddle with his remains so awfully guarded by a malediction; and lest any of the idle or the curious, or any collector of relics, should be tempted to commit depredations, the old sexton kept watch over the place for two days, until the vault was finished and the aperture closed again. He told me that he had made bold to look in at the hole, but could see neither coffin nor bones; nothing but dust. It was something, I thought, to have seen the dust of Shakespeare.

Next to this grave are those of his wife, his favorite daughter, Mrs. Hall, and others of his family. On a tomb close by, also, is a full-length effigy of his old friend John Combe of usurious memory; on whom he is said to have written a ludicrous epitaph. There are other monuments around, but the mind refuses to dwell on any thing that is not connected with Shakespeare. His idea pervades the place; the whole pile seems but as his mausoleum. The feelings, no longer checked and thwarted by doubt, here indulge in perfect confidence:

other traces of him may be false or dubious, but here is palpable evidence and absolute certainty. As I trod the sounding pavement, there was something intense and thrilling in the idea, that, in very truth, the remains of Shakespeare were mouldering beneath my feet. It was a long time before I could prevail upon myself to leave the place; and as I passed through the churchyard, I plucked a branch from one of the yew trees, the only relic that I have brought from Stratford.

I had now visited the usual objects of a pilgrim's devotion, but I had a desire to see the old family seat of the Lucy's, at Charlecot, and to ramble through the park where Shakespeare, in company with some of the roysters of Stratford, committed his youthful offence of deer-stealing. In this hare-brained exploit we are told that he was taken prisoner, and carried to the keeper's lodge, where he remained all night in doleful captivity. When brought into the presence of Sir Thomas Lucy, his treatment must have been galling and humilating; for it so wrought upon his spirit as to produce a rough pasquinade, which was affixed to the park gate at Charlecot.*

This flagitious attack upon the dignity of the knight so incensed him, that he applied to a lawyer at Warwick to put the severity of the laws in force against the rhyming deerstalker. Shakespeare did not wait to brave the united puissance of a knight of the shire and a country

---

*The following is the only stanza extant of this lampoon:—

> A parliament member, a justice of peace,
> At home a poor scarecrow, at London an asse,
> If lowsie is Lucy, as some volke miscalle it,
> Then Lucy is lowsie, whatever befall it.
>   He thinks himself great;
>   Yet an asse in his state,
> We allow by his ears but with asses to mate,
> If Lucy is lowsie, as some volke miscalle it,
> Then sing lowsie Lucy whatever befall it.

attorney. He forthwith abandoned the pleasant banks of the Avon and his paternal trade; wandered away to London; became a hanger-on to the theatres; then an actor; and, finally, wrote for the stage; and thus, through the persecution of Sir Thomas Lucy, Stratford lost an indifferent wool-comber, and the world gained an immortal poet. He retained, however, for a long time, a sense of the harsh treatment of the Lord of Charlecot, and revenged himself in his writings; but in the sportive way of a good-natured mind. Sir Thomas is said to be the original Justice Shallow, and the satire is slyly fixed upon him by the justice's armorial bearings, which, like those of the knight, had white luces* in the quarterings.

Various attempts have been made by his biographers to soften and explain away this early transgression of the poet; but I look upon it as one of those thoughtless exploits natural to his situation and turn of mind. Shakespeare, when young, had doubtless all the wildness and irregularity of an ardent, undisciplined, and undirected genius. The poetic temperament has naturally something in it of the vagabond. When left to itself it runs loosely and wildly, and delights in every thing eccentric and licentious. It is often a turn-up of a die, in the gambling freaks of fate, whether a natural genius shall turn out a great rogue or a great poet; and had not Shakespeare's mind fortunately taken a literary bias, he might have as daringly transcended all civil, as he has all dramatic laws.

I have little doubt that, in early life, when running, like an unbroken colt, about the neighborhood of Stratford, he was to be found in the company of all kinds of odd, anomalous characters; that he associated

*The luce is a pike or jack, and abounds in the Avon about Charlecot.

with all the madcaps of the place, and was one of those
unlucky urchins, at mention of whom old men shake
their heads, and predict that they will one day come to
the gallows. To him the poaching in Sir Thomas Lucy's
park was doubtless like a foray to a Scottish knight, and
struck his eager, and, as yet untamed, imagination, as
something delightfully adventurous.*

The old mansion of Charlecot and its surrounding
park still remain in the possession of the Lucy family,
and are peculiarly interesting, from being connected
with this whimsical but eventful circumstance in the
scanty history of the bard. As the house stood but little
more than three miles' distance from Stratford, I

*A proof of Shakespeare's random habits and associates in his
youthful days may be found in a traditionary anecdote, picked up at
Stratford by the elder Ireland, and mentioned in his "Picturesque
Views on the Avon."

About seven miles from Stratford lies the thirsty little market town
of Bedford, famous for its ale. Two societies of the village yeomanry
used to meet, under the appellation of the Bedford topers, and to
challenge the lovers of good ale of the neighboring villages to a contest
of drinking. Among others, the people of Stratford were called out to
prove the strength of their heads; and in the number of the champions
was Shakespeare, who, in spite of the proverb that "they who drink
beer will think beer," was as true to his ale as Falstaff to his sack. The
chivalry of Stratford was staggered at the first onset, and sounded a
retreat while they had yet legs to carry them off the field. They had
scarcely marched a mile when, their legs failing them, they were
forced to lie down under a crab-tree, where they passed the night. It is
still standing, and goes by the name of Shakespeare's tree.

In the morning his companions awaked the bard, and proposed
returning to Bedford, but he declined, saying he had had enough,
having drank with

> Piping Pebworth, Dancing Marston,
> Haunted Hilbro', Hungry Grafton,
> Dudging Exhall, Papist Wicksford,
> Beggarly Broom, and Drunken Bedford.

"The villages here alluded to," says Ireland, "still bear the epithets
thus given them: the people of Pebworth are still famed for their skill
on the pipe and tabor; Hilborough is now called Haunted Hilborough;
and Grafton is famous for the poverty of its soil."

resolved to pay it a pedestrian visit, that I might stroll leisurely through some of those scenes from which Shakespeare must have derived his earliest ideas of rural imagery.

The country was yet naked and leafless; but English scenery is always verdant, and the sudden change in the temperature of the weather was surprising in its quickening effects upon the landscape. It was inspiring and animating to witness this first awakening of spring; to feel its warm breath stealing over the senses; to see the moist mellow earth beginning to put forth the green sprout and the tender blade; and the trees and shrubs, in their reviving tints and bursting buds, giving the promise of returning foliage and flower. The cold snowdrop, that little borderer on the skirts of winter, was to be seen with its chaste white blossoms in the small gardens before the cottages. The bleating of the newdropt lambs was faintly heard from the fields. The sparrow twittered about the thatched eaves and budding hedges; the robin threw a livelier note into his late querulous wintry strain; and the lark, springing up from the reeking bosom of the meadow, towered away into the bright fleecy cloud, pouring forth torrents of melody. As I watched the little songster, mounting up higher and higher, until his body was a mere speck on the white bosom of the cloud, while the ear was still filled with his music, it called to mind Shakespeare's exquisite little song in *Cymbeline*:

> Hark! hark! the lark at heaven's gate sings,
>   And Phœbus 'gins arise,
> His steeds to water at those springs,
>   On chaliced flowers that lies.
>
> And winking mary-buds begin
>   To ope their golden eyes;
> With every thing that pretty bin,
>   My lady sweet arise!

Indeed the whole country about here is poetic ground: every thing is associated with the idea of Shakespeare. Every old cottage that I saw, I fancied into some resort of his boyhood, where he had acquired his intimate knowledge of rustic life and manners, and heard those legendary tales and wild superstitions which he has woven like witchcraft into his dramas. For in his time, we are told, it was a popular amusement in winter evenings "to sit round the fire, and tell merry tales of errant knights, queens, lovers, lords, ladies, giants, dwarfs, thieves, cheaters, witches, fairies, goblins, and friars."*

My route for a part of the way lay in sight of the Avon, which made a variety of the most fancy doublings and windings through a wide and fertile valley; sometimes glittering from among willows, which fringed its borders; sometimes disappearing among groves, or beneath green banks; and sometimes rambling out into full view, and making an azure sweep round a slope of meadow land. This beautiful bosom of country is called the Vale of the Red Horse. A distant line of undulating blue hills seems to be its boundary, whilst all the soft intervening landscape lies in a manner enchained in the silver links of the Avon.

After pursuing the road for about three miles, I turned off into a footpath, which led along the borders of fields, and under hedgerows to a private gate of the park; there was a stile, however, for the benefit of the pedestrian; there being a public right of way through

---

*Scott, in his "Discoverie of Witchcraft," enumerates a host of these fireside fancies. "And they have so fraid us with bull-beggars, spirits, witches, urchins, elves, hags, fairies, satyrs, pans, faunes, syrens, kit with the can sticke, tritons, centaurs, dwarfes, giantes, imps, calcars, conjurors, nymphes, changelings, incubus, Robin-good-fellow, the spoorne, the mare, the man in the oke, the hell-waine, the fier drake, the puckle, Tom Thombe, hobgoblins, Tom Tumbler, boneless, and such other bugs, that we were afraid of our own shadowes."

the grounds. I delight in these hospitable estates, in which every one has a kind of property—at least as far as the footpath is concerned. It in some measure reconciles a poor man to his lot, and, what is more, to the better lot of his neighbor, thus to have parks and pleasure-grounds thrown open for his recreation. He breathes the pure air as freely, and lolls as luxuriously under the shade, as the lord of the soil; and if he has not the privilege of calling all that he sees his own, he has not, at the same time, the trouble of paying for it, and keeping it in order.

I now found myself among noble avenues of oaks and elms, whose vast size bespoke the growth of centuries. The wind sounded solemnly among their branches, and the rooks cawed from their hereditary nests in the tree tops. The eye ranged through a long lessening vista, with nothing to interrupt the view but a distant statue; and a vagrant deer stalking like a shadow across the opening.

There is something about these stately old avenues that has the effect of Gothic architecture, not merely from the pretended similarity of form, but from their bearing the evidence of long duration, and of having had their origin in a period of time with which we associate ideas of romantic grandeur. They betoken also the long-settled dignity, and proudly-concentrated independence of an ancient family; and I have heard a worthy but aristocratic old friend observe, when speaking of the sumptuous palaces of modern gentry, that "money could do much with stone and mortar, but, thank Heaven, there was no such thing as suddenly building up an avenue of oaks."

It was from wandering in early life among this rich scenery, and about the romantic solitudes of the ad-

joining park of Fullbroke, which then formed a part of
the Lucy estate, that some of Shakespeare's commentators have supposed he derived his noble forest meditations of Jaques, and the enchanting woodland pictures
in *As You Like It*. It is in lonely wanderings through
such scenes, that the mind drinks deep but quiet
draughts of inspiration, and becomes intensely sensible of the beauty and majesty of nature. The imagination kindles into reverie and rapture; vague but exquisite images and ideas keep breaking upon it; and we
revel in a mute and almost incommunicable luxury of
thought. It was in some such mood, and perhaps under
one of those very trees before me, which threw their
broad shades over the grassy banks and quivering
waters of the Avon, that the poet's fancy may have sallied
forth into that little song which breathes the very soul of
a rural voluptuary:

> Under the green wood tree,
> Who loves to lie with me,
> And tune his merry throat
> Unto the sweet bird's note,
> Come hither, come hither, come hither.
> Here shall he see
> No enemy,
> But winter and rough weather.

I had now come in sight of the house. It is a large
building of brick, with stone quoins, and is in the Gothic
style of Queen Elizabeth's day, having been built in the
first year of her reign. The exterior remains very nearly
in its original state, and may be considered a fair
specimen of the residence of a wealthy country gentleman of those days. A great gateway opens from the park
into a kind of courtyard in front of the house, ornamented with a grass-plot, shrubs, and flower-beds. The
gateway is in imitation of the ancient barbacan; being a

kind of outpost, and flanked by towers; though evidently for mere ornament, instead of defence. The front of the house is completely in the old style; with stone-shafted casements, a great bow-window of heavy stone-work, and a portal with armorial bearings over it, carved in stone. At each corner of the building is an octagon tower, surmounted by a gilt ball and weather-cock.

The Avon, which winds through the park, makes a bend just at the foot of a gently-sloping bank, which sweeps down from the rear of the house. Large herds of deer were feeding or reposing upon its borders; and swans were sailing majestically upon its bosom. As I contemplated the venerable old mansion, I called to mind Falstaff's encomium on Justice Shallow's abode, and the affected indifference and real vanity of the latter:

"*Falstaff.* You have a goodly dwelling and a rich.
Shallow. Barren, barren, barren; beggars all, beggars all, Sir John! Marry, good air."

What have may have been the joviality of the old mansion in the days of Shakespeare, it had now an air of stillness and solitude. The great iron gateway that opened into the courtyard was locked; there was no show of servants bustling about the place; the deer gazed quietly at me as I passed, being no longer harried by the moss-troopers of Stratford. The only sign of domestic life that I met with was a white cat, stealing with wary look and stealthy pace towards the stables, as if on some nefarious expedition. I must not omit to mention the carcass of a scoundrel crow which I saw suspended against the barn wall, as it shows that the Lucys still inherit that lordly abhorrence of poachers, and maintain that rigorous exercise of territorial power which was so strenuously manifested in the case of the bard.

After prowling about for some time, I at length found my way to a lateral portal, which was the everyday entrance to the mansion. I was courteously received by a worthy old housekeeper, who, with the civility and comunicativeness of her order, showed me the interior of the house. The greater part has undergone alterations, and been adapted to modern tastes and modes of living: there is a fine old oaken staircase; and the great hall, that noble feature in an ancient manor-house, still retains much of the appearance it must have had in the days of Shakespeare. The ceiling is arched and lofty; and at one end is a gallery in which stands an organ. The weapons and trophies of the chase, which formerly adorned the hall of a country gentleman, have made way for family portraits. There is a wide hospitable fireplace, calculated for an ample old-fashioned wood fire, formerly the rallying-place of winter festivity. On the opposite side of the hall is the huge Gothic bow-window, with stone shafts, which looks out upon the courtyard. Here are emblazoned in stained glass the armorial bearings of the Lucy family for many generations, some being dated in 1558. I was delighted to observe in the quarterings the three *white luces*, by which the character of Sir Thomas was first identified with that of Justice Shallow. They are mentioned in the first scene of the *Merry Wives of Windsor*, where the Justice is in a rage with Falstaff for having "beaten his men, killed his deer, and broken into his lodge." The poet had no doubt the offences of himself and his comrades in mind at the time, and we may suppose the family pride and vindictive threats of the puissant Shallow to be a caricature of the pompous indignation of Sir Thomas.

"*Shallow.* Sir Hugh, persuade me not: I will make a Star-Chamber matter of it; if he were twenty John Falstaffs, he shall not abuse Sir Robert Shallow, Esq.

Slender. In the county of Gloster, justice of peace, and *coram.*

Shallow. Ay, cousin Slender, and *custalorum.*

Slender. Ay, and *ratalorum* too, and a gentleman born, master parson; who writes himself *Armigero* in any bill, warrant, quittance, or obligation, *Armigero.*

Shallow. Ay, that I do; and have done any time these three hundred years.

Slender. All his successors gone before him have done't, and all his ancestors that come after him may; they may give the dozen *white luces* in their coat. * * * * *

Shallow. The council shall hear it; it is a riot.

Evans. It is not meet the council hear of a riot; there is no fear of Got in a riot; the council, hear you, shall desire to hear the fear of Got, and not to hear a riot; take your vizaments in that.

Shallow. Ha! o' my life, if I were young again, the sword should end it!"

Near the window thus emblazoned hung a portrait by Sir Peter Lely, of one of the Lucy family, a great beauty of the time of Charles the Second; the old housekeeper shook her head as she pointed to the picture, and informed me that this lady had been sadly addicted to cards, and had gambled away a great portion of the family estate, among which was that part of the park where Shakespeare and his comrades had killed the deer. The lands thus lost had not been entirely regained by the family even at the present day. It is but justice to this recreant dame to confess that she had a surpassingly fine hand and arm.

The picture which most attracted my attention was a great painting over the fireplace, containing likenesses of Sir Thomas Lucy and his family, who inhabited the hall in the latter part of Shakespeare's lifetime. I at first thought that it was the vindictive knight himself, but the housekeeper assured me that it was his son; the only likeness extant of the former being an effigy upon his tomb in the church of the neighboring hamlet of Charlecot.* The picture gives a lively idea of the costume and manners of the time. Sir Thomas is dressed in ruff and doublet; white shoes with roses in them; and has a peaked yellow, or, as Master Slender would say, "a cane-colored beard." His lady is seated on the opposite side of the picture, in wide ruff and long stomacher, and the children have a most venerable stiffness and formality of dress. Hounds and spaniels are mingled in the family group; a hawk is seated on his perch in the foreground, and one of the children holds a bow;—all intimating the knight's skill in hunting, hawking, and archery—so indispensable to an accomplished gentleman in those days.†

*This effigy is in white marble, and represents the Knight in complete armor. Near him lies the effigy of his wife, and on her tomb is the following inscription; which, if really composed by her husband, places him quite above the intellectual level of Master Shallow:

Here lyeth the Lady Joyce Lucy wife of Sr Thomas Lucy of Charlecot in ye county of Warwick, Knight, Daughter and heir of Thomas Acton of Sutton in ye county of Worcester Esquire who departed out of this wretched world to her heavenly kingdom ye 10 day of February in ye yeare of our Lord God 1595 and of her age 60 and three. All the time of her lyfe a true and faythful servant of her good God, never detected of any cryme or vice. In religion most sounde, in love to her husband most faythful and true. In friendship most constant; to what in trust was committed unto her most secret. In wisdom excelling. In governing of her house, bringing up of youth in ye fear of God that did converse with her moste rare and singular. A great maintayner of hospitality. Greatly esteemed of her betters; misliked of none unless of the envyous. When all is spoken that can be saide a woman so garnished with virtue as not to be bettered and hardly to be equalled by any. As shee lived most virtuously so shee died most Godly. Set downe by him yt best did knowe what hath byn written to be true.

                                        Thomas Lucye

†Bishop Earle, speaking of the country gentleman of his time, observes, "his housekeeping is seen much in the different families of dogs, and serving-men attendant on their kennels; and the deepness of their throats is the depth of his discourse. A hawk he esteems the

I regretted to find that the ancient furniture of the hall had disappeared; for I had hoped to meet with the stately elbow-chair of carved oak, in which the country squire of former days was wont to sway the sceptre of empire over his rural domains; and in which it might be presumed the redoubted Sir Thomas sat enthroned in awful state when the recreant Shakespeare was brought before him. As I like to deck out pictures for my own entertainment, I pleased myself with the idea that this very hall had been the scene of the unlucky bard's examination on the morning after his captivity in the lodge. I fancied to myself the rural potentate, surrounded by his body-guard of butler, pages, and blue-coated serving-men, with their badges; while the luckless culprit was brought in, forlorn and chopfallen, in the custody of gamekeepers, huntsmen, and whippers-in, and followed by a rabble rout of country clowns. I fancied bright faces of curious housemaids peeping from the half-opened doors; while from the gallery the fair daughters of the knight leaned gracefully forward, eyeing the youthful prisoner with that pity "that dwells in womanhood." Who would have thought that this poor varlet, thus trembling before the brief authority of a country squire, and the sport of rustic boors, was soon to become the delight of princes, the theme of all tongues and ages, the dictator to the human mind, and was to confer immortality on his oppressor by a caricature and a lampoon!

---

true burden of nobility, and is exceedingly ambitious to seem delighted with the sport, and have his fist gloved with his jesses." And Gilpin, in his description of a Mr. Hastings, remarks, "he kept all sorts of hounds that ran buck, fox, hare, otter, and badger; and had hawks of all kinds both long and short winged. His great hall was commonly strewed with marrow-bones, and full of hawk perches, hounds, spaniels, and terriers. On a broad hearth, paved with brick, lay some of the choicest terriers, hounds, and spaniels."

I was now invited by the butler to walk into the garden, and I felt inclined to visit the orchard and arbor where the justice treated Sir John Falstaff and Cousin Silence "to a last year's pippin of his own grafting, with a dish of caraways;" but I had already spent so much of the day in my ramblings that I was obliged to give up any further investigations. When about to take my leave I was gratified by the civil entreaties of the housekeeper and butler, that I would take some refreshment: an instance of good old hospitality which, I grieve to say, we castle-hunters seldom meet with in modern days. I make no doubt it is a virtue which the present representative of the Lucy's inherits from his ancestors; for Shakespeare, even in his caricature, makes Justice Shallow importunate in this respect, as witness his pressing instances to Falstaff.

"By cock and pye, sir, you shall not away to-night * * * I will not excuse you; you shall not be excused; excuses shall not be admitted; there is no excuse shall serve; you shall not be excused * * *. Some pigeons, Davy; a couple of short-legged hens; a joint of mutton; and any pretty little tiny kickshaws, tell William Cook."

I now bade a reluctant farewell to the old hall. My mind had become so completely possessed by the imaginary scenes and characters connected with it, that I seemed to be actually living among them. Everything brought them as it were before my eyes; and as the door of the dining-room opened, I almost expected to hear the feeble voice of Master Silence quavering forth his favorite ditty:

"'Tis merry in hall, when beards wag all,
And welcome merry shrove-tide!"

On returning to my inn, I could not but reflect on the singular gift of the poet; to be able thus to spread the magic of his mind over the very face of nature; to give to things and places a charm and character not their own, and to turn this "working-day world" into a perfect fairy land. He is indeed the true enchanter, whose spell operates, not upon the senses, but upon the imagination and the heart. Under the wizard influence of Shakespeare I had been walking all day in a complete delusion. I had surveyed the landscape through the prism of poetry, which tinged every object with the hues of the rainbow. I had been surrounded with fancied beings; with mere airy nothings, conjured up by poetic power; yet which, to me, had all the charm of reality. I had heard Jaques soliloquize beneath his oak; had beheld the fair Rosalind and her companion adventuring through the woodlands; and, above all, had been once more present in spirit with fat Jack Falstaff and his contemporaries, from the august Justice Shallow, down to the gentle Master Slender and the sweet Anne Page. Ten thousand honors and blessings on the bard who has thus gilded the dull realities of life with innocent illusions; who has spread exquisite and unbought pleasures in my chequered path; and beguiled my cheerful sympathies of social life!

As I crossed the bridge over the Avon on my return, I paused to contemplate the distant church in which the poet lies buried, and could not but exult in the malediction, which has kept his ashes undisturbed in its quiet and hallowed vaults. What honor could his name have derived from being mingled in dusty companionship with the epitaphs and escutcheons and venal eulogiums of a titled multitude? What would a crowded corner in Westminster Abbey have been, compared with this reverend pile, which seems to stand in beautiful loneliness as his sole mausoleum! The solicitude about the grave may be but the offspring of an over-wrought sensibility; but human nature is made up of foibles and prejudices; and its best and tenderest affections are mingled with these factitious feelings. He who has sought renown about the world, and has reaped a full harvest of worldly favor, will find, after all, that there is no love, no admiration, no applause, so sweet to the soul as that which springs up in his native place. It is there that he seeks to be gathered in peace and honor among his kindred and his early friends. And when the weary heart and failing head begin to warn him that the evening of life is drawing on, he turns as fondly as does the infant to the mother's arms, to sink to sleep in the bosom of the scene of his childhood.

How would it have cheered the spirit of the youthful bard when, wandering forth in disgrace upon a doubtful world, he cast back a heavy look upon his paternal home, could he have foreseen that, before many years, he should return to it covered with renown; that his name should become the boast and glory of his native place; that his ashes should be religiously guarded as its most precious treasure; and that its lessening spire, on which his eyes were fixed in tearful contemplation, should one day become the beacon, towering amidst the gentle landscape, to guide the literary pilgrim of every nation to his tomb!

TRAITS OF INDIAN CHARACTER

"I appeal to any white man if ever he entered Logan's cabin hungry, and he gave him not to eat; if ever he came cold and naked, and he clothed him not."

SPEECH OF AN INDIAN CHIEF

THERE IS something in the character and habits of the North American savage, taken in connection with the scenery over which he is accustomed to range, its vast lakes, boundless forests, majestic rivers, and trackless plains, that is, to my mind, wonderfully striking and sublime. He is formed for the wilderness, as the Arab is for the desert. His nature is stern, simple, and enduring; fitted to grapple with difficulties, and to support privations. There seems but little soil in his heart for the support of the kindly virtues; and yet, if we would but take the trouble to penetrate through that proud stoicism and habitual taciturnity, which lock up his character from casual observation, we should find him linked to his fellow-man of civilized life by more of those sympathies and affections than are usually ascribed to him.

It has been the lot of the unfortunate aborigines of America, in the early periods of colonization, to be doubly wronged by the white men. They have been dispossessed of their hereditary possessions by mercenary and frequently wanton warfare, and their characters have been traduced by bigoted and interested writers. The colonist often treated them like beasts of the forest; and the author has endeavored to justify him in his outrages. The former found it easier to exterminate than to civilize; the latter to vilify than to discriminate. The appellations of savage and pagan were

299

deemed sufficient to sanction the hostilities of both; and thus the poor wanderers of the forest were persecuted and defamed, not because they were guilty, but because they were ignorant.

The rights of the savage have seldom been properly appreciated or respected by the white man. In peace he has too often been the dupe of artful traffic; in war he has been regarded as a ferocious animal, whose life or death was a question of mere precaution and convenience. Man is cruelly wasteful of life when his own safety is endangered, and he is sheltered by impunity; and little mercy is to be expected from him, when he feels the sting of the reptile and is conscious of the power to destroy.

The same prejudices, which were indulged thus early, exist in common circulation at the present day. Certain learned societies have, it is true, with laudable diligence, endeavored to investigate and record the real characters and manners of the Indian tribes; the American government, too, has wisely and humanely exerted itself to inculcate a friendly and forbearing spirit towards them, and to protect them from fraud and injustice.* The current opinion of the Indian character, however, is too apt to be formed from the miserable hordes which infest the frontiers, and hang on the skirts of the settlements. These are too commonly composed of degenerate beings, corrupted and enfeebled by the vices of society, without being benefited by its civilization. That proud independence, which formed the main pillar of savage

*The American government has been indefatigable in its exertions to ameliorate the situation of the Indians, and to introduce among them the arts of civilization, and civil and religious knowledge. To protect them from the frauds of the white traders, no purchase of land from them by individuals is permitted; nor is any person allowed to receive lands from them as a present, without the express sanction of government. These precautions are strictly enforced.

virtue, has been shaken down, and the whole moral fabric lies in ruins. Their spirits are humiliated and debased by a sense of inferiority, and their native courage cowed and daunted by the superior knowledge and power of their enlightened neighbors. Society has advanced upon them like one of those withering airs that will sometimes breed desolation over a whole region of fertility. It has enervated their strength, multiplied their diseases, and superinduced upon their original barbarity the low vices of artificial life. It has given them a thousand superfluous wants, whilst it has diminished their means of mere existence. It has driven before it the animals of the chase, who fly from the sound of the axe and the smoke of the settlement, and seek refuge in the depths of remoter forests and yet untrodden wilds. Thus do we too often find the Indians on our frontiers to be the mere wrecks and remnants of once powerful tribes, who have lingered in the vicinity of the settlements, and sunk into precarious and vagabond existence. Poverty, repining and hopeless poverty, a canker of the mind unknown in savage life, corrodes their spirits, and blights every free and noble quality of their natures. They become drunken, indolent, feeble, thievish, and pusillanimous. They loiter like vagrants about the settlements, among spacious dwellings replete with elaborate comforts, which only render them sensible of the comparative wretchedness of their own condition. Luxury spreads its ample board before their eyes; but they are excluded from the banquet. Plenty revels over the fields; but they are starving in the midst of its abundance; the whole wilderness has blossomed into a garden; but they feel as reptiles that infest it.

How different was their state while yet the undisputed lords of the soil! Their wants were few, and the means of gratification within their reach. They saw every one around them sharing the same lot, enduring the same hardships, feeding on the same aliments, arrayed in the same rude garments. No roof then rose, but was open to the homeless stranger; no smoke curled among the trees, but he was welcome to sit down by its fire, and join the hunter in his repast. "For," says an old historian of New England, "their life is so void of care, and they are so loving also, that they make use of those things they enjoy as common goods, and are therein so compassionate, that rather than one should starve through want, they would starve all; thus they pass their time merrily, not regarding our pomp, but are better content with their own, which some men esteem so meanly of." Such were the Indians, whilst in the pride and energy of their primitive natures: they resembled those wild plants, which thrive best in the shades of the forest, but shrink from the hand of cultivation, and perish beneath the influence of the sun.

In discussing the savage character, writers have been too prone to indulge in vulgar prejudice and passionate exaggeration, instead of the candid temper of true philosophy. They have not sufficiently considered the peculiar circumstances in which the Indians have been placed, and the peculiar principles under which they have been educated. No being acts more rigidly from rule than the Indian. His whole conduct is regulated according to some general maxims early implanted in his mind. The moral laws that govern him are, to be sure, but few; but then he conforms to them all;—the white man abounds in laws of religion, morals, and manners, but how many does he violate?

A frequent ground of accusation against the Indians is their disregard of treaties, and the treachery and wantonness with which, in time of apparent peace, they will suddenly fly to hostilities. The intercourse of the white men with the Indians, however, is too apt to be cold, distrustful, oppressive, and insulting. They seldom treat them with that confidence and frankness which are indispensable to real friendship; nor is sufficient caution observed not to offend against those feelings of pride or superstition, which often prompts the Indian to hostility quicker than mere considerations of interest. The solitary savage feels silently, but acutely. His sensibilities are not diffused over so wide a surface as those of the white man; but they run in steadier and deeper channels. His pride, his affections, his superstitions, are all directed towards fewer objects; but the wounds inflicted on them are proportionably severe, and furnish motives of hostility which we cannot sufficiently appreciate. Where a community is also limited in number, and forms one great patriarchal family, as in an Indian tribe, the injury of an individual is the injury of the whole; and the sentiment of vengeance is almost instantaneously diffused. One council fire is sufficient for the discussion and arrangement of a plan of hostilities. Here all the fighting men and sages assemble. Eloquence and superstition combine to inflame the minds of the warriors. The orator awakens their martial ardor, and they are wrought up to a kind of religious desperation, by the visions of the prophet and the dreamer.

An instance of one of those sudden exasperations, arising from a motive peculiar to the Indian character, is extant in an old record of the early settlement of Massachusetts. The planters of Plymouth had defaced the monuments of the dead at Passonagessit, and had plundered the grave of the Sachem's mother of some skins with which it had been decorated. The Indians are remarkable for the reverence which they entertain for the sepulchres of their kindred. Tribes that have passed generations exiled from the abodes of their ancestors, when by chance they have been travelling in the vicinity, have been known to turn aside from the highway, and, guided by wonderfully accurate tradition, have crossed the country for miles to some tumulus, buried perhaps in woods, where the bones of their tribe were anciently deposited; and there have passed hours in silent meditation. Influenced by this sublime and holy feeling, the Sachem, whose mother's tomb had been violated, gathered his men together, and addressed them in the following beautifully simple and pathetic harangue; a curious specimen of Indian eloquence, and an affecting instance of filial piety in a savage.

"When last the glorious light of all the sky was underneath this globe, and birds grew silent, I began to settle, as my custom is, to take repose. Before mine eyes were fast closed, methought I saw a vision, at which my spirit was much troubled; and trembling at that doleful sight, a spirit cried aloud, 'Behold, my son, whom I have cherished, see the breasts that gave thee suck, the hands that lapped thee warm, and fed thee oft. Canst thou forget to take revenge of those wild people who have defaced my monument in a despiteful manner, disdaining our antiquities and honorable customs? See, now, the Sachem's grave lies like the common people, defaced by an ignoble race. Thy mother doth complain, and implores thy aid against this thievish people, who have newly intruded on our land. If this be suffered, I shall not rest quiet in my everlasting habitation.' This said, the spirit vanished, and I, all in a sweat, not able scarce to speak, began to get some strength, and recollect my spirits that were fled, and determined to demand your counsel and assistance."

I have adduced this anecdote at some length, as it tends to show how these sudden acts of hostility, which have been attributed to caprice and perfidy, may often arise from deep and generous motives, which our inattention to Indian character and customs prevents our properly appreciating.

Another ground of violent outcry against the Indians is their barbarity to the vanquished. This had its origin partly in policy and partly in superstition. The tribes, though sometimes called nations, were never so formidable in their numbers, but that the loss of several warriors was sensibly felt; this was particularly the case when they had been frequently engaged in warfare; and many an instance occurs in Indian history, where a tribe, that had long been formidable to its neighbors, has been broken up and driven away, by the capture and massacre of its principal fighting men. There was a strong temptation, therefore, to the victor to be merciless; not so much to gratify any cruel revenge, as to provide for future security. The Indians had also the superstitious belief, frequent among barbarous nations, and prevalent also among the ancients, that the manes of their friends who had fallen in battle were soothed by the blood of the captives. The prisoners, however, who are not thus sacrificed, are adopted into their families in the place of the slain, and are treated with the confidence and affection of relatives and friends; nay, so hospitable and tender is their entertainment, that when the alternative is offered them, they will often prefer to remain with their adopted brethren, rather than return to the home and the friends of their youth.

The cruelty of the Indians towards their prisoners has been heightened since the colonization of the whites. What was formerly a compliance with policy and superstition, has been exasperated into a gratification of vengeance. They cannot but be sensible that the white men are the usurpers of their ancient dominion, the cause of their degradation, and the gradual destroyers of their race. They go forth to battle, smarting with injuries and indignities which they have individually suffered, and they are driven to madness and despair by the wide-spreading desolation, and the overwhelming ruin of European warfare. The whites have too frequently set them an example of violence, by burning their villages, and laying waste their slender means of subsistence, and yet they wonder that savages do not show moderation and magnanimity towards those who have left them nothing but mere existence and wretchedness.

We stigmatize the Indians, also, as cowardly and treacherous, because they use stratagem in warfare, in preference to open force; but in this they are fully justified by their rude code of honor. They are early taught that stratagem is praiseworthy; the bravest warrior thinks it no disgrace to lurk in silence, and take every advantage of his foe: he triumphs in the superior craft and sagacity by which he has been enabled to surprise and destroy an enemy. Indeed, man is naturally more prone to subtlety than open valor, owing to his physical weakness in comparison with other animals. They are endowed with natural weapons of defense: with horns, with tusks, with hoofs, and talons; but man has to depend on his superior sagacity. In all his encounters with these, his proper enemies, he resorts to stratagem; and when he perversely turns his hostility against his fellow-man, he at first continues the same subtle mode of warfare.

The natural principle of war is to do the most harm to our enemy with the least harm to ourselves; and this of course is to be effected by stratagem. That chivalrous courage which induces us to despise the suggestions of prudence, and to rush in the face of certain danger, is the offspring of society, and produced by education. It is honorable, because it is in fact the triumph of lofty sentiment over an instinctive repugnance to pain, and over those yearnings after personal ease and security, which society has condemned as ignoble. It is kept alive by pride and the fear of shame; and thus the dread of real evil is overcome by the superior dread of an evil which exists but in the imagination. It has been cherished and stimulated also by various means. It has been the theme of spirit-stirring song and chivalrous story. The poet and minstrel have delighted to shed round it the splendors of fiction; and even the historian has forgotten the sober gravity of narration, and broken forth into enthusiasm and rhapsody in its praise. Triumphs and gorgeous pageants have been its reward; monuments, on which art has exhausted its skill, and opulence its treasures, have been erected to perpetuate a nation's gratitude and admiration. Thus artificially excited, courage has risen to an extraordinary and factitious degree of heroism; and arrayed in all the glorious "pomp and circumstance of war," this turbulent quality has even been able to eclipse many of those quiet, but invaluable virtues, which silently ennoble the human character, and swell the tide of human happiness.

But if courage intrinsically consists in the defiance of danger and pain, the life of the Indian is a continual exhibition of it. He lives in a state of perpetual hostility and risk. Peril and adventure are congenial to his nature; or rather seem necessary to arouse his faculties and to give an interest to his existence. Surrounded by hostile tribes, whose mode of warfare is by ambush and surprisal, he is always prepared for fight, and lives with his weapons in his hands. As the ship careers in fearful singleness through the solitudes of ocean—as the bird mingles among clouds and storms, and wings its way, a mere speck, across the pathless fields of air—so the

Indian holds his course, silent, solitary, but undaunted, through the boundless bosom of the wilderness. His expeditions may vie in distance and danger with the pilgrimage of the devotee, or the crusade of the knight-errant. He traverses vast forests, exposed to the hazards of lonely sickness, of lurking enemies, and pining famine. Stormy lakes, those great inland seas, are no obstacles to his wanderings: in his light canoe of bark he sports, like a feather, on their waves, and darts, with the swiftness of an arrow, down the roaring rapids of the rivers. His very subsistence is snatched from the midst of toil and peril. He gains his food by the hardships and dangers of the chase; he wraps himself in the spoils of the bear, the panther, and the buffalo, and sleeps among the thunders of the cataract.

No hero of ancient or modern days can surpass the Indian in his lofty contempt of death, and the foritude with which he sustains its cruellest infliction. Indeed we here behold him rising superior to the white man, in consequence of his peculiar education. The latter rushes to glorious death at the cannon's mouth; the former calmly contemplates its approach, and triumphantly endures it, amidst the varied torments of surrounding foes and the protracted agonies of fire. He even takes a pride in taunting his persecutors, and provoking their ingenuity of torture; and as the devouring flames prey on his very vitals, and the flesh shrinks from the sinews, he raises his last song of triumph, breathing the defiance of an unconquered heart, and invoking the spirits of his fathers to witness that he died without a groan.

Notwithstanding the obloquy with which the early historians have overshadowed the characters of the unfortunate natives, some bright gleams occasionally break through, which throw a degree of melancholy lustre on their memories. Facts are occasionally to be met with in the rude annals of the eastern provinces, which, though recorded with the coloring of prejudice and bigotry, yet speak for themselves; and will be dwelt on with applause and sympathy, when prejudice shall have passed away.

In one of the homely narratives of the Indian wars in New England, there is a touching account of the desolation carried into the tribe of the Pequod Indians. Humanity shrinks from the cold-blooded detail of indiscriminate butchery. In one place we read of the surprisal of an Indian fort in the night, when the wigwams were wrapped in flames, and the miserable inhabitants shot down and slain in attempting to escape, "all being despatched and ended in the course of an hour." After a series of similar transactions, "our soldiers," as the historian piously observes, "being resolved by God's assistance to make a final destruction of them," the unhappy savages being hunted from their homes and fortresses, and pursued with fire and sword, a scanty, but gallant band, the sad remnant of the Pequod warriors, with their wives and children, took refuge in a swamp.

Burning with indignation, and rendered sullen by despair; with hearts bursting with grief at the destruction of their tribe, and spirits galled and sore at the fancied ignominy of their defeat, they refused to ask their lives at the hands of an insulting foe, and preferred death to submission.

As the night drew on they were surrounded in their dismal retreat, so as to render escape impracticable. Thus situated, their enemy "plied them with shot all the time, by which means many were killed and buried in the mire." In the darkness and fog that preceded the dawn of day some few broke through the besiegers and escaped into the woods; "the rest were left to the conquerors, of which many were killed in the swamp, like sullen dogs who would rather, in their self-willedness and madness, sit still and be shot through, or cut to pieces," than implore for mercy. When the day broke upon this handful of forlorn but dauntless spirits, the soldiers, we are told, entering the swamp, "saw several heaps of them sitting close together, upon whom they discharged their pieces, laden with ten or twelve pistol bullets at a time, putting the muzzles of the pieces under the boughs, within a few yards of them; so as, besides those that were found dead, many more were killed and sunk into the mire, and never were minded more by friend or foe."

Can any one read this plain unvarnished tale, without admiring the stern resolution, the unbending pride, the loftiness of spirit, that seemed to nerve the hearts of these self-taught heroes, and to raise them above the instinctive feelings of human nature? When the Gauls laid waste the city of Rome, they found the senators clothed in their robes, and seated with stern tranquillity in their curule chairs; in this manner they suffered death without resistance or even supplication. Such conduct was, in them, applauded as noble and magnanimous; in the hapless Indian it was reviled as obstinate and sullen! How truly are we the dupes of show and circumstance! How different is virtue, clothed in purple and enthroned in state, from virtue, naked and destitute, and perishing obscurely in a wilderness!

But I forbear to dwell on these gloomy pictures. The eastern tribes have long since disappeared; the forests that sheltered them have been laid low, and scarce any traces remain of them in the thickly-settled states of New England, excepting here and there the Indian name of a village or a stream. And such must, sooner or later, be the fate of those other tribes which skirt the frontiers, and have occasionally been inveigled from their forests to mingle in the wars of white men. In a little while, and they will go the way that their brethren have gone before. The few hordes which still linger about the shores of Huron and Superior, and the tributary streams of the Mississippi, will share the fate of those tribes that once spread over Massachusetts and Connecticut, and lorded it along the proud banks of the Hudson; of that gigantic race said to have existed on the borders of the Susquehanna; and of those various nations that flourished about the Potomac and the Rappahannock, and that peopled the forests of the vast valley of Shenandoah. They will vanish like a vapor from the face of the earth; their very history will be lost in forgetfulness; and "the places that now know them will know them no more for ever." Or if, perchance, some dubious memorial of them should survive, it may be in the romantic dreams of the poet, to people in imagination his glades and groves, like the fauns and satyrs and sylvan deities of antiquity. But should he venture upon the dark story of their wrongs and wretchedness; should he tell how they were invaded, corrupted, despoiled, driven from their native abodes and the sepulchres of their fathers, hunted like wild beasts about the earth, and sent down with violence and butchery to the grave, posterity will either turn with horror and incredulity from the tale, or blush with indignation at the inhumanity of their forefathers. "We are driven back," said an old warrior, "until we can retreat no farther—our hatchets are broken, our bows are snapped, our fires are nearly extinguished—a little longer, and the white man will cease to persecute us—for we shall cease to exist!"

PHILIP OF POKANOKET

AN INDIAN MEMOIR

As monumental bronze unchanged his look:
A soul that pity touch'd, but never shook:
Train'd from his tree-rock'd cradle to his bier
The fierce extremes of good and ill to brook
Impassive—fearing but the shame of fear—
A stoic of the woods—a man without a tear.

CAMPBELL

IT IS TO BE regretted that those early writers, who treated of the discovery and settlement of America, have not given us more particular and candid accounts of the remarkable characters that flourished in savage life. The scanty anecdotes which have reached us are full of peculiarity and interest; they furnish us with nearer glimpses of human nature, and show what man is in a comparatively primitive state, and what he owes to civilization. There is something of the charm of discovery in lighting upon these wild and unexplored tracts of human nature; in witnessing, as it were, the native growth of moral sentiment, and perceiving those generous and romantic qualities which have been artificially cultivated by society, vegetating in spontaneous hardihood and rude magnificence.

In civilized life, where the happiness, and indeed almost the existence, of man depends so much upon the opinion of his fellow-men, he is constantly acting a studied part. The bold and peculiar traits of native character are refined away, or softened down by the levelling influence of what is termed good-breeding; and he practises so many petty deceptions, and affects so many genereous sentiments, for the pupuses of popularity, that it is difficult to distinguish his real from his artificial character. The Indian, on the contrary, free from the restraints and refinements of polished life, and, in a great degree, a solitary and independent being, obeys the impulses of his inclination or the dictates of his judgment; and thus the attributes of his nature, being freely indulged, grow singly great and striking. Society is like a lawn, where every roughness is smoothed, every bramble eradicated, and where the eye is delighted by the smiling verdure of a velvet surface; he, however, who would study nature in its wildness and variety, must plunge into the forest, must explore the glen, must stem the torrent, and dare the precipice.

These reflections arose on casually looking through a volume of early colonial history, wherein are recorded, with great bitterness, the outrages of the Indians, and their wars with the settlers of New England. It is painful to perceive even from these partial narratives, how the footsteps of civilization may be traced in the blood of the aborigines; how easily the colonists were moved to hostility by the lust of conquest; how merciless and exterminating was their warfare. The imagination shrinks at the idea, how many intellectual beings were hunted from the earth, how many brave and noble hearts, of nature's sterling coinage, were broken down and trampled in the dust!

Such was the fate of PHILIP OF POKANOKET, an Indian warrior, whose name was once a terror throughout Massachusetts and Connecticut. He was the most distinguished of a number of contemporary Sachems who reigned over the Pequods, the Narragansets, the Wampanoags, and the other eastern tribes, at the time of the first settlement of New England; a band of native untaught heroes, who made the most generous struggle of which human nature is capable; fighting to the last gasp in the cause of their country, without a hope of victory or a thought of renown. Worthy of an age of poetry, and fit subjects for local story and romantic fiction, they have left scarcely any authentic traces on the page of history, but stalk, like gigantic shadows, in the dim twilight of tradition.*

When the pilgrims, as the Plymouth settlers are called by their descendants, first took refuge on the shores of the New World, from the religious persecutions of the Old, their situation was to the last degree gloomy and disheartening. Few in number, and that number rapidly perishing away through sickness and hardships; surrounded by a howling wilderness and savage tribes; exposed to the rigors of an almost arctic winter, and the vicissitudes of an ever-shifting climate; their minds were filled with doleful forebodings, and nothing preserved them from sinking into despondency but the strong excitement of religious enthusiasm. In this forlorn situation they were visited by Massasoit, chief Sagamore of the Wampanoags, a powerful chief, who reigned over a great extent of country. Instead of taking advantage of the scanty number of the strangers, and expelling them from his territories, into which they had intruded, he seemed at once to conceive for them a generous friendship, and extended towards them the rites of primitive hospitality. He came early in the spring to their settlement of New Plymouth, attended by a mere handful of followers, entered into a solemn league of peace and amity; sold them a portion of the soil, and promised to secure for them the good-will of his savage allies. Whatever may be said of Indian perfidy, it is certain that the integrity and good faith of Massasoit have never been impeached. He continued a firm and

*While correcting the proof sheets of this article, the author is informed that a celebrated English poet has nearly finished an heroic poem on the story of Philip of Pokanoket.

magnanimous friend of the white men; suffering them to extend their possessions, and to strengthen themselves in the land; and betraying no jealousy of their increasing power and prosperity. Shortly before his death he came once more to New Plymouth, with his son Alexander, for the purpose of renewing the covenant of peace, and of securing it to his posterity.

At this conference he endeavored to protect the religion of his forefathers from the encroaching zeal of the missionaries; and stipulated that no further attempt should be made to draw off his people from their ancient faith; but, finding the English obstinately opposed to any such condition, he mildly relinquished the demand. Almost the last act of his life was to bring his two sons, Alexander and Philip (as they had been named by the English), to the residence of a principal settler, recommending mutual kindness and confidence; and entreating that the same love and amity which had existed between the white men and himself might be continued afterwards with his children. The good old Sachem died in peace, and was happily gathered to his fathers before sorrow came upon his tribe; his children remained behind to experience the ingratitude of white men.

His eldest son, Alexander, succeeded him. He was of a quick and impetuous temper, and proudly tenacious of his hereditary rights and dignity. The intrusive policy and dictatorial conduct of the strangers excited his indignation; and he beheld with uneasiness their exterminating wars with the neighboring tribes. He was doomed soon to incur their hostility, being accused of plotting with the Narragansets to rise against the English and drive them from the land. It is impossible to say whether this accusation was warranted by facts or was grounded on mere suspicion. It is evident, however, by the violent and overbearing measures of the settlers, that they had by this time begun to feel conscious of the rapid increase of their power, and to grow harsh and inconsiderate in their treatment of the natives. They despatched an armed force to seize upon Alexander, and to bring him before their courts. He was traced to his woodland haunts, and surprised at a hunting house, where he was reposing with a band of his followers, unarmed, after the toils of the chase. The suddenness of his arrest, and the outrage offered to his sovereign dignity, so preyed upon the irascible feelings of this proud savage, as to throw him into a raging fever. He was permitted to return home, on condition of sending his son as a pledge for his reappearance; but the blow he had received was fatal, and before he had reached his home he fell a victim to the agonies of a wounded spirit.

The successor of Alexander was Metacomet, or King Philip, as he was called by the settlers, on account of his lofty spirit and ambitious temper. These, together with his well known energy and enterprise, had rendered him an object of great jealousy and apprehension, and he was accused of having always cherished a secret and implacable hostility towards the whites. Such may very probably, and very naturally, have been the case. He considered them as originally but mere intruders into the country, who had presumed upon indulgence, and were extending an influence baneful to savage life. He saw the whole race of his countrymen melting before them from the face of the earth; their territories slipping from their hands, and their tribes becoming feeble, scattered and dependent. It may be said that the soil was originally purchased by the settlers; but who does not know the nature of Indian purchases, in the early periods of colonization? The Europeans always made thrifty bargains through their superior adroitness in traffic; and they gained vast accessions of territory by easily provoked hostilities. An uncultivated savage is never a nice inquirer into the refinements of law, by which an injury may be gradually and legally inflicted. Leading facts are all by which he judges; and it was enough for Philip to know that before the intrusion of the Europeans his countrymen were lords of the soil, and that now they were becoming vagabonds in the land of their fathers.

But whatever may have been his feelings of general hostility, and his particular indignation at the treatment of his brother, he suppressed them for the present, renewed the contract with the settlers, and resided peaceably for many years at Pokanoket, or, as it was called by the English, Mount Hope,* the ancient seat of dominion of his tribe. Suspicions, however, which were at first but vague and indefinite, began to acquire form and substance; and he was at length charged with attempting to instigate the various Eastern tribes to rise at once, and, by a simultaneous effort, to throw off the yoke of their oppressors. It is difficult at this distant period to assign the proper credit due to these early accusations against the Indians. There was a proneness to suspicion, and an aptness to acts of violence, on the part of the whites, that gave weight and importance to every idle tale. Informers abounded where talebearing met with countenance and reward; and the sword was readily unsheathed when its success was certain, and it carved out empire.

The only positive evidence on record against Philip is the accusation of one Sausaman, a renegade Indian, whose natural cunning had been quickened by a partial education which he had received among the settlers. He changed his faith and his allegiance two or three times,

*Now Bristol, Rhode Island.

with a facility that evinced the looseness of his principles. He had acted for some time as Philip's confidential secretary and counsellor, and had enjoyed his bounty and protection. Finding, however, that the clouds of adversity were gathering round his patron, he abandoned his service and went over to the whites; and, in order to gain their favor, charged his former benefactor with plotting against their safety. A rigorous investigation took place. Philip and several of his subjects submitted to be examined, but nothing was proved against them. The settlers, however, had now gone too far to retract; they had previously determined that Philip was a dangerous neighbor; they had publicly evinced their distrust; and had done enough to insure his hostility; according, therefore, to the usual mode of reasoning in these cases, his destruction had become necessary to their security. Sausaman, the treacherous informer, was shortly afterwards found dead, in a pond, having fallen a victim to the vengeance of his tribe. Three Indians, one of whom was a friend and counsellor of Philip, were apprehended and tried, and, on the testimony of one very questionable witness, were condemned and executed as murderers.

This treatment of his subjects, and ignominious punishment of his friend, outraged the pride and exasperated the passions of Philip. The bolt which had fallen thus at his very feet awakened him to the gathering storm, and he determined to trust himself no longer in the power of the white men. The fate of his insulted and broken-hearted brother still rankled in his mind; and he had a further warning in the tragical story of Miantonimo, a great Sachem of the Narragansets, who, after manfully facing his accusers before a tribunal of the colonists, exculpating himself from a charge of conspiracy, and receiving assurances of amity, had been perfidiously despatched at their instigation. Philip, therefore, gathered his fighting men about him; persuaded all strangers that he could, to join his cause; sent the women and children to the Narragansets for safety; and wherever he appeared, was continually surrounded by armed warriors.

When the two parties were thus in a state of distrust and irritation, the least spark was sufficient to set them in a flame. The Indians, having weapons in their hands, grew mischievous, and committed various petty depredations. In one of their maraudings a warrior was fired on and killed by a settler. This was the signal for open hostilies; the Indians pressed to revenge the death of their comrade, and the alarm of war resounded through the Plymouth colony.

In the early chronicles of these dark and melancholy times we meet with many indications of the diseased state of the public mind. The gloom of religious abstraction, and the wildness of their situation, among trackless forests and savage tribes, had disposed the colonists to superstitious fancies, and had filled their imaginations with the frightful chimeras of witchcraft and spectrology. They were much given also to a belief in omens. The troubles with Philip and his Indians were preceded, we are told, by a variety of those awful warnings which forerun great and public calamities. The perfect form of an Indian bow appeared in the air at New Plymouth, which was looked upon by the inhabitants as a "prodigious apparition." At Hadley, Northampton, and other towns in their neighborhood, "was heard the report of a great piece of ordnance, with a shaking of the earth and a considerable echo."* Others where alarmed on a still, sunshiny morning by the discharge of guns and muskets; bullets seemed to

*The Rev. Increase Mather's *History.*

whistle past them, and the noise of drums resounded in the air, seeming to pass away to the westward; others fancied that they heard the galloping of horses over their heads; and certain monstrous births, which took place about the time, filled the superstitious in some towns with doleful forebodings. Many of these portentous sights and sounds may be ascribed to natural phenomena: to the northern lights which occur vividly in those latitudes; the meteors which explode in the air; the casual rushing of a blast through the top branches of the forest; the crash of fallen trees or disrupted rocks; and to those other uncouth sounds and echoes which will sometimes strike the ear so strangely amidst the profound stillness of woodland solitudes. These may have startled some melancholy imaginations, may have been exaggerated by the love for the marvellous, and listened to with that avidity with which we devour whatever is fearful and mysterious. The universal currency of these superstitious fancies, and the grave record made of them by one of the learned men of the day, are strongly characteristic of the times.

The nature of the contest that ensued was such as too often distinguishes the warfare between civilized men and savages. On the part of the whites it was conducted with superior skill and success; but with a wastefulness of the blood, and a disregard of the natural rights of their antagonists; on the part of the Indians it was waged with the desperation of men fearless of death, and who had nothing to expect from peace, but humiliation, dependence, and decay.

The events of the war are transmitted to us by a worthy clergyman of the time; who dwells with horror and indignation on every hostile act of the Indians, however justifiable, whilst he mentions with applause the most sanguinary atrocities of the whites. Philip is reviled as a murderer and a traitor; without considering that he was a true born prince, gallantly fighting at the head of his subjects to avenge the wrongs of his family; to retrieve the tottering power of his line; and to deliver his native land from the oppression of usurping strangers.

The project of a wide and simultaneous revolt, if such had really been formed, was worthy of a capacious mind, and, had it not been prematurely discovered, might have been overwhelming in its consequences. The war that actually broke out was but a war of detail, a mere succession of casual exploits and unconnected enterprises. Still it sets forth the military genius and daring prowess of Philip; and wherever, in the prejudiced and passionate narrations that have been given of it, we can arrive at simple facts, we find him displaying a vigorous mind, a fertility of expedients, a contempt of suffering and hardship, and an unconquerable resolution, that command our sympathy and applause.

Driven from his paternal domains of Mount Hope, he threw himself into the depths of those vast and trackless forests that skirted the settlements, and were almost impervious to any thing but a wild beast, or an Indian. Here he gathered together his forces, like the storm accumulating its stores of mischief in the bosom of the thunder cloud, and would suddenly emerge at a time and place least expected, carrying havoc and dismay into the villages. There were now and then indications of these impending ravages, that filled the minds of the colonists with awe and apprehension. The report of a distant gun would perhaps be heard from the solitary woodland, where there was known to be no white man; the cattle which had been wandering in the woods would sometimes return home wounded; or an Indian or two would be seen lurking about the skirts of the forests, and suddenly disappearing; as the lightning will sometimes be seen playing silently about the edge of the cloud that is brewing up the tempest.

Though sometimes pursued and even surrounded by the settlers, yet Philip as often escaped almost miraculously from their toils, and, plunging into the wilderness, would be lost to all search or inquiry, until he again emerged at some far distant quarter, laying the country desolate. Among his strongholds, were the great swamps or morasses, which extend in some parts of New England; composed of loose bogs of deep black mud; perplexed with thickets, brambles, rank weeds, the shattered and mouldering trunks of fallen trees, overshadowed by lugubrious hemlocks. The uncertain footing and the tangled mazes of these shaggy wilds, rendered them almost impracticable to the white man, though the Indian could thrid their labyrinths with the agility of a deer. Into one of these, the great swamp of Pocasset Neck, was Philip once driven with a band of his followers. The English did not dare to pursue him, fearing to venture into these dark and frightful recesses, where they might perish in fens and miry pits, or be shot down by lurking foes. They therefore invested the entrance to the Neck, and began to build a fort, with the thought of starving out the foe; but Philip and his warriors wafted themselves on a raft over an arm of the sea, in the dead of the night, leaving the women and children behind; and escaped away to the westward, kindling the flames of war among the tribes of Massachusetts and the Nipmuck country, and threatening the colony of Connecticut.

In this way Philip became a theme of universal apprehension. The mystery in which he was enveloped exaggerated his real terrors. He was an evil that walked in darkness; whose coming none could foresee, and against which none knew when to be on the alert. The whole country abounded with rumors and alarms. Philip seemed almost possessed of ubiquity; for, in whatever part of the widely-extended frontier an irruption from the forest took place, Philip was said to be its leader. Many superstitious notions also were circulated concerning him. He was said to deal in necromancy, and to be attended by an old Indian witch or prophetess, whom he consulted, and who assisted him by her charms and incantations. This indeed was frequently the case with Indian chiefs; either through their own credulity, or to act upon that of their followers: and the influence of the prophet and the dreamer over Indian superstition has been fully evidenced in recent instances of savage warfare.

At the time that Philip effected his escape from Pocasset, his fortunes were in a desperate condition. His forces had been thinned by repeated fights, and he had lost almost the whole of his resources. In this time of adversity he found a faithful friend in Canonchet, chief Sachem of all the Narragansets. He was the son and heir of Miantonimo, the great Sachem, who, as already mentioned, after an honorable acquittal of the charge of conspiracy, had been privately put to death at the perfidious instigations of the settlers. "He was the heir," says the old chronicler, "of all his father's pride and insolence, as well as of his malice towards the English"— he certainly was the heir of his insults and injuries, and the legitimate avenger of his murder. Though he had forborne to take an active part in this hopeless war, yet he received Philip and his broken forces with open arms, and gave them the most generous countenance and support. This at once drew upon him the hostility of the English; and it was determined to strike a signal blow that should involve both the Sachems in one common ruin. A great force was therefore gathered together from Massachusetts, Plymouth, and Connecticut, and was sent into the Narraganset country in the depth of winter, when the swamps, being frozen and leafless, could be traversed with comparative facility, and would no longer afford dark and impenetrable fastnesses to the Indians.

Apprehensive of attack, Canonchet had conveyed the greater part of his stores, together with the old, the infirm, the women and children of his tribe, to a strong fortress; where he and Philip had likewise drawn up the flower of their forces. This fortress, deemed by the Indians impregnable, was situated upon a rising mound or kind of island, of five or six acres, in the midst of a swamp; it was constructed with a degree of judgment and skill vastly superior to what is usually displayed in Indian fortification, and indicative of the martial genius of these two chieftains.

Guided by a renegade Indian, the English penetrated, through December snows, to this stronghold, and came upon the garrison by surprise. The fight was fierce and tumultuous. The assailants were repulsed in their first attack, and several of their bravest officers were shot down in the act of storming the fortress sword in hand. The assault was renewed with greater success. A lodgment was effected. The Indians were driven from one post to another. They disputed their ground inch by inch, fighting with the fury of despair. Most of their veterans were cut to pieces; and after a long and bloody battle, Philip and Canonchet, with a handful of surviving warriors, retreated from the fort, and took refuge in the thickets of the surrounding forest.

The victors set fire to the wigwams and the fort; the whole was soon in a blaze; many of the old men, the women and the children perished in the flames. This last outrage overcame even the stoicism of the savage. The neighboring woods resounded with the yells of rage and despair, uttered by the fugitive warriors, as they beheld the destruction of their dwellings, and heard the agonizing cries of their wives and offspring. "The burning of the wigwams," says a contemporary writer, "the shrieks and cries of the women and children, and the yelling of the warriors, exhibited a most horrible and affecting scene, so that it greatly moved some of the soldiers." The same writer cautiously adds, "they were in *much doubt* then, and afterwards seriously inquired, whether burning their enemies alive could be consistent with humanity, and the benevolent principles of the Gospel."*

The fate of the brave and generous Canonchet is worthy of particular mention: the last scene of his life is one of the noblest instances on record of Indian magnanimity.

Broken down in his power and resources by this signal defeat, yet faithful to his ally, and to the hapless cause which he had espoused, he rejected all overtures of peace, offered on condition of betraying Philip and his followers, and declared that "he would fight it out to the last man, rather than become a servant to the English." His home being destroyed; his country harassed and laid waste by the incursions of the conquerors; he was obliged to wander away to the banks of the Connecticut; where he formed a rallying point to the whole body of western Indians, and laid waste several of the English settlements.

Early in the spring he departed on a hazardous expedition, with only thirty chosen men, to penetrate to Seaconck, in the vicinity of Mount Hope, and to procure seed corn to plant for the sustenance of his troops. This

*MS. of the Rev. W. Ruggles.

little band of adventurers had passed safely through the Pequod country, and were in the center of the Narraganset, resting at some wigwams near Pawtucket River, when an alarm was given of an approaching enemy. Having but seven men by him at the time, Canonchet despatched two of them to the top of a neighboring hill, to bring intelligence of the foe.

Panic-struck by the appearance of a troop of English and Indians rapidly advancing, they fled in breathless terror past their chieftain, without stopping to inform him of the danger. Canonchet sent another scout, who did the same. He then sent two more, one of whom, hurrying back in confusion and affright, told him that the whole British army was at hand. Canonchet saw there was no choice but immediate flight. He attempted to escape round the hill, but was perceived and hotly pursued by the hostile Indians and a few of the fleetest of the English. Finding the swiftest pursuer close upon his heels, he threw off, first his blanket, then his silver-laced coat and belt of peag, by which his enemies knew him to be Canonchet, and redoubled the eagerness of pursuit.

At length, in dashing through the river, his foot slipped upon a stone, and he fell so deep as to wet his gun. This accident so struck him with despair, that, as he afterwards confessed, "his heart and his bowels turned within him, and he became like a rotten stick, void of strength."

To such a degree was he unnerved, that, being seized by a Pequod Indian within a short distance of the river, he made no resistance, though a man of great vigor of body and boldness of heart. But on being made prisoner the whole pride of his spirit arose within him; and from that moment, we find, in the anecdotes given by his enemies, nothing but repeated flashes of elevated and prince-like heroism. Being questioned by one of the English who first came up with him, and who had not attained his twenty-second year, the proud-hearted warrior, looking with lofty contempt upon his youthful countenance, replied, "You are a child—you cannot understand matters of war—let your brother or your chief come—him will I answer."

Though repeated offers were made to him of his life, on condition of submitting with his nation to the English, yet he rejected them with disdain, and refused to send any proposals of the kind to the great body of his subjects; saying, that he knew none of them would comply. Being reproached with his breach of faith towards the whites; his boast that he would not deliver up a Wampanoag nor the paring of a Wampanoag's nail; and his threat that he would burn the English alive in their houses; he disdained to justify himself, haughtily answering that others were as forward for the war as himself, and "he desired to hear no more thereof."

So noble and unshaken a spirit, so true a fidelity to his cause and his friend, might have touched the feelings of the generous and the brave; but Canonchet was an Indian—a being towards whom war had no courtesy, humanity no law, religion no compassion—he was condemned to die. The last words of him that are recorded, are worthy the greatness of his soul. When sentence of death was passed upon him, he observed "that he liked it well, for he should die before his heart was soft, or he had spoken any thing unworthy of himself." His enemies gave him the death of a soldier, for he was shot at Stoningham, by three young Sachems of his own rank.

The defeat at the Narraganset fortress, and the death of Canonchet, were fatal blows to the fortunes of King Philip. He made an ineffectual attempt to raise a head of war, by stirring up the Mohawks to take arms; but though possessed of the native talents of a statesman, his arts were counteracted by the superior arts of his enlightened enemies, and the terror of their warlike skill began to subdue the resolution of the neighboring tribes. The unfortunate chieftain saw himself daily stripped of power, and his ranks rapidly thinning around him. Some were suborned by the whites; others fell victims to hunger and fatigue, and to the frequent attacks by which they were harassed. His stores were all captured; his chosen friends were swept away from before his eyes; his uncle was shot down by his side; his sister was carried into captivity; and in one of his narrow escapes he was compelled to leave his beloved wife and only son to the mercy of the enemy. "His ruin," says the historian, "being thus gradually carried on, his misery was not prevented, but augmented thereby; being himself made acquainted with the sense and experimental feeling of the captivity of his children, loss of friends, slaughter of his subjects, bereavement of all family relations, and being stripped of all outward comforts, before his own life should be taken away."

To fill up the measure of his misfortunes, his own followers began to plot against his life, that by sacrificing him they might purchase dishonorable safety. Through treachery a number of his faithful adherents, the subjects of Wetamoe, an Indian princess of Pocasset, a near kinswoman and confederate of Philip, were betrayed into the hands of the enemy. Wetamoe was among them at the time, and attempted to make her escape by crossing a neighboring river: either exhausted by swimming, or starved by cold and hunger, she was found dead and naked near the water side. But persecution ceased not at the grave. Even death, the refuge of the wretched, where the wicked commonly cease from troubling, was no protection to this outcast female, whose great crime was affectionate fidelity to her kinsman and her friend. Her corpse was the object of unmanly and dastardly vengeance; the head was severed from the body and set upon a pole, and was thus exposed at Taunton, to the view of her captive subjects. They immediately recognized the features of their unfortunate queen, and were so affected at this barbarous spectacle, that we are told they broke forth into the "most horrid and diabolical lamentations."

However Philip had borne up against the complicated miseries and misfortunes that surrounded him, the treachery of his followers seemed to wring his heart and reduce him to despondency. It is said that "he never rejoiced afterwards, nor had success in any of his designs." The spring of hope was broken—the ardor of enterprise was extingushed—he looked around, and all was danger and darkness; there was no eye to pity, nor any arm that could bring deliverance. With a scanty band of followers, who still remained true to his desperate fortunes, the unhappy Philip wandered back to the vicinity of Mount Hope, the ancient dwelling of his fathers. Here he lurked about, like a spectre, among the scenes of former power and prosperity, now bereft of home, of family and friend. There needs no better picture of his destitute and piteous situation, than that furnished by the homely pen of the chronicler, who is unwarily enlisting the feelings of the reader in favor of the hapless warrior whom he reviles. "Philip," he says, "like a savage wild beast, having been hunted by the English forces through the woods, above a hundred miles backward and forward, at last was driven to his own den upon Mount Hope, where he retired, with a few of his best friends, into a swamp, which proved but a prison to keep him fast till the messengers of death came by divine permission to execute vengeance upon him."

Even in this last refuge of desperation and despair, a sullen grandeur gathers round his memory. We picture him to ourselves seated among his care-worn followers, brooding in silence over his blasted fortunes, and acquiring a savage sublimity from the wildness and dreariness of his lurking-place. Defeated, but not dismayed—crushed to the earth, but not humiliated—he seemed to grow more haughty beneath disaster, and to experience a fierce satisfaction in draining the last dregs of bitterness. Little minds are tamed and subdued by misfortune; but great minds rise above it. The very idea of submission awakened the fury of Philip, and he smote to death one of his followers, who proposed an expedient of peace. The brother of the victim made his escape, and in revenge betrayed the retreat of his chieftain. A body of white men and Indians were immediately despatched to the swamp where Philip lay crouched, glaring with fury and despair. Before he was aware of their approach, they had begun to surround him. In a little while he saw five of his trustiest followers laid dead at his feet; all resistance was vain; he rushed forth from his covert, and made a headlong attempt to escape, but was shot through the heart by a renegade Indian of his own nation.

Such is the scanty story of the brave, but unfortunate King Philip; persecuted while living, slandered and dishonored when dead. If, however, we consider even the prejudiced anecdotes furnished us by his enemies, we may perceive in them traces of amiable and lofty character sufficient to awaken sympathy for his fate, and respect for his memory. We find that, amidst all the harassing cares and ferocious passions of constant warfare, he was alive to the softer feelings of connubial love and paternal tenderness, and to the generous sentiment of friendship. The captivity of his "beloved wife and only son" are mentioned with exultation as causing him poignant misery: the death of any near friend is triumphantly recorded as a new blow on his sensibilities; but the treachery and desertion of many of his followers, in whose affections he had confided, is said to have desolated his heart, and to have bereaved him of all further comfort. He was a patriot attached to his native soil—a prince true to his subjects, and indignant of their wrongs—a soldier, daring in battle, firm in adversity, patient of fatigue, of hunger, of every variety of bodily suffering, and ready to perish in the cause he had espoused. Proud of heart, and with an untamable love of natural liberty, he preferred to enjoy it among the beasts of the forests or in the dismal and famished recesses of swamps and morasses, rather than bow his haughty spirit to submission, and live dependent and despised in the ease and luxury of the settlements. With heroic qualities and bold achievements that would have graced a civilized warrior, and have rendered him the theme of the poet and the historian; he lived a wanderer and a fugitive in his native land, and went down, like a lonely bark foundering amid darkness and tempest— without a pitying eye to weep his fall, or a friendly hand to record his struggle.

JOHN BULL

An old song, made by an aged old pate,
Of an old worshipful gentleman who had a great estate,
That kept a brave old house at a bountiful rate,
And an old porter to relieve the poor at his gate.
With an old study fill'd full of learned old books,
With an old reverend chaplain, you might know him by his looks,
With an old buttery hatch worn quite off the hooks,
And an old kitchen that maintained half-a-dozen old cooks.
                    Like an old courtier, etc.

                                            OLD SONG

THERE IS no species of humor in which the English more excel, than that which consists in caricaturing and giving ludicrous appellations, or nicknames. In this way they have whimsically designated, not merely individuals, but nations; and, in their fondness for pushing a joke, they have not spared even themselves. One would think that, in personifying itself, a nation would be apt to picture something grand, heroic, and imposing; but it is characteristic of the peculiar humor of the English, and of their love for what is blunt, comic, and familiar, that they have embodied their national oddities in the figure of a sturdy, corpulent old fellow, with a three-cornered hat, red waistcoat, leather breeches, and stout oaken cudgel. Thus they have taken a singular delight in exhibiting their most private foibles in a laughable point of view; and have been so successful in their delineations, that there is scarcely a being in actual existence more absolutely present to the public mind than that eccentric personage, John Bull.

Perhaps the continual contemplation of the character thus drawn of them has contributed to fix it upon the nation; and thus to give reality to what at first may have been painted in a great measure from the imagination.

Men are apt to acquire peculiarities that are continually ascribed to them. The common orders of English seem wonderfully captivated with the *beau ideal* which they have formed of John Bull, and endeavor to act up to the broad caricature that is perpetually before their eyes. Unluckily, they sometimes make their boasted Bull-ism an apology for their prejudice or grossness; and this I have especially noticed among those truly homebred and genuine sons of the soil who have never migrated beyond the sound of Bow-bells. If one of these should be a little uncouth in speech, and apt to utter impertinent truths, he confesses that he is a real John Bull, and always speaks his mind. If he now and then flies into an unreasonable burst of passion about trifles, he observes, that John Bull is a choleric old blade, but then his passion is over in a moment, and he bears no malice. If he betrays a coarseness of taste, and an insensibility to foreign refinements, he thanks heaven for his ignorance—he is a plain John Bull, and has no relish for frippery and nicknacks. His very proneness to be gulled by strangers, and to pay extravagantly for absurdities, is excused under the plea of munificence—for John is always more generous than wise.

Thus, under the name of John Bull, he will contrive to argue every fault into a merit, and will frankly convict himself of being the honestest fellow in existence.

However little, therefore, the character may have suited in the first instance, it has gradually adapted itself to the nation, or rather they have adapted themselves to each other; and a stranger who wishes to study English peculiarities, may gather much valuable information from the innumerable portraits of John Bull, as exhibited in the windows of the caricature-shops. Still, however, he is one of those fertile humorists, that are continually throwing out new portraits, and presenting different aspects from different points of view; and, often as he has been described, I cannot resist the temptation to give a slight sketch of him, such as he has met my eye.

John Bull, to all appearance, is a plain downright matter-of-fact fellow, with much less of poetry about him than rich prose. There is little of romance in his nature, but a vast deal of strong natural feeling. He excels in humor more than in wit; is jolly rather than gay; melancholy rather than morose; can easily be moved to a sudden tear or surprised into a broad laugh; but he loathes sentiment, and has no turn for light pleasantry. He is a boon companion, if you allow him to have his humor, and to talk about himself; and he will stand by a friend in a quarrel, with life and purse, however soundly he may be cudgelled.

In this last respect, to tell the truth, he has a propensity to be somewhat too ready. He is a busy-minded personage, who thinks not merely for himself and family, but for all the country round, and is most generously disposed to be everybody's champion. He is continually volunteering his services to settle his neighbors' affairs, and takes it in great dudgeon if they engage in any matter of consequence without asking his advice; though he seldom engages in any friendly office of the kind without finishing by getting into a squabble with all parties, and then railing bitterly at their ingratitude. He unluckily took lessons in his youth in the noble science of defense, and having accomplished himself in the use of his limbs and his weapons, and become a perfect master at boxing and cudgel-play, he has had a troublesome life of it ever since. He cannot hear of a quarrel between the most distant of his neighbors, but he begins incontinently to fumble with the head of his cudgel, and consider whether his interest or honor does not require that he should meddle in the broil. Indeed he has extended his relations of pride and policy so completely over the whole country, that no event can take place, without infringing some of his finely-spun rights and dignities. Couched in his little domain, with these filaments stretching forth in every direction, he is like some choleric, bottle-bellied old spider, who has woven his web over a whole chamber, so that a fly cannot buzz, nor a breeze blow, without startling his repose, and causing him to sally forth wrathfully from his den.

Though really a good-hearted, good-tempered old fellow at bottom, yet he is singularly fond of being in the midst of contention. It is one of his peculiarities, however, that he only relishes the beginning of an affray; he always goes into a fight with alacrity, but comes out of it grumbling even when victorious; and though no one fights with more obstinacy to carry a contested point, yet, when the battle is over, and he comes to the reconciliation, he is so much taken up with the mere shaking of hands, that he is apt to let his antagonist pocket all that they have been quarreling about. It is not, therefore, fighting that he ought so much to be on his guard against, as making friends. It is difficult to cudgel him out of a farthing; but put him in a good humor, and you may bargain him out of all the money in his pocket. He is like a stout ship, which will weather the roughest storm uninjured, but roll its masts overboard in the succeeding calm.

He is a little fond of playing the magnifico abroad; of pulling out a long purse; flinging his money bravely about at boxing matches, horse races, cock fights, and carrying a high head among "gentlemen of the fancy," but immediately after one of these fits of extravagance, he will be taken with violent qualms of economy; stop short at the most trivial expenditure; talk desperately of being ruined and brought upon the parish; and, in such moods, will not pay the smallest tradesman's bill, without violent altercation. He is in fact the most punctual and discontented paymaster in the world; drawing his coin out of his breeches pocket with infinite reluctance; paying to the uttermost farthing, but accompanying every guinea with a growl.

With all his talk of economy, however, he is a bountiful provider, and a hospitable housekeeper. His economy is of a whimsical kind, its chief object being to devise how he may afford to be extravagant; for he will begrudge himself a beefsteak and pint of port one day, that he may roast an ox whole, broach a hogshead of ale, and treat all his neighbors on the next.

His domestic establishment is enormously expensive; not so much from any great outward parade, as from the great consumption of solid beef and pudding; the vast number of followers he feeds and clothes; and his singular disposition to pay hugely for small services. He is a most kind and indulgent master, and, provided his servants humor his peculiarities, flatter his vanity a little now and then, and do not peculate grossly on him before his face, they may manage him to perfection. Everything that lives on him seems to thrive and grow fat. His house-servants are well paid, and pampered, and have little to do. His horses are sleek and lazy, and prance slowly before his state carriage; and his house-dogs sleep quietly about the door, and will hardly bark at a house-breaker.

His family mansion is an old castellated manor-house, gray with age, and of a most venerable, though weather-beaten appearance. It has been built upon no regular plan, but is a vast accumulation of parts, erected in various tastes and ages. The center bears evident traces of Saxon achitecture, and is as solid as ponderous stone and old English oak can make it. Like all the relics of that style, it is full of obscure passages, intricate mazes, and dusky chambers; and though these have been partially lighted up in modern days, yet there are many places where you must still grope in the dark. Additions have been made to the original edifice from time to time, and great alterations have taken place; towers and battlements have been erected during wars and tumults: wings built in time of peace; and out-houses, lodges, and offices, run up according to the whim or convenience of different generations, until it has become one of the most spacious, rambling tenements imaginable. An entire wing is taken up with the family chapel, a reverend pile, that must have been exceedingly sumptuous, and, indeed, in spite of having been altered and simplified at various periods, has still a look of solemn religious pomp. Its walls within are storied with the monuments of John's ancestors; and it is snugly fitted with soft cushions and well-lined chairs, where such of his family as are inclined to church services, may doze comfortably in the discharge of their duties.

To keep up this chapel has cost John much money; but he is stanch in his religion, and piqued in his zeal, from the circumstance that many dissenting chapels have been erected in his vicinity, and several of his neighbors, with whom he has had quarrels, are strong papists.

To do the duties of the chapel he maintains, at a large expense, a pious and portly family chaplain. He is a most learned and decorous personage, and a truly well-bred Christian, who always backs the old gentleman in his opinions, winks discreetly at his little peccadilloes, rebukes the children when refractory, and is of great use in exhorting the tenants to read their Bibles, say their prayers, and, above all, to pay their rents punctually, and without grumbling.

The family apartments are in a very antiquated taste, somewhat heavy, and often inconvenient, but full of the solemn magnificence of former times; fitted up with rich, though faded, tapestry, unwieldy furniture, and loads of massy gorgeous old plate. The vast fireplaces, ample kitchens, extensive cellars, and sumptuous banqueting halls, all speak of the roaring hospitality of days of yore, of which the modern festivity at the manorhouse is but a shadow. There are, however, complete suites of rooms apparently deserted and time-worn; and towers and turrets that are tottering to decay; so that in high winds there is danger of their tumbling about the ears of the household.

John has frequently been advised to have the old edifice thoroughly overhauled; and to have some of the useless parts pulled down, and the others strengthened with their materials; but the old gentleman always grows testy on this subject. He swears the house is an excellent house—that it is tight and weather proof, and not to be shaken by tempests—that it has stood for several hundred years, and, therefore, is not likely to tumble down now—that as to its being inconvenient, his family is accustomed to the inconveniences, and would not be comfortable without them—that as to its unwieldy size and irregular construction, these result from its being the growth of centuries, and being improved by the wisdom of every generation—that an old family, like his, requires a large house to dwell in; new, upstart families may live in modern cottages and snug boxes; but an old English family should inhabit an old English manorhouse. If you point out any part of the building as superfluous, he insists that it is material to the strength or decoration of the rest, and the harmony of the whole; and swears that the parts are so built into each other that if you pull down one, you run the risk of having the whole about your ears.

The secret of the matter is, that John has a great disposition to protect and patronize. He thinks it indispensable to the dignity of an ancient and honorable family, to be bounteous in its appointments, and to be eaten up by dependents; and so, partly from pride, and partly from kind-heartedness, he makes it a rule always to give shelter and maintenance to his superannuated servants.

The consequence is, that, like many other venerable family establishments, his manor is encumbered by old retainers whom he cannot turn off, and an old style which he cannot lay down. His mansion is like a great hospital of invalids, and, with all its magnitude, is not a whit too large for its inhabitants. Not a nook or corner but is of use in housing some useless personage. Groups of veteran beef-eaters, gouty pensioners, and retired heroes of the buttery and the larder, are seen lolling about its walls, crawling over its lawns, dozing under its trees, or sunning themselves upon the benches at its doors. Every office and out-house is garrisoned by these supernumeraries and their families; for they are amazingly prolific, and when they die off, are sure to leave John a legacy of hungry mouths to be provided for. A mattock cannot be struck against the most mouldering tumble-down tower, but out pops, from some cranny or loop-hole, the gray pate of some superannuated hanger-on, who has lived at John's expense all his life, and makes the most grievous outcry at their pulling down the roof from over the head of a worn-out servant of the family. This is an appeal that John's honest heart never can withstand; so that a man, who has faithfully eaten his beef and pudding all his life, is sure to be rewarded with a pipe and tankard in his old days.

A great part of his park, also, is turned into paddocks, where his broken-down chargers are turned loose to graze undisturbed for the remainder of their existence—a worthy example of grateful recollection, which if some of his neighbors were to imitate, would not be to their discredit. Indeed, it is one of his great pleasures to point out these old steeds to his visitors, to dwell on their good qualities, extol their past services, and boast, with some little vainglory, of the perilous adventures and hardy exploits through which they have carried him.

He is given, however, to indulge his veneration for family usages, and family incumbrances, to a whimsical extent. His manor is infested by gangs of gypsies; yet he will not suffer them to be driven off, because they have infested the place time out of mind, and been regular poachers upon every generation of the family. He will scarcely permit a dry branch to be lopped from the great trees that surround the house, lest it should molest the rooks, that have bred there for centuries. Owls have taken possession of the dovecote; but they are hereditary owls, and must not be disturbed. Swallows have nearly choked up every chimney with their nests; martins build in every frieze and cornice; crows flutter about the towers, and perch on every weather-cock; and old gray-headed rats may be seen in every quarter of the house, running in and out of their holes undauntedly in broad daylight. In short, John has such a reverence for every thing that has been long in the family, that he will not hear even of abuses being reformed, because they are good old family abuses.

All these whims and habits have concurred wofully to drain the old gentleman's purse; and as he prides himself on punctuality in money matters, and wishes to maintain his credit in the neighborhood, they have caused him great perplexity in meeting his engagements. This, too, has been increased by the altercations and heart-burnings which are continually taking place in his family. His children have been brought up to different callings, and are of different ways of thinking; and as they have always been allowed to speak their minds freely, they do not fail to exercise the privilege most clamorously in the present posture of his affairs. Some stand up for the honor of the race, and are clear that the old establishment should be kept up in all its state, whatever may be the cost; others, who are more prudent and considerate, entreat the old gentleman to retrench his expenses, and to put his whole system of housekeeping on a more moderate footing. He has, indeed, at times, seemed inclined to listen to their opinions, but their wholesome advice has been completely defeated by the obstreperous conduct of one of his sons. This is a noisy, rattle-pated fellow, of rather low habits, who neglects his business to frequent ale-houses—is the orator of village clubs, and a complete oracle among the poorest of his father's tenants. No sooner does he hear any of his brothers mention reform or retrenchment, than up he jumps, takes the words out of their mouths, and roars out for an overturn. When his tongue is once going nothing can stop it. He rants about the room; hectors the old man about his spend-thrift practices; ridicules his tastes and pursuits; insists that he shall turn the old servants out of doors; give the broken-down horses to the hounds; send the fat chap-lain packing, and take a field-preacher in his place—nay, that the whole family mansion shall be levelled with the ground, and a plain one of brick and mortar built in its place. He rails at every social entertainment and family festivity, and skulks away growling to the ale-house whenever an equipage drives up to the door. Though constantly complaining of the emptiness of his purse, yet he scruples not to spend all his pocket-money in these tavern convocations, and even runs up scores for the liquor over which he preaches about his father's extravagance.

It may readily be imagined how little such thwarting agrees with the old cavalier's fiery temperament. He has become so irritable, from repeated crossings, that the mere mention of retrenchment or reform is a signal for a brawl between him and the tavern oracle. As the latter is too sturdy and refractory for paternal discipline, having grown out of all fear of the cudgel, they have frequent scenes of wordy warfare, which at times run so high, that John is fain to call in the aid of his son Tom, an officer who has served abroad, but is at present living at home, on half-pay. This last is sure to stand by the old gentleman, right or wrong; likes nothing so much as a racketing, roystering life; and is ready at a wink or nod, to out sabre, and flourish it over the orator's head, if he dares to array himself against paternal authority.

These family dissensions, as usual, have got abroad, and are rare food for scandal in John's neighborhood. People begin to look wise, and shake their heads, whenever his affairs are mentioned. They all "hope that matters are not so bad with him as represented; but when a man's own children begin to rail at his extravagance, things must be badly managed. They understand he is mortgaged over head and ears, and is continually dabbling with money lenders. He is certainly an open-handed old gentleman, but they fear he has lived too fast; indeed, they never knew any good come of this fondness for hunting, racing, revelling and prize-fighting. In short, Mr. Bull's estate is a very fine one, and has been in the family a long time; but, for all that, they have known many finer estates come to the hammer."

What is worst of all, is the effect which these pecuniary embarrassments and domestic feuds have had on the poor man himself. Instead of that jolly round corporation, and smug rosy face, which he used to present, he has of late become as shrivelled and shrunk as a frost-bitten apple. His scarlet gold-laced waistcoat, which bellied out so bravely in those prosperous days when he sailed before the wind, now hangs loosely about him like a mainsail in a calm. His leather breeches are all in folds and wrinkles, and apparently have much ado to hold up the boots that yawn on both sides of his once sturdy legs.

Instead of strutting about as formerly, with his three-cornered hat on one side; flourishing his cudgel, and bringing it down every moment with a hearty thump upon the ground; looking every one sturdily in the face, and trolling out a stave of a catch or a drinking song; he now goes about whistling thoughtfully to himself, with his head drooping down, his cudgel tucked under his arm, and his hands thrust to the bottom of his breeches pockets, which are evidently empty.

Such is the plight of honest John Bull at present; yet for all this the old fellow's spirit is as tall and as gallant as ever. If you drop the least expression of sympathy or concern, he takes fire in an instant; swears that he is the richest and stoutest fellow in the country; talks of laying out large sums to adorn his house or buy another estate; and with a valiant swagger and grasping of his cudgel, longs exceedingly to have another bout at quarter-staff.

Though there may be something rather whimsical in all this, yet I confess I cannot look upon John's situation without strong feelings of interest. With all his odd humors and obstinate prejudices, he is a sterling-hearted old blade. He may not be so wonderfully fine a fellow as he thinks himself, but he is at least twice as good as his neighbors represent him. His virtues are all his own; all plain, homebred, and unaffected. His very faults smack of the raciness of his good qualities. His extravagance savors of his generosity; his quarrel-someness of his courage; his credulity of his open faith; his vanity of his pride; and his bluntness of his sincerity. They are all the redundancies of a rich and liberal character. He is like his own oak, rough without, but sound and solid within; whose bark abounds with excrescences in proportion to the growth and graudeur of the timber; and whose branches make a fearful groaning and murmuring in the least storm, from their very magnitude and luxuriance. There is something, too, in the appearance of his old family mansion that is extremely poetical and picturesque; and, as long as it can be rendered comfortably habitable, I should almost tremble to see it meddled with, during the present conflict of tastes and opinions. Some of his advisers are no doubt good architects, that might be of service; but many, I fear, are mere levellers, who, when they had once got to work with their mattocks on this venerable edifice, would never stop until they had brought it to the ground, and perhaps buried themselves among the ruins. All that I wish is, that John's present troubles may teach him more prudence in future. That he may cease to distress his mind about other people's affairs; that he may give up the fruitless attempt to promote the good of his neighbors, and the peace and happiness of the world, by dint of the cudgel; that he may remain quietly at home; gradually get his house into repair; cultivate his rich estate according to his fancy; husband his income—if he thinks proper; bring his unruly children into order—if he can; renew the jovial scenes of ancient prosperity; and long enjoy, on his paternal lands, a green, an honorable, and a merry old age.

THE PRIDE OF THE VILLAGE

> May no wolfe howle; no screech owle stir
> A wing about thy sepulchre!
> No boysterous winds or stormes come hither,
>   To starve or wither
> Thy soft sweet earth! but, like a spring,
> Love kept it ever flourishing.
>
> HERRICK

I N THE course of an excursion through one of the remote counties of England, I had struck into one of those crossroads that lead through the more secluded parts of the country, and stopped one afternoon at a village, the situation of which was beautifully rural and retired. There was an air of primitive simplicity about its inhabitants, not to be found in the villages which lie on the great coach-roads. I determined to pass the night there, and, having taken an early dinner, strolled out to enjoy the neighboring scenery.

My ramble, as is usually the case with travellers, soon led me to the church, which stood at a little distance from the village. Indeed, it was an object of some curiosity, its old tower being completely overrun with ivy, so that only here and there a jutting buttress, an angle of gray wall, or a fantastically carved ornament, peered through the verdant covering. It was a lovely evening. The early part of the day had been dark and showery, but in the afternoon it had cleared up; and though sullen clouds still hung overhead, yet there was a broad tract of golden sky in the west, from which the setting sun gleamed through the dripping leaves, and lit up all nature with a melancholy smile. It seemed like the parting hour of a good Christian, smiling on the sins and sorrows of the world, and giving, in the serenity of his decline, an assurance that he will rise again in glory.

I had seated myself on a half-sunken tombstone, and was musing, as one is apt to do at this sober-thoughted hour, on past scenes and early friends—on those who were distant and those who were dead—and indulging in that kind of melancholy fancying, which has in it something sweeter even than pleasure. Every now and then, the stroke of a bell from the neighboring tower fell on my ear; its tones were in unison with the scene, and, instead of jarring, chimed in with my feelings; and it was some time before I recollected that it must be tolling the knell of some new tenant of the tomb.

Presently I saw a funeral train moving across the village green; it wound slowly along a lane; was lost, and reappeared through the breaks of the hedges, until it passed the place where I was sitting. The pall was supported by young girls, dressed in white; and another, about the age of seventeen, walked before, bearing a chaplet of white flowers; a token that the deceased was a young and unmarried female. The corpse was followed by the parents. They were a venerable couple of the better order of peasantry. The father seemed to repress his feelings; but his fixed eye, contracted brow, and deeply-furrowed face, showed the struggle that was passing within. His wife hung on his arm, and wept aloud with the convulsive burst of a mother's sorrow.

I followed the funeral into the church. The bier was placed in the center aisle, and the chaplet of white flowers, with a pair of white gloves, were hung over the seat which the deceased had occupied.

Everyone knows the soul-subduing pathos of the funeral service; for who is so fortunate as never to have followed some one he has loved to the tomb? but when performed over the remains of innocence and beauty, thus laid low in the bloom of existence—what can be more affecting? At that simple, but most solemn consignment of the body to the grave—"Earth to earth—ashes to ashes—dust to dust!"—the tears of the youthful companions of the deceased flowed unrestrained. The father still seemed to struggle with his feelings, and to comfort himself with the assurance, that the dead are blessed which die in the Lord; but the mother only thought of her child as a flower of the field cut down and withered in the midst of its sweetness; she was like Rachel, "mourning over her children, and would not be comforted."

On returning to the inn, I learned the whole story of the deceased. It was a simple one, and such as has often been told. She had been the beauty and pride of the village. Her father had once been an opulent farmer, but was reduced in circumstances. This was an only child, and brought up entirely at home, in the simplicity of rural life. She had been the pupil of the village pastor, the favorite lamb of his little flock. The good man watched over her education with paternal care; it was limited, and suitable to the sphere in which she was to move; for he only sought to make her an ornament to her station in life, not to raise her above it. The tenderness and indulgence of her parents, and the exemption from all ordinary occupations, had fostered a natural grace and delicacy of character, that accorded with the fragile loveliness of her form. She appeared like some tender plant of the garden, blooming accidentally amid the hardier natives of the fields.

The superiority of her charms was felt and acknowledged by her companions, but without envy; for it was surpassed by the unassuming gentleness and winning kindness of her manners. It might be truly said of her:

> "This is the prettiest low-born lass, that ever
> Ran on the green-sward; nothing she does or seems,
> But smacks of something greater than herself;
> Too noble for this place."

The village was one of those sequestered spots, which still retain some vestiges of old English customs. It had its rural festivals and holiday pastimes, and still kept up some faint observance of the once popular rites of May. These, indeed, had been promoted by its present pastor, who was a lover of old customs, and one of those simple Christians that think their mission fulfilled by promoting joy on earth and good-will among mankind. Under his auspices the May-pole stood from year to year in the center of the village green; on May-day it was decorated with garlands and streamers; and a queen or lady of the May was appointed, as in former times, to preside at the sports, and distribute the prizes and rewards. The picturesque situation of the village, and the fancifulness of its rustic fêtes, would often attract the notice of casual visitors. Among these, on one May-day, was a young officer, whose regiment had been recently quartered in the neighborhood. He was charmed with the native taste that pervaded this village pageant; but, above all, with the dawning loveliness of the queen of May. It was the village favorite, who was crowned with flowers, and blushing and smiling in all the beautiful confusion of girlish diffidence and delight. The artlessness of rural habits enabled him readily to make her acquaintance; he gradually won his way into her intimacy; and paid his court to her in that unthinking way in which young officers are too apt to trifle with rustic simplicity.

There was nothing in his advances to startle or alarm. He never even talked of love: but there are modes of making it more eloquent than language, and which convey it subtilely and irresistibly to the heart. The beam of the eye, the tone of voice, the thousand tendernesses which emanate from every word, and look, and action—these form the true eloquence of love, and can always be felt and understood, but never described. Can we wonder that they should readily win a heart, young, guileless, and susceptible? As to her, she loved almost unconsciously; she scarcely inquired what was the growing passion that was absorbing every thought and feeling, or what were to be its consequences. She, indeed, looked not to the future. When present, his looks and words occupied her whole attention; when absent, she thought but of what had passed at their recent interview. She would wander with him through the green lanes and rural scenes of the vicinity. He taught her to see new beauties in nature; he talked in the language of polite and cultivated life, and breathed into her ear the witcheries of romance and poetry.

Perhaps there could not have been a passion, between the sexes, more pure than this innocent girl's. The gallant figure of her youthful admirer, and the splendor of his military attire, might at first have charmed her eye; but it was not these that had captivated her heart. Her attachment had something in it of idolatry. She looked up to him as to a being of a superior order. She felt in his society the enthusiasm of a mind naturally delicate and poetical, and now first awakened to a keen perception of the beautful and grand. Of the sordid distinctions of rank and fortune she thought nothing; it was the difference of intellect, of demeanor, of manners, from those of the rustic society to which she had been accustomed, that elevated him in her opinion. She would listen to him with charmed ear and downcast look of mute delight, and her cheek would mantle with enthusiasm; or if ever she ventured a shy glance of timid admiration, it was as quickly withdrawn, and she would sigh and blush at the idea of her comparative unworthiness.

Her lover was equally impassioned; but his passion was mingled with feelings of a coarser nature. He had begun the connection in levity; for he had often heard his brother officers boast of their village conquests, and thought some triumph of the kind necessary to his reputation as a man of spirit. But he was too full of youthful fervor. His heart had not yet been rendered sufficiently cold and selfish by a wandering and a dissipated life: it caught fire from the very flame it sought to kindle; and before he was aware of the nature of his situation, he became really in love.

What was he to do? There were the old obstacles which so incessantly occur in these heedless attachments. His rank in life—the prejudices of titled connections—his dependence upon a proud and unyielding father—all forbade him to think of matrimony—but when he looked down upon this innocent being, so tender and confiding, there was a purity in her manners, a blamelessness in her life, and a beseeching modesty in her looks that awed down every licentious feeling. In vain did he try to fortify himself by a thousand heartless examples of men of fashion; and to chill the glow of generous sentiment with that cold derisive levity with which he had heard them talk of female virtue: whenever he came into her presence, she was still surrounded by that mysterious but impassive charm of virgin purity in whose hallowed sphere no guilty thought can live.

The sudden arrival of orders for the regiment to repair to the continent completed the confusion of his mind. He remained for a short time in a state of the most painful irresolution; he hesitated to communicate the tidings, until the day for marching was at hand; when he gave her the intelligence in the course of an evening ramble.

The idea of parting had never before occurred to her. It broke in at once upon her dream of felicity; she looked upon it as a sudden and insurmountable evil, and wept with the guileless simplicity of a child. He drew her to his bosom, and kissed the tears from her soft cheek; nor did he meet with a repulse, for these are moments of mingled sorrow and tenderness, which hallow the caresses of affection. He was naturally impetuous; and the sight of beauty, apparently yielding in his arms, the confidence of his power over her, and the dread of losing her for ever, all conspired to overwhelm his better feelings—he ventured to propose that she should leave her home, and be the companion of his fortunes.

He was quite a novice in seduction, and blushed and faltered at his own baseness; but so innocent of mind was his intended victim, that she was at first at a loss to comprehend his meaning; and why she should leave her native village, and the humble roof of her parents. When at last the nature of his proposal flashed upon her pure mind, the effect was withering. She did not weep—she did not break forth into reproach—she said not a word—but she shrunk back aghast as from a viper; gave him a look of anguish that pierced to his very soul; and, clasping her hands in agony, fled, as if for refuge, to her father's cottage.

The officer retired, confounded, humiliated, and repentant. It is uncertain what might have been the result of the conflict of his feelings, had not his thoughts been diverted by the bustle of departure. New scenes, new pleasures, and new companions, soon dissipated his self-reproach, and stifled his tenderness; yet, amidst the stir of camps, the revelries of garrisons, the array of armies, and even the din of battles, his thoughts would sometimes steal back to the scenes of rural quiet and village simplicity—the white cottage—the footpath along the silver brook and up the hawthorn hedge, and the little village maid loitering along it, leaning on his arm, and listening to him with eyes beaming with unconscious affection.

The shock which the poor girl had received, in the destruction of all her ideal world, had indeed been cruel. Faintings and hysterics had at first shaken her tender frame, and were succeeded by a settled and pining melancholy. She had beheld from her window the march of the departing troops. She had seen her faithless lover borne off, as if in triumph, amidst the sound of drum and trumpet, and the pomp of arms. She strained a last aching gaze after him, as the morning sun glittered about his figure, and his plume waved in the breeze; he passed away like a bright vision from her sight, and left her all in darkness.

It would be trite to dwell on the particulars of her after story. It was, like other tales of love, melancholy. She avoided society, and wandered out alone in the walks she had most frequented with her lover. She sought, like the stricken deer, to weep in silence and loneliness, and brood over the barbed sorrow that rankled in her soul. Sometimes she would be seen late of an evening sitting in the porch of the village church; and the milkmaids, returning from the fields, would now and then overhear her singing some plaintive ditty in the hawthorn walk. She became fervent in her devotions at church; and as the old people saw her approach, so wasted away, yet with a hectic gloom, and that hallowed air which melancholy diffuses round the form, they would make way for her, as for something spiritual, and, looking after her, would shake their heads in gloomy foreboding.

She felt a conviction that she was hastening to the tomb, but looked forward to it as a place of rest. The silver cord that had bound her to existence was loosed, and there seemed to be no more pleasure under the sun. If ever her gentle bosom had entertained resentment against her lover, it was extinguished. She was incapable of angry passions; and in a moment of saddened tenderness, she penned him a farewell letter. It was couched in the simplest language, but touching from its very simplicity. She told him that she was dying, and did not conceal from him that his conduct was the cause. She even depicted the sufferings which she had experienced; but concluded with saying, that she could not die in peace, until she had sent him her forgiveness and her blessing.

By degrees her strength declined, that she could no longer leave the cottage. She could only totter to the window, where, propped up in her chair, it was her enjoyment to sit all day and look out upon the landscape. Still she uttered no complaint, nor imparted to anyone the malady that was preying on her heart. She never even mentioned her lover's name; but would lay her head on her mother's bosom and weep in silence. Her poor parents hung, in mute anxiety, over this fading blossom of their hopes, still flattering themselves that it might again revive to freshness, and that the bright unearthly bloom which sometimes flushed her cheek might be the promise of returning health.

In this way she was seated between them one Sunday afternoon; her hands were clasped in theirs, the lattice was thrown open, and the soft air that stole in brought with it the fragrance of the clustering honeysuckle which her own hands had trained round the window.

Her father had just been reading a chapter in the Bible; it spoke of the vanity of worldly things, and of the joys of heaven; it seemed to have diffused comfort and serenity through her bosom. Her eye was fixed on the distant village church; the bell had tolled for the evening service; the last villager was lagging into the porch; and every thing had sunk into that hallowed stillness peculiar to the day of rest. Her parents were gazing on her with yearning hearts. Sickness and sorrow, which pass so roughly over some faces, had given to hers the expression of a seraph's. A tear trembled in her soft blue eyes. Was she thinking of her faithless lover? Or were her thoughts wandering to that distant church-yard, into whose bosom she might soon be gathered?

Suddenly the clang of hoofs was heard—a horseman galloped to the cottage—he dismounted before the window—the poor girl gave a faint exclamation, and sunk back in her chair: it was her repentant lover! He rushed into the house, and flew to clasp her to his bosom; but her wasted form—her deathlike countenance—so wan, yet so lovely in its desolation—smote him to the soul, and he threw himself in agony at her feet. She was too faint to rise—she attempted to extend her trembling hand—her lips moved as if she spoke, but no word was articulated—she looked down upon him with a smile of unutterable tenderness—and closed her eyes forever!

Such are the particulars which I gathered of this village story. They are but scanty, and I am conscious have little novelty to recommend them. In the present rage also for strange incident and high-seasoned narrative, they may appear trite and insignificant, but they interested me strongly at the time; and, taken in connection with the affecting ceremony which I had just witnessed, left a deeper impression on my mind than many circumstances of a more striking nature. I have passed through the place since, and visited the church again, from a better motive than mere curiosity. It was a wintry evening; the trees were stripped of their foliage; the churchyard looked naked and mournful, and the wind rustled coldly through the dry grass. Evergreens, however, had been planted about the grave of the village favorite, and osiers were bent over it to keep the turf uninjured.

The church door was open, and I stepped in. There hung the chaplet of flowers and the gloves, as on the day of the funeral; the flowers were withered, it is true, but care seemed to have been taken that no dust should soil their whiteness. I have seen many monuments, where art has exhausted its powers to awaken the sympathy of the spectator, but I have met with none that spoke more touchingly to my heart, than this simple but delicate memento of departed innocence.

THE ANGLER

This day dame Nature seem'd in love,
The lusty sap began to move,
Fresh juice did stir th' embracing vines
And birds had drawn their valentines.
The jealous trout that low did lie,
Rose at a well-dissembled flie.
There stood my friend, with patient skill,
Attending of his trembling quill.
SIR H. WOTTON

I T IS said that many an unlucky urchin is induced to run away from his family, and betake himself to a seafaring life, from reading the history of Robinson Crusoe; and I suspect that, in like manner, many of those worthy gentlemen who are given to haunt the sides of pastoral streams with angle rods in hand, may trace the origin of their passion to the seductive pages of honest Izaak Walton. I recollect studying his *Compleat Angler* several years since, in company with a knot of friends in America, and moreover that we were all completely bitten with the angling mania. It was early in the year; but as soon as the weather was auspicious, and that the spring began to melt into the verge of summer, we took rod in hand and sallied into the country, as stark mad as was ever Don Quixote from reading books of chivalry.

One of our party had equalled the Don in the fullness of his equipments: being attired cap-a-pie for the enterprise. He wore a broad-skirted fustian coat, perplexed with half a hundred pockets; a pair of stout shoes, and leathern gaiters; a basket slung on one side for fish; a patent rod, a landing net, and a score of other inconveniences, only to be found in the true angler's armory. Thus harnessed for the field, he was as great a matter of stare and wonderment among the country folk, who had never seen a regular angler, as was the steel-clad hero of La Mancha among the goatherds of the Sierra Morena.

Our first essay was along a mountain brook, among the highlands of the Hudson; a most unfortunate place for the execution of those piscatory tactics which had been invented along the velvet margins of quiet English rivulets. It was one of those wild streams that lavish, among our romantic solitudes, unheeded beauties, enough to fill the sketch-book of a hunter of the picturesque. Sometimes it would leap down rocky shelves, making small cascades, over which the trees threw their broad balancing sprays, and long nameless weeds hung in fringes from the impending banks, dripping with diamond drops. Sometimes it would brawl and fret along a ravine in the matted shade of a forest, filling it with murmurs; and, after this termagant career, would steal forth into open day with the most placid demure face imaginable; as I have seen some pestilent shrew of a housewife, after filling her home with uproar and ill-humor, come dimpling out of doors, swimming and courtesying, and smiling upon all the world.

How smoothly would this vagrant brook glide, at such times, through some bosom of green meadow-land among the mountains; where the quiet was only interrupted by the occasional tinkling of a bell from the lazy cattle among the clover, or the sound of a woodcutter's axe from the neighboring forest.

For my part, I was always a bungler at all kinds of sport that required either patience or adroitness, and had not angled above half an hour before I had completely "satisfied the sentiment," and convinced myself of the truth of Izaak Walton's opinion, that angling is something like poetry—a man must be born to it. I hooked myself instead of the fish; tangled my line in every tree; lost my bait; broke my rod; until I gave up the attempt in despair, and passed the day under the trees, reading old Izaak; satisfied that it was his fascinating vein of honest simplicity and rural feeling that had betwiched me, and not the passion for angling. My companions, however, were more persevering in their delusion. I have them at this moment before my eyes, stealing along the border of the brook, where it lay open to the day, or was merely fringed by shrubs and bushes. I see the bittern rising with hollow scream as they break in upon his rarely-invaded haunt; the kingfisher watching them suspiciously from his dry tree that overhangs the deep black mill-pond, in the gorge of the hills; the tortoise letting himself slip sideways from off the stone or log on which he is sunning himself; and the panic-struck frog plumping in headlong as they approach, and spreading an alarm throughout the watery world around.

I recollect also, that, after toiling and watching and creeping about for the greater part of a day, with scarcely any success, in spite of all our admirable apparatus, a lubberly country urchin came down from the hills with a rod made from a branch of a tree, a few yards of twine, and, as Heaven shall help me! I believe, a crooked pin for a hook, baited with a vile earthworm—and in half an hour caught more fish than we had nibbles throughout the day!

But, above all, I recollect, the "good, honest, wholesome, hungry" repast, which we made under a beech-tree, just by a spring of pure sweet water that stole out of the side of a hill; and how, when it was over, one of the party read old Izaak Walton's scene with the milkmaid, while I lay on the grass and built castles in a bright pile of clouds, until I fell asleep. All this may appear like mere egotism; yet I cannot refrain from uttering these recollections, which are passing like a strain of music over my mind, and have been called up by an agreeable scene which I witnessed not long since.

In a morning's stroll along the banks of the Alun, a beautiful little stream which flows down from the Welsh hills and throws itself into the Dee, my attention was attracted to a group seated on the margin. On approaching, I found it to consist of a veteran angler and two rustic disciples. The former was an old fellow with a wooden leg, with clothes very much but very carefully patched, betokening poverty, honestly come by, and decently maintained. His face bore the marks of former storms, but present fair weather; its furrows had been worn into an habitual smile; his iron-gray locks hung about his ears, and he had altogether the good-humored air of a constitutional philosopher who was disposed to take the world as it went. One of his companions was a ragged wight, with the skulking look of an arrant poacher, and I'll warrant could find his way to any gentleman's fishpond in the neighborhood in the darkest night. The other was a tall, awkward, country lad, with a lounging gait, and apparently somewhat of a rustic beau. The old man was busy in examining the maw of a trout which he had just killed, to discover by its contents what insects were seasonable for bait; and was lecturing on the subject to his companions, who appeared to listen with infinite deference. I have a kind feeling towards all "brothers of the angle," ever since I read Izaak Walton. They are men he affirms, of a "mild, sweet, and peaceable spirit;" and my esteem for them has been increased since I met with an old "Tretyse of fishing with the Angle," in which are set forth many of the maxims of their inoffensive fraternity. "Take good hede," sayeth this honest little tretyse, "that in going about your disportes ye open no man's gates but that ye shet them again. Also ye shall not use this forsayd crafti disport for no covetousness to the encreasing and sparing of your money only, but principally for your solace, and to cause the helth of your body and specyally of your soule"*

I thought that I could perceive in the veteran angler before me an exemplification of what I had read; and there was a cheerful contentedness in his looks that quite drew me towards him. I could not but remark the gallant manner in which he stumped from one part of the brook to another; waving his rod in the air, to keep the line from dragging on the ground, or catching among the bushes; and the adroitness with which he would throw his fly to any particular place; sometimes skimming it lightly along a little rapid; sometimes casting it into one of those dark holes made by a twisted root or overhanging bank, in which the large trout are apt to lurk. In the meanwhile he was giving instructions to his two disciples; showing them the manner in which they should handle their rods, fix their flies, and play them along the surface of the stream. The scene brought to my mind the instructions of the sage Piscator to his scholar. The country around was of that pastoral kind which Walton is fond of describing. It was a part of the great plain of Cheshire, close by the beautiful vale of Gessford, and just where the inferior Welsh hills begin

* From this same treatise, it would appear that angling is a more industrious and devout employment than it is generally considered.— "For when ye purpose to go on your disportes in fishynge ye will not desyre greatlye many persons with you, which might let you of your game. And that ye may serve God devoutly in sayinge effectually your customable prayers. And thus doying, ye shall eschew and also avoyde many vices, as ydelnes, which is principall cause to induce man to many other vices, as it is right well known."

to swell up from among fresh-smelling meadows. The day, too, like that recorded in his work, was mild and sunshiny, with now and then a soft-dropping shower, that sowed the whole earth with diamonds.

I soon fell into conversation with the old angler, and was so much entertained that, under pretext of receiving insructions in his art, I kept company with him almost the whole day; wandering along the banks of the stream, and listening to his talk. He was very communicative, having all the easy garrulity of cheerful old age; and I fancy was a little flattered by having an opportunity of displaying his piscatory lore; for who does not like now and then to play the sage?

He had been much of a rambler in his day, and had passed some years of his youth in America, particularly in Savannah, where he had entered into trade, and had been ruined by the indiscretion of a partner. He had afterwards experienced many ups and downs in life, until he got into the navy, where his leg was carried away by a cannon ball, at the battle of Camperdown. This was the only stroke of real good fortune he had ever experienced, for it got him a pension, which, together with some small paternal property, brought him in a revenue of nearly forty pounds. On this he retired to his native village, where he lived quietly and independently; and devoted the remainder of his life to the "noble art of angling."

I found that he had read Izaak Walton attentively, and he seemed to have imbibed all his simple frankness and prevalent good-humor. Though he had been sorely buffeted about the world, he was satisfied that the world, in itself, was good and beautiful. Though he had been as roughly used in different countries as a poor sheep that is fleeced by every hedge and thicket, yet he spoke of every nation with candor and kindness, appearing to look only on the good side of things: and, above all, he was almost the only man I had ever met with who had been an unfortunate adventurer in America, and had honesty and magnanimity enough to take the fault to his own door, and not to curse the country. The lad that was receiving his instructions, I learned, was the son and heir apparent of a fat old widow who kept the village inn, and of course a youth of some expectation, and much courted by the idle gentlemanlike personages of the place. In taking him under his care, therefore, the old man had probably an eye to a privileged corner in the tap-room, and an occasional cup of cheerful ale free of expense.

There is certainly something in angling, if we could forget, which anglers are apt to do, the cruelties and tortures inflicted on worms and insects, that tends to produce a gentleness of spirit, and a pure serenity of mind. As the English are methodical even in their recreations, and are the most scientific of sportsmen, it has been reduced among them to perfect rule and system. Indeed it is an amusement peculiarly adapted to the mild and highly-cultivated scenery of England, where every roughness has been softened away from the landscape. It is delightful to saunter along those limpid streams which wander, like veins of silver, through the bosom of this beautiful country; leading one through a diversity of small home scenery; sometimes winding through ornamented grounds; sometimes brimming along through rich pasturage, where the fresh green is mingled with sweet-smelling flowers; sometimes venturing in sight of villages and hamlets, and then running capriciously away into shady retirements. The sweetness and serenity of nature, and the quiet watchfulness of the sport, gradually bring on pleasant fits of musing; which are now and then agreeably interrupted by the song of a bird, the distant whistle of the peasant, or perhaps the vagary of some fish, leaping out of the still water, and skimming transiently about its glassy surface. "When I would beget content," says Izaak Walton, "and increase confidence in the power and wisdom and providence of Almighty God, I will walk the meadows by some gliding stream, and there contemplate the lilies that take no care, and those very many other little living creatures that are not only created, but fed (man knows not how) by the goodness of the God of nature, and therefore trust in him."

I cannot forbear to give another quotation from one of those ancient champions of angling, which breathes the same innocent and happy spirit:

> Let me live harmlessly, and near the brink
> Of Trent or Avon have a dwelling-place,
> Where I may see my quill, or cork, down sink,
> With eager bite of pike, or bleak, or dace;
> And on the world and my Creator think:
> Whilst some men strive ill-gotten goods t' embrace;
> And others spend their time in base excess
> Of wine, or worse, in war, or wantonness.
>
> Let them that will, these pastimes still pursue,
> And on such pleasing fancies feed their fill;
> So I the fields and meadows green may view,
> And daily by fresh rivers walk at will,
> Among the daisies and the violets blue,
> Red hyacinth and yellow daffodil.*

On parting with the old angler I inquired after his place of abode, and happening to be in the neighborhood of the village a few evenings afterwards, I had the curiosity to seek him out. I found him living in a small cottage, containing only one room, but a perfect curiosity in its method and arrangement. It was on the skirts of

*J. Davors.

the village, on a green bank, a little back from the road, with a small garden in front, stocked with kitchen herbs, and adorned with a few flowers. The whole front of the cottage was overrun with a honeysuckle. On the top was a ship for a weather-cock. The interior was fitted up in a truly nautical style, his ideas of comfort and convenience having been acquired on the berth-deck of a man-of-war. A hammock was slung from the ceiling, which, in the daytime, was lashed up so as to take but little room. From the center of the chamber hung a model of a ship, of his own workmanship. Two or three chairs, a table, and a large sea-chest, formed the principal movables. About the wall were stuck up naval ballads, such as Admiral Hosier's Ghost, All in the Downs, and Tom Bowline, intermingled with pictures of sea-fights, among which the battle of Camperdown held a distinguished place. The mantel-piece was decorated with sea-shells; over which hung a quadrant, flanked by two woodcuts of most bitter-looking naval commanders. His implements for angling were carefully disposed on nails and hooks about the room. On a shelf was arranged his library, containing a work on angling, much worn, a Bible covered with canvas, an odd volume or two of voyages, a nautical almanac, and a book of songs.

His family consisted of a large black cat with one eye, and a parrot which he had caught and tamed, and educated himself, in the course of one of his voyages; and which uttered a variety of sea phrases with the hoarse brattling tone of a veteran boatswain. The establishment reminded me of that of the renowned Robinson Crusoe; it was kept in neat order, everything being "stowed away" with the regularity of a ship of war; and he informed me that he "scoured the deck every morning, and swept it between meals."

I found him seated on a bench before the door,

smoking his pipe in the soft evening sunshine. His cat was purring soberly on the threshold, and his parrot describing some strange evolutions in an iron ring that swung in the center of his cage. He had been angling all day, and gave me a history of his sport with as much minuteness as a general would talk over a campaign; being particularly animated in relating the manner in which he had taken a large trout, which had completely tasked all his skill and wariness, and which he had sent as a trophy to mine hostess of the inn.

How comforting it is to see a cheerful and contented old age; and to behold a poor fellow, like this, after being tempest-tossed through life, safely moored in a snug and quiet harbor in the evening of his days! His happiness, however, sprung from within himself, and was independent of external circumstances; for he had that inexhaustible good-nature, which is the most precious gift of Heaven; spreading itself like oil over the troubled sea of thought, and keeping the mind smooth and equable in the roughest weather.

On inquiring further about him, I learned that he was a universal favorite in the village, and the oracle of the tap-room; where he delighted the rustics with his songs, and, like Sinbad, astonished them with his stories of strange lands, and shipwrecks, and sea-fights. He was much noticed too by gentlemen sportsmen of the neighborhood; had taught several of them the art of angling; and was a privileged visitor to their kitchens. The whole tenor of his life was quiet and inoffensive, being principally passed about the neighboring streams, when the weather and season were favorable; and at other times he employed himself at home, preparing his fishing tackle for the next campaign, or manufacturing rods, nets, and flies, for his patrons and pupils among the gentry.

He was a regular attendant at church on Sundays, though he generally fell asleep during the sermon. He had made it his particular request that when he died he should be buried in a green spot, which he could see from his seat in church, and which he had marked out ever since he was a boy, and had thought of when far from home on the raging sea, in danger of being food for the fishes—it was the spot where his father and mother had been buried.

I have done, for I fear that my reader is growing weary; but I could not refrain from drawing the picture of this worthy "brother of the angle;" who has made me more than ever in love with the theory, though I fear I shall never be adroit in the practice of his art; and I will conclude this rambling sketch in the words of honest Izaak Walton, by craving the blessing of St. Peter's master upon my reader, "and upon all that are true lovers of virtue; and dare trust in his providence; and be quiet; and go a angling."

THE LEGEND OF SLEEPY
HOLLOW

FOUND AMONG THE PAPERS OF THE LATE
DIEDRICH KNICKERBOCKER

A pleasing land of drowsy head it was,
  Of dreams that wave before the half-shut eye;
And of gay castles in the clouds that pass,
  For ever flushing round a summer sky.

CASTLE OF INDOLENCE

IN THE bosom of one of those spacious coves which indent the eastern shore of the Hudson, at that broad expansion of the river denominated by the ancient Dutch navigators the Tappan Zee, and where they always prudently shortened sail, and implored the protection of St. Nicholas when they crossed, there lies a small market-town or rural port, which by some is called Greensburgh, but which is more generally and properly known by the name of Tarry Town. This name was given, we are told, in former days, by the good house-wives of the adjacent country, from the inveterate propensity of their husbands to linger about the village tavern on market days. Be that as it may, I do not vouch for the fact, but merely advert to it, for the sake of being precise and authentic. Not far from this village, perhaps about two miles, there is a little valley, or rather lap of land, among high hills, which is one of the quietest places in the whole world. A small brook glides through it, with just murmur enough to lull one to repose; and the occasional whistle of a quail, or tapping of a woodpecker, is almost the only sound that ever breaks in upon the uniform tranquillity.

I recollect that, when a stripling, my first exploit in

squirrel-shooting was in a grove of tall walnut-trees that shades one side of the valley. I had wandered into it at noon time, when all nature is peculiarly quiet, and was startled by the roar of my own gun, as it broke the Sabbath stillness around, and was prolonged and reverberated by the angry echoes. If ever I should wish for a retreat, whither I might steal from the world and its distractions, and dream quietly away the remnant of a troubled life, I know of none more promising than this little valley.

From the listless repose of the place, and the peculiar character of its inhabitants, who are descendants from the original Dutch settlers, this sequestered glen has long been known by the name of SLEEPY HOLLOW, and its rustic lads are called the Sleepy Hollow Boys throughout all the neighboring country. A drowsy, dreamy influence seems to hang over the land, and to pervade the very atmosphere. Some say that the place was bewitched by a high German doctor, during the early days of the settlement; others, that an old Indian chief, the prophet or wizard of his tribe, held his powwows there before the country was discovered by Master Hendrick Hudson. Certain it is, the place still continues under the sway of some witching power, that holds a spell over the minds of the good people, causing them to walk in a continual reverie. They are given to all kinds of marvellous beliefs; are subject to trances and visions; and frequently see strange sights, and hear music and voices in the air. The whole neighborhood abounds with local tales, haunted spots, and twilight superstitions; stars shoot and meteors glare oftener across the valley than in any other part of the country, and the nightmare, with her whole ninefold, seems to make it the favorite scene of her gambols.

The dominant spirit, however, that haunts this enchanted region, and seems to be commander-in-chief of all the powers of the air, is the apparition of a figure on horseback without a head. It is said by some to be the ghost of a Hessian trooper, whose head had been carried away by a cannon-ball, in some nameless battle during the revolutionary war; and who is ever and anon seen by the country folk, hurrying along in the gloom of night, as if on the wings of the wind. His haunts are not confined to the valley, but extend at times to the adjacent roads, and especially to the vicinity of a church at no great distance. Indeed, certain of the most authentic historians of those parts, who have been careful in collecting and collating the floating facts concerning this spectre, allege that the body of the trooper, having been buried in the church-yard, the ghost rides forth to the scene of battle in nightly quest of his head; and that the rushing speed with which he sometimes passes along the Hollow, like a midnight blast, is owing to his being belated, and in a hurry to get back to the church-yard before daybreak.

Such is the general purport of this legendary superstition, which has furnished materials for many a wild story in that region of shadows; and the spectre is known, at all the country firesides, by the name of the Headless Horseman of Sleepy Hollow.

It is remarkable that the visionary propensity I have mentioned is not confined to the native inhabitants of the valley, but is unconsciously imbibed by every one who resides there for a time. However wide awake they may have been before they entered that sleepy region, they are sure, in a little time, to inhale the witching influence of the air, and begin to grow imaginative—to dream dreams, and see apparitions.

I mention this peaceful spot with all possible laud; for it is in such little retired Dutch valleys, found here and there embosomed in the great State of New York, that population, manners, and customs, remain fixed; while the great torrent of migration and improvement, which is making such incessant changes in other parts of this restless country, sweeps by them unobserved. They are like those little nooks of still water which border a rapid stream; where we may see the straw and bubble riding quietly at anchor, or slowly revolving in their mimic harbor, undisturbed by the rush of the passing current. Though many years have elapsed since I trod the drowsy shades of Sleepy Hollow, yet I question whether I should not still find the same trees and the same families vegetating in its sheltered bosom.

In this by-place of nature, there abode, in a remote period of American history, that is to say, some thirty years since, a worthy wight of the name of Ichabod Crane; who sojourned, or, as he expressed it, "tarried," in Sleepy Hollow, for the purpose of instructing the children of the vicinity. He was a native of Connecticut; a State which supplies the Union with pioneers for the mind as well as for the forest, and sends forth yearly its legions of frontier woodsmen and country schoolmasters. The cognomen of Crane was not inapplicable to his person. He was tall, but exceedingly lank, with narrow shoulders, long arms and legs, hands that dangled a mile out of his sleeves, feet that might have served for shovels, and his whole frame most loosely hung together. His head was small, and flat at top, with huge ears, large green glassy eyes, and a long snipe nose, so that it looked like a weather-cock, perched upon his spindle neck, to tell which way the wind blew. To see him striding along the profile of a hill on a windy day, with his clothes bagging and fluttering about him, one might have mistaken him for the genius of famine descending upon the earth, or some scarecrow eloped from a cornfield.

His school-house was a low building of one large room, rudely constructed of logs; the windows partly glazed, and partly patched with leaves of old copy-books. It was most ingeniously secured at vacant hours, by a withe twisted in the handle of the door, and stakes set against the window shutters; so that, though a thief might get in with perfect ease, he would find some embarrassment in getting out; an idea most probably borrowed by the architect, Yost Van Houten, from the mystery of an eel-pot. The school-house stood in a rather lonely but pleasant situation, just at the foot of a woody hill, with a brook running close by, and a formidable birch tree growing at one end of it. From hence the low murmur of his pupils' voices, conning over their lessons, might be heard in a drowsy summer's day, like the hum of a bee-hive; interrupted now and then by the authoritative voice of the master, in the tone of menace or command; or peradventure, by the appalling sound of the birch, as he urged some tardy loiterer along the flowery path of knowledge. Truth to say, he was a conscientious man, and ever bore in mind the golden maxim, "Spare the rod and spoil the child." Ichabod Crane's scholars certainly were not spoiled.

I would not have it imagined, however, that he was one of those cruel potentates of the school, who joy in the smart of their subjects; on the contrary, he administered justice with discrimination rather than severity; taking the burthen off the backs of the weak, and laying it on those of the strong. Your mere puny stripling, that winced at the least flourish of the rod, was passed by with indulgence; but the claims of justice were satisfied by inflicting a double portion on some little, tough, wrong-headed, broad-skirted Dutch urchin, who sulked and swelled and grew dogged and sullen beneath the birch. All this he called "doing his duty by their parents;" and he never inflicted a chastisement without following it by the assurance, so consolatory to the smarting urchin, that "he would remember it, and thank him for it the longest day he had to live."

When school hours were over, he was even the companion and playmate of the larger boys; and on holiday afternoons would convoy some of the smaller ones home, who happened to have pretty sisters, or good housewives for mothers, noted for the comforts of the cupboard. Indeed it behooved him to keep on good terms with his pupils. The revenue arising from his school was small, and would have been scarcely sufficient to furnish him with daily bread, for he was a huge feeder, and though lank, had the dilating powers of an anaconda; but to help out his maintenance, he was, according to country custom in those parts, boarded and lodged at the houses of the farmers, whose children he instructed. With these he lived successively a week at a time; thus going the rounds of the neighborhood, with all his worldly effects tied up in a cotton handkerchief.

That all this might not be too onerous on the purses of his rustic patrons, who are apt to consider the costs of schooling a grievous burden, and schoolmasters as mere drones, he had various ways of rendering himself both useful and agreeable. He assisted the farmers occasionally in the lighter labors of their farms; helped to make hay; mended the fences; took the horses to water; drove the cows from pasture; and cut wood for the winter fire. He laid aside, too, all the dominant dignity and absolute sway with which he lorded it in his little empire, the school, and became wonderfully gentle and ingratiating. He found favor in the eyes of the mothers, by petting the children, particularly the youngest; and like the lion bold, which whilom so magnanimously the lamb did hold, he would sit with a child on one knee, and rock a cradle with his foot for whole hours together.

In addition to his other vocations, he was the singing-master of the neighborhood, and picked up many bright shillings by instructing the young folks in psalmody. It was a matter of no little vanity to him, on Sundays, to take his station in front of the church gallery, with a band of chosen singers; where, in his own mind, he completely carried away the palm from the parson. Certain it is, his voice resounded far above all the rest of the congregation; and there are peculiar quavers still to be heard in that church, and which may even be heard half a mile off, quite to the opposite side of the mill-pond, on a still Sunday morning, which are said to be legitimately descended from the nose of Ichabod Crane. Thus, by divers little make-shifts in that ingenious way which is commonly denominated "by hook and by crook," the worthy pedagogue got on tolerably enough, and was thought, by all who understood nothing of the labor of headwork, to have a wonderfully easy life of it.

The schoolmaster is generally a man of some importance in the female circle of a rural neighborhood; being considered a kind of idle gentlemanlike personage, of vastly superior taste and accomplishments to the rough country swains, and, indeed, inferior in learning only to the parson. His appearance, therefore, is apt to occasion some little stir at the teatable of a farmhouse, and the addition of a supernumerary dish of cakes or sweet-meats, or, peradventure, the parade of a silver tea-pot. Our man of letters, therefore, was peculiarly happy in the smiles of all the country damsels. How he would figure among them in the churchyard, between services on Sundays! gathering grapes for them from the wild vines that overrun the surrounding trees; reciting for their amusement all the epitaphs on the tombstones; or sauntering, with a whole bevy of them, along the banks of the adjacent millpond; while the more bashful country bumpkins hung sheepishly back, envying his superior elegance and address.

From his half itinerant life, also, he was a kind of travelling gazette, carrying the whole budget of local gossip from house to house; so that his appearance was always greeted with satisfaction. He was, moreover, esteemed by the women as a man of great erudition, for he had read several books quite through, and was a perfect master of Cotton Mather's *History of New England Witchcraft*, in which, by the way, he most firmly and potently believed.

He was, in fact, an odd mixture of small shrewdness and simple credulity. His appetite for the marvellous, and his powers of digesting it, were equally extraordinary; and both had been increased by his residence in this spellbound region. No tale was too gross or monstrous for his capacious swallow. It was often his delight, after his school was dismissed in the afternoon, to stretch himself on the rich bed of clover, bordering the little brook that whimpered by his school-house, and there con over old Mather's direful tales, until the gathering dusk of the evening made the printed page a mere mist before his eyes. Then, as he wended his way, by swamp and stream and awful woodland, to the farmhouse where he happened to be quartered, every sound of nature, at that witching hour, fluttered his

excited imagination: the moan of the whip-poor-will*
from the hill-side; the boding cry of the tree-toad, that
harbinger of storm; the dreary hooting of the screech-
owl, or the sudden rustling in the thicket of birds
frightened from their roost. The fire-flies, too, which
sparkled most vividly in the darkest places, now and
then startled him, as one of uncommon brightness
would stream across his path; and if, by chance, a huge
blockhead of a beetle came winging his blundering flight
against him, the poor varlet was ready to give up the
ghost, with the idea that he was struck with a witch's
token. His only resource on such occasions, either to
drown thought, or drive away evil spirits, was to sing
psalm tunes; and the good people of Sleepy Hollow, as
they sat by their doors of an evening, were often filled
with awe, at hearing his nasal melody, "in linked
sweetness long drawn out," floating from the distant hill,
or along the dusky road.

Another of his sources of fearful pleasure was to pass
long winter evenings with the old Dutch wives, as they
sat spinning by the fire, with a row of apples roasting
and spluttering along the hearth, and listen to their
marvellous tales of ghosts and goblins, and haunted
fields, and haunted brooks, and haunted bridges, and
haunted houses, and particularly of the headless horseman, or galloping Hessian of the Hollow, as they
sometimes called him. He would delight them equally by
his anecdotes of witchcraft, and of the direful omens
and portentous sights and sounds in the air, which
prevailed in the earlier times of Connecticut; and would
frighten them woefully with speculations upon comets
and shooting stars; and with the alarming fact that the

*The whip-poor-will is a bird which is only heard at night. It receives
its name from its note, which is thought to resemble those words.

world did absolutely turn round, and that they were half the time topsy-turvy!

But if there was a pleasure in all this, while snugly cuddling in the chimney corner of a chamber that was all of a ruddy glow from the crackling wood fire, and where, of course, no spectre dared to show his face, it was dearly purchased by the terrors of his subsequent walk homewards. What fearful shapes and shadows beset his path amidst the dim and ghastly glare of a snowy night! With what wistful look did he eye every trembling ray of light streaming across the waste fields from some distant window! How often was he appalled by some shrub covered with snow, which, like a sheeted spectre, beset his very path! How often did he shrink with curdling awe at the sound of his own steps on the frosty crust beneath his feet; and dread to look over his shoulder, lest he should behold some uncouth being tramping close behind him! And how often was he thrown into complete dismay by some rushing blast, howling among the trees, in the idea that it was the Galloping Hessian on one of his nightly scourings!

All these, however, were mere terrrors of the night, phantoms of the mind that walk in darkness; and though he had seen many spectres in his time, and been more than once beset by Satan in divers shapes, in his lonely perambulations, yet daylight put an end to all these evils; and he would have passed a pleasant life of it, in despite of the devil and all his works, if his path had not been crossed by a being that causes more perplexity to mortal man than ghosts, goblins, and the whole race of witches put together, and that was—a woman.

Among the musical disciples who assembled, one evening in each week, to receive his instructions in psalmody, was Katrina Van Tassel, the daughter and only child of a substantial Dutch farmer. She was a blooming lass of fresh eighteen; plump as a partridge; ripe and melting and rosy cheeked as one of her father's peaches, and universally famed, not merely for her beauty, but her vast expectations. She was withal a little of a coquette, as might be perceived even in her dress, which was a mixture of ancient and modern fashions, as most suited to set off her charms. She wore the ornaments of pure yellow gold, which her great-great-grandmother had brought over from Saardam; the tempting stomacher of the olden time; and withal a provokingly short petticoat, to display the prettiest foot and ankle in the country round.

Ichabod Crane had a soft and foolish heart towards the sex; and it is not to be wondered at, that so tempting a morsel soon found favor in his eyes; more especially after he had visited her in her paternal mansion. Old Baltus Van Tassel was a perfect picture of a thriving, contented, liberal-hearted farmer. He seldom, it is true, sent either his eyes or his thoughts beyond the boundaries of his own farm; but within those everything was snug, happy, and well-conditioned. He was satisfied with his wealth, but not proud of it; and piqued himself upon the hearty abundance, rather than the style in which he lived. His stronghold was situated on the banks of the Hudson, in one of those green, sheltered, fertile nooks, in which the Dutch farmers are so fond of nestling. A great elm-tree spread its broad branches over it; at the foot of which bubbled up a spring of the softest and sweetest water, in a little well, formed of a barrel; and then stole sparkling away through the grass, to a neighboring brook, that bubbled along among alders and dwarf willows. Hard by the farmhouse was a vast barn, that might have served for a church; every window and crevice of which seemed bursting forth with the treasures of the farm; the flail was busily resounding within it from morning to night; swallows and martins skimmed twittering about the eaves; and rows of pigeons, some with one eye turned up, as if watching the weather, some with their heads under their wings, or buried in their bosoms, and others swelling, and cooing, and bowing about their dames, were enjoying the sunshine on the roof. Sleek unwieldly porkers were grunting in the repose and abundance of their pens; whence sallied forth, now and then, troops of sucking pigs, as if to snuff the air. A stately squadron of snowy geese were riding in an adjoining pond, convoying whole fleets of ducks; regiments of turkeys were gobbling through the farmyard, and guinea fowls fretting about it, like ill-tempered housewives, with their peevish discontented cry. Before the barn door strutted the gallant cock, that pattern of a husband, a warrior, and a fine gentleman, clapping his burnished wings, and crowing in the pride and gladness of his heart— sometimes tearing up the earth with his feet, and then generously calling his ever-hungry family of wives and children to enjoy the rich morsel which he had discovered.

The pedagogue's mouth watered, as he looked upon this sumptuous promise of luxurious winter fare. In his devouring mind's eye, he pictured to himself every roasting pig running about with a pudding in his belly, and an apple in his mouth; the pigeons were snugly put to bed in a comfortable pie, and tucked in with a coverlet of crust; the geese were swimming in their own gravy; and the ducks pairing cosily in dishes, like snug married couples, with a decent competency of onion sauce. In the porkers he saw carved out the future sleek side of bacon, and juicy relishing ham; not a turkey but he beheld daintily trussed up, with its gizzard under its wing, and, peradventure, a necklace of savory sausages;

and even bright chanticleer himself lay sprawling on his back, in a side-dish, with uplifted claws, as if craving that quarter which his chivalrous spirit disdained to ask while living.

As the enraptured Ichabod fancied all this, and as he rolled his great green eyes over the fat meadow-lands, the rich fields of wheat, of rye, of buckwheat, and Indian corn, and the orchards burthened with ruddy fruit, which surrounded the warm tenement of Van Tassel, his heart yearned after the damsel who was to inherit these domains, and his imagination expanded with the idea, how they might be readily turned into cash, and the money investd in immense tracts of wild land, and shingle palaces in the wilderness. Nay, his busy fancy already realized his hopes, and presented to him the blooming Katrina, with a whole family of children, mounted on the top of a wagon loaded with household trumpery, with pots and kettles dangling beneath; and he beheld himself bestriding a pacing mare, with a colt at her heels, setting out for Kentucky, Tennessee, or the Lord knows where.

When he entered the house the conquest of his heart was complete. It was one of those spacious farmhouses, with high-ridged, but lowly-sloping roofs, built in the style handed down from the first Dutch settlers; the low projecting eaves forming a piazza along the front, capable of being closed up in bad weather. Under this were flung flails, harness, various utensils of husbandry, and nets for fishing in the neighboring river. Benches were built along the sides for summer use; and a great spinning-wheel at one end, and a churn at the other, showed the various uses to which this important porch might be devoted. From this piazza the wondering Ichabod entered the hall, which formed the center of the mansion and the place of usual residence. Here, rows of resplendent pewter, ranged on a long dresser, dazzled his eyes. In one corner stood a huge bag of wool ready to be spun; in another a quantity of linsey-woolsey just from the loom; ears of Indian corn, and strings of dried apples and peaches, hung in gay festoons along the walls, mingled with the gaud of red peppers; and a door left ajar gave him a peep into the best parlor, where the claw-footed chairs, and dark mahogany tables, shone like mirrors; and irons, with their accompanying shovel and tongs, glistened from their covert of asparagus tops; mock-oranges and conch-shells decorated the mantel-piece; strings of various colored birds' eggs were suspended above it: a great ostrich egg was hung from the centre of the room, and a corner cupboard, knowingly left open, displayed immense treasures of old silver and well-mended china.

From the moment Ichabod laid his eyes upon these regions of delight, the peace of his mind was at an end, and his only study was how to gain the affections of the peerless daughter of Van Tassel. In this enterprise, however, he had more real difficulties than generally fell to the lot of a knight-errant of yore, who seldom had any thing but giants, enchanters, fiery dragons, and such like easily-conquered adversaries, to contend with; and had to make his way merely through gates of iron and brass, and walls of adamant, to the castle keep, where the lady of his heart was confined; all which he achieved as easily as a man would carve his way to the center of a Christmas pie; and then the lady gave him her hand as a matter of course. Ichabod, on the contrary, had to win his way to the heart of a country coquette, beset with a labyrinth of whims and caprices, which were forever presenting new difficulties and impediments; and he had to encounter a host of fearful adversaries of real flesh and blood, the numerous rustic admirers, who beset every portal to her heart; keeping a watchful and angry eye upon each other, but ready to fly out in the common cause against any new competitor.

Among these the most formidable was a burly, roaring, roystering blade, of the name of Abraham, or, according to the Dutch abbreviation, Brom Van Brunt, the hero of the country round, which rang with his feats of strength and hardihood. He was broad-shouldered and double-jointed, with short curly black hair, and a bluff, but not unpleasant countenance, having a mingled air of fun and arrogance. From his Herculean frame and great powers of limb, he had received the nickname of BROM BONES, by which he was universally known. He was famed for great knowledge and skill in horsemanship, being as dexterous on horseback as a Tartar. He was foremost at all races and cock-fights; and, with the ascendency which bodily strength acquires in rustic life, was the umpire in all disputes, setting his hat on one side, and giving his decisions with an air and tone admitting of no gainsay or appeal. He was always ready for either a fight or a frolic; but had more mischief than ill-will in his composition; and, with all his overbearing roughness, there was a strong dash of waggish good humor at bottom. He had three or four boon companions, who regarded him as their model, and at the head of whom he scoured the country, attending every scene of feud or merriment for miles round. In cold weather he was distinguished by a fur cap, surmounted with a flaunting fox's tail; and when the folks at a country gathering descried this well-known crest at a distance, whisking about among a squad of hard riders, they always stood by for a squall. Sometimes his crew would be heard dashing along past the farmhouses at midnight, with whoop and halloo, like a troop of Don Cossacks; and the old dames, startled out of their sleep, would listen for a moment till the hurry-scurry had clattered by, and then exclaim, "Ay, there goes Brom Bones and his gang!" The neighbors looked upon him with a mixture of awe, admiration, and good will; and when any madcap prank, or rustic brawl, occurred in the vicinity, always shook their heads, and warranted Brom Bones was at the bottom of it.

This rantipole hero had for some time singled out the blooming Katrina for the object of his uncouth gallantries, and though his amorous toyings were something like the gentle caresses and endearments of a bear, yet it was whispered that she did not altogether discourage his hopes. Certain it is, his advances were signals for rival candidates to retire, who felt no inclination to cross a lion in his amours; insomuch, that when his horse was seen tied to Van Tassel's paling, on a Sunday night, a sure sign that his master was courting, or, as it is termed, "sparking," within, all other suitors passed by in despair, and carried the war into other quarters.

Such was the formidable rival with whom Ichabod Crane had to contend, and, considering all things, a stouter man than he would have shrunk from the competition, and a wiser man would have despaired. He had, however, a happy mixture of pliability and perseverance in his nature; he was in form and spirit like a supple-jack—yielding, but tough; though he bent, he never broke; and though he bowed beneath the slightest pressure, yet, the moment it was away—jerk! he was as erect, and carried his head as high as ever.

To have taken the field openly against his rival would have been madness; for he was not a man to be thwarted in his amours, any more than that stormy lover, Achilles. Ichabod, therefore, made his advances in a quiet and gently-insinuating manner. Under cover of his character of singing-master, he made frequent visits at the farmhouse; not that he had any thing to apprehend from the meddlesome interference of parents, which is so often a stumbling-block in the path of lovers. Balt Van Tassel was an easy indulgent soul; he loved his daughter better even than his pipe, and, like a reasonable man and an excellent father, let her have her way in every thing. His notable little wife, too, had enough to do to attend to her housekeeping and manage her poultry; for, as she sagely observed, ducks and geese are foolish things, and must be looked after, but girls can take care of themselves. Thus while the busy dame bustled about the house, or plied her spinning-wheel at one end of the piazza, honest Balt would sit smoking his evening pipe at the other, watching the achievements of a little wooden warrior, who, armed with a sword in each hand, was most valiantly fighting the wind on the pinnacle of the barn. In the mean time, Ichabod would carry on his suit with the daughter by the side of the spring under the great elm, or sauntering along in the twilight, that hour so favorable to the lover's eloquence.

I profess not to know how women's hearts are wooed and won. To me they have always been matters of riddle and admiration. Some seem to have but one vulnerable point, or door of access; while others have a thousand avenues, and may be captured in a thousand different ways. It is a great triumph of skill to gain the former, but a still greater proof of generalship to maintain possession of the latter, for the man must battle for his fortress at every door and window. He who wins a thousand common hearts is therefore entitled to some renown; but he who keeps undisputed sway over the heart of a coquette, is indeed a hero. Certain it is, this was not the case with the redoubtable Brom Bones; and from the moment Ichabod Crane made his advances, the interests of the former evidently declined; his horse was no longer seen tied at the palings on Sunday nights, and a deadly feud gradually arose between him and the preceptor of Sleepy Hollow.

Brom, who had a degree of rough chivalry in his nature, would fain have carried matters to open warfare, and have settled their pretensions to the lady, according to the mode of those most concise and simple reasoners, the knights-errant of yore—by single combat; but Ichabod was too conscious of the superior might of his adversary to enter the lists against him: he had overheard a boast of Bones, that he would "double the schoolmaster up, and lay him on a shelf of his own school-house;" and he was too wary to give him an opportunity. There was something extremely provoking in this obstinately pacific system; it left Brom no alternative but to draw upon the funds of rustic waggery in his disposition, and to play off boorish practical jokes upon his rival. Ichabod became the object of whimsical persecution of Bones, and his gang of rough riders. They harried his hitherto peaceful domains; smoked out his singing school, by stopping up the chimney; broke into the school-house at night, in spite of its formidable fastenings of withe and window stakes, and turned everything topsy-turvy: so that the poor schoolmaster began to think all the witches in the country held their meetings there. But what was still more annoying, Brom took all opportunities of turning him into ridicule in presence of his mistress, and had a scoundrel dog whom he taught to whine in the most ludicrous manner, and introduced as a rival of Ichabod's to instruct her in psalmody.

In this way matters went on for some time, without producing any material effect on the relative situation of the contending powers. On a fine autumnal afternoon, Ichabod, in pensive mood, sat enthroned on the lofty stool whence he usually watched all the concerns of his little literary realm. In his hand he swayed a ferule, that sceptre of despotic power; the birch of justice reposed on three nails, behind the throne, a constant terror to evil doers; while on the desk before him might be seen sundry contraband articles and prohibited weapons, detected upon the persons of idle urchins; such as half-munched apples, popguns, whirligigs, fly-cages, and whole legions of rampant little paper game-cocks. Apparently there had been some appalling act of justice recently inflicted, for his scholars were all busily intent upon their books, or slyly whispering behind them with one eye kept upon the master; and a kind of buzzing stillness reigned throughout the schoolroom. It was suddenly interrupted by the appearance of a negro, in tow-cloth jacket and trowsers, a round-crowned fragment of a hat, like the cap of Mercury, and mounted on the back of a ragged, wild, half-broken colt, which he managed with a rope by way of halter. He came clattering up to the school door with an invitation to Ichabod to attend a merrymaking or "quilting frolic," to be held that evening at Mynheer Van Tassel's; and having delivered his message with that air of importance, and effort at fine language, which a negro is apt to display on petty embassies of the kind, he dashed over the brook, and was seen scampering away up the hollow, full of the importance and hurry of his mission.

All was now bustle and hubbub in the late quiet schoolroom. The scholars were hurried through their lessons, without stopping at trifles; those who were nimble skipped over half with impunity, and those who were tardy, had a smart application now and then in the rear, to quicken their speed, or help them over a tall word. Books were flung aside without being put away on the shelves, inkstands were overturned, benches thrown down, and the whole school was turned loose an hour before the usual time, bursting forth like a legion of young imps, yelping and racketing about the green, in joy of their early emancipation.

The gallant Ichabod now spent at least an extra half hour at his toilet, brushing and furbishing up his best, and indeed only suit of rusty black, and arranging his looks by a bit of broken looking-glass, that hung up in the school-house. That he might make his appearance before his mistress in the true style of a cavalier, he borrowed a horse from the farmer with whom he was domiciliated, a choleric old Dutchman, of the name of Hans Van Ripper, and, thus gallantly mounted, issued forth, like a knight-errant in quest of adventures. But it is meet I should, in the true spirit of romantic story, give some account of the looks and equipment of my hero and his steed. The animal he bestrode was a broken-down plough-horse, that had outlived almost every thing but his viciousness. He was gaunt and shagged, with a ewe neck and a head like a hammer; his rusty mane and tail were tangled and knotted with burrs; one eye had lost its pupil, and was glaring and spectral; but the other had the gleam of a genuine devil in it. Still he must have had fire and mettle in his day, if we may judge from the name he bore of Gunpowder. He had, in fact, been a favorite steed of his master's, the choleric Van Ripper, who was a furious rider, and had infused, very probably, some of his own spirit into the animal; for, old and broken-down as he looked, there was more of the lurking devil in him than in any young filly in the country.

Ichabod was a suitable figure for such a steed. He rode with short stirrups, which brought his knees nearly up to the pommel of the saddle; his sharp elbows stuck out like grasshoppers'; he carried his whip perpendicularly in his hand, like a sceptre, and, as his horse jogged on, the motion of his arms was not unlike the flapping of a pair of wings. A small wool hat rested on the top of his nose, for so his scanty strip of forehead might be called; and the skirts of his black coat fluttered out almost to the horse's tail. Such was the appearance of Ichabod and his steed, as they shambled out of the gate of Hans Van Ripper, and it was altogether such an apparition as is seldom to be met with in broad daylight.

It was, as I have said, a fine autumnal day, the sky was clear and serene, and nature wore that rich and golden livery which we always associate with the idea of abundance. The forests had put on their sober brown and yellow, while some trees of the tenderer kind had been nipped by the frosts into brilliant dyes of orange, purple, and scarlet. Streaming files of wild ducks began to make their appearance high in the air; the bark of the squirrel might be heard from the groves of beech and hickory nuts, and the pensive whistle of the quail at intervals from the neighboring stubble-field.

The small birds were taking their farewell banquets. In the fulness of their revelry, they fluttered, chirping and frolicking, from bush to bush, and tree to tree, capricious from the very profusion and variety around them. There was the honest cock-robin, the favorite game of stripling sportsmen, with its loud querulous note; and the twittering blackbirds flying in sable clouds; and the golden-winged woodpecker, with his crimson crest, his broad black gorget, and splendid plumage; and the cedar bird, with its red-tipped wings and yellow-tipt tail, and its little monteiro cap of feathers; and the blue jay, that noisy coxcomb, in his gay light-blue coat and white under-clothes; screaming and chattering, nodding and bobbing and bowing, and pretending to be on good terms with every songster of the grove.

As Ichabod jogged slowly on his way, his eye, ever open to every symptom of culinary abundance, ranged with delight over the treasures of jolly autumn. On all sides he beheld vast store of apples; some hanging in oppressive opulence on the trees; some gathered into baskets and barrels for the market; others heaped up in rich piles for the cider-press. Farther on he beheld great fields of Indian corn, with its golden ears peeping from their leafy coverts, and holding out the promise of cakes and hasty pudding; and the yellow pumpkins lying beneath them, turning up their fair round bellies to the sun, and giving ample prospects of the most luxurious of pies; and anon he passed the fragrant buckwheat fields, breathing the odor of the bee-hive, and as he beheld them, soft anticipations stole over his mind of dainty slapjacks, well buttered, and garnished with honey or treacle, by the delicate little dimpled hand of Katrina Van Tassel.

Thus feeding his mind with many sweet thoughts and "sugared suppositions," he journeyed along the sides of a range of hills which look out upon some of the goodliest scenes of the mighty Hudson. The sun gradually wheeled his broad disk down into the west. The wide bosom of the Tappan Zee lay motionless and glassy, excepting that here and there a gentle undulation waved and prolonged the blue shadow of the distant mountain. A few amber clouds floated in the sky, without a breath of air to move them. The horizon was of a fine golden tint, changing gradually into a pure apple green, and from that into the deep blue of the midheaven. A slanting ray lingered on the woody crests of the precipices that overhung some parts of the river, giving greater depth to the dark-gray and purple of their rocky sides. A sloop was loitering in the distance, dropping slowly down with the tide, her sail hanging uselessly against the mast; and as the reflection of the sky gleamed along the still water, it seemed as if the vessel was suspended in the air.

It was toward evening that Ichabod arrived at the castle of the Heer Van Tassel, which he found thronged with the pride and flower of the adjacent country. Old farmers, a spare leathern-faced race, in homespun coats and breeches, blue stockings, huge shoes, and magnificent pewter buckles. Their brisk, withered little dames, in close crimped caps, long-waisted shortgowns, homespun petticoats, with scissors and pincushions, and gay calico pockets hanging on the outside. Buxom lasses, almost as antiquated as their mothers, excepting where a straw hat, a fine ribbon, or perhaps a white frock, gave symptoms of city innovation. The sons, in short square-skirted coats with rows of stupendous brass buttons, and their hair generally queued in the fashion of the times, especially if they could procure an eel-skin for the purpose, it being esteemed, throughout the country, as a potent nourisher and strengthener of the hair.

Brom Bones, however, was the hero of the scene, having come to the gathering on his favorite steed Daredevil, a creature, like himself, full of mettle and mischief, and which no one but himself could manage. He was, in fact, noted for preferring vicious animals, given to all kinds of tricks, which kept the rider in constant risk of his neck, for he held a tractable well-broken horse as unworthy of a lad of spirit.

Fain would I pause to dwell upon the world of charms that burst upon the enraptured gaze of my hero, as he entered the state parlor of Van Tassel's mansion. Not those of the bevy of buxom lasses, with their luxurious display of red and white; but the ample charms of a genuine Dutch country tea-table, in the sumptuous time of autumn. Such heaped-up platters of cakes of various and almost indescribable kinds, known only to experienced Dutch housewives! There was the doughty dough-nut, the tenderer oly koek, and the crisp and crumbling cruller; sweet cakes and short cakes, ginger cakes and honey cakes, and the whole family of cakes. And then there were apple pies and peach pies and pumpkin pies; besides slices of ham and smoked beef; and moreover delectable dishes of preserved plums, and peaches, and pears, and quinces; not to mention broiled shad and roasted chickens; together with bowls of milk and cream, all mingled higgledy-piggledy, pretty much as I have enumerated them, with the motherly tea-pot sending up its clouds of vapor from the midst—Heaven bless the mark! I want breath and time to discuss this banquet as it deserves, and am too eager to get on with my story. Happily, Ichabod Crane was not in so great a hurry as his historian, but did ample justice to every dainty.

He was a kind and thankful creature, whose heart dilated in proportion as his skin was filled with good cheer; and whose spirits rose with eating as some men's do with drink. He could not help, too, rolling his large eyes round him as he ate, and chuckling with the possibility that he might one day be lord of all this scene of almost unimaginable luxury and splendor. Then, he thought, how soon he'd turn his back upon the old school-house; snap his fingers in the face of Hans Van Ripper, and every other niggardly patron, and kick any itinerant pedagogue out of doors that should dare to call him comrade!

Old Baltus Van Tassel moved about among his guests with a face dilated with content and good humor, round and jolly as the harvest moon. His hospitable attentions were brief, but expressive, being confined to a shake of the hand, a slap on the shoulder, a loud laugh, and a pressing invitation to "fall to, and help themselves."

And now the sound of the music from the common room, or hall, summoned to the dance. The musician was an old grayheaded negro, who had been the itinerant orchestra of the neighborhood for more than half a century. His instrument was as old and battered as himself. The greater part of the time he scraped on two or three strings, accompanying every movement of the bow with a motion of the head; bowing almost to the ground, and stamping with his foot whenever a fresh couple were to start.

Ichabod prided himself upon his dancing as much as upon his vocal powers. Not a limb, not a fibre about him was idle; and to have seen his loosely hung frame in full motion, and clattering about the room, you would have thought Saint Vitus himself, that blessed patron of the dance, was figuring before you in person. He was the admiration of all the negroes; who, having gathered, of all ages and sizes, from the farm and the neighborhood, stood forming a pyramid of shining black faces at every door and window, gazing with delight at the scene, rolling their white eyeballs, and showing grinning rows of ivory from ear to ear. How could the flogger of urchins be otherwise than animated and joyous? The lady of his heart was his partner in the dance, and smiling graciously in reply to all his amorous oglings; while Brom Bones, sorely smitten with love and jealousy, sat brooding by himself in one corner.

When the dance was at an end, Ichabod was attracted to a knot of the sager folks, who, with old Van Tassel, sat smoking at one end of the piazza, gossiping over former times, and drawing out long stories about the war.

This neighborhood, at the time of which I am speaking, was one of those highly-favored places which abound with chronicle and great men. The British and American line had run near it during the war; it had, therefore, been the scene of marauding, and infested with refugees, cow-boys, and all kinds of border chivalry. Just sufficient time had elapsed to enable each storyteller to dress up his tale with a little becoming fiction, and, in the indistinctness of his recollection, to make himself the hero of every exploit.

There was the story of Doffue Martling, a large blue-bearded Dutchman, who had nearly taken a British frigate with an old iron nine-pounder from a mud breastwork, only that his gun burst at the sixth discharge. And there was an old gentleman who shall be nameless, being too rich a mynheer to be lightly mentioned, who, in the Battle of White Plains, being an excellent master of defense, parried a musket ball with a small sword, insomuch that he absolutely felt it whiz round the blade, and glance off at the hilt: in proof of which, he was ready at any time to show the sword, with the hilt a little bent. There were several more that had been equally great in the field, not one of whom but was persuaded that he had a considerable hand in bringing the war to a happy termination.

But all these were nothing to the tales of ghosts and apparitions that succeeded. The neighborhood is rich in legendary treasures of the kind. Local tales and superstitions thrive best in these sheltered long-settled retreats; but are trampled under foot by the shifting throng that forms the population of most of our country places. Besides, there is no encouragement for ghosts in most of our villages, for they have scarcely had time to finish their first nap, and turn themselves in their graves, before their surviving friends have travelled away from the neighborhood; so that when they turn out at night to walk their rounds, they have no acquaintance left to call upon. This is perhaps the reason why we so seldom hear of ghosts except in our long-established Dutch communities.

The immediate cause, however, of the prevalence of supernatural stories in these parts, was doubtless owing to the vicinity of Sleepy Hollow. There was a contagion in the very air that blew from that haunted region; it breathed forth an atmosphere of dreams and fancies infecting all the land. Several of the Sleepy Hollow people were present at Van Tassel's, and, as usual, were doling out their wild and wonderful legends. Many dismal tales were told about funeral trains, and mourning cries and wailings heard and seen about the great tree where the unfortunate Major André was taken, and which stood in the neighborhood. Some mention was made also of the woman in white, that haunted the dark glen at Raven Rock, and was often heard to shriek on winter nights before a storm, having perished there in the snow. The chief part of the stories, however, turned upon the favorite spectre of Sleepy Hollow, the headless horseman, who had been heard several times of late, patrolling the country; and, it was said, tethered his horse nightly among the graves in the churchyard.

The sequestered situation of this church seems always to have made it a favorite haunt of troubled spirits. It stands on a knoll, surrounded by locust-trees and lofty elms, from among which its decent whitewashed walls shine modestly forth, like Christian purity beaming through the shades of retirement. A gentle slope descends from it to a silver sheet of water, bordered by high trees, between which, peeps may be caught at the blue hills of the Hudson. To look upon its grass-grown yard, where the sunbeams seem to sleep so quietly, one would think that there at least the dead might rest in peace. On one side of the church extends a wide woody dell, along which raves a large brook among broken rocks and trunks of fallen trees. Over a deep black part of the stream, not far from the church, was formerly thrown a wooden bridge; the road that led to it, and the bridge itself, were thickly shaded by overhanging trees, which cast a gloom about it, even in the daytime; but occasioned a fearful darkness at night. This was one of the favorite haunts of the headless horseman; and the place where he was most frequently encountered. The tale was told of old Brouwer, a most heretical disbeliever in ghosts, how he met the horseman returning from his foray into Sleepy Hollow, and was obliged to get up behind him; how they galloped over bush and brake, over hill and swamp, until they reached the bridge; when the horseman suddenly turned into a skeleton, threw old Brouwer into the brook, and sprang away over the tree-tops with a clap of thunder.

This story was immediately matched by a thrice marvellous adventure of Brom Bones, who made light of the galloping Hessian as an arrant jockey. He affirmed that, on returning one night from the neighboring village of Sing Sing, he had been overtaken by this midnight trooper; that he had offered to race with him for a bowl of punch, and should have won it too, for Daredevil beat the goblin horse all hollow, but, just as they came to the church-bridge, the Hessian bolted, and vanished in a flash of fire.

All these tales, told in the drowsy undertone with which men talk in the dark, the countenances of the listeners only now and then receiving a casual gleam from the glare of a pipe, sank deep in the mind of Ichabod. He repaid them in kind with large extracts from his invaluable author, Cotton Mather, and added many marvellous events that had taken place in his native State of Connecticut, and fearful sights which he had seen in his nightly walks about Sleepy Hollow.

The revel now gradually broke up. The old farmers gathered together their families in their wagons, and were heard for some time rattling along the hollow roads, and over the distant hills. Some of the damsels mounted on pillions behind their favorite swains, and their light-hearted laughter, mingling with the clatter of hoofs, echoed along the silent woodlands, sounding fainter and fainter until they gradually died away—and the late scene of noise and frolic was all silent and deserted. Ichabod only lingered behind, according to the custom of country lovers, to have a tête-à-tête with the heiress, fully convinced that he was now on the high road to success. What passed at this interview I will not pretend to say, for in fact I do not know. Something, however, I fear me, must have gone wrong, for he certainly sallied forth, after no very great interval, with an air quite desolate and chop-fallen.—Oh these women! these women! Could that girl have been playing off any of her coquettish tricks? Was her encouragement of the poor pedagogue all a mere sham to secure her conquest of his rival? Heaven only knows, not I!—Let it suffice to say, Ichabod stole forth with the air of one who had been sacking a hen-roost, rather than a fair lady's heart. Without looking to the right or left to notice the scene of rural wealth, on which he had so often gloated, he went straight to the stable, and with several hearty cuffs and kicks, roused his steed most uncourteously from the comfortable quarters in which he was soundly sleeping, dreaming of mountains of corn and oats, and whole valleys of timothy and clover.

It was the very witching time of night that Ichabod, heavy-hearted and crest-fallen, pursued his travel homewards, along the sides of the lofty hills which rise above Tarry Town, and which he had traversed so cheerily in the afternoon. The hour was as dismal as himself. Far below him, the Tappan Zee spread its dusky and indistinct waste of waters, with here and there the tall mast of a sloop, riding quietly at anchor under the land. In the dead hush of midnight, he could even hear the barking of the watchdog from the opposite shore of the Hudson; but it was so vague and faint as only to give an idea of his distance from this faithful companion of man. Now and then, too, the long-drawn crowing of a cock, accidentally awakened, would sound far, far off, from some farmhouse away among the hills—but it was like a dreaming sound in his ear. No signs of life occurred near him, but occasionally the melancholy chirp of a cricket, or perhaps the guttural twang of a bull-frog, from a neighboring marsh, as if sleeping uncomfortably, and turning suddenly in his bed.

All the stories of ghosts and goblins that he had heard in the afternoon, now came crowding upon his recollection. The night grew darker and darker; the stars seemed to sink deeper in the sky, and driving clouds occasionally hid them from his sight. He had never felt so lonely and dismal. He was, moreover, approaching the very place where many of the scenes of the ghost stories had been laid. In the center of the road stood an enormous tulip-tree, which towered like a giant above all the other trees of the neighborhood, and formed a kind of landmark. Its limbs were gnarled, and fantastic, large enough to form trunks for ordinary trees, twisting down almost to the earth, and rising again into the air. It was connected with the tragical story of the unfortunate André, who had been taken prisoner hard by; and was universally known by the name of MajorAndré's tree. The common people regarded it with a mixture of respect and superstition, partly out of sympathy for the fate of its ill-starred namesake, and partly from the tales of strange sights and doleful lamentations told concerning it.

As Ichabod approached this fearful tree, he began to whistle: he thought his whistle was answered—it was but a blast sweeping sharply through the dry branches. As he approached a little nearer, he thought he saw something white, hanging in the midst of the tree—he paused and ceased whistling; but on looking more narrowly, perceived that it was a place where the tree had been scathed by lightning, and the white wood laid bare. Suddenly he heard a groan—his teeth chattered and his knees smote against the saddle: it was but the rubbing of one huge bough upon another, as they were swayed about by the breeze. He passed the tree in safety, but new perils lay before him.

About two hundred yards from the tree a small brook crossed the road, and ran into a marshy and thickly-wooded glen, known by the name of Wiley's swamp. A few rough logs, laid side by side, served for a bridge over this stream. On that side of the road where the brook entered the wood, a group of oaks and chestnuts, matted thick with wild grapevines, threw a cavernous gloom over it. To pass this bridge was the severest trial. It was at this identical spot that the unfortunate André was captured, and under the covert of those chestnuts and vines were the sturdy yeomen concealed who surprised him. This has ever since been considered a haunted stream, and fearful are the feelings of the schoolboy who has to pass it alone after dark.

As he approached the stream his heart began to thump; he summoned up, however, all his resolution, gave his horse half a score of kicks in the ribs, and attempted to dash briskly across the bridge; but instead of starting forward, the perverse old animal made a lateral movement, and ran broadside against the fence. Ichabod, whose fears increased with the delay, jerked the reins on the other side, and kicked lustily with the contrary foot: it was all in vain; his steed started, it is true, but it was only to plunge to the opposite side of the road into a thicket of brambles and alder bushes. The schoolmaster now bestowed both whip and heel upon the starveling ribs of old Gunpowder, who dashed forward, snuffling and snorting, but came to a stand just by the bridge, with a suddenness that had nearly sent his rider sprawling over his head. Just at this moment a plashy tramp by the side of the bridge caught the sensitive ear of Ichabod. In the dark shadow of the grove, on the margin of the brook, he beheld something huge, misshapen, black and towering. It stirred not, but seemed gathered up in the gloom, like some gigantic monster ready to spring upon the traveller.

The hair of the affrighted pedagogue rose upon his head with terror. What was to be done? To turn and fly was now too late; and besides, what chance was there of escaping ghost or goblin, if such it was, which could ride upon the wings of the wind? Summoning up, therefore, a show of courage, he demanded in stammering accents—"Who are you?" He received no reply. He repeated his demand in a still more agitated voice. Still there was no answer. Once more he cudgelled the sides of the inflexible Gunpowder, and, shutting his eyes, broke forth with involuntary fervor into a psalm tune. Just then the shadowy object of alarm put itself in motion, and, with a scramble and a bound, stood at once in the middle of the road. Though the night was dark and dismal, yet the form of the unknown might now in some degree be ascertained. He appeared to be a horseman of large dimensions, and mounted on a black horse of powerful frame. He made no offer of molestation or sociability, but kept aloof on one side of the road, jogging along on the blind side of old Gunpowder, who had now got over his fright and waywardness.

Ichabod, who had no relish for this strange midnight companion, and bethought himself of the adventure of Brom Bones with the Galloping Hessian, now quickened his steed, in hopes of leaving him behind. The stranger, however, quickened his horse to an equal pace. Ichabod pulled up, and fell into a walk, thinking to lag behind— the other did the same. His heart began to sink within him; he endeavored to resume his psalm tune, but his parched tongue clove to the roof of his mouth, and he could not utter a stave. There was something in the moody and dogged silence of this pertinacious companion, that was mysterious and appalling. It was soon fearfully accounted for. On mounting a rising ground, which brought the figure of his fellow-traveller in relief against the sky, gigantic in height, and muffled in a cloak, Ichabod was horror-struck, on perceiving that he was headless! But his horror was still more increased, on observing that the head, which should have rested on his shoulders, was carried before him on the pommel of the saddle: his terror rose to desperation; he rained a shower of kicks and blows upon Gunpowder, hoping, by a sudden movement, to give his companion the slip— but the spectre started full jump with him. Away then they dashed, through thick and thin; stones flying, and sparks flashing at every bound. Ichabod's flimsy garments fluttered in the air, as he stretched his long lank body away over his horse's head, in the eagerness of his flight.

They had now reached the road which turns off to Sleepy Hollow; but Gunpowder, who seemed possessed with a demon, instead of keeping up it, made an opposite turn, and plunged headlong down hill to the left. This road leads through a sandy hollow, shaded by trees for about a quarter of a mile, where it crosses the bridge famous in goblin story, and just beyond swells the green knoll on which stands the whitewashed church.

As yet the panic of the steed had given his unskillful rider an apparent advantage in the chase; but just as he had got halfway through the hollow, the girths of the saddle gave way, and he felt it slipping from under him. He seized it by the pommel, and endeavored to hold it firm, but in vain; and had just time to save himself by clasping old Gunpowder round the neck, when the saddle fell to the earth, and he heard it trampled under foot by his pursuer. For a moment the terror of Hans Van Ripper's wrath passed across his mind—for it was his Sunday saddle; but this was no time for petty fears; the goblin was hard on his haunches; and (unskillful rider that he was!) he had much ado to maintain his seat; sometimes slipping on one side, sometimes on another, and sometimes jolted on the high ridge of his horse's back-bone, with a violence that he verily feared would cleave him asunder.

An opening in the trees now cheered him with the hopes that the church bridge was at hand. The wavering reflection of a silver star in the bosom of the brook told him that he was not mistaken. He saw the walls of the church dimly glaring under the trees beyond. He recollected the place where Brom Bones's ghostly competitor had disappeared. "If I can but reach that bridge," thought Ichabod, "I am safe." Just then he heard the black steed panting and blowing close behind him; he even fancied that he felt his hot breath. Another convulsive kick in the ribs, and old Gunpowder sprang upon the bridge; he thundered over the resounding planks; he gained the opposite side; and now Ichabod cast a look behind to see if his pursuer should vanish, according to rule, in a flash of fire and brimstone. Just then he saw the goblin rising in his stirrups, and in the very act of hurling his head at him. Ichabod endeavored to dodge the horrible missile, but too late. It encountered his cranium with a tremendous crash—he was tumbled headlong into the dust, and Gunpowder, the black steed, and the goblin rider, passed by like a whirlwind.

The next morning the old horse was found without his saddle, and with the bridle under his feet, soberly cropping the grass at his master's gate. Ichabod did not make his appearance at breakfast—dinner-hour came, but no Ichabod. The boys assembled at the schoolhouse, and strolled idly about the banks of the brook; but no schoolmaster. Hans Van Ripper now began to feel some uneasiness about the fate of poor Ichabod, and his saddle. An inquiry was set on foot, and after diligent investigation they came upon his traces. In one part of the road leading to the church was found the saddle trampled in the dirt; the tracks of horses' hoofs deeply dented in the road, and evidently at furious speed, were traced to the bridge, beyond which, on the bank of a broad part of the brook, where the water ran deep and black, was found the hat of the unfortunate Ichabod, and close beside it a shattered pumpkin.

The brook was searched, but the body of the schoolmaster was not to be discovered. Hans Van Ripper, as executor of his estate, examined the bundle which contained all his worldly effects. They consisted of two shirts and a half; two stocks for the neck; a pair or two of worsted stockings; an old pair of corduroy small-clothes; a rusty razor; a book of psalm tunes, full of dogs' ears; and a broken pitchpipe. As to the books and furniture of the school-house, they belonged to the community, excepting Cotton Mather's *History of Witchcraft*, a *New*

England Almanac, and a book of dreams and fortune-telling; in which last was a sheet of foolscap much scribbled and blotted in several fruitless attempts to make a copy of verses in honor of the heiress of Van Tassel. These magic books and the poetic scrawl were forthwith consigned to the flames by Hans Van Ripper; who from that time forward determined to send his children no more to school; observing, that he never knew any good come of this same reading and writing. Whatever money the schoolmaster possessed, and he had received his quarter's pay but a day or two before, he must have had about his person at the time of his disappearance.

The mysterious event caused much speculation at the church on the folloing Sunday. Knots of gazers and gossips were collected in the churchyard, at the bridge, and at the spot where the hat and pumpkin had been found. The stories of Brouwer, of Bones, and a whole budget of others, were called to mind; and when they had diligently considered them all, and compared them with the symptoms of the present case, they shook their heads, and came to the conclusion that Ichabod had been carried off by the galloping Hessian. As he was a bachelor, and in nobody's debt, nobody troubled his head anymore about him. The school was removed to a different quarter of the hollow, and another pedagogue reigned in his stead.

It is true, an old farmer, who had been down to New York on a visit several years after, and from whom this account of the ghostly adventure was received, brought home the intelligence that Ichabod Crane was still alive; that he had left the neighborhood, partly through fear of the goblin and Hans Van Ripper, and partly in mortification at having been suddenly dismissed by the heiress; that he had changed his quarters to a distant part of the country; had kept school and studied law at the same time, had been admitted to the bar, turned politician, electioneered, written for the newspapers, and finally had been made a justice of the Ten Pound Court. Brom Bones too, who shortly after his rival's disappearance conducted the blooming Katrina in triumph to the altar, was observed to look exceedingly knowing whenever the story of Ichabod was related, and always burst into a hearty laugh at the mention of the pumpkin; which led some to suspect that he knew more about the matter than he chose to tell.

The old country wives, however, who are the best judges of these matters, maintain to this day that Ichabod was spirited away by supernatural means; and it is a favorite story often told about the neighborhood round the winter evening fire. The bridge became more than ever an object of superstitious awe, and that may be the reason why the road has been altered of late years, so as to approach the church by the border of the mill-pond. The school-house being deserted, soon fell to decay, and was reported to be haunted by the ghost of the unfortunate pedagogue; and the ploughboy, loitering homeward of a still summer evening, has often fancied his voice at a distance, chanting a melancholy psalm tune among the tranquil solitudes of Sleepy Hollow.

POSTSCRIPT
FOUND IN THE HANDWRITING OF MR. KNICKERBOCKER

The preceding Tale is given, almost in the precise words in which I heard it related at a Corporation meeting of the ancient city of Manhattoes, at which were present many of its sagest and most illustrious burghers. The narrator was a pleasant, shabby, gentlemanly old fellow, in pepper-and-salt clothes, with a sadly humorous face; and one whom I strongly suspected of being poor—he made such efforts to be entertaining. When his story was concluded, there was much laughter and approbation, particularly from two or three deputy aldermen, who had been asleep the greater part of the time. There was, however, one tall, dry-looking old gentleman, with beetling eyebrows, who maintained a grave and rather severe face throughout; now and then folding his arms, inclining his head, and looking down upon the floor, as if turning a doubt over in his mind. He was one of your wary men, who never laugh, but upon good grounds—when they have reason and the law on their side. When the mirth of the rest of the company had subsided, and silence was restored, he leaned one arm on the elbow of his chair, and, sticking the other akimbo, demanded, with a slight but exceeding sage motion of the head, and contraction of the brow, what was the moral of the story, and what it went to prove?

The story-teller, who was just putting a glass of wine to his lips, as a refreshment after his toils, paused for a moment, looked at his inquirer with an air of infinite deference, and, lowering the glass slowly to the table, observed, that the story was intended most logically to prove:

"That there is no situation in life but has its advantages and pleasures—provided we will but take a joke as we find it.

"That, therefore, he that runs races with goblin troopers is likely to have rough riding of it.

"Ergo, for a country schoolmaster to be refused the hand of a Dutch heiress, is a certain step to high preferment in the state."

The cautious old gentleman knit his brows tenfold closer after this explanation, being sorely puzzled by the ratiocination of the syllogism; while, methought, the one in pepper-and-salt eyed him with something of a triumphant leer. At length, he observed, that all this was very well, but still he thought the story a little on the extravagant—there were one or two points on which he had his doubts.

"Faith, sir," replied the story-teller, "as to that matter, I don't believe one-half of it myself."

D. K.

L'ENVOY*

Go, little booke, God send thee good passage,
And specially let this be thy prayere,
Unto them all that thee will read or hear,
Where thou art wrong, after their help to call,
Thee to correct in any part or all.
CHAUCER'S *Belle Dame sans Mercie*

IN concluding a second volume of the Sketch Book, the Author cannot but express his deep sense of the indulgence with which his first has been received, and of the liberal disposition that has been evinced to treat him with kindness as a stranger. Even the critics, whatever may be said of them by others, he has found to be a singularly gentle and good-natured race; it is true that each has in turn objected to some one or two articles, and that these individual exceptions, taken in the aggregate, would amount almost to a total condemnation of his work; but then he has been consoled by observing, that what one has particularly censured another has as particularly praised; and thus, the encomiums being set off against the objections, he finds his work, upon the whole, commended far beyond its deserts.

He is aware that he runs a risk of forfeiting much of this kind favor by not following the counsel that has been liberally bestowed upon him; for where abundance of valuable advice is given gratis, it may seem a man's own fault if he should go astray. He can only say, in his vindication, that he faithfully determined, for a time, to govern himself in his second volume by the opinions passed upon his first; but he was soon brought to a stand by the contrariety of excellent counsel. One kindly

*Closing the second volume of the London edition.

advised him to avoid the ludicrous; another to shun the pathetic; a third assured him that he was tolerable at description, but cautioned him to leave narrative alone; while a fourth declared that he had a very pretty knack at turning a story, and was really entertaining when in a pensive mood, but was grievously mistaken if he imagined himself to possess a spirit of humor.

Thus perplexed by the advice of his friends, who each in turn closed some particular path, but left him all the world beside to range in, he found that to follow all their counsels would, in fact, be to stand still. He remained for a time sadly embarrassed; when, all at once, the thought struck him to ramble on as he had begun; that his work being miscellaneous, and written for different humors, it could not be expected that any one would be pleased with the whole; but that if it should contain something to suit each new reader, his end would be completely answered. Few guests sit down to a varied table with an equal appetite for every dish. One has an elegant horror of a roasted pig; another holds a curry or a devil in utter abomination; a third cannot tolerate th ancient flavor of venison and wildfowl; and a fourth, of truly masculine stomach, looks with sovereign contempt on those knick-knacks, here and there dished up for t e ladies. Thus each article is condemned in its turn; and yet, amidst this variety of appetites, seldom does a d sh go away from the table without being tasted and relished by some one or other of the guests.

With these considerations he ventures to serve up this second volume in the same heterogeneous way with his first; simply requesting the reader, if he should find here and there something to please him, to rest assured that it was written expressly for intelligent readers like himself; but entreating him, should he find anything to dislike, to tolerate it, as one of those articles which the author has been obliged to write for readers of a less refined taste.

To be serious. The author is conscious of the numerous faults and imperfections of his work and well aware how little he is disciplined and accomplished in the arts of authorship. His deficiencies are also increased by a diffidence arising from his peculiar situation. He finds himself writing in a strange land, and appearing before a public which he has been accustomed, from childhood, to regard with the highest feelings of awe and reverence. He is full of solicitude to deserve their approbation, yet finds that very solicitude continually embarrassing his powers, and depriving him of that ease and confidence which are necessary to successful exertion. Still the kindness with which he is treated encourages him to go on, hoping that in time he may acquire a steadier footing; and thus he proceeds, half venturing, half shrinking, surprised at his own good fortune, and wondering at his own temerity.

A Tour on the
Prairies
(1835)

INTRODUCTION

H AVING, since my return to the United States, made a wide and varied tour, for the gratification of my curiosity, it has been supposed that I did it for the purpose of writing a book; and it has more than once been intimated in the papers, that such a work was actually in the press, containing scenes and sketches of the Far West.

These announcements, gratuitously made for me before I had put pen to paper, or even contemplated any thing of the kind, have embarrassed me exceedingly. I have been like a poor actor who finds himself announced for a part he had no thought of playing, and his appearance expected on the stage before he has committed a line to memory.

I have always had a repugnance, amounting almost to disability, to write in the face of expectation; and, in the present instance, I was expected to write about a region fruitful of wonders and adventures, and which had already been made the theme of spirit-stirring narratives from able pens; yet about which I had nothing wonderful or adventurous to offer.

Since such, however, seems to be the desire of the public, and that they take sufficient interest in my wanderings to deem them worthy of recital, I have hastened, as promptly as possible, to meet in some degree, the expectation which others have excited. For this purpose, I have, as it were, plucked a few leaves out of my memorandum book, containing a month's foray beyond the outposts of human habitation, into the wilderness of the Far West. It forms, indeed, but a small portion of an extensive tour; but it is an episode, complete as far as it goes. As such, I offer it to the public, with great diffidence. It is a simple narrative of every day occurrences; such as happens to everyone who travels the prairies. I have no wonders to describe, nor any moving accidents by flood or field to narrate; and as to those who look for a marvellous or adventurous story at my hands, I can only reply in the words of the weary knife-grinder: "Story! God bless you, I have none to tell, sir."

CHAPTER I

THE PAWNEE HUNTING GROUNDS—TRAVELLING COMPANIONS—A COMMISSIONER—A VIRTUOSO—A SEEKER OF ADVENTURES—A GIL BLAS OF THE FRONTIER—A YOUNG MAN'S ANTICIPATIONS OF PLEASURE

IN THE often vaunted regions of the Far West, several hundred miles beyond the Mississippi, extends a vast tract of uninhabited country, where there is neither to be seen the log house of the white man, nor the wigwam of the Indian. It consists of great grassy plains, interspersed with forests and groves, and clumps of trees, and watered by the Arkansas, the grand Canadian, the Red River, and their tributary streams. Over these fertile and verdant wastes still roam the elk, the buffalo, and the wild horse, in all their native freedom. These, in fact, are the hunting grounds of the various tribes of the Far West. Hither repair the Osage, the Creek, the Delaware and other tribes that have linked themselves with civilization, and live within the vicinity of the white settlements. Here resort also, the Pawnees, the Comanches, and other fierce, and as yet independent tribes, the nomads of the prairies, or the inhabitants of the skirts of the Rocky Mountains. The regions I have mentioned form a debatable ground of these warring and vindictive tribes; none of them presume to erect a permanent habitation within its borders. Their hunters and "Braves" repair thither in numerous bodies during the season of game, throw up their transient hunting camps, consisting of light bowers covered with bark and skins, commit sad havoc among the innumerable herds that graze the prairies, and having loaded themselves with venison and buffalo meat, warily retire from the dangerous neighborhood. These expeditions partake, always, of a warlike character; the hunters are all armed for action, offensive and defensive, and are bound to incessant vigilance. Should they, in their excursions, meet the hunters of an adverse tribe, savage conflicts take place. Their encampments, too, are always subject to be surprised by wandering war parties, and their hunters, when scattered in pursuit of game, to be captured or massacred by lurking foes. Mouldering skulls and skeletons, bleaching in some dark ravine, or near the traces of a hunting camp, occasionally mark the scene of a foregone act of blood, and let the wanderer know the dangerous nature of the region he is traversing. It is the purport of the following pages to narrate a month's excursion to these noted hunting grounds, through a tract of country which had not as yet been explored by white men.

It was early in October, 1832, that I arrived at Fort Gibson, a frontier post of the Far West, situated on the Neosho, or Grand River, near its confluence with the Arkansas. I had been travelling for a month past, with a small party from St. Louis, up the banks of the Missouri, and along the frontier line of agencies and missions, that extends from the Missouri to the Arkansas. Our party was headed by one of the Commissioners appointed by the government of the United States to superintend the settlement of the Indian tribes migrating from the east to the west of the Mississippi. In the discharge of his duties, he was thus visiting the various outposts of civilization.

And here let me bear testimony to the merits of this worthy leader of our little band. He was a native of one of the towns of Connecticut, a man in whom a course of legal practice and political life had not been able to vitiate an innate simplicity and benevolence of heart. The greater part of his days had been passed in the bosom of his family and the society of deacons, elders, and selectmen, on the peaceful banks of the Connecticut; when suddenly he had been called to mount his steed, shoulder his rifle, and mingle among stark hunters, backwoodsmen, and naked savages, on the trackless wilds of the Far West.

Another of my fellow-travellers was Mr. L., an Englishman by birth, but descended from a foreign stock; and who had all the buoyancy and accommodating spirit of a native of the Continent. Having rambled over many countries, he had become to a certain degree, a citizen of the world, easily adapting himself to any change. He was a man of a thousand occupations; a botanist, a geologist, a hunter of beetles and butterflies, a musical amateur, a sketcher of no mean pretensions, in short, a complete virtuoso; added to which, he was a very indefatigable, if not always a very successful, sportsman. Never had a man more irons in the fire, and, consequently, never was man more busy nor more cheerful.

My third fellow-traveller was one who had accompanied the former from Europe, and travelled with him as his Telemachus; being apt, like his prototype, to give occasional perplexity and disquiet to his Mentor. He was a young Swiss Count, scarce twenty-one years of age, full of talent and spirit, but galliard in the extreme, and prone to every kind of wild adventure.

Having made this mention of my comrades, I must not pass over unnoticed, a personage of inferior rank, but of all-pervading and prevalent importance: the squire, the groom, the cook, the tent man, in a word, the factotum, and, I may add, the universal meddler and marplot of our party. This was a little swarthy meagre, French creole, named Antoine, but familiarly dubbed Tonish: a kind of Gil Blas of the frontiers, who had passed a scrambling life, sometimes among white men, sometimes among Indians; sometimes in the employ of traders, missionaries, and Indian agents; sometimes mingling with the Osage hunters. We picked him up at St. Louis, near which he has a small farm, an Indian wife, and a brood of half-blood children. According to his own account, however, he had a wife in every tribe; in fact, if all this little vagabond said of himself were to be believed, he was without morals, without caste, without creed, without country, and even without language; for he spoke a jargon of mingled French, English, and Osage. He was, withal, a notorious braggart, and a liar of the first water. It was amusing to hear him vapor and gasconade about his terrible exploits and hairbreadth escapes in war and hunting. In the midst of his volubility, he was prone to be seized by a spasmodic gasping, as if the springs of his jaws were suddenly unhinged; but I am apt to think it was caused by some falsehood that stuck in his throat, for I generally remarked, that immediately afterwards there bolted forth a lie of the first magnitude.

Our route had been a pleasant one, quartering ourselves, occasionally, at the widely separated establishments of the Indian missionaries, but in general camping out in the fine groves that border the streams, and sleeping under cover of a tent. During the latter part of our tour we had pressed forward in hopes of arriving in time at Fort Gibson, to accompany the Osage hunters on their autumnal visit to the buffalo prairies. Indeed the imagination of the young Count had become completely excited on the subject. The grand scenery and wild habits of the prairie had set his spirits madding, and the stories that little Tonish told him of Indian braves and Indian beauties, of hunting buffaloes and catching wild horses, had set him all agog for a dash into savage life. He was a bold and hard rider, and longed to be scouring the hunting grounds. It was amusing to hear his youthful anticipations of all that he was to see, and do, and enjoy, when mingling among the Indians and participating in their hardy adventures; and it was still more amusing to listen to the gasconadings of little Tonish, who volunteered to be his faithful squire in all his perilous undertakings; to teach him how to catch the wild horse, bring down the buffalo, and win the smiles of Indian princesses—"And if we can only get sight of a prairie on fire!" said the young Count—"By Gar, I'll set one on fire myself!" cried the little Frenchman.

CHAPTER II

ANTICIPATIONS DISAPPOINTED—NEW PLANS—PREPARATIONS TO JOIN AN EXPLORING PARTY—DEPARTURE FROM FORT GIBSON— FORDING OF THE VERDIGRIS—AN INDIAN CAVALIER

THE anticipations of a young man are prone to meet with disappointment. Unfortunately for the Count's scheme of wild campaigning, before we reached the end of our journey, we heard that the Osage hunters had set forth upon their expedition to the buffalo grounds. The Count still determined, if possible, to follow on their track and overtake them, and for this purpose stopped short at the Osage Agency, a few miles distant from Fort Gibson, to make inquiries and preparations. His travelling companion, Mr. L., stopped with him; while the Commissioner and myself proceeded to Fort Gibson, followed by the faithful and veracious Tonish. I hinted to him his promises to follow the Count in his campaignings, but I found the little varlet had a keen eye to self-interest. He was aware that the Commissioner, from his official duties, would remain for a long time in the country, and be likely to give him permanent employment, while the sojourn of the Count would be but transient. The gasconading of the little braggart was suddenly therefore at an end. He spoke not another word to the young Count about Indians, buffaloes, and wild horses, but putting himself tacitly in the train of the Commissioner, jogged silently after us to the garrison.

On arriving at the fort, however, a new chance presented itself for a cruise on the prairies. We learnt that a company of mounted rangers, or riflemen, had departed but three days previous, to make a wide exploring tour, from the Arkansas to the Red River, including a part of the Pawnee hunting grounds, where no party of white men had as yet penetrated. Here, then, was an opportunity of ranging over those dangerous and interesting regions under the safeguard of a powerful escort; for the Commissioner, in virtue of his office, could claim the service of this newly-raised corps of riflemen, and the country they were to explore was destined for the settlement of some of the migrating tribes connected with his mission.

Our plan was promptly formed and put into execution. A couple of Creek Indians were sent off express, by the commander of Fort Gibson, to overtake the rangers and bring them to a halt until the Commissioner and his party should be able to join them. As we should have a march of three or four days through a wild country, before we could overtake the company of rangers, an escort of fourteen mounted riflemen, under the command of a lieutenant, was assigned us.

We sent word to the young Count and Mr. L. at the Osage Agency, of our new plan and prospects, and invited them to accompany us. The Count, however, could not forego the delights he had promised himself in mingling with absolutely savage life. In reply, he agreed to keep with us until we should come upon the trail of the Osage hunters, when it was his fixed resolve to strike off into the wilderness in pursuit of them; and his faithful mentor, though he grieved at the madness of the scheme, was too staunch a friend to desert him. A general rendezvous of our party and escort was appointed, for the following morning, at the Agency.

We now made all arrangements for prompt departure. Our baggage had hitherto been transported on a light wagon, but we were now to break our way through an untravelled country, cut up by rivers, ravines, and thickets, where a vehicle of the kind would be a complete impediment. We were to travel on horseback, in hunters' style, and with as little encumbrance as possible. Our baggage, therefore, underwent a rigid and most abstemious reduction. A pair of saddlebags, and those by no means crammed, sufficed for each man's scanty wardrobe, and, with his great coat were to be carried upon the steed he rode. The rest of the baggage was placed on pack-horses. Each one had a bear-skin and a couple of blankets for bedding, and there was a tent to shelter us in case of sickness or bad weather. We took care to provide ourselves with flour, coffee, and sugar, together with a small supply of salt pork for emergencies; for our main subsistence we were to depend upon the chase.

Such of our horses as had not been tired out in our recent journey, were taken with us as pack-horses, or supernumeraries; but as we were going on a long and rough tour, where there would be occasional hunting, and where, in case of meeting with hostile savages, the safety of the rider might depend upon the goodness of his steed, we took care to be well mounted. I procured a stout silver-gray; somewhat rough, but stanch and powerful; and retained a hardy pony which I had hitherto ridden, and which, being somewhat jaded, was suffered to ramble along with the pack-horses, to be mounted only in case of emergency.

All these arrangements being made, we left Fort Gibson, on the morning of the tenth of October, and crossing the river in the front of it, set off for the rendezvous at the Agency. A ride of a few miles brought us to the ford of the Verdigris, a wild rocky scene overhung with forest trees. We descended to the bank of the river and crossed in straggling file, the horses stepping cautiously from rock to rock, and in a manner feeling about for a foothold beneath the rushing and brawling stream.

Our little Frenchman, Tonish, brought up the rear with the pack-horses. He was in high glee, having experienced a kind of promotion. In our journey hitherto he had driven the wagon, which he seemed to consider a very inferior employ; now he was master of the horse. He sat perched like a monkey behind the pack on one of the horses; he sang, he shouted, he yelped like an Indian, and ever and anon blasphemed the loitering pack-horses in his jargon of mingled French, English and Osage, which not one of them could understand.

As we were crossing the ford we saw on the opposite shore a Creek Indian on horseback. He had paused to reconnoitre us from the brow of a rock, and formed a picturesque object, in unison with the wild scenery around him. He wore a bright blue hunting-shirt trimmed with scarlet fringe; a gaily-colored handkerchief was bound round his head something like a turban, with one end hanging down beside his ear; he held a long rifle in his hand, and looked like a wild Arab on the prowl. Our loquacious and ever-meddling little Frenchman called out to him in his Babylonish jargon, but the savage having satisfied his curiosity tossed his hand in the air, turned the head of his steed, and galloping along the shore soon disappeared among the trees.

CHAPTER III

AN INDIAN AGENCY—RIFLEMEN—OSAGES, CREEKS, TRAPPERS,
DOGS, HORSES, HALF-BREEDS—BEATTE, THE HUNTSMAN

HAVING crossed the ford, we soon reached the Osage Agency where Col. Choteau has his offices and magazines, for the dispatch of Indian affairs, and the distribution of presents and supplies. It consisted of a few log houses on the banks of the river, and presented a motley frontier scene. Here was our escort awaiting our arrival; some were on horseback, some on foot, some seated on the trunks of fallen trees, some shooting at a mark. They were a heterogeneous crew; some in frock-coats made of green blankets; others in leathern hunting-shirts, but the most part in marvellously ill-cut garments, much the worse for wear, and evidently put on for rugged service.

Near by these was a group of Osages: stately fellows; stern and simple in garb and aspect. They wore no ornaments; their dress consisted merely of blankets, leggins, and moccasins. Their heads were bare; their hair was cropped close, excepting a bristling ridge on the top, like the crest of a helmet, with a long scalp lock hanging behind. They had fine Roman countenances, and broad deep chests; and, as they generally wore their blankets wrapped round their loins, so as to leave the bust and arms bare, they looked like so many noble bronze figures. The Osages are the finest looking Indians I have ever seen in the West. They had not yielded sufficiently, as yet, to the influence of civilization to lay by their simple Indian garb, or to lose the habits of the hunter and the warrior; and their poverty prevents their indulging in much luxury of apparel.

In contrast to these was a gaily-dressed party of Creeks. There is something, at the first glance, quite oriental in the appearance of this tribe. They dress in calico hunting shirts, of various brilliant colors, decorated with bright fringes, and belted with broad girdles, embroidered with beads: they have leggins of dressed deer skins, or of green or scarlet cloth, with embroidered knee-bands and tassels: their moccasins are fancifully wrought and ornamented, and they wear gaudy handkerchiefs tastefully bound round their heads.

Beside these, there was a sprinkling of trappers, hunters, half-breeds, creoles, negroes of every hue; and all that other rabble rout of nondescript beings that keep about the frontiers, between civilized and savage life, as those equivocal birds, the bats, hover about the confines of light and darkness.

The little hamlet of the Agency was in a complete bustle; the blacksmith's shed, in particular, was a scene of preparation; a strapping negro was shoeing a horse; two half-breeds were fabricating iron spoons in which to melt lead for bullets. An old trapper, in leathern hunting frock and moccasins, had placed his rifle against a work-bench, while he superintended the operation, and gossiped about his hunting exploits; several large dogs were lounging in and out of the shop, or sleeping in the sunshine, while a little cur, with head cocked on one side, and one ear erect, was watching, with that curiosity common to little dogs, the process of shoeing the horse, as if studying the art, or waiting for his turn to be shod.

We found the Count and his companion, the Virtuoso, ready for the march. As they intended to overtake the Osages, and pass some time in hunting the buffalo and the wild horse, they had provided themselves accordingly; having, in addition to the steeds which they used for travelling, others of prime quality which were to be led when on the march, and only to be mounted for the chase.

They had, moreover, engaged the services of a young man named Antoine, a half-breed of French and Osage origin. He was to be a kind of Jack-of-all-work; to cook, to hunt, and to take care of the horses; but he had a vehement propensity to do nothing, being one of the worthless brood engendered and brought up among the missions. He was, moreover, a little spoiled by being really a handsome young fellow, an Adonis of the frontier, and still worse by fancying himself highly connected, his sister being concubine to an opulent white trader!

For our own parts, the Commissioner and myself were desirous, before setting out, to procure another attendant well versed in wood craft, who might serve us as a hunter; for our little Frenchman would have his hands full when in camp, in cooking, and on the march, in taking care of the pack-horses. Such a one presented himself, or rather was recommended to us, in Pierre Beatte, a half-breed of French and Osage parentage. We were assured that he was acquainted with all parts of the country, having traversed it in all directions, both in hunting and war parties; that he would be of use both as guide and interpreter, and that he was a first-rate hunter.

I confess I did not like his looks when he was first presented to me. He was lounging about, in an old hunting frock and metasses or leggins, of deer skin, soiled and greased, and almost japanned by constant use. He was apparently about thirty-six years of age, square and strongly built. His features were not bad, being shaped not unlike those of Napoleon, but sharpened up, with high Indian cheek bones. Perhaps the dusky greenish hue of his complexion, aided his resemblance to an old bronze bust I had seen of the Emperor. He had, however, a sullen, saturnine expression, set off by a slouched woolen hat, and elf locks that hung about his ears.

Such was the appearance of the man, and his manners were equally unprepossessing. He was cold and laconic; made no promises or professions; stated the terms he required for the services of himself and his horse, which we thought rather high, but showed no disposition to abate them, nor any anxiety to secure our employ. He had altogether more of the red than the white man in his composition; and, as I had been taught to look upon all half-breeds with distrust, as an uncertain and faithless race, I would gladly have dispensed with the services of Pierre Beatte. We had no time, however, to look out for any one more to our taste, and had to make an arrangement with him on the spot. He then set about making his preparations for the journey, promising to join us at our evening's encampment.

One thing was yet wanting to fit me out for the Prairies—a thoroughly trustworthy steed: I was not yet mounted to my mind. The gray I had bought, though strong and serviceable, was rough. At the last moment I succeeded in getting an excellent animal; a dark bay; powerful, active, generous-spirited, and in capital condition. I mounted him with exultation, and transferred the silver gray to Tonish, who was in such ecstasies at finding himself so completely *en Cavalier,* that I feared he might realize the ancient and well-known proverb of "a beggar on horseback."

CHAPTER IV

THE DEPARTURE

THE long-drawn notes of a bugle gave the signal for departure. The rangers filed off in a straggling line of march through the woods: we were soon on horseback and following on, but were detained by the irregularity of the pack-horses. They were unaccustomed to keep the line, and straggled from side to side among the thickets, in spite of all the pesting and bedeviling of Tonish; who, mounted on his gallant gray, with a long rifle on his shoulder, worried after them, bestowing a superabundance of dry blows and curses.

We soon, therefore, lost sight of our escort, but managed to keep on their track, thridding lofty forests, and entangled thickets, and passing by Indian wigwams and negro huts, until towards dusk we arrived at a frontier farm-house, owned by a settler of the name of Berryhill. It was situated on a hill, below which the rangers had encamped in a circular grove, on the margin of a stream. The master of the house received us civilly but could offer us no accommodation, for sickness prevailed in his family. He appeared himself to be in no very thriving condition, for though bulky in frame, he had a sallow, unhealthy complexion, and a whiffling double voice, shifting abruptly from a treble to a thorough-bass.

Finding his log house was a mere hospital, crowded with invalids, we ordered our tent to be pitched in the farm-yard.

We had not been long encamped, when our recently engaged attendant, Beatte, the Osage half-breed, made his appearance. He came mounted on one horse and leading another, which seemed to be well packed with supplies for the expedition. Beatte was evidently an "old soldier," as to the art of taking care of himself and looking out for emergencies. Finding that he was in government employ, being engaged by the Commissioner, he had drawn rations of flour and bacon, and put them up so as to be weather-proof. In addition to the horse for the road, and for ordinary service, which was a rough, hardy animal, he had another for hunting. This was of a mixed breed like himself, being a cross of the domestic stock with the wild horse of the prairies; and a noble steed it was, of generous spirit, fine action, and admirable bottom. He had taken care to have his horses well shod at the Agency. He came prepared at all points for war or hunting: his rifle on his shoulder, his powder-horn and bullet-pouch at his side, his hunting-knife stuck in his belt, and coils of cordage at his saddle bow, which we were told were lariats, or noosed cords, used in catching the wild horse.

Thus equipped and provided, an Indian hunter on a prairie is like a cruiser on the ocean, perfectly independent of the world, and competent to self-protection and self-maintenance. He can cast himself loose from every one, shape his own course, and take care of his own fortunes. I thought Beatte seemed to feel his independence, and to consider himself superior to us all, now that we were launching into the wilderness. He maintained a half proud, half sullen look, and great taciturnity; and his first care was to unpack his horses and put them in safe quarters for the night. His whole demeanor was in perfect contrast to our vaporing, chattering, bustling little Frenchman. The latter too, seemed jealous of this new-comer. He whispered to us that these half-breeds were a touchy, capricious people, little to be depended upon. That Beatte had evidently come prepared to take care of himself, and that, at any moment in the course of our tour, he would be liable to take some sudden disgust or affront, and abandon us at a moment's warning: having the means of shifting for himself, and being perfectly at home on the prairies.

CHAPTER V

FRONTIER SCENES—A LYCURGUS OF THE BORDER—LYNCH'S LAW —THE DANGER OF FINDING A HORSE—THE YOUNG OSAGE

ON THE following morning (Oct. 11) we were on the march by half-past seven o'clock, and rode through deep rich bottoms of alluvial soil, overgrown with redundant vegetation, and trees of an enormous size. Our route lay parallel to the west bank of the Arkansas, on the borders of which river, near the confluence of the Red Fork, we expected to overtake the main body of rangers. For some miles the country was sprinkled with Creek villages and farm-houses; the inhabitants of which appeared to have adopted, with considerable facility, the rudiments of civilization, and to have thriven in consequence. Their farms were well stocked, and their houses had a look of comfort and abundance.

We met with numbers of them returning from one of their grand games of ball, for which their nation is celebrated. Some were on foot, some on horseback; the latter, occasionally, with gaily-dressed females behind them. They are a well-made race, muscular and closely knit, with well-turned thighs and legs. They have a Gypsy fondness for brilliant colors and gay decorations, and are bright and fanciful objects when seen at a distance on the prairies. One had a scarlet handkerchief bound round his head, surmounted with a tuft of black feathers like a cock's tail. Another had a white handkerchief, with red feathers; while a third, for want of a plume, had stuck in his turban a brilliant bunch of sumach.

On the verge of the wilderness we paused to inquire our way at a log house, owned by a white settler or squatter, a tall raw-boned old fellow, with red hair, a lank lantern visage, and an inveterate habit of winking with one eye, as if every thing he said was of knowing import. He was in a towering passion. One of his horses was missing; he was sure it had been stolen in the night by a straggling party of Osages encamped in a neighboring swamp; but he would have satisfaction! He would make an example of the villains. He had accordingly caught down his rifle from the wall, that invariable enforcer of right or wrong upon the frontiers, and, having saddled his steed, was about to sally forth on a foray into the swamp; while a brother squatter with rifle in hand, stood ready to accompany him.

We endeavored to calm the old campaigner of the

prairies, by suggesting that his horse might have strayed into the neighboring woods; but he had the frontier propensity to charge everything to the Indians, and nothing could dissuade him from carrying fire and sword into the swamp.

After riding a few miles further we lost the trail of the main body of rangers, and became perplexed by a variety of tracks made by the Indians and settlers. At length coming to a log house, inhabited by a white man, the very last on the frontier, we found that we had wandered from our true course. Taking us back for some distance, he again brought us to the right trail; putting ourselves upon which, we took our final departure, and launched into the broad wilderness.

The trail kept on like a straggling footpath, over hill and dale, through brush and brake, and tangled thicket, and open prairie. In traversing the wilds it is customary for a party either of horse or foot to follow each other in single file like the Indians; so that the leaders break the way for those who follow, and lessen their labor and fatigue. In ths way, also, the number of a party is concealed, the whole leaving but one narrow well trampled track to mark their course.

We had not long regained the trail, when, on emerging from a forest, we beheld our raw-boned, hard-winking, hard-riding knight-errant of the frontier, descending the slope of a hill, followed by his companion in arms. As he drew near to us, the gauntness of his figure and ruefulness of his aspect reminded me of the description of La Mancha, and he was equally bent on affairs of doughty enterprise, being about to penetrate the thickets of the perilous swamp, within which the enemy lay ensconced.

While we were holding a parley with him on the slope of the hill, we descried an Osage on horseback issuing out of a skirt of wood about half a mile off, and leading a horse by a halter. The latter was immediately recognized by our hard-winking friend as the steed of which he was in quest. As the Osage drew near, I was struck with his appearance. He was about nineteen or twenty years of age, but well grown, with the fine Roman countenance common to his tribe, and as he rode with his blanket wrapped round his loins, his naked bust would have furnished a model for a statuary. He was mounted on a beautiful piebald horse, a mottled white and brown, of the wild breed of the prairies, decorated with a broad collar, from which hung in front a tuft of horse-hair dyed of a bright scarlet.

The youth rode slowly up to us with a frank open air, and signified by means of our interpreter Beatte, that the horse he was leading had wandered to their camp, and he was now on his way to conduct him back to his owner.

I had expected to witness an expression of gratitude on the part of our hard-favored cavalier, but to my surprise the old fellow broke out into a furious passion. He declared that the Indians had carried off his horse in the night, with the intention of bringing him home in the morning, and claiming a reward for finding him; a common practice, as he affirmed, among the Indians. He was, therefore, for tying the young Indian to a tree and giving him a sound lashing; and was quite surprised at the burst of indignation which this novel mode of requiting a service drew from us. Such, however, is too often the administration of law on the frontier, "Lynch's law," as it is technically termed, in which the plaintiff is apt to be witness, jury, judge, and executioner, and the defendant to be convicted and punished on mere presumption; and in this way, I am convinced, are occasioned many of those heart-burnings and resentments among the Indians, which lead to retaliation, and end in Indian wars. When I compared the open, noble countenance and frank demeanor of the young Osage, with the sinister visage and high-handed conduct of the frontiersman, I felt little doubt on whose back a lash would be most meritoriously bestowed.

Being thus obliged to content himself with the recovery of his horse, without the pleasure of flogging the finder into the bargain, the old Lycurgus, or rather Draco, of the frontier, set off growling on his return homeward, followed by his brother squatter.

As for the youthful Osage, we were all prepossessed in his favor; the young Count especially, with the sympathies proper to his age and incident to his character, had taken quite a fancy to him. Nothing would suit but he must have the young Osage as a companion and squire in his expedition into the wilderness. The youth was easily tempted, and, with the prospect of a safe range over the buffalo prairies and the promise of a new blanket, he turned his bridle, left the swamp and the encampment of his friends behind him, and set off to follow the Count in his wanderings in quest of the Osage hunters.

Such is the glorious independence of man in a savage state. This youth, with his rifle, his blanket, and his horse, was ready at a moment's warning to rove the world; he carried all his worldly effects with him, and in the absence of artificial wants, possessed the great secret of personal freedom. We of society are slaves, not so much to others as to ourselves; our superfluities are the chains that bind us, impeding every movement of our bodies and thwarting every impulse of our souls. Such, at least, were my speculations at the time, though I am not sure but that they took their tone from the enthusiasm of the young Count, who seemed more enchanted than ever with the wild chivalry of the prairies, and talked of putting on the Indian dress and adopting the Indian habits during the time he hoped to pass with the Osages.

CHAPTER VI

TRAIL OF THE OSAGE HUNTERS—DEPARTURE OF THE COUNT AND HIS PARTY—A DESERTED WAR CAMP—A VAGRANT DOG—THE ENCAMPMENT

IN THE course of the morning the trail we were pursuing was crossed by another, which struck off through the forest to the west in a direct course for the Arkansas River. Beatte, our half-breed, after considering it for a moment, pronounced it the trail of the Osage hunters; and that it must lead to the place where they had forded the river on their way to the hunting grounds.

Here then the young Count and his companion came to a halt and prepared to take leave of us. The most experienced frontiersmen in the troop remonstrated on the hazard of the undertaking. They were about to throw themselves loose in the wilderness, with no other guides, guards, or attendants, than a young ignorant half-breed, and a still younger Indian. They were embarrassed by a pack-horse and two led horses, with which they would have to make their way through matted forests, and across rivers and morasses. The Osages and Pawnees were at war, and they might fall in with some warrior party of the latter, who are ferocious foes; besides, their small number, and their valuable horses would form a great temptation to some of the straggling bands of Osages loitering about the frontier, who might rob them of their horses in the night, and leave them destitute and on foot in the midst of the prairies.

Nothing, however, could restrain the romantic ardor of the Count for a campaign of buffalo hunting with the Osages, and he had a game spirit that seemed always stimulated by the idea of danger. His travelling companion, of discreeter age and calmer temperament, was convinced of the rashness of the enterprise; but he could not control the impetuous zeal of his youthful friend and he was too loyal to leave him to pursue his hazardous scheme alone. To our great regret, therefore, we saw them abandon the protection of our escort, and strike off on their hap-hazard expedition. The old hunters of our party shook their heads, and our half-breed, Beatte, predicted all kinds of trouble to them; my only hope was, that they would soon meet with perplexities enough to cool the impetuosity of the young Count, and induce him to rejoin us. With this idea we travelled slowly, and made a considerable halt at noon. After resuming our march, we came in sight of the Arkansas. It presented a broad and rapid stream, bordered by a beach of fine sand, overgrown with willows and cotton-wood trees. Beyond the river, the eye wandered over a beautiful champaign country, of flowery plains and sloping uplands, diversified by groves and clumps of trees, and long screens of woodland; the whole wearing the aspect of complete, and even ornamental cultivation, instead of native wildness. Not far from the river, on an open eminence, we passed through the recently deserted camping place of an Osage war party. The frames of the tents or wigwams remained, consisting of poles bent into an arch, with each end stuck into the ground: these are intertwined with twigs and branches, and covered with bark and skins. Those experienced in Indian lore, can ascertain the tribe, and whether on a hunting or a warlike expedition, by the shape and disposition of the wigwams. Beatte pointed out to us, in the present skeleton camp, the wigwam in which the chiefs had held their consultations round the council-fire; and an open area, well trampled down, on which the grand war-dance had been performed.

Pursuing our journey, as we were passing through a forest, we were met by a forlorn, half-famished dog, who came rambling along the trail, with inflamed eyes, and bewildered look. Though nearly trampled upon by the foremost rangers, he took notice of no one, but rambled heedlessly among the horses. The cry of "mad dog" was immediately raised, and one of the rangers levelled his rifle, but was stayed by the ever-ready humanity of the Commissioner. "He is blind!" said he. "It is the dog of some poor Indian, following his master by the scent. It would be a shame to kill so faithful an animal." The ranger shouldered his rifle, the dog blundered blindly through the cavalcade unhurt, and keeping his nose to the ground, continued his course along the trail, affording a rare instance of a dog surviving a bad name.

About three o'clock, we came to a recent camping-place of the company of rangers: the brands of one of their fires were still smoking; so that, according to the opinion of Beatte, they could not have passed on above a day previously. As there was a fine stream of water close by, and plenty of pea-vines for the horses, we encamped here for the night.

We had not been here long, when we heard a halloo from a distance, and beheld the young Count and his party advancing through the forest. We welcomed them to the camp with heart-felt satisfaction; for their departure upon so hazardous an expedition had caused us great uneasiness. A short experiment had convinced them of the toil and difficulty of inexperienced travellers like themselves making their way through the wilderness with such a train of horses, and such slender attendance. Fortunately, they determined to rejoin us before nightfall; one night's camping out might have cost them their horses. The Count had prevailed upon his protegee and esquire, the young Osage, to continue with him, and still calculated upon achieving great exploits with his assistance, on the buffalo prairies.

CHAPTER VII

NEWS OF THE RANGERS—THE COUNT AND HIS INDIAN SQUIRE—
HALT IN THE WOODS—WOODLAND SCENE—OSAGE VILLAGE—OSAGE
VISITORS AT OUR EVENING CAMP

IN THE morning early, the two Creeks who had been sent express by the commander of Fort Gibson, to stop the company of rangers, arrived at our encampment on their return. They had left the company encamped about fifty miles distant, in a fine place on the Arkansas, abounding in game, where they intended to await our arrival. This news spread animation throughout our party, and we set out on our march at sunrise, with renewed spirit.

In mounting our steeds, the young Osage attempted to throw a blanket upon his wild horse. The fine, sensitive animal took fright, reared and recoiled. The attitudes of the wild horse and the almost naked savage, would have formed studies for a painter or a statuary.

I often pleased myself in the course of our march,

with noticing the appearance of the young Count and his newly-enlisted follower, as they rode before me. Never was preux chevalier better suited with an esquire. The Count was well mounted, and as I have before observed, was a bold and graceful rider. He was fond, too, of caracoling his horse, and dashing about in the buoyancy of youthful spirits. His dress was a gay Indian hunting frock of dressed deer skin, setting well to the shape, dyed of a beautiful purple, and fancifully embroidered with silks of various colors; as if it had been the work of some Indian beauty, to decorate a favorite chief. With this he wore leathern pantaloons and moccasons, a foraging cap, and a double-barrelled gun slung by a bandoleer athwart his back: so that he was quite a picturesque figure as he managed gracefully his spirited steed.

The young Osage would ride close behind him on his wild and beautifully mottled horse, which was decorated with crimson tufts of hair. He rode with his finely shaped head and bust naked; his blanket being girt round his waist. He carried his rifle in one hand, and managed his horse with the other, and seemed ready to dash off at a moment's warning, with his youthful leader, on any madcap foray or scamper. The Count, with the sanguine anticipations of youth, promised himself many hardy adventures and exploits in company with his youthful "brave," when we should get among the buffaloes, in the Pawnee hunting grounds.

After riding some distance, we crossed a narrow, deep stream, upon a solid bridge, the remains of an old beaver dam; the industrious community which had constructed it had all been destroyed. Above us, a streaming flight of wild geese, high in air, and making a vociferous noise, gave note of the waning year.

About half past ten o'clock we made a halt in a forest,

where there was abundance of the pea-vine. Here we turned the horses loose to graze. A fire was made, water procured from an adjacent spring, and in a short time our little Frenchman, Tonish, had a pot of coffee prepared for our refreshment. While partaking of it, we were joined by an old Osage, one of a small hunting party who had recently passed this way. He was in search of his horse, which had wandered away, or been stolen. Our half-breed, Beatte, made a wry face on hearing of Osage hunters in this direction. "Until we pass those hunters," said he, "we shall see no buffaloes. They frighten away every thing like a prairie on fire."

The morning repast being over, the party amused themselves in various ways. Some shot with their rifles at a mark, others lay asleep half buried in the deep bed of foliage, with their heads resting on their saddles; others gossiped round the fire at the foot of a tree, which sent up wreaths of blue smoke among the branches. The horses banqueted luxuriously on the pea-vines, and some lay down and rolled amongst them.

We were overshadowed by lofty trees, with straight, smooth trunks, like stately columns; and as the glancing rays of the sun shone through the transparent leaves, tinted with the many-colored hues of autumn, I was reminded of the effect of sunshine among the stained windows and clustering columns of a Gothic cathedral. Indeed there is a grandeur and solemnity in our spacious forests of the West, that awaken in me the same feeling I have experienced in those vast and venerable piles, and the sound of the wind sweeping through them, supplies occasionally the deep breathings of the organ.

About noon the bugle sounded to horse, and we were again on the march, hoping to arrive at the encampment of the rangers before night; as the old Osage had assured us it was not above ten or twelve miles distant. In our course through a forest, we passed by a lonely pool, covered with the most magnificent water-lilies I had ever beheld; among which swam several wood-ducks, one of the most beautiful of water-fowl, remarkable for the gracefulness and brilliancy of its plumage.

After proceeding some distance farther, we came down upon the banks of the Arkansas, at a place where tracks of numerous horses, all entering the water, showed where a party of Osage hunters had recently crossed the river on their way to the buffalo range. After letting our horses drink in the river, we continued along its bank for a space, and then across prairies, where we saw a distant smoke, which we hoped might proceed from the encampment of the rangers. Following what we supposed to be their trail, we came to a meadow in which were a number of horses grazing: they were not, however, the horses of the troop. A little farther on, we reached a straggling Osage village, on the banks of the Arkansas. Our arrival created quite a sensation. A number of old men came forward and shook hands with us all severally; while the women and children huddled together in groups, staring at us wildly, chattering and laughing among themselves. We found that all the young men of the village had departed on a hunting expedition, leaving the women and children and old men behind. Here the Commissioner made a speech from on horseback; informing his hearers of the purport of his mission, to promote a general peace among the tribes of the West, and urging them to lay aside all warlike and bloodthirsty notions, and not to make any wanton attacks upon the Pawnees. This speech being interpreted by Beatte, seemed to have a most pacifying effect upon the multitude, who promised faithfully that, as far as in them lay, the peace should not be disturbed;

and indeed their age and sex gave some reason to trust that they would keep their word.

Still hoping to reach the camp of the rangers before nightfall, we pushed on until twilight, when we were obliged to halt on the borders of a ravine. The rangers bivouaced under trees, at the bottom of the dell, while we pitched our tent on a rocky knoll near a running stream. The night came on dark and overcast, with flying clouds, and much appearance of rain. The fires of the rangers burnt brightly in the dell, and threw strong masses of light upon the robber-looking groups that were cooking, eating and drinking around them. To add to the wildness of the scene, several Osage Indians, visitors from the village we had passed, were mingled among the men. Three of them came and seated themselves by our fire. They watched every thing that was going on round them in silence, and looked like figures of monumental bronze. We gave them food, and, what they most relished, coffee; for the Indians partake in the universal fondness for this beverage, which pervades the West. When they had made their supper they stretched themselves, side by side, before the fire, and began a low nasal chant, drumming with their hands upon their breasts, by way of accompaniment. Their chant seemed to consist of regular staves, every one terminating, not in a melodious cadence, but in the abrupt interjection huh! uttered almost like a hiccup. This chant, we were told by our interpreter, Beatte, related to ourselves, our appearance, our treatment of them, and all that they knew of our plans. In one part they spoke of the young Count, whose animated character and eagerness for Indian enterprise had struck their fancy, and they indulged in some waggery about him and the young Indian beauties, that produced great merriment among our half-breeds.

This mode of improvising is common throughout the savage tribes; and in this way, with a few simple inflections of the voice, they chant all their exploits in war and hunting, and occasionally indulge in a vein of comic humor and dry satire, to which the Indians appear to me much more prone than is generally imagined.

In fact, the Indians that I have had an opportunity of seeing in real life, are quite different from those described in poetry. They are by no means the stoics that they are represented; taciturn, unbending, without a tear or a smile. Taciturn they are, it is true, when in company with white men, whose good-will they distrust, and whose language they do not understand; but the white man is equally taciturn under like circumstances. When the Indians are among themselves, however, there cannot be greater gossips. Half their time is taken up in talking over their adventures in war and hunting, and in telling whimsical stories. They are great mimics and buffoons, also, and entertain themselves excessively at the expense of the whites with whom they have associated, and who have supposed them impressed with profound respect for their grandeur and dignity. They are curious observers, noting everything in silence, but with a keen and watchful eye; occasionally exchanging a glance or a grunt with each other, when any thing particularly strikes them: but reserving all comments until they are alone. Then it is that they give full scope to criticism, satire, mimicry, and mirth.

In the course of my journey along the frontier, I have had repeated opportunities of noticing their excitability and boisterous merriment at their games; and have occasionally noticed a group of Osages sitting round a fire until a late hour of the night, engaged in the most animated and lively conversation; and at times making the woods resound with peals of laughter. As to tears, they have them in abundance, both real and affected; at times they make a merit of them. No one weeps more bitterly or profusely at the death of a relative or friend: and they have stated times when they repair to howl and lament at their graves. I have heard doleful wailings at daybreak, in the neighboring Indian villages, made by some of the inhabitants, who go out at that hour into the fields, to mourn and weep for the dead: at such times, I am told, the tears will stream down their cheeks in torrents.

As far as I can judge, the Indian of poetical fiction is like the shepherd of pastoral romance, a mere personification of imaginary attributes.

The nasal chant of our Osage guests gradually died away; they covered their heads with their blankets and fell fast asleep, and in a little while all was silent, excepting the pattering of scattered rain-drops upon our tent.

In the morning our Indian visitors breakfasted with us, but the young Osage who was to act as esquire to the Count in his knight-errantry on the prairies, was no-where to be found. His wild horse, too, was missing, and, after many conjectures, we came to the conclusion that he had taken "Indian leave" of us in the night. We afterwards ascertained that he had been persuaded so to do by the Osages we had recently met with; who had represented to him the perils that would attend him in an expedition to the Pawnee hunting grounds, where he might fall into the hands of the implacable enemies of his tribe; and, what was scarcely less to be apprehended, the annoyances to which he would be subjected from the capricious and overbearing conduct of the white men; who, as I have witnessed in my own short experience, are prone to treat the poor Indians as little better than brute animals. Indeed, he had had a specimen of it himself in the narrow escape he made from the inflic- tion of "Lynch's law," by the hard-winking worthy of the frontier, for the flagitious crime of finding a stray horse.

The disappearance of the youth was generally regret- ted by our party, for we had all taken a great fancy to him from his handsome, frank, and manly appearance, and the easy grace of his deportment. He was indeed a native-born gentleman. By none, however, was he so much lamented as by the young Count, who thus suddenly found himself deprived of his esquire. I regretted the departure of the Osage for his own sake, for we should have cherished him throughout the expedition, and I am convinced, from the munificent spirit of his patron, he would have returned to his tribe laden with wealth of beads and trinkets and Indian blankets.

CHAPTER VIII

THE HONEY CAMP

THE weather, which had been rainy in the night, having held up, we resumed our march at seven o'clock in the morning, in confident hope of soon arriving at the encampment of the rangers. We had not ridden above three or four miles when we came to a large tree which had recently been felled by an axe, for the wild honey contained in the hollow of its trunk, several broken flakes of which still remained. We now felt sure that the camp could not be far distant. About a couple of miles further some of the rangers set up a shout, and pointed to a number of horses grazing in a woody bottom. A few paces brought us to the brow of an elevated ridge, whence we looked down upon the encampment. It was a wild bandit, or Robin Hood, scene. In a beautiful open forest, traversed by a running stream, were booths of bark and branches, and tents of blankets, temporary shelters from the recent rain, for the rangers commonly bivouac in the open air. There were groups of rangers in every kind of uncouth garb. Some were cooking at large fires made at the feet of trees, some were stretching and dressing deer skins; some were shooting at a mark, and some lying about on the grass. Venison jerked, and hung on frames, was drying over the embers in one place; in another lay carcasses recently brought in by the hunters. Stacks of rifles were leaning against the trunks of the trees, and saddles, bridles, and powder-horns hanging above them, while the horses were grazing here and there among the thickets.

Our arrival was greeted with acclamation. The rangers crowded about their comrades to inquire the news from the fort; for our own part, we were received in frank simple hunter's style by Captain Bean, the commander of the company; a man about forty years of age, vigorous and active. His life had been chiefly passed on the frontier, occasionally in Indian warfare, so that he was a thorough woodsman, and a first-rate hunter. He was equipped in character; in leathern hunting shirt and leggings, and a leathern foraging cap.

While we were conversing with the Captain, a veteran huntsman approached, whose whole appearance struck me. He was of the middle size, but tough and weather-proved; a head partly bald and garnished with loose iron-gray locks, and a fine black eye, beaming with youthful spirit. His dress was similar to that of the Captain, a rifle shirt and leggings of dressed deer skin, that had evidently seen service; a powder-horn was slung by his side, a hunting knife stuck in his belt, and in his hand was an ancient and trusty rifle, doubtless as dear to him as a bosom friend. He asked permission to go hunting, which was readily granted. "That's old Ryan," said the Captain, when he had gone; "there's not a better hunter in the camp; he's sure to bring in game."

In a little while our pack-horses were unloaded and turned loose to revel among the pea-vines. Our tent was pitched; our fire made; the half of a deer had been sent to us from the Captain's lodge; Beatte brought in a couple of wild turkeys; the spits were laden, and the camp-kettle crammed with meat; and to crown our luxuries, a basin filled with great flakes of delicious honey, the spoils of a plundered bee-tree, was given us by one of the rangers.

Our little Frenchman, Tonish, was in an ecstasy, and tucking up his sleeves to the elbows, set to work to make a display of his culinary skill, on which he prided himself almost as much as upon his hunting, his riding, and his warlike prowess.

CHAPTER IX

A BEE HUNT

THE beautiful forest in which we were encamped abounded in bee-trees; that is to say, trees in the decayed trunks of which wild bees had established their hives. It is surprising in what countless swarms the bees have overspread the Far West within but a moderate number of years. The Indians consider them the harbinger of the white man, as the buffalo is of the red man; and say that in proportion as the bee advances, the Indian and buffalo retire. We are always accustomed to associate the hum of the bee-hive with the farmhouse and flower-garden, and to consider those industrious little animals as connected with the busy haunts of man, and I am told that the wild bee is seldom to be met with at any great distance from the frontier. They have been the heralds of civilization, steadfastly preceding it as it advanced from the Atlantic borders, and some of the ancient settlers of the West pretend to give the very year when the honey-bee first crossed the Mississippi. The Indians with surprise found the mouldering trees of their forests suddenly teeming with ambrosial sweets, and nothing, I am told, can exceed the greedy relish with which they banquet for the first time upon this unbought luxury of the wilderness.

At present the honey-bee swarms in myriads, in the noble groves and forests which skirt and intersect the prairies, and extend along the alluvial bottoms of the rivers. It seems to me as if these beautiful regions answer literally to the description of the land of promise, "a land flowing with milk and honey;" for the rich pasturage of the prairies is calculated to sustain herds of cattle as countless as the sands upon the sea-shore, while the flowers with which they are enamelled render them a very paradise for the nectar-seeking bee.

We had not been long in the camp when a party set out in quest of a bee-tree; and, being curious to witness the sport, I gladly accepted an invitation to accompany them. The party was headed by a veteran bee-hunter, a tall lank fellow in homespun garb that hung loosely about his limbs, and a straw hat shaped not unlike a bee-hive; a comrade, equally uncouth in garb, and without a hat, straddled along at his heels, with a long rifle on his shoulder. To these succeeded half a dozen others, some with axes and some with rifles, for no one stirs far from the camp without his firearms, so as to be ready either for wild deer or wild Indian.

After proceeding some distance we came to an open glade on the skirts of the forest. Here our leader halted, and then advanced quietly to a low bush, on the top of which I perceived a piece of honey-comb. This I found was the bait or lure for the wild bees. Several were humming about it, and diving into its cells. When they had laden themselves with honey they would rise into the air, and dart off in a straight line, almost with the velocity of a bullet. The hunters watched attentively the course they took, and then set off in the same direction, stumbling along over twisted roots and fallen trees, with their eyes turned up to the sky. In this way they traced the honey-laden bees to their hive, in the hollow trunk of a blasted oak, where, after buzzing about for a moment, they entered a hole about sixty feet from the ground.

Two of the bee-hunters now plied their axes vigorously at the foot of the tree to level it with the ground. The mere spectators and amateurs, in the meantime, drew off to a cautious distance, to be out of the way of the falling of the tree and the vengeance of its inmates. The jarring blows of the axe seemed to have no effect in alarming or disturbing this most industrious community. They continued to ply at their usual occupations, some arriving full freighted into port, others sallying forth on new expeditions, like so many merchantmen in a money-making metropolis, little suspicious of impending bankruptcy and downfall. Even a loud crack which announced the disrupture of the trunk, failed to divert their attention from the intense pursuit of gain; at length down came the tree with a tremendous crash bursting open from end to end, and displaying all the hoarded treasures of the commonwealth.

One of the hunters immediately ran up with a whisp of lighted hay as a defence against the bees. The latter, however, made no attack and sought no revenge; they seemed stupefied by the catastrophe and unsuspicious of its cause, and remained crawling and buzzing about the ruins without offering us any molestation. Every one of the party now fell to, with spoon and hunting knife, to scoop out the flakes of honey-comb with which the hollow trunk was stored. Some of them were of old date and a deep brown color, others were beautifully white, and the honey in their cells was almost limpid. Such of the combs as were entire were placed in camp kettles to be conveyed to the encampment; those which had been shivered in the fall were devoured upon the spot. Every stark bee-hunter was to be seen with a rich morsel in his hand, dripping about his fingers, and disappearing as rapidly as a cream tart before the holiday appetite of a schoolboy.

Nor was it the bee-hunters alone that profited by the downfall of this industrious community; as if the bees would carry through the similitude of their habits with those of laborious and gainful man, I beheld numbers from rival hives, arriving on eager wing, to enrich themselves with the ruins of their neighbors. These busied themselves as eagerly and cheerfully as so many wreckers on an Indiaman that has been driven on shore; plunging into the cells of the broken honey-combs, banqueting greedily on the spoil, and then winging their way full freighted to their homes. As to the poor proprietors of the ruin, they seemed to have no heart to do any thing, not even to taste the nectar that flowed around them; but crawled backwards and forwards, in vacant desolation, as I have seen a poor fellow with his

hands in his pockets, whistling vacantly and despondingly about the ruins of his house that had been burnt.

It is difficult to describe the bewilderment and confusion of the bees of the bankrupt hive who had been
absent at the time of the catastrophe, and who arrived
from time to time, with full cargoes from abroad. At first
they wheeled about in the air, in the place where the
fallen tree had once reared its head, astonished at
finding it all a vacuum. At length, as if comprehending
their disaster, they settled down in clusters on a dry
branch of a neighboring tree, whence they seemed to
contemplate the prostrate ruin, and to buzz forth
doleful lamentations over the downfall of their republic.
It was a scene on which the "melancholy Jacques" might
have moralized by the hour.

We now abandoned the place, leaving much honey in
the hollow of the tree. "It will all be cleared off by
varmint," said one of the rangers. "What vermin?" asked
I. "Oh, bears, and skunks, and racoons, and 'possums.
The bears is the knowingest varmint for finding out a
bee-tree in the world. They'll gnaw for days together at
the trunk till they make a hole big enough to get in their
paws, and then they'll haul out honey, bees and all."

CHAPTER X

O N returning to the camp, we found it a scene of the
greatest hilarity. Some of the rangers were shooting at a mark, others were leaping, wrestling, and
playing at prison bars. They were mostly young men, on
their first expedition, in high health and vigor, and
buoyant with anticipations; and I can conceive nothing
more likely to set the youthful blood into a flow, than a
wild wood life of the kind, and the range of a magnificent wilderness, abounding with game, and fruitful of
adventure. We send our youth abroad to grow luxurious
and effeminate in Europe; it appears to me, that a
previous tour on the prairies would be more likely to
produce that manliness, simplicity, and self-depend-
ence, most in unison with our political institutions.

While the young men were engaged in these boisterous amusements, a graver set, composed of the Captain,
the Doctor and other sages and leaders of the camp,
were seated or stretched out on the grass, round a
frontier map, holding a consultation about our position,
and the course we were to pursue.

Our plan was to cross the Arkansas just above where
the Red Fork falls into it, then to keep westerly, until we
should pass through a grand belt of open forest, called
the Cross Timber, which ranges nearly north and south
from the Arkansas to Red River; after which, we were to
keep a southerly course towards the latter river.

Our half-breed, Beatte, being an experienced Osage
hunter, was called into the consultation. "Have you ever

hunted in this direction?" said the Captain. "Yes," was the laconic reply.

"Perhaps, then, you can tell us in which direction lies the Red Fork?"

"If you keep along yonder, by the edge of the prairie, you will come to a bald hill, with a pile of stones upon it."

"I have noticed that hill as I was hunting," said the Captain.

"Well! those stones were set up by the Osages as a landmark: from that spot you may have a sight of the Red Fork."

"In that case," cried the Captain, "we shall reach the Red Fork to-morrow; then cross the Arkansas above it, into the Pawnee country, and then in two days we shall crack buffalo bones!"

The idea of arriving at the adventurous hunting grounds of the Pawnees, and of coming upon the traces of the buffaloes, made every eye sparkle with animation. Our further conversation was interrupted by the sharp report of a rifle at no great distance from the camp.

"That's old Ryan's rifle," exclaimed the Captain; "there's a buck down, I'll warrant!" nor was he mistaken; for, before long, the veteran made his appearance, calling upon one of the younger rangers to return with him, and aid in bringing home the carcass.

The surrounding country, in fact, abounded with game, so that the camp was overstocked with provisions, and, as no less than twenty bee-trees had been cut down in the vicinity, every one revelled in luxury. With the wasteful prodigality of hunters, there was a continual feasting, and scarce any one put by provision for the morrow. The cooking was conducted in hunters' style: the meat was stuck upon tapering spits of dogwood, which were thrust perpendicularly into the ground, so as to sustain the joint before the fire, where it was roasted or broiled with all its juices retained in it in a manner that would have tickled the palate of the most experienced gourmand. As much could not be said in favor of the bread. It was little more than a paste made of flour and water, and fried like fritters, in lard; though some adopted a ruder style, twisting it round the ends of sticks and thus roasting it before the fire. In either way, I have found it extremely palatable on the prairies. No one knows the true relish of food until he has a hunter's appetite.

Before sunset, we were summoned by little Tonish to a sumptuous repast. Blankets had been spread on the ground near to the fire, upon which we took our seats. A large dish, or bowl, made from the root of a maple tree, and which we had purchased at the Indian village, was placed on the ground before us, and into it were emptied the contents of one of the camp kettles, consisting of a wild turkey hashed, together with slices of bacon and lumps of dough. Beside it was placed another bowl of similar ware, containing an ample supply of fritters. After we had discussed the hash, two wooden spits, on which the ribs of a fat buck were broiling before the fire, were removed and planted in the ground before us, with a triumphant air, by little Tonish. Having no dishes, we had to proceed in hunters' style, cutting off strips and slices with our hunting-knives, and dipping them in salt and pepper. To do justice to Tonish's cookery, however, and to the keen sauce of the prairies, never have I tasted venison so delicious. With all this, our beverage was coffee, boiled in a camp kettle, sweetened with brown sugar, and drunk out of tin cups: and such was the style of our banqueting throughout this expedition, whenever provisions were plenty, and as long as flour and coffee and sugar held out.

As the twilight thickened into night, the sentinels were marched forth to their stations around the camp; an indispensable precaution in a country infested by Indians. The encampment now presented a picturesque appearance. Camp fires were blazing and smouldering here and there among the trees, with groups of rangers round them; some seated or lying on the ground, others standing in the ruddy glare of the flames, or in shadowy relief. At some of the fires there was much boisterous mirth, where peals of laughter were mingled with loud ribald jokes and uncouth exclamations; for the troop was evidently a raw, undisciplined band, levied among the wild youngsters of the frontier, who had enlisted, some for the sake of roving adventure, and some for the purpose of getting a knowledge of the country. Many of them were the neighbors of their officers, and accustomed to regard them with the familiarity of equals and companions. None of them had any idea of the restraint and decorum of a camp, or ambition to acquire a name for exactness in a profession in which they had no intention of continuing.

While this boisterous merriment prevailed at some of the fires, there suddenly rose a strain of nasal melody from another, at which a choir of "vocalists" were uniting their voices in a most lugubrious psalm tune. This was led by one of the lieutenants; a tall, spare man, who we were informed had officiated as schoolmaster, singing-master, and occasionally as Methodist preacher, in one of the villages of the frontier. The chant rose solemnly and sadly in the night air, and reminded me of the description of similar canticles in the camps of the Covenanters; and, indeed, the strange medley of figures and faces and uncouth garbs, congregated together in our troop, would not have disgraced the banners of Praise-God Barebones.

In one of the intervals of this nasal psalmody, an amateur owl, as if in competition, began his dreary hooting. Immediately there was a cry throughout the camp of "Charley's owl! Charley's owl!" It seems this "obscure bird" had visited the camp every night, and had been fired at by one of the sentinels, a half-witted lad, named Charley; who, on being called up for firing when on duty, excused himself by saying, that he understood that owls made uncommonly good soup.

One of the young rangers mimicked the cry of this bird of wisdom, who, with a simplicity little consonant with his character, came hovering within sight, and alighted on the naked branch of a tree, lit up by the blaze of our fire. The young Count immediately seized his fowling-piece, took fatal aim, and in a twinkling the poor bird of ill omen came fluttering to the ground. Charley was now called upon to make and eat his dish of owl-soup, but declined, as he had not shot the bird.

In the course of the evening, I paid a visit to the Captain's fire. It was composed of huge trunks of trees, and of sufficient magnitude to roast a buffalo whole. Here were a number of the prime hunters and leaders of the camp, some sitting, some standing, and others lying on skins or blankets before the fire, telling old frontier stories about hunting and Indian warfare.

As the night advanced, we perceived above the trees to the west, a ruddy glow flushing up the sky.

"That must be a prairie set on fire by the Osage hunters," said the Captain.

"It is at the Red Fork," said Beatte, regarding the sky. "It seems but three miles distant, yet it perhaps is twenty."

About half past eight o'clock, a beautiful pale light gradually sprang up in the east, a precursor of the rising moon. Drawing off from the Captain's lodge, I now prepared for the night's repose. I had determined to abandon the shelter of the tent, and henceforth to bivouac like the rangers. A bear-skin spread at the foot of a tree was my bed, with a pair of saddle-bags for a pillow. Wrapping myself in blankets, I stretched myself on this hunter's couch, and soon fell into a sound and sweet sleep, from which I did not awake until the bugle sounded at daybreak.

CHAPTER XI

BREAKING UP OF THE ENCAMPMENT—PICTURESQUE MARCH—GAME—CAMP SCENES—TRIUMPH OF A YOUNG HUNTER—ILL SUCCESS OF OLD HUNTERS—FOUL MURDER OF A POLECAT

OCT. 14. At the signal-note of the bugle, the sentinels and patrols marched in from their stations around the camp and were dismissed. The rangers were roused from their night's repose, and soon a bustling scene took place. While some cut wood, made fires, and prepared the morning's meal, others struck their foul-weather shelters of blankets, and made every preparation for departure; while others dashed about, through brush and brake, catching the horses and leading or driving them into camp.

During all this bustle the forest rang with whoops, and shouts, and peals of laughter; when all had breakfasted, packed up their effects and camp equipage, and loaded the pack-horses, the bugle sounded to saddle and mount. By eight o'clock the whole troop set off in a long straggling line, with whoop and halloo, intermingled with many an oath at the loitering pack-horses, and in a little while the forest, which for several days had been the scene of such unwonted bustle and uproar, relapsed into its primeval solitude and silence.

It was a bright sunny morning, with a pure transparent atmosphere that seemed to bathe the very heart with gladness. Our march continued parallel to the Arkansas, through a rich and varied country; sometimes we had to break our way through alluvial bottoms matted with redundant vegetation, where the gigantic trees were entangled with grape-vines, hanging like cordage from their branches; sometimes we coasted along sluggish brooks, whose feebly-trickling current just served to link together a succession of glassy pools, imbedded like mirrors in the quiet bosom of the forest, reflecting its autumnal foliage, and patches of the clear blue sky. Sometimes we scrambled up broken and rocky hills, from the summits of which we had wide views stretching on one side over distant prairies diversified by groves and forests, and on the other ranging along a line of blue and shadowy hills beyond the waters of the Arkansas.

The appearance of our troop was suited to the country; stretching along in a line of upwards of half a mile in length, winding among brakes and bushes, and up and down the defiles of the hills: the men in every kind of uncouth garb, with long rifles on their shoulders, and mounted on horses of every color. The pack-horses, too, would incessantly wander from the line of march, to crop the surrounding herbage, and were banged and beaten back by Tonish and his half-breed compeers, with volleys of mongrel oaths. Every now and then the notes of the bugle from the head of the column, would echo through the woodlands and along the hollow glens, summoning up stragglers, and announcing the line of march. The whole scene reminded me of the description given of bands of buccaneers penetrating the wilds of South America, on their plundering expeditions against the Spanish settlements.

At one time we passed through a luxuriant bottom of meadow bordered by thickets, where the tall grass was pressed down into numerous "deer beds," where those animals had couched the preceding night. Some oak trees also bore signs of having been clambered by bears, in quest of acorns, the marks of their claws being visible in the bark.

As we opened a glade of this sheltered meadow, we beheld several deer bounding away in wild affright, until, having gained some distance, they would stop and gaze back, with the curiosity common to this animal, at the strange intruders into their solitudes. There was immediately a sharp report of rifles in every direction, from the young huntsmen of the troop, but they were too eager to aim surely, and the deer, unharmed, bounded away into the depths of the forest.

In the course of our march we struck the Arkansas, but found ourselves still below the Red Fork, and, as the river made deep bends, we again left its banks and continued through the woods until nearly eight o'clock, when we encamped in a beautiful basin bordered by a fine stream, and shaded by clumps of lofty oaks.

The horses were now hobbled, that is to say, their fore legs were fettered with cords or leathern straps, so as to impede their movements, and prevent their wandering from the camp. They were then turned loose to graze. A number of rangers, prime hunters, started off in different directions in search of game. There was no whooping nor laughing about the camp as in the morning; all were either busy about the fires preparing the evening's repast, or reposing upon the grass. Shots were soon heard in various directions. After a time a huntsman rode into the camp with the carcass of a fine buck hanging across his horse. Shortly afterwards came in a couple of stripling hunters on foot, one of whom bore on his shoulders the body of a doe. He was evidently proud of his spoil, being probably one of his first achievements, though he and his companion were much bantered by their comrades, as young beginners who hunted in partnership.

Just as the night set in, there was a great shouting at one end of the camp, and immediately afterwards a body of young rangers came parading round the various fires, bearing one of their comrades in triumph on their shoulders. He had shot an elk for the first time in his life, and it was the first animal of the kind that had been killed on this expedition. The young huntsman, whose name was M'Lellan, was the hero of the camp for the night, and was the "father of the feast" into the bargain; for portions of his elk were soon roasting at every fire.

The other hunters returned without success. The captain had observed the tracks of a buffalo, which must have passed within a few days, and had tracked a bear for some distance until the foot-prints had disappeared. He had seen an elk too, on the banks of the Arkansas, which walked out on a sand-bar of the river, but before he could steal round through the bushes to get a shot, it had re-entered the woods.

Our own hunter, Beatte, returned silent and sulky, from an unsuccessful hunt. As yet he had brought us in nothing, and we had depended for our supplies of venison upon the Captain's mess. Beatte was evidently mortified, for he looked down with contempt upon the rangers, as raw and inexperienced woodsmen, but little skilled in hunting; they, on the other hand, regarded Beatte with no very complacent eye, as one of an evil breed, and always spoke of him as "the Indian."

Our little Frenchman Tonish also, by his incessant boasting and chattering, and gasconading, in his balderdashed dialect, had drawn upon himself the ridicule of many of the wags of the troop, who amused themselves at his expense in a kind of raillery by no means remarkable for its delicacy; but the little varlet was so completely fortified by vanity and self-conceit, that he was invulnerable to every joke. I must confess, however, that I felt a little mortified at the sorry figure our retainers were making among these moss-troopers of the frontier. Even our very equipments came in for a share of unpopularity, and I heard many sneers at the double-barrelled guns with which we were provided against smaller game; the lads of the West holding "shot-guns," as they call them, in great contempt, thinking grouse, partridges, and even wild turkeys as beneath their serious attention, and the rifle the only firearm worthy of a hunter.

I was awakened before daybreak the next morning, by the mournful howling of a wolf, who was skulking about the purlieus of the camp, attracted by the scent of venison. Scarcely had the first gray streak of dawn appeared, when a youngster at one of the distant lodges, shaking off his sleep, crowed in imitation of a cock, with a loud clear note and prolonged cadence, that would have done credit to the most veteran chanticleer. He was immediately answered from another quarter, as if from a rival rooster. The chant was echoed from lodge to lodge, and followed by the cackling of hens, quacking of ducks, gabbling of turkeys, and grunting of swine, until we seemed to have been transported into the midst of a farmyard, with all its inmates in full concert around us.

After riding a short distance this morning, we came upon a well-worn Indian track, and following it, scrambled to the summit of a hill, whence we had a wide prospect over a country diversified by rocky ridges and waving lines of upland, and enriched by groves and clumps of trees of varied tuft and foliage. At a distance to the west, to our great satisfaction, we beheld the Red Fork rolling its ruddy current to the Arkansas, and found that we were above the point of junction. We now descended and pushed forward, with much difficulty, through the rich alluvial bottom that borders the Arkansas. Here the trees were interwoven with grape-vines, forming a kind of cordage, from trunk to trunk and limb to limb; there was a thick undergrowth, also, of bush and bramble, and such an abundance of hops, fit for gathering, that it was difficult for our horses to force their way through.

The sod was imprinted in many places with the tracks of deer, and the claws of bears were to be traced on various trees. Every one was on the look-out in the hope of starting some game, when suddenly there was a bustle and a clamor in a distant part of the line. A bear! a bear! was the cry. We all pressed forward to be present at the sport, when to my infinite, though whimsical chagrin, I found it to be our two worthies, Beatte and Tonish, perpetrating a foul murder on a polecat, or skunk! The animal had ensconced itself beneath the trunk of a fallen tree, whence it kept up a vigorous defence in its peculiar style, until the surrounding forest was in a high state of fragrance.

Gibes and jokes now broke out on all sides at the expense of the Indian hunter, and he was advised to wear the scalp of the skunk as the only trophy of his prowess. When they found, however, that he and Tonish were absolutely bent upon bearing off the carcass as a peculiar dainty, there was a universal expression of disgust; and they were regarded as little better than cannibals.

Mortified at this ignominious debut of our two hunters, I insisted upon their abandoning their prize and
resuming their march. Beatte complied with a dogged,
discontented air, and lagged behind muttering to himself. Tonish, however, with his usual buoyancy, consoled
himself by vociferous eulogies on the richness and
delicacy of a roasted polecat, which he swore was
considered the daintiest of dishes by all experienced
Indian gourmands. It was with difficulty I could silence
his loquacity by repeated and peremptory commands. A
Frenchman's vivacity however, if repressed in one way,
will break out in another, and Tonish now eased off his
spleen by bestowing volleys of oaths and dry blows on
the pack-horses. I was likely to be no gainer in the end,
by my opposition to the humors of these varlets, for
after a time, Beatte, who had lagged behind, rode up to
the head of the line to resume his station as a guide, and
I had the vexation to see the carcass of his prize,
stripped of its skin, and looking like a fat sucking pig,
dangling behind his saddle. I made a solemn vow,
however, in secret, that our fire should not be disgraced
by the cooking of that polecat.

CHAPTER XII

THE CROSSING OF THE ARKANSAS

W E HAD now arrived at the river, about a quarter of a
mile above the junction of the Red Fork; but the
banks were steep and crumbling, and the current was
deep and rapid. It was impossible, therefore, to cross at
this place; and we resumed our painful course through
the forest, dispatching Beatte ahead, in search of a

fording place. We had proceeded about a mile further, when he rejoined us, bringing intelligence of a place hard by, where the river, for a great part of its breadth, was rendered fordable by sand-bars, and the remainder might easily be swam by the horses.

Here, then, we made a halt. Some of the rangers set to work vigorously with their axes, felling trees on the edge of the river, wherewith to form rafts for the transportation of their baggage and camp equipage. Others patrolled the banks of the river farther up, in hopes of finding a better fording place; being unwilling to risk their horses in the deep channel.

It was now that our worthies, Beatte and Tonish, had an opportunity of displaying their Indian adroitness and resource. At the Osage village which we had passed a day or two before, they had procured a dry buffalo skin. This was now produced; cords were passed through a number of small eyelet holes with which it was bordered, and it was drawn up, until it formed a kind of deep trough. Sticks were then placed athwart it on the inside, to keep it in shape; our camp equipage and a part of our baggage were placed within, and the singular bark was carried down the bank and set afloat. A cord was attached to the prow, which Beatte took between his teeth, and throwing himself into the water, went ahead, towing the bark after him; while Tonish followed behind, to keep it steady and to propel it. Part of the way they had foothold, and were enabled to wade, but in the main current they were obliged to swim. The whole way, they whooped and yelled in the Indian style, until they landed safely on the opposite shore.

The Commissioner and myself were so well pleased with this Indian mode of ferriage, that we determined to trust ourselves in the buffalo hide. Our companions, the Count and Mr. L., had proceeded with the horses, along the river bank, in search of a ford which some of the rangers had discovered, about a mile and a half distant. While we were waiting for the return of our ferryman, I happened to cast my eyes upon a heap of luggage under a bush, and descried the sleek carcass of the polecat, snugly trussed up, and ready for roasting before the evening fire. I could not resist the temptation to plump it into the river, when it sunk to the bottom like a lump of lead; and thus our lodge was relieved from the bad odor which this savory viand had threatened to bring upon it.

Our men having recrossed with their cockle-shell bark, it was drawn on shore, half filled with saddles, saddlebags, and other luggage, amounting to a hundred weight; and being again placed in the water, I was invited to take my seat. It appeared to me pretty much like the embarkation of the wise men of Gotham, who went to sea in a bowl: I stepped in, however, without hesitation, though as cautiously as possible, and sat down on top of the luggage, the margin of the hide sinking to within a hand's breadth of the water's edge. Rifles, fowling-pieces, and other articles of small bulk, were then handed in, until I protested against receiving any more freight. We then launched forth upon the stream, the bark being towed as before.

It was with a sensation half serious, half comic, that I found myself thus afloat, on the skin of a buffalo, in the midst of a wild river, surrounded by wilderness, and towed along by a half savage, whooping and yelling like a devil incarnate. To please the vanity of little Tonish, I discharged the double-barrelled gun, to the right and left, when in the centre of the stream. The report echoed along the woody shores, and was answered by shouts from some of the rangers, to the great exultation of the little Frenchman, who took to himself the whole glory of this Indian mode of navigation.

Our voyage was accomplished happily; the Commissioner was ferried across with equal success, and all our effects were brought over in the same manner. Nothing could equal the vainglorious vaporing of little Tonish, as he strutted about the shore, and exulted in his superior skill and knowledge, to the rangers. Beatte, however, kept his proud, saturnine look, without a smile. He had a vast contempt for the ignorance of the rangers, and felt that he had been undervalued by them. His only observation was, "Dey now see de Indian good for someting, anyhow!"

The broad, sandy shore where we had landed, was intersected by innumerable tracks of elk, deer, bears, racoons, turkeys, and water-fowl. The river scenery at this place was beautifully diversified, presenting long, shining reaches, bordered by willows and cotton-wood trees; rich bottoms, with lofty forests; among which towered enormous plane trees, and the distance was closed in by high embowered promontories. The foliage had a yellow autumnal tint, which gave to the sunny landscape the golden tone of one of the landscapes of Claude Lorraine. There was animation given to the scene, by a raft of logs and branches, on which the Captain and his prime companion, the Doctor, were ferrying their effects across the stream; and by a long line of rangers on horseback, fording the river obliquely, along a series of sand-bars, about a mile and a half distant.

CHAPTER XIII

THE CAMP OF THE GLEN

CAMP GOSSIP—PAWNEES AND THEIR HABITS—A HUNTER'S ADVEN-
TURE—HORSES FOUND, AND MEN LOST

BEING joined by the Captain and some of the rangers, we struck into the woods for about half a mile, and then entered a wild, rocky dell, bordered by two lofty ridges of limestone, which narrowed as we advanced, until they met and united; making almost an angle. Here a fine spring of water rose among the rocks, and fed a silver rill that ran the whole length of the dell, freshening the grass with which it was carpeted.

In this rocky nook we encamped, among tall trees. The rangers gradually joined us, straggling through the forest singly or in groups; some on horseback, some on foot, driving their horses before them, heavily laden with baggage, some dripping wet, having fallen into the river; for they had experienced much fatigue and trouble from the length of the ford, and the depth and rapidity of the stream. They looked not unlike banditti returning with their plunder, and the wild dell was a retreat worthy to receive them. The effect was heightened after dark, when the light of the fires was cast upon rugged looking groups of men and horses; with baggage tumbled in heaps, rifles piled against the trees, and saddles, bridles, and powder-horns hanging about their trunks.

At the encampment we were joined by the young Count and his companion, and the young half-breed, Antoine, who had all passed successfully by the ford. To my annoyance, however, I discovered that both of my horses were missing. I had supposed them in the charge of Antoine: but he, with characteristic carelessness, had paid no heed to them, and they had probably wandered from the line on the opposite side of the river. It was arranged that Beatte and Antoine should recross the river at an early hour of the morning, in search of them.

A fat buck, and a number of wild turkeys being brought into the camp, we managed, with the addition of a cup of coffee, to make a comfortable supper; after which, I repaired to the Captain's lodge, which was a kind of council fire and gossiping place for the veterans of the camp.

As we were conversing together, we observed, as on former nights, a dusky, red glow in the west, above the summits of the surrounding cliffs. It was again attributed to Indian fires on the prairies; and supposed to be on the western side of the Arkansas. If so, it was thought they must be made by some party of Pawnees, as the Osage hunters seldom ventured in that quarter. Our half-breeds, however, pronounced them Osage fires; and that they were on the opposite side of the Arkansas.

The conversation now turned upon the Pawnees, into whose hunting grounds we were about entering. There is always some wild untamed tribe of Indians, who form, for a time, the terror of a frontier, and about whom all kinds of fearful stories are told. Such, at present, was the case with the Pawnees, who rove the regions between the Arkansas and the Red River, and the prairies of Texas. They were represented as admirable horsemen, and always on horseback; mounted on fleet and hardy steeds, the wild race of the prairies. With these they roam the great plains that extend about the Arkansas, the Red River, and through Texas, to the Rocky Mountains; sometimes engaged in hunting the deer and buffalo, sometimes in warlike and predatory expeditions; for, like their counterparts, the sons of Ishmael, their hand is against every one, and every one's hand against them. Some of them have no fixed habitation, but dwell in tents of skins, easily packed up and transported, so that they are here to-day, and away, no one knows where, to-morrow.

One of the veteran hunters gave several anecdotes of their mode of fighting. Luckless, according to his account, is the band of weary traders or hunters descried by them, in the midst of a prairie. Sometimes, they will steal upon them by stratagem, hanging with one leg over the saddle, and their bodies concealed; so that their troop at a distance has the appearance of a gang of wild horses. When they have thus gained sufficiently upon the enemy, they will suddenly raise themselves in their saddles, and come like a rushing blast, all fluttering with feathers, shaking their mantles, brandishing their weapons, and making hideous yells. In this way, they seek to strike a panic into the horses, and put them to the scamper, when they will pursue and carry them off in triumph.

The best mode of defence, according to this veteran woodsman, is to get into the covert of some wood, or thicket; or if there be none at hand, to dismount, tie the horses firmly head to head in a circle, so that they cannot break away and scatter, and resort to the shelter of a ravine, or make a hollow in the sand, where they may be screened from the shafts of the Pawnees. The latter chiefly use the bow and arrow, and are dexterous archers; circling round and round their enemy, and launching their arrows when at full speed. They are chiefly formidable on the prairies, where they have free career for their horses, and no trees to turn aside their arrows. They will rarely follow a flying enemy into the forest.

Several anecdotes also were given of the secrecy and

caution with which they will follow, and hang about the camp of an enemy, seeking a favorable moment for plunder or attack.

"We must now begin to keep a sharp look-out," said the Captain. "I must issue written orders, that no man shall hunt without leave, or fire off a gun, on pain of riding a wooden horse with a sharp back. I have a wild crew of young fellows, unaccustomed to frontier service. It will be difficult to teach them caution. We are now in the land of a silent, watchful, crafty people, who, when we least suspect it, may be around us, spying out all our movements, and ready to pounce upon all stragglers."

"How will you be able to keep your men from firing, if they see game while strolling round the camp?" asked one of the rangers.

"They must not take their guns with them unless they are on duty, or have permission."

"Ah, Captain!" cried the ranger, "that will never do for me. Where I go, my rifle goes. I never like to leave it behind; it's like a part of myself. There's no one will take such care of it as I, and there's nothing will take such care of me as my rifle."

"There's truth in all that," said the Captain, touched by a true hunter's sympathy. "I've had my rifle pretty nigh as long as I have had my wife, and a faithful friend it has been to me."

Here the Doctor, who is as keen a hunter as the Captain, joined in the conversation: "A neighbor of mine says, next to my rifle, I'd as leave lend you my wife."

"There's few," observed the Captain, "that take care of their rifles as they ought to be taken care of."

"Or of their wives either," replied the Doctor, with a wink.

"That's a fact," rejoined the Captain.

Word was now brought that a party of four rangers, headed by "Old Ryan," were missing. They had separated from the main body, on the opposite side of the river, when searching for a ford, and had straggled off, nobody knew whither. Many conjectures were made about them, and some apprehensions expressed for their safety.

"I should send to look after them," said the Captain, "but old Ryan is with them, and he knows how to take care of himself and of them too. If it were not for him, I would not give much for the rest; but he is as much at home in the woods or on a prairie, as he would be in his own farmyard. He's never lost, wherever he is. There's a good gang of them to stand by one another; four to watch and one to take care of the fire."

"It's a dismal thing to get lost at night in a strange and wild country," said one of the younger rangers.

"Not if you have one or two in company," said an older one. "For my part, I could feel as cheerful in this hollow as in my own home, if I had but one comrade to take turns to watch and keep the fire going. I could lie here for hours, and gaze up to that blazing star there, that seems to look down into the camp as if it were keeping guard over it."

"Aye, the stars are a kind of company to one, when you have to keep watch alone. That's a cheerful star, too, somehow; that's the evening star, the planet Venus they call it, I think."

"If that's the planet Venus," said one of the council, who, I believe, was the psalm-singing schoolmaster, "it bodes us no good; for I recollect reading in some book that the Pawnees worship that star, and sacrifice their prisoners to it. So I should not feel the better for the sight of that star in this part of the country."

"Well," said the sergeant, a thorough-bred woodsman,

"star or no star, I have passed many a night alone in a wilder place than this, and slept sound too, I'll warrant you. Once, however, I had rather an uneasy time of it. I was belated in passing through a tract of wood, near the Tombigbee River; so I struck a light, made a fire, and turned my horse loose, while I stretched myself to sleep. By and by, I heard the wolves howl. My horse came crowding near me for protection, for he was terribly frightened. I drove him off, but he returned, and drew nearer and nearer, and stood looking at me and at the fire, and dozing, and nodding, and tottering on his fore feet, for he was powerful tired. After a while, I heard a strange dismal cry. I thought at first it might be an owl. I heard it again, and then I knew it was not an owl, but must be a panther. I felt rather awkward, for I had no weapon but a double-bladed penknife. I however prepared for defence in the best way I could, and piled up small brands from the fire, to pepper him with, should he come nigh. The company of my horse now seemed a comfort to me; the poor creature laid down beside me and soon fell asleep, being so tired. I kept watch, and nodded and dozed, and started awake, and looked round, expecting to see the glaring eyes of the panther close upon me; but somehow or other, fatigue got the better of me, and I fell asleep outright. In the morning I found the tracks of a panther within sixty paces. They were as large as my two fists. He had evidently been walking backwards and forwards, trying to make up his mind to attack me; but luckily, he had not courage."

Oct. 16. I awoke before daybreak. The moon was shining feebly down into the glen, from among light drifting clouds; the camp fires were nearly burnt out, and the men lying about them, wrapped in blankets. With the first streak of day, our huntsman, Beatte, with Antoine, the young half-breed, set off to recross the river, in search of the stray horses, in company with several rangers who had left their rifles on the opposite shore. As the ford was deep, and they were obliged to cross in a diagonal line, against a rapid current, they had to be mounted on the tallest and strongest horses.

By eight o'clock, Beatte returned. He had found the horses, but had lost Antoine. The latter, he said, was a boy, a greenhorn, that knew nothing of the woods. He had wandered out of sight of him, and got lost. However, there were plenty more for him to fall in company with, as some of the rangers had gone astray also, and old Ryan and his party had not returned.

We waited until the morning was somewhat advanced, in hopes of being rejoined by the stragglers, but they did not make their appearance. The Captain observed, that the Indians on the opposite side of the river, were all well disposed to the whites so that no serious apprehensions need be entertained for the safety of the missing. The greatest danger was, that their horses might be stolen in the night by straggling Osages. He determined, therefore, to proceed, leaving a rear-guard in the camp, to await their arrival.

I sat on a rock that overhung the spring at the upper part of the dell, and amused myself by watching the changing scene before me. First, the preparations for departure. Horses driven in from the purlieus of the camp; rangers riding about among rocks and bushes in quest of others that had strayed to a distance; the bustle of packing up camp equipage, and the clamor after kettles and frying-pans borrowed by one mess from another, mixed up with oaths and exclamations at restive horses, or others that had wandered away to graze after being packed: among which the voice of our little Frenchman, Tonish, was particularly to be distinguished.

The bugle sounded the signal to mount and march. The troop filed off in irregular line down the glen, and through the open forest, winding and gradually disappearing among the trees, though the clamor of voices and the notes of the bugle could be heard for some time afterwards. The rear-guard remained under the trees in the lower part of the dell, some on horseback, with their rifles on their shoulders; others seated by the fire or lying on the ground, gossiping in a low, lazy tone of voice, their horses unsaddled, standing and dozing around; while one of the rangers, profiting by this interval of leisure, was shaving himself before a pocket mirror stuck against the trunk of a tree.

The clamor of voices and the notes of the bugle at length died away, and the glen relapsed into quiet and silence, broken occasionally by the low murmuring tone of the group around the fire, or the pensive whistle of some laggard among the trees; or the rustling of yellow leaves, which the lightest breath of air brought down in wavering showers, a sign of the departing glories of the year.

CHAPTER XIV

DEER SHOOTING—LIFE ON THE PRAIRIES—BEAUTIFUL ENCAMP-
MENT—HUNTER'S LUCK—ANECDOTES OF THE DELAWARES AND
THEIR SUPERSTITIONS

HAVING passed through the skirt of woodland bordering the river, we ascended the hills, taking a westerly course through an undulating country of "oak openings," where the eye stretched over wide tracts of hill and dale, diversified by forests, groves, and clumps of trees. As we were proceeding at a slow pace, those who were at the head of the line descried four deer grazing on a grassy slope about half a mile distant. They apparently had not perceived our approach, and continued to graze in perfect tranquillity. A young ranger obtained permission from the Captain to go in pursuit of them, and the troop halted in lengthened line, watching him in silence. Walking his horse slowly and cautiously, he made a circuit until a screen of wood intervened between him and the deer. Dismounting then, he left his horse among the trees, and creeping round a knoll, was hidden from our view. We now kept our eyes intently fixed on the deer, which continued grazing, unconscious of their danger. Presently there was the sharp report of a rifle; a fine buck made a convulsive bound and fell to the earth; his companions scampered off. Immediately our whole line of march was broken; there was a helter-skelter galloping of the youngsters of the troop, eager to get a shot at the fugitives; and one of the most conspicuous personages in the chase was our little Frenchman Tonish on his silver-gray; having abandoned his pack-horses at the first sight of the deer. It was some time before our scattered forces coud be recalled by the bugle, and our march resumed.

Two or three times in the course of the day we were interrupted by hurry-scurry scenes of the kind. The young men of the troop were full of excitement on entering an unexplored country abounding in game, and they were too little accustomed to discipline or restraint to be kept in order. No one, however, was more unmanageable than Tonish. Having an intense conceit of his skill as a hunter, and an irrepressible passion for display, he was continually sallying forth, like an ill-broken hound, whenever any game was started, and had as often to be whipped back.

At length his curiosity got a salutary check. A fat doe came bounding along in full view of the whole line. Tonish dismounted, levelled his rifle, and had a fair shot. The doe kept on. He sprang upon his horse, stood up on the saddle like a posture-master, and continued gazing after the animal as if certain to see it fall. The doe, however, kept on its way rejoicing; a laugh broke out along the line, the little Frenchman slipped quietly into his saddle, began to belabor and blaspheme the wandering pack-horses, as if they had been to blame, and for some time we were relieved from his vaunting and vaporing.

In one place of our march we came to the remains of an old Indian encampment, on the banks of a fine stream, with the moss-grown skulls of deer lying here and there about it. As we were in the Pawnee country, it was supposed, of course, to have been a camp of those formidable rovers; the Doctor, however, after considering the shape and disposition of the lodges, pronounced it the camp of some bold Delawares, who had probably made a brief and dashing excursion into these dangerous hunting grounds.

Having proceeded some distance further, we observed a couple of figures on horseback, slowly moving parallel to us along the edge of a naked hill about two miles distant; and apparently reconnoitring us. There was a halt, and much gazing and conjecturing. Were they Indians? If Indians, were they Pawnees? There is something exciting to the imagination and stirring to the feelings, while traversing these hostile plains, in seeing a horseman prowling along the horizon. It is like descrying a sail at sea in time of war, when it may be either a privateer or a pirate. Our conjectures were soon set at rest by reconnoitring the two horsemen through a small spy-glass, when they proved to be two of the men we had left at the camp, who had set out to rejoin us, and had wandered from the track.

Our march this day was animating and delightful. We were in a region of adventure; breaking our way through a country hitherto untrodden by white men, excepting perchance by some solitary trapper. The weather was in its perfection, temperate, genial and enlivening; a deep blue sky with a few light feathery clouds, an atmosphere of perfect transparency, an air pure and bland, and a glorious country spreading out far and wide in the golden sunshine of an autumnal day; but all silent, lifeless, without a human habitation, and apparently without a human inhabitant! It was as if a ban hung over this fair but fated region. The very Indians dared not abide here, but made it a mere scene of perilous enterprise, to hunt for a few days, and then away.

After a march of about fifteen miles west we encamped in a beautiful peninsula, made by the windings and doublings of a deep, clear, and almost motionless brook, and covered by an open grove of lofty and magnificent trees. Several hunters immediately started forth in quest of game before the noise of the camp should frighten it from the vicinity. Our man, Beatte, also took his rifle and went forth alone, in a different course from the rest.

For my own part, I laid on the grass under the trees, and built castles in the clouds, and indulged in the very luxury of rural repose. Indeed I can scarcely conceive a kind of life more calculated to put both mind and body in a healthful tone. A morning's ride of several hours diversified by hunting incidents; an encampment in the afternoon under some noble grove on the borders of a stream; an evening banquet of venison, fresh killed, roasted, or broiled on the coals; turkeys just from the thickets and wild honey from the trees; and all relished with an appetite unknown to the gourmets of the cities. And at night—such sweet sleeping in the open air, or waking and gazing at the moon and stars, shining between the trees!

On the present occasion, however, we had not much reason to boast of our larder. But one deer had been killed during the day, and none of that had reached our lodge. We were fain, therefore, to stay our keen appetites by some scraps of turkey brought from the last encampment, eked out with a slice or two of salt pork. This scarcity, however, did not continue long. Before dark a young hunter returned well laden with spoil. He had shot a deer, cut it up in an artist-like style, and, putting the meat in a kind of sack made of the hide, had slung it across his shoulder and trudged with it to camp.

Not long after, Beatte made his appearance with a fat doe across his horse. It was the first game he had brought in, and I was glad to see him with a trophy that might efface the memory of the polecat. He laid the carcass down by our fire without saying a word, and then turned to unsaddle his horse; nor could any questions from us about his hunting draw from him more than laconic replies. If Beatte, however, observed this Indian taciturnity about what he had done, Tonish made up for it by boasting of what he meant to do. Now that we were in a good hunting country he meant to take the field, and, if we would take his word for it, our lodge would henceforth be overwhelmed with game. Luckily his talking did not prevent his working, the doe was skilfully dissected, several fat ribs roasted before the fire, the coffee kettle replenished, and in a little while we were enabled to indemnify ourselves luxuriously for our late meagre repast.

The Captain did not return until late, and he returned empty handed. He had been in pursuit of his usual game, the deer, when he came upon the tracks of a gang of about sixty elk. Having never killed an animal of the kind, and the elk being at this moment an object of ambition among all the veteran hunters of the camp, he abandoned his pursuit of the deer, and followed the newly-discovered track. After some time he came in sight of the elk, and had several fair chances of a shot, but was anxious to bring down a large buck which kept in the advance. Finding at length there was danger of the whole gang escaping him, he fired at a doe. The shot took effect, but the animal had sufficient strength to keep on for a time with its companions. From the tracks of blood he felt confident it was mortally wounded, but evening came on, he could not keep the trail, and had to give up the search until morning.

Old Ryan and his little band had not yet rejoined us, neither had our young half-breed Antoine made his appearance. It was determined, therefore, to remain at our encampment for the following day, to give time for all stragglers to arrive.

The conversation this evening, among the old huntsmen, turned upon the Delaware tribe, one of whose encampments we had passed in the course of the day; and anecdotes were given of their prowess in war and dexterity in hunting. They used to be deadly foes of the Osages, who stood in great awe of their desperate valor, though they were apt to attribute it to a whimsical cause. "Look at the Delawares," would they say, "dey got short leg—no can run—must stand and fight a great heap." In fact the Delawares are rather short legged, while the Osages are remarkable for length of limb.

The expeditions of the Delawares, whether of war or hunting, are wide and fearless; a small band of them will penetrate far into these dangerous and hostile wilds, and will push their encampments even to the Rocky Mountains. This daring temper may be in some measure encouraged by one of the superstitions of their creed. They believe that a guardian spirit, in the form of a great eagle, watches over them, hovering in the sky, far out of sight. Sometimes, when well pleased with them, he wheels down into the lower regions, and may be seen circling with widespread wings against the white clouds; at such times the seasons are propitious, the corn grows finely, and they have great success in hunting. Sometimes, however, he is angry, and then he vents his rage in the thunder, which is his voice, and the lightning, which is the flashing of his eye, and strikes dead the object of his displeasure.

The Delawares make sacrifices to this spirit, who occasionally lets drop a feather from his wing in token of satisfaction. These feathers render the wearer invisible, and invulnerable. Indeed, the Indians generally consider the feathers of the eagle possessed of occult and sovereign virtues.

At one time a party of the Delawares, in the course of a bold excursion into the Pawnee hunting grounds, were surrounded on one of the great plains, and nearly destroyed. The remnant took refuge on the summit of one of those isolated and conical hills which rise almost like artificial mounds, from the midst of the prairies. Here the chief warrior, driven almost to despair, sacrificed his horse to the tutelar spirit. Suddenly an enormous eagle, rushing down from the sky, bore off the victim in his talons, and mounting into the air, dropped a quill feather from his wing. The chief caught it up with joy, bound it to his forehead, and, leading his followers down the hill, cut his way through the enemy with great slaughter, and without any one of his party receiving a wound.

CHAPTER XV

WITH THE morning dawn, the prime hunters of the camp were all on the alert, and set off in different directions, to beat up the country for game. The Captain's brother, Sergeant Bean, was among the first, and returned before breakfast with success, having killed a fat doe, almost within the purlieus of the camp.

When breakfast was over, the Captain mounted his horse, to go in quest of the elk which he had wounded on the preceding evening; and which, he was persuaded, had received its death wound. I determined to join him in the search, and we accordingly sallied forth together, accompanied also by his brother, the sergeant, and a lieutenant. Two rangers followed on foot, to bring home the carcass of the doe which the sergeant had killed. We had not ridden far, when we came to where it lay, on the side of a hill, in the midst of a beautiful woodland scene. The two rangers immediately fell to work, with true hunters' skill to dismember it, and prepare it for transportation to the camp, while we continued on our course. We passed along sloping hill sides, among skirts of thicket and scattered forest trees, until we came to a place where the long herbage was pressed down with numerous elk beds. Here the Captain had first roused the gang of elks, and, after looking about diligently for a little while, he pointed out their "trail," the foot-prints of which were as large as those of horned cattle. He now put himself upon the track, and went quietly forward, the rest of us following him in Indian file. At length he halted at the place where the elk had been when shot at. Spots of blood on the surrounding herbage showed that the shot had been effective. The wounded animal had evidently kept for some distance with the rest of the herd, as could be seen by sprinklings of blood here and there, on the shrubs and weeds bordering the trail. These at length suddenly disappeared. "Somewhere hereabout," said the Captain, "the elk must have turned off from the gang. Whenever they feel themselves mortally wounded, they will turn aside, and seek some out-of-the-way place to die alone."

There was something in this picture of the last moments of a wounded deer, to touch the sympathies of one not hardened to the gentle disports of the chase; such sympathies, however, are but transient. Man is naturally an animal of prey; and, however changed by civilization, will readily relapse into his instinct for destruction. I found my ravenous and sanguinary propensities daily growing stronger upon the prairies.

After looking about for a little while, the Captain succeeded in finding the separate trail of the wounded elk, which turned off almost at right angles from that of the herd, and entered an open forest of scattered trees. The traces of blood became more faint and rare, and occurred at greater distances; at length they ceased altogether, and the ground was so hard, and the herbage so much parched and withered, that the footprints of the animal could no longer be perceived.

"The elk must lie somewhere in this neighborhood," said the Captain, "as you may know by those turkey-buzzards wheeling about in the air; for they always hover in that way above some carcass. However, the dead elk cannot get away, so let us follow the trail of the living ones; they may have halted at no great distance, and we may find them grazing, and get another crack at them."

We accordingly returned, and resumed the trail of the elks, which led us a straggling course over hill and dale, covered with scattered oaks. Every now and then we would catch a glimpse of a deer bounding away across some glade of the forest, but the Captain was not to be diverted from his elk hunt by such inferior game. A large flock of wild turkeys, too, were roused by the trampling of our horses; some scampered off as fast as their long legs could carry them; others fluttered up into the trees, where they remained with outstretched necks, gazing at us. The Captain would not allow a rifle to be discharged at them, lest it should alarm the elk, which he hoped to find in the vicinity. At length we came to where the forest ended in a steep bank, and the Red Fork wound its way below us, between broad sandy shores. The trail descended the bank, and we could trace it, with our eyes, across the level sands, until it terminated in the river, which, it was evident, the gang had forded on the preceding evening.

"It is needless to follow on any further," said the Captain. "The elk must have been much frightened, and, after crossing the river, may have kept on for twenty miles without stopping."

Our little party now divided, the lieutenant and sergeant making a circuit in quest of game, and the Captain and myself taking the direction of the camp. On our way, we came to a buffalo track, more than a year old. It was not wider than an ordinary footpath, and worn deep into the soil; for these animals follow each other in single file. Shortly afterwards, we met two rangers on foot, hunting. They had wounded an elk, but he had escaped; and in pursuing him, had found the one shot by the Captain on the preceding evening. They turned back, and conducted us to it. It was a noble animal, as large as a yearling heifer, and lay in an open part of the forest, about a mile and a half distant from the place where it had been shot. The turkey buzzards, which we had previously noticed, were wheeling in the air above it. The observation of the Captain seemed verified. The poor animal, as life was ebbing away, had apparently abandoned its unhurt companions, and turned aside to die alone.

The Captain and the two rangers forthwith fell to work, with their hunting-knives, to flay and cut up the carcass. It was already tainted on the inside, but ample collops were cut from the ribs and haunches, and laid in a heap on the outstretched hide. Holes were then cut along the border of the hide, raw thongs were passed through them, and the whole drawn up like a sack, which was swung behind the Captain's saddle. All this while, the turkey-buzzards were soaring overhead, waiting for our departure, to swoop down and banquet on the carcass.

The wreck of the poor elk being thus dismantled, the Captain and myself mounted our horses, and jogged back to the camp, while the two rangers resumed their hunting.

On reaching the camp, I found there our young half-breed, Antoine. After separating from Beatte, in the search after the stray horses on the other side of the Arkansas, he had fallen upon a wrong track, which he followed for several miles, when he overtook old Ryan and his party, and found he had been following their traces.

They all forded the Arkansas about eight miles above our crossing place, and found their way to our late encampment in the glen, where the rear-guard we had left behind was waiting for them. Antoine, being well mounted, and somewhat impatient to rejoin us, had pushed on alone, following our trail, to our present encampment, and bringing the carcass of a young bear which he had killed.

Our camp, during the residue of the day, presented a mingled picture of bustle and repose. Some of the men were busy round the fires, jerking and roasting venison and bear's meat, to be packed up as a future supply. Some were stretching and dressing the skins of the animals they had killed; others were washing their clothes in the brook, and hanging them on the bushes to dry; while many were lying on the grass, and lazily gossiping in the shade. Every now and then a hunter would return, on horseback or on foot, laden with game, or empty handed. Those who brought home any spoil, deposited it at the Captain's fire, and then filed off to their respective messes, to relate their day's exploits to their companions. The game killed at this camp consisted of six deer, one elk, two bears, and six or eight turkeys.

During the last two or three days, since their wild Indian achievement in navigating the river, our retainers had risen in consequence among the rangers; and now I found Tonish making himself a complete oracle among some of the raw and inexperienced recruits, who had never been in the wilderness. He had continually a knot hanging about him, and listening to his extravagant tales about the Pawnees, with whom he pretended to have had fearful encounters. His representations, in fact, were calculated to inspire his hearers with an awful idea of the foe into whose lands they were intruding. According to his accounts, the rifle of the white man was no match for the bow and arrow of the Pawnee. When the rifle was once discharged, it took time and trouble to load it again, and in the mean time the enemy could keep on launching his shafts as fast as he could draw his bow. Then the Pawnee, according to Tonish, could shoot, with unerring aim, three hundred yards, and send his arrow clean through and through a buffalo;

nay, he had known a Pawnee shaft pass through one buffalo and wound another. And then the way the Pawnees sheltered themselves from the shots of their enemy: they would hang with one leg over the saddle, crouching their bodies along the opposite side of their horse, and would shoot their arrows from under his neck, while at full speed!

If Tonish was to be believed, there was peril at every step in these debateable grounds of the Indian tribes. Pawnees lurked unseen among the thickets and ravines. They had their scouts and sentinels on the summit of the mounds which command a view over the prairies, where they lay crouched in the tall grass; only now and then raising their heads to watch the movements of any war or hunting party that might be passing in lengthened line below. At night, they would lurk round an encampment; crawling through the grass, and imitating the movements of a wolf, so as to deceive the sentinel on the outpost, until, having arrived sufficiently near, they would speed an arrow through his heart, and retreat undiscovered. In telling his stories, Tonish would appeal from time to time to Beatte, for the truth of what he said; the only reply would be a nod or shrug of the shoulders; the latter being divided in mind between a distaste for the gasconading spirit of his comrade, and a sovereign contempt for the inexperience of the young rangers in all that he considered true knowledge.

CHAPTER XVI

O CT. 18. We prepared to march at the usual hour, but word was brought to the Captain that three of the rangers, who had been attacked with the measles, were unable to proceed, and that another one was missing. The last was an old frontiersman, by the name of Sawyer, who had gained years without experience and having sallied forth to hunt, on the preceding day, had probably lost his way on the prairies. A guard of ten men was, therefore, left to take care of the sick, and wait for the straggler. If the former recovered sufficiently in the course of two or three days, they were to rejoin the main body, otherwise to be escorted back to the garrison.

Taking our leave of the sick camp, we shaped our course westward, along the heads of small streams, all wandering, in deep ravines, towards the Red Fork. The land was high and undulating, or "rolling," as it is termed in the West; with a poor hungry soil mingled with the sandstone, which is unusual in this part of the country, and checkered with harsh forests of post-oak and black-jack.

In the course of the morning, I received a lesson on the importance of being chary of one's steed on the prairies. The one I rode surpassed in action most horses of the troop, and was of great mettle and a generous spirit. In crossing the deep ravines, he would scramble up the steep banks like a cat, and was always for leaping the narrow runs of water. I was not aware of the impudence of indulging him in such exertions, until, in leaping him across a small brook, I felt him immediately

483

falter beneath me. He limped forward a short distance, but soon fell stark lame, having sprained his shoulder. What was to be done? He could not keep up with the troop, and was too valuable to be abandoned on the prairie. The only alternative was to send him back to join the invalids in the sick camp, and to share their fortunes. Nobody, however, seemed disposed to lead him back, although I offered a liberal reward. Either the stories of Tonish, about the Pawnees had spread an apprehension of lurking foes and imminent perils on the prairies; or there was a fear of missing the trail and getting lost. At length two young men stepped forward and agreed to go in company, so that, should they be benighted on the prairies, there might be one to watch while the other slept.

The horse was accordingly consigned to their care, and I looked after him with a rueful eye, as he limped off, for it seemed as if, with him, all strength and buoyancy had departed from me.

I looked round for a steed to supply his place, and fixed my eyes upon the gallant gray which I had transferred at the Agency to Tonish. The moment, however, that I hinted about his dismounting and taking up with the supernumerary pony, the little varlet broke out into vociferous remonstrances and lamentations, gasping and almost strangling, in his eagerness to give vent to them. I saw that to unhorse him would be to prostrate his spirit and cut his vanity to the quick. I had not the heart to inflict such a wound, or to bring down the poor devil from his transient vainglory; so I left him in possession of his gallant gray; and contented myself with shifting my saddle to the jaded pony.

I was now sensible of the complete reverse to which a horseman is exposed on the prairies. I felt how completely the spirit of the rider depended upon his steed. I had hitherto been able to make excursions at will from the line, and to gallop in pursuit of any object of interest or curiosity. I was now reduced to the tone of the jaded animal I bestrode, and doomed to plod on patiently and slowly after my file leader. Above all, I was made conscious how unwise it is, on expeditions of the kind, where a man's life may depend upon the strength, and speed, and freshness of his horse, to task the generous animal by any unnecessary exertion of his powers.

I have observed that the wary and experienced huntsman and traveller of the prairies is always sparing of his horse, when on a journey; never, except in emergency, putting him off of a walk. The regular journeyings of frontiersmen and Indians, when on a long march, seldom exceed above fifteen miles a day, and are generally about ten or twelve, and they never indulge in capricious galloping. Many of those, however, with whom I was travelling were young and inexperienced, and full of excitement at finding themselves in a country abounding with game. It was impossible to retain them in the sobriety of a march, or to keep them to the line. As we broke our way through the coverts and ravines, and the deer started up and scampered off to the right and left, the rifle balls would whiz after them, and our young hunters dash off in pursuit. At one time they made a grand burst after what they supposed to be a gang of bears, but soon pulled up on discovering them to be black wolves, prowling in company.

After a march of about twelve miles we encamped, a little after mid-day, on the borders of a brook which loitered through a deep ravine. In the course of the afternoon old Ryan, the Nestor of the camp, made his appearance, followed by his little band of stragglers. He was greeted with joyful acclamations, which showed the estimation in which he was held by his brother woodmen. The little band came laden with venison; a fine haunch of which the veteran hunter laid, as a present, by the Captain's fire.

Our men, Beatte and Tonish, both sallied forth, early in the afternoon, to hunt. Towards evening the former returned, with a fine buck across his horse. He laid it down, as usual, in silence, and proceeded to unsaddle and turn his horse loose. Tonish came back without any game, but with much more glory, having made several capital shots, though unluckily the wounded deer had all escaped him.

There was an abundant supply of meat in the camp; for besides other game, three elk had been killed. The wary and veteran woodmen were all busy jerking meat, against a time of scarcity; the less experienced revelled in present abundance, leaving the morrow to provide for itself.

On the following morning, (Oct. 19) I succeeded in changing my pony and a reasonable sum of money for a strong and active horse. It was a great satisfaction to find myself once more tolerably well mounted. I perceived, however, that there would be little difficulty in making a selection from among the troop, for the rangers had all that propensity for "swapping," or, as they term it, "trading," which pervades the West. In the course of our expedition, there was scarce a horse, rifle, powder-horn, or blanket, that did not change owners several times; and one keen "trader" boasted of having by dint of frequent bargains changed a bad horse into a good one, and put a hundred dollars in his pocket.

The morning was lowering and sultry, with low muttering of distant thunder. The change of weather had its effect upon the spirits of the troop. The camp was unusually sober and quiet; there was none of the accustomed farmyard melody of crowing and cackling at daybreak; none of the bursts of merriment, the loud jokes and banterings, that had commonly prevailed during the bustle of equipment. Now and then might be heard a short strain of a song, a faint laugh, or a solitary whistle; but, in general, every one went silently and doggedly about the duties of the camp or the preparations for departure.

When the time arrived to saddle and mount, five horses were reported as missing; although all the woods and thickets had been beaten up for some distance round the camp. Several rangers were dispatched to "skir" the country round in quest of them. In the meantime, the thunder continued to growl, and we had a passing shower. The horses, like their riders, were affected by the change of weather. They stood here and there about the camp, some saddled and bridled, others loose, but all spiritless and dozing, with stooping head, one hind leg partly drawn up so as to rest on the point of the hoof, and the whole hide reeking with the rain, and sending up wreaths of vapor. The men, too, waited in listless groups the return of their comrades who had gone in quest of the horses; now and then turning up an anxious eye to the drifting clouds, which boded an approaching storm. Gloomy weather inspires gloomy thoughts. Some expressed fears that we were dogged by some party of Indians, who had stolen the horses in the night. The most prevalent apprehension, however, was, that they had returned on their traces to our last encampment, or had started off on a direct line for Fort Gibson. In this respect, the instinct of horses is said to resemble that of the pigeon. They will strike for home by a direct course, passing through tracts of wilderness which they have never before traversed.

After delaying until the morning was somewhat advanced, a lieutenant with a guard was appointed to await the return of the rangers, and we set off on our day's journey, considerably reduced in numbers; much, as I thought, to the discomposure of some of the troop, who intimated that we might prove too weak-handed in case of an encounter with the Pawnees.

CHAPTER XVII

THUNDER-STORM ON THE PRAIRIES—THE STORM ENCAMPMENT—
NIGHT SCENE—INDIAN STORIES—A FRIGHTENED HORSE

OUR MARCH for a part of the day, lay a little to the south of west through straggling forests of the kind of low scrubbed trees already mentioned, called "post-oaks," and "black-jacks." The soil of these "oak barrens" is loose and unsound; being little better at times than a mere quicksand, in which, in rainy weather, the horse's hoof slips from side to side, and now and then sinks in a rotten, spongy turf, to the fetlock. Such was the case at present in consequence of successive thunder-showers, through which we draggled along in dogged silence. Several deer were roused by our approach, and scudded across the forest glades; but no one, as formerly, broke the line of march to pursue them. At one time, we passed the bones and horns of a buffalo, and at another time a buffalo track, not above three days old. These signs of the vicinity of this grand game of the prairies, had a reviving effect on the spirits of our huntsmen; but it was of transient duration.

In crossing a prairie of moderate extent, rendered little better than a slippery bog by the recent showers, we were overtaken by a violent thunder-gust. The rain came rattling upon us in torrents, and spattered up like steam along the ground; the whole landscape was suddenly wrapped in gloom that gave a vivid effect to the intense sheets of lightning, while the thunder seemed to burst over our very heads, and was reverberated by the groves and forests that checkered and skirted the prairie. Man and beast were so pelted, drenched, and confounded, that the line was thrown in complete confusion; some of the horses were so frightened as to be almost unmanageable, and our scattered cavalcade looked like a tempest-tossed fleet, driving hither and thither, at the mercy of wind and wave.

At length, at half past two o'clock, we came to a halt, and gathering together our forces, encamped in an open and lofty grove, with a prairie on one side and a stream on the other. The forest immediately rang with the sound of the axe, and the crash of falling trees. Huge fires were soon blazing; blankets were stretched before them, by way of tents; booths were hastily reared of bark and skins; every fire had its group drawn close round it, drying and warming themselves, or preparing a comforting meal. Some of the rangers were discharging and cleaning their rifles, which had been exposed to the rain; while the horses, relieved from their saddles and burdens, rolled in the wet grass.

The showers continued from time to time, until late in the evening. Before dark, our horses were gathered in and tethered about the skirts of the camp, within the outposts, through fear of Indian prowlers, who are apt to take advantage of stormy nights for their depredations and assaults. As the night thickened, the huge fires became more and more luminous; lighting up masses of the overhanging foliage, and leaving other parts of the grove in deep gloom. Every fire had its goblin group around it, while the tethered horses were dimly seen, like spectres, among the thickets; excepting that here and there a gray one stood out in bright relief.

The grove, thus fitfully lighted up by the ruddy glare of the fires, resembled a vast leafy dome, walled in by opaque darkness but every now and then two or three quivering flashes of lightning in quick succession, would suddenly reveal a vast champaign country, where fields and forests, and running streams, would start, as it were, into existence for a few brief seconds, and, before the eye could ascertain them, vanish again into gloom.

A thunder-storm on a prairie, as upon the ocean, derives grandeur and sublimity from the wild and boundless waste over which it rages and bellows. It is not surprising that these awful phenomena of nature should be objects of superstitious reverence to the poor savages, and that they should consider the thunder the angry voice of the Great Spirit. As our half-breeds sat gossiping round the fire, I drew from them some of the notions entertained on the subject by their Indian friends. The latter declare that extinguished thunder-bolts are sometimes picked up by hunters on the prairies, who use them for the heads of arrows and lances, and that any warrior thus armed is invincible. Should a thunder-storm occur, however, during battle, he is liable to be carried away by the thunder, and never heard of more.

A warrior of the Konza tribe, hunting on a prairie, was overtaken by a storm, and struck down senseless by the thunder. On recovering, he beheld the thunderbolt lying on the ground, and a horse standing beside it. Snatching up the bolt, he sprang upon the horse, but found, too late, that he was astride of the lightning. In an instant he was whisked away over prairies and forests, and streams and deserts, until he was flung senseless at the foot of the Rocky Mountains; whence, on recovering, it took him several months to return to his own people.

This story reminded me of an Indian tradition, related by a traveller, of the fate of a warrior who saw the thunder lying upon the ground, with a beautifully wrought moccason on each side of it. Thinking he had found a prize, he put on the moccasons but they bore him away to the land of spirits, whence he never returned.

These are simple and artless tales, but they had a wild and romantic interest heard from the lips of half-savage narrators round a hunter's fire, in a stormy night, with a forest on one side and a howling waste on the other; and where, peradventure, savage foes might be lurking in the outer darkness.

Our conversation was interrupted by a loud clap of thunder followed immediately by the sound of a horse galloping off madly into the waste. Every one listened in mute silence. The hoofs resounded vigorously for a time, but grew fainter and fainter until they died away in remote distance.

When the sound was no longer to be heard, the listeners turned to conjecture what could have caused the sudden scamper. Some thought the horse had been startled by the thunder; others, that some lurking Indian had galloped off with him. To this it was objected, that the usual mode with the Indians is to steal quietly upon the horse, take off his fetters, mount him gently, and walk him off as silently as possible, leading off others, without any unusual stir or noise to disturb the camp.

On the other hand, it was stated as a common practice with the Indians, to creep among a troop of horses when grazing at night, mount one quietly, and then start off suddenly at full speed. Nothing is so contagious among horses as a panic; one sudden break-away of this kind, will sometimes alarm the whole troop, and they will set off, helter-skelter, after the leader.

Everyone who had a horse grazing on the skirts of the camp was uneasy, lest his should be the fugitive; but it was impossible to ascertain the fact until morning. Those who had tethered their horses felt more secure; though horses thus tied up, and limited to a short range at night, are apt to fall off in flesh and strength, during a long march; and many of the horses of the troop already gave signs of being wayworn.

After a gloomy and unruly night, the morning dawned bright and clear, and a glorious sunrise transformed the whole landscape, as if by magic. The late dreary wilderness brightened into a fine open country, with stately groves, and clumps of oaks of a gigantic size, some of which stood singly, as if planted for ornament and shade, in the midst of rich meadows; while our horses, scattered about, and grazing under them, gave to the whole the air of a noble park. It was difficult to realize the fact that we were so far in the wilds beyond the residence of man. Our encampment, alone, had a savage appearance; with its rude tents of skins and blankets, and its columns of blue smoke rising among the trees.

The first care in the morning, was to look after our horses. Some of them had wandered to a distance, but all were fortunately found; even the one whose clattering hoofs had caused such uneasiness in the night. He had come to a halt about a mile from the camp, and was found quietly grazing near a brook. The bugle sounded for departure about half past eight. As we were in greater risk of Indian molestation the farther we advanced, our line was formed with more precision than heretofore. Everyone had his station assigned him, and was forbidden to leave in pursuit of game, without special permission. The pack-horses were placed in the center of the line, and a strong guard in the rear.

CHAPTER XVIII

A GRAND PRAIRIE—CLIFF CASTLE—BUFFALO TRACKS—DEER HUNTED BY WOLVES—CROSS TIMBER

AFTER a toilsome march of some distance through a country cut up by ravines and brooks, and entangled by thickets, we emerged upon a grand prairie. Here one of the characteristic scenes of the Far West broke upon us. An immense extent of grassy, undulating, or, as it is termed, rolling country, with here and there a clump of trees, dimly seen in the distance like a ship at sea; the landscape deriving sublimity from its vastness and simplicity. To the southwest, on the summit of a hill, was a singular crest of broken rocks, resembling a ruined fortress. It reminded me of the ruin of some Moorish castle, crowning a height in the midst of a lonely Spanish landscape. To this hill we gave the name of Cliff Castle.

The prairies of these great hunting regions differed in the character of their vegetation from those through which I had hitherto passed. Instead of a profusion of tall flowering plants and long flaunting grasses, they were covered with a shorter growth of herbage called buffalo grass, somewhat coarse, but, at the proper seasons, affording excellent and abundant pasturage. At present it was growing wiry, and in many places was too much parched for grazing.

The weather was verging into that serene but some-what arid season called the Indian Summer. There was a smoky haze in the atmosphere that tempered the brightness of the sunshine into a golden tint, softening the features of the landscape, and giving a vagueness to the outlines of distant objects. This haziness was daily increasing, and was attributed to the burning of distant prairies by the Indian hunting parties.

We had not gone far upon the prairie before we came to where deeply-worn footpaths were seen traversing the country; sometimes two or three would keep on parallel to each other, and but a few paces apart. These were pronounced to be traces of buffaloes, where large droves had passed. There were tracks also of horses, which were observed with some attention by our experienced hunters. They could not be the tracks of wild horses, as there were no prints of the hoofs of colts; all were full-grown. As the horses evidently were not shod, it was concluded they must belong to some hunting party of Pawnees. In the course of the morning, the tracks of a single horse, with shoes, were discovered. This might be the horse of a Cherokee hunter, or perhaps a horse stolen from the whites of the frontier. Thus, in traversing these perilous wastes, every foot-print and dint of hoof becomes matter of cautious inspection and shrewd surmise; and the question con-tinually is, whether it be the trace of friend or foe, whether of recent or ancient date, and whether the being that made it be out of reach, or liable to be ecnountered.

We were getting more and more into the game country: as we proceeded, we repeatedly saw deer to the right and left, bounding off for the coverts; but their appearance no longer excited the same eagerness to pursue. In passing along a slope of the prairie, between two rolling swells of land, we came in sight of a genuine natural hunting match. A pack of seven black wolves and one white one were in full chase of a buck, which they had nearly tired down. They crossed the line of our march without apparently perceiving us; we saw them have a fair run of nearly a mile, gaining upon the buck until they were leaping upon his haunches, when he plunged down a ravine. Some of our party galloped to a rising ground commanding a view of the ravine. The poor buck was completely beset, some on his flanks, some at his throat: he made two or three struggles and desperate bounds, but was dragged down, over-powered, and torn to pieces. The black wolves, in their ravenous hunger and fury, took no notice of the distant group of horsemen; but the white wolf, apparently less game, abandoned the prey, and scampered over hill and dale, rousing various deer that were crouched in the hollows, and which bounded off likewise in different directions. It was altogether a wild scene, worthy of the "hunting grounds."

We now came once more in sight of the Red Fork, winding its turbid course between well-wooded hills, and through a vast and magnificent landscape. The prairies bordering on the rivers are always varied in this way with woodland, so beautifully interspersed as to appear to have been laid out by the hand of taste; and they only want here and there a village spire, the battlements of a castle, or the turrets of an old family mansion rising from among the trees, to rival the most ornamented scenery of Europe.

About mid-day we reached the edge of that scattered belt of forest land, about forty miles in width, which stretches across the country from north to south, from the Arkansas to the Red River, separating the upper from the lower prairies, and commonly called the "Cross

Timber." On the skirts of this forest land, just on the edge of a prairie, we found traces of a Pawnee encampment of between one and two hundred lodges, showing that the party must have been numerous. The skull of a buffalo lay near the camp, and the moss which had gathered on it proved that the encampment was at least a year old. About half a mile off we encamped in a beautiful grove watered by a fine spring and rivulet. Our day's journey had been about fourteen miles.

In the course of the afternoon we were rejoined by two of Lieutenant King's party, which we had left behind a few days before, to look after stray horses. All the horses had been found, though some had wandered to the distance of several miles. The lieutenant, with seventeen of his companions, had remained at our last night's emcampment to hunt, having come upon recent traces of buffalo. They had also seen a fine wild horse, which, however, had galloped off with a speed that defied pursuit.

Confident anticipations were now indulged, that on the following day we should meet with buffalo, and perhaps with wild horses, and every one was in spirits. We needed some excitement of the kind, for our young men were growing weary of marching and encamping under restraint, and provisions this day were scanty. The Captain and several of the rangers went out hunting, but brought home nothing but a small deer and a few turkeys. Our two men, Beatte and Tonish, likewise went out. The former returned with a deer athwart his horse, which, as usual, he laid down by our lodge, and said nothing. Tonish returned with no game, but with his customary budget of wonderful tales. Both he and the deer had done marvels. Not one had come within the lure of his rifle without being hit in a mortal part, yet, strange to say, every one had kept on his way without flinching. We all determined that, from the accuracy of his aim Tonish must have shot with charmed balls, but that every deer had a charmed life. The most important intelligence brought by him, however, was, that he had seen the fresh tracks of several wild horses. He now considered himself upon the eve of great exploits, for there was nothing upon which he glorified himself more than his skill in horse-catching.

CHAPTER XIX

HUNTERS' ANTICIPATIONS—THE RUGGED FORD—A WILD HORSE

OCT. 21. This morning the camp was in a bustle at an early hour: the expectation of falling in with buffalo in the course of the day roused every one's spirit. There was a continual cracking of rifles, that they might be reloaded: the shot was drawn off from double-barrelled guns, and balls were substituted. Tonish, however, prepared chiefly for a campaign against wild horses. He took the field, with a coil of cordage hung at his saddle-bow, and a couple of white wands, something like fishing-rods, eight or ten feet in length, with forked ends. The coil of cordage thus used in hunting the wild horse, is called a lariat, and answers to the laso of South America. It is not flung, however, in the graceful and dexterous Spanish style. The hunter, after a hard chase, when he succeeds in getting almost head and head with the wild horse, hitches the running noose of the lariat over his head by means of the forked stick; then letting him have the full length of the cord, plays him like a fish, and chokes him into subjection.

All this Tonish promised to exemplify to our full

satisfaction; we had not much confidence in his success, and feared he might knock up a good horse in a headlong gallop after a bad one: for, like all the French creoles, he was a merciless hard rider. It was determined, therefore, to keep a sharp eye upon him, and to check his sallying propensities.

We had not proceeded far on our morning's march, when we were checked by a deep stream, running along the bottom of a thickly-wooded ravine. After coasting it for a couple of miles we came to a fording place; but to get down to it was the difficulty, for the banks were steep and crumbling, and overgrown with forest trees, mingled with thickets, brambles, and grapevines. At length the leading horseman broke his way through the thicket, and his horse, putting his feet together, slid down the black crumbling bank, to the narrow margin of the stream; then floundering across, with mud and water up to the saddle-girths, he scrambled up the opposite bank, and arrived safe on level ground. The whole line followed pell-mell after the leader, and pushing forward in close order, Indian file, they crowded each other down the bank and into the stream. Some of the horsemen missed the ford, and were soused over head and ears; one was unhorsed, and plumped head foremost into the middle of the stream: for my own part, while pressed forward, and hurried over the bank by those behind me, I was interrupted by a grape-vine, as thick as a cable, which hung in a festoon as low as the saddle-bow, and, dragging me from the saddle, threw me among the feet of the trampling horses. Fortunately, I escaped without injury, regained my steed, crossed the stream without further difficulty, and was enabled to join in the merriment occasioned by the ludicrous disasters of the fording.

It is at passes like this that occur the most dangerous

ambuscades and sanguinary surprises of Indian war-fare. A party of savages well placed among the thickets, might have made sad havoc among our men, while entangled in the ravine.

We now came out upon a vast and glorious prairie, spreading out beneath the golden beams of an autumnal sun. The deep and frequent traces of buffalo, showed it to be one of their favorite grazing grounds; yet none were to be seen. In the course of the morning, we were overtaken by the lieutenant and seventeen men, who had remained behind, and who came laden with the spoils of buffaloes; having killed three on the preceding day. One of the rangers, however, had little luck to boast of; his horse having taken fright at sight of the buf-faloes, thrown his rider, and escaped into the woods.

The excitement of our hunters, both young and old, now rose almost to fever height; scarce any of them having ever encountered any of this far-famed game of the prairies. Accordingly, when in the course of the day the cry of buffalo! buffalo! rose from one part of the line, the whole troop were thrown in agitation. We were just then passing through a beautiful part of the prairie, finely diversified by hills and slopes, and woody dells, and high, stately groves. Those who had given the alarm, pointed out a large black-looking animal, slowly moving along the side of a rising ground, about two miles off. The ever-ready Tonish jumped up, and stood with his feet on the saddle, and his forked sticks in his hands, like a posture-master or scaramouch at a circus, just ready for a feat of horsemanship. After gazing at the animal for a moment, which he could have seen full as well without rising from his stirrups, he pronounced it a wild horse; and dropping again into his saddle, was about to dash off full tilt in pursuit, when, to his inexpressible chagrin, he was called back, and ordered to keep to his post, in rear of the baggage horses.

The Captain and two of his officers now set off to reconnoitre the game. It was the intention of the Captain, who was an admirable marksman, to endeavor to crease the horse; that is to say, to hit him with a rifle ball in the ridge of the neck. A wound of this kind paralyzes a horse for a moment; he falls to the ground, and may be secured before he recovers. It is a cruel expedient, however, for an ill-directed shot may kill or maim the noble animal.

As the Captain and his companions moved off laterally and slowly, in the direction of the horse, we continued our course forward; watching intently, however, the movements of the game. The horse moved quietly over the profile of the rising ground, and disappeared behind it. The Captain and his party were likewise soon hidden by an intervening hill.

After a time, the horse suddenly made his appearance to our right, just ahead of the line, emerging out of a small valley, on a brisk trot; having evidently taken the alarm. At sight of us, he stopped short, gazed at us for an instant with surprise, then tossing up his head, trotted off in fine style, glancing at us first over one shoulder, then over the other, his ample mane and tail streaming in the wind. Having dashed through a skirt of thicket, that looked like a hedge-row, he paused in the open field beyond, glanced back at us again, with a beautiful bend of the neck, snuffed the air, and then tossing his head again, broke into a gallop, and took refuge in a wood.

It was the first time I had ever seen a horse scouring his native wilderness in all the pride and freedom of his nature. How different from the poor, mutilated, harnessed, checked, reined-up victim of luxury, caprice, and avarice, in our cities!

After travelling about fifteen miles, we encamped about one o'clock, that our hunters might have time to procure a supply of provisions. Our encampment was in a spacious grove of lofty oaks and walnuts, free from under wood, on the border of a brook. While unloading the pack-horses, our little Frenchman was loud in his complaints at having been prevented from pursuing the wild horse, which he would certainly have taken. In the meantime, I saw our half-breed, Beatte, quietly saddle his best horse, a powerful steed of a half savage race, hang a lariat at the saddle-bow, take a rifle and forked stick in hand, and, mounting, depart from the camp without saying a word. It was evident he was going off in quest of the wild horse, but was disposed to hunt alone.

CHAPTER XX

THE CAMP OF THE WILD HORSE

HUNTERS' STORIES—HABITS OF THE WILD HORSE—THE HALF-BREED AND HIS PRIZE—A HORSE CHASE—A WILD SPIRIT TAMED

WE HAD encamped in a good neighborhood for game, as the reports of rifles in various directions speedily gave notice. One of our hunters soon returned with the meat of a doe, tied up in the skin, and slung across his shoulders. Another brought a fat buck across his horse. Two other deer were brought in, and a number of turkeys. All the game was thrown down in front of the Captain's fire, to be portioned out among the various messes. The spits and camp kettles were soon in full employ, and throughout the evening there was a scene of hunters' feasting and profusion.

We had been disappointed this day in our hopes of meeting with buffalo, but the sight of the wild horse had been a great novelty, and gave a turn to the conversation of the camp for the evening. There were several anecdotes told of a famous gray horse, which has ranged the prairies of this neighborhood for six or seven years, setting at naught every attempt of the hunters to capture him. They say he can pace and rack (or amble) faster than the fleetest horses can run. Equally marvellous accounts were given of a black horse on the Brassos, who grazed the prairies on that river's banks in the Texas. For years he out-stripped all pursuit. His fame spread far and wide; offers were made for him to the amount of a thousand dollars; the boldest and most hard-riding hunters tried incessantly to make prize of him, but in vain. At length he fell a victim to his gallantry, being decoyed under a tree by a tame mare, and a noose dropped over his head by a boy perched among the branches.

The capture of the wild horse is one of the most favorite achievements of the prairie tribes; and, indeed, it is from this source that the Indian hunters chiefly supply themselves. The wild horses which range those vast grassy plains, extending from the Arkansas to the Spanish settlements, are of various forms and colors, betraying their various descents. Some resemble the common English stock, and are probably descended from horses which have escaped from our border settlements. Others are of a low but strong make, and are supposed to be of the Andalusian breed, brought out by the Spanish discoverers.

Some fanciful speculatists have seen in them descendants of the Arab stock, brought into Spain from Africa, and thence transferred to this country; and have pleased themselves with the idea, that their sires may have been of the pure coursers of the desert, that once bore Mahomet and his warlike disciples across the sandy plains of Arabia.

The habits of the Arab seem to have come with the steed. The introduction of the horse on the boundless prairies of the Far West, changed the whole mode of living of their inhabitants. It gave them that facility of rapid motion, and of sudden and distant change of place, so dear to the roving propensities of man. Instead of lurking in the depths of gloomy forests, and patiently threading the mazes of a tangled wilderness on foot, like his brethren of the north, the Indian of the West is a rover of the plain; he leads a brighter and more sunshiny life; almost always on horseback, on vast flowery prairies and under cloudless skies.

I was lying by the Captain's fire, late in the evening, listening to stories about those coursers of the prairies, and weaving speculations of my own, when there was a clamor of voices and a loud cheering at the other end of the camp; and word was passed that Beatte, the half-breed, had brought in a wild horse.

In an instant every fire was deserted; the whole camp crowded to see the Indian and his prize. It was a colt about two years old, well grown, finely limbed, with bright prominent eyes, and a spirited yet gentle de-meanor. He gazed about him with an air of mingled stupefaction and surprise, at the men, the horses, and the camp-fires; while the Indian stood before him with folded arms, having hold of the other end of the cord which noosed his captive, and gazing on him with a most imperturbable aspect. Beatte as I have before observed, has a greenish olive complexion, with a strongly marked countenance, not unlike the bronze casts of Napoleon;

and as he stood before his captive horse, with folded arms and fixed aspect, he looked more like a statue than a man.

If the horse, however, manifested the least restiveness, Beatte would immediately worry him with the lariat, jerking him first on one side, then on the other, so as almost to throw him on the ground; when he had thus rendered him passive, he would resume his statue-like attitude and gaze at him in silence.

The whole scene was singularly wild; the tall grove, partially illumined by the flashing fires of the camp, the horses tethered here and there among the trees, the carcasses of deer hanging around, and in the midst of all, the wild huntsman and his wild horse, with an admiring throng of rangers, almost as wild.

In the eagerness of their excitement, several of the young rangers sought to get the horse by purchase or barter, and even offered extravagant terms; but Beatte declined all their offers. "You give great price now;" said he, "to-morrow you be sorry, and take back, and say d—d Indian!"

The young men importuned him with questions about the mode in which he took the horse, but his answers were dry and laconic; he evidently retained some pique at having been undervalued and sneered at by them; and at the same time looked down upon them with contempt as greenhorns, little versed in the noble science of woodcraft.

Afterwards, however, when he was seated by our fire, I readily drew from him an account of his exploit; for, though taciturn among strangers, and little prone to boast of his actions, yet his taciturnity, like that of all Indians, had its times of relaxation.

He informed me, that on leaving the camp, he had returned to the place where we had lost sight of the wild horse. Soon getting upon its track, he followed it to the banks of the river. Here, the prints being more distinct in the sand, he perceived that one of the hoofs was broken and defective, so he gave up the pursuit.

As he was returning to the camp, he came upon a gang of six horses, which immediately made for the river. He pursued them across the stream, left his rifle on the river bank, and putting his horse to full speed, soon came up with the fugitives. He attempted to noose one of them, but the lariat hitched on one of his ears, and he shook it off. The horses dashed up a hill, he followed hard at their heels, when, of a sudden, he saw their tails whisking in the air, and they plunging down a precipice. It was too late to stop. He shut his eyes, held in his breath, and went over with them—neck or nothing. The descent was between twenty and thirty feet, but they all came down safe upon a sandy bottom.

He now succeeded in throwing his noose round a fine young horse. As he galloped alongside of him, the two horses passed each side of a sapling, and the end of the lariat was jerked out of his hand. He regained it, but an intervening tree obliged him again to let it go. Having once more caught it, and coming to a more open country, he was enabled to play the young horse with the line until he gradually checked and subdued him, so as to lead him to the place where he had left his rifle.

He had another formidable difficulty in getting him across the river, where both horses stuck for a time in the mire, and Beatte was nearly unseated from his saddle by the force of the current and the struggles of his captive. After much toil and trouble, however, he got across the stream, and brought his prize safe into camp.

For the remainder of the evening, the camp remained in a high state of excitement; nothing was talked of but the capture of wild horses; every youngster of the troop was for this harum-scarum kind of chase; every one promised himself to return from the campaign in triumph, bestriding one of these wild coursers of the prairies. Beatte had suddenly risen to great importance; he was the prime hunter, the hero of the day. Offers were made him by the best mounted rangers, to let him ride their horses in the chase, provided he would give them a share of the spoil. Beatte bore his honors in silence, and closed with none of the offers. Our stammering, chattering, gasconading little Frenchman, however, made up for his taciturnity, by vaunting as much upon the subject as if it were he that had caught the horse. Indeed he held forth so learnedly in the matter, and boasted so much of the many horses he had taken, that he began to be considered an oracle; and some of the youngsters were inclined to doubt whether he were not superior even to the taciturn Beatte.

The excitement kept the camp awake later than usual. The hum of voices, interrupted by occasional peals of laughter, was heard from the groups around the various fires, and the night was considerably advanced before all had sunk to sleep.

With the morning dawn the excitement revived, and Beatte and his wild horse were again the gaze and talk of the camp. The captive had been tied all night to a tree among the other horses. He was again led forth by Beatte, by a long halter or lariat, and, on his manifesting the least restiveness, was, as before, jerked and worried into passive submission. He appeared to be gentle and docile by nature, and had a beautifully mild expression of the eye. In his strange and forlorn situation, the poor animal seemed to seek protection and companionship in the very horse which had aided to capture him.

Seeing him thus gentle and tractable, Beatte, just as we were about to march, strapped a light pack upon his back, by way of giving him the first lesson in servitude. The native pride and independence of the animal took fire at this indignity. He reared, and plunged, and kicked, and tried in every way to get rid of the degrading burden. The Indian was too potent for him. At every paroxysm he renewed the discipline of the halter, until the poor animal, driven to despair, threw himself prostrate on the ground, and lay motionless, as if acknowledging himself vanquished. A stage hero, representing the despair of a captive prince, could not have played his part more dramatically. There was absolutely a moral grandeur in it.

The imperturbable Beatte folded his arms, and stood for a time, looking down in silence upon his captive; until seeing him perfectly subdued, he nodded his head slowly, screwed his mouth into a sardonic smile of triumph, and, with a jerk of the halter, ordered him to rise. He obeyed, and from that time forward offered no resistance. During that day he bore his pack patiently, and was led by the halter; but in two days he followed voluntarily at large among the supernumerary horses of the troop.

I could not but look with compassion upon this fine young animal, whose whole course of existence had been so suddenly reversed. From being a denizen of these vast pastures, ranging at will from plain to plain and mead to mead, cropping of every herb and flower, and drinking of every stream, he was suddenly reduced to perpetual and painful servitude, to pass his life under the harness and the curb, amid, perhaps, the din and dust and drudgery of cities. The transition in his lot was such as sometimes takes place in human affairs, and in the fortunes of towering individuals—one day, a prince of the prairies—the next day, a pack-horse!

CHAPTER XXI

WE LEFT the camp of the wild horse about a quarter before eight, and, after steering nearly south for three or four miles, arrived on the banks of the Red Fork, about seventy-five miles, as we supposed, above its mouth. The river was about three hundred yards wide, wandering among sand-bars and shoals. Its shores, and the long sandy banks that stretched out into the stream, were printed, as usual, with the traces of various animals that had come down to cross it, or to drink its waters.

Here we came to a halt, and there was much consultation about the possibility of fording the river with safety, as there was an apprehension of quicksands. Beatte, who had been somewhat in the rear, came up while we were debating. He was mounted on his horse of the half-wild breed, and leading his captive by the bridle. He gave the latter in charge to Tonish, and without saying a word, urged his horse into the stream, and crossed it in safety. Every thing was done by this man in a similar way, promptly, resolutely, and silently, without a previous promise or an after vaunt.

The troop now followed the lead of Beatte, and reached the opposite shore without any mishap, though one of the pack horses wandering a little from the track, came near being swallowed up in a quicksand, and was with difficulty dragged to land.

After crossing the river, we had to force our way, for nearly a mile, through a thick canebrake, which, at first sight, appeared an impervious mass of reeds and brambles. It was a hard struggle; our horses were often to the saddle-girths in mire and water, and both horse and horseman harassed and torn by bush and brier. Falling, however, upon a buffalo track, we at length extricated ourselves from this morass, and ascended a ridge of land, where we beheld a beautiful open country before us; while to our right, the belt of forest land, called "The Cross Timber," continued stretching away to the southward, as far as the eye could reach. We soon abandoned the open country, and struck into the forest land. It was the intention of the Captain to keep on southwest by south, and traverse the Cross Timber diagonally, so as to come out upon the edge of the great western prairie. By thus maintaining something of a southerly direction, he trusted, while he crossed the belt of the forest, he would at the same time approach the Red River.

The plan of the Captain was judicious; but he erred from not being informed of the nature of the country. Had he kept directly west, a couple of days would have carried us through the forest land, and we might then have had an easy course along the skirts of the upper prairies, to Red River; by going diagonally, we were kept for many weary days toiling through a dismal series of rugged forests.

The Cross Timber is about forty miles in breadth, and stretches over a rough country of rolling hills, covered with scattered tracts of post-oak and black-jack; with some intervening valleys, which at proper seasons, would afford good pasturage. It is very much cut up by deep ravines, which, in the rainy seasons, are the beds of temporary streams, tributary to the main rivers, and these are called "branches." The whole tract may present a pleasant aspect in the fresh time of the year, when the ground is covered with herbage; when the trees are in their green leaf, and the glens are enlivened by running streams. Unfortunately, we entered it too late in the season. The herbage was parched; the foliage of the scrubby forests was withered; the whole woodland prospect, as far as the eye could reach, had a brown and arid hue. The fires made on the prairies by the Indian hunters, had frequently penetrated these forests, sweeping in light transient flames along the dry grass, scorching and calcining the lower twigs and branches of the trees, and leaving them black and hard, so as to tear the flesh of man and horse that had to scramble through them. I shall not easily forget the mortal toil, and the vexations of flesh and spirit, that we underwent occasionally, in our wanderings through the Cross Timber. It was like struggling through forests of cast iron.

After a tedious ride of several miles, we came out upon an open tract of hill and dale, interspersed with woodland. Here we were roused by the cry of buffalo! buffalo! The effect was something like that of the cry of a sail! a sail! at sea. It was not a false alarm. Three or four of those enormous animals were visible to our sight grazing on the slope of a distant hill.

There was a general movement to set off in pursuit, and it was with some difficulty that the vivacity of the younger men of the troop could be restrained. Leaving orders that the line of march should be preserved, the Captain and two of his officers departed at a quiet pace, accompanied by Beatte, and by the ever-forward Tonish; for it was impossible any longer to keep the little Frenchman in check, being half crazy to prove his skill and prowess in hunting the buffalo.

The intervening hills soon hid from us both the game and the huntsmen. We kept on our course in quest of a camping place, which was difficult to be found; almost all the channels of the streams being dry, and the country being destitute of fountain heads.

After proceeding some distance, there was again a cry

of buffalo, and two were pointed out on a hill to the left. The Captain being absent, it was no longer possible to restrain the ardor of the young hunters. Away several of them dashed, full speed, and soon disappeared over the ravines: the rest kept on, anxious to find a proper place for encampment.

Indeed we now began to experience the disadvantages of the season. The pasturage of the prairies was scanty and parched; the pea-vines which grew in the woody bottoms were withered, and most of the "branches" or streams were dried up. While wandering in this perplexity, we were overtaken by the Captain and all his party, except Tonish. They had pursued the buffalo for some distance without getting within shot, and had given up the chase, being fearful of fatiguing their horses, or being led off too far from camp. The little Frenchman, however, had galloped after them at headlong speed, and the last they saw of him, he was engaged, as it were, yard-arm and yard-arm, with a great buffalo bull, firing broadsides into him. "I tink dat little man crazy—somehow," observed Beatte, dryly.

CHAPTER XXII

THE ALARM CAMP

WE NOW came to a halt, and had to content ourselves with an indifferent encampment. It was in a grove of scrub-oaks, on the borders of a deep ravine, at the bottom of which were a few scanty pools of water. We were just at the foot of a gradually-sloping hill covered with half-withered grass, that afforded meagre pasturage. In the spot where we had encamped, the grass was high and parched. The view around us was circumscribed and much shut in by gently-swelling hills.

Just as we were encamping, Tonish arrived, all glorious, from his hunting match; his white horse hung all round with buffalo meat. According to his own account, he had laid low two mighty bulls. As usual, we deducted one half from his boastings; but, now that he had something real to vaunt about, there was no restraining the valor of his tongue.

After having in some measure appeased his vanity by boasting of his exploit, he informed us that he had observed the fresh track of horses, which, from various circumstances, he suspected to have been made by some roving band of Pawnees. This caused some little uneasiness. The young men who had left the line of march in pursuit of the two buffaloes, had not yet rejoined us: apprehensions were expressed that they might be waylaid and attacked. Our veteran hunter, old Ryan, also, immediately on our halting to encamp, had gone off on foot, in company with a young disciple. "Dat old man will have his brains knocked out by de Pawnees yet," said Beatte. "He tink he know every ting, but he don't know Pawnees, anyhow."

Taking his rifle, the Captain repaired on foot to reconnoitre the country from the naked summit of one of the neighboring hills. In the meantime, the horses were hobbled and turned loose to graze; and wood was cut, and fires made, to prepare the evening's repast.

Suddenly there was an alarm of fire in the camp! The flames from one of the kindling fires had caught to the tall dry grass: a breeze was blowing; there was danger that the camp would soon be wrapped in a light blaze. "Look to the horses!" cried one; "drag away the baggage!" cried another. "Take care of the rifles and powder-horns!" cried a third. All was hurry-scurry and uproar. The horses dashed wildly about: some of the men snatched away rifles and powder-horns, others dragged off saddles and saddle-bags. Meantime, no one thought of quelling the fire, nor indeed knew how to quell it. Beatte, however, and his comrades attacked it in the Indian mode, beating down the edges of the fire with blankets and horse-cloths, and endeavoring to prevent its spreading among the grass; the rangers followed their example, and in a little while the flames were happily quelled.

The fires were now properly kindled on places from which the dry grass had been cleared away. The horses were scattered about a small valley, and on the sloping hill-side, cropping the scanty herbage. Tonish was preparing a sumptuous evening's meal from his buffalo meat, promising us a rich soup and a prime piece of roast beef: but we were doomed to experience another and more serious alarm.

There was an indistinct cry from some rangers on the summit of the hill, of which we could only distinguish the words, "The horses! the horses! get in the horses!"

Immediately a clamor of voices arose; shouts, questions, replies, were all mingled together, so that nothing could be clearly understood, and every one drew his own inference.

"The Captain has started buffaloes," cried one, "and wants horses for the chase." Immediately a number of rangers seized their rifles, and scampered for the hill-top. "The prairie is on fire beyond the hill," cried another; "I see the smoke—the Captain means we shall drive the horses beyond the brook."

By this time a ranger from the hill had reached the skirts of the camp. He was almost breathless, and could only say that the Captain had seen Indians at a distance.

"Pawnees! Pawnees!" was now the cry among our

wild-headed youngsters. "Drive the horses into the camp!" cried one. "Saddle the horses!" cried another. "Form the line!" cried a third. There was now a scene of clamor and confusion that baffles all description. The rangers were scampering about the adjacent field in pursuit of their horses. One might be seen tugging his steed along by a halter; another without a hat, riding bare-backed; another driving a hobbled horse before him, that made awkward leaps like a kangaroo.

The alarm increased. Word was brought from the lower end of the camp that there was a band of Pawnees in a neighboring valley. They had shot old Ryan through the head, and were chasing his companion. "No, it was not old Ryan that was killed—it was one of the hunters that had been after the two buffaloes." "There are three hundred Pawnees just beyond the hill," cried one voice. "More, more!" cried another.

Our situation, shut in among hills, prevented our seeing to any distance, and left us a prey to all these rumors. A cruel enemy was supposed to be at hand, and an immediate attack apprehended. The horses by this time were driven into the camp, and were dashing about among the fires, and trampling upon the baggage. Everyone endeavored to prepare for action; but here was the perplexity. During the late alarm of fire, the saddles, bridles, rifles, powder-horns, and other equipments, had been snatched out of their places, and thrown helter-skelter among the trees.

"Where is my saddle?" cried one. "Has any one seen my rifle?" cried another. "Who will lend me a ball?" cried a third, who was loading his piece. "I have lost my bullet pouch." "For God's sake help me to girth this horse!" cried another; "he's so restive I can do nothing with him." In his hurry and worry, he had put on the saddle the hind part before!

Some affected to swagger and talk bold; others said nothing, but went on steadily, preparing their horses and weapons, and on these I felt the most reliance. Some were evidently excited and elated with the idea of an enounter with Indians; and none more so than my young Swiss fellow traveller, who had a passion for wild adventure. Our man, Beatte, led his horses in the rear of the camp, placed his rifle against a tree, then seated himself by the fire in perfect silence. On the other hand, little Tonish, who was busy cooking, stopped every moment from his work to play the fanfaron, singing, swearing, and affecting an unusual hilarity, which made me strongly suspect that there was some little fright at bottom, to cause all this effervescence.

About a dozen of the rangers, as soon as they could saddle their horses, dashed off in the direction in which the Pawnees were said to have attacked the hunters. It was now determined in case our camp should be assailed, to put our horses in the ravine in rear, where they would be out of danger from arrow or rifle ball, and to take our stand within the edge of the ravine. This would serve as a trench, and the trees and thickets with which it bordered, would be sufficient to turn aside any shaft of the enemy. The Pawnees, beside, are wary of attacking any covert of the kind; their warfare, as I have already observed, lies in the open prairie, where, mounted upon their fleet horses, they can swoop like hawks upon their enemy, or wheel about him and discharge their arrows. Still I could not but perceive, that, in case of being attacked by such a number of these well-mounted and warlike savages as were said to be at hand, we should be exposed to considerable risk from the inexperience and want of discipline of our newly-raised rangers, and from the very courage of many of the younger ones who seemed bent on adventure and exploit.

By this time the Captain reached the camp, and everyone crowded round him for information. He informed us, that he had proceeded some distance on his reconnoitring expedition, and was slowly returning towards the camp, along the brow of a naked hill, when he saw something on the edge of a parallel hill, that looked like a man. He paused, and watched it; but it remained so perfectly motionless, that he supposed it a bush, or the top of some tree beyond the hill. He resumed his course, when it likewise began to move in a parallel direction. Another form now rose beside it, of someone who had either been lying down, or had just ascended the other side of the hill. The Captain stopped and regarded them; they likewise stopped. He then lay down upon the grass, and they began to walk. On his rising, they again stopped, as if watching him. Knowing that the Indians are apt to have their spies and sentinels thus posted on the summit of naked hills, commanding extensive prospects, his doubts were increased by the suspicious movements of these men. He now put his foraging cap on the end of his rifle, and waved it in the air. They took no notice of the signal. He then walked on, until he entered the edge of a wood, which concealed him from their view. Stopping out of sight for a moment, he again looked forth, when he saw the two men passing swiftly forward. As the hill on which they were walking made a curve toward that on which he stood, it seemed as if they were endeavoring to head him before he should reach the camp. Doubting whether they might not belong to some large party of Indians, either in ambush or moving along the valley beyond the hill, the Captain hastened his steps homeward, and, descrying some rangers on an eminence between him and the camp, he called out to them to pass the word to have the horses driven in, as these are generally the first objects of Indian depredation.

Such was the origin of the alarm which had thrown the camp in commotion. Some of those who heard the Captain's narration, had no doubt that the men on the hill were Pawnee scouts, belonging to the band that had waylaid the hunters. Distant shots were heard at intervals, which were supposed to be fired by those who had sallied out to rescue their comrades. Several more rangers, having completed their equipments, now rode forth in the direction of the firing; others looked anxious and uneasy.

"If they are as numerous as they are said to be," said one, "and as well mounted as they generally are, we shall be a bad match for them with our jaded horses."

"Well," replied the Captain, "we have a strong encampment, and can stand a siege."

"Ay, but they may set fire to the prairie in the night and burn us out of our encampment."

"We will then set up a counter-fire!"

The word was now passed that a man on horseback approached the camp.

"It is one of the hunters! It is Clements! He brings buffalo meat!" was announced by several voices as the horseman drew near.

It was, in fact, one of the rangers who had set off in the morning in pursuit of the two buffaloes. He rode into the camp, with the spoils of the chase hanging round his horse, and followed by his companions, all sound and unharmed, and equally well laden. They proceeded to give an account of a grand gallop they had had after the two buffaloes, and how many shots it had cost them to bring one to the ground.

"Well, but the Pawnees—the Pawnees—where are the Pawnees?"

"What Pawnees?"

"The Pawnees that attacked you."

"No one attacked us."

"But have you seen no Indians on your way?"

"Oh yes, two of us got to the top of a hill to look out for the camp, and saw a fellow on an opposite hill cutting queer antics, who seemed to be an Indian."

"Pshaw! that was I!" said the Captain.

Here the bubble burst. The whole alarm had risen from this mutual mistake of the Captain and the two rangers. As to the report of the three hundred Pawnees and their attack on the hunters, it proved to be a wanton fabrication, of which no further notice was taken; though the author deserved to have been sought out, and severely punished.

There being no longer any prospect of fighting, every one now thought of eating; and here the stomachs throughout the camp were in unison. Tonish served up to us his promised regale of buffalo soup and buffalo beef. The soup was peppered most horribly, and the roast beef proved the bull to have been one of the patriarchs of the prairies; never did I have to deal with a tougher morsel. However, it was our first repast on buffalo meat, so we ate it with a lively faith; nor would our little Frenchman allow us any rest, until he had extorted from us an acknowledgment of the excellence of his cookery; though the pepper gave us the lie in our throats.

The night closed in without the return of old Ryan and his companion. We had become accustomed, however, to the aberrations of this old cock of the woods, and no further solicitude was expressed on his account.

After the fatigues and agitations of the day, the camp

soon sunk into a profound sleep, excepting those on guard, who were more than usually on the alert; for the traces recently seen of Pawnees, and the certainty that we were in the midst of their hunting grounds, excited to constant vigilance. About half past ten o'clock we were all startled from sleep, by a new alarm. A sentinel had fired off his rifle and run into camp, crying that there were Indians at hand.

Every one was on his legs in an instant. Some seized their rifles; some were about to saddle their horses; some hastened to the Captain's lodge, but were ordered back to their respective fires. The sentinel was examined. He declared he had seen an Indian approach, crawling along the ground; whereupon he had fired upon him, and run into camp. The Captain gave it as his opinion, that the supposed Indian was a wolf; he reprimanded the sentinel for deserting his post, and obliged him to return to it. Many seemed inclined to give credit to the story of the sentinel; for the events of the day had predisposed them to apprehend lurking foes and sudden assaults during the darkness of the night. For a long time they sat round their fires, with rifle in hand carrying on low, murmuring conversations, and listening for some new alarm. Nothing further, however, occurred; the voices gradually died away; the gossipers nodded and dozed, and sunk to rest; and, by degrees, silence and sleep once more stole over the camp.

CHAPTER XXIII

ON MUSTERING our forces in the morning (Oct. 23) old Ryan and his comrade were still missing; but, the Captain had such perfect reliance on the skill and resources of the veteran woodsman, that he did not think it necessary to take any measures with respect to him.

Our march this day lay through the same kind of rough rolling country; checkered by brown dreary forests of post-oak, and cut up by deep dry ravines. The distant fires were evidently increasing on the prairies. The wind had been at northwest for several days; and the atmosphere had become so smoky, as in the height of Indian summer, that it was difficult to distinguish objects at any distance.

In the course of the morning, we crossed a deep stream with a complete beaver dam, above three feet high, making a large pond, and doubtless containing several families of that industrious animal, though not one showed his nose above water. The Captain would not permit this amphibious commonwealth to be disturbed.

We were now continually coming upon the tracks of buffaloes and wild horses; those of the former, tended invariably to the south, as we could perceive by the direction of the trampled grass. It was evident, we were on the great highway of these migratory herds, but that they had chiefly passed to the southward.

Beatte, who generally kept a parallel course several hundred yards distant from our line of march, to be on

the look-out for game, and who regarded every track
with the knowing eye of an Indian, reported that he had
come upon a very suspicious trail. There were the tracks
of men who wore Pawnee moccasons. He had scented
the smoke of mingled sumach and tobacco, such as the
Indians use. He had observed tracks of horses, mingled
with those of a dog; and a mark in the dust where a cord
had been trailed along; probably the long bridle, one
end of which the Indian horsemen suffer to trail on the
ground. It was evident, they were not the tracks of wild
horses. My anxiety began to revive about the safety of
our veteran hunter Ryan, for I had taken a great fancy
to this real old Leatherstocking; everyone expressed a
confidence, however, that wherever Ryan was, he was
safe, and knew how to take care of himself.

We had accomplished the greater part of a weary day's
march, and were passing through a glade of the oak
openings, when we came in sight of six wild horses,
among which I especially noticed two very handsome
ones, a gray and a roan. They pranced about, with heads
erect, and long flaunting tails, offering a proud contrast
to our poor, spiritless, travel-tired steeds. Having reconnoitred us for a moment, they set off at a gallop, passed
through a woody dingle, and in a little while emerged
once more to view, trotting up a slope about a mile
distant.

The sight of these horses was again a sore trial to the
vaporing Tonish, who had his lariat and forked stick
ready, and was on the point of launching forth in
pursuit, on his jaded horse, when he was again ordered
back to the pack-horses.

After a day's journey of fourteen miles in a southwest
direction, we encamped on the banks of a small clear
stream, on the northern border of the Cross Timbers;
and on the edge of those vast prairies, that extend away

to the foot of the Rocky Mountains. In turning loose the horses to graze, their bells were stuffed with grass to prevent their tinkling, lest it might be heard by some wandering horde of Pawnees.

Our hunters now went out in different directions, but without much success, as but one deer was brought into the camp. A young ranger had a long story to tell of his adventures. In skirting the thickets of a deep ravine he had wounded a buck, which he plainly heard to fall among the bushes. He stopped to fix the lock of his rifle, which was out of order, and to reload it; then advancing to the edge of the thicket, in quest of his game, he heard a low growling. Putting the branches aside, and stealing silently forward, he looked down into the ravine and beheld a huge bear dragging the carcass of the deer along the dry channel of a brook, and growling and snarling at four or five officious wolves, who seemed to have dropped in to take supper with him.

The ranger fired at the bear, but missed him. Bruin maintained his ground and his prize, and seemed disposed to make battle. The wolves, too, who were evidently sharp set, drew off to but a small distance. As night was coming on, the young hunter felt dismayed at the wildness and darkness of the place, and the strange company he had fallen in with; so he quietly withdrew, and returned empty handed to the camp, where, having told his story, he was heartily bantered by his more experienced comrades.

In the course of the evening, old Ryan came straggling into the camp, followed by his disciples, and as usual was received with hearty gratulations. He had lost himself yesterday, when hunting, and camped out all night, but had found our trail in the morning, and followed it up. He had passed some time at the beaver dam, admiring the skill and solidity with which it had been constructed. "These beavers," said he, "are industrious little fellows. They are the knowingest varmint as I know; and I'll warrant the pond was stocked with them."

"Aye," said the Captain, "I have no doubt most of the small rivers we have passed are full of beaver. I would like to come and trap on these waters all winter."

"But would you not run the chance of being attacked by Indians?" asked one of the company.

"Oh, as to that, it would be safe enough here, in the winter time. There would be no Indians here until spring. I should want no more than two companions. Three persons are safer than a large number for trapping beaver. They can keep quiet, and need seldom fire a gun. A bear would serve them for food, for two months, taking care to turn every part of it to advantage."

A consultation was now held as to our future progress. We had thus far pursued a western course; and, having traversed the Cross Timber, were on the skirts of the Great Western Prairie. We were still, however, in a very rough country, where food was scarce. The season was so far advanced that the grass was withered, and the prairies yielded no pasturage. The pea-vines of the bottoms, also, which had sustained our horses for some part of the journey, were nearly gone, and for several days past the poor animals had fallen off woefully both in flesh and spirit. The Indian fires on the prairies were approaching us from north and south, and west; they might spread also from the east, and leave a scorched desert between us and the frontier, in which our horses might be famished.

It was determined, therefore, to advance no further to the westward, but to shape our course more to the east, so as to strike the north fork of the Canadian, as soon as possible, where we hoped to find abundance of young cane; which, at this season of the year, affords the most nutritious pasturage for the horses; and, at the same time, attracts immense quantities of game. Here then we fixed the limits of our tour to the Far West, being within little more than a day's march of the boundary line of Texas.

CHAPTER XXIV

SCARCITY OF BREAD—RENCONTRE WITH BUFFALOES—WILD TUR-
KEYS—FALL OF A BUFFALO BULL

THE MORNING broke bright and clear, but the camp had nothing of its usual gaiety. The concert of the farmyard was at an end; not a cock crew, nor dog barked; nor was there either singing or laughing; every one pursued his avocations quietly and gravely. The novelty of the expedition was wearing off. Some of the young men were getting as way-worn as their horses; and most of them, unaccustomed to the hunter's life, began to repine at its privations. What they most felt was the want of bread, their rations of flour having been exhausted for several days. The old hunters, who had often experienced this want, made light of it; and Beatte, accustomed when among the Indians to live for months without it, considered it a mere article of luxury. "Bread," he would say scornfully, "is only fit for a child."

About a quarter before eight o'clock, we turned our backs upon the Far West, and set off in a southeast course, along a gentle valley. After riding a few miles, Beatte, who kept parallel with us, along the ridge of a naked hill to our right, called out and made signals, as if something were coming round the hill to intercept us. Some who were near me cried out that it was a party of Pawnees. A skirt of thickets hid the approach of the supposed enemy from our view. We heard a trampling among the brushwood. My horse looked toward the place, snorted and pricked up his ears, when presently a couple of large huge buffalo bulls, who had been alarmed by Beatte, came crashing through the brake, and making directly towards us. At sight of us they wheeled round, and scuttled along a narrow defile of the hill. In an instant half a score of rifles cracked off; there was a universal whoop and halloo, and away went half the troop, helter-skelter in pursuit, and myself among the number. The most of us soon pulled up, and gave over a chase which led through birch and brier, and break-neck ravines. Some few of the rangers persisted for a time; but eventually joined the line, slowly lagging one after another. One of them returned on foot; he had been thrown while in full chase; his rifle had been broken in the fall, and his horse, retaining the spirit of the rider, had kept on after the buffalo. It was a melancholy predicament to be reduced to, without horse or weapon in the midst of the Pawnee hunting grounds.

For my own part, I had been fortunate enough recently, by a further exchange, to get possession of the best horse in the troop; a full-blooded sorrel of excellent bottom, beautiful form, and most generous qualities.

In such a situation, it almost seems as if a man changes his nature with his horse. I felt quite like another being, now that I had an animal under me, spirited yet gentle, docile to a remarkable degree, and easy, elastic, and rapid in all his movements. In a few days he became almost as much attached to me as a dog; would follow me when I dismounted, would come to me in the morning to be noticed and caressed; and would put his muzzle between me and my book, as I sat reading at the foot of a tree. The feeling I had for this my dumb companion of the prairies gave me some faint idea of that attachment the Arab is said to entertain for the horse that has borne him about the deserts.

After riding a few miles further, we came to a fine meadow with a broad clear stream winding through it, on the banks of which there was excellent pasturage. Here we at once came to a halt, in a beautiful grove of elms, on the site of an old Osage encampment. Scarcely had we dismounted, when a universal firing of rifles took place upon a large flock of turkeys, scattered about the grove, which proved to be a favorite roosting-place for these simple birds. They flew to the trees, and sat perched upon their branches, stretching out their long necks, and gazing in stupid astonishment, until eighteen of them were shot down.

In the height of the carnage, word was brought that there were four buffaloes in a neighboring meadow. The turkeys were now abandoned for nobler game. The tired horses were again mounted, and urged to the chase. In a little while we came in sight of the buffaloes, looking like brown hillocks among the long green herbage. Beatte endeavored to get ahead of them and turn them towards us, that the inexperienced hunters might have a chance. They ran round the base of a rocky hill that hid us from the sight. Some of us endeavored to cut across the hill, but became entrapped in a thick wood, matted with grape-vines. My horse, who, under his former rider had hunted the buffalo, seemed as much excited as myself, and endeavored to force his way through the bushes. At length we extricated ourselves, and galloping over the hill, I found our little Frenchman Tonish curvetting on horseback round a great buffalo which he had wounded too severely to fly, and which he was keeping employed until we should come up. There was a mixture of the grand and the comic, in beholding this tremendous animal and his fantastic assailant. The buffalo stood with his shagged front always presented to his foe; his mouth open, his tongue parched, his eyes like coals of fire, and his tail erect with rage; every now and then he would make a faint rush upon his foe, who easily evaded his attack, capering and cutting all kinds of antics before him.

We now made repeated shots at the buffalo, but they glanced into his mountain of flesh without proving mortal. He made a slow and grand retreat into the shallow river, turning upon his assailants whenever they pressed upon him; and when in the water, took his stand there as if prepared to sustain a siege. A rifle ball, however, more fatally lodged, send a tremor through his frame. He turned and attempted to wade across the stream, but after tottering a few paces, slowly fell upon his side and expired. It was the fall of a hero, and we felt somewhat ashamed of the butchery that had effected it; but, after the first shot or two, we had reconciled it to our feelings, by the old plea of putting the poor animal out of his misery.

Two other buffaloes were killed this evening, but they were all bulls, the flesh of which is meagre and hard, at this season of the year. A fat buck yielded us more savory meat for our evening's repast.

CHAPTER XXV

W E LEFT the buffalo camp about eight o'clock, and had a toilsome and harassing march of two hours, over ridges of hills, covered with a ragged meagre forest of scrub-oaks, and broken by deep gullies. Among the oaks I observed many of the most diminutive size; some not above a foot high, yet bearing abundance of small acorns. The whole of the Cross Timber, in fact, abounds with mast. There is a pine-oak which produces an acorn pleasant to the taste, and ripening early in the season.

About ten o'clock in the morning, we came to where this line of rugged hills swept down into a valley, through which flowed the north fork of the Red River. A beautiful meadow about half a mile wide, enamelled with yellowed autumnal flowers, stretched for two or three miles along the foot of the hills, bordered on the opposite side by the river, whose banks were fringed with cotton-wood trees, the bright foliage of which refreshed and delighted the eye, after being wearied by the contemplation of monotonous wastes of brown forest.

The meadow was finely diversified by groves and clumps of trees, so happily dispersed, that they seemed as if set out by the hand of art. As we cast our eyes over this fresh and delightful valley, we beheld a troop of wild horses, quietly grazing on a green lawn, about a mile distant to our right, while to our left, at nearly the same distance, were several buffaloes; some feeding, others reposing and ruminating among the high rich herbage, under the shade of a clump of cotton-wood trees. The whole had the appearance of a broad beautiful tract of pasture land, on the highly ornamented estate of some gentleman farmer, with his cattle grazing about the lawns and meadows.

A council of war was now held, and it was determined to profit by the present favorable opportunity, and try our hand at the grand manœuvre, which is called ringing the wild horse. This requires a large party of horsemen, well-mounted. They extend themselves in each direction, singly, at certain distances apart, and gradually form a ring of two or three miles in circumference, so as to surround the game. This has to be done with extreme care, for the wild horse is the most readily alarmed inhabitant of the prairie, and can scent a hunter at a great distance, if to windward.

The ring being formed, two or three ride towards the horses who start off in an opposite direction. Whenever they approach the bounds of the ring, however, a huntsman presents himself and turns them from their course. In this way, they are checked and driven back at every point; and kept galloping round and round this magic circle, until, being completely tired down, it is easy for the hunters to ride up bside them, and throw the lariat over their heads. The prime horses of most speed, courage, and bottom, however, are apt to break through and escape, so that, in general, it is the second-rate horses that are taken.

Preparations were now made for a hunt of the kind. The pack-horses were taken into the woods and firmly tied to trees, lest, in a rush of the wild horses, they should break away with them. Twenty-five men were then sent under the command of a lieutenant, to steal along the edge of the valley within the strip of wood that skirted the hills. They were to station themselves about fifty yards apart, within the edge of the woods, and not advance or show themselves until the horse dashed in that direction. Twenty-five men were sent across the valley, to steal in like manner along the river bank that bordered the opposite side, and to station themselves among the trees. A third party, of about the same number, was to form a line, stretching across the lower part of the valley, so as to connect the two wings. Beatte and our other half-breed Antoine, together with the ever-officious Tonish, were to make a circuit through the woods, so as to get to the upper part of the valley, in the rear of the horses, and to drive them forward into the kind of sack that we had formed, while the two wings should join behind them and make a complete circle.

The flanking parties were quietly extending themselves, out of sight, on each side of the valley, and the residue were stretching themselves, like the links of a chain, across it, when the wild horses gave signs that they scented an enemy; snuffing the air, snorting, and looking about. At length they pranced off slowly toward the river, and disappeared behind a green bank. Here, had the regulations of the chase been observed, they would have been quietly checked and turned back by the advance of a hunter from among the trees; unluckily, however, we had our wildfire Jack-o-lantern little Frenchman to deal with. Instead of keeping quietly up the right side of the valley, to get above the horses, the moment he saw them move toward the river, he broke out of the covert of woods, and dashed furiously across the plain in pursuit of them, being mounted on one of the led horses belonging to the Count. This put an end to all system. The half-breeds and half-score of rangers joined in the chase. Away they all went over the green bank; in a moment or two the wild horses reappeared, and came thundering down the valley, with Frenchman, half-breeds, and rangers galloping and yelling like devils behind them. It was in vain that the line drawn across the valley attempted to check and turn back the fugitives. They were too hotly pressed by their pursuers; in their panic they dashed through the line, and clattered down the plain. The whole troop joined in the headlong chase, some of the rangers without hats or caps, their hair flying about their ears, others with handkerchiefs tied round their heads. The buffaloes, who had been calmly ruminating among the herbage, heaved up their huge forms, gazed for a moment with astonishment at the tempest that came scouring down the meadow, then turned and took to heavy-rolling flight. They were soon overtaken: the promiscuous throng were pressed together by the contracting sides of the valley, and away they went, pell-mell, hurry-scurry, wild buffalo, wild horse, wild huntsman, with clang and clatter, and whoop and halloo, that made the forests ring.

At length the buffaloes turned into a green brake on the river bank, while the horses dashed up a narrow defile of the hills, with their pursuers close at their heels. Beatte passed several of them, having fixed his eye upon a fine Pawnee horse that had his ears slit, and saddle marks upon his back. He pressed him gallantly, but lost him in the woods. Among the wild horses was a fine black mare, far gone with foal. In scrambling up the defile, she tripped and fell. A young ranger sprang from his horse, and seized her by the mane and muzzle. Another ranger dismounted, and came to his assistance. The mare struggled fiercely, kicking and biting, and striking with her fore feet but a noose was slipped over her head, and her struggles were in vain. It was some time, however, before she gave over rearing and plunging, and lashing out with her feet on every side. The two rangers then led her along the valley by two long lariats which enabled them to keep at a sufficient distance on each side to be out of the reach of her hoofs, and whenever she struck out in one direction, she was jerked in the other. In this way her spirit was gradually subdued.

As to little Scaramouch Tonish, who had marred the whole scene by his precipitancy, he had been more successful than he deserved, having managed to catch a beautiful cream-colored colt, about seven months old, which had not strength to keep up with its companions. The mercurial little Frenchman was beside himself with exultation. It was amusing to see him with his prize. The colt would rear and kick, and struggle to get free, when Tonish would take him about the neck, wrestle with him, jump on his back, and cut as many antics as a monkey with a kitten. Nothing surprised me more, however, than to witness how soon these animals, thus taken from the unbounded freedom of the prairie, yielded to the dominion of man. In the course of two or three days the mare and colt went with the led horses and became quite docile.

CHAPTER XXVI

FORDING OF THE NORTH FORK—DREARY SCENERY OF THE CROSS TIMBER—SCAMPER OF HORSES IN THE NIGHT—OSAGE WAR PARTY— EFFECTS OF A PEACE HARANGUE—BUFFALO—WILD HORSE

RESUMING our march, we forded the North Fork a rapid stream and of a purity seldom to be found in the rivers of the prairies. It evidently had its sources in high land, well supplied with springs. After crossing the river, we again ascended among hills, from one of which we had an extensive view over this belt of cross timber, and a cheerless prospect it was; hill beyond hill, forest beyond forest, all of one sad russet hue—excepting that here and there a line of green cotton-wood trees, sycamores, and willows, marked the course of some streamlet through a valley. A procession of buffaloes, moving slowly up the profile of one of those distant hills, formed a characteristic object in the savage scene. To the left, the eye stretched beyond this rugged wilderness of hills, and ravines, and ragged forests, to a prairie about ten miles off, extending in a clear blue line along the horizon. It was like looking from among rocks and breakers upon a distant tract of tranquil ocean. Unluckily, our route did not lie in that direction; we still had to traverse many a weary mile of the "cross timber."

We encamped towards evening in a valley, beside a scanty pool, under a scattered grove of elms, the upper branches of which were fringed with tufts of the mystic mistletoe. In the course of the night, the wild colt whinnied repeatedly; and about two hours before day, there was a sudden *stampedo,* or rush of horses, along the purlieus of the camp, with a snorting and neighing, and clattering of hoofs, that startled most of the rangers from their sleep, who listened in silence, until the sound died away like the rushing of a blast. As usual, the noise was at first attributed to some party of marauding Indians, but as the day dawned, a couple of wild horses were seen in a neighboring meadow, which scoured off on being approached. It was now supposed that a gang of them had dashed through our camp in the night. A general mustering of our horsses took place, many were found scattered to a considerable distance, and several were not to be found. The prints of their hoofs, however, appeared deeply dinted in the soil, leading off at full speed into the waste, and their owners, putting themselves on the trail, set off in weary search of them.

We had a ruddy daybreak, but the morning gathered

up gray and lowering, with indications of an autumnal storm. We resumed our march silently and seriously, through a rough and cheerless country, from the highest points of which we could descry large prairies, stretching indefinitely westward. After travelling for two or three hours, as we were traversing a withered prairie, resembling a great brown heath, we beheld seven Osage warriors approaching at a distance. The sight of any human being in this lonely wilderness was interesting; it was like speaking a ship at sea. One of the Indians took the lead of his companions, and advanced towards us with head erect, chest thrown forward, and a free and noble mien. He was a fine-looking fellow, dressed in scarlet frock and fringed leggins of deer skin. His head was decorated with a white tuft, and he stepped forward with something of a martial air, swaying his bow and arrows in one hand.

We held some conversation with him through our interpreter, Beatte, and found that he and his companions had been with the main part of their tribe hunting the buffalo, and had met with great success; and he informed us, that in the course of another day's march, we would reach the prairies on the banks of the Grand Canadian, and find plenty of game. He added, that as their hunt was over, and the hunters on their return homeward, he and his comrades had set out on a war party, to waylay and hover about some Pawnee camp, in hopes of carrying off scalps or horses.

By this time his companions, who at first stood aloof, joined him. Three of them had indifferent fowling-pieces; the rest were armed with bows and arrows. I could not but admire the finely shaped heads and busts of these savages, and their graceful attitudes and expressive gestures, as they stood conversing with our interpreter, and surrounded by a cavalcade of rangers. We endeavored to get one of them to join us, as we were desirous of seeing him hunt the buffalo with his bow and arrow. He seemed at first inclined to do so, but was dissuaded by his companions.

The worthy Commissioner now remembered his mission as pacificator, and made a speech, exhorting them to abstain from all offensive acts against the Pawnees; informing them of the plan of their father at Washington, to put an end to all war among his red children; and assuring them that he was sent to the frontier to establish a universal peace. He told them, therefore, to return quietly to their homes, with the certainty that the Pawnees would no longer molest them, but would soon regard them as brothers.

The Indians listened to the speech with their customary silence and decorum; after which, exchanging a few words among themselves, they bade us farewell, and pursued their way across the prairie.

Fancying that I saw a lurking smile in the countenance of our interpreter, Beatte, I privately inquired what the Indians had said to each other after hearing the speech. The leader, he said, had observed to his companions, that, as their great father intended so soon to put an end to all warfare, it behooved them to make the most of the little time that was left them. So they had departed, with redoubled zeal, to pursue their project of horse stealing!

We had not long parted from the Indians before we discovered three buffaloes among the thickets of a marshy valley to our left. I set off with the Captain and several rangers, in pursuit of them. Stealing through a straggling grove, the Captain, who took the lead, got within rifle shot, and wounded one of them in the flank. They all three made off in headlong panic, through thickets and brushwood, and swamp and mire, bearing down every obstacle by their immense weight. The

Captain and rangers soon gave up a chase which threatened to knock up their horses; I had got upon the traces of the wounded bull, however, and was in hopes of getting near enough to use my pistols, the only weapons with which I was provided; but before I could effect it, he reached the foot of a rocky hill, covered with post-oak and brambles, and plunged forward, dashing and crashing along, with neck or nothing fury, where it would have been madness to have followed him.

The chase had led me so far on one side that it was some time before I regained the trail of our troop. As I was slowly ascending a hill, a fine black mare came prancing round the summit, and was close to me before she was aware. At sight of me she started back, then turning, swept at full speed down into the valley, and up the opposite hill, with flowing mane and tail, and action free as air. I gazed after her as long as she was in sight, and breathed a wish that so glorious an animal might never come under the degrading thraldom of whip and curb, but remain a free rover of the prairies.

CHAPTER XXVII

FOUL WEATHER ENCAMPMENT—ANECDOTES OF BEAR HUNTING—
INDIAN NOTIONS ABOUT OMENS—SCRUPLES RESPECTING THE DEAD

O N overtaking the troop, I found it encamping in a rich bottom of woodland, traversed by a small stream, running between deep crumbling banks. A sharp cracking off of rifles was kept up for some time in various directions, upon a numerous flock of turkeys, scampering among the thickets, or perched upon the trees. We had not been long at a halt, when a drizzling rain ushered in the autumnal storm that had been brewing. Preparations were immediately made to weather it; our tent was pitched, and our saddles, saddlebags, packages of coffee, sugar, salt, and everything else that could be damanged by the rain, were gathered under its shelter. Our men, Beatte, Tonish, and Antoine, drove stakes with forked ends into the ground, laid poles across them for rafters, and thus made a shed or pent-house, covered with bark and skins, sloping towards the wind, and open towards the fire. The rangers formed similar shelters of bark and skins, or of blankets stretched on poles, supported by forked stakes, with great fires in front.

These precautions were well-timed. The rain set in sullenly and steadily, and kept on, with slight intermissions, for two days. The brook which flowed peaceably on our arrival, swelled into a turbid and boiling torrent, and the forest became little better than a mere swamp. The men gathered under their shelters of skins and blankets, or sat cowering round their fires; while columns of smoke curling up among the trees, and diffusing themselves in the air, spread a blue haze through the woodland. Our poor, way-worn horses, reduced by weary travel and scanty pasturage, lost all remaining spirit, and stood, with drooping heads, flagging ears, and half-closed eyes, dozing and steaming in the rain; while the yellow autumnal leaves, at every shaking of the breeze, came wavering down around them.

Notwithstanding the bad weather, however, our hunters were not idle, but during the intervals of the rain, sallied forth on horseback to prowl through the woodland. Every now and then the sharp report of a distant rifle boded the death of a deer. Venison in abundance was brought in. Some busied themselves under the sheds, flaying and cutting up the carcasses, or round the fires with spits and camp kettles, and a rude kind of feasting, or rather gormandizing, prevailed throughout the camp. The axe was continually at work, and wearied the forest with its echoes. Crash! some mighty tree would come down; in a few minutes its limbs would be blazing and crackling on the huge camp fires, with some luckless deer roasting before it that had once sported beneath its shade.

The change of weather had taken sharp hold of our little Frenchman. His meagre frame, composed of bones and whipcord, was racked with rheumatic pains and twinges. He had the toothache—the earache—his face was tied up—he had shooting pains in every limb: yet all seemed but to increase his restless activity, and he was in an incessant fidget about the fire, roasting, and stewing, and groaning, and scolding, and swearing.

Our man Beatte returned grim and mortified, from hunting. He had come upon a bear of formidable dimensions, and wounded him with a rifle shot. The bear took to the brook, which was swollen and rapid. Beatte dashed in after him and assailed him in the rear with his hunting knife. At every blow the bear turned furiously upon him, with a terrific display of white teeth. Beatte, having a foothold in the brook, was enabled to push him off with his rifle, and, when he turned to swim, would flounder after, and attempt to hamstring him. The bear, however, succeeded in scrambling off among the thickets, and Beatte had to give up the chase.

This adventure, if it produced no game, brought up at least several anecdotes, round the evening fire, relative to bear hunting, in which the grizzly bear figured conspicuously. This powerful and ferocious animal is a favorite theme of hunter's story, both among red and white men; and his enormous claws are worn round the neck of an Indian brave, as a trophy more honorable than a human scalp. He is now scarcely seen below the upper prairies, and the skirts of the Rocky Mountains. Other bears are formidable when wounded and provoked, but seldom make battle when allowed to escape. The grizzly bear, alone, of all the animals of our western wilds, is prone to unprovoked hostility. His prodigious size and strength make him a formidable opponent; and his great tenacity of life often baffles the skill of the hunter, notwithstanding repeated shots of the rifle and wounds of the hunting knife.

One of the anecdotes related on this occasion gave a picture of the accidents and hard shifts, to which our frontier rovers are inured. A hunter, while in pursuit of a deer, fell into one of those deep funnel-shaped pits, formed on the prairies by the settling of the waters after heavy rains, and known by the name of sink-holes. To his great horror, he came in contact, at the bottom, with a huge grizzly bear. The monster grappled him; a deadly contest ensued, in which the poor hunter was severely torn and bitten, and had a leg and an arm broken, but succeeded in killing his rugged foe. For several days he remained at the bottom of the pit, too much crippled to move, and subsisting on the raw flesh of the bear, during which time he kept his wounds open, that they might heal gradually and effectually. He was at length enabled to scramble to the top of the pit, and so out upon the open prairie. With great difficulty he crawled to a ravine, formed by a stream, then nearly dry. Here he took a delicious draught of water, which infused new life into him; then dragging himself along from pool to pool, he supported himself by small fish and frogs.

One day he saw a wolf hunt down and kill a deer in the neighboring prairie. He immediately crawled forth from the ravine, drove off the wolf, and, lying down beside the carcass of the deer, remained there until he made several hearty meals, by which his strength was much recruited.

Returning to the ravine, he pursued the course of the brook, until it grew to be a considerable stream. Down this he floated, until he came to where it emptied into the Mississippi. Just at the mouth of the stream, he found a forked tree, which he launched with some difficulty, and, getting astride of it, committed himself to the current of the mighty river. In this way he floated along, until he arrived opposite the fort at Council Bluffs. Fortunately he arrived there in the daytime, otherwise he might have floated unnoticed, past this solitary post, and perished in the idle waste of waters. Being descried from the fort, a canoe was sent to his relief, and he was brought to shore more dead than alive, where he soon recovered from his wounds, but remained maimed for life.

Our man Beatte had come out of his contest with the bear, very much worsted and discomfited. His drenching in the brook, together with the recent change of weather, had brought on rheumatic pains in his limbs, to which he is subject. Though ordinarily a fellow of undaunted spirit, and above all hardship, yet he now sat down by the fire, gloomy and dejected, and for once gave way to repining. Though in the prime of life, and of a robust frame, and apparently iron constitution, yet, by his own account he was little better than a mere wreck. He was, in fact, a living monument of the hardships of wild frontier life. Baring his left arm, he showed it warped and contracted by a former attack of rheumatism; a malady with which the Indians are often afflicted; for their exposure to the vicissitudes of the elements does not produce that perfect hardihood and insensibility to the changes of the seasons that many are apt to imagine. He bore the scars of various maims and bruises; some received in hunting, some in Indian warfare. His right arm had been broken by a fall from his horse; at another time his steed had fallen with him, and crushed his left leg.

"I am all broke to pieces and good for nothing;" said he, "I no care now what happen to me any more." "However," added he, after a moment's pause, "for all that, it would take a pretty strong man to put me down, anyhow."

I drew from him various particulars concerning himself, which served to raise him in my estimation. His residence was on the Neosho, in an Osage hamlet or neighborhood, under the superintendence of a worthy missionary from the banks of the Hudson, by the name of Requa, who was endeavoring to instruct the savages in the art of agriculture, and to make husbandmen and herdsmen of them. I had visited this agricultural mission of Requa in the course of my recent tour along the frontier, and had considered it more likely to produce solid advantages to the poor Indians, than any of the mere praying and preaching missions along the border.

In this neighborhood, Pierre Beatte had his little farm, his Indian wife, and his half-breed children; and aided Mr. Requa in his endeavors to civilize the habits, and meliorate the condition of the Osage tribe. Beatte had been brought up a Catholic, and was inflexible in his religious faith; he could not pray with Mr. Requa, he said, but he could work with him, and he evinced a zeal for the good of his savage relations and neighbors. Indeed, though his father had been French, and he himself had been brought up in communion with the whites, he evidently was more of an Indian in his tastes, and his heart yearned towards his mother's nation.

When he talked to me of the wrongs and insults that the poor Indians suffered in their intercourse with the rough settlers on the frontiers; when he described the precarious and degraded state of the Osage tribe, diminished in numbers, broken in spirit, and almost living on sufferance in the land where they once figured so heroically, I could see his veins swell, and his nostrils distend with indignation; but he would check the feeling with a strong exertion of Indian self-command and, in a manner, drive it back into his bosom.

He did not hesitate to relate an instance wherein he had joined his kindred Osages, in pursuing and avenging themselves on a party of white men who had committed a flagrant outrage upon them; and I found, in the encounter that took place, Beatte had shown himself the complete Indian.

He had more than once accompanied his Osage relations in their wars with the Pawnees, and related a skirmish which took place on the borders of these very hunting grounds, in which several Pawnees were killed. We should pass near the place, he said, in the course of our tour, and the unburied bones and skulls of the slain were still to be seen there. The surgeon of the troop, who was present at our conversation, pricked up his ears at this intelligence. He was something of a phrenologist, and offered Beatte a handsome reward if he would procure him one of the skulls.

Beatte regarded him for a moment with a look of stern surprise.

"No!" said he at length, "dat too bad! I have heart strong enough—I no care kill, but *let the dead alone!*"

He added, that once in travelling with a party of white men, he had slept in the same tent with a doctor, and found that he had a Pawnee skull among his baggage: he at once renounced the doctor's tent, and his fellowship. "He try to coax me," said Beatte, "but I say no, we must part—I no keep such company."

In the temporary depression of his spirits, Beatte gave way to those superstitious forebodings to which Indians are prone. He had sat for some time, with his cheek upon his hand, gazing into the fire. I found his thoughts were wandering back to his humble home, on the banks of the Neosho; he was sure, he said, that he should find some one of his family ill, or dead, on his return: his left eye had twitched and twinkled for two days past; an omen which always boded some misfortune of the kind.

Such are the trival circumstances which, when magnified into omens, will shake the souls of these men of iron. The least sign of mystic and sinister portent is sufficient to turn a hunter or a warrior from his course, or to fill his mind with apprehensions of impending evil. It is this superstitious propensity, common to the solitary and savage rovers of the wilderness, that gives such powerful influence to the prophet and the dreamer.

The Osages, with whom Beatte had passed much of his life, retain these superstitious fancies and rites in much of their original force. They all believe in the existence of the soul after its separation from the body, and that it carries with it all its mortal tastes and habitudes. At an Osage village in the neighborhood of Beatte, one of the chief warriors lost an only child, a beautiful girl, of a very tender age. All her playthings were buried with her. Her favorite little horse, also, was killed, and laid in the grave beside her, that she might have it to ride in the land of spirits.

I will here add a little story, which I picked up in the course of my tour through Beatte's country, and which illustrates the superstitions of his Osage kindred. A large party of Osages had been encamped for some time on the borders of a fine stream called the Nickanansa.

Among them was a young hunter, one of the bravest and most graceful of the tribe, who was to be married to an Osage girl, who, for her beauty, was called the Flower of the Prairies. The young hunter left her for a time among her relatives in the encampment, and went to St. Louis, to dispose of the products of his hunting, and purchase ornaments for his bride. After an absence of some weeks, he returned to the banks of the Nickanansa, but the camp was no longer there; the bare frames of the lodges and the brands of extinguished fires alone marked the place. At a distance he beheld a female seated, as if weeping, by the side of the stream. It was his affianced bride. He ran to embrace her, but she turned mournfully away. He dreaded lest some evil had befallen the camp.

"Where are our people?" cried he.

"They are gone to the banks of the Wagrushka."

"And what art thou doing here alone?"

"Waiting for thee."

"Then let us hasten to join our people on the banks of the Wagrushka."

He gave her his pack to carry, and walked ahead, according to the Indian custom.

They came to where the smoke of the distant camp was seen rising from the woody margin of the stream. The girl seated herself at the foot of a tree. "It is not proper for us to return together," said she; "I will wait here."

The young hunter proceeded to the camp alone, and was received by his relations with gloomy countenances.

"What evil has happened," said he, "that ye are all so sad?"

No one replied.

He turned to his favorite sister, and bade her go forth, seek his bride, and conduct her to the camp.

"Alas!" cried she, "how shall I seek her? She died a few days since."

The relations of the young girl now surrounded him, weeping and wailing; but he refused to believe the dismal tidings. "But a few moments since," cried he, "I left her alone and in health, come with me, and I will conduct you to her."

He led the way to the tree where she had seated herself, but she was no longer there, and his pack lay on the ground. The fatal truth struck him to the heart; he fell to the ground dead.

I give this simple little story almost in the words in which it was related to me, as I lay by the fire in an evening encampment on the banks of the haunted stream where it is said to have happened.

CHAPTER XXVIII

A SECRET EXPEDITION—DEER BLEATING—MAGIC BALLS

ON THE following morning we were rejoined by the rangers who had remained at the last encampment, to seek for the stray horses. They had tracked them for a considerable distance through bush and brake, and across streams, until they found them cropping the herbage on the edge of a prairie. Their heads were in the direction of the fort, and they were evidently grazing their way homeward, heedless of the unbounded freedom of the prairie so suddenly laid open to them.

About noon the weather held up, and I observed a mysterious consultation going on between our half-breeds and Tonish; it ended in a request that we would dispense with the services of the latter for a few hours, and permit him to join his comrades in a grand foray. We objected that Tonish was too much disabled by aches and pains for such an undertaking; but he was wild with eagerness for the mysterious enterprise, and, when permission was given him, seemed to forget all his ailments in an instant.

In a short time the trio were equipped and on horseback; with rifles on their shoulders and handkerchiefs twisted round their heads, evidently bound for a grand scamper. As they passed by the different lodges of the camp, the vainglorious little Frenchman could not help boasting to the right and left of the great things he was about to achieve; though the taciturn Beatte, who rode in advance, would every now and then check his horse, and look back at him with an air of stern rebuke. It was hard, however, to make the loquacious Tonish play "Indian."

Several of the hunters, likewise, sallied forth, and the prime old woodman, Ryan, came back early in the afternoon, with ample spoil, having killed a buck and two fat does. I drew near to a group of rangers that had gathered round him as he stood by the spoil, and found they were discussing the merits of a stratagem sometimes used in deer hunting. This consists in imitating, with a small instrument called a bleat, the cry of the fawn, so as to lure the doe within reach of the rifle. There are bleats of various kinds, suited to calm or windy weather, and to the age of the fawn. The poor animal, deluded by them, in its anxiety about its young, will sometimes advance close up to the hunter. "I once bleated a doe," said a young hunter, "until it came with twenty yards of me, and presented a sure mark. I levelled my rifle three times, but had not the heart to shoot, for the poor doe looked so wistfully, that it in a manner made my heart yearn. I thought of my own mother, and how anxious she used to be about me when I was a child; so to put an end to the matter, I gave a halloo, and started the doe out of rifle shot in a moment."

"And you did right," cried honest old Ryan. "For my part, I never could bring myself to bleating deer. I've been with hunters who had bleats, and have made them throw them away. It is a rascally trick to take advantage of a mother's love for her young."

Towards evening, our three worthies returned from their mysterious foray. The tongue of Tonish gave notice of their approach, long before they came in sight; for he was vociferating at the top of his lungs, and rousing the attention of the whole camp. The lagging gait and reeking flanks of their horses, gave evidence of hard riding; and, on nearer approach, we found them hung round with meat, like a butcher's shambles. In fact they had been scouring an immense prairie that extended beyond the forest, and which was covered with herds of buffalo. Of this prairie, and the animals upon it, Beatte had received intelligence a few days before, in his conversation with the Osages: but had kept the information a secret from the rangers, that he and his comrades might have the first dash at the game. They had contented themselves with killing four; though, if Tonish might be believed, they might have slain them by scores.

These tidings, and the buffalo meat brought home in evidence, spread exultation through the camp, and every one looked forward with joy to a buffalo hunt on the prairies. Tonish was again the oracle of the camp, and held forth by the hour to a knot of listeners, crouched round the fire, with their shoulders up to their ears. He was now more boastful than ever of his skill as a marksman. All his want of success in the early part of our march, he attributed to being "out of luck," if not "spellbound;" and finding himself listened to with apparent credulity, gave an instance of the kind, which he declared had happened to himself, but which was evidently a tale picked up among his relations, the Osages.

According to this account, when about fourteen years of age, as he was one day hunting, he saw a white deer come out from a ravine. Crawling near to get a shot, he beheld another and another come forth, until there were seven, all as white as snow. Having crept sufficiently near, he singled one out and fired, but without effect; the deer remained unfrightened. He loaded and fired again, and again he missed. Thus he continued firing and missing until all his ammunition was expended, and the deer remained without a wound. He returned home despairing of his skill as a marksman, but was consoled by an old Osage hunter. These white deer, said he, have a charmed life, and can only be killed by bullets of a particular kind.

The old Indian cast several balls for Tonish, but would not suffer him to be present on the occasion, nor inform him of the ingredients and mystic ceremonials.

Provided with these balls, Tonish again set out in quest of the white deer, and succeeded in finding them. He tried at first with ordinary balls, but missed as before. A magic ball, however, immediately brought a fine buck to the ground. Whereupon the rest of the herd immediately disappeared and were never seen again.

Oct. 29. The morning opened gloomy and lowering; but towards eight o'clock the sun struggled forth and lighted up the forest, and the notes of the bugle gave signal to prepare for marching. Now began a scene of bustle, and clamor, and gayety. Some were scampering and brawling after their horses, some were riding in bare-backed, and driving in the horses of their comrades. Some were stripping the poles of the wet blankets that had served for shelters; others packing up with all possible dispatch, and loading the baggage horses as they arrived, while others were cracking off their damp rifles and charging them afresh, to be ready for the sport.

About ten o'clock we began our march. I loitered in the rear of the troop as it forded the turbid brook and defiled through the labyrinths of the forest. I always felt disposed to linger until the last straggler disappeared among the trees and the distant note of the bugle died upon the ear, that I might behold the wilderness relapsing into silence and solitude. In the present instance, the deserted scene of our late bustling encampment had a forlorn and desolate appearance. The surrounding forest had been in many places trampled into a quagmire. Trees felled and partly hewn in pieces, and scattered in huge fragments; tent-poles stripped of their covering; smouldering fires, with great morsels of roasted venison and buffalo meat, standing in wooden spits before them, hacked and slashed by the knives of hungry hunters; while around were strewed the hides, the horns, the antlers and bones of buffaloes and deer, with uncooked joints, and unplucked turkeys, left behind with that reckless improvidence and wastefulness which young hunters are apt to indulge when in a neighborhood where game abounds. In the meantime a score or two of turkey-buzzards, or vultures, were already on the wing, wheeling their magnificent flight high in the air, and preparing for a descent upon the camp as soon as it should be abandoned.

CHAPTER XXIX

AFTER proceeding about two hours in a southerly direction, we emerged towards mid-day from the dreary belt of the Cross Timber, and to our infinite delight beheld "the great Prairie," stretching to the right and left before us. We could distinctly trace the meandering course of the Main Canadian, and various smaller streams, by the strips of green forest that bordered them. The landscape was vast and beautiful. There is always an expansion of feeling in looking upon these boundless and fertile wastes; but I was doubly conscious of it after emerging from our "close dungeon of innumerous boughs."

From a rising ground Beatte pointed out the place where he and his comrades had killed the buffaloes; and we beheld several black objects moving in the distance, which he said were part of the herd. The Captain determined to shape his course to a woody bottom about a mile distant, and to encamp there for a day or two, by way of having a regular buffalo hunt, and getting a supply of provisions. As the troop defiled along the slope of the hill towards the camping ground, Beatte proposed to my messmates and myself, that we should put ourselves under his guidance, promising to take us where we should have plenty of sport. Leaving the line of march, therefore, we diverged towards the prairie; traversing a small valley, and ascending a gentle swell of land. As we reached the summit, we beheld a gang of wild horses about a mile off. Beatte was immediately on the alert, and no longer thought of buffalo hunting. He was mounted on his powerful half-wild horse, with a lariat coiled at the saddle-bow, and set off in pursuit;

while we remained on a rising ground watching his manœuvres with great solicitude. Taking advantage of a strip of woodland, he stole quietly along, so as to get close to them before he was perceived. The moment they caught sight of him a grand scamper took place. We watched him skirting along the horizon like a privateer in full chase of a merchantman; at length he passed over the brow of a ridge, and down into a shallow valley; in a few moments he was on the opposite hill, and close upon one of the horses. He was soon head and head, and appeared to be trying to noose his prey; but they both disappeared again below the hill, and we saw no more of them. It turned out afterwards that he had noosed a powerful horse, but could not hold him, and had lost his lariat in the attempt.

While we were waiting for his return, we perceived two buffalo bulls descending a slope, towards a stream, which wound through a ravine fringed with trees. The young Count and myself endeavored to get near them under cover of the trees. They discovered us while we were yet three or four hundred yards off, and turning about, retreated up the rising ground. We urged our horses across the ravine, and gave chase. The immense weight of head and shoulders causes the buffalo to labor heavily up hill; but it accelerates his descent. We had the advantage, therefore, and gained rapidly upon the fugitives, though it was difficult to get our horses to approach them, their very scent inspiring them with terror. The Count, who had a double-barrelled gun loaded with ball, fired, but it missed. The bulls now altered their course, and galloped down hill with head-long rapidity. As they ran in different directions, we each singled one and separated. I was provided with a brace of veteran brass-barrelled pistols, which I had borrowed at Fort Gibson, and which had evidently seen some service. Pistols are very effective in buffalo hunting, as the hunter can ride up close to the animal, and fire at it while at full speed; whereas the long heavy rifles used on the frontier, cannot be easily managed, nor discharged with accurate aim from horseback. My object, therefore, was to get within pistol shot of the buffalo. This was no very easy matter. I was well mounted on a horse of excellent speed and bottom, that seemed eager for the chase, and soon overtook the game; but the moment he came nearly parallel, he would keep sheering off, with ears forked and pricked forward, and every symptom of aversion and alarm. It was no wonder. Of all animals, a buffalo, when close pressed by the hunter, has an aspect the most diabolical. His two short black horns curve out of a huge frontlet of shaggy hair; his eyes glow like coals; his mouth is open, his tongue parched and drawn up into a half crescent; his tail is erect, and tufted and whisking about in the air, he is a perfect picture of mingled rage and terror.

It was with difficulty I urged my horse sufficiently near, when, taking aim, to my chagrin, both pistols missed fire. Unfortunately the locks of these veteran weapons were so much worn, that in the gallop, the priming had been shaken out of the pans. At the snapping of the last pistol I was close upon the buffalo, when, in his despair, he turned round with a sudden snort and rushed upon me. My horse wheeled about as if on a pivot, made a convulsive spring, and, as I had been leaning on one side with pistol extended, I came near being thrown at the feet of the buffalo.

Three or four bounds of the horse carried us out of the reach of the enemy; who, having merely turned in desperate self-defense, quickly resumed his flight. As soon as I could gather in my panic-stricken horse, and prime the pistols afresh, I again spurred in pursuit of the buffalo, who had slackened his speed to take breath. On my approach he again set off full tilt, heaving himself forward with a heavy rolling gallop, dashing with head-long precipitation through brakes and ravines, while several deer and wolves, startled from their coverts by his thundering career, ran helter-skelter to right and left across the waste.

A gallop across the prairies in pursuit of game is by no means so smooth a career as those may imagine, who have only the idea of an open level plain. It is true, the prairies of the hunting ground are not so much entangled with flowering plants and long herbage as the lower prairies, and are principally covered with short buffalo grass; but they are diversified by hill and dale, and where most level, are apt to be cut up by deep rifts and ravines, made by torrents after rains; and which, yawning from an even surface, are almost like pitfalls in the way of the hunter, checking him suddenly, when in full career, or subjecting him to the risk of limb and life. The plains, too, are beset by burrowing holes of small animals, in which the horse is apt to sink to the fetlock, and throw both himself and his rider. The late rain had covered some parts of the prairie, where the ground was hard, with a thin sheet of water, through which the horse had to splash his way. In other parts there were innumerable shallow hollows, eight or ten feet in diameter, made by the buffaloes, who wallow in sand and mud like swine. These being filled with water, shone like mirrors, so that the horse was continually leaping over them or springing on one side. We had reached, too, a rough part of the prairie, very much broken and cut up, the buffalo, who was running for life, took no heed to his course, plunging down break-neck ravines, where it was necessary to skirt the borders in search of a safer descent. At length we came to where a winter stream had torn a deep chasm across the whole prairie, leaving open jagged rocks, and forming a long glen bordered by steep crumbling cliffs of mingled stone and clay. Down one of these the buffalo flung himself, half tumbling, half leaping, and then scuttled along the bottom; while I, seeing all further pursuit useless, pulled up, and gazed quietly after him from the border of the cliff, until he disappeared amidst the windings of the ravine.

Nothing now remained but to turn my steed and rejoin my companions. Here at first was some little difficulty. The ardor of the chase had betrayed me into a long, heedless gallop. I now found myself in the midst of a lonely waste, in which the prospect was bounded by undulating swells of land, naked and uniform, where, from the deficiency of landmarks and distinct features, an inexperienced man may become bewildered, and lose his way as readily as in the wastes of the ocean. The day, too, was overcast, so that I could not guide myself by the sun; my only mode was to retrace the track my horse had made in coming, though this I would often lose sight of, where the ground was covered with parched herbage.

To one unaccustomed to it, there is something inexpressibly lonely in the solitude of a prairie. The loneliness of a forest seems nothing to it. There the view is shut in by trees, and the imagination is left free to picture some livelier scene beyond. But here we have an immense extent of landscape without a sign of human existence. We have the consciousness of being far, far beyond the bounds of human habitation; we feel as if moving in the midst of a desert world. As my horse lagged slowly back over the scenes of our late scamper, and the delirium of the chase had passed away, I was peculiarly sensible to these circumstances. The silence of the waste was now and then broken by a cry of a distant flock of pelicans, stalking like spectres about a shallow pool; sometimes by the sinister croaking of a raven in the air while occasionally a scoundrel wolf would scour off from before me; and, having attained a safe distance, would sit down and howl and whine with tones that gave a dreariness to the surrounding solitude.

After pursuing my way for some time, I descried a horseman on the edge of a distant hill, and soon recognized him to be the Count. He had been equally unsuccessful with myself; we were shortly after rejoined by our worthy comrade, the Virtuoso, who, with spectacles on nose, had made two or three ineffectual shots from horseback.

We determined not to seek the camp until we had made one more effort. Casting our eyes about the surrounding waste, we descried a herd of buffalo about two miles distant, scattered apart, and quietly grazing near a small strip of trees and bushes. It required but little stretch of fancy to picture them so many cattle grazing on the edge of a common, and that the grove might shelter some lowly farmhouse.

We now formed our plan to circumvent the herd, and by getting on the other side of them, to hunt them in the direction where we knew our camp to be situated: otherwise, the pursuit might take us to such a distance as to render it impossible to find our way back before nightfall. Taking a wide circuit therefore, we moved slowly and cautiously, pausing occasionally, when we saw any of the herd desist from grazing. The wind fortunately set from them, otherwise they might have scented us and have taken the alarm. In this way, we succeeded in getting round the herd without disturbing it. It consisted of about forty head, bulls, cows and calves. Separating to some distance from each other, we now approached slowly in a parallel line, hoping by degrees to steal near without exciting attention. They began, however, to move off quietly, stopping at every step or two to graze, when suddenly a bull that, unobserved by us, had been taking his siesta under a clump of trees to our left, roused himself from his lair, and hastened to join his companions. We were still at a considerable distance, but the game had taken the alarm. We quickened our pace, they broke into a gallop, and now commenced a full chase.

As the ground was level, they shouldered along with great speed, following each other in a line; two or three bulls bringing up the rear, the last of whom, from his enormous size and venerable frontlet, and beard of sunburnt hair, looked like the patriarch of the herd; and as if he might long have reigned the monarch of the prairie.

There is a mixture of the awful and the comic in the look of these huge animals, as they bear their great bulk forwards, with an up and down motion of the unwieldy head and shoulders; their tail cocked up like the cue of Pantaloon in a pantomime, the end whisking about in a fierce yet whimsical style, and their eyes glaring venomously with an expression of fright and fury.

For some time I kept parallel with the line, without being able to force my horse within pistol shot, so much had he been alarmed by the assault of the buffalo in the preceding chase. At length I succeeded, but was again balked by my pistols missing fire. My companions, whose horses were less fleet, and more way worn, could not overtake the herd; at length Mr. L., who was in the rear of the line, and losing ground, levelled his double-barrelled gun, and fired a long raking shot. It struck a buffalo just above the loins, broke its back-bone, and brought it to the ground. He stopped and alighted to dispatch his prey, when borrowing his gun, which had yet a charge remaining in it, I put my horse to his speed, again overtook the herd which was thundering along, pursued by the Count. With my present weapon there was no need of urging my horse to such close quarters; galloping along parallel, therefore, I singled out a buffalo, and by a fortunate shot brought it down on the spot. The ball had struck a vital part; it could not move from the place where it fell, but lay there struggling in mortal agony, while the rest of the herd kept on their headlong career across the prairie.

Dismounting, I now fettered my horse to prevent his straying; and advanced to contemplate my victim. I am nothing of a sportsman; I had been prompted to this unwonted exploit by the magnitude of the game, and the excitement of an adventurous chase. Now that the excitement was over, I could not but look with commiseration upon the poor animal that lay struggling and bleeding at my feet. His very size and importance, which had before inspired me with eagerness, now increased my compunction. It seemed as if I had inflicted pain in proportion to the bulk of my victim, and as if there were a hundred-fold greater waste of life than there would have been in the destruction of an animal of inferior size.

To add to these after-qualms of conscience, the poor animal lingered in his agony. He had evidently received a mortal wound, but death might be long in coming. It would not do to leave him here to be torn piecemeal, while yet alive, by the wolves that had already snuffed his blood, and were skulking and howling at a distance, and waiting for my departure; and by the ravens that were flapping about, croaking dismally in the air. It became now an act of mercy to give him his quietus, and put him out of his misery. I primed one of the pistols, therefore and advanced close up to the buffalo. To inflict a wound thus in cold blood, I found a totally different thing from firing in the heat of the chase. Taking aim, however, just behind the fore-shoulder, my pistol for once proved true; the ball must have passed through the heart, for the animal gave one convulsive throe and expired.

While I stood meditating and moralizing over the wreck I had so wantonly produced, with my horse grazing near me, I was rejoined by my fellow-sportsman, the Virtuoso; who, being a man of universal adroitness, and withal, more experienced and hardened in the gentle art of "venerie," soon managed to carve out the tongue of the buffalo, and delivered it to me to bear back to the camp as a trophy.

CHAPTER XXX

A COMRADE LOST—A SEARCH FOR THE CAMP—THE COMMISSIONER, THE WILD HORSE, AND THE BUFFALO—A WOLF SERENADE

OUR solicitude was now awakened for the young Count. With his usual eagerness and impetuosity he had persisted in urging his jaded horse in pursuit of the herd, unwilling to return without having likewise killed a buffalo. In this way he had kept on following them, hither and thither, and occasionally firing an ineffectual shot, until by degrees horseman and herd became indistinct in the distance, and at length swelling ground and strips of trees and thickets hid them entirely from sight.

By the time my friend, the amateur, joined me, the young Count had been long lost to view. We held a consultation on the matter. Evening was drawing on.

Were we to pursue him, it would be dark before we should overtake him, granting we did not entirely lose trace of him in the gloom. We should then be too much bewildered to find our way back to the encampment; even now, our return would be difficult. We determined, therefore, to hasten to the camp as speedily as possible, and send out our half-breeds, and some of the veteran hunters, skilled in cruising about the prairies, to search for our companion.

We accordingly set forward in what we supposed to be the direction of the camp. Our weary horses could hardly be urged beyond a walk. The twilight thickened upon us; the landscape grew gradually indistinct; we tried in vain to recognize various landmarks which we had noted in the morning. The features of the prairies are so similar as to baffle the eye of any but an Indian, or a practised woodman. At length night closed in. We hoped to see the distant glare of camp fires; we listened to catch the sound of the bells about the necks of the grazing horses. Once or twice we thought we distinguished them; we were mistaken. Nothing was to be heard but a monotonous concert of insects, with now and then the dismal howl of wolves mingling with the night breeze. We began to think of halting for the night, and bivouacking under the lee of some thicket. We had implements to strike a light; there was plenty of firewood at hand, and the tongues of our buffaloes would furnish us with a repast.

Just as we were preparing to dismount, we heard the report of a rifle, and shortly after, the notes of the bugle, calling up the night guard. Pushing forward in that direction, the camp fires soon broke on our sight, gleaming at a distance from among the thick groves of an alluvial bottom.

As we entered the camp, we found it a scene of rude

hunters' revelry and wassail. There had been a grand day's sport, in which all had taken a part. Eight buffaloes had been killed; roaring fires were blazing on every side; all hands were feasting upon roasted joints, broiled marrow-bones, and the juicy hump, far-famed among the epicures of the prairies. Right glad were we to dismount and partake of the sturdy cheer, for we had been on our weary horses since morning without tasting food.

As to our worthy friend, the Commissioner, with whom we had parted company at the outset of this eventful day, we found him lying in a corner of the tent, much the worse for wear, in the course of a successful hunting match.

It seems that our man, Beatte, in his zeal to give the Commissioner an opportunity of distinguishing himself, and gratifying his hunting propensities, had mounted him upon his half-wild horse, and started him in pursuit of a huge buffalo bull, that had already been frightened by the hunters. The horse, which was fearless as his owner, and, like him, had a considerable spice of devil in his composition, and who, beside, had been made familiar with the game, no sooner came in sight and scent of the buffalo than he set off full speed, bearing the involuntary hunter hither and thither, and whither he would not—up hill and down hill—leaping pools and brooks—dashing through glens and gullies, until he came up with the game. Instead of sheering off, he crowded upon the buffalo. The Commissioner, almost in self-defense, discharged both barrels of a double-barrelled gun into the enemy. The broadside took effect, but was not mortal. The buffalo turned furiously upon his pursuer: the horse, as he had been taught by his owner, wheeled off. The buffalo plunged after him. The worthy Commissioner, in great extremity, drew his sole pistol from his holster, fired it off as a stern-chaser, shot the buffalo full in the breast, and brought him lumbering forward to the earth.

The Commissioner returned to camp, lauded on all sides for his signal exploit; but grievously battered and way-worn. He had been a hard rider per force, and a victor in spite of himself. He turned a deaf ear to all compliments and congratulations; had but little stomach for the hunter's fare placed before him, and soon retreated to stretch his limbs in the tent, declaring that nothing should tempt him again to mount that half-devil Indian horse, and that he had enough of buffalo hunting for the rest of his life.

It was too dark now to send any one in search of the young Count. Guns, however, were fired, and the bugle sounded from time to time, to guide him to the camp, if by chance he should straggle within hearing; but the night advanced without his making his appearance. There was not a star visible to guide him, and we concluded that wherever he was, he would give up wandering in the dark, and bivouack until daybreak.

It was a raw, overcast night. The carcasses of the buffaloes killed in the vicinity of the camp had drawn about it an unusual number of wolves, who kept up the most forlorn concert of whining yells, prolonged into dismal cadences and inflexions, literally converting the surrounding waste into a howling wilderness. Nothing is more melancholy than the midnight howl of a wolf on a prairie. What rendered the gloom and wildness of the night and the savage concert of the neighboring waste the more dreary to us was the idea of the lonely and exposed situation of our young and inexperienced comrade. We trusted, however, that on the return of daylight, he would find his way back to the camp, and then all the events of the night would be remembered only as so many savory gratifications of his passion for adventure.

CHAPTER XXXI

A HUNT FOR A LOST COMRADE

THE morning dawned, and an hour or two passed without any tidings of the Count. We began to feel uneasiness lest, having no compass to aid him, he might perplex himself and wander in some opposite direction. Stragglers are thus often lost for days; what made us the more anxious about him was, that he had no provisions with him, was totally unversed in "wood craft," and liable to fall into the hands of some lurking or straggling party of savages.

As soon as our people, therefore, had made their breakfast, we beat up for volunteers for a cruise in search of the Count. A dozen of the rangers, mounted on some of the best and freshest horses, and armed with rifles, were soon ready to start; our half-breeds Beatte and Antoine also, with our little mongrel Frenchman, were zealous in the cause; so Mr. L. and myself taking the lead, to show the way to the scene of our little hunt, where we had parted company with the Count, we all set out across the prairie. A ride of a couple of miles brought us to the carcasses of the two buffaloes we had killed. A legion of ravenous wolves were already gorging upon them. At our approach they reluctantly drew off, skulking with a caitiff look to the distance of a few hundred yards, and there awaiting our departure, that they might return to their banquet.

I conducted Beatte and Antoine to the spot whence the young Count had continued the chase alone. It was like putting hounds upon the scent. They immediately distinguished the track of his horse amidst the trampings of the buffaloes, and set off at a round pace, following with the eye in nearly a straight course, for upwards of a mile, when they came to where the herd had divided, and run hither and thither about a meadow. Here the track of the horse's hoofs wandered and doubled and often crossed each other; our half-breeds were like hounds at fault. While we were at a halt, waiting until they should unravel the maze, Beatte suddenly gave a short Indian whoop, or rather yelp, and pointed to a distant hill. On regarding it attentively, we perceived a horseman on the summit. "It is the Count!" cried Beatte, and set off at full gallop, followed by the whole company. In a few moments he checked his horse. Another figure on horseback had appeared on the brow of the hill. This completely altered the case. The Count had wandered off alone; no other person had been missing from the camp. If one of these horsemen were indeed the Count, the other must be an Indian. If an Indian, in all probability a Pawnee. Perhaps they were both Indians; scouts of some party lurking in the vicinity. While these and other suggestions were hastily discussed, the two horsemen glided down from the profile of the hill, and we lost sight of them. One of the rangers suggested that there might be a straggling party of Pawnees behind the hill, and that the Count might have fallen into their hands. The idea had an electric effect upon the little troop. In an instant every horse was at full speed, the half-breeds leading the way; the young rangers as they rode set up wild yelps of exultation at the thoughts of having a brush with the Indians. A neck or nothing gallop brought us to the skirts of the hill, and revealed our mistake. In a ravine we found the two horsemen standing by the carcass of a buffalo which they had killed. They proved to be two rangers, who, unperceived, had left the camp a little before us, and had come here in a direct line, while we had made a wide circuit about the prairie.

This episode being at an end, and the sudden excitement being over, we slowly and coolly retraced our steps to the meadow, but it was some time before our half-breeds could again get on the track of the Count. Having at length found it, they succeeded in following it through all its doublings, until they came to where it was no longer mingled with the tramp of buffaloes, but became single and separate, wandering here and there about the prairies, but always tending in a direction opposite to that of the camp. Here the Count had evidently given up the pursuit of the herd, and had endeavored to find his way to the encampment, but had become bewildered as the evening shades thickened around him, and had completely mistaken the points of the compass.

In all this quest our half-breeds displayed that quickness of eye, in following up a track, for which Indians are so noted. Beatte, especially, was as stanch as a veteran hound. Sometimes he would keep forward on an easy trot; his eyes fixed on the ground a little ahead of his horse, clearly distinguishing prints in the herbage which to me were invisible, excepting on the closest inspection. Sometimes he would pull up and walk his horse slowly, regarding the ground intensely, where to my eye nothing was apparent. Then he would dismount, lead his horse by the bridle, and advance cautiously step by step, with his face bent towards the earth, just catching, here and there, a casual indication of the vaguest kind to guide him onward. In some places where the soil was hard, and the grass withered, he would lose the track entirely, and wander backwards and forwards, and right and left, in search of it; returning occasionally to the place where he had lost sight of it, to take a new departure. If this failed he would examine the banks of the neighboring streams, or the sandy bottoms of the ravines, in hopes of finding tracks where the Count had crossed. When he again came upon the track, he would remount his horse, and resume his onward course. At length, after crossing a stream, in the crumbling banks of which the hoofs of the horse were deeply dented, we came upon a high dry prairie, where our half-breeds were completely baffled. Not a footprint was to be discerned, though they searched in every direction; and Beatte at length coming to a pause shook his head despondingly.

Just then a small herd of deer, roused from a neighboring ravine, came bounding by us. Beatte sprang from his horse, levelled his rifle, and wounded one slightly, but without bringing it to the ground. The report of the rifle was almost immediately followed by a long halloo from a distance. We looked around but could see nothing. Another long halloo was heard, and at length a horseman was descried, emerging out of a skirt of forest. A single glance showed him to be the young Count; there was a universal shout and scamper, everyone setting off full gallop to greet him. It was a joyful meeting to both parties; for, much anxiety had been felt by us all on account of his youth and inexperience, and for his part, with all his love of adventure, he seemed right glad to be once more among his friends.

As we supposed, he had completely mistaken his course on the preceding evening, and had wandered about until dark, when he thought of bivouacing. The night was cold, yet he feared to make a fire, lest it might betray him to some lurking party of Indians. Hobbling his horse with his pocket handkerchief, and leaving him to graze on the margin of the prairie, he clambered into a tree, fixed his saddle in the fork of the branches, and placing himself securely with his back against the trunk, prepared to pass a dreary and anxious night, regaled occasionally with the howlings of the wolves. He was agreeably disappointed. The fatigue of the day soon brought on a sound sleep; he had delightful dreams about his home in Switzerland, nor did he wake until it was broad daylight.

He then descended from his roosting-place, mounted his horse, and rode to the naked summit of a hill, whence he beheld a trackless wilderness around him, but, at no great distance, the Grand Canadian, winding its way between borders of forest land. The sight of this river consoled him with the idea that, should he fail in finding his way back to the camp, or, in being found by some party of his comrades, he might follow the course of the stream, which could not fail to conduct him to some frontier post, or Indian hamlet. So closed the events of our hap-hazard buffalo hunt.

CHAPTER XXXII

A REPUBLIC OF PRAIRIE DOGS

ON returning from our expedition in quest of the young Count, I learned that a burrow, or village, as it is termed, of prairie dogs had been discovered on the level summit of a hill, about a mile from the camp. Having heard much of the habits and peculiarities of these little animals, I determined to pay a visit to the community. The prairie dog is, in fact, one of the curiosities of the Far West, about which travellers delight to tell marvellous tales, endowing him at times with something of the politic and social habits of a rational being, and giving him systems of civil government and domestic economy, almost equal to what they used to bestow upon the beaver.

The prairie dog is an animal of the coney kind, and about the size of a rabbit. He is of a sprightly mercurial nature; quick, sensitive, and somewhat petulant. He is very gregarious living in large communities, sometimes of several acres in extent where innumerable little heaps of earth show the entrances to the subterranean cells of the inhabitants, and the well-beaten tracks, like lanes and streets, show their mobility and restlessness. According to the accounts given of them, they would seem to be continually full of sport, business, and public affairs; whisking about hither and thither, as if on gossiping visits to each other's houses, or congregating in the cool of the evening, or after a shower, and gambolling together in the open air. Some times, especially when the moon shines, they pass half the night in revelry, barking or yelping with short, quick, yet weak tones, like those of very young puppies. While in the height of their playfulness and clamor, however, should there be the least alarm, they all vanish into their cells in an instant, and the village remains blank and silent. In case they are hard pressed by their pursuers, without any hope of escape, they will assume a pugnacious air, and a most whimsical look of impotent wrath and defiance.

The prairie dogs are not permitted to remain sole and undisturbed inhabitants of their own homes. Owls and rattlesnakes are said to take up their abodes with them;

but whether as invited guests or unwelcome intruders, is a matter of controversy. The owls are of a peculiar kind, and would seem to partake of the character of the hawk; for they are taller and more erect on their legs, more alert in their looks and rapid in their flight than ordinary owls, and do not confine their excursions to the night, but sally forth in broad day.

Some say that they only inhabit cells which the prairie dogs have deserted, and suffered to go to ruin, in consequence of the death in them of some relative; for they would make out this little animal to be endowed with keen sensibilities, that will not permit it to remain in the dwelling where it has witnessed the death of a friend. Other fanciful speculators represent the owl as a kind of housekeeper to the prairie dog; and, from having a note very similar, insinuate that it acts, in a manner, as family preceptor, and teaches the young litter to bark.

As to the rattlesnake, nothing satisfactory has been asertained of the part he plays in this most interesting household; though he is considered as little better than a sycophant and sharper, that winds himself into the concerns of the honest, credulous little dog, and takes him in most sadly. Certain it is, if he acts as toad-eater, he occasionally solaces himself with more than the usual perquisites of his order; as he is now and then detected with one of the younger members of the family in his maw.

Such are a few of the particulars that I could gather about the domestic economy of this little inhabitant of the prairies, who, with his pigmy republic, appears to be a subject of much whimsical speculation and burlesque remarks, among the hunters of the Far West.

It was towards evening that I set out with a companion, to visit the village in question. Unluckily, it had been invaded in the course of the day by some of the rangers, who had shot two or three of its inhabitants, and thrown the whole sensitive community in confusion. As we approached, we could perceive numbers of the inhabitants seated at the entrance of their cells, while sentinels seemed to have been posted on the outskirts, to keep a look-out. At sight of us, the picket guards scampered in and gave the alarm; whereupon every inhabitant gave a short welp, or bark, and dived into his hole, his heels twinkling in the air as if he had thrown a somerset.

We traversed the whole village, or republic, which covered an area of about thirty acres; but not a whisker of an inhabitant was to be seen. We probed their cells as far as the ramrods of our rifles would reach, but could unearth neither dog, nor owl, nor rattlesnake. Moving quietly to a little distance, we lay down upon the ground, and watched for a long time, silent and motionless. By and by, a cautious old burgher would slowly put forth the end of his nose, but instantly draw it in again. Another, at a greater distance, would emerge entirely; but, catching a glance of us, would throw a somerset, and plunge back again into his hole. At length, some who resided on the opposite side of the village, taking courage from the continued stillness, would steal forth, and hurry off to a distant hole, the residence possibly of some family connection, or gossiping friend, about whose safety they were solicitous, or with whom they wished to compare notes about the late occurrences.

Others, still more bold, assembled in little knots, in the streets and public places, as if to discuss the recent outrages offered to the commonwealth, and the atrocious murders of their fellow-burghers.

We rose from the ground and moved forward, to take a nearer view of these public proceedings, when, yelp! yelp! yelp!—there was a shrill alarm passed from mouth to mouth; the meetings suddenly dispersed; feet twinkled in the air in every direction; and in an instant all had vanished into the earth.

The dusk of the evening put an end to our observations, but the train of whimsical comparisons produced in my brain by the moral attributes which I had heard given to these little politic animals, still continued after my return to camp; and late in the night, as I lay awake after all the camp was asleep, and heard in the stillness of the hour, a faint clamor of shrill voices from the distant village, I could not help picturing to myself the inhabitants gathered together in noisy assemblage, and windy debate, to devise plans for the public safety, and to vindicate the invaded nights and insulted dignity of the republic.

CHAPTER XXXIII

A COUNCIL IN THE CAMP—REASONS FOR FACING HOMEWARDS—
HORSES LOST—DEPARTURE WITH A DETACHMENT ON THE HOME-
WARD ROUTE—SWAMP—WILD HORSE—CAMP SCENE BY NIGHT—
THE OWL, HARBINGER OF DAWN

WHILE breakfast was preparing, a council was held as to our future movements. Symptoms of discontent had appeared for a day or two past, among the rangers, most of whom, unaccustomed to the life of the prairies, had become impatient of its privations, as well as the restraints of the camp. The want of bread had been felt severely, and they were wearied with constant travel. In fact, the novelty and excitement of the expedition were at an end. They had hunted the deer, the bear, the elk, the buffalo, and the wild horse, and had no further object of leading interest to look forward to. A general inclination prevailed, therefore, to turn homewards.

Grave reasons disposed the Captain and his officers to adopt this resolution. Our horses were generally much jaded by the fatigues of travelling and hunting, and had fallen away sadly for want of good pasturage, and from being tethered at night, to protect them from Indian depredations. The late rains, too, seemed to have washed away the nourishment from the scanty herbage that remained; and since our encampment during the storm, our horses had lost flesh and strength rapidly. With every possible care, horses, accustomed to grain, and to the regular and plentiful nourishment of the stable and the farm, lose heart and condition in travelling on the prairies. In all expeditions of the kind we were engaged in, the hardy Indian horses, which are generally mustangs, or a cross of the wild breed, are to be preferred. They can stand all fatigues, hardships, and privations, and thrive on the grasses and wild herbage of the plains.

Our men, too, had acted with little forethought; galloping off whenever they had a chance, after the game that we encountered while on the march. In this way they had strained and wearied their horses, instead of husbanding their strength and spirits. On a tour of the kind, horses should as seldom as possible be put off of a quiet walk; and the average day's journey should not exceed ten miles.

We had hoped, by pushing forward, to reach the bottoms of the Red River, which abound with young cane, a most nourishing forage for cattle at this season of the year. It would now take us several days to arrive there, and in the meantime many of our horses would probably give out. It was the time, too, when hunting parties of Indians set fire to the prairies; the herbage, throughout this part of the country, was in that parched state, favorable to combustion, and there was daily more and more risk that the prairies between us and the fort would be set on fire by some of the return parties of Osages, and a scorched desert left for us to traverse. In a word, we had started too late in the season, or loitered too much in the early part of our march, to accomplish our originally-intended tour; and there was imminent hazard, if we continued on, that we should lose the greater part of our horses; and, besides suffering various other inconveniences, be obliged to return on foot. It was determined, therefore, to give up all further progress, and, turning our faces to the southeast, to make the best of our way back to Fort Gibson.

This resolution being taken, there was an immediate eagerness to put it into operation. Several horses, however, were missing, and among others those of the Captain and the Surgeon. Persons had gone in search of them, but the morning advanced without any tidings of them. Our party in the meantime, being all ready for a march, the Commissioner determined to set off in the advance, with his original escort of a lieutenant and fourteen rangers, leaving the Captain to come on at his convenience, with the main body. At ten o'clock, we accordingly started, under the guidance of Beatte, who had hunted over this part of the country, and knew the direct route to the garrison.

For some distance we skirted the prairie, keeping a southeast direction; and in the course of our ride we saw a variety of wild animals, deer, white and black wolves, buffaloes, and wild horses. To the latter, our half-breeds and Tonish gave ineffectual chase, only serving to add to the weariness of their already jaded steeds. Indeed it is rarely that any but the weaker and least fleet of the wild horses are taken in these hard racings; while the horse of the huntsman is prone to be knocked up. The latter, in fact, risks a good horse to catch a bad one. On this occasion, Tonish, who was a perfect imp on horseback, and noted for ruining every animal he bestrode, succeeded in laming and almost disabling the powerful gray on which we had mounted him at the outset of our tour.

After proceeding a few miles, we left the prairie, and struck to the east, taking what Beatte pronounced an old Osage war-track. This led us through a rugged tract of country; overgrown with scrubbed forests and entangled thickets and intersected by deep ravines, and brisk-running streams, the sources of Little River. About three o'clock, we encamped by some pools of water in a small valley, having come about fourteen miles. We had brought on a supply of provisions from our last camp, and supped heartily upon stewed buffalo meat, roasted venison, beignets, or fritters of flour fried in bear's lard, and tea made of a species of the golden-rod, which we had found, throughout our whole route, almost as grateful a beverage as coffee. Indeed our coffee, which, as long as it held out, had been served up with every meal, according to the custom of the West, was by no means a beverage to boast of. It was roasted in a frying-pan, without much care, pounded in a leathern bag, with a round stone, and boiled in our prime and almost only kitchen utensil, the camp kettle, in "branch" or brook water; which, on the prairies, is deeply colored by the soil, of which it always holds abundant particles in a state of solution and suspension. In fact, in the course of our tour, we had tasted the quality of every variety of soil, and the draughts of water we had taken might vie in diversity of color, if not of flavor, with the tinctures of an apothecary's shop. Pure, limpid water is a rare luxury on the prairies, at least at this season of the year. Supper over, we placed sentinels about our scanty and diminished camp, spread our skins and blankets under the trees, now nearly destitute of foliage, and slept soundly until morning.

We had a beautiful daybreak. The camp again resounded with cheerful voices; every one was animated with the thoughts of soon being at the fort, and revelling on bread and vegetables. Even our saturnine man, Beatte, seemed inspired on this occasion; and as he drove up the horses for the march, I heard him singing, in nasal tones, a most forlorn Indian ditty. All this transient gaiety, however, soon died away amidst the fatigues of our march, which lay through the same kind of rough, hilly, thicketed country as that of yesterday. In the course of the morning we arrived at the valley of the Little River, where it wound through a broad bottom of alluvial soil. At present it had overflowed its banks, and inundated a great part of the valley. The difficulty was to distinguish the stream from the broad sheets of water it had formed, and to find a place where it might be forded; for it was in general deep and miry, with abrupt crumbling banks. Under the pilotage of Beatte, therefore, we wandered for some time among the links made by this winding stream, in what appeared to us a trackless labyrinth of swamps, thickets, and standing pools. Sometimes our jaded horses dragged their limbs forward with the utmost difficulty, having to toil for a great distance, with the water up to the stirrups, and beset at the bottom with roots and creeping plants. Sometimes we had to force our way through dense thickets of brambles and grapevines, which almost pulled us out of our saddles. In one place, one of the pack-horses sunk in the mire and fell on his side, so as to be extricated with great difficulty. Wherever the soil was bare, or there was a sand-bank, we beheld innumerable tracks of bears, wolves, wild horses, turkeys, and water-fowl; showing the abundant sport this valley might afford to the huntsman. Our men, however, were sated with hunting, and too weary to be excited by these signs, which in the outset of our tour would have put them in a fever of anticipation. Their only desire at present was to push on doggedly for the fortress.

At length we succeeded in finding a fording place, where we all crossed Little River, with the water and mire to the saddle-girths, and then halted for an hour and a half, to overhaul the wet baggage, and give the horses time to rest.

On resuming our march, we came to a pleasant little meadow, surrounded by groves of elms and cotton-wood trees, in the midst of which was a fine black horse grazing. Beatte, who was in the advance, beckoned us to halt, and, being mounted on a mare, approached the horse gently, step by step, imitating the whinny of the animal with admirable exactness. The noble courser of the prairie gazed for a time, snuffed the air, neighed, pricked up his ears, and pranced round and round the mare in gallant style; but kept at too great a distance for Beatte to throw the lariat. He was a magnificent object, in all the pride and glory of his nature. It was admirable to see the lofty and airy carriage of his head; the freedom of every movement; the elasticity with which he trod the meadow. Finding it impossible to get within noosing distance, and seeing that the horse was receding and growing alarmed, Beatte slid down from his saddle, levelled his rifle across the back of his mare, and took aim, with the evident intention of creasing him. I felt a throb of anxiety for the safety of the noble animal, and called out to Beatte to desist. It was too late; he pulled the trigger as I spoke; luckily he did not shoot with his usual accuracy, and I had the satisfaction to see the coal-black steed dash off unharmed into the forest.

On leaving this valley, we ascended among broken hills and rugged, ragged forests, equally harassing to horse and rider. The ravines, too, were of red clay, and often so steep, that in descending, the horses would put their feet together and fairly slide down, and then scramble up the opposite side like cats. Here and there among the thickets in the valleys, we met with sloes and persimmon, and the eagerness with which our men broke from the line of march, and ran to gather these poor fruits, showed how much they craved some vege-table condiment, after living so long exclusively on animal food.

About half past three we encamped near a brook in a meadow where there was some scanty herbage for our half-famished horses. As Beatte had killed a fat doe in the course of the day, and one of our company a fine turkey, we did not lack for provisions.

It was a splendid autumnal evening. The horizon, after sunset, was of a clear apple green, rising into a delicate lake which gradually lost itself in a deep purple blue. One narrow streak of cloud, of a mahogany color, edged with amber and gold, floated in the west, and just beneath it was the evening star, shining with the pure brilliancy of a diamond. In unison with this scene, there was an evening concert of insects of various kinds, all blended and harmonized into one sober and somewhat melancholy note, which I have always found to have a soothing effect upon the mind, disposing it to quiet musings.

The night that succeeded was calm and beautiful. There was a faint light from the moon, now in its second quarter, and after it had set, a fine starlight, with shooting meteors. The wearied rangers, after a little murmuring conversation round their fires, sank to rest at an early hour, and I seemed to have the whole scene to myself. It is delightful in thus bivouacking on the prairies, to lie awake and gaze at the stars; it is like watching them from the deck of a ship at sea, when at one view we have the whole cope of heaven. One realizes, in such lonely scenes, that companionship with these beautiful luminaries which made astronomers of the eastern shepherds, as they watched their flocks by night. How often, while contemplating their mild and benignant radiance, I have called to mind the exquisite text of Job, "Canst thou bind the secret influences of the Pleiades, or loose the bands of Orion?" I do not know why it was, but I felt this night unusually affected by the solemn magnificence of the firmament; and seemed, as I lay thus under the open vault of heaven, to inhale with the pure untainted air, an exhilarating buoyancy of spirit, and, as it were, an ecstasy of mind. I slept and waked alternately; and when I slept, my dreams partook of the happy tone of my waking reveries. Towards morning, one of the sentinels, the oldest man in the troop, came and took a seat near me: he was weary and sleepy, and impatient to be relieved. I found he had been gazing at the heavens also, but with different feelings.

"If the stars don't deceive me," said he, "it is near daybreak."

"There can be no doubt of that," said Beatte, who lay close by. "I heard an owl just now."

"Does the owl, then, hoot towards daybreak?" asked I.

"Aye, sir, just as the cock crows."

This was a useful habitude of the bird of wisdom, of which I was not aware. Neither the stars nor owl deceived their votaries. In a short time there was a faint streak of light in the east.

CHAPTER XXXIV

T HE country through which we passed this morning
(Nov. 2), was less rugged, and of more agreeable
aspect than that we had lately traversed. At eleven
o'clock, we came out upon an extensive prairie, and
about six miles to our left beheld a long line of green
forest, marking the course of the north fork of the
Arkansas. On the edge of the prairie, and in a spacious
grove of noble trees which overshadowed a small brook,
were the traces of an old Creek hunting camp. On the
bark of the trees were rude delineations of hunters and
squaws, scrawled with charcoal; together with various
signs and heiroglyphics, which our half-breeds interpreted as indicating that from this encampment the
hunters had returned home.

In this beautiful camping ground we made our mid-
day halt. While reposing under the trees, we heard a
shouting at no great distance, and presently the Captain
and the main body of rangers, whom we had left behind
two days since, emerged from the thickets, and crossing
the brook, were joyfully welcomed into the camp. The
Captain and the Doctor had been unsuccessful in the
search after their horses, and were obliged to march for
the greater part of the time on foot; yet they had come
on with more than ordinary speed.

We resumed our march about one o'clock, keeping
easterly, and approaching the north fork obliquely; it
was late before we found a good camping place; the
beds of the streams were dry, the prairies, too, had been
burnt in various places, by Indian hunting parties. At

length we found water in a small alluvial bottom, where there was tolerable pasturage.

On the following morning, there were flashes of lightning in the east, with low, rumbling thunder, and clouds began to gather about the horizon. Beatte prognosticated rain, and that the wind would veer to the north. In the course of our march, a flock of brant were seen overhead, flying from the north. "There comes the wind!" said Beatte; and, in fact, it began to blow from that quarter almost immediately, with occasional flurries of rain. About half past nine o'clock, we forded the north fork of the Canadian, and encamped about one, that our hunters might have time to beat up the neighborhood for game; for a serious scarcity began to prevail in the camp. Most of the rangers were young, heedless, and inexperienced, and could not be prevailed upon, while provisions abounded, to provide for the future, by jerking meat, or carrying away any on their horses. On leaving an encampment, they would leave quantities of meat lying about, trusting to Providence and their rifles for a future supply. The consequence was that any temporary scarcity of game, or ill luck in hunting, produced almost a famine in the camp. In the present instance, they had left loads of buffalo meat at the camp on the great prairie; and, having ever since been on a forced march, leaving no time for hunting, they were now destitute of supplies, and pinched with hunger. Some had not eaten any thing since the morning of the preceding day. Nothing would have persuaded them when revelling in the abundance of the buffalo encampment that they would so soon be in such famishing plight.

The hunters returned with indifferent success. The game had been frightened away from this part of the country, by Indian hunting parties, which had preceded us. Ten or a dozen wild turkeys were brought in, but not a deer had been seen. The rangers began to think turkeys and even prairie hens deserving of attention; game which they had hitherto considered unworthy of their rifles.

The night was cold and windy, with occasional sprinklings of rain; but we had roaring fires to keep us comfortable. In the night, a flight of wild geese passed over the camp, making a great cackling in the air; symptoms of approaching winter.

We set forward at an early hour the next morning, in a northeast course, and came upon the trace of a party of Creek Indians, which enabled our poor horses to travel with more ease. We entered upon a fine champaign country. From a rising ground we had a noble prospect, over extensive prairies, finely diversified by groves and tracts of woodland, and bounded by long lines of distant hills, all clothed with the rich mellow tints of autumn. Game, too, was more plenty. A fine buck sprang up from among the herbage on our right, and dashed off at full speed; but, a young ranger by the name of Childers, who was on foot, levelled his rifle, discharged a ball that broke the neck of the bounding deer, and sent him tumbling head over heels forward. Another buck and a doe, beside several turkeys were killed before we came to a halt, so that the hungry mouths of the troop were once more supplied.

About three o'clock we encamped in a grove after a forced march of twenty-five miles, that had proved a hard trial to the horses. For a long time after the head of the line had encamped, the rest kept straggling in, two and three at a time; one of our pack-horses had given out, about nine miles back and a pony belonging to Beatte, shortly after. Many of the other horses looked so gaunt and feeble, that doubts were entertained of their being able to reach the fort. In the night, there was heavy rain, and the morning dawned cloudy and dismal. The camp resounded, however, with something of its former gaiety. The rangers had supped well, and were renovated in spirits, anticipating a speedy arrival at the garrison. Before we set forward on our march, Beatte returned, and brought his pony to the camp with great difficulty. The pack-horse, however, was completely knocked up and had to be abandoned. The wild mare, too, had cast her foal, through exhaustion, and was not in a state to go forward. She and the pony, therefore, were left at this encampment, where there was water and good pasturage, and where there would be a chance of their reviving, and being afterwards sought out and brought to the garrison.

We set off about eight o'clock, and had a day of weary and harassing travel; part of the time over rough hills, and part over rolling prairies. The rain had rendered the soil slippery and plashy, so as to afford unsteady foothold. Some of the rangers dismounted, their horses having no longer strength to bear them. We made a halt in the course of the morning, but the horses were too tired to graze. Several of them laid down, and there was some difficulty in getting them on their feet again. Our troop presented a forlorn appearance, straggling slowly along, in a broken and scattered line, that extended over hill and dale, for three miles and upwards, in groups of three and four widely apart; some on horseback, some on foot, with a few laggards far in the rear. About four o'clock, we halted for the night in a spacious forest, beside a deep narrow river, called the Little North Fork, or Deep Creek. It was late before the main part of the troop straggled into the encampment, many of the horses having given out. As this stream was too deep to be forded, we waited until the next day to devise means to cross it, but our half-breeds swam the horses of our party to the other side in the evening, as they would have better pasturage, and the stream was evidently swelling. The night was cold and unruly; the wind sounding hoarsely through the forest and whirling about the dry leaves. We made long fires of great trunks of trees, which diffused something of consolation if not cheerfulness around.

The next morning there was general permission given to hunt until twelve o'clock; the camp being destitute of provisions. The rich woody bottom in which we were encamped, abounded with wild turkeys, of which a considerable number were killed. In the meantime, preparations were made for crossing the river, which had risen several feet during the night; and it was determined to fell trees for the purpose, to serve as bridges.

The Captain and Doctor, and one or two other leaders of the camp, versed in woodcraft, examined with learned eye the trees growing on the river bank, until they singled out a couple of the largest size, and most suitable inclinations. The axe was then vigorously applied to their roots, in such a way as to insure their falling directly across the stream. As they did not reach to the opposite bank, it was necessary for some of the men to swim across and fell trees on the other side, to meet them. They at length succeeded in making a precarious footway across the deep and rapid current, by which the baggage could be carried over: but it was necessary to grope our way, step by step, along the trunks and main branches of the trees, which for a part of the distance were completely submerged, so that we were to our waists in water. Most of the horses were then swam across, but some of them were too weak to brave the current, and evidently too much knocked up to bear any further travel. Twelve men, therefore, were left at the encampment to guard these horses, until by repose and good pasturage they should be sufficiently recovered to complete their journey; and the Captain engaged to send the men a supply of flour and other necessaries, as soon as we should arrive at the Fort.

CHAPTER XXXV

A LOOK-OUT FOR LAND—HARD TRAVELLING AND HUNGRY HALT-ING—A FRONTIER FARMHOUSE—ARRIVAL AT THE GARRISON

IT WAS a little after one o'clock when we again resumed our weary wayfaring. The residue of that day and the whole of the next were spent in toilsome travel. Part of the way was over stony hills, part across wide prairies, rendered spongy and miry by the recent rain, and cut up by brooks swollen into torrents. Our poor horses were so feeble that it was with difficulty we could get them across the deep ravines and turbulent streams. In traversing the miry plains, they slipped and staggered at every step, and most of us were obliged to dismount and walk for the greater part of the way. Hunger prevailed throughout the troop; every one began to look anxious and haggard, and to feel the growing length of each additional mile. At one time, in crossing a hill, Beatte climbed a high tree, commanding a wide prospect, and took a look-out, like a mariner from the mast-head at sea. He came down with cheering tidings. To the left he had beheld a line of forest stretching across the country, which he knew to be the woody border of the Arkansas; and at a distance he had recognized certain landmarks, from which he concluded that we could not be above forty miles distant from the fort. It was like the welcome cry of land to tempest-tossed mariners.

In fact we soon after saw smoke rising from a woody glen at a distance. It was supposed to be made by a hunting-party of Creek or Osage Indians from the neighborhood of the fort, and was joyfully hailed as a harbinger of man. It was now confidently hoped that we would soon arrive among the frontier hamlets of Creek Indians, which are scattered along the skirts of the un-inhabited wilderness; and our hungry rangers trudged forward with reviving spirit, regaling themselves with savory anticipations of farmhouse luxuries, and enumerating every article of good cheer, until their mouths fairly watered at the shadowy feasts thus con-jured up.

A hungry night, however, closed in upon a toilsome day. We encamped on the border of one of the tributary streams of the Arkansas, amidst the ruins of a stately grove that had been riven by a hurricane. The blast had torn its way through the forest in a narrow column, and its course was marked by enormous trees shivered and splintered, and upturned, with their roots in the air: all lay in one direction, like so many brittle reeds broken and trodden down by the hunter.

Here was fuel in abundance, without the labor of the axe: we had soon immense fires blazing and sparkling in the frosty air, and lighting up the whole forest; but, alas! we had no meat to cook at them. The scarcity in the camp almost amounted to famine. Happy was he who had a morsel of jerked meat, or even the half-picked bones of a former repast. For our part, we were more lucky at our mess than our neighbors; one of our men having shot a turkey. We had no bread to eat with it, nor salt to season it withal. It was simply boiled in water; the

latter was served up as soup, and we were fain to rub
each morsel of the turkey on the empty salt-bag, in
hopes some saline particle might remain to relieve its
insipidity.

The night was biting cold; the brilliant moonlight
sparkled on the frosty crystals which covered every
object around us. The water froze beside the skins on
which we bivouacked, and in the morning I found the
blanket in which I was wrapped covered with a hoar
frost; yet I had never slept more comfortably.

After a shadow of a breakfast, consisting of turkey
bones and a cup of coffee without sugar, we decamped
at an early hour; for hunger is a sharp quickener on a
journey. The prairies were all gemmed with frost, that
covered the tall weeds and glistened in the sun. We saw
great flights of prairie hens, or grouse, that hovered
from tree to tree, or sat in rows along the naked
branches, waiting until the sun should melt the frost
from the weeds and herbage. Our rangers no longer
despised such humble game, but turned from the ranks
in pursuit of a prairie hen as eagerly as they formerly
would go in pursuit of a deer.

Every one now pushed forward, anxious to arrive at
some human habitation before night. The poor horses
were urged beyond their strength, in the thought of
soon being able to indemnify them for present toil, by
rest and ample provender. Still the distsances seemed to
stretch out more than ever, and the blue hills, pointed
out as landmarks on the horizon, to recede as we
advanced. Every step became a labor; every now and
then a miserable horse would give out and lie down. His
owner would raise him by main strength, force him
forward to the margin of some stream, where there
might be a scanty border of herbage, and then abandon
him to his fate. Among those that were thus left on the

way was one of the led horses of the Count; a prime hunter, that had taken the lead of every thing in the chase of the wild horses. It was intended, however, as soon as we should arrive at the fort, to send out a party provided with corn, to bring in such of the horses as should survive.

In the course of the morning, we came upon Indian tracks, crossing each other in various directions, a proof that we must be in the neighborhood of human habitations. At length, on passing through a skirt of wood, we beheld two or three log houses, sheltered under lofty trees on the border of a prairie, the habitations of Creek Indians, who had small farms adjacent. Had they been sumptuous villas, abounding with the luxuries of civilization, they could not have been hailed with greater delight.

Some of the rangers rode up to them in quest of food: the greater part, however, pushed forward in search of the habitation of a white settler, which we were told was at no great distance. The troop soon disappeared among the trees, and I followed slowly in their track; for my once fleet and generous steed faltered under me, and was just able to drag one foot after the other, yet I was too weary and exhausted to spare him.

In this way we crept on, until, on turning a thick clump of trees, a frontier farmhouse suddenly presented itself to view. It was a low tenement of logs, overshadowed by great forest trees, but it seemed as if a very region of Cocaigne prevailed around it. Here was a stable and barn, and granaries teeming with abundance, while legions of grunting swine, gobbling turkeys, cackling hens and strutting roosters, swarmed about the farmyard.

My poor jaded and half-famished horse raised his head and pricked up his ears at the well-known sights

and sounds. He gave a chuckling inward sound, something like a dry laugh; whisked his tail, and made great
leeway toward a corn-crib, filled with golden ears of
maize, and it was with some difficulty that I could
control his course, and steer him up to the door of the
cabin. A single glance within was sufficient to raise every
gastronomic faculty. There sat the Captain of the
rangers and his officers, round a three-legged table,
crowned by a broad and smoking dish of boiled beef and
turnips. I sprang off my horse in an instant, cast him
loose to make his way to the corn-crib, and entered this
palace of plenty. A fat good-humored negress received
me at the door. She was the mistress of the house, the
spouse of the white man, who was absent. I hailed her as
some swart fairy of the wild, that had suddenly conjured
up a banquet in the desert; and a banquet was it in good
sooth. In a twinkling, she lugged from the fire a huge
iron pot, that might have rivalled one of the famous
flesh-pots of Egypt, or the witches' caldron in *Macbeth*.
Placing a brown earthen dish on the floor, she inclined
the corpulent caldron on one side, and out leaped
sundry great morsels of beef, with a regiment of turnips
tumbling after them, and a rich cascade of broth
overflowing the whole. This she handed me with an
ivory smile that extended from ear to ear; apologizing
for our humble fare, and the humble style in which it
was served up. Humble fare! humble style! Boiled beef
and turnips, and an earthen dish to eat them from! To
think of apologizing for such magnificent slices of bread
and butter! Head of Apicius, what a banquet!

"The rage of hunger" being appeased, I began to
think of my horse. He, however like an old campaigner,
had taken good care of himself. I found him paying
assiduous attention to the crib of Indian corn, and
dexterously drawing forth and munching the ears that

protruded between the bars. It was with great regret that I interrupted his repast, which he abandoned with a heavy sigh, or rather a rumbling groan. I was anxious, however, to rejoin my travelling companions, who had passed by the farmhouse without stopping, and proceeded to the banks of the Arkansas; being in hopes of arriving before night at the Osage Agency. Leaving the Captain and his troop, therefore, amidst the abundance of the farm, where they had determined to quarter themselves for the night, I bade adieu to our sable hostess, and again pushed forward.

A ride of about a mile brought me to where my comrades were waiting on the banks of the Arkansas, which here poured along between beautiful forests. A number of Creek Indians, in their brightly colored dresses, looking like so many gay tropical birds, were busy aiding our men to transport the baggage across the river in a canoe. While this was doing, our horses had another regale from two great cribs heaped up with ears of Indian corn, which stood near the edge of the river. We had to keep a check upon the poor half-famished animals, lest they should injure themselves by their voracity.

The baggage being all carried to the opposite bank, we embarked in the canoe, and swam our horses across the river. I was fearful, lest in their enfeebled state, they should not be able to stem the current; but their banquet of Indian corn had already infused fresh life and spirit into them, and it would appear as if they were cheered by the instinctive consciousness of their approach to home, where they would soon be at rest, and in plentiful quarters; for no sooner had we landed and resumed our route, then they set off on a hand-gallop, and continued so for a great part of seven miles, that we had to ride through the woods.

It was an early hour in the evening when we arrived at the Agency, on the banks of the Verdigris River, whence we had set off about a month before. Here we passed the night comfortably quartered; yet, after having been accustomed to sleep in the open air, the confinement of a chamber was, in some respects, irksome. The atmosphere seemed close, and destitute of freshness; and when I woke in the night and gazed about me upon complete darkness, I missed the glorious companionship of the stars.

The next morning after breakfast, I again set forward in company with the worthy Commissioner, for Fort Gibson, where we arrived much tattered, travel-stained and weather-beaten, but in high health and spirits—and thus ended my foray into the Pawnee Hunting Grounds.

Salmagundi;
or, the Whim-Whams
and Opinions of
Launcelot Langstaff, Esq.,
and Others
(1807–1808)

NO. I—SATURDAY,
JANUARY 24, 1807

As everybody knows, or ought to know, what a SALMAGUND is, we shall spare ourselves the trouble of an explanation; besides, we despise trouble as we do everything low and mean, and hold the man who would incur it unnecessarily as an object worthy our highest pity and contempt. Neither will we puzzle our heads to give an account of ourselves, for two reasons; first, because it is nobody's business; secondly, because if it were, we do not hold ourselves bound to attend to anybody's business but our own; and even *that* we take the liberty of neglecting when it suits our inclination. To these we might add a third, that very few men *can* give a tolerable account of themselves, let them try ever so hard; but this reason, we candidly avow, would not hold good with ourselves.

There are, however, two or three pieces of information which we bestow gratis on the public, chiefly because it suits our own pleasure and convenience that they should be known, and partly because we do not wish that there should be any ill will between us at the commencement of our acquaintance.

Our intention is simply to instruct the young, reform the old, correct the town, and castigate the age; this is an arduous task, and therefore we undertake it with confidence. We intend for this purpose to present a striking picture of the town; and as everybody is anxious to see his own phiz on canvas, however stupid or ugly it may be, we have no doubt but the whole town will flock to our exhibition. Our picture will necessarily include a vast variety of figures; and should any gentleman or lady be displeased with the inveterate truth of their likenesses, they may ease their spleen by laughing at those of their neighbors—this being what *we* understand by *poetical justice*.

Like all true and able editors, we consider ourselves infallible; and therefore, with the customary diffidence of our brethren of the quill, we shall take the liberty of interfering in all matters either of a public or private nature. We are critics, amateurs, dilettanti and cognoscenti; and as we know "by the pricking of our thumbs," that every opinion which we may advance in either of those characters will be correct, we are determined, though it may be questioned, contradicted, or even controverted, yet it shall never be revoked.

We beg the public particularly to understand that we solicit no patronage. We are determined, on the contrary, that the patronage shall be entirely on our side. We have nothing to do with the pecuniary concerns of the paper; its success will yield us neither pride nor profit—nor will its failure occasion to us either loss or mortification. We advise the public, therefore, to purchase our numbers merely for their own sakes; if they do not, let them settle the affair with their consciences and posterity.

To conclude, we invite all editors of newspaper and literary journals to praise us heartily in advance, as we assure them that we intend to deserve their praises. To our next-door neighbor, "Town," we hold out a hand of amity, declaring to him that, after ours, his paper will stand the best chance for immortality. We proffer an exchange of civilities: he shall furnish us with notices of epic poems and tobacco; and we, in return, will enrich him with original speculations on all manner of subjects, together with "the rummaging of my grandfather's mahogany chest of drawers," "the life and amours of mine Uncle John," "anecdotes of the Cockloft family," and learned quotations from that unheard of writer of folios, Linkum Fidelius.

PUBLISHER'S NOTICE

SHAKESPEARE GALLERY, NEW YORK

T HIS WORK will be published and sold by D. Longworth. It will be printed on hot-pressed vellum paper, as that is held in highest estimation for buckling up young ladies' hair—a purpose to which similar works are usually appropriated; it will be a small, neat, duodecimo size, so that when enough numbers are written, it may form a volume sufficiently portable to be carried in old ladies' pockets and young ladies' workbags.

As the above work will not come out at stated periods, notice will be given when another number will be published. The price will depend on the size of the number, and must be paid on delivery. The publisher professes the same sublime contempt for money as his authors. The liberal patronage bestowed by his discerning fellow-citizens on various works of taste which he has published, has left him no *inclination* to ask for further favors at their hands, and he publishes this work in the mere hope of requiting their bounty.*

*It was not originally the intention of the authors to insert the above address in the work; but, unwilling that a *morceau* so precious should be lost to posterity, they have been induced to alter their minds. This will account for any repetition of idea that may appear in the introductory essay.

FROM THE ELBOW-CHAIR
OF LAUNCELOT
LANGSTAFF, ESQ.

W E WERE a considerable time in deciding whether we should be at the pains of introducing ourselves to the public. As we care for nobody, and as we are not yet at the bar, we do not feel bound to hold up our hands and answer to our names.

Willing, however, to gain at once that frank, confidential footing, which we are certain of ultimately possessing in this, doubtless, "best of all possible cities;" and anxious to spare its worthy inhabitants the trouble of making a thousand *wise* conjectures, not one of which would be worth a tobacco-stopper, we have thought it in some degree a necessary exertion of charitable condescension to furnish them with a slight clue to the truth.

Before we proceed further, however, we advise everybody, man, woman, and child, that can read, or get any friend to read for them, to purchase this paper—not that we write for money, for, in common with all philosophical wiseacres, from Solomon downward, we hold it in supreme contempt. The public are welcome to buy this work, or not, just as they choose. If it be purchased freely, so much the better for the public—and the publisher—we gain not a stiver. If it be not purchased we give fair warning—we shall burn all our essays, critiques, and epigrams, in one promiscuous blaze; and, like the books of the sibyls and the Alexandrian library, they will be lost forever to posterity. For the sake, therefore, of our publisher, for the sake of the public, and for the sake of the public's children to the nineteenth generation, we advise them to purchase our paper. We beg the respectable old matrons of this city not to be alarmed at the appearance we make; we are none of those outlandish geniuses who swarm in New York, who live by their wits, or rather by the little wit of their neighbors, and who spoil the genuine honest American tastes of their daughters with French slops and fricasseed sentiment.

We have said we do not write for money—neither do we write for fame; we know too well the variable nature of public opinion, to build our hopes upon it—we *care* not what the public think of us, and we suspect, before we reach the tenth number, they will not *know* what to think of us. In two words, we write for no other earthly purpose but to please ourselves—and this we shall be sure of doing, for we are all three of us determined beforehand to be pleased with what we write. If, in the course of this work, we edify, and instruct, and amuse the public, so much the better for the public; but we frankly acknowledge that so soon as we get tired of reading our own works, we shall discontinue them without the least remorse, whatever the public may think of it. While we continue to go on, we will go on merrily: if we moralize, it shall be but seldom; and, on all occasions, we shall be more solicitous to make our readers laugh than cry; for we are laughing philosophers, and clearly of opinion that wisdom, true wisdom, is a plump, jolly dame, who sits in her arm-chair, laughs right merrily at the farce of life—and takes the world as it goes.

We intend particularly to notice the conduct of the fashionable world; nor in this shall we be governed by that carping spirit with which narrow-minded bookworm cynics squint at the little extravagances of the ton; but with that liberal toleration which actuates every man of fashion. While we keep more than a Cerberus watch over the guardian rules of female delicacy and decorum, we shall not discourage any little sprightliness of demeanor, or innocent vivacity of character. Before we advance one line further, we must let it be understood, as our firm opinion, void of all prejudice or partiality, that the ladies of New York are the fairest, the finest, the most accomplished, the most bewitching, the most ineffable beings that walk, creep, crawl, swim, fly, float, or vegetate in any or all of the four elements; and that they only want to be cured of certain whims, eccentricities, and unseemly conceits, by our superintending cares, to render them absolutely perfect. They will, therefore, receive a large portion of those attentions directed to the fashionable world; nor will the gentlemen who *doze* away their time in the circles of the *haut-ton*, escape our currying. We mean those stupid fellows who sit stock-still upon their chairs, without saying a word, and then complain how —— stupid it was at Mrs. —— party.

This department will be under the peculiar direction and control of ANTHONY EVERGREEN, gent., to whom all communications on this subject are to be addressed. This gentleman, from his long experience in the routine of balls, tea-parties, and assemblies, is eminently qualified for the task he has undertaken. He is a kind of patriarch in the fashionable world; and has seen generation after generation pass away into the silent tomb of matrimony while he remains unchangeably the same. He can recount the amours and courtships of the fathers, mothers, uncles and aunts, and even the grandames, of all the belles of the present day—provided their pedigrees extend so far back without being lost in obscurity. As, however, treating of pedigrees is rather an ungrateful task in this city, and as we mean to be perfectly good-natured, he has promised to be cautious in this particular. He recollects perfectly the time when young ladies used to go sleigh-riding, at night, without their mammas or grandmammas; in short without being matronized at all: and can relate a thousand pleasant stories about Kissing-bridge. He likewise remembers the time when ladies paid tea-visits, at three in the afternoon, and returned before dark to see that the house was shut up and the servants on duty. He has often played cricket in the orchard in the rear of old Vauxhall, and remembers when the Bull's Head was quite out of town. Though he was slowly and gradually given into modern fashions, and still flourishes in the *beau-monde*, yet he seems a little prejudiced in favor of the dress and manners of the *old school;* and his chief commendation of a new mode is, "that it is the same good old fashion we had before the war." It has cost us much trouble to make him confess that a cotillon is superior to a minuet, or an unadorned crop to a pig-tail and powder. Custom and fashion have, however, had more effect on him than all our lectures; and he tempers, so happily, the grave and ceremonious gallantry of the old school with the "hail-fellow" familiarity of the new, that, we trust, on a little acquaintance, and making allowance for his old-fashioned prejudices, he will become a very considerable favorite with our readers—if not, the worse for themselves—as they will have to endure his company.

In the territory of criticism, WILLIAM WIZARD, Esq., has undertaken to preside; and though we may all dabble in it a little by turns, yet we have willingly ceded to him all discretionary powers in this respect. Though Will has not had the advantage of an education at Oxford or Cambridge, or even at Edinburgh or Aberdeen, and though he is but little versed in Hebrew, yet we have no doubt he will be found fully competent to the undertaking. He has improved his taste by a long residence abroad, particularly at Canton, Calcutta, and the gay and polished court of Haiti. He has also had an opportunity of seeing the best singing-girls and trage-dians of China, is a great connoisseur in mandarine dresses, and porcelain, and particularly values himself on his intimate knowledge of the buffalo, and war-dances of the northern Indians. He is likewise promised the assistance of a gentleman, lately from London, who was born and bred in that centre of science and *bon goût*, the vicinity of Fleet Market, where he has been edified, man and boy, these six-and-twenty years, with the harmonious jingle of Bow-bells. His taste, therefore, has attained to such an exquisite pitch of refinement that there are few exhibitions of any kind which do not put him in a fever. He has assured Will, that if Mr. Cooper emphasizes "*and*" instead of "*but*," or Mrs. Oldmixon pins her kerchief a hair's breadth awry—or Mrs. Darley offers to dare to look less than the "daughter of a senator of Venice"— the standard of a senator's daugh-ter being exactly six feet—they shall all hear of it in good time. We have, however, advised Will Wizard to keep his friend in check, lest, by opening the eyes of the public to the wretchedness of the actors by whom they have hitherto been entertained, he might cut off one source of amusement from out fellow-citizens. We hereby give notice, that we have taken the whole corps, from the manager in his mantle of gorgeous copperlace to honest *John* in his green coat and black breeches, under our wing—and woe be unto him who injures a hair of their heads. As we have no design against the patience of our fellow citizens, we shall not dose them with copious draughts of theatrical criticism; we well know that they have already been well physicked with them of late; our theatrics shall take up but a small part of our paper; nor shall they be altogether confined to the stage, but extend from time to time to those incorrigible offenders against the peace of society, the stage-critics, who not unfrequently create the fault they find, in order to yield an opening for their witticisms—censure an actor for a gesture he never made, or an emphasis he never gave; and, in their attempt to show off *new readings*, make the sweet swan of Avon cackle like a goose. If any one should feel himself offended by our remarks, let him attack us in return—we shall not wince from the combat. If his passes be successful, we will be the first to cry out, a hit! a hit! and we doubt not we shall frequently lay ourselves open to the weapons of our assailants. But let them have a care how they run a tilting with us; they have to deal with stubborn foes, who can bear a world of pummelling; we will be relentless in our vengeance, and will fight "till from our bones the flesh be hack't."

What other subjects we shall include in the range of our observations, we have not determined, or rather we shall not trouble ourselves to detail. The public have already more information concerning us, than we intended to impart. We owe them no favors, neither do we ask any. We again advise them, for their own sakes, to read our papers when they come out. We recommend to all mothers to purchase them for their daughters, who will be taught the true line of propriety, and the most advisable method of managing their beaux. We advise all daughters to purchase them for the sake of their mothers, who shall be initiated into the arcana of the bon-ton, and cured of all those rusty old notions which they acquired during the last century: parents shall be taught how to govern their children, girls how to get husbands, and old maids how to do without them.

As we do not measure our wits by the yard or the bushel, and as they do not flow periodically nor constantly, we shall not restrict out paper as to size or the time of its appearance. It will be published whenever we have sufficient matter to constitute a number, and the size of the number shall depend on the stock in hand. This will best suit our negligent habits, and leave us that full liberty and independence which is the joy and pride of our souls. As we have before hinted, that we do not concern ourselves about the pecuniary matters of our paper, we leave its price to be regulated by our publisher: only recommending him, for his own interest, and the honor of its authors, not to sell their invaluable productions too cheap.

Is there any one who wishes to know more about us?—let him read SALMAGUNDI, and grow wise apace. Thus much we will say—there are three of us, "Bardolph, Peto, and I," all townsmen good and true—many a time and oft have we three amused the town without its knowing to whom it was indebted; and many a time have we seen the midnight lamp twinkle faintly on our studious phizes, and heard the morning salutation of "past three o'clock," before we sought our pillows. The result of these midnight studies is now offered to the public; and little as we care for the opinion of this exceedingly stupid world, we shall take care, as far as lies in our careless natures, to fulfill the promises made in this introduction; if we do not, we shall have so many examples to justify us, that we feel little solicitude on that account.

THEATRICS—CONTAINING THE QUINTESSENCE OF MODERN CRITICISM

BY WILLIAM WIZARD, ESQ.

*M*ACBETH was performed to a very crowded house, and much to our satisfaction. As, however, our neighbor TOWN has been very voluminous already in his criticisms on this play, we shall make but few remarks. Having never seen KEMBLE in this character, we are absolutely at a loss to say whether Mr. COOPER performed it well or not. We think, however, there was an error in his *costume*, as the learned Linkum Fidelius is of opinion, that in the time of Macbeth the Scots did not wear sandals, but wooden shoes. Macbeth also was noted for wearing his jacket open, that he might play the Scotch fiddle more conveniently—that being a hereditary accomplishment in the Glamis family.

We have seen this character performed in China, by the celebrated Chow-Chow, the Roscius of that great empire, who in the dagger scene always electrified the audience by blowing his nose like a trumpet. Chow-Chow, in compliance with the opinion of the sage Linkum Fidelius, performed *Macbeth* in wooden shoes; this gave him an opportunity of producing great effect, for on first seeing the "air-drawn dagger," he always cut a prodigious high caper, and kicked his shoes into the pit at the heads of the critics; whereupon the audience were marvellously delighted, flourished their hands, and stroked their whiskers three times, and the matter was carefully recorded in the next number of a paper called the *flim-flam*.

We were much pleased with Mrs. VILLIERS as Lady

MACBETH; but we think she would have given a greater effect to the night scene, if, instead of holding the candle in her hand, or setting it down on the table, which is sagaciously censured by neighbor Town, she had stuck it in her night-cap. This would have been extremely picturesque, and would have marked more strongly the derangement of her mind.

Mrs. Villiers, however, is not by any means large enough for the character: Lady Macbeth having been, in our opinion, a woman of extraordinary size, and of the race of the giants, not withstanding what she says of her "little hand—" which being said in her sleep passes for nothing. We should be happy to see this character in the hands of the lady who played Glumdalca, queen of the giants, in Tom Thumb; she is exactly of imperial dimensions; and, provided she is well shaved, of a most interesting physiognomy: as she appears likewise to be a lady of some nerve, I dare engage she will read a letter about witches vanishing in air, and such *common occurrences*, without being unnaturally surprised, to the annoyance of honest "Town."

We are happy to observe that Mr. Cooper profits by the instructions of friend Town, and does not dip the daggers in blood so deep as formerly by a matter of an inch or two. This was a violent outrage upon our `immortal bard. We differ with Mr. Town in his *reading* of the words "this is a *sorry sight*." We are of opinion the force of the sentence should be thrown on the word *sight*, because Macbeth having been, shortly before, most confoundedly humbugged with an aërial dagger, was in doubt whether the daggers actually in his hands were real, or whether they were not mere shadows, or as the old English *may* have termed it, *syghtes*; (this, at any rate, will establish our skill in *new readings*.) Though we differ in this respect from our neighbor Town, yet we heartily agree with him in censuring Mr. Cooper for omitting that passage so remarkable for "beauty of imagery," etc., beginning with "and pity like a naked new-born babe," etc. It is one of those passages of Shakespeare which should always be retained, for the purpose of showing how sometimes that great poet could talk like a buzzard; or, to speak more plainly, like the famous mad poet, Nat Lee.

As it is the first duty of a friend to advise—and as we profess and do actually feel a friendship for honest "Town," we warn him never, in his criticisms, to meddle with a lady's "petticoats," or to quote Nic Bottom. In the first instance he may "catch a tartar;" and in the second, the ass's head may rise up in judgment against him; and when it is once afloat there is no knowing where some unlucky hand may place it. We would not, for all the money in our pockets, see Town flourishing his critical quill under the auspices of an ass's head, like the great Franklin in his *Montero Cap*.

NEW YORK ASSEMBLY

BY ANTHONY EVERGREEN, GENT.

THE assemblies this year have gained a great accession of beauty. Several brilliant stars have risen from the East and from the North, to brighten the firmament of fashion; among the number I have discovered *another planet*, which rivals even Venus in lustre, and I claim equal honor with Herschel for my discovery. I shall take some future opportunity to describe this planet, and the numerous satellites which revolve around it.

At the last assembly the company began to make some show about eight, but the most fashionable delayed their appearance until about nine—nine being the number of the muses, and therefore, the best possible hour for beginning to exhibit the graces. (This is meant for a pretty play upon words, and I assure my readers that I think it very tolerable.)

Poor WILL HONEYCOMB, whose memory I hold in special consideration, even with his half century of experience, would have been puzzled to point out the humors of a lady by her prevailing colors; for the "rival queens" of fashion, Mrs. TOOLE and Madame BOUCHARD, appeared to have exhausted their wonderful inventions in the different disposition, variation, and combination of tints and shades. The philosopher who maintained that black was white, and that, of course, there was no such color as white, might have given some color to his theory on this occasion, by the absence of poor forsaken white muslin. I was, however, much pleased to see that red maintains its ground against all other colors, because red is the color of Mr. Jefferson's * * * *, Tom Paine's nose, and my slippers.*

*In this instance, as well as on several other occasions, a little innocent pleasantry is indulged at Mr. Jefferson's expense. The allusion made here is to the red velvet small clothes with which the President, in defiance of good taste, used to attire himself on levee days and other public occasions.

In one of his splenetic moods in Virginia, John Randolph once vented his complaint of Jefferson, with an allusion to the old scandal. "I cannot live," said he, "in this miserable undone country, where, as the Turks follow their sacred standard, which is a pair of Mahomet's green breeches, we are governed by the old red breeches of that prince of projectors, St. Thomas of Cantingbury; and surely, Becket himself never had more pilgrims at his shrine, than the saint of Monticello."

As for the proboscis of Paine, "I shall secure him to a nicety," said Jarvis, when he was about to take the bust of Paine, now in the New York Historical Society, "if I can get plaster enough for his carbuncled nose." Dr. Francis, who relates the anecdote in one of the interesting

Let the grumbling smellfungi of this world, who cultivate taste among books, cobwebs, and spiders, rail at the extravagance of the age; for my part, I was delighted with the magic of the scene, and as the ladies tripped through the mazes of the dance, sparkling and glowing and dazzling, I, like the honest Chinese, thanked them heartily for the jewels and finery with which they loaded themselves, merely for the entertainment of bystanders, and blessed my stars that I was a bachelor.

The gentlemen were considerably numerous, and being, as usual, equipped in their appropriate black uniforms, constituted a sable regiment, which contributed not a little to the brilliant gaiety of the ballroom. I must confess I am indebted for this remark to our friend the cockney, Mr. 'SBIDLIKENSFLASH, or 'Sbidlikens, as he is called for shortness. He is a fellow of infinite verbosity—stands in high favor—with himself—and, like Caleb Quotem, is "up to everything." I remember when a comfortable, plump-looking citizen led into the room a fair damsel, who looked for all the world like the personification of a rainbow; 'Sbidlikens observed that it reminded him of a fable, which he had read somewhere, of the marriage of an honest painstaking snail, who had once walked six feet in an hour for a wager, to a butterfly whom he used to gallant by the elbow, with the aid of much puffing and exertion. On being called upon to tell where he had come across the story, 'Sbidlikens absolutely refused to answer.

It would but be repeating an old story to say, that the ladies of New York dance well—and well may they,

historical sketches which he has given to the public, also furnishes a couplet sung by the boys in the streets.

"Tom Paine is come from far, from far;
His nose is like a blazing star!"

since they learn it scientifically, and begin their lessons before they have quit their swaddling clothes. The immortal DUPORT has usurped despotic sway over all the female heads and heels in this city;—horn-books, primers, and pianos are neglected, to attend to his positions; and poor CHILTON, with his pots, and kettles, and chemical crockery, finds him a more potent enemy than the whole collective force of the "North River Society."* 'Sbidlikens insists that this dancing mania will inevitably continue as long as a dancing-master will charge the fashionable price of five-and-twenty dollars a quarter, and all other accomplishments are so vulgar as to be attainable at "half the money;" but I put no faith in 'Sbidlikens' candor in this particular. Among his infinitude of endowments, he is but a poor proficient in dancing; and though he often flounders through a cotillon, yet he never cut a pigeonwing in his life.

In my mind there's no position more positive and unexceptionable than that most Frenchmen, dead or alive, are born dancers. I came pounce upon this discovery at the assembly, and I immediately noted it down in my register of indisputable facts; the public shall know all about it. As I never dance cotillons, holding them to be monstrous distorters of the human frame, and tantamount in their operations to being broken and dislocated on the wheel, I generally take occasion, while they are going on, to make my remarks on the company. In the course of these observations I was struck with the energy and eloquence of sundry limbs, which seemed to be flourishing about without appertaining to anybody. After much investigation and difficulty I, at length, traced them to their respective

*An imaginary association, the object of which was to set the North River (the Hudson) on fire. A number of young men of some fashion, little talent, and great pretension, were ridiculed as members.

owners, whom I found to be all Frenchmen to a man. Art may have meddled somewhat in these affairs, but nature certainly did more. I have since been considerably employed in calculations on this subject; and by the most accurate computation I have determined, that a Frenchman passes at least three-fifths of his time between the heavens and the earth, and partakes eminently of the nature of a gossamer or soap-bubble. One of these jack-o'-lantern heroes, in taking a figure, which neither Euclid nor Pythagoras himself could demonstrate, unfortunately wound himself—I mean his feet—his better part—into a lady's cobweb muslin robe; but perceiving it at the instant, he set himself a spinning the other way, like a top, unravelled his step, without omitting one angle or curve, and extricated himself without breaking a thread of the lady's dress! He then sprung up, like a sturgeon, crossed his feet four times, and finished this wonderful evolution by quivering his left leg, as a cat does her paw when she has accidentally dipped it in water. No man, "of woman born," who was not a Frenchman, or a mountebank, could have done the like.

Among the new faces, I remarked a blooming nymph, who has brought a fresh supply of roses from the country to adorn the wreath of beauty, where lilies too much predominate. As I wish well to every sweet face under heaven, I sincerely hope her roses may survive the frosts and dissipations of winter, and lose nothing by a comparison with the loveliest offerings of the spring. 'Sbidlikens, to whom I made similar remarks, assured me that they were very just, and very prettily expressed; and that the lady in question was a prodigious fine piece of flesh and blood. Now, could I find it in my heart to baste these cockneys like their own roast beef—they can make no distinction between a fine woman and a fine horse.

I would praise the sylph-like grace with which another young lady acquitted herself in the dance, but that she excels in far more valuable accomplishments. Who praises the rose for its beauty, even though it is beautiful?

The company retired at the customary hour to the supper-room, where the tables were laid out with their usual splendor and profusion. My friend, 'Sbidlikens, with the native forethought of a cockney, had carefully stowed his pocket with cheese and crackers, that he might not be tempted again to venture his limbs in the crowd of hungry fair ones who throng the supper-room door: his precaution was unnecessary, for the company entered the room with surprising order and decorum. No gowns were torn—no ladies fainted—no noses bled—nor was there any need of the interference of either managers or peace officers.

Diedrich
Knickerbocker's
A History of New York
(1809)

ACCOUNT OF THE
AUTHOR

I T WAS some time, if I recollect right, in the early part of the autumn of 1808, that a stranger applied for lodgings at the Independent Columbian Hotel in Mulberry street, of which I am landlord. He was a small, brisk-looking old gentleman, dressed in a rusty black coat, a pair of olive velvet breeches, and a small cocked hat. He had a few gray hairs plaited and clubbed behind, and his beard seemed to be of some eight-and-forty hours' growth. The only piece of finery which he bore about him was a bright pair of square silver shoebuckles, and all his baggage was contained in a pair of saddle-bags, which he carried under his arm. His whole appearance was something out of the common run; and my wife, who is a very shrewd body, at once set him down for some eminent country schoolteacher.

As the Independent Columbian Hotel is a very small house, I was a little puzzled at first where to put him; but my wife, who seemed taken with his looks, would needs put him in her best chamber, which is genteelly set off with the profiles of the whole family, done in black, by those two great painters, Jarvis and Wood; and commands a very pleasant view of the new grounds on the Collect, together with the rear of the Poor House and Bridewell, and a full front of the Hospital; so that it is the cheerfullest room in the whole house.

During the whole time that he stayed with us, we found him a very worthy good sort of an old gentleman, though a little queer in his ways. He would keep in his room for days together, and if any of the children cried, or made a noise about his door, he would bounce out in a great passion, with his hands full of papers, and say something about "deranging his ideas;" which made my wife believe sometimes that he was not altogether *compos*. Indeed, there was more than one reason to make her think so, for his room was always covered with scraps of paper and old mouldy books, laying about at sixes and sevens, which he would never let anybody touch; for he said he had laid them all away in their proper places, so that he might know where to find them; though for that matter, he was half his time worrying about the house in search of some book or writing which he had carefully put out of the way. I shall never forget what a pother he once made, because my wife cleaned out his room when his back was turned, and put every thing to rights; for he swore he would never be able to get his papers in order again in a twelve-month. Upon this my wife ventured to ask him what he did with so many books and papers; and he told her, that he was "seeking for immortality;" which made her think more than ever, that the poor old gentleman's head was a little cracked.

He was a very inquisitive body, and when not in his room was continually poking about town, hearing all the news, and prying into every thing that was going on: this was particularly the case about election time, when he did nothing but bustle about from poll to poll, attending all ward meetings, and committee rooms; though I could never find that he took part with either side of the question. On the contrary, he would come home and rail at both parties with great wrath—and plainly proved one day, to the satisfaction of my wife and three old ladies who were drinking tea with her, that the two parties were like two rogues, each tugging at a skirt of the nation; and that in the end they would tear the very coat off its back, and expose its nakedness. Indeed he was an oracle among the neighbors, who would collect around him to hear him talk of an afternoon, as he smoked his pipe on the bench before the door; and I really believe he would have brought over the whole neighborhood to his own side of the question, if they could ever have found out what it was.

He was very much given to argue, or, as he called it, *philosophize,* about the most trifling matter; and to do him justice, I never knew anybody that was a match for him, except it was a grave-looking old gentleman who called now and then to see him, and often posed him in an argument. But this is nothing surprising, as I have since found out this stranger is the city librarian; who, of course, must be a man of great learning: and I have my doubts if he had not some hand in the following history.

As our lodger had been a long time with us, and we had never received any pay, my wife began to be somewhat uneasy, and curious to find out who and what he was. She accordingly made bold to put the question to his friend, the librarian, who replied in his dry way that he was one of the *literati,* which she supposed to mean some new party in politics. I scorn to push a lodger for his pay; so I let day after day pass on without dunning the old gentleman for a farthing: but my wife, who always takes these matters on herself, and is, as I said, a shrewd kind of a woman, at last got out of patience, and hinted, that she thought it high time "some people should have a sight of some people's money." To which the old gentleman replied, in a mighty touchy manner, that she need not make herself uneasy, for that he had a treasure there, (pointing to his saddlebags) worth her whole house put together. This was the only answer we could ever get from him; and as my wife, by some of those odd ways in which women find out every thing, learnt that he was of very great connections, being related to the Knickerbockers of Scaghtikoke, and cousin-german to the congressman of that name, she did not like to treat him uncivilly. What is more, she even offered, merely by way of making things easy, to let him live scot-free, if he would teach the children their letters; and to try her best and get her neighbors to send their children also: but the old gentleman took it in such dudgeon, and seemed so affronted at being taken for a schoolmaster, that she never dared to speak on the subject again.

About two months ago, he went out of a morning, with a bundle in his hand, and has never been heard of since. All kinds of inquiries were made after him, but in vain. I wrote to his relations at Scaghtikoke, but they sent for answer, that he had not been there since the year before last, when he had a great dispute with the congressman about politics, and left the place in a huff, and they had neither heard nor seen any thing of him from that time to this. I must own I felt very much worried about the poor old gentleman, for I thought something bad must have happened to him, that he should be missing so long, and never return to pay his bill. I therefore advertised him in the newspapers, and though my melancholy advertisement was published by several humane printers, yet I have never been able to learn any thing satisfactory about him.

My wife now said it was high time to take care of ourselves, and see if he had left any thing behind in his room, that would pay us for his board and lodging. We found nothing, however, but some old books and musty writings, and his saddle-bags; which, being opened in the presence of the librarian, contained only a few articles of worn-out clothes, and a large bundle of blotted paper. On looking over this, the librarian told us he had no doubt it was the treasure which the old gentleman had spoken about; as it proved to be a most excellent and faithful HISTORY OF NEW YORK, which he advised us by all means to publish: assuring us that it would be so eagerly bought up by a discerning public, that he had no doubt it would be enough to pay our arrears ten times over. Upon this we got a very learned schoolmaster, who teaches our children, to prepare it for the press, which he accordingly has done; and has, moreover, added to it a number of valuable notes of his own.

This, therefore, is a true statement of my reasons for having this work printed, without waiting for the consent of the author: and I here declare, that if he ever returns, (though I much fear some unhappy accident has befallen him,) I stand ready to account with him like a true and honest man. Which is all at present,

From the public's humble servant,

SETH HANDASIDE

Independent Columbian Hotel, New York.

BOOK IV

CONTAINING THE CHRONICLES OF THE REIGN OF WILLIAM THE TESTY

CHAPTER I

SHOWING THE NATURE OF HISTORY IN GENERAL; CONTAINING FARTHERMORE THE UNIVERSAL ACQUIREMENTS OF WILLIAM THE TESTY, AND HOW A MAN MAY LEARN SO MUCH AS TO RENDER HIMSELF GOOD FOR NOTHING

WHEN THE lofty Thucydides is about to enter upon his description of the plague that desolated Athens, one of his modern commentators assures the reader, that the history is now going to be exceeding solemn, serious, and pathetic; and hints, with that air of chuckling gratulation with which a good dame draws forth a choice morsel from a cupboard to regale a favorite, that this plague will give his history a most agreeable variety.

In like manner did my heart lap within me, when I came to the dolorous dilemma of Fort Goed Hoop, which I at once perceived to be the forerunner of a series of great events and entertaining disasters. Such are the true subjects for the historic pen. For what is history, in fact, but a kind of Newgate calendar, a register of the crimes and miseries that man has inflicted on his fellow-man? It is a huge libel on human nature, to which we industriously add page after page, volume after volume, as if we were building up a monument to the honor, rather than the infamy of our species. If we turn over the pages of these chronicles that man has written of himself, what are the characters dignified by the appellation of great, and held up to the admiration of posterity? Tyrants, robbers, conquerors, renowned only for the magnitude of their misdeeds, and the stupendous wrongs and miseries they have inflicted on mankind—warriors, who have hired themselves to the trade of blood, not from motives of virtuous patriotism, or to protect the injured and defenceless, but merely to gain the vaunted glory of being adroit and successful in massacring their fellow-beings! What are the great events that constitute a glorious era? The fall of empires—the desolation of happy countries—splendid cities smoking in their ruins—the proudest works of art tumbled in the dust—the shrieks and groans of whole nations ascending unto heaven!

It is thus the historian may be said to thrive on the miseries of mankind, like birds of prey which hover over the field of battle, to fatten on the mighty dead. It was observed by a great projector of inland lock navigation, that rivers, lakes, and oceans, were only formed to feed canals. In like manner I am tempted to believe, that plots, conspiracies, wars, victories, and massacres, are ordained by Providence only as food for the historian.

It is a source of great delight to the philosopher, in studying the wonderful economy of nature, to trace the mutual dependencies of things, how they are created reciprocally for each other, and how the most noxious and apparently unnecessary animal has its uses. Thus those swarms of flies, which are so often execrated as useless vermin, are created for the sustenance of spiders—and spiders, on the other hand, are evidently made to devour flies. So those heroes who have been such scourges to the world, were bounteously provided as themes for the poet and historian, while the poet and the historian were destined to record the achievements of heroes!

These, and many similar reflections, naturally arose in my mind, as I took up my pen to commence the reign of William Kieft: for now the stream of our history, which hitherto has rolled in a tranquil current, is about to depart forever from its peaceful haunts, and brawl through many a turbulent and rugged scene.

As some sleek ox, sunk in the rich repose of a clover-field, dozing and chewing the cud, will bear repeated blows before it raises itself; so the province of Nieuw Nederlandts, having waxed fat under the drowsy reign of the Doubter, needed cuffs and kicks to rouse it into action. The reader will now witness the manner in which a peaceful community advances towards a state of war; which is apt to be like the approach of a horse to a drum, with much prancing and little progress, and too often with the wrong end foremost.

Wilhelmus Kieft, who, in 1634, ascended the gubernatorial chair (to borrow a favorite though clumsy appellation of modern phraseologists), was of a lofty descent, his father being inspector of wind-mills in the ancient town of Saardam; and our hero, we are told, when a boy, made very curious investigations into the nature and operation of these machines, which was one reason why he afterwards came to be so ingenious a governor. His name, according to the most authentic etymologists, was a corruption of Kyver; that is to say, a *wrangler* or *scolder;* and expressed the characteristic of his family, which, for nearly two centuries, had kept the windy town of Saardam in hot water, and produced more tartars and brimstones than any ten families in the place; and so truly did he inherit this family peculiarity, that he had not been a year in the government of the province, before he was universally denominated William the Testy. His appearance answered to his name. He was a brisk, wiry, waspish little old gentleman; such a one as may now and then be seen stumping about our city in a broad-skirted coat with huge buttons, a cocked hat stuck on the back of his head, and a cane as high as his chin. His face was broad, but his features were sharp; his cheeks were scorched into a dusky red, by two fiery little gray eyes; his nose turned up, and the corners of his mouth turned down, pretty much like the muzzle of an irritable pug-dog.

I have heard it observed by a profound adept in human physiology, that if a woman waxes fat with the progress of years, her tenure of life is somewhat precarious, but if haply she withers as she grows old, she lives forever. Such promised to be the case with William the Testy, who grew tough in proportion as he dried .He had withered, in fact, not through the process of years, but through the tropical fervor of his soul, which burnt like a vehement rush-light in his bosom; inciting him to incessant broils and bickerings. Ancient traditions speak much of his learning, and of the gallant inroads he had made into the dead languages, in which he had made captive a host of Greek nouns and Latin verbs; and brought off rich booty in ancient saws and apothegms; which he was wont to parade in his public harangues, as a triumphant general of yore, his *spolia opima*. Of metaphysics he knew enough to confound all hearers and himself into the bargain. In logic, he knew the whole family of syllogisms and dilemmas, and was so proud of his skill that he never suffered even a self-evident fact to pass unargued. It was observed, however, that he seldom got into an argument without getting into a perplexity, and then into a passion with his adversary for not being convinced gratis.

He had, moreover, skirmished smartly on the frontiers of several of the sciences, was fond of experimental philosophy, and prided himself upon inventions of all kinds. His abode, which he had fixed at a Bowerie or country-seat at a short distance from the city, just at what is now called Dutch-street, soon abounded with proofs of his ingenuity: patent smoke-jacks that required a horse to work them; Dutch ovens that roasted meat without fire; carts that went before the horses; weather-cocks that turned against the wind; and other wrong-headed contrivances that astonished and confounded all beholders. The house, too, was beset with paralytic cats and dogs, the subjects of his experimental philosophy; and the yelling and yelping of the latter unhappy victims of science, while aiding in the pursuit of knowledge, soon gained for the place the name of "Dog's Misery," by which it continues to be known even at the present day.

It is in knowledge as in swimming; he who flounders and splashes on the surface, makes more noise, and attracts more attention, than the pearl-diver who quietly dives in quest of treasures to the bottom. The vast acquirements of the new governor were the theme of marvel among the simple burghers of New Amsterdam; he figured about the place as learned a man as a Bonze at Pekin, who has mastered one half of the Chinese alphabet: and was unanimously pronounced a "universal genius!"

I have known in my time many a genius of this stamp; but, to speak my mind freely, I never knew one who, for the ordinary purposes of life, was worth his weight in straw. In this respect, a little sound judgment and plain common sense is worth all the sparkling genius that ever wrote poetry or invented theories. Let us see how the universal acquirements of William the Testy aided him in the affairs of government.

CHAPTER II

N O SOONER had this bustling little potentate been
blown by a whiff of fortune into the seat of
government than he called his council together to make
them a speech on the state of affairs.

Caius Gracchus, it is said, when he harangued the
Roman populace, modulated his tone by an oratorical
flute or pitchpipe; Wilhelmus Kieft, not having such an
instrument at hand, availed himself of that musical
organ or trump which nature has implanted in the midst
of a man's face; in other words, he preluded his address
by a sonorous blast of the nose; a preliminary flourish
much in vogue among public orators.

He then commenced by expressing his humble sense
of his utter unworthiness of the high post to which he
had been appointed; which made some of the simple
burghers wonder why he undertook it, not knowing that
it is a point of etiquette with a public orator never to
enter upon office without declaring himself unworthy to
cross the threshold. He then proceeded in a manner
highly classic and erudite to speak of government
generally, and of the governments of ancient Greece in
particular; together with the wars of Rome and Car-
thage; and the rise and fall of sundry outlandish
empires which the worthy burghers had never read nor
heard of. Having thus, after the manner of your learned
orator, treated of things in general, he came by a
natural, roundabout transition, to the matter in hand,
namely, the daring aggressions of the Yankees.

As my readers are well aware of the advantage a

potentate has of handling his enemies as he pleases in his speeches and bulletins, where he has the talk all on his own side, they may rest assured that William the Testy did not let such an opportunity escape of giving the Yankees what is called "a taste of his quality." In speaking of their inroads into the territories of their High Mightinesses, he compared them to the Gauls who desolated Rome; the Goths and Vandals who overran the fairest plains of Europe; but when he came to speak of the unparalleled audacity with which they of Weathersfield had advanced their patches up to the very walls of Fort Goed Hoop, and threatened to smother the garrison in onions, tears of rage started into his eyes, as though he nosed the very offense in question.

Having thus wrought up his tale to a climax, he assumed a most belligerent look, and assured the council that he had devised an instrument, potent in its effects, and which he trusted would soon drive the Yankees from the land. So saying, he thrust his hand into one of the deep pockets of his broad-skirted coat and drew forth, not an infernal machine, but an instrument in writing, which he laid with great emphasis upon the table.

The burghers gazed at it for a time in silent awe, as a wary housewife does at a gun, fearful it may go off half-cocked. The document in question had a sinister look, it is true; it was crabbed in text, and from a broad red ribbon dangled the great seal of the province, about the size of a buckwheat pancake. Still, after all, it was but an instrument in writing. Herein, however, existed the wonder of the invention. The document in question was a PROCLAMATION, ordering the Yankees to depart instantly from the territories of their High Mightinesses under pain of suffering all the forfeitures and punishments in such case made and provided. It was on the moral effect of this formidable instrument that Wilhelmus Kieft calculated; pledging his valor as a governor that, once fulminated against the Yankees, it would, in less than two months, drive every mother's son of them across the borders.

The council broke up in perfect wonder, and nothing was talked of for some time among the old men and women of New Amsterdam but the vast genius of the governor, and his new and cheap mode of fighting by proclamation.

As to Wilhelmus Kieft, having dispatched his proclamation to the frontiers, he put on his cocked hat and corduroy small-clothes, and mounting a tall raw-boned charger, trotted out to his rural retreat of Dog's Misery. Here, like the good Numa, he reposed from the toils of state, taking lessons in government, not from the nymph Egeria, but from the honored wife of his bosom; who was one of that class of females sent upon the earth a little after the flood, as a punishment for the sins of mankind, and commonly known by the appellation of *knowing women*. In fact, my duty as an historian obliges me to make known a circumstance which was a great secret at the time, and consequently was not a subject of scandal at more than half the tea-tables in New Amsterdam, but which, like many other great secrets, has leaked out in the lapse of years—and this was, that Wilhelmus the Testy, though one of the most potent little men that ever breathed, yet submitted at home to a species of government, neither laid down in Aristotle nor Plato; in short, it partook of the nature of a pure, unmixed tyranny, and is familiarly denominated *petticoat government*, an absolute sway, which, although exceedingly common in these modern days, was very rare among the ancients, if we may judge from the rout made about the domestic economy of honest Socrates; which is the only ancient case on record.

The great Kieft, however, warded off all the sneers and sarcasms of his particular friends, who are ever ready to joke with a man on sore points of the kind, by alleging that it was a government of his own election, to which he submitted through choice; adding at the same time a profound maxim which he had found in an ancient author, that "he who would aspire to *govern,* should first learn to *obey.*"

CHAPTER III

IN WHICH ARE RECORDED THE SAGE PROJECTS OF A RULER OF UNIVERSAL GENIUS—THE ART OF FIGHTING BY PROCLAMATION—AND HOW THAT THE VALIANT JACOBUS VAN CURLET CAME TO BE FOULLY DISHONORED AT FORT GOED HOOP

NEVER was a more comprehensive, a more expeditious, or, what is still better, a more economical measure devised, than this of defeating the Yankees by proclamation—an expedient, likewise, so gentle and humane, there were ten chances to one in favor of its succeeding, but then there was one chance to ten that it would not succeed—as the ill-natured fates would have it, that single chance carried the day! The proclamation was perfect in all its parts, well-constructed, well-written, well-sealed, and well-published—all that was wanting to insure its effect was, that the Yankees should stand in awe of it; but, provoking to relate, they treated it with the most absolute contempt, applied it to an unseemly purpose, and thus did the first warlike proclamation come to a shameful end—a fate which I am credibly informed has befallen but too many of its successors.

So far from abandoning the country, those varlets continued their encroachments, squatting along the green banks of the Varsche river, and founding Hartford, Stamford, New Haven, and other border towns. I have already shown how the onion patches of Pyquag were an eyesore to Jacobus Van Curlet and his garrison; but now these moss-troopers increased in their atrocities, kidnapping hogs, impounding horses, and sometimes grievously rib-roasting their owners. Our worthy forefathers could scarcely stir abroad without danger of being outjockeyed in horseflesh, or taken in in bargaining; while, in their absence, some daring Yankee peddler would penetrate to their household, and nearly ruin the good housewives with tin-ware and wooden bowls.

I am well aware of the perils which environ me in this part of my history. While raking, with curious hand but pious heart, among the mouldering remains of former days, anxious to draw therefrom the honey of wisdom, I may fare somewhat like that valiant worthy, Samson, who, in meddling with the carcass of a dead lion, drew a swarm of bees about his ears. Thus, while narrating the many misdeeds of the Yanokie or Yankee race, it is ten chances to one but I offend the morbid sensibilities of certain of their unreasonable descendants, who may fly out and raise such a buzzing about this unlucky head of mine, that I shall need the tough hide of an Achilles, or an Orlando Furioso, to protect me from their stings.

Should such be the case, I should deeply and sincerely lament—not my misfortune in giving offence—but the wrong-headed perverseness of an ill-natured generation, in taking offence at any thing I say. That their ancestors did use my ancestors ill is true, and I am very sorry for it. I would, with all my heart, the fact were otherwise; but as I am recording the sacred events of history, I'd not bate one nail's breadth of the honest truth, though I were sure the whole edition of my work would be bought up and burnt by the common hangman of Connecticut. And in sooth, now that these testy gentlemen have drawn me out, I will make bold to go farther, and observe that this is one of the grand purposes for which we impartial historians are sent into the world—to redress wrongs and render justice on the heads of the guilty. So that, though a powerful nation may wrong its neighbors with temporary impunity, yet sooner or later an historian springs up, who wreaks ample chastisement on it in return.

Thus these moss-troopers of the east little thought, I'll warrant it, while they were harassing the inoffensive province of Nieuw Nederlands, and driving its unhappy governor to his wit's end, that an historian would ever arise, and give them their own, with interest. Since, then, I am but performing my bounden duty as an historian, in avenging the wrongs of our revered ancestors, I shall make no further apology, and, indeed, when it is considered that I have all these ancient borderers of the east in my power, and at the mercy of my pen, I trust that it will be admitted I conduct myself with great humanity and moderation.

It was long before William the Testy could be persuaded that his much vaunted war measure was ineffectual; on the contrary, he flew in a passion whenever it was doubted, swearing that though slow in operating, yet when it once began to work, it would soon purge the land of these invaders. When convinced, at length, of the truth, like a shrewd physician, he attributed the failure to the quantity, not the quality of the medicine, and resolved to double the dose. He fulminated, therefore, a second proclamation more vehement than the first, forbidding all intercourse with these Yankee intruders; ordering the Dutch burghers on the frontiers to buy none of their pacing horses, measly pork, apple sweetmeats, Weathersfield onions, or wooden bowls, and to furnish them with no supplies of gin, gingerbread, or sourcraut.

Another interval elapsed, during which the last proclamation was as little regarded as the first, and the non-intercourse was especially set at naught by the young folks of both sexes, if we may judge by the active bundling which took place along the borders.

At length one day the inhabitants of New Amsterdam were aroused by a furious barking of dogs, great and small, and beheld, to their surprise, the whole garrison of Fort Goed Hoop straggling into town all tattered and wayworn, with Jacobus Van Curlet at their head, bringing the melancholy intelligence of the capture of Fort Goed Hoop by the Yankees.

The fate of this important fortress is an impressive warning to all military commanders. It was neither carried by storm nor famine; nor was it undermined; nor bombarded; nor set on fire by red-hot shot; but was taken by a stratagem no less singular than effectual, and which can never fail of success, whenever an opportunity occurs of putting it in practice.

It seems that the Yankees had received intelligence that the garrison of Jacobus Van Curlet had been reduced nearly one-eighth by the death of two of his most corpulent soldiers, who had overeaten themselves on fat salmon caught in the Varsche river. A secret expedition was immediately set on foot to surprise the fortress. The crafty enemy knowing the habits of the garrison to sleep soundly after they had eaten their dinners and smoked their pipes, stole upon them at the noontide of a sultry summer's day, and surprised them in the midst of their slumbers.

In an instant the flag of their High Mightinesses was lowered, and the Yankee standard elevated in its stead, being a dried codfish, by way of a spread eagle. A strong garrison was appointed, of long-sided, hard-fisted Yankees, with Weathersfield onions for cockades and feathers. As to Jacobus Van Curlet and his men, they were seized by the nape of the neck, conducted to the gate, and one by one dismissed with a kick in the crupper, as Charles XII, dismissed the heavy-bottomed Russians at the battle of Narva; Jacobus Van Curlet receiving two kicks in consideration of his official dignity.

CHAPTER IV

CONTAINING THE FEARFUL WRATH OF WILLIAM THE TESTY, AND THE ALARM OF NEW AMSTERDAM—HOW THE GOVERNOR DID STRONGLY FORTIFY THE CITY—OF THE RISE OF ANTHONY THE TRUMPETER, AND THE WINDY ADDITION TO THE ARMORIAL BEARINGS OF NEW AMSTERDAM

LANGUAGE cannot express the awful ire of William the Testy on hearing of the catastrophe at Fort Goed Hoop. For three good hours his rage was too great for words, or rather the words were too great for him, (being a very small man), and he was nearly choked by the misshapen, nine-cornered Dutch oaths and epithets which crowded at once into his gullet. At length his words found vent, and for three days he kept up a constant discharge, anathematizing the Yankees, man, woman, and child, for a set of dieven, schobbejacken, deugenieten, twistzoekeren, blaes-kaken, loosen-schalken, kakken-bedden, and a thousand other names, of which, unfortunately for posterity, history does not make mention. Finally, he swore that he would have nothing more to do with such a squatting, bundling, guessing, questioning, swapping, pumpkin-eating, molasses-daubing, shingle-splitting, cider-watering, horse-jockeying, notion-peddling crew—that they might stay at Fort Goed Hoop and rot, before he would dirty his hands by attempting to drive them away; in proof of which he ordered the new-raised troops to be marched forthwith into winter quarters, although it was not as yet quite mid-summer. Great despondency now fell upon the city of New Amsterdam. It was feared that the conquerors of Fort Goed Hoop, flushed with victory and apple-brandy, might march on to the capital, take it by storm, and annex the whole province to Connecticut. The name of Yankee became as terrible among the Nieuw Nederlanders as was that of Gaul among the ancient Romans; insomuch that the good wives of the Manhattoes used it as a bugbear wherewith to frighten their unruly children.

Everybody clamored around the governor, imploring him to put the city in a complete posture of defence, and he listened to their clamors. Nobody could accuse William the Testy of being idle in time of danger, or at any other time. He was never idle, but then he was often busy to very little purpose. When a youngling he had been impresssed with the words of Solomon, "Go to the ant, thou sluggard, observe her ways and be wise," in conformity to which he had ever been of a restless, ant-like turn; hurrying hither and thither, nobody knew why or wherefore, busying himself about small matters with an air of great importance and anxiety, and toiling at a grain of mustard-seed in the full conviction that he was moving a mountain. In the present instance, he called in all his inventive powers to his aid, and was continually pondering over plans, making diagrams, and worrying about with a troop of workmen and projectors at his heels. At length, after a world of consultation and contrivance, his plans of defence ended in rearing a great flag-staff in the centre of the fort, and perching a wind-mill on each bastion.

These warlike preparations in some measure allayed the public alarm, especially after an additional means of securing the safety of the city had been suggested by the governor's lady. It had already been hinted in this most authentic history, that in the domestic establishment of William the Testy "the gray mare was the better horse;" and, in governing the governor, governed the province, which might thus be said to be under petticoat government.

Now it came to pass, that about this time there lived in the Manhattoes a jolly, robustious trumpeter, named Antony Van Corlear, famous for his long wind; and who, as the story goes, could twang so potently upon his instrument, that the effect upon all within hearing was like that ascribed to the Scotch bagpipe when it sings right lustily i' the nose.

This sounder of brass was moreover a lusty bachelor, with a pleasant, burly visage, a long nose, and huge whiskers. He had his little *bowerie*, or retreat in the country, where he led a roystering life, giving dances to the wives and daughters of the burghers of the Manhattoes, insomuch that he became a prodigious favorite with all the women, young and old. He is said to have been the first to collect that famous toll levied on the fair sex at Kissing Bridge, on the highway to Hellgate.

To this sturdy bachelor the eyes of all the women were turned in this time of darkness and peril, as the very man to second and carry out the plans of defence of the governor. A kind of petticoat council was forthwith held at the government house, at which the governor's lady presided; and this lady, as has been hinted, being all potent with the governor, the result of these councils was the elevation of Antony the Trumpeter to the post of commandant of wind-mills and champion of New Amsterdam.

The city being thus fortified and garrisoned, it would have done one's heart good to see the governor snapping his fingers and fidgeting with delight, as the trumpeter strutted up and down the ramparts twanging defiance to the whole Yankee race, as does a modern editor to all the principalities and powers on the other side of the Atlantic. In the hands of Antony Van Corlear this windy instrument appeared to him as potent as the horn of the paladin Astolpho, or even the more classic horn of Alecto; nay, he had almost the temerity to compare it with the rams' horns celebrated in holy writ, at the very sound of which the walls of Jericho fell down.

Be all this as it may, the apprehensions of hostilities from the east gradually died away. The Yankees made no further invasion; nay, they declared they had only taken possession of Fort Goed Hoop as being erected within their territories. So far from manifesting hostility, they continued to throng to New Amsterdam with the most innocent countenances imaginable, filling the market with their notions, being as ready to trade with the Nederlanders as ever—and not a whit more prone to get to the windward of them in a bargain.

The old wives of the Manhattoes who took tea with the governor's lady attributed all this affected moderation to the awe inspired by the military preparations of the governor, and the windy prowess of Antony the Trumpeter.

There were not wanting illiberal minds, however, who sneered at the governor for thinking to defend his city as he governed it, by mere wind; but William Kieft was not to be jeered out of his wind-mills—he had seen them perched upon the ramparts of his native city of Saardam, and was persuaded they were connected with the great science of defence; nay, so much piqued was he by having them made a matter of ridicule, that he introduced them into the arms of the city, where they remain to this day, quartered with the ancient beaver of the Manhattoes, an emblem and memento of his policy.

I must not omit to mention that certain wise old burghers of the Manhattoes, skilful in expounding signs and mysteries, after events have come to pass, consider this early intrusion of the wind-mill into the escutcheon of our city, which before had been wholly occupied by the beaver, as portentous of its after fortune, when the quiet Dutchman would be elbowed aside by the enterprising Yankee, and patient industry overtopped by windy speculation.

Tales of
The Alhambra
(1832)

THE BALCONY

I HAVE spoken of a balcony of the central window of the Hall of Ambassadors. It served as a kind of observatory, where I used often to take my seat, and consider not merely the heaven above but the earth beneath. Besides the magnificent prospect which it commanded of mountain, valley, and vega, there was a little busy scene of human life laid open to inspection immediately below. At the foot of the hill was an alameda, or public walk, which, though not so fashionable as the more modern and splendid paseo of the Xenil, still boasted a varied and picturesque concourse. Hither resorted the small gentry of the suburbs, together with priests and friars, who walked for appetite and digestion; majos and majas, the beaux and belles of the lower classes, in their Andalusian dresses; swaggering contrabandistas, and sometimes half-muffled and mysterious loungers of the higher ranks, on some secret assignation.

It was a moving picture of Spanish life and character, which I delighted to study; and as the astronomer has his grand telescope with which to sweep the skies, and, as it were, bring the stars nearer for his inspection, so I had a smaller one, of pocket size, for the use of my observatory, with which I could sweep the regions below, and bring the countenances of the motley groups so close as almost, at times, to make me think I could divine their conversation by the play and expression of their features. I was thus, in a manner, an invisible observer, and, without quitting my solitude, could throw myself in an instant into the midst of society, a rare advantage to one of somewhat shy and quiet habits, and fond, like myself, of observing the drama of life without becoming an actor in the scene.

There was a considerable suburb lying below the Alhambra, filling the narrow gorge of the valley, and extending up the opposite hill of the Albaycin. Many of the houses were built in the Moorish style, round patios, or courts, cooled by fountains and open to the sky; and as the inhabitants passed much of their time in these courts, and on the terraced roofs during the summer season, it follows that many a glance at their domestic life might be obtained by an aerial spectator like myself, who could look down on them from the clouds.

I enjoyed, in some degree, the advantages of the student in the famous old Spanish story, who beheld all Madrid unroofed for his inspection; and my gossiping squire, Mateo Ximenes, officiated occasionally as my Asmodeus, to give me anecdotes of the different mansions and their inhabitants.

I preferred, however, to form conjectural histories for myself, and thus would sit for hours, weaving, from casual incidents and indications passing under my eye, a whole tissue of schemes, intrigues, and occupations of the busy mortals below. There was scarce a pretty face or a striking figure that I daily saw, about which I had not thus gradually framed a dramatic story, though some of my characters would occasionally act in direct opposition to the part assigned them, and disconcert the whole drama. Reconnoitring one day with my glass the streets of the Albaycin, I beheld the procession of a novice about to take the veil; and remarked several circumstances which excited the strongest sympathy in the fate of the youthful being thus about to be consigned to a living tomb. I ascertained to my satisfaction that she was beautiful; and, from the paleness of her cheek, that she was a victim, rather than a votary. She was arrayed in bridal garments, and decked with a chaplet of white flowers, but her heart evidently revolted at this mockery of a spiritual union, and yearned after its earthly loves. A tall stern-looking man walked near her in the procession; it was, of course, the tyrannical father, who, from some bigoted or sordid motive, had compelled this sacrifice. Amid the crowd was a dark handsome youth, in Andalusian garb, who seemed to fix on her an eye of agony. It was doubtless the secret lover from whom she was for ever to be separated. My indignation rose as I noted the malignant expression painted on the countenances of the attendant monks and friars. The procession arrived at the chapel of the convent; the sun gleamed for the last time upon the chaplet of the poor novice, as she crossed the fatal threshold, and disappeared within the building. The throng poured in with cowl, and cross, and minstrelsy; the lover paused for a moment at the door. I could divine the tumult of his feelings; but he mastered them, and entered. There was a long interval—I pictured to myself the scene passing within; the poor novice despoiled of her transient finery, and clothed in the conventual garb; the bridal chaplet taken from her brow, and her beautiful head shorn of its long silken tresses. I heard her murmur the irrevocable vow. I saw her extended on a bier; the death-pall spread over her; the funeral service performed that proclaimed her dead to the world; her sighs were drowned in the deep tones of the organ, and the plaintive requiem of the nuns; the father looked on, unmoved, without a tear; the lover—no—my imagination refused to portray the anguish of the lover—there the picture remained a blank.

After a time the throng again poured forth, and dispersed various ways, to enjoy the light of the sun and mingle with the stirring scenes of life; but the victim, with her bridal chaplet, was no longer there. The door of the convent closed that severed her from the world for ever. I saw the father and the lover issue forth; they were in earnest conversation. The latter was vehement in his gesticulations; I expected some violent termination to my drama; but an angle of a building interfered and closed the scene. My eye afterwards was frequently turned to that convent with painful interest. I remarked late at night a solitary light twinkling from a remote lattice of one of its towers. "There," said I, "the unhappy nun sits weeping in her cell, while perhaps her lover paces the street below in unavailing anguish."

The officious Mateo interrupted my meditations and destroyed in an instant the cobweb tissue of my fancy. With his usual zeal he had gathered facts concerning the scene, which put my fictions all to flight. The heroine of my romance was neither young nor handsome; she had no lover; she had entered the convent of her own free will, as a respectable asylum, and was one of the most cheerful residents within its walls.

It was some little while before I could forgive the wrong done me by the nun in being thus happy in her cell, in contradiction to all the rules of romance; I diverted my spleen, however, by watching, for a day or two, the pretty coquetries of a dark-eyed brunette, who, from the covert of a balcony shrouded with flowering shrubs and a silken awning, was carrying on a mysterious correspondence with a handsome, dark, well-whiskered cavalier, who lurked frequently in the street beneath her window. Sometimes I saw him at an early hour, stealing forth wrapped to the eyes in a mantle. Sometimes he loitered at a corner, in various disguises, apparently waiting for a private signal to slip into the house. Then there was the tinkling of a guitar at night, and a lantern shifted from place to place in the balcony. I imagined another intrigue like that of Almaviva; but was again disconcerted in all my suppositions. The supposed lover turned out to be the husband of the lady, and a noted contrabandista; and all his mysterious signs and movements had doubtless some smuggling scheme in view.

I occasionally amused myself with noting from this balcony the gradual changes of the scenes below, according to the different stages of the day.

Scarce has the gray dawn streaked the sky, and the earliest cock crowed from the cottages of the hill-side, when the suburbs give sign of reviving animation; for the fresh hours of dawning are precious in the summer season in a sultry climate. All are anxious to get the start of the sun, in the business of the day. The muleteer drives forth his loaded train for the journey; the traveller slings his carbine behind his saddle, and mounts his steed at the gate of the hostel; the brown peasant from the country urges forward his loitering beasts, laden with panniers of sunny fruit and fresh dewy vegetables; for already the thrifty housewives are hastening to the market.

The sun is up and sparkles along the valley, tipping the transparent foliage of the groves. The matin bells resound melodiously through the pure bright air, announcing the hour of devotion. The muleteer halts his burdened animals before the chapel, thrusts his staff through his belt behind, and enters with hat in hand, smoothing his coal-black hair, to hear a mass, and put up a prayer for a prosperous wayfaring across the sierra. And now steals forth on fairy foot the gentle Señora, in trim basquiña, with restless fan in hand, and dark eye flashing from beneath the gracefully folded mantilla; she seeks some well-frequented church to offer up her morning orisons; but the nicely-adjusted dress, the dainty shoe and cobweb stocking, the raven tresses exquisitely braided, the fresh plucked rose, gleaming among them like a gem, show that earth divides with Heaven the empire of her thoughts. Keep an eye upon her, careful mother, or virgin aunt, or vigilant duenna, whichever you be, that walk behind!

As the morning advances, the din of labor augments on every side; the streets are thronged with man, and steed, and beast of burden, and there is a hum and murmur, like the surges of the ocean. As the sun ascends to his meridian the hum and bustle gradually decline; at the height of noon there is a pause. The panting city sinks into lassitude, and for several hours there is a general repose. The windows are closed, the curtains drawn; the inhabitants retired into the coolest recesses of their mansions; the full-fed monk snores in his dormitory; the brawny porter lies stretched on the pavement beside his burden; the peasant and the laborer sleep beneath the trees of the Alameda, lulled by the sultry chirping of the locust. The streets are deserted, except by the water-carrier, who refreshes the ear by proclaiming the merits of his sparkling beverage, "colder than the mountain snow (*mas fria que la nieve*)."

As the sun declines, there is again a gradual reviving, and when the vesper bell rings out his sinking knell, all nature seems to rejoice that the tyrant of the day has fallen. Now begins the bustle of enjoyment, when the citizens pour forth to breathe the evening air, and revel away the brief twilight in the walks and gardens of the Darro and Xenil.

As night closes, the capricious scene assumes new features. Light after light gradually twinkles forth; here a taper from a balconied window; there a votive lamp before the image of a Saint. Thus, by degrees, the city emerges from the pervading gloom, and sparkles with scattered lights, like the starry firmament. Now break forth from court and garden, and street and lane, the tinkling of innumerable guitars, and the clicking of castañets; blending, at this lofty height, in a faint but general concert. "Enjoy the moment," is the creed of the gay and amorous Andalusian, and at no time does he practise it more zealously than in the balmy nights of summer, wooing his mistress with the dance, the love ditty, and the passionate serenade.

GOVERNOR MANCO AND THE SOLDIER

WHILE Governor Manco, or "the one-armed," kept up a show of military state in the Alhambra, he became nettled at the reproaches continually cast upon his fortress, of being a nestling place of rogues and contrabandistas. On a sudden, the old potentate determined on reform, and setting vigorously to work, ejected whole nests of vagbonds out of the fortress and the gipsy caves with which the surrounding hills are honeycombed. He sent out soldiers, also, to patrol the avenues and footpaths, with orders to take up all suspicious persons.

One bright summer morning, a patrol, consisting of the testy old corporal who had distinguished himself in the affair of the notary, a trumpeter and two privates, was seated under the garden wall of the Generalife, beside the road which leads down from the mountain of the sun, when they heard the tramp of a horse, and a male voice singing in rough, though not unmusical tones, an old Castilian campaigning song.

Presently they beheld a sturdy, sunburnt fellow, clad in the ragged garb of a foot-soldier, leading a powerful

Arabian horse, caparisoned in the ancient Moresco fashion.

Astonished at the sight of a strange soldier descending, steed in hand, from that solitary mountain, the corporal stepped forth and challenged him.

"Who goes there?"

"A friend."

"Who and what are you?"

"A poor soldier just from the wars, with a cracked crown and empty purse for a reward."

By this time they were enabled to view him more narrowly. He had a black patch across his forehead, which, with a grizzled beard, added to a certain daredevil cast of countenance, while a slight squint threw into the whole an occasional gleam of roguish good humor.

Having answered the questions of the patrol, the soldier seemed to consider himself entitled to make others in return. "May I ask," said he, "what city is that which I see at the foot of the hill?"

"What city!" cried the trumpeter; "come, that's too bad. Here's a fellow lurking about the mountain of the sun, and demands the name of the great city of Granada!"

"Granada! Madre di Dios! can it be possible?"

"Perhaps not!" rejoined the trumpeter; "and perhaps you have no idea that yonder are the towers of the Alhambra."

"Son of a trumpet," replied the stranger, "do not trifle with me; if this be indeed the Alhambra, I have some strange matters to reveal to the governor."

"You will have an opportunity," said the corporal, "for we mean to take you before him." By this time the trumpeter had seized the bridle of the steed, the two privates had each secured an arm of the soldier, the corporal put himself in front, gave the word, "Forward —march!" and away they marched for the Alhambra.

The sight of a ragged foot-soldier and a fine Arabian horse, brought in captive by the patrol, attracted the attention of all the idlers of the fortress, and of those gossip groups that generally assemble about wells and fountains at early dawn. The wheel of the cistern paused in its rotations, and the slipshod servant-maid stood gaping, with pitcher in hand, as the corporal passed by with his prize. A motley train gradually gathered in the rear of the escort.

Knowing nods and winks and conjectures passed from one to another. "It is a deserter," said one; "A contrabandista," said another; "A bandalero," said a third; until it was affirmed that a captain of a desperate band of robbers had been captured by the prowess of the corporal and his patrol. "Well, well," said the old crones, one to another, "captain or not, let him get out of the grasp of old Governor Manco if he can, though he is but one-handed."

Governor Manco was seated in one of the inner halls of the Alhambra, taking his morning's cup of chocolate in company with his confessor, a fat Franciscan friar, from the neighboring convent. A demure, dark-eyed damsel of Malaga, the daughter of his housekeeper, was attending upon him. The world hinted that the damsel, who, with all her demureness, was a sly buxom baggage, had found out a soft spot in the iron heart of the old governor, and held complete control over him. But let that pass—the domestic affairs of these mighty potentates of the earth should not be too narrowly scrutinized.

When word was brought that a suspicious stranger had been taken lurking about the fortress, and was actually in the outer court, in durance of the corporal, waiting the pleasure of his excellency, the pride and

stateliness of office swelled the bosom of the governor.
Giving back his chocolate cup into the hands of the
demure damsel, he called for his basket-hilted sword,
girded it to his side, twirled up his mustaches, took his
seat in a large high-backed chair, assumed a bitter and
forbidding aspect, and ordered the prisoner into his
presence. The soldier was brought in, still closely
pinioned by his captors, and guarded by the corporal.
He maintained, however, a resolute self-confident air,
and returned the sharp, scrutinizing look of the governor with an easy squint, which by no means pleased the
punctilious old potentate.

"Well, culprit," said the governor, after he had regarded him for a moment in silence, "what have you to say
for yourself—who are you?"

"A soldier, just from the wars, who has brought away
nothing but scars and bruises."

"A soldier—humph—a foot-soldier by your garb. I
understand you have a fine Arabian horse. I presume
you brought him too from the wars, besides your scars
and bruises."

"May it please your excellency, I have something
strange to tell about the horse. Indeed I have one of the
most wonderful things to relate. Something too that
concerns the security of this fortress, indeed of all
Granada. But it is a matter to be imparted only to your
private ear, or in presence of such only as are in your
confidence."

The governor considered for a moment, and then
directed the corporal and his men to withdraw, but to
post themselves outside of the door, and be ready at a
call. "This holy friar," said he, "is my confessor, you may
say any thing in his presence—and this damsel," nodding towards the handmaid, who had loitered with an

air of great curiosity, "this damsel is of great secrecy and discretion, and to be trusted with anything."

The soldier gave a glance between a squint and a leer at the demure handmaid. "I am perfectly willing," said he, "that the damsel should remain."

When all the rest had withdrawn, the soldier commenced his story. He was a fluent, smooth-tongued varlet, and had a command of language above his apparent rank.

"May it please your excellency," said he, "I am, as I before observed, a soldier, and have seen some hard service, but my term of enlistment being expired, I was discharged, not long since, from the army at Valladolid, and set out on foot for my native village in Andalusia. Yesterday evening the sun went down as I was traversing a great dry plain of Old Castile."

"Hold," cried the governor, "what is this you say? Old Castile is some two or three hundred miles from this."

"Even so," replied the soldier, coolly; "I told your excellency I had strange things to relate; but not more strange than true; as your excellency will find, if you will deign me a patient hearing."

"Proceed, culprit," said the governor, twirling up his mustaches.

"As the sun went down," continued the soldier. "I cast my eyes about in search of quarters for the night, but as far as my sight could reach, there were no signs of habitation. I saw that I should have to make my bed on the naked plain, with my knapsack for a pillow; but your excellency is an old soldier, and knows that to one who has been in the wars, such a night's lodging is no great hardship."

The governor nodded assent, as he drew his pocket handkerchief out of the basket-hilt, to drive away a fly that buzzed about his nose.

"Well, to make a long story short," continued the soldier, "I trudged forward for several miles until I came to a bridge over a deep ravine, through which ran a little thread of water, almost dried up by the summer heat. At one end of the bridge was a Moorish tower, the upper end all in ruins, but a vault in the foundation quite entire. Here, thinks I, is a good place to make a halt; so I went down to the stream, took a hearty drink, for the water was pure and sweet, and I was parched with thirst; then, opening my wallet, I took out an onion and a few crusts, which were all my provisions, and seating myself on a stone on the margin of the stream, began to make my supper; intending afterwards to quarter myself for the night in the vault of the tower; and capital quarters they would have been for a campaigner just from the wars, as your excellency, who is an old soldier, may suppose."

"I have put up gladly with worse in my time," said the governor, returning his pocket-handkerchief into the hilt of his sword.

"While I was quietly crunching my crust," pursued the soldier, "I heard something stir within the vault; I listened—it was the tramp of a horse. By and by a man came forth from a door in the foundation of the tower, close by the water's edge, leading a powerful horse by the bridle. I could not well make out what he was by the starlight. It had a suspicious look to be lurking among the ruins of a tower, in that wild solitary place. He might be a mere wayfarer, like myself; he might be a contrabandista; he might be a bandalero! what of that? thank heaven and my poverty, I had nothing to lose; so I sat still and munched my crust.

"He led his horse to the water, close by where I was sitting, so that I had a fair opportunity of reconnoitering him. To my surprise he was dressed in a Moorish garb, with a cuirass of steel, and a polished skull-cap that I distinguished by the reflection of the stars upon it. His horse, too, was harnessed in the Moresco fashion, with great shovel stirrups. He led him, as I said, to the side of the stream, into which the animal plunged his head almost to the eyes, and drank until I thought he would have burst.

"'Comrade,' said I, 'your steed drinks well; it's a good sign when a horse plunges his muzzle bravely into the water.'

"'He may well drink,' said the stranger, speaking with a Moorish accent; 'it is a good year since he had his last draught.'

"'By Santiago,' said I, 'that beats even the camels I have seen in Africa. But come, you seem to be something of a soldier, will you sit down and take part of a soldier's fare?' In fact, I felt the want of a companion in this lonely place, and was willing to put up with an infidel. Besides, as your excellency well knows, a soldier is never very particular about the faith of his company, and soldiers of all countries are comrades on peaceable ground."

The governor again nodded assent.

"Well as I was saying, I invited him to share my supper, such as it was, for I could not do less in common hospitality. 'I have no time to pause for meat or drink,' said he, 'I have a long journey to make before morning.'

"'In which direction?' said I.

"'Andalusia,' said he.

"'Exactly my route,' said I, 'so, as you won't stop and eat with me, perhaps you will let me mount and ride with you. I see your horse is of a powerful frame, I'll warrant he'll carry double.'

"'Agreed,' said the trooper; and it would not have been civil and soldierlike to refuse, especially as I had

offered to share my supper with him. So up he mounted, and up I mounted behind him.

"'Hold fast,' said he, 'my steed goes like the wind.'

"'Never fear me,' said I, and so off we set.

"From a walk the horse soon passed to a trot, from a
trot to a gallop, and from a gallop to a harum-scarum
scamper. It seemed as if rocks, trees, houses, every
thing, flew hurry-scurry behind us.

"'What town is this?' said I.

"'Segovia,' said he; and before the word was out of his
mouth, the towers of Segovia were out of sight. We
swept up the Guadarama mountains, and down by the
Escurial; and we skirted the walls of Madrid, and we
scoured away across the plains of La Mancha. In this
way we went up hill and down dale, by towers and cities,
all buried in deep sleep, and across mountains, and
plains, and rivers, just glimmering in the starlight.

"To make a long story short, and not to fatigue your
excellency, the trooper suddenly pulled up on the side
of a mountain. 'Here we are,' said he, 'at the end of our
journey.' I looked about, but could see no signs of
habitation; nothing but the mouth of a cavern. While I
looked I saw multitudes of people in Moorish dresses,
some on horseback, some on foot, arriving as if borne by
the wind from all points of the compass and hurrying
into the mouth of the cavern like bees into a hive. Before
I could ask a question the trooper struck his long
Moorish spurs into the horse's flanks, and dashed in with
the throng. We passed along a steep winding way, that
descended into the very bowels of the mountain. As we
pushed on, a light began to glimmer up, by little and
little, like the first glimmerings of day, but what caused it
I could not discern. It grew stronger and stronger, and
enabled me to see every thing around. I now noticed, as
we passed along, great caverns, opening to the right and

left, like halls in an arsenal. In some there were shields, and helmets, and cuirasses, and lances, and scimitars, hanging against the walls; in others there were great heaps of warlike munitions, and camp equipage lying upon the ground.

"It would have done your excellency's heart good, being an old soldier, to have seen such grand provision for war. Then, in other caverns, there were long rows of horsemen armed to the teeth, with lances raised and banners unfurled, all ready for the field; but they all sat motionless in their saddles like so many statues. In other halls were warriors sleeping on the ground beside their horses, and foot-soldiers in groups ready to fall into the ranks. All were in old-fashioned Moorish dresses and armor.

"Well, your excellency, to cut a long story short, we at length entered an immense cavern, or I may say palace, of grotto work, the walls of which seemed to be veined with gold and silver, and to sparkle with diamonds and sapphires and all kinds of precious stones. At the upper end sat a Moorish king on a golden throne, with his nobles on each side, and a guard of African blacks with drawn scimitars. All the crowd that continued to flock in, and amounted to thousands and thousands, passed one by one before his throne, each paying homage as he passed. Some of the multitude were dressed in magnificent robes, without stain or blemish and sparkling with jewels; others in burnished and enamelled armor; while others were in mouldered and mildewed garments, and in armor all battered and dented and covered with rust.

"I had hitherto held my tongue, for your excellency well knows it is not for a soldier to ask many questions when on duty, but I could keep silent no longer.

"'Prithee, comrade,' said I, 'what is the meaning of all this?'

"'This,' said the trooper, 'is a great and fearful mystery. Know, O Christian, that you see before you the court and army of Boabdil the last king of Granada.'

"'What is this you tell me?' cried I, 'Boabdil and his court were exiled from the land hundreds of years agone, and all died in Africa.'

"'So it is recorded in your lying chronicles,' replied the Moor, 'but know that Boabdil and the warriors who made the last struggle for Granada were all shut up in the mountain by powerful enchantment. As for the king and army that marched forth from Granada at the time of the surrender, they were a mere phantom train of spirits and demons, permitted to assume those shapes to deceive the Christian sovereigns. And furthermore let me tell you, friend, that all Spain is a country under the power of enchantment. There is not a mountain cave, not a lonely watchtower in the plains, nor ruined castle on the hills, but has some spell-bound warriors sleeping from age to age within its vaults, until the sins are expiated for which Allah permitted the dominion to pass for a time out of the hands of the faithful. Once every year, on the eve of St. John, they are released from enchantment, from sunset to sunrise, and permitted to repair here to pay homage to their sovereign! and the crowds which you beheld swarming into the cavern are Moslem warriors from their haunts in all parts of Spain. For my own part you saw the ruined tower of the bridge in Old Castile, where I have now wintered and summered for many hundred years, and where I must be back again by daybreak. As to the battalions of horse and foot which you beheld drawn up in array in the neighboring caverns, they are the spell-bound warriors of Granada. It is written in the book of fate, that when the enchantment is broken, Boabdil will descend from the mountain at the head of this army, resume his throne in the Alhambra and his sway of Granada, and gathering together the enchanted warriors, from all parts of Spain, will reconquer the Peninsula and restore it to Moslem rule.'

"'And when shall this happen?' said I.

"'Allah alone knows: we had hoped the day of deliverance was at hand; but there reigns at present a vigilant governor in the Alhambra, a staunch old soldier, well known as Governor Manco. While such a warrior holds command of the very outpost, and stands ready to check the first irruption from the mountain, I fear Boabdil and his soldiery must be content to rest upon their arms.'"

Here the governor raised himself somewhat perpendicularly, adjusted his sword, and twirled up his mustaches.

"To make a long story short, and not to fatigue your excellency, the trooper, having given me this account, dismounted from his steed.

"'Tarry here,' said he, 'and guard my steed while I go and bow the knee to Boabdil.' So saying, he strode away among the throng that pressed forward to the throne.

"'What's to be done?' thought I, when thus left to myself, 'shall I wait here until this infidel returns to whisk me off on his goblin steed, the Lord knows where; or shall I make the most of my time and beat a retreat from this hobgoblin community?' A soldier's mind is soon made up, as your excellency well knows. As to the horse, he belonged to an avowed enemy of the faith and the realm, and was a fair prize according to the rules of war. So hoisting myself from the crupper into the saddle, I turned the reins, struck the Moorish stirrups into the sides of the steed, and put him to make the best of his way out of the passage by which he had entered. As we scoured by the halls where the Moslem horsemen sat in motionless battalions, I thought I heard the clang of armor and a hollow murmur of voices. I gave the steed another taste of the stirrups and doubled my speed. There was now a sound behind me like a rushing blast; I heard the clatter of a thousand hoofs; a countless throng overtook me. I was borne along in the press, and hurled forth from the mouth of the cavern, while thousands of shadowy forms were swept off in every direction by the four winds of heaven.

"In the whirl and confusion of the scene I was thrown senseless to the earth. When I came to myself I was lying on the brow of a hill, with the Arabian steed standing beside me; for in falling, my arm had slipped within the bridle, which, I presume prevented his whisking off to Old Castile.

"Your excellency may easily judge of my surprise, on looking round, to behold hedges of aloes and Indian figs and other proofs of a southern climate, and to see a great city below me, with towers and palaces, and a grand cathedral.

"I descended the hill cautiously, leading my steed, for I was afraid to mount him again, lest he should play me some slippery trick. As I descended I met with your patrol, who let me into the secret that it was Granada that lay before me; and that I was actually under the walls of the Alhambra, the fortress of the redoubted Governor Manco, the terror of all enchanted Moslems. When I heard this, I determined at once to seek your excellency to inform you of all that I had seen, and to warn you of the perils that surround and undermine you, that you may take measures in time to guard your fortress, and the kingdom itself, from this intestine army that lurks in the very bowels of the land."

"And prithee, friend, you who are a veteran campaigner, and have seen so much service," said the governor, "how would you advise me to proceed, in order to prevent this evil?"

"It is not for a humble private of the ranks," said the soldier, modestly, "to pretend to instruct a commander of your excellency's sagacity, but it appears to me that your excellency might cause all the caves and entrances into the mountains to be walled up with solid mason work, so that Boabdil and his army might be completely corked up in their subterranean habitation. If the good father, too," added the soldier, reverently bowing to the friar, and devoutly crossing himself, "would consecrate the barricadoes with his blessing, and put up a few crosses and relics and images of saints, I think they might withstand all the power of infidel enchantments."

"They doubtless would be of great avail," said the friar.

The governor now placed his arm a-kimbo, with his hand resting on the hilt of his Toledo, fixed his eye upon the soldier, and gently wagging his head from one side to the other,

"So, friend," said he, "then you really suppose I am to be gulled with this cock-and-bull story about enchanted mountains and enchanted Moors? Hark ye, culprit!— not another word. An old soldier you may be, but you'll find you have an older soldier to deal with, and one not easily outgeneralled. Ho! guards there! put this fellow in irons."

The demure handmaid would have put in a word in favor of the prisoner, but the governor silenced her with a look.

As they were pinioning the soldier, one of the guards felt something of bulk in his pocket, and drawing it forth, found a long leathern purse that appeared to be well-filled. Holding it by one corner, he turned out the contents upon the table before the governor, and never did freebooter's bag make more gorgeous delivery. Out tumbled rings, and jewels, and rosaries of pearls, and sparkling diamond crosses, and a profusion of ancient golden coin, some of which fell jingling to the floor, and rolled away to the uttermost parts of the chamber.

For a time the functions of justice were suspended; there was a universal scramble after the glittering fugitives. The governor alone, who was imbued with true Spanish pride, maintained his stately decorum, though his eye betrayed a little anxiety until the last coin and jewel were restored to the sack.

The friar was not so calm; his whole face glowed like a furnace, and his eyes twinkled and flashed at sight of the rosaries and crosses.

"Sacrilegious wretch that thou art!" exclaimed he; "what church or sanctuary hast thou been plundering of these sacred relics?"

"Neither one nor the other, holy father. If they be sacrilegious spoils, they must have been taken, in times long past, by the infidel trooper I have mentioned. I was just going to tell his excellency when he interrupted me, that on taking possession of the trooper's horse, I unhooked a leathern sack which hung at the saddle-bow, and which I presume contained the plunder of his campaignings in days of old, when the Moors overran the country."

"Mighty well; at present you will make up your mind to take up your quarters in a chamber of the vermilion tower, which, though not under a magic spell, will hold you as safe as any cave of your enchanted Moors."

"Your excellency will do as you think proper," said the prisoner, coolly. "I shall be thankful to your excellency for any accommodation in the fortress. A soldier who has been in the wars, as your excellency well knows, is not particular about his lodgings: provided I have a snug dungeon and regular rations, I shall manage to make myself comfortable. I would only entreat that while your excellency is so careful about me, you would have an eye to your fortress, and think on the hint I dropped about stopping up the entrances to the mountain."

Here ended the scene. The prisoner was conducted to a strong dungeon in the vermilion tower, the Arabian steed was led to his excellency's stable, and the trooper's sack was deposited in his excellency's strong box. To the latter, it is true, the friar made some demur, questioning whether the sacred relics, which were evidently sacrilegious spoils, should not be placed in custody of the church; but as the governor was peremptory on the subject, and was absolute lord in the Alhambra, the friar discreetly dropped the discussion, but determined to convey intelligence of the fact to the church dignitaries in Granada.

To explain these prompt and rigid measures on the part of old Governor Manco, it is proper to observe, that about this time the Alpuxarra mountains in the neighborhood of Granada were terribly infested by a gang of robbers, under the command of a daring chief named Manuel Borasco, who were accustomed to prowl about the country, and even to enter the city in various disguises, to gain intelligence of the departure of convoys of merchandise, or travellers with well-lined purses, whom they took care to waylay in distant and solitary passes of the road. These repeated and daring outrages had awakened the attention of government, and the commanders of the various posts had received instructions to be on the alert, and to take up all suspicious stragglers. Governor Manco was particularly zealous in consequence of the various stigmas that had been cast upon his fortress, and he now doubted not he had entrapped some formidable desperado of this gang.

In the mean time the story took wind, and became the talk, not merely of the fortress, but of the whole city of Granada. It was said that the noted robber Manuel Borasco, the terror of the Alpuxarras, had fallen into the clutches of old Governor Manco, and been cooped up by him in a dungeon of the vermilion towers; and every one who had been robbed by him flocked to recognize the marauder. The vermilion towers, as is well known, stand apart from the Alhambra on a sister hill, separated from the main fortress by the ravine down which passes the main avenue. There were no outer walls, but a sentinel patrolled before the tower. The window of the chamber in which the soldier was confined was strongly grated, and looked upon a small esplanade. Here the good folks of Granada repaired to gaze at him, as they would at a laughing hyena, grinning through the cage of a menagerie. Nobody, however, recognized him for Manuel Borasco, for that terrible robber was noted for a ferocious physiognomy, and had by no means the good-humored squint of the prisoner. Visitors came not merely from the city, but from all parts of the country; but nobody knew him, and there began to be doubts in the minds of the common people whether there might not be some truth in his story. That Boabdil and his army were shut up in the mountain was an old tradition which many of the ancient inhabitants had heard from their fathers. Numbers went up to the mountain of the sun, or rather of St. Elena, in search of the cave mentioned by the soldier; and saw and peeped into the deep dark pit, descending, no one knows how far, into the mountain, and which remains there to this day—the fabled entrance to the subterranean abode of Boabdil.

By degrees the soldier became popular with the common people. A freebooter of the mountains is by no means the opprobrious character in Spain that a robber is in any other country: on the contrary, he is a kind of chivalrous personage in the eyes of the lower classes. There is always a disposition, also, to cavil at the conduct of those in command, and many began to murmur at the high-handed measures of old Governor Manco, and to look upon the prisoner in the light of a martyr.

The soldier, moreover, was a merry, waggish fellow that had a joke for every one who came near his window, and a soft speech for every female. He had procured an old guitar also, and would sit by his window and sing ballads and love-ditties to the delight of the women of the neighborhood, who would assemble on the esplanade in the evening and dance boleros to his music. Having trimmed off his rough beard, his sunburnt face found favor in the eyes of the fair, and the demure handmaid of the governor declared that his squint was perfectly irresistible. This kind-hearted damsel had from the first evinced a deep sympathy in his fortunes, and having in vain tried to mollify the governor, had set to work privately to mitigate the rigor of his dispensations. Every day she brought the prisoner some crumbs of comfort which had fallen from the governor's table, or been abstracted from his larder, together with, now and then, a consoling bottle of choice Val de Peñas, or rich Malaga.

While this petty treason was going on, in the very center of the old governor's citadel, a storm of open war was brewing up among his external foes. The circumstance of a bag of gold and jewels having been found upon the person of the supposed robber, had been reported, with many exaggerations, in Granada. A question of territorial jurisdiction was immediately started by the governor's inveterate rival, the captain-general. He insisted that the prisoner had been captured without the precincts of the Alhambra, and within the rules of his authority. He demanded his body therefore, and the *spolia opima* taken with him. Due information having been carried likewise by the friar to the grand inquisitor of the crosses and rosaries, and other relics contained in the bag, he claimed the culprit as having been guilty of sacrilege, and insisted that his plunder was due to the church, and his body to the next auto da fe. The feuds ran high; the governor was furious, and swore, rather than surrender his captive, he would hang him up within the Alhambra, as a spy caught within the purlieus of the fortress.

The captain-general threatened to send a body of soldiers to transfer the prisoner from the vermilion tower to the city. The grand inquisitor was equally bent upon dispatching a number of the familiars of the Holy Office. Word was brought late at night to the governor of these machinations. "Let them come," said he, "they'll find me beforehand with them; he must rise bright and early who would take in an old soldier." He accordingly issued orders to have the prisoner removed, at daybreak, to the donjon keep within the walls of the Alhambra. "And d'ye hear, child," said he to his demure handmaid, "tap at my door, and wake me before cock-crowing, that I may see to the matter myself."

The day dawned, the cock crowed, but nobody tapped at the door of the governor. The sun rose high above the mountaintops, and glittered in at his casement, ere the governor was awakened from his morning dreams by his veteran corporal, who stood before him with terror stamped upon his iron visage.

"He's off! he's gone!" cried the corporal, gasping for breath.

"Who's off—who's gone?"

"The soldier—the robber—the devil, for aught I know; his dungeon is empty, but the door locked: no one knows how he has escaped out of it."

"Who saw him last?"

"Your handmaid, she brought him his supper."

"Let her be called instantly."

Here was new matter of confusion. The chamber of the demure damsel was likewise empty, her bed had not been slept in: she had doubtless gone off with the culprit, as she had appeared, for some days past, to have frequent conversations with him.

This was wounding the old governor in a tender part, but he had scarce time to wince at it, when new misfortunes broke upon his view. On going into his cabinet he found his strong box open, the leather purse of the trooper abstracted, and with it, a couple of corpulent bags of doubloons.

But how, and which way had the fugitives escaped? An old peasant who lived in a cottage by the road-side, leading up into the Sierra, declared that he had heard the tramp of a powerful steed just before daybreak, passing up into the mountains. He had looked out at his casement, and could just distinguish a horseman, with a female seated before him.

"Search the stables!" cried Governor Manco. The stables were searched; all the horses were in their stalls, excepting the Arabian steed. In his place was a stout cudgel tied to the manger, and on it a label bearing these words, "A gift to Governor Manco, from an Old Soldier."